EXPLORING WORLD HISTORY

GLOBE BOOK COMPANY
A Division of Simon & Schuster
Paramus, New Jersey

SOL HOLT

Sol Holt has made many contributions to social studies education over the course of his professional career. He has been a social studies teacher in New York City high schools, served as social studies department chairman for twenty-five years, trained hundreds of teachers in social studies methods, and has been author or co-author of texts in geography, economics and history.

JOHN R. O'CONNOR

John R. O'Connor taught social studies for many years before becoming a principal in the New York City school system. He is widely known for his lectures and articles on reading skills in the social studies. In addition to this book, John R. O'Connor has co-authored other Globe textbooks: *Exploring United States History*, *Exploring American Citizenship*, *Unlocking Social Studies Skills*, and *Exploring the Urban World*. He has edited Globe's *Exploring American History*, *Exploring a Changing World*, and *Exploring the Non-Western World*.

Acknowledgments for printed matter begin on page 751.
Acknowledgments for photographs begin on page 752.

ISBN: 835-90644-2

Printed in the United States of America
    5 6 7 8 9 10   98 99 00 01

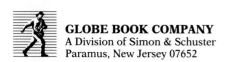

GLOBE BOOK COMPANY
A Division of Simon & Schuster
Paramus, New Jersey 07652

CONSULTANTS

Professor Diane Barnes
Professional Assistant to the Teachers of
  Secondary Schools Programs
University of Southern Maine
Gorham, Maine

Dr. Burton F. Beers
Professor of History
North Carolina State University
Raleigh, North Carolina

Professor Bud Burkhard
Professorial Lecturer in History
Georgetown University
Washington, D.C.

Dr. Harold Marcus
Professor of History and African Studies
Associate Director of African Studies Center
Michigan State University
East Lansing, Michigan

Dr. Laurence Michalak
Vice-Chairman, Center for Middle Eastern Studies
University of California at Berkeley
Berkeley, California

Dr. Blaise Nagy, Ph.D.
Associate Professor of Classics
College of the Holy Cross
Worcester, Massachusetts

Timothy Plummer
Director of Education and Communications
The Asia Society
New York, New York

Dr. James Reardon-Anderson
Sun Yat-sen Professor of China Studies
School of Foreign Service
Georgetown University
Washington, D.C.

Dr. Donald Schwartz
Social Science Credential Coordinator
California State University at Long Beach
Long Beach, California

Dr. Paul Varley
Professor of East Asian Languages and Cultures
Columbia University
New York, New York

Dr. James Wilke
Professor of History
University of California at Los Angeles
Los Angeles, California

Barbara Winslow
Adjunct Lecturer of Women's Studies
City University of New York
Adjunct Lecturer in History
City University of New York, Baruch College
New York, New York

REVIEWERS

Beth Bagwell
Social Studies Teacher
Miami-Palmetto High School
Miami, Florida

Carlos Chavez
Social Studies Teacher
Albuquerque High School
Albuquerque, New Mexico

Loyal L. Darr
Supervisor of Social Studies, K through 12
Denver Public Schools
Denver, Colorado

Adrian Davis
Social Studies Teacher
Redford High School
Detroit, Michigan

Irene Frias
English and Social Studies Teacher
Powell Junior High School
Mesa, Arizona

Elliot Kraut
Division Coordinator of Social Studies
Staples High School
Westport, Connecticut

Dr. Dana Kurfman
Supervisor of Social Studies, K through 12
Prince George's County Public School System
Prince George's County, Maryland

Beverly Stebbins
Social Studies Teacher
Arlington High School
Arlington, Texas

Judith Walsh
Associate Professor of Comparative Humanities
State University of New York at Old Westbury
Old Westbury, New York

Deborah Washington
Humanities Department Chair
Dorchester High School
Dorchester, Massachusetts

T ake charge of your studies.

You'll learn more and get the most enjoyment from reading about world history when you know how to use this book. Read these six pages first. They'll show you the best way to use all the study aids and Special Features you'll find in EXPLORING WORLD HISTORY.

Take a good look at the two pages that start each Unit. They'll give you a better understanding of what you'll be learning in the Unit.

The Unit title and the list of Chapter titles give you a quick outline of the people, places, and events you'll be studying.

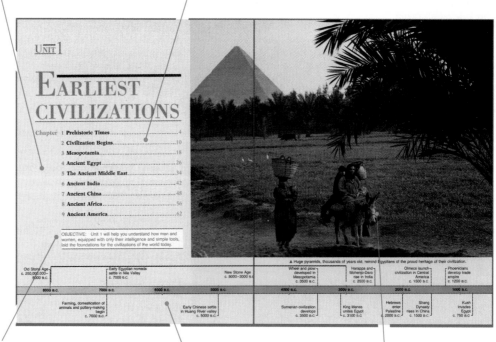

A Huge pyramids, thousands of years old, remind Egyptians of the proud heritage of their civilization.

Read the Unit Objective. It will give you a good idea of what you should think about as you read the Unit and help you relate the Chapters to one another.

The Unit Time Line shows the time span and the major historical events covered in the Unit.

Pictures at the beginning of each Unit introduce scenes and people from history and give you a feeling for the time and place you'll meet in the Unit.

Every Chapter begins
with an Objective that poses
an important question.
Focus on answering
the question as you read, and
you'll develop a good
understanding of the Chapter.

Key History Words
you should know are highlighted
in boldface type.

The Introduction to
the Chapter helps you relate
history to your own
experience and to events
around the world.

Colored triangles mark
critical thinking questions
that will involve you
in the readings.

CHAPTER 4

Ancient Egypt

OBJECTIVE: What were the key strengths of ancient Egyptian civilization that allowed it to last for 3,000 years?

▶ 1. Did your community ever suffer a flood during which you had to move up onto drier ground and clean up slimy mud afterwards? Or did your community ever suffer a drought during which you had to be careful of water use? If you have ever experienced such troubles, they will give you some idea of the challenges faced by the people of ancient Egypt. Droughts and floods along the great Nile River were a regular part of Egyptian life. The Egyptians lived in a hot, dry desert where it almost never rains. Each year, without any rain falling over Egypt, the Nile would overflow, flooding the lands near it and leaving behind a layer of rich soil. Why is Egypt sometimes called "the

▲ An Egyptian farmer lifts water from the Nile River for irrigation. Irrigated agriculture flourished in Egypt more than 4,000 years ago.

gift of the Nile"? The ancient Egyptians believed that the crocodile god called Sobek gave the Nile the power to rise. What they did not know was that summer rains come each year to the Ethiopian highlands. The lessons that Egyptians learned about cop-

ing with their drought-stricken land and life-giving floods laid the foundations for one of the earliest and greatest civilizations.

THE NILE VALLEY: Why did early civilization in Egypt develop in the Nile River valley?

2. The dry desert (DEZ-urt) land of Egypt is located in the northeastern part of Africa. The Nile River flows south to north through Egypt, bringing rich soil along with water to the desert land. Today dams control the river's flooding. However, in ancient times the Nile River would rise every year in July and by September would flood the flatland of the Nile valley. The harvest of crops each year depended on how well the Nile had flooded. Egypt's farmers also dug ditches and canals to water their crops.

3. About 7000 B.C., nomadic people moved into the Nile valley and began to farm the rich soil. By about 3500 B.C., they were living in a number of small villages and growing wheat, barley, and vegetables. Gradually these villages were united under a single government. Each of the early villages in Egypt had its own ruler. Then the rulers of certain villages gained control over other villages. After many hundreds of years, the villages were joined together to form two kingdoms. Finally about 3100 B.C., King Menes united Egypt into one great kingdom.

4. Pharaoh (FAIR-oh) was the title given to the rulers of ancient Egypt. The title comes from the Egyptian word for palace. King Menes began the first dynasty (DY-nus-tee), or family of rulers. During the next 3,000 years, Egypt had 31 dynasties of pharaohs. All but one of these rulers were men.

5. The resources of the Nile River valley and the surrounding desert and seas helped the ancient Egyptian kingdom in other ways besides farming. The valley of the Nile had large supplies of limestone and sandstone. How might these have helped the Egyptians to construct buildings? Even more important, the deserts surrounding the Nile valley protected Egypt from attack

by other peoples. The Mediterranean Sea and the Red Sea also helped to protect it. These deserts and seas formed natural barriers that defended Egypt from invasion for thousands of years. Look at the map on page 29 and locate these deserts and bodies of water. Why do you think it was difficult for enemy peoples to cross the deserts and seas?

6. Because their land was well protected, the Egyptians did not need large armies. Instead, they used their wealth, their resources, and their skills to build a great civilization that lasted more than 3,000 years.

EGYPT'S RELIGION: What were the Egyptians' religious beliefs, and why were they so important in Egypt's civilization?

7. The Egyptians believed in many gods. Egyptians worshiped the sun god Amon-Re; Osiris, the god of the Nile; Isis, the mother goddess; and many others. They believed these gods brought them large crops and good harvests. In fact, Egyptians believed that the gods decided everything that happened to them and their families.

8. Central to the Egyptian religion was the belief in life after death. Egyptians believed that those who had lived good lives would be rewarded with pleasant, happy lives in the next world. Egyptians also believed that they would need their body as a home for their soul in the next world. As a result, Egyptians preserved the bodies of the dead. The preserved body is called a mummy (MUM-ee).

SPOTLIGHT ON SOURCES

9. All Egyptians planned for the afterlife, but the way the pharaohs prepared was the most elaborate and costly. The pharaohs had huge tombs built for them. The tombs were filled with all the rich treasures the pharaohs believed they would need on their journey to the next world. Their tombs were piled high with food, furniture, jewelry, and other valuable goods. Written messages to

	Old Kingdom begins 2700 B.C.	New Kingdom begins 1560 B.C.	Hatshepsut takes power 1489 B.C.
3500 B.C.	3000 B.C.	2500 B.C.	2000 B.C.	1500 B.C.	1000 B.C.
King Menes unites Egypt 3100 B.C.		Middle Kingdom begins 2000 B.C.	Egyptian power declines 1100 B.C.

26

27

Each Section in the Chapter
begins with an
important question to direct
your reading. Finding
the answer to that question
helps you understand what you've read.

You can find the main idea
of every paragraph in
the first or second sentence.

Study the Chapter Time Line.
It's a great way
to preview and recall key
events and dates from
the Chapter.

Special Features show world history in action.

Every Chapter is filled with interesting details on the people, places, and ideas that have shaped history. As you read the Features, you'll build social studies skills and master important facts from the Chapter, too.

A Geographic View of History— Explore the relationship between geography and history. You'll see how understanding geography helps you understand the course of history.

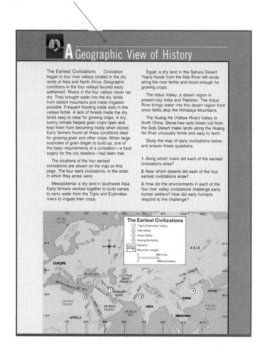

Skill Builder/Maps— Maps are important in studying history, and you'll find opportunities like these to practice and improve your skills at reading and using maps.

Spotlight on Sources—
History comes alive as you read the actual ideas and views of people who have influenced history.

The Arts and Artifacts—
You can visit the Russian ballet, learn how churches were built in the Middle Ages, and tour the Coliseum and the Taj Mahal. You'll do all this and more as you discover the art created by people of different lands and times.

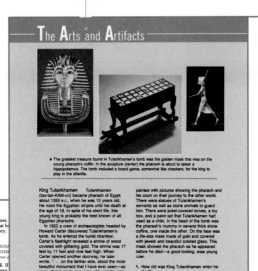

People in History—
History is filled with extraordinary people. You'll learn how their ideas and actions affected the course of history.

Daily life in...
As you read about events and people that make history, you'll also get a close-up view of the day-to-day lives of people from those same lands and times.

Check your understanding and develop skills.

Two pages of review and skill-building activities at the end of each Chapter and again at the end of each Unit help you check what you've learned. Review pages will help you master the important information from the Chapter or Unit, develop proper study habits, and build history skills.

Begin your review with a check of the Key History Words you learned in the Chapter.

In the first Skill Builder section, you review the content of the Chapter and practice your history study skills.

Use the Study Hints to improve your understanding of the Chapter and to help you get better grades on tests.

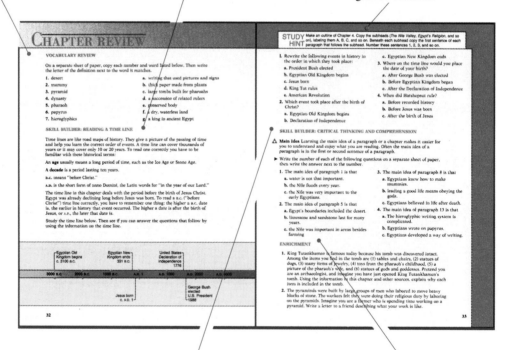

A second Skill Builder section challenges you to think critically about what you've learned in the Chapter.

Learn more about world history by making your own discoveries. Enrichment activities take what you've learned in the chapter and ask you to use it in new, creative ways.

The activities in the
Unit Review cover all the
Chapters together,
so you'll see how they connect
to each other. First
read the Summary to help you
remember important
information you read
in the Unit.

The first Skill Builder
section uses maps and graphs
to review important
places, empires, and historical
trends in the Unit.

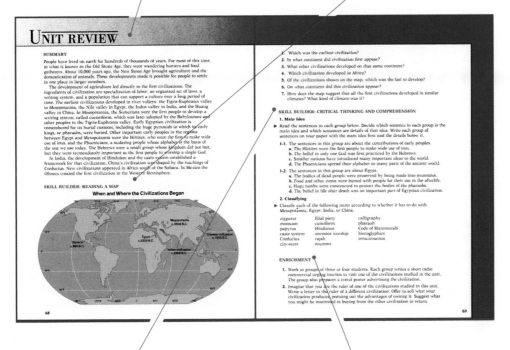

The second Skill Builder
section applies your critical
thinking skills to
people, places, and events
throughout the Unit.

Enrichment activities
challenge you to explore facts
and ideas from the Unit
in greater depth. For some
activities, you will
have to look for information
in places other than
your textbook.

CONTENTS

LIST OF MAPS

PEOPLE IN HISTORY

Daily life in...

1

UNIT 1

ESL/LEP Strategy: Help students learn new words by creating Guesstimate Dictionaries. First, ask students to guess the meanings of new words or terms. Then, have them look up the words in a dictionary and compare their own definitions to the dictionary definitions. Finally, invite students to share their dictionaries with the class.

EARLIEST CIVILIZATIONS

OBJECTIVE: Unit 1 will help you understand how men and women, equipped with only their intelligence and simple tools, laid the foundations for the civilizations of the world today.

Old Stone Age
c. 2,500,000–
8000 B.C.

Early Egyptian nomads
settle in Nile Valley
c. 7000 B.C.

New Stone Age
c. 8000–3000 B.C.

| 8000 B.C. | 7000 B.C. | 6000 B.C. | 5000 B.C. |

Farming, domestication of
animals and pottery-making
begin
c. 7000 B.C.

Early Chinese settle
in Huang River valley
c. 5000 B.C.

▲ Huge pyramids, thousands of years old, remind Egyptians of the proud heritage of their civilization.

Wheel and plow
developed in
Mesopotamia
c. 3500 B.C.

Harappa and
Mohenjo-Daro
rise in India
c. 2500 B.C.

Olmecs launch
civilization in Central
America
c. 1500 B.C.

Phoenicians
develop trade
empire
c. 1200 B.C.

| 4000 B.C. | 3000 B.C. | 2000 B.C. | 1000 B.C. |

Sumerian civilization
develops
c. 3500 B.C.

King Menes
unites Egypt
c. 3100 B.C.

Hebrews
enter
Palestine
c. 2000 B.C.

Shang
Dynasty
rises in China
c. 1500 B.C.

Kush
invades
Egypt
c. 750 B.C.

CHAPTER 1

Prehistoric Times

▲ Two archaeologists explore the ruins of an ancient building. Archaeological finds offer important clues to life in prehistoric times.

OBJECTIVE: What was life like before written history?

1. No one knows for certain when the first human beings appeared on earth. Although scientists now believe that the story of humankind begins well over a million years ago, little is known about the lives of our ancient ancestors. Often, people's ideas about **prehistoric** (pree-hiss-TOH-rik) times, or the period of time before written history, are colored by comic strips, television cartoons, or science fiction. People imagine heavy-browed cavemen and women who wear hairy animal skins and carry clubs. The cave dwellers may be huddled together in some dark cave while giant dinosaurs battle to the death outside. In fact, the last of the dinosaurs disappeared tens of millions of years before the first human being walked on earth. Although prehistoric people never had to flee from the hungry tyrannosaurus rex, their lives were not easy. As you learn about prehistoric

Oldest human fossils found 3,200,000 B.C.	Beginning of Old Stone Age (Paleolithic) 2,500,000 B.C.		Prehistoric humans master fire c. 750,000 B.C.	End of last Ice Age 10,000 B.C.
3,000,000 B.C.	**2,000,000 B.C.**		**1,000,000 B.C.**	**A.D. 1**
	First stone tools are used 2,500,000 B.C.			End of Old Stone Age 8000 B.C.

Ask: What do you think the prehistoric people looked like and how do you think they lived? On what are these impressions based?

times, you will realize that our ancient past is at least as amazing as any science fiction story.

ARCHAEOLOGISTS AND ANTHROPOLOGISTS: How do we know about prehistoric people?

2. If prehistory is the time before people began to keep written records, how does anyone know what really happened then? Fortunately, **archaeologists** (ahr-kee-AHL-uh-jists) have found pieces of the puzzle that tell something about the people who lived thousands of years ago. Archaeologists make a scientific study of the material remains of past human life and activities. Often they find the material remains by digging and sifting through soils where ancient people probably lived. The artifacts archaeologists find include bones, tools, and other objects, and serve as clues in revealing how our ancestors may have looked and behaved.

3. Other scientists, called **anthropologists** (an-throh-PAHL-uh-jists), study human beings and how they interact with their environment and with each other. Anthropologists also study the culture of humans. Until about 50 years ago, people could do little more than guess the age of the ancient objects they found buried in the earth. Today, scientists have several different ways to help them figure out how old things are. One way, for example, is carbon dating, which can be used with items that contain the element carbon, such as wood or bones. By measuring the radioactivity of the carbon, scientists can tell the age of an object many thousands of years old.

4. Every archaeological find is like a new piece of a jigsaw puzzle with most of the pieces still missing. When scientists study prehistory, they use the limited pieces of the puzzle to try to paint a picture of an entire way of life. Archaeologists have learned a great deal about the kinds of tools and pottery that people used thousands of years ago. However, they can only guess what thoughts may have passed through the minds of the people who made and used those objects. What can bits of stone and clay reveal about the beliefs of ancient peoples? Seeking out new clues and using them to solve the puzzle of prehistoric life are the excitement and challenge of archeology.

SPOTLIGHT ON SOURCES

5. One of the best ways you can learn about the thoughts and feelings of any group of people is by studying the art they produce. Fortunately, the people of the **Paleolithic** (pay-lee-oh-LITH-ik), or "Old Stone," Age left behind many beautiful works of art. The paintings and carved figures they created many thousands of years ago tell us that these prehistoric people could create works of great power. After studying the famous prehistoric cave paintings at Lascaux in France, Dr. Annette

Daily life in . . .

Prehistoric people found time to do more than look for food. They decorated their clothing with colorful beads and seemed to enjoy wearing necklaces and bracelets of shells, teeth, ivory, and stone. People today wonder at the skillful carvings and wall murals left behind by our "primitive" ancestors. Archaeologists can only guess what part music may have played in the lives of prehistoric people. However, bone whistles were made in Africa at least 65,000 years ago. Other instruments included drums made from logs and rattles made from gourds. Our ancestors also took the time to bury their dead. The burial of tools and food with bodies suggests that prehistoric people may have believed in life after death.

Activity: Have students read about the pioneering work of archaeologists Louis and Mary Leakey.

Ask: Why do you think prehistoric people painted on cave walls? Explain "sympathetic magic."

Laming-Empelaire, a noted archaeologist, wrote:

> The mentality of Paleolithic man was far more complex than is generally supposed and . . . the scope of his artistic inspiration [ideas] extended [stretched] far beyond a daily preoccupation [thought] with the hunt and its quarry [prey]. If these paintings and engravings do indeed illustrate [show] myths of very great antiquity [ancient times], they may represent man's first attempt to express his vision [view] of the world and the relationship of one living creature with another.
>
> *Lascaux: Paintings and Engravings,* Annette Laming-Empelaire

CLIMATE AND GEOGRAPHY: What role did the environment play in shaping the prehistoric world?

6. The story of humankind begins over two million years ago with the Old Stone Age. At least four times during this age, **glaciers**, or sheets of ice, covered parts of Europe, Asia, and North America. The last ice sheet began to melt about 12,000 years ago. Water from this melting ice formed great river valleys as it flowed to the sea. Glaciers are now seen only in the cold mountain and polar regions.

7. Changes in geography and climate played an important role in shaping prehistoric life. During the Ice Age, Africa was free of ice. Great herds of animals lived there

SKILL BUILDER/MAPS The Continents and Oceans

Ice sheets covered much of the earth during the Ice Age. The ice sheets locked up so much water that sea level fell and "land bridges" connected all the continents.

1. What continents had the oldest prehuman and humanlike fossils?

2. What continents had human inhabitants 10,000 years ago?

3. How do you think early humans crossed into the Americas from Asia?

4. How do you think early humans reached Australia?

Prehistoric Humans

▲ Prehumans (lived 14 to 2.5 million years ago)

— Greatest extent of ice in Ice Age

▲ Humanlike (lived 2 million to 1 million years ago)

▲ Neanderthal (lived 250,000 to 40,000 years ago)

Present-day land masses and coastlines

▲ Homo erectus (lived 1.5 millon to 300,000 years ago)

▲ Earliest modern humans (lived 40,000 to 10,000 years ago)

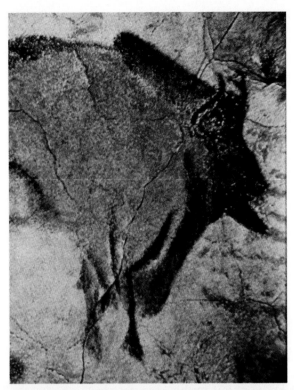

▲ Prehistoric cave paintings like this lifelike bison tell how skilled and observant early humans were.

and supplied the first human hunters with plenty of meat. As the ice melted, the hunting and gathering way of life of early humans gradually spread north from Africa throughout Asia and Europe. Many centuries later, some Asian people entered the Americas by a land bridge that once connected Siberia and Alaska. Others traveled to Australia and the Pacific Islands. Although people first lived in the milder regions of the planet, they proved that they could adapt to a wide variety of conditions. By the end of the Ice Age, people were living on nearly every landmass on earth.

8. People who lived during the last fifty thousand years of the Old Stone Age probably looked very much as people do today. They also had the same basic human needs. They needed to find ways of getting enough food to eat, staying warm and dry, and protecting themselves from danger. What are some of your basic human needs?

9. The ability to make tools gave early humans a special advantage over other animals sharing the environment. Axes made of stone were used to dig for food, cut wood, and scrape animal hides. As time went on, people also learned to use materials such as animal bones to make knives, spears, arrowheads, fishing-hooks, and bows and arrows. Such tools helped early humans hunt animals much larger and stronger than themselves.

10. People in the Old Stone Age were **nomads** (NOH-madz), or wanderers. They traveled from place to place in search of wild grains and fruits and animals to hunt. The struggle for survival taught them the advantages of living and working together. Soon language developed as a way of sharing thoughts and experiences.

11. Human life greatly improved after the discovery of fire some 750,000 years ago. Control of fire allowed early humans to keep warm and cook food. Fire was also used to hunt wild animals and to keep them out of the caves where early humans lived. With a burning hearth to provide heat and light, a cave could become a home and not merely a shelter for the night. Control of light and warmth also allowed people to gather together at night. As they gathered to share stories about the past and make plans for the future, their language grew richer.

OUTLOOK

12. The Old Stone Age gradually came to an end about 12,000 years ago. As the last glacier retreated and the earth grew warmer, many people settled in what had been ice-covered northern regions of the world. When mammoths and other large animals became extinct, people began to depend more on small game, fish, and wild plants for their survival. The human population had increased greatly over the centuries, and people had learned to live and work together in small communities. What do you think the next step might have been in the development of human life?

CHAPTER REVIEW

VOCABULARY REVIEW

Write each of the following sentences on a sheet of paper. Then fill in the blank with the word that best completes each sentence.

1. Time before written history is _____.

2. _____ study the life and culture of ancient peoples by digging for ancient cities and artifacts.

3. _____ study myths, customs, and social interactions of ancient people.

4. The _____ period is also known as the Old Stone Age.

5. A _____ is a large mass of ice.

6. _____ are members of a tribe that moves about in search of food.

a. glacier

b. anthropologists

c. archaeologists

d. prehistoric

e. nomads

f. Paleolithic

g. Old Stone Age

SKILL BUILDER: SOURCES OF INFORMATION

Historians are like detectives as they look for information about the past. Fossils, paintings, and buried cities are the things they study to learn about prehistoric people who left no written records. If you want to know about prehistoric people, the best way would be to examine some of these **firsthand sources of information**, such as fossils and paintings. Since these sources are not easily available to you, you must use **secondhand information**, such as photographs and books.

People's ability to speak and write has been a useful historical tool for unearthing information about the past. Historians, or people who write history, may depend upon earlier historians for information, or they may look at other written records from the past. Sometimes the language of a place gives more information than the human remains, tools, and statues uncovered from long ago.

An excellent firsthand source, which can also be called an **original source**, is a record of events written by a person who actually took part in the events. Those who saw something happen and wrote about it are among our best sources of information.

Very often, however, there are two eyewitnesses to the same event. They may give completely different accounts of what happened. Did you ever hear two witnesses to an argument tell who started it? Do you always agree with the umpire in a baseball game? Historians face this kind of problem when they study different accounts of the same event and try to decide which is the correct one. They must decide which sources are most reliable.

For example, imagine that you wanted to learn about two astronauts in orbit around the moon who are having trouble with the oxygen system in their spacecraft. Some of the sources of information about this event would be:

a. the report of the astronauts from the spacecraft

b. the report of the space controllers on the ground in touch with the astronauts

c. a television discussion of the trouble

d. a report by a friend who tells you about the trouble

e. a newspaper story of the trouble in the spacecraft

8

1. Which of these is the best source of information?

2. Which is the next best source?

3. Which source is the least reliable?

4. Why might several people seeing the same event give different accounts of what happened?

SKILL BUILDER: CRITICAL THINKING AND COMPREHENSION

▲ Main Idea

The main idea is the most important idea in a paragraph. It tells what the paragraph is about. Often the main idea is in the first sentence of the paragraph. Sometimes the main idea can be found in another sentence of the paragraph.

Supporting details tell more about the main idea. They support the main idea or make it stronger. They help to prove that the main idea of the paragraph is true.

Read the following paragraph:

> Mary Leakey is a well-known British archaeologist who has studied the prehistoric life of ancient Africa. While searching in Tanzania in 1959, she found a humanlike skull that is thought to be 1.8 million years old. Later, in Kenya, she and her husband, Louis, discovered fragments of a jaw and teeth thought to be 14 million years old.

Notice that the main idea of the paragraph is the first sentence. These details support the main idea:

She found a humanlike skull that is about 1.8 million years old.

She found fragments of a jaw and teeth thought to be 14 million years old.

When reading a chapter or other material that contains many facts, look for the main ideas and supporting details.

▶ What is the main idea of paragraph 11 in the chapter you have just read?

   a. Later, these people mastered the art of starting fires as they were needed.

   b. Human life was strongly affected by the discovery of fire some 750,000 years ago.

   c. Control of light and warmth also allowed people to extend their days.

ENRICHMENT

1. Prepare a report on Paleolithic art. What sort of art did prehistoric people make? What was the subject matter of their art? What do you think their purpose was in creating art?

2. Make a drawing, painting, or diorama to illustrate a scene of family life in the Old Stone Age.

CHAPTER 2

Civilization Begins

▲ The lives of these Mongol nomads are similar to those of herders in the New Stone Age, when the first civilizations were beginning to appear.

OBJECTIVE: What is civilization?

1. At some time, you have probably heard someone tell a rude or impolite person to behave like a civilized human being. We all know that we are expected to behave in a civilized manner, but what does it actually mean to be "civilized"? The word **civilization** (siv-uh-luh-ZAY-shun) comes from a Latin word *civilis,* which refers to a community of citizens or a city. A civilization usually has four ingredients: the specialization of labor, an organized set of laws, a writing system, and a population that can support a **culture** (KUL-chur) over a long period of time. Culture is the way of life of a group of people, often including music, art, and writings. Long before there were cities, human beings had begun to learn ways of living and working together. As time went by, people slowly gave up their nomadic way of life and settled into permanent communities. Some of these small, loosely

		Earliest settlements of New Stone Age c. 8000 B.C.		Pottery and weaving c. 7000 B.C.		Neolithic or New Stone Age ends c. 4000 B.C.
Sewing begins c. 11,000 B.C.						
12,000 B.C.	**10,000 B.C.**	**8000 B.C.**		**6000 B.C.**		**4000 B.C.**
Bow and arrow invented c. 11,000 B.C.		Domestication of animals; wheat grown in Middle East c. 8000 B.C.		Metal working begins in Asia c. 6500 B.C.		Potter's wheel used in Mesopotamia c. 3500 B.C.

10

organized tribal villages grew into great cities. The rise of civilization had begun.

AGRICULTURE: What role did farming play in the beginning of civilization?

2. Human beings had come a long way over the thousands of years of the Old Stone Age. The people who lived 12,000 years ago were masters of the basic rules of survival. They were highly skilled in hunting and gathering and had developed ways of dealing with wild animals and harsh weather. In many places the end of the last Ice Age brought warmer weather, increased rainfall, and a longer growing season. Where food was plentiful, people settled in one place for longer periods of time.

3. The Old Stone Age slowly came to an end around 8000 B.C. as more people turned from food gathering to food raising. No one knows exactly how the idea of farming first came about. Perhaps the idea of planting crops started when someone noticed what happened to seeds when they were dropped on fertile soil. Sometimes the seeds sprouted and grew into new plants that produced food. This discovery of farming gave early people some control over their food supply for the first time in history.

4. Farming seems to have begun around 7000 B.C. in the Middle East. From there, it quickly spread to the continents of Europe and Africa. Wheat, barley, lentils, and peas were among the first farm crops. Before long, Asians were growing yams and rice while people in the Americas turned to beans and corn.

5. The change from hunting and gathering to an agricultural way of life did not happen overnight. Farming could not have started without the established success of the hunters and gatherers. The farmers still depended upon hunting and gathering for most of their food supply. The first farmers were probably women who planted seeds near their caves or in a patch of cleared ground.

6. The **domestication** (duh-mes-tih-KAY-shun), or taming, of animals began at about the same time that farming first appeared. Just as people had learned to control the growth of wild plants, they learned to control animals. For example, they could have a steady supply of milk and meat by herding sheep and goats. Later, pigs, cattle, and dogs were domesticated as well. The idea of keeping dogs and other animals as pets also arose at this time. Before long, dogs were being used to help in the hunt and to round up other animals on the farm.

SPOTLIGHT ON SOURCES

7. Sheep bones nearly 11,000 years old have been found in some ancient human settlements in the Middle East. Scientists still debate whether dogs, sheep, or goats were the first animals to be domesticated.

Daily life in . . .

Çatal Hüyük, a settlement in what is now Turkey, was one of the first towns in the world. Nearly 6,000 people lived in about 1,000 mudbrick houses squeezed into an area of about 30 acres. The people who lived there 8000 years ago irrigated the land they farmed and raised cattle. They were also active in trade and industry. These skilled woodworkers, weavers, and potters brought in most of their raw materials from outlying villages. Art and religion played an important role in their lives. Shrine rooms were built for the practice of religion that centered on a supreme Mother Goddess. Beautiful sculptures, wall paintings, and ceremonial objects have been unearthed by archaeologists at this ancient site. These artifacts tell about a highly complex Neolithic culture on the doorstep of civilization.

ESL/LEP Strategy: Have students reread paragraph 3. Review any difficult words in the paragraph. Then, ask students to draw a picture that illustrates the main idea. You may wish to display art in class.

11

In his book *On Farming*, written in the first century B.C., Marcus Terentius Varro, a great scholar of ancient Rome, expressed his opinion.

> There is reason to believe that amongst animals sheep were the first to be adopted, on account of their usefulness and gentle nature, because they are extremely gentle and especially fitted for association with man's life, for through them milk and cheese were added to his food, while for his body they furnished clothing in the shape of skins.
>
> —from *On Farming*, Marcus Terentius Varro

▶ How do you think New Stone Age humans domesticated sheep?

8. As more and more prehistoric people took to farming or became better at it, new ways of living began to develop. Prehistoric farmers learned to use fertilizers to enrich the soil. They also learned to dig **irrigation** (ihr-uh-GAY-shun) ditches to bring water to land that would otherwise be too dry for raising crops. To irrigate means to supply with water. Farmers soon discovered that a

forked stick could be drawn through the ground to plant seeds. Later, a larger piece of wood, used as a plow, was attached to a rope pulled by cattle. Although caves were still sometimes used for shelter, many prehistoric people began building homes because they could settle in one place. Their houses were made of wood, mud, or straw. Homes were built close together, and people began thinking of themselves as members of a community. Villages and towns arose as more and more people began living together in permanent settlements.

NEW WAYS OF LIVING: How did life change in the New Stone Age?

9. The **Neolithic** (nee-oh-LITH-ik), or "New Stone," Age was characterized by the invention of many new and improved tools. Sandstone was used to polish and sharpen the cutting edge of stone blades. The resulting tools were far better than the primitive flints used throughout the Old Stone Age. How do you think the idea of boring a hole ◀ through the center of an ax head came about? The idea of attaching a handle to

▼ Archaeologists have built this model of part of the village of Çatal Hüyük. The houses were built so close together that they were entered by wooden ladders to their flat roofs.

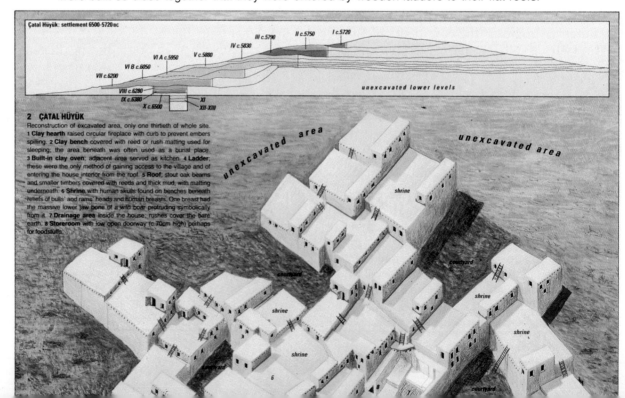

Çatal Hüyük: settlement 6500-5720 BC

I c.5720
II c.5750
III c.5790
IV c.5830
V c.5880
VI A c.5950
VI B c.6050
VII c.6200
VIII c.6280
IX c.6380
X c.6500
XI
XII-XIII

unexcavated lower levels

2 ÇATAL HÜYÜK
Reconstruction of excavated area, only one thirtieth of whole site. **1 Clay hearth** raised circular fireplace with curb to prevent embers spilling. **2 Clay bench** covered with reed or rush matting used for sleeping; the area beneath was often used as a burial place. **3 Built-in clay oven**; adjacent area served as kitchen. **4 Ladder**; these were the only method of gaining access to the village and of entering the house interior from the roof. **5 Roof**; stout oak beams and smaller timbers covered with reeds and thick mud, with matting underneath. **6 Shrine** with human skulls found on benches beneath reliefs of bulls' and rams' heads and human breasts. One breast had the massive lower jaw bone of a wild boar protruding symbolically from it. **7 Drainage area** inside the house; rushes cover the bare earth. **8 Storeroom** with low open doorway (c.70cm high) perhaps for foodstuffs.

unexcavated area

shrine

courtyard

▲ Throughout history, people have invented new tools to help them in their work. These tools are from the New Stone Age. Can you tell (or guess) for what each was used?

to an ax head was a giant step forward in the history of toolmaking. Saws, wedges, chisels, and other new tools made woodworking easier. Wooden hoes and stone sickles made farming easier. Prehistoric people also began to use stone to grind the various grains that had become an important part of the human diet. What reasons did these people have for developing new tools?

10. Cloth-weaving and pottery-making were two other skills developed during the New Stone Age. Animal skins had become more scarce as hunting became a less important part of daily life. Cloth woven from wool or flax was a great improvement over hides and pelts as clothing material. Pottery making began around 7000 B.C. when people discovered how to bake clay to make bowls, dishes, and cooking utensils. Pottery making took less time and energy than carving household objects out of solid stone. The invention of the potter's wheel was probably the first important step toward the use of the wheel for carts. By studying fragments of pottery, called **shards** (SHARDZ),

archaeologists have learned a great deal about ancient settlements and migration routes. The patterns and colors used in the pottery give archaeologists clues to specific times and places. Why do you think this ◀ is so? Because of the clues it provides, pottery has been called the "alphabet of archaeology."

11. With the production of cloth and pottery came increased trade and the specialization of labor. Farming was now a source of food, so prehistoric people did not have to spend all day in search of food. They were able to specialize in particular jobs. Some people continued to work as farmers. Others became weavers, potters, or flint miners. A **barter economy** (BAHR-tur ih-KAH-nuh-mee) arose, which means that people exchanged their goods and services directly, without using money. Soon distant groups of people began to trade with one another. People called **merchants** (MUR-chunts) became necessary to arrange the exchange of goods between villages. Merchants are people who buy and sell goods for profit. As trade expanded, boat-building became an

Ask: Why was the first pottery probably made by women?
Background: The potter's wheel was probably the first wheel used by prehistoric people. The wheel would soon replace the rolling log as a means of moving carts pulled by powerful animals.

13

The Earliest Civilizations Civilization began in four river valleys located in the dry lands of Asia and North Africa. Geographic conditions in the four valleys favored early settlement. Rivers in the four valleys never ran dry. They brought water into the dry lands from distant mountains and made irrigation possible. Frequent flooding made soils in the valleys fertile. A lack of forests made the dry lands easy to clear for growing crops. A dry, sunny climate helped grain crops ripen and kept them from becoming moldy when stored. Early farmers found all these conditions ideal for growing grain and other crops. When large surpluses of grain began to build up, one of the basic requirements of a civilization—a food supply for the city dwellers—had been met.

The locations of the four earliest civilizations are shown on the map on this page. The four early civilizations, in the order in which they arose were:

Mesopotamia: a dry land in southwest Asia. Early farmers worked together to build canals to carry water from the Tigris and Euphrates rivers to irrigate their crops.

Egypt: a dry land in the Sahara Desert. Yearly floods from the Nile River left lands along the river fertile and moist enough for growing crops.

The Indus Valley: a desert region in present-day India and Pakistan. The Indus River brings water into this desert region from snow fields atop the Himalaya Mountains.

The Huang He (Yellow River) Valley in North China. Stone-free soils blown out from the Gobi Desert make lands along the Huang He River unusually fertile and easy to farm.

Study the map of early civilizations below and answer these questions.

1. Along which rivers did each of the earliest civilizations arise?

2. Near which deserts did each of the four earliest civilizations arise?

3. How did the environments in each of the four river valley civilizations challenge early human settlers? How did early humans respond to the challenge?

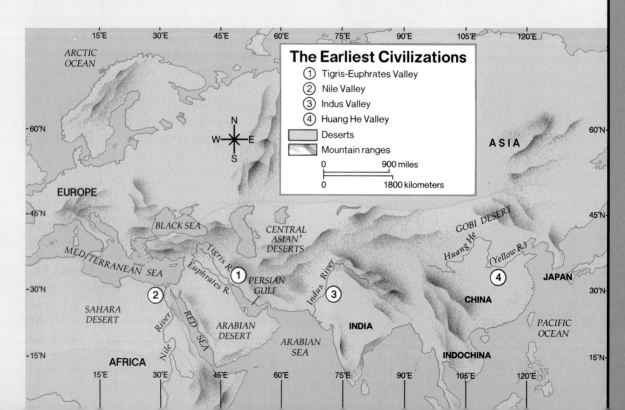

The Earliest Civilizations
① Tigris-Euphrates Valley
② Nile Valley
③ Indus Valley
④ Huang He Valley
▢ Deserts
▨ Mountain ranges

0 — 900 miles
0 — 1800 kilometers

▲ The fertile land of the Nile River valley is in stark contrast to the desert that surrounds it. Why did all of the earliest civilizations begin in surroundings like these?

important industry, and the first roads appeared. Food could be grown in one place and shipped to another in exchange for hand-crafted textiles, beautifully decorated pottery, and copper trinkets.

12. The craft of metalworking was just beginning at the very end of the New Stone Age. Before long, people would learn to combine copper with other substances to make new, harder metals called **alloys** (AL-oyz). A mix of copper and tin, called bronze, was one of the first alloys. With bronze, people could make stronger tools, fancier jewelry, and deadlier weapons.

13. Large permanent settlements changed the way in which people set up rules. At first, village elders may have kept the peace by using tribal traditions to settle arguments. As the population grew, however, disagreements also grew more numerous. Religious leaders and warrior chiefs stepped in to explain customs and make them into law. In some places a class of full-time soldiers arose to enforce those laws. As warfare between settlements became more common, small villages began banding together for protection. Cities grew larger, and local leaders were replaced by powerful kings. Increasingly, community decisions were made by some people while the work was carried out by others.

OUTLOOK

14. The New Stone Age drew to a close about six thousand years ago. By then many people lived in cities. As society grew more complex, the need to keep records arose. Property owners wanted to make lists of their holdings. Merchants wanted to make lists of their goods and keep track of their trading activities. Kings wanted to list the people under their rule for taxation and military service. Priests wanted to write down religious traditions. With the coming of fixed settlements, word-of-mouth was not enough to keep important information. The invention of writing marked the end of the prehistoric era. Why do you suppose ◀ history is said to begin with the invention of writing?

15

CHAPTER REVIEW

VOCABULARY REVIEW

Write each number and word or phrase on a piece of paper. Write the letter of the definition next to the word or phrase it matches.

1. domestication
2. irrigation
3. shards
4. alloy
5. civilization
6. merchants
7. barter economy
8. culture

a. a man-made system of moving water from one place to another
b. a mixture of metals
c. the exchange of goods and services without using money
d. taming
e. pottery fragments
f. a community of citizens with a writing system, an organized set of laws, specialization of labor, and the ability to support a culture over a long period of time
g. people who buy and sell goods for profit
h. the way of life of a group of people, including their art and music

SKILL BUILDER: PREVIEWING

How do you choose a book from the library to read? Chances are, you leaf through it first to get an idea of what it is about. When you look over a book or selection quickly, before reading it, you are **previewing** that book or selection. Previewing is a skill that helps you figure out what a book or selection is going to be about.

There are some steps you can follow when you preview a selection.

1. The **title** of the selection or chapter tells you what the selection is about. Look at this first.
2. Read any headings that are printed in boldface type. They may help you to better understand what the selection is about.
3. Pay attention to key words or phrases that are boldfaced in a selection. They will give you more information about the selection.
4. While reading the section headings or topic sentences, think of some questions that the selection might answer.

Practice the steps of previewing by applying them to Chapter 3, **Mesopotamia**.

1. Write the title of the chapter.
2. Write the objective of the chapter.
3. Write each subhead of the chapter.
4. Locate and list the vocabulary words.
5. Read the first sentence of each paragraph. Then write two questions for each paragraph you think the paragraph will answer.

Save the questions you have written to use for further reference.

SKILL BUILDER: CRITICAL THINKING AND COMPREHENSION

▲ Main Idea

The main idea is the most important idea of a paragraph. The main idea tells what the paragraph is about. The supporting details give more information about the main idea. These details help to prove that the main idea is true.

▶ Find the main idea for each paragraph listed. Rewrite each main idea and the paragraph number it matches.

1. The Neolithic, or "New Stone," Age was characterized by the invention of many new and improved tools.

2. With the production of cloth and pottery came increased trade and the specialization of labor.

3. Large permanent settlements changed the way people set up community rules.

4. The New Stone Age drew to a close about 6,000 years ago.

Paragraph Number

a. 11

b. 3

c. 9

d. 13

e. 14

Look at the supporting details below. After reading them, write a main idea that they can support.

5. As farming appeared, people became more self-sufficient.

6. People had to learn how to control animals. They could have a steady supply of milk and meat if their animals were tamed.

7. Farmers soon discovered how to use fertilizers, dig irrigation ditches, and build their own homes.

8. Animal skins became less important in daily life because hunting as a way of life declined.

ENRICHMENT

1. Imagine that you live in an ancient town at the dawn of civilization. The ruler of your town has asked for suggestions on how to make life better for the people in the community. Write a speech in which you explain how the specialization of labor and the creation of a barter economy would help to improve the lives of people in your town.

2. Write a story about a family living in the New Stone Age. Show how family life might have been affected by the change from hunting and gathering to an agricultural way of life.

3. Work with two or three other students. Invent a tool of the kind that might have been used for hunting in the Old Stone Age or for agriculture in the New Stone Age. Then prepare an advertisement for the tool. Brag about what the tool does, and tell why it is an improvement over what had been done before. Your advertisement can be a full-page magazine ad, or it can be a one-minute radio or television commercial.

CHAPTER 3

Mesopotamia

▲ The Tigris and Euphrates rivers join at Qurna in the dry lands of present-day Iraq. This area is often called the "cradle of civilization."

OBJECTIVE: How are the Mesopotamian civilizations and the civilizations of today similar?

1. Think about all the writing there is in the world around you. At this very moment you are reading words that are part of a writing system that millions of people use ▶ every day. In what other ways is writing ▶ important to your life? Has writing helped you to figure out a computer game, or find your way by subway or bus, or correctly use medicine? Obviously, you live in a world that depends on writing as a basic means of communication. The first writing was developed almost 5,000 years ago by a people called the Sumerians. The Sumerians developed a system of writing to keep daily records of trade and land exchanges. Before long they used writing to record Sumerian laws and religious beliefs. Other groups of people adapted the Sumerian writing system for their own languages. After reading many Sumerian records, archaeologists and historians have decided that the Sumerians were probably the founders of the first civilization.

	Sumerian civilization begins c. 3500 B.C.			Hammurabi rules Babylon c. 1792–1750 B.C.		Persian empire extends power over Mesopotamia c. 530 B.C.
3500 B.C.	**3000 B.C.**	**2500 B.C.**	**2000 B.C.**	**1500 B.C.**	**1000 B.C.**	**500 B.C.**
	First written documents 3200–2850 B.C.	Sumerian city-states develop c. 3000 B.C.	Babylonians invade Mesopotamia c. 2000 B.C.		Assyrians defeat Babylonians c. 900 B.C.	Assyrian capital of Nineveh is sacked c. 612 B.C.

MESOPOTAMIA: Why were different groups of people drawn to the valley of Mesopotamia?

▶ **2.** The Sumerian civilization began in the Middle East in a valley between the Tigris and Euphrates rivers. Can you find the Tigris and Euphrates rivers on the map on page 21? Into what body of water do these rivers flow? The valley is called Mesopotamia, meaning "land between the rivers." Mesopotamia was part of the **Fertile Crescent**, an area of land that stretched from the Persian Gulf to the Mediterranean Sea.

3. The Mesopotamian valley provided several important natural resources for survival of the Sumerians. One resource was the abundant supply of water from the rivers. A second resource was a natural supply of food that included fish, wildfowl, and dates from the date palm tree. A third resource was soil, which was used for both growing crops and making bricks and pottery.

4. From about 3500 B.C. to about 530 B.C., at least seven different groups of people ruled the Mesopotamian valley. The most important were the Sumerians and the Babylonians. The Sumerians were the first people to build a civilization in Mesopotamia. The other groups that invaded Mesopotamia were probably attracted to the region by its wealthy cities and its abundant supplies of food and water. Look at the
▶ map of Mesopotamia on page 21. Were there any natural barriers to protect Mesopotamia from invasions?

THE SUMERIANS: How did the Sumerians create a civilization?

5. Among the key ingredients of a civilization is specialization of labor. The most important and first labor skill the Sumerians developed was the ability to farm. They grew crops such as grains and **dates**. A date is a sweet, fleshy fruit with a hard seed in the center. The Sumerians became so skilled at growing crops that fewer people were needed to work in the fields. As the food supply increased, some people became available to do other kinds of work and develop other skills. Potters invented the potter's wheel to spin clay into beautifully shaped pottery. Other Sumerians made sailboats, wheeled carts, animal-drawn plows, medicines, and cosmetics. Still others became government leaders and religious leaders. Some Sumerians who had learned how to read and write became scribes. Scribes kept daily records, mostly on the amount of food that was harvested and how it was used. Sumerian builders built thick walls around their cities for protection and large temples for worship. They also built canals that brought water to their crops and helped to control the flood waters. These irrigation systems turned dry lands into green fields.

6. The second key ingredient of a civilization is a system of writing. It would be difficult to have an organized society with-
◀ out a system of writing. Why do you think this is so? The Sumerians developed the first system of writing that was more than just pictures. Their writing is called **cuneiform** (kyoo-NEE-uh-form). The wedge-shaped cuneiform symbols were made with a reed, called a stylus, pressed on wet clay tablets. The clay tablets were then dried in the sun or baked over fire until they were hard. About one-half million of these clay tablets have lasted for thousands of years and can be read today. They tell us that the Sumerians had an organized way of gathering, sorting, and trading food and other goods. These records tell us, too, about Sumerian government, religion, wars, and building projects. The records also tell us that the scribes were trained in schools set up in the temples.

7. The third key ingredient of a civilization is government with an organized set of laws. This government rules from a central place, such as a city, a palace, or a temple. The Sumerian civilization was organized into 12 separate units called **city-states**. Each city-state ruled the city and its surrounding farmland. Sumerians believed that each city-state belonged to a god or goddess that owned the land and controlled the yearly floods. Each city-state built a

Background: Point out to students that dates were an excellent supplement to the Sumerian diet because the dates ripened at the season when other crops were at their lowest supply.

19

▲ Temple towers, or ziggurats, were the largest buildings in ancient Mesopotamia, and they were important centers for government and religion. This reconstructed ziggurat is at Ur.

ziggurat (ZIG-oo-rat), or temple, to honor its god or goddess. Made of sun-baked clay, the pyramid-shaped ziggurats were the largest buildings in the city-states. The Sumerians believed that the gods and goddesses controlled everything that happened in their lives. As a result, the religious leaders were powerful in the city-states. For example, they controlled the land, collected and stored the crops, and owned large herds of sheep and cattle.

8. The king was also an important leader in each city-state. Historians believe that the powerful role of the king developed because of disagreements among the city-

▶ states. What kinds of things do you suppose the city-states might disagree about? The king became the military leader of the city-state. He trained the citizens to fight for their city and led them into battle. The king probably also oversaw the production of spears, shields, and other military equipment and the building of walls around the central city.

9. The last ingredient of a civilization is a culture supported by a large population

over a long period of time. Why do you ◀ think the Sumerian civilization lasted so long? As the Sumerians improved their food production, their population grew. As the population grew, rich landowners often moved to the central city for protection from raiders. As the cities grew, so did trade, specialization of labor, and the need for laws. The ability to read and write helped to unify the culture, laws, and traditions of the Sumerians. Because the Sumerians had developed this well-ordered society, their city-states and cultures lasted for nearly 1,000 years.

BABYLON: What have archaeologists learned about the Babylonians?

10. With no natural barriers to keep invaders out, the Sumerian city-states were subjected to a series of invasions after 2300 B.C. When the invaders took over the Sumerian lands, they probably hoped to become part of the Sumerian way of life. What happened instead was that each group of

Ask: Have you ever heard of the "Hanging Gardens of Babylon"? The Hanging Gardens were called one of the wonders of the ancient world.

invaders created a new civilization, borrowing much from the earlier ones in the process. The first successful invader was Sargon of Akkad. Sargon was a brilliant soldier who established a large empire. After his death, however, the Sumerians regained control of their land.

11. About 2,000 B.C., new invaders established Babylon (BAB-ih-lahn) as the center of their rule. By 1700 B.C., Babylon ruled most of Mesopotamia. Although the Babylonians took over Mesopotamia, they did not completely destroy the old Sumerian culture. In fact, they adopted much of the Sumerian way of life. One of the most important things they adopted was cuneiform. Babylonian scribes wrote volumes of new texts. They also recopied Sumerian texts.

12. From the supply of tablets that were preserved, much has been learned about the Babylonians. For example, their society was well organized. The soldiers, priests of high rank, and the landowners were the most important members of society. Next came the craftspeople, traders, and farmers. At the bottom of society were the poor people and the slaves (who had originally been prisoners of war). The tablets also show that the Babylonians were probably the first to understand and use the principles of algebra and geometry.

13. The king who had the greatest influence on Babylon was Hammurabi, who came to power in 1792 B.C. The strength of his rule grew out of his wish to promote justice, destroy wicked people, and protect weak people from strong people. To do this, Hammurabi had 282 laws written on clay tablets. Those laws are called the **Code of Hammurabi** (KOHD uv hah-moo-RAH-bee), and they were displayed throughout Babylon. In this way the people of Babylon understood the laws and what would happen if they failed to obey the laws. Many of the laws in the Code of Hammurabi were based on older laws. Hammurabi, however, was the first ruler to organize these laws into a complete system.

▼ The great Mesopotamian civilizations arose at the eastern end of the Fertile Crescent. What two rivers helped make Mesopotamia fertile?

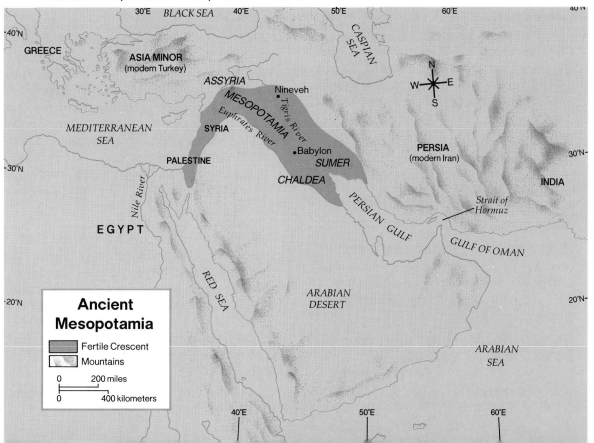

Ancient Mesopotamia

Fertile Crescent
Mountains

0   200 miles
0   400 kilometers

▲ The sculpture atop a pillar with the Code of Hammurabi shows the king receiving symbols of authority from the Mesopotamian sun god.

SPOTLIGHT ON SOURCES

14. The Code of Hammurabi covered such things as trade agreements, family problems, actions against people or property, and rules about land use. Compare the following with modern laws.

> If a builder builds a house . . . and does not make the construction [building] firm, and the house that he has built collapses [falls down] and causes a death, that builder shall be put to death.
>
> If a man, in a case [trial] utters [speaks] against the witness and does not prove the testimony he has given [tell the truth] in a case involving life, that man shall be put to death.
>
> If a son strikes his father, they shall cut off his [the son's] fingers.
>
> —*From The Code of Hammurabi*

How do you think people in the United States today would react to these laws?

THE ASSYRIANS: How were the Assyrians different from the Sumerians and Babylonians?

15. From the end of Hammurabi's rule in 1750 B.C. until about 900 B.C., Mesopotamia was raided and ruled by different groups of people. Each group brought its own traditions to add to the culture of Babylon. Then, about 900 B.C., Babylon was conquered by the Assyrians.

16. Assyria was a land to the north of Mesopotamia. Unlike the Mesopotamians, the Assyrians did not have to deal with irrigation and conflicts over water rights. Their crops were nourished by rainfall. Assyria was also a major trading center. Metals and textiles were regularly traded in Assyria and brought great wealth to the Assyrians. With a plentiful supply of metals, the Assyrians became skilled at metalcrafting. Why did their skill in metal crafting give the Assyrians an advantage in war?

17. From about 900 B.C. to about 630 B.C., Assyria's warlike people built a large empire. The well-trained Assyrian army included soldiers who rode into battle on chariots. The Assyrians used spears, swords, and arrows that were made of iron. They wore metal helmets and chest guards to protect themselves in battle. How do you think these new military and metalworking skills helped the Assyrians to conquer Mesopotamia? The Assyrians also used terror as a weapon. They treated the people they captured cruelly. They beheaded enemy chiefs and made slaves of many soldiers they conquered in battle.

18. The Assyrian capital was the walled city of Nineveh (NIN-uh-vuh). There the Assyrians built large palaces decorated with stone carvings showing religious **rites** (RYTS) and their army in battle. A rite is a formal, serious custom. In Nineveh one of the Assyrian rulers built a library in which he kept more than 22,000 clay tablets. These tablets, written in cuneiform, helped to

Activity: Some students might like to research and draw Assyrian weapons and chariots to display. Keep the illustrations and have students compare weapons among cultures and across the centuries.

preserve the records of Sumeria and Babylon.

19. The Assyrian Empire at its height lasted for only about 100 years. Assyrian rulers were cruel and harsh, which caused the people they had conquered to revolt. In 612 B.C., Nineveh was captured by the Chaldeans (KAL-dee-unz) and the Medes (MEEDZ), who then divided up the Assyrian Empire. Led by King Nebuchadrezzar (neb-yuh-kud-REZ-ur), the Chaldeans now ruled Mesopotamia, where they rebuilt the Babylonian Empire. The Medes took control of the lands north of Mesopotamia.

THE PERSIANS: How did the Persians unite and rule their vast empire in the Middle East?

20. About 530 B.C., the Persians began to build one of the largest empires yet established in the ancient Middle East. The Persians were a group of nomads who settled in present-day Iran, the land to the east of Mesopotamia. Led by their ruler, Cyrus the Great, the Persians defeated the Medes in 550 B.C. Then, in 539 B.C., they defeated the Chaldeans and made Babylon a part of the Persian Empire. The Persians also conquered other lands until, at the peak of their power, they ruled an empire reaching from Greece all the way to India.

21. The Persians were skillful rulers whose empire lasted for more than 200 years. Darius I made the huge empire easier to rule by dividing it into 20 **satrapies** (SAY-truh-peez), or provinces. The conquered peoples were allowed to keep their own religions, languages, and customs. However, ruling so many different peoples was a difficult task. Therefore, Darius I organized a group of loyal spies who watched for unrest in the empire. To help unite the empire, the Persians built roads and set up a unified system of laws, taxes, and money. Darius I also had a system of roads built that improved communication and trade in the empire. The king's messengers raced along these roads. Their horses ▶ were the first to wear horseshoes. Why was the horseshoe an important invention?

▲ The Assyrians' warlike ways are reflected in their art. Here an Assyrian sculpture shows a king attacking a lion.

OUTLOOK

22. The Sumerians of Mesopotamia established the first great civilization. They had a well-organized system of laws, the first writing system, and an excellent system of record keeping. The Sumerians also had a strong belief in their gods. Even though their land was conquered by a series of invaders, many of the Sumerian ideas and ways lasted and spread to other groups of people. Some of the Sumerian traditions were adopted and improved by other groups of people. As you study the history of the world, you will discover that the traditions of some peoples have lasted to today. The traditions of other peoples may be gone forever. Why do you think some ◀ traditions are saved and copied, while others are not? Can you think of an American ◀ tradition that has been copied by other nations?

23

CHAPTER REVIEW

1. Fertile Crescent
2. date
3. scribe
4. cuneiform
5. city-state
6. ziggurat
7. Code of Hammurabi
8. chariot
9. rite
10. satrapies

a. a person who records information
b. a type of fruit popular in the Middle East
c. a ritual or ceremony
d. an ancient temple
e. a type of writing which uses wedge-shaped marks
f. a set of laws developed by a Mesopotamian king
g. an independent urban area which controls the surrounding land
h. governors of ancient Persian provinces
i. an area of rich land between the Persian Gulf and the Mediterranean Sea

SKILL BUILDER: READING A TABLE

Use the table to help you complete each sentence that follows the table.

THE SUMERIANS AND THE ELEMENTS OF CIVILIZATION

Specialization of labor	A System of writing	Organized government ruling from a central place	A culture supported by a large population over a long period of time
Farmers Construction workers	cuneiform wedge-shaped stylus	Twelve city-states Religious leaders ziggurats	The Sumerian civilization lasted 1000 years
Religious leaders Government leaders Potters Carpenters Pharmacists Scribes Cosmeticians	clay tablets scribes	Kings Laws Military	No census taken but population large enough to support twelve city-states.

1. The title of the table is _____ .
2. The four elements of civilization are _____ .
3. You know that the Sumerians had specialization of labor because _____ .
4. The tools the Sumerians needed to write with were _____ .
5. Two types of Sumerian leaders were _____ and _____ .
6. The Sumerian civilization lasted _____ .

24

SKILL BUILDER: CRITICAL THINKING AND COMPREHENSION

1. Main Idea

The main idea tells what a paragraph is about. Often the main idea is the first sentence of a paragraph. There are usually details in a paragraph that support the main idea. Locating the main idea and supporting details of a paragraph is a great study aid.

1-1. Match each main idea to the correct paragraph number.

Main Idea	Paragraph Number
a. The Mesopotamian Valley provided several important natural resources for survival.	8
	18
	21
b. The Assyrian capital was the walled city of Nineveh.	12
	3
	10
c. The king was also an important leader in each city-state.	
d. The Persians were skillful rulers whose empire lasted for more than 200 years.	
e. From the supply of tablets that were preserved, much has been learned about the Babylonians.	

1-2. Reread the text and write the main idea for each group of supporting details:

a. Abundant supply of water, natural supply of food, soil used both for growing crops and making bricks and pottery.

d. Tigris and Euphrates rivers, "land between the rivers," part of the Fertile Crescent.

b. Wanted to promote justice and protect weak people, developed a code of laws; people understood the laws and the punishment.

e. Grew crops, invented the potter's wheel; made sailboats and plows; had government leaders and religious leaders; had scribes; built city walls and canals.

c. Well-trained army, chariots, spears, swords, arrows, helmets and chest guards; terror was a weapon.

ENRICHMENT

1. Use library reference materials to help you draw three symbols of the Mesopotamian culture. The symbols might include cuneiform, a ziggurat, an irrigated field, a Mesopotamian god, or a diagram of a city-state.

2. The Assyrians and Persians were two powerful groups of invaders who took over Mesopotamia. Use library reference materials to help you research how this group of invaders fit the four ingredients of a civilization. Create a table similar to the one about the Sumerians.

CHAPTER 4

Ancient Egypt

OBJECTIVE: What were the key strengths of ancient Egyptian civilization that allowed it to last for 3,000 years?

▶ **1.** Did your community ever suffer a flood during which you had to move up onto drier ground and clean up slimy mud afterwards? Or did your community ever suffer a drought during which you had to be careful of water use? If you have ever experienced such troubles, they will give you some idea of the challenges faced by the people of ancient Egypt. Droughts and floods along the great Nile River were a regular part of Eygptian life. The Eyptians lived in a hot, dry desert where it almost never rains. Each year, without any rain falling over Egypt, the Nile would overflow, flooding the lands near it and leaving behind a layer of rich
▶ soil. Why is Egypt sometimes called "the

▲ An Egyptian farmer lifts water from the Nile River for irrigation. Irrigated agriculture flourished in Egypt more than 4,000 years ago.

gift of the Nile"? The ancient Egyptians believed that the crocodile god called Sobek gave the Nile the power to rise. What they did not know was that summer rains come each year to the Ethiopian highlands. The lessons that Egyptians learned about cop-

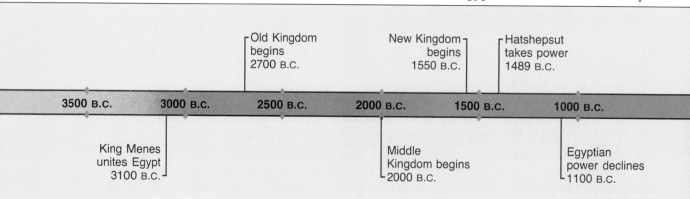

		Old Kingdom begins 2700 B.C.		New Kingdom begins 1550 B.C.	Hatshepsut takes power 1489 B.C.	
3500 B.C.	3000 B.C.	2500 B.C.	2000 B.C.	1500 B.C.	1000 B.C.	
	King Menes unites Egypt 3100 B.C.		Middle Kingdom begins 2000 B.C.		Egyptian power declines 1100 B.C.	

ing with their drought-stricken land and life-giving floods laid the foundations for one of the earliest and greatest civilizations.

THE NILE VALLEY: Why did early civilization in Egypt develop in the Nile River valley?

2. The dry **desert** (DEZ-urt) land of Egypt is located in the northeastern part of Africa. The Nile River flows south to north through Egypt, bringing rich soil along with water to the desert land. Today dams control the river's flooding. However, in ancient times the Nile River would rise every year in July and by September would flood the flatland of the Nile valley. The harvest of crops each year depended on how much water the Nile brought. Egypt's farmers also dug ditches and canals to water their crops.

3. About 7000 B.C., nomadic people moved into the Nile valley and began to farm the rich soil. By about 3500 B.C., they were living in a number of small villages and growing wheat, barley, and vegetables. Gradually these villages were united under a single government. Each of the early villages in Egypt had its own ruler. Then the rulers of certain villages gained control over other villages. After many hundreds of years, the villages were joined together to form two kingdoms. Finally about 3100 B.C., King Menes (MEE-neez) united Egypt into one great kingdom.

4. **Pharoah** (FAIR-oh) was the title given to the rulers of ancient Egypt. The title comes from the Egyptian word for palace. King Menes began the first **dynasty** (DY-nus-tee), or family of rulers. During the next 3,000 years, Egypt had 31 dynasties of pharaohs. All but one of these rulers were men.

5. The resources of the Nile River valley and the surrounding desert and seas helped the ancient Egyptian kingdom in other ways besides farming. The valley of the Nile had large supplies of limestone and sandstone. How might these have helped the Egyptians to construct buildings? Even more important, the deserts surrounding the Nile valley protected Egypt from attack

by other peoples. The Mediterranean Sea and the Red Sea also helped to protect it. These deserts and seas formed natural barriers that defended Egypt from invasion for thousands of years. Look at the map on page 29 and locate these deserts and bodies of water. Why do you think it was difficult for enemy peoples to cross the deserts and seas?

6. Because their land was well protected, the Egyptians did not need large armies. Instead, they used their wealth, their resources, and their skills to build a great civilization that lasted more than 3,000 years.

EGYPT'S RELIGION: What were the Egyptians' religious beliefs, and why were they so important in Egypt's civilization?

7. The Egyptians believed in many gods. Egyptians worshiped the sun god Amon-Re; Osiris, the god of the Nile; Isis, the mother goddess; and many others. They believed these gods brought them large crops and good harvests. In fact, Egyptians believed that the gods decided everything that happened to them and their families.

8. Central to the Egyptian religion was the belief in life after death. Egyptians believed that those who had lived good lives would be rewarded with pleasant, happy lives in the next world. Egyptians also believed that they would need their bodies as homes for their souls in the next world. As a result, Egyptians preserved the bodies of the dead. The preserved body is called a **mummy** (MUM-ee).

SPOTLIGHT ON SOURCES

9. All Egyptians planned for the afterlife, but the way the pharaohs prepared was the most elaborate and costly. The pharaohs had huge tombs built for themselves. The tombs were filled with all the treasures the pharaohs believed they would need on their journey to the next world. Their tombs were piled high with food, furniture, jewelry, and other valuable goods. Written messages to

Activity: Have students read about the Egyptian gods. Students, individually or in small groups, can report about individual gods to the class.

27

the gods told about the dead person's good qualities. Here is part of one of these messages:

> Hail to Thee, Great God, Lord of Truth and Justice! . . . I bring unto you Truth . . . . I have not oppressed the poor . . . . I have not laid labor upon any free man beyond that which he wrought [did] for himself . . . . I have not caused the slave to be ill-treated of his master. I have not starved any man, I have not made any to weep, I have not assassinated [killed] any man . . . . I have not committed treason against any. I have not [reduced in any way] the supplies of the temple . . . . I have not taken away milk from the mouths of sucklings [babies] . . . . I am pure. I am pure. I am pure.
>
> From *Our Oriental Heritage*, by Will Durant

▶ What do you think a modern version of this message might say?

10. Wall paintings in the tomb told about the lives of the pharaoh's and their courts. Much of what is now known about Egypt comes from these tombs. Some tombs were carved out of hillsides in the desert. Other tombs were built in secret hiding places in the **pyramids** of ancient Egypt. A pyramid has a square ground plan with outside walls that form four triangles that meet in a point
▶ at the top. Why do you think the pyramids are still standing today?

EGYPT'S GOVERNMENT: What were the powers of the pharaohs, and how did these rulers govern Egypt?

11. The Egyptians believed that each pharaoh was a god on earth. The pharaohs had complete power over their people and government. As gods, they owned all the land and the crops that grew on it. Each pharaoh made all the laws and was the chief judge. The pharaoh also was the high priest who was able to gain the favor of the sun god and other gods for the people.

12. The pharaohs' duty was to care for the people and to protect them by using

▲ The pyramid of Khafre, the second largest of the great pyramids, has towered over the Egyptian desert for nearly 5,000 years.

great power wisely. Priests and high officials helped the pharaohs to govern Egypt. Some of these officials served the pharaohs at court. Others governed different parts of the kingdom. The Egyptian people gave a large amount of their crops to the pharaohs as taxes. They also had a duty to work for the pharaohs by helping to build religious temples and tombs.

EGYPTIAN CIVILIZATION: What were some of the greatest achievements of the Egyptians?

13. The Egyptians were among the first people to work out a system of writing. This writing, called **hieroglyphics** (hy-roh-GLIF-iks), used about 500 pictures and signs to stand for words and sounds. Egyptians used reed brushes and ink to write these hieroglyphics on scrolls, or rolls, of **papyrus** (puh-PY-rus). Papyrus was thick paper

Ask: Why were all Egyptian tombs, including the great pyramids, built in the desert? [Fertile land in the Nile valley was too scarce and valuable to be used for this purpose.]

28

made from plants that grew along the Nile River. Like the Sumerians, Egyptian priests set up schools in the temples to train the scribes.

14. The Egyptians were the greatest builders in the ancient world. Today the 80 pyramids that still stand along the Nile are known throughout the world. The huge pyramid of Pharaoh Khufu at Giza is still the largest structure ever built. This pyramid is nearly 500 feet (152 meters) high, or about as high as a 50-story building. It covers as much land as 12 football fields. This great pyramid at Giza took 100,000 workers nearly 20 years to finish. About 2.3 million huge blocks of limestone were used to build it. Each of these limestone blocks weighed about 2.5 tons. The workers who built the pyramid had to push and pull these huge, heavy blocks of stone by using their muscle power. Most of the workers who built the pyramids were ordinary Egyptian farmers. They performed this labor as a religious duty for the pharaoh.

15. The Egyptians were skilled at measuring time. They developed one of the most accurate calendars in the ancient world. The year was divided into 12 months of 30 days each. The extra 5 days were used as holidays and religious feasts. The Egyptians used this calendar to tell them when the Nile would flood, when to plant crops, and when to harvest them. Egypt's calendar is the basis of the calendar used today.

16. The Egyptians also invented ways to measure land. Each year the Nile floods washed away many of the markers used to show the land boundaries. To remedy this situation, Egyptians developed skillful ways to **survey** (sur–VAY), or to measure, the land. How do people survey land today? ◄

17. Some of the earliest discoveries in medicine were made by the Egyptians. They studied the human body and learned how to mend broken bones. They also discovered how to treat certain illnesses by using herbs. The Egyptians were one of the first people to perform surgery.

EGYPT'S KINGDOMS: What were the three major periods of Egypt's history, and what changes took place in Egypt in these years?

18. Historians divide Egypt's history into three major periods: the Old Kingdom, the Middle Kingdom, and the New Kingdom. The Old Kingdom in Egypt lasted from about 2700 B.C. to 2200 B.C.. In this great period of Egyptian civilization, the largest

SKILL BUILDER/MAPS
Understanding Rivers

The Nile River brings lifegiving waters to the deserts of Egypt from the mountains of Central Africa.

1. Into what sea does the Nile River empty?
2. Does the Nile River flow northwards or southwards? How can you tell?
3. What two headwaters join to form the Nile in Nubia?
4. Which of the two Nile headwaters contributes a steadier flow of water throughout the year? Why?

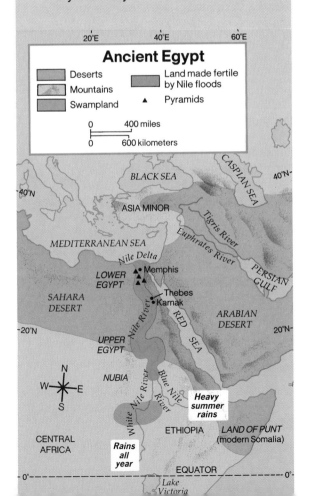

Ancient Egypt

Deserts
Mountains
Swampland
Land made fertile by Nile floods
▲ Pyramids

0   400 miles
0   600 kilometers

29

The Arts and Artifacts

▲ The greatest treasure found in Tutankhamen's tomb was the golden mask that was on the young pharaoh's coffin. In the sculpture (right), the pharaoh is about to spear a hippopotamus. The tomb included a board game, somewhat like checkers, for the king to play in the afterlife.

King Tutankhamen   Tutankhamen (toot-ahnk-AH-mun) became pharaoh of Egypt about 1355 B.C., when he was 10 years old. He ruled the Egyptian empire until his death at the age of 18. In spite of his short life, this young king is probably the best known to us of all Egyptian pharaohs.

In 1922 a crew of archaeologists headed by Howard Carter discovered Tutankhamen's tomb. As he entered the burial chamber, Carter's flashlight revealed a shrine of wood covered with glittering gold. The shrine was 17 feet by 11 feet and nine feet high. When Carter opened another doorway, he later wrote, ". . . on the farther side, stood the most beautiful monument that I have ever seen—so lovely that it made one gasp with wonder and admiration."

The tomb held gold-covered chariots, a solid gold throne, and jewelry set with precious stones. The walls of the tomb were painted with pictures showing the pharaoh and his court on their journey to the other world. There were statues of Tutankhamen's servants as well as stone animals to guard him. There were jewel-covered knives, a toy box, and a paint set that Tutankhamen had used as a child. In the heart of the tomb was the pharaoh's mummy in several thick stone coffins, one inside the other. On the face was a life-size mask made of gold and covered with jewels and beautiful colored glass. This mask showed the pharaoh as he appeared before he died—a good-looking, wise young ruler.

1. How long did King Tutankhamen rule?

2. How does the description of this tomb support what you read in Paragraph 9?

3. How has the discovery of this tomb helped people learn about Egyptian civilization?

pyramids were built for the powerful pharoahs.

19. The Middle Kingdom, which began in 2000 B.C., lasted for nearly 200 years, until about 1800 B.C.. During this time, a new dynasty of pharaohs from Thebes ruled Egypt. These pharaohs reunited the people after a period of civil war. The pharoahs made Egyptian farming and trade prosper again. After the Middle Kingdom ended, Egypt was controlled for a time by foreign invaders called the **Hyksos** (HIK-sohz). The Hyksos finally were driven out about l570 B.C..

20. The New Kingdom, which lasted from about 1550 B.C. to 331 B.C., was the peak of Egypt's power. During this period most pharaohs were skilled rulers. They increased Egypt's trade with nearby lands and made Egypt a wealthy and powerful land once more. The capital at Thebes became the greatest city of the ancient world. The new dynasty also decided that Egypt must build a strong army. The pharaohs were determined to prevent invasions by peoples coming from the Middle East across the Sinai peninsula into Egypt. Study the map on page 29 to find the lands Egypt conquered. The Egyptians built an **empire** (EM-pyr)to protect their own land. An empire is a large area of land ruled by a conquering nation.

▲ Hatshepsut ruled as pharaoh of Egypt for 20 years. The temples that she ordered to be built were among the most beautiful in Egypt.

art and sculpture of ancient Egypt was created while Hatshepsut was pharaoh.

22. After 1100 B.C., Egypt's once mighty empire was attacked by invaders. Several peoples, including the Assyrians and the Persians, invaded Egypt from the Middle East. Finally, in 331 B.C., Alexander the Great of Greece conquered Egypt and ended the 3,000-year-old rule of the pharaohs.

PEOPLE IN HISTORY

21. **Hatshepsut** (hat-SHEP-soot) was one of the most important rulers in the period of the New Kingdom. When Hatshepsut's father died, her brother was expected to become pharaoh. However, Hatshepsut, with the help of priests and powerful court nobles, was made pharaoh instead. Queen Hatshepsut ruled from 1489 B.C. to 1469 B.C.. She was the first woman ruler of any civilization in the ancient world. During her years as pharaoh, Egypt enjoyed peace and prosperity. Hatshepsut increased Egypt's wealth by sending trading ships down the Red Sea to East Africa. Some of the finest

OUTLOOK

23. The civilization of ancient Egypt developed in the Nile River valley. The waters of the Nile allowed the Egyptians to live and prosper in this hot, dry land of North Africa. The people of Egypt learned they could depend on the Nile's yearly floods to grow the food they needed. Therefore, Egyptians felt safe and secure in their land. As a result they developed a way of looking at life that seems very modern. They thought that their life was good, and they believed that their conduct shaped their future. Do you think most Americans today have these same feelings about their lives?

Background: Historians have yet to learn just who the Hyksos were. There is no firm evidence that would relate them to any of the known peoples of the ancient Middle East.

31

CHAPTER REVIEW

VOCABULARY REVIEW

On a separate sheet of paper, copy each number and word listed below. Then write the letter of the definition next to the word it matches.

1. desert
2. mummy
3. pyramid
4. dynasty
5. pharaoh
6. papyrus
7. hieroglyphics

a. writing that used pictures and signs
b. thick paper made from plants
c. large tombs built for pharoahs
d. a succession of related rulers
e. preserved body
f. a dry, waterless land
g. a king in ancient Egypt

SKILL BUILDER: READING A TIME LINE

Time lines are like road maps of history. They give a picture of the passing of time and help you learn the correct order of events. A time line can cover thousands of years or it may cover only 10 or 20 years. To read one correctly you have to be familiar with these historical terms:

An **age** usually means a long period of time, such as the Ice Age or Stone Age.

A **decade** is a period lasting ten years.

B.C. means "before Christ."

A.D. is the short form of anno Domini, the Latin words for "in the year of our Lord."

The time line in this chapter deals with the period before the birth of Jesus. Egypt was already declining long before Jesus was born. To read a B.C. ("before Christ") time line correctly, you have to remember one thing: the higher a B.C. date is, the earlier in history that event occurred. The higher a date is after the birth of Jesus, or A.D., the later that date is.

Study the time line below. Then see if you can answer the questions that follow by using the information on the time line.

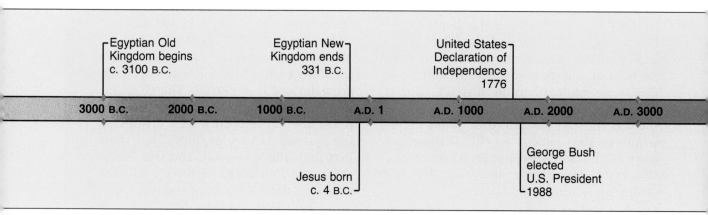

Egyptian Old Kingdom begins c. 3100 B.C.

Egyptian New Kingdom ends 331 B.C.

United States Declaration of Independence 1776

3000 B.C.   2000 B.C.   1000 B.C.   A.D. 1   A.D. 1000   A.D. 2000   A.D. 3000

Jesus born c. 4 B.C.

George Bush elected U.S. President 1988

Make an outline of Chapter 4. Copy the subheads (*The Nile Valley, Egypt's Religion*, and so on), labeling them A, B, C, and so on. Beneath each subhead copy the first sentence of each paragraph that follows the subhead. Number these sentences 1, 2, 3, and so on.

1. Rewrite the following events in history in the order in which they took place:
   a. President Bush elected
   b. Egyptian Old Kingdom begins
   c. Jesus born
   d. King Tut rules
   e. American Revolution

2. Which event took place after the birth of Christ?
   a. Egyptian Old Kingdom begins
   b. Declaration of Independence
   c. Egyptian New Kingdom ends

3. Where on the time line would you place the date of your birth?
   a. After George Bush was elected
   b. Before Egyptian Kingdom began
   c. After the Declaration of Independence

4. When did Hatshepsut rule?
   a. Before recorded history
   b. Before Jesus was born
   c. After the birth of Jesus

SKILL BUILDER: CRITICAL THINKING AND COMPREHENSION

Main Idea Learning the main idea of a paragraph or a chapter makes it easier for you to understand and enjoy what you are reading. Often the main idea of a paragraph is in the first or second sentence of a paragraph.

▶ Write the number of each of the following questions on a separate sheet of paper, then write the answer next to the number.

1. The main idea of paragraph 1 is that
   a. water is not that important.
   b. the Nile floods every year.
   c. the Nile was very important to the early Egyptians.

2. The main idea of paragraph 5 is that
   a. Egypt's boundaries included the desert.
   b. limestone and sandstone last for many years.
   c. the Nile was important in areas besides farming

3. The main idea of paragraph 8 is that
   a. Egyptians knew how to make mummies.
   b. leading a good life means obeying the gods.
   c. Egyptians believed in life after death.

4. The main idea of paragraph 13 is that
   a. The hieroglyphic writing system is complicated.
   b. Egyptians wrote on papyrus.
   c. Egyptians developed a way of writing.

ENRICHMENT

1. King Tutankhamen is famous today because his tomb was discovered intact. Among the items you find in the tomb are (1) tables and chairs, (2) statues of dogs, (3) many items of jewelry, (4) toys from the pharaoh's childhood, (5) a picture of the pharaoh's wife, and (6) statues of gods and goddesses. Pretend you are an archaeologist, and imagine you have just opened King Tutankhamen's tomb. Using the information in this chapter and other sources, explain why each item is included in the tomb.

2. The pyraminds were built by large groups of men who labored to move heavy blocks of stone. The workers felt they were doing their religious duty by laboring on the pyramids. Imagine you are a farmer who is spending time working on a pyramid. Write a letter to a friend describing what your work is like.

CHAPTER 5

The Ancient Middle East

OBJECTIVE: How do some of the important achievements of the Hittites, the Phoenicians, and the Hebrews influence your life today?

1. From the hills of Asia Minor to the Dead Sea is only about 600 miles—less than the distance between New York and Chicago. But between 1600 B.C. and 1200 B.C. three remarkable peoples arose in that region. Though the area was small, these people were strikingly different. Each one created something that changed the world forever, and each one's contribution reflected the values they placed highest. The Hittites were a warlike people whose secret can be summed up in one word: iron. They were the first people to make it and then turn it into deadly weapons. Farther south

▲ The Phoenicians were great traders and sailors. Their ships carried cargoes throughout the ancient Mediterranean world.

were the Phoenicians, who were shipbuilders and traders. The Phoenicians were the greatest traders that the world had known up to that time. To keep track of their ventures, they gave the world its first widely

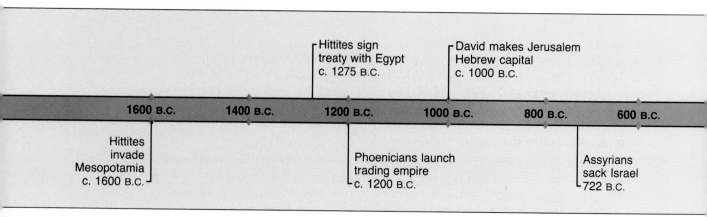

Hittites sign
treaty with Egypt
c. 1275 B.C.

David makes Jerusalem
Hebrew capital
c. 1000 B.C.

1600 B.C.	1400 B.C.	1200 B.C.	1000 B.C.	800 B.C.	600 B.C.

Hittites
invade
Mesopotamia
c. 1600 B.C.

Phoenicians launch
trading empire
c. 1200 B.C.

Assyrians
sack Israel
722 B.C.

used alphabet. Farthest south, the Hebrews created a nation, not of warriors or traders, but of religious thinkers. They were the first people to believe there was only one God, and they set down their beliefs in a book that is as important today as ever, the Bible.

THE HITTITES: How did the Hittites become a powerful nation?

2. The Hittites were a people who lived in Asia Minor, a region to the north of Mesopotamia. About 1600 B.C. the Hittites invaded Mesopotamia. They soon conquered Babylonia and other parts of the Middle East. By 1450 B.C. the Hittites had set up a powerful kingdom, with their capital at Hattushash in Asia Minor. Study the map on page 36 and locate the Hittite kingdom.

3. One of the most important achievements of the Hittites was the discovery of how to make iron weapons and tools. The Hittites were the first people to conquer their enemies by using iron spears and axes. Iron was a harder metal than the bronze and copper used by most ancient people at that time. The homeland of the Hittites in Asia Minor had large amounts of iron ore. ▶ What advantages would iron have over other metals? In time, the use of iron spread to other peoples and brought changes not only in warfare but also in daily life.

4. The Hittites were one of the first people to use horses in warfare. The horses pulled **chariots** (CHAIR-ee-uts), two-wheeled carts in which two men could stand. One man drove the horses. The other man shot arrows from his bow, which he could do very quickly because both hands were free. These swift horse-drawn chariots and their deadly iron weapons helped the Hittites conquer Babylonia and Syria. Syria is a land in the upper Euphrates Valley and in nearby coastal areas of the Mediterranean Sea.

5. For many years, the Hittites and the Egyptians fought bloody battles for control of Syria. Both the Hittite empire and the Egyptian empire had strong armies. Finally, about 1270 B.C., these two empires signed a **treaty** to end their fighting. A treaty is a written agreement between rulers or governments. This treaty is one of the oldest known.

6. By the time the treaty was signed, the wars with the Egyptians had weakened the Hittite kingdom. In addition, other peoples began to use iron instead of bronze to make weapons. About 1200 B.C., the Hittite homeland was conquered by invading tribes who came into Asia Minor from southeast Europe. Egypt, also, lost control of the lands it ruled in the ancient Middle East. As a result, other peoples now became important in the ancient Middle East. Between about 1200 B.C. and 700 B.C., the achievements of two of these peoples, the Phoenicians and the Hebrews, had lasting effects on later civilizations.

THE PHOENICIANS: How did the Phoenician city-states gain control of trade in the Mediterranean and set up colonies along its shores?

7. The Phoenicians lived in small city-states along the eastern coast of the Mediterranean Sea. Phoenicia was a land of hills and mountains with little fertile soil for farming. The mountains in the east kept the Phoenicians from moving inland. Therefore, from early times, the Phoenicians depended on the sea for their living. The Phoenicians obtained wood for building ships from the thick forests that grew on their eastern mountains. The seaport cities of Sidon, Tyre, and Byblos became important city-states, but they never united.

8. Beginning about 1200 B.C., the Phoenicians became the greatest trading people of the ancient Middle East. Fast-moving Phoenician ships powered by sails and oars carried goods the entire length of the Mediterranean Sea. They traded furniture and lumber made from hard cedar wood. Phoenician woolen cloth was also in great demand. The market for this cloth became even greater after the Phoenicians invented a purple dye to color it. The foul-smelling dye came from a kind of snail that lived

Ask: Why do you think some historians refer to the Mediterranean as a "Phoenician Lake"?

only along the Phoenician coast. Purple cloth cost so much that only very wealthy people in other lands could afford to buy it. As a result, "royal purple" became the color that kings and queens most often wore. In addition, skilled Phoenician crafts workers made beautiful glassware, jewelry, and metal goods. Phoenician merchants also traded goods from other lands. Tyre and the other Phoenician city-states grew wealthy from this trade.

9. As their trade expanded, Phoenician merchants founded **colonies** (KOL-uh-neez) in many parts of the Mediterranean. Colonies are settlements in other lands. Most of these colonies were started as trading posts where Phoenician ships could sell or exchange their goods. Some of these trading posts grew into important trading cities that included large areas of land along the Mediterranean Sea. The Phoenicians founded colonies on the islands of Cyprus,

▲ The Hittites were the first people to use iron weapons. Why do you think iron weapons gave the Hittites an advantage over their enemies?

▼ The Hittites were the first powerful people to occupy Asia Minor. Phoenicia and the Hebrew kingdoms appeared later.

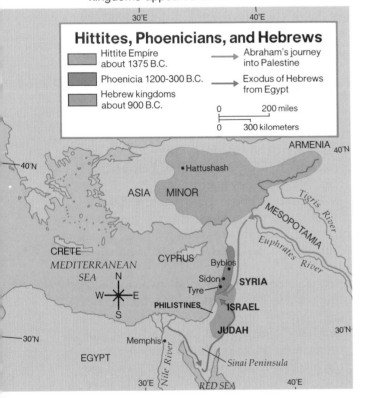

Hittites, Phoenicians, and Hebrews

Hittite Empire about 1375 B.C.
Phoenicia 1200-300 B.C.
Hebrew kingdoms about 900 B.C.
→ Abraham's journey into Palestine
→ Exodus of Hebrews from Egypt
0   200 miles
0   300 kilometers

Sicily, and Sardinia, and as far west as Gibraltar. The greatest of the Phoenician colonies was Carthage in North Africa. Carthage was founded about 814 B.C. For the next 600 years, Carthage controlled most of the trade in the western half of the Mediterranean Sea.

10. The most important Phoenician contribution to our civilization was the alphabet. The Phoenician system of writing was an alphabet with only 22 characters. It was much simpler than the Sumerian or the Egyptian systems, both of which had more than 500 characters. What would be the advantage of this simpler system? Phoenician traders used this alphabet to keep records of the goods they traded. Their wide use of the alphabet also spread it to other lands. The Greeks and later the Romans copied this alphabet with slight changes. In time, this slightly changed Phoenician alphabet became the one used today in most of the world.

Activity: To help students understand the daring of the Phoenician sailors, have them use the Atlas map on pages 722–723 to trace the route from Phoenicia (1) through the Strait of Gibraltar into the Atlantic Ocean; (2) to England; (3) to India; (4) around the coast of Africa.

36

11. The Hebrews came from Mesopotamia into Palestine, a land south of Phoenicia, about 2000 B.C. Abraham was the leader of the Hebrew tribes during this journey to Palestine. Palestine, or Canaan (KAY-nun), as this land also was called, was located at the land bridge, or meeting point, between Egypt and the rest of the ancient Middle East. In about 1730 B.C., the Hyksos crossed Canaan to invade Egypt. When other peoples, such as the Hittites, the Assyrians, and the Persians, invaded Egypt in later years, they marched through Canaan and conquered its people, too. Yet in times of peace, merchants from other lands brought their camels carrying goods to trade into Canaan. In this way the Hebrew tribes learned many of the ideas and achievements of the peoples of Mesopotamia and Egypt.

12. The religion of the Hebrews is known as **Judaism** (JOOD-uh-iz-um). Judaism later became a major world religion. Although Judaism developed over many centuries, its central belief remained the same. The Hebrews were the first people to believe in one God. They believed that God would take care of them if they remained faithful to Him as His chosen people.

13. The Old Testament tells that about 1700 B.C. some Hebrew tribes left Canaan, or Palestine, to settle in Egypt. They and their descendants lived there for about 400 years, until Pharaoh Ramses II made slaves of them. According to the Old Testament, a great Hebrew leader named Moses finally forced Ramses II to free the Hebrews.

14. Moses led the Hebrew people on the Exodus, or journey out of Egypt, across the Sinai desert, and back to Canaan. However, some of the people feared to return to Canaan. They believed their lives would be better if they returned to the rich, fertile valley of the Nile. It was at this time that Moses announced the Ten Commandments, the set of basic religious laws of Judaism. The Hebrews believed that God had given these laws to Moses. They also believed that

Moses had made a **covenant** with God. A covenant (KUV-uh-nunt) is an agreement that must be obeyed. In this covenant God promised the Hebrews a new land in Canaan. The story of the Exodus is told in the Old Testament of the Bible.

SPOTLIGHT ON SOURCES

15. The Ten Commandments were the religious laws that the Hebrew people believed God required them to obey. Here are the first three of these commandments:

God Spoke, and these were his words:

I am the Lord your God who brought you out of Egypt, out of the land of slavery.

[1] You shall have no other god to set against Me.

▼ According to the Bible, Moses climbed a mountain alone. He returned with the Ten Commandments, which God had written on two stone tablets.

Activity: Have students use the map on page 361 to trace the route of the Hebrews on their flight from Egypt.

37

[2] You shall not make a carved image for yourself nor the likeness of anything in the heavens above, or on the earth below, or in the waters under the earth. You shall not bow down to them or worship them . . .

[3] You shall not make wrong use of the name of the Lord your God . . .

The New English Bible, Exodus 20:1–7

▶ What do these three commandments tell you about the Hebrew religion? Do you know any of the other commandments?

16. The Hebrews faced a long and difficult journey across the hot desert of the Sinai Peninsula on their return to Canaan about 1200 B.C.. When they finally arrived in Canaan, the Hebrews had to fight wars with several groups of people living there. Of these, the most powerful were the Philistines, a seafaring people who had settled along the coast. The Bible tells of many battles with the Philistines. In one of these battles, a gigantic Philistine leader named Goliath was slain by David, a young shepherd boy from Bethlehem armed only with a slingshot. The name Palestine, which often is used to identify this area, derives from these people.

17. These bitter struggles for control of the land along the Jordan River lasted more than 100 years. Finally, about 1025 B.C., the twelve Hebrew tribes set up the kingdom of Israel, with Saul as the first king. Saul was succeeded by David. Under both kings, the small kingdom increased its power and expanded its borders. About 1000 B.C., David conquered the city of Jerusalem and made it the capital of Israel. David was Israel's greatest king, and he left a strong kingdom to his successor, his son Solomon.

PEOPLE IN HISTORY

18. Solomon ruled from about 960 B.C. to 930 B.C. Solomon was the most powerful of Israel's rulers. During his rule, Solomon built up the army to protect Israel from the Philistines. Solomon also improved Israel's relations with other nearby peoples. For example, he encouraged trade with the Phoenician city-states, and with Egypt he organized a system for trading horses and chariots. In addition, Solomon built new cities, new roads, and several palaces to show Israel's growing power. His most important work was the great temple he built in Jerusalem.

19. Solomon caused unrest among the people of Israel by making them pay heavy taxes for his buildings and the army. Many people disliked these taxes and wanted their tribes to gain back their independence. What do you think happened after ◀ Solomon died about 930 B.C.? When the revolt of the people ended, Israel was split into two parts. The northern part became the new kingdom of Israel. The southern part was the kingdom of Judah (JOOD-uh). The two kingdoms were too weak to defend themselves against the powerful new empires that now arose in the ancient Middle East.

20. The Hebrew kingdoms of Israel and Judah were attacked by large and powerful empires. In 722 B.C. Assyrian armies conquered Israel. The Assyrians took the ten tribes of Israel away into slavery and brought new people to settle the land. The two tribes that remained were called **Jews,** after the name of their kingdom of Judah. The kingdom of Judah lasted longer than Israel. Then it, too, was overrun in 586 B.C., by the Chaldeans. The Chaldeans were a people who had conquered Mesopotamia and set up their capital at Babylon. Nebuchadrezzar, the Chaldean ruler, took the Jews to Babylon, where they lived many years as slaves.

21. When the Persian ruler Cyrus conquered Babylon about fifty years later, he allowed the Jews to return to Judah. There, in and around Jerusalem, the Jews lived for many centuries. Most of the time, however, the land was ruled by foreign powers. Yet Judaism, the religion of the Jews, became a force in the ancient Middle East. Later it also became a vital part of the two other

Background: Historians have never been able to determine what happened to the ten tribes of Hebrews taken from Israel by the Assyrians. They have been identified as early Americans, Gypsies, and other peoples whose background historians cannot fathom.

great religions that developed in the Middle East, Christianity and Islam.

JUDAISM: What were the teachings of Judaism, and why did these beliefs make it one of the world's great religions?

22. The greatest contribution of Hebrew culture was Judaism. The major beliefs of this religion are found in the Old Testament of the Bible. The first five books of the Old Testament are known as the Torah. These books contain the laws of Judaism, including the Ten Commandments. Other books contain history, poetry, and the writings of the Hebrew prophets, or religious thinkers.

23. Judaism became so important as a great world religion because the Hebrews were the first people whose religion was based on a belief in one God. This belief in a single god is known as **monotheism** (MAH-no-thee-iz-um). The Hebrews believed that **Yahweh** (YAH-weh), or God, created the world and cared for all its people. The Hebrews believed that God had created all people in His own image. They believed that God was like a wise and loving father who wanted His children to lead good lives. For this reason, God had given Moses the Ten Commandments as rules for people to follow. The Hebrews also believed that the writings of the prophets in the Old Testament could help them live as God wanted them to do. These prophets were great religious thinkers who helped the Hebrews learn the ideas of Judaism. The prophets taught that God was loving, merciful, and just, and that God wanted people to act the same way, too. Thus, Judaism, the religion of the Hebrews, centered on the belief in one God and the rules that God expected people to follow.

▲ Jerusalem's Western Wall, at the right, is the holiest place in Judaism. It is the only remaining part of the ancient temple of Solomon.

OUTLOOK

24. The Hittites, the Hebrews, and the Phoenicians were conquered by the armies of several mighty empires that took control of the Middle East. Yet the Phoenicians and the Hebrews made contributions to the world that continued long after their lands were taken over by other people. Both the seafaring skills and the alphabet of the Phoenicians were passed on to other peoples who followed. The religion of the Hebrews became especially important. Its beliefs became part of two other great religions, Christianity and Islam. Long after the Hebrew people left Canaan, or Palestine, their religion remained a great force in their lives. The Jewish people who are the descendants of the Hebrews always hoped to return to Palestine some day. Finally, in 1948, the Jewish people established an independent nation in Israel. What do you ◄ think caused the Jewish people to found their new nation in this land of the Middle East? What does this tell you about the power of history and religion in people's lives?

39

CHAPTER REVIEW

VOCABULARY REVIEW

In your notebook, copy the following vocabulary words. Use your glossary to find their definitions. Then use each word in a sentence.

1. treaty
2. colonies
3. alphabet
4. Judaism
5. monotheism
6. cedar

SKILL BUILDER: FOLLOWING DIRECTIONS

When taking a test, applying for a job, or just getting from one place to another, following directions is important. Directions are usually given in logical order. That is, each step in a series of directions leads you to the next step. Read the series of directions below. Then, on a separate sheet of paper, write what is missing from the directions.

1. How to fix a bicycle's flat tire.

   a. Remove the old inner tube from the wheel.

   b. Place the old inner tube in a pan of water.

   c. Squeeze inner tube to find leak.

   d. Place inner tube in tire.

   e. Place both on bicycle.

Several steps are missing from the series of directions above. If you tried to follow them, you'd of course fail to repair your bike. It also is important that you follow them in a logical order. Below are a series of directions for using a bow and arrow. On a separate sheet of paper, copy the directions, then place them in a logical order.

2. How to use a bow and arrow.

   a. Shoot the arrow.

   b. Place arrow in bowstring by fitting arrow's notch to the string.

   c. Select an arrow.

   d. While holding arrow and bowstring, pull back bow string.

   e. Lift bow and aim.

3. Follow the directions given in lines **a** to **f** to spell out an idea from Chapter 5. Write your sentence on a separate sheet of paper.

   a. Write the first two words in paragraph 4.

   b. Write the first two words in paragraph 7.

   c. Write the last word in line 1, column 1, page 37. Then write the first two words in the same line.

   d. Write the second word in line 2, paragraph 20.

   e. Write the fourth word in line 1, paragraph 23. Then write the seventh word in line 8 of that same paragraph.

   f. Write the first four words in the last line of column 1, page 39.

STUDY HINT Write a one-page summary of the chapter, presenting its main points. Then exchange summaries with another student. Talk about each other's summaries. Do the facts agree? Is everything important included? Make any needed changes in your summary.

SKILL BUILDER: CRITICAL THINKING AND COMPREHENSION

1. Classifying

▶ On a separate sheet of paper, copy the following chart. Use the information below to complete the chart.

Group of People	Major Contributions

Phoenicians
Hittites
horse-drawn war chariots
the alphabet
trading colonies
Hebrews
Belief in one god
ironworking
purple dye
Old Testament

2. Main Idea

Each group of people studied in this chapter had special qualities and made special contributions. Read the first sentence in paragraphs 3, 6, and 11. In your notebook, write the main idea of each paragraph.

ENRICHMENT

1. Read about the Hebrews' flight from Egypt, as told in Exodus, the second book in the Bible. Write a short essay describing the problems faced by these people.
2. The Hittites were able to extend their power because they used iron. Can you think of other examples in history of how new inventions helped a group of people gain power? Some examples of such inventions might be the steam engine, gunpowder, or airplanes.
3. Use encyclopedias and other reference works to find out more about transportation in the ancient Middle East. Make a series of drawings showing different types of ships, chariots, and animals used to transport goods and people. Which types of transportation are still in use today?
4. The alphabet used in modern English has 26 letters. Design an alphabet that uses only 20 letters. Which letters would be the best choices to leave out? Write a short paragraph using this new alphabet. Be sure to include some words that would need respelling because of the letters you omitted. Then ask one of your classmates to read the paragraph.
5. In an encyclopedia or other reference work, read about the Phoenician voyages of exploration. Choose one of these voyages to prepare a report about. In your report, include a map showing the route of the voyage. Then write a report on the voyage in the form of a diary of one of the sailors on the ship.

CHAPTER 6

Ancient India

▲ Mohenjo-Daro was one of the centers of the Indus Valley civilization. The great city probably fell to invading Aryans about 1500 B.C.

OBJECTIVE: In what ways did the civilization of ancient India help build the foundation of India's culture today?

▶ **1.** Can you imagine living in a family whose members have been silver crafters or traders for centuries? For many people in India, the only available work was the kind their parents did. The people they were allowed to marry had to be someone from the same kind of family. If you were a tax collector, your children and your children's children would be tax collectors as well.

▶ How would you feel living in such a system? What if you wanted to be a doctor but, because of your family, you had to become a government official? In this chapter you will learn about the origins of the caste system. The caste system defines each per-

son's role in society. No matter how hardworking, a person has virtually no chance of making a better life for himself or herself. You are born into a caste, and you stay there until you die.

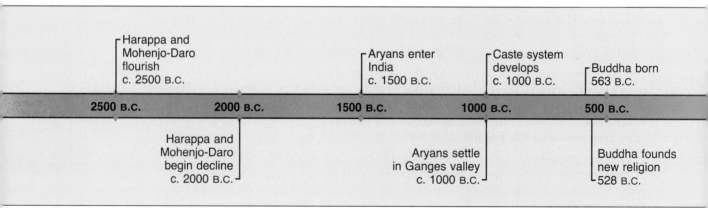

	Harappa and Mohenjo-Daro flourish c. 2500 B.C.		Aryans enter India c. 1500 B.C.	Caste system develops c. 1000 B.C.	Buddha born 563 B.C.
2500 B.C.	**2000 B.C.**	**1500 B.C.**	**1000 B.C.**		**500 B.C.**
	Harappa and Mohenjo-Daro begin decline c. 2000 B.C.		Aryans settle in Ganges valley c. 1000 B.C.		Buddha founds new religion 528 B.C.

INDIA'S GEOGRAPHY: How did India's rivers, mountains, and climate affect India's ancient civilization?

2. India is a large triangle-shaped land located in southern Asia. India is surrounded by the waters of the Arabian Sea, the Indian Ocean, and the Bay of Bengal. In the north are the rugged Hindu Kush Mountains and the towering Himalaya Mountains, the highest in the world. The Indus River and the Ganges River flow from these mountains across India's broad northern plains. Study the map on page 44 and locate these major features of India's geography. The waters around India and most of the northern mountains protected India from invading peoples. Only the Hindu Kush Mountains in the northwest had passes through which invaders could enter India. ► Why would this fact be important to people who lived in the Indus River Valley?

3. Climate has a very important effect on people's lives in India. The climate in the fertile northern plains along the Indus River and the Ganges River is very hot and dry in the summer. The people there depend on the **monsoons** (mahn-SOONZ) to bring them the rain they need to grow their crops. The monsoons are strong winds that bring heavy rains in the summer. The monsoon winds in the winter bring dry, cool weather.

HARAPPA AND MOHENJO-DARO: Why were these cities important in the early Indus valley civilization?

4. The first Indian civilization developed in the valley of the Indus River, in what is now Pakistan. The civilization began to take shape about 2500 B.C. By 2200 B.C., it was centered in two important cities, Harappa and Mohenjo-Daro, which were among the largest in the ancient world. These cities had paved streets, brick houses, shops, and public buildings built with hardened bricks. Wealthy people sometimes lived in houses that were two or three stories high. Skilled craft workers in these cities wove cotton cloth and made pottery, jewelry, and furniture. Outside the cities most of the people in the Indus valley were farmers. They raised wheat, barley, cotton, and fruit on farmlands near the cities. Traders carried these crops and cotton cloth to trade for goods with the Sumerian city-states of Mesopotamia.

5. The Indus valley civilization began to weaken between 2000 B.C. and 1500 B.C. Some historians think that floods or an earthquake may have weakened the Indus cities. Other historians believe invaders conquered and killed or drove away the Indus valley people.

THE ARYANS: What ideas about society and religion developed in ancient India during the Aryan civilization?

6. About 1500 B.C., tribes of nomads invaded India through passes in the Hindu Kush Mountains. These Aryan [AR-ee-un) tribes were skilled and brave fighters. With their bronze weapons and horse-drawn chariots, they were more powerful than the Dravidians (druh-VID-ee-unz) who then lived in the Indus Valley. The Aryans soon conquered the Dravidians of northern India. However, some of the Dravidians moved to southern India and set up kingdoms there. The Aryans also moved eastward. By 1000 B.C., they ruled nearly all of the fertile plains of northern India. There, in the valley of the Ganges River, they settled and developed India's second great civilization.

7. As their civilization developed, the Aryans formed small states by joining together the villages in each area. A **rajah** (RAJ-uh) ruled each state with the help of a group of warriors. A rajah was the leader of a tribe chosen by the warriors. Some of the most powerful rajahs established strong states that later became independent kingdoms. However, the villages in each state were allowed to govern most of their own affairs.

8. Under the Aryans, India's society soon became organized into a **caste system** (KAST SIS-tum). In a caste system people are divided into several separate groups

Background: Scientists are still unsure who built the cities of Harappa and Mohenjo-Daro. Oddly enough, evidence of a more primitive civilization has been found above the advanced ruins.

43

based on who their parents are. Some castes are considered better than others, but no one may ever leave his or her caste. Many people of India still follow this caste system today. Soon after the Aryans settled in India, they decided that they should not allow their tribes to mix with the Dravidians. They began to treat the Dravidians as a separate and inferior group. Four separate castes gradually developed. The top three castes originally were made up of Aryans. The highest were priests and religious teachers; then came warriors, and finally merchants and traders. The fourth caste was formed for the Dravidians. At the bottom was another group called the **pariahs** (puh-RY-uz). The pariahs were not part of society at all. The pariahs were also known as "untouchables," since a pariah's touch was believed to make other people impure.

9. The caste system became more rigid over the years. Each person belonged to the same caste as his or her parents. People could not move to a different caste or marry a member of another caste. Each caste had strict rules about its members' behavior and religious duties. There also were rules about the ways caste members could earn money and even about the food they could eat. In time the castes themselves became divided into many smaller groups. The caste system shaped every aspect of people's lives in India.

HINDUISM: What were the beliefs of Hinduism, and how did this religion shape the lives of the people of India?

10. An important new religion called **Hinduism** (HIN-doo-iz-um) began during the years of the Aryan civilization in India. Hinduism teaches that few people end their earthly life when they die. Instead, they are reborn and must live again in the world in a new earthly body. This rebirth is known as **reincarnation** (ree-in-kar-NAY-shun). A person who has lived a good life will be reborn into a higher caste. A person who has lived

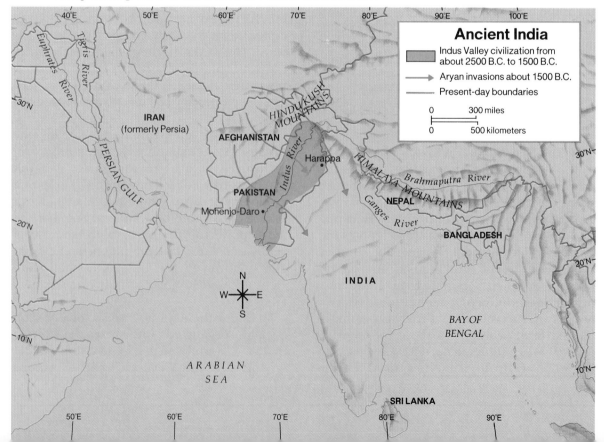

▼ The Indus Valley civilization is the oldest known urban civilization of the Indian subcontinent. Along which great river did it develop? When did it flourish?

Ask: Who do you think would favor the caste system in Indian society? Which caste would probably be most opposed to the caste system?

▲ Shiva is one of the leading Hindu gods. Here, in the form of four-armed Nataraja, or Lord of the Cosmic Dance, he dances atop a demon.

PEOPLE IN HISTORY

12. The most important person who tried to reform, or change, certain Hindu practices was **Siddartha Gautama** (sih-DAR-tuh GOW-tuh-muh). Gautama was a wealthy young prince who was born in northern India in 563 B.C. When he was 29 he left his palace to learn how his people lived. Seeing poor, sick, and hungry people changed Gautama's life. He became so unhappy about people's suffering and pain that he decided to give up his wealth and his family to find the causes of people's suffering. After six years, Gautama found the truth he was seeking. His followers began calling him the Buddha, meaning "the Enlightened One."

13. The Buddha taught that a person can find salvation by following the Middle Way, Buddha's guide to ways of thinking and behaving. People are to act unselfishly toward others and treat all others fairly and equally. Leading lives based on goodness and love will end suffering and evil in the world. When salvation is achieved, a person's soul finds lasting peace called **nirvana** (nur-VAH-nuh). These religious beliefs taught by the Buddha are called **Buddhism** (BOO-diz-um). Buddhism soon became a major religion in Asia. It is still one of the most important world religions today.

a bad life will be reborn into a lower caste or perhaps as an animal. Hinduism teaches that a person's soul may have to be reborn many times until it reaches perfection. Once perfection is achieved, the soul escapes from the life of the earth. Perfection and the rejection of earthly things end the cycle of birth, death, and rebirth.

11. Hindu beliefs strengthened the caste system because they taught that people must accept the caste into which they are born. They have a duty to accept it, because their caste is the result of all their good and bad actions in their past life. If people accept their caste in this life, they will be rewarded with a higher caste in the next life.

OUTLOOK

14. The civilizations of ancient India were among the greatest of the ancient world. Although the Indus valley civilization built important cities, they disappeared by 1500 B.C. The Aryan civilization that followed from 1500 B.C. to 500 B.C. has shaped life in India until the present day. The caste system and the beliefs of Hinduism and Buddhism are the most important and lasting contributions of Aryan civilization. How does your knowledge of the caste system and Buddhism better help you to understand the Indian nation today?

CHAPTER REVIEW

On a separate sheet of paper, rewrite each sentence filling in the blank with the correct vocabulary word.

a. monsoons
b. rajah
c. caste system

d. pariahs
e. Hinduism
f. reincarnation

g. nirvana
h. Buddhism

1. Followers of this religion seek _____ , a state of lasting peace.

2. The _____ teaches that everyone has a place in society based on family occupation.

3. A _____ was an Indian ruler of a small state.

4. The _____ bring India heavy winds, rain and cool weather.

5. People who are untouchables are called _____ .

6. The Middle Way is taught by people who practice _____ .

7. The caste system is followed by people who practice _____ .

8. The idea of being reborn in a new earthly body is called _____ .

SKILL BUILDER: READING A TIME LINE

1. Historians use several terms to indicate periods of years. For example, *century* means 100 years; *decade* means ten years; and an *age* or *era* means a long period of time. The time line below is divided into centuries. Use the time line to copy the events below in their correct order.

a. Buddha born
b. Carthage founded
c. Aryans settle in Ganges Valley
d. Buddha founds new religion
e. Caste system begun
f. Assyrians sack Israel

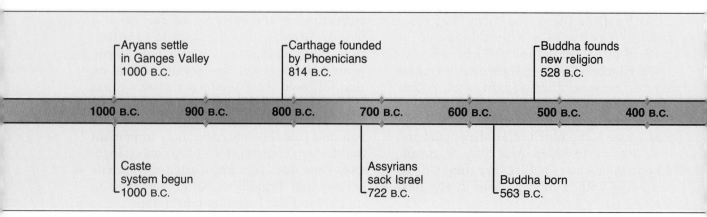

Aryans settle in Ganges Valley 1000 B.C.

Carthage founded by Phoenicians 814 B.C.

Buddha founds new religion 528 B.C.

| 1000 B.C. | 900 B.C. | 800 B.C. | 700 B.C. | 600 B.C. | 500 B.C. | 400 B.C. |

Caste system begun 1000 B.C.

Assyrians sack Israel 722 B.C.

Buddha born 563 B.C.

2. Answer the questions below by using information from the time line.

  a. About what year did the caste system begin?

  b. When was Israel conquered?

  c. How old was Buddha when he founded Buddhism?

  d. About how many years after the caste system began was Buddha born?

  e. In what century was Carthage founded?

SKILL BUILDER: CRITICAL THINKING AND COMPREHENSION

1. Classifying:

Study the chart below. Complete the chart by using information from the chapter.

GEOGRAPHIC FEATURES OF INDIA

Rivers	Mountains	Surrounding Waters

Look at paragraphs 11, 12, and 13.

  a. What is the main idea of paragraph 11?

  b. In what paragraph is the Middle Way discussed?

  c. In what sentence is the main idea of paragraph 12 discussed?

  d. What religion is discussed in paragraph 11?

ENRICHMENT

  1. The pariahs, or untouchables, performed certain jobs in Indian society. What were those jobs? Research and write down what the untouchables did.

  2. Buddhism has grown to be an important religion in Asia. Look up Buddhism in an encyclopedia. Make a list of the nations that have large Buddhist populations. Identify the nations on a map.

CHAPTER 7

Ancient China

▲ Rice, cultivated by hand in China since ancient times, is still the chief food crop produced in China today.

OBJECTIVE: What early ideas and experiences helped to make Chinese civilization the oldest surviving culture?

▶ **1.** Would you carry your grandmother around on your back if she could not walk?
▶ Would you give up your food so that your parents could eat? Maybe you have to think a moment before answering those questions. In many modern societies, parents consider the needs of their children to be more important than their own. In ancient China, however, one of the strongest ideals was respect for parents and other older people. Possibly the worst thing Chinese people could do was to show disrespect for their parents. This respect extended also to their ancestors. When Chinese people did something wrong, they faced more than

punishment. They faced the shame of knowing that they had brought disrespect upon their elders. Although many young Chinese no longer believe in this ideal, respect for

				Shang dynasty begins c. 1500 B.C.	Confucius born 551 B.C.	
5000 B.C.	**4000 B.C.**	**3000 B.C.**	**2000 B.C.**		**1000 B.C.**	A.D. 1
	Early Chinese civilization begins c. 5000 B.C.		Huang river civilization develops c. 3000 B.C.		Zhou dynasty replaces Shangs c. 1027 B.C.	

48

elders is still part of traditional Chinese culture. The strength of the idea reflects the strength of Chinese civilization, the oldest culture that still exists.

CHINA'S GEOGRAPHY: How did China's land and location help shape its ancient civilization?

2. One important reason why Chinese civilization has lasted is China's geography. China is a huge land that covers much of eastern Asia. Yet most of its land is mountains or deserts. Only the river valleys of China have the rich soil and good climate that people need for farming. The three great river valleys in China are formed by the Huang River, the Yangtze River, and the Xi River. Locate these river valleys on the map on page 50. These three valleys are the part of China where most of that nation's 1.1 billion people live today.

3. China's geography provides natural barriers against invasions. In western China are the Kunlun, Himalaya, and other rugged mountains. Dry, treeless plains cover a large part of western China. Mountains and tropical jungles separate southern China from Southeast Asia. The huge Gobi Desert, mountain ranges, and plains form China's northern borders. To the east lies the Pacific Ocean.

4. Early invaders could reach China only from the north. Several times the nomad peoples who lived in Mongolia and Manchuria invaded China by crossing the Gobi Desert or the northern plains. Sometimes these invaders were able to place themselves at the head of the Chinese government. Yet as soon as they did, they began to follow the customs and ideas of the Chinese. In this way China and its people were able to preserve their civilization for thousands of years. Why do you think invaders ◄ adopted Chinese culture?

THE HUANG RIVER VALLEY: How did early Chinese civilization begin?

5. The early Chinese first settled along the Huang River—also called the Yellow River—about 5000 B.C. Hundreds of years later, farming villages were built there. By about 3000 B.C. Chinese farmers were growing grain in the valley's rich soil. They also were raising cattle and sheep. Like the Egyptians along the Nile River, the people in the Huang valley learned how to build dikes to control river floods. They also built ditches and canals to irrigate their fields. The Huang River was not as regular as the Nile in ancient Egypt. Some years the Huang did not flood. In other years the Huang's floods broke through the dikes along its banks and destroyed crops as well as whole villages. For this reason the Chinese named the Huang the River of Sorrows. Why do you think people continued to ◄ live near this dangerous river?

Daily life in . . .

During the Zhou Dynasty nearly all of China's people were farmers. Chinese farm families were **extended families**. This meant that the family included grandparents, parents, children, sons and their wives, unmarried daughters, and often other relatives as well. In years when crops were poor, many farm families went hungry and suffered hard times. Even so, the use of the iron plow and hoe helped increase the output of crops under the Zhou Dynasty. The use of oxen to plow fields increased China's wheat and millet crops. These crops supplied most of the food the people ate. As farming improved, the size of China's population grew. With the increasing cultivation of rice, which was now grown in the Yangtze River valley, China's population grew even more.

49

6. China's first dynasty of rulers began in the Huang River valley, where early farming villages were governed by local leaders. After hundreds of years these villages grew into small cities and towns. In about 1500 B.C. the Shang kings set up their government in one of these cities and became China's first dynasty of rulers. At first they ruled only the part of the Huang River valley around the city of Anyang. While most of the Huang valley lands were still controlled by local leaders, they promised to help defend Shang land against nomad invaders. In time of war the Shang king would command all the local armies. The Shang armies used wheeled chariots and bronze weapons to defeat their enemies.

7. Slowly, the Shang rulers gained power over the local leaders and ruled more and more land. As the Chinese population grew, the people spread south into the fertile Chang River valley. By 1200 B.C., the Shang kings had become powerful rulers. But powerful nobles combined with invaders from the northwest to eventually drive the Shang rulers from power.

THE ZHOU DYNASTY: What important changes took place in China during the Zhou Dynasty?

8. About 1027 B.C., the Zhou Dynasty replaced the Shang. The Zhou were invaders from northwest China. Like most conquerors of China, they soon adopted China's culture and way of life. The Zhou Dynasty set up its capital at Luoyang (luh-woh-YAN). The Zhou kings ruled China for the next 800 years.

9. The Zhou kings had overturned the Shang dynasty with the help of nearby Chinese city-states. The nobles who ruled these city-states remained powerful. These nobles ruled in the name of the king, but they were so powerful that they really were independent of him.

▼ Ancient China's Shang dynasty was centered along the Huang river valley. What geographic features protected and favored those early Chinese settlements?

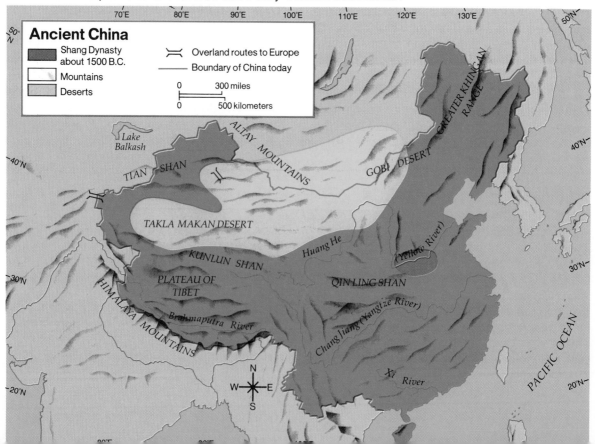

Ancient China

- Shang Dynasty about 1500 B.C.
- Mountains
- Deserts

⨝ Overland routes to Europe
— Boundary of China today

0   300 miles
0   500 kilometers

Lake Balkash
ALTAY MOUNTAINS
TIAN SHAN
GOBI DESERT
GREATER KHINGAN RANGE
TAKLA MAKAN DESERT
KUNLUN SHAN
Huang He
Yellow River
PLATEAU OF TIBET
QIN LING SHAN
HIMALAYA MOUNTAINS
Brahmaputra River
Chang Jiang (Yangtze River)
Xi River
PACIFIC OCEAN

▲ Women prepare newly woven silk in this old Chinese painting. Silk cloth was a valuable trading item in China as early as the Zhou Dynasty.

10. The Zhou kingdom was greatly weakened when the nobles of several small kingdoms began fighting wars among themselves. ▶ Why would this kind of fighting weaken a country? By the 400s B.C., the Zhou rulers controlled only their own city-state. The rest of China was ruled by many powerful nobles. These years of fighting among the kingdoms and of the growing weakness of the Zhou Dynasty are called the Years of the Warring States. Yet, in spite of the endless wars and great unrest, Chinese civilization reached new heights during the Zhou Dynasty.

11. Important new ideas about government began during the Zhou Dynasty. The Zhou rulers helped develop a view of China's government called the **Mandate of Heaven.** The Mandate of Heaven meant that each of China's dynasties received its power, or mandate (MAN-dayt), from the gods. The dynasty could rule only so long as it kept the mandate. Then the gods would give the mandate to a new dynasty. Every dynasty began when a strong ruler defeated the last king of the old dynasty. This new leader then started his own dynasty.

12. The Mandate of Heaven became an important and lasting belief in Chinese thinking and religion. When a ruler did not govern wisely, the Chinese believed he had lost his mandate to rule from the gods. When this happened, the people had the right to rebel and to set up a new dynasty. When the people were able to overthrow a ruler, this proved that he had lost the Mandate of Heaven. ◀ How would you compare this system to that in the United States?

THE FAMILY: Why was the family the backbone of Chinese Civilization?

13. China's unity and strength in the Zhou Dynasty depended on the family, which was the backbone of Chinese society. Religious beliefs increased the importance of the family. One of the main beliefs of Chinese religion was **ancestor worship.** Ancestor worship means honoring members of the family who had lived in the past. The members of every Chinese family believed that they had a special link with their an-

Activity: Discuss ancestor worship with students. Ask the students whether they think that ancestor worship is sensible, or that the young people in a society come first.

cestors. Their ancestors were powerful spirits who could help them find favor with the gods. Priests wrote messages on bones and shells asking people's ancestors to help their living descendants. The Chinese people also asked their ancestors' spirits to tell them what would happen in the future.

NEW DEVELOPMENTS: What were the early achievements of Chinese civilization?

14. Chinese writing was invented during the Shang dynasty, between 1500 B.C. and about 1000 B.C.. Priests' messages to people's ancestors on animal bones and shells were the most important examples of this writing. At first Chinese writing, like Mesopotamian writing, used signs, or symbols, to represent a word. Later these signs were put together to form new words as the Chinese language grew. In this way Chinese writing grew from about 3,500 symbols in the Shang dynasty to more than 50,000

▼ Confucius's thoughts on social behavior and government have guided the development of Chinese civilization for centuries.

symbols today. How would you feel about having to learn 50,000 symbols in order to write? Chinese writing soon came to be written in ink on silk cloth. This kind of writing, called **calligraphy** (kuh-LIG-ruh-fee), became a beautiful form of Chinese art. In ancient China, only persons who were highly trained and skilled in calligraphy were able to write. As a result, few Chinese people could hope to learn to read and write.

15. The Chinese people made other important achievements during the Shang dynasty. They invented a calendar during these early years to help them know when to plant and harvest their crops. With some changes this calendar was used in China for nearly 3,000 years. What other early civilization developed a calendar? Artisans and skilled crafts workers produced lovely jewelry and figures of animals carved in ivory and jade stone. Delicate silk cloth and fine clay pottery were produced. Bronze vases, often in the form of animals, were the greatest achievement of Shang art. Many of these wonderful bronze works were used in religious ceremonies.

16. During the Zhou Dynasty, which followed the Shang, production of silk and other goods increased. Artisans and crafts workers made pottery, cooking vessels, and other products people needed. At the same time new groups of people became important in China's growing cities and towns. Merchants who traded these goods became important, and cities became centers of trade. Most of this trade took place within China. The chief goods traded were silk cloth, jade and ivory jewelry, wooden furniture, bronze vases, pottery, and iron tools. During the Zhou Dynasty traders began to use coins as a way to trade for goods. Why do you think people didn't continue simply to exchange goods?

PEOPLE IN HISTORY

17. Out of the unrest and disorder in China during the Zhou Dynasty, a remark-

able man named Confucius appeared. Confucius was the most important thinker in all of Chinese history. Confucius was born in 551 B.C. and had a difficult childhood. Because his father died when Confucius was very young, Confucius was raised only by his mother. They were poor, but Confucius worked hard and managed to get a good education. As a young man he became an official in his own city-state of Lu. There Confucius became worried about the growing disorder and wars among China's city-states. When he was forced to leave Lu, Confucius became a teacher. He spent the next 14 years urging the rulers of the city-states to end their wars and follow peaceful ways. He also began to teach his ideas to many students who came to seek his views.

18. Confucius believed that during the Shang dynasty China had been strong and powerful because the rulers had governed wisely. The Chinese people had enjoyed peace and order because they had obeyed their kings and respected their families. Confucius believed that China would find true peace and happiness only when the people once more followed these same rules of conduct.

19. Confucius clearly described the ways people should act in all of their relationships. These rules set forth the proper way to behave among family members and among people in society. They also taught the proper relations between the ruler and his people. All people in society must treat each other with kindness, trust, and respect. In each family, children must obey their parents, wives must obey their husbands, and younger people must obey and respect older people. Since the family was the center of Chinese society, obedience, respect for authority, and loyalty were the duties of all family members. A central idea of Confucius teachings was **filial piety** (FIL-ee-ul PY-uh-tee). This meant that children and young people must honor and love their parents and all older family members. Confucius's teachings about the family and filial piety tied all families closer together.

▶ How would these teachings strengthen the Chinese reverence for ancestors and belief in ancestor worship?

20. Confucius also taught that in a good society people must have a strong government. This required that the people trust and obey their ruler. The ruler, in turn, had a duty to protect, educate, and care for his people. If every person followed these rules of conduct, all people would have happy lives in a peaceful society.

21. The teachings of Confucius were not accepted by the rulers of the warring city-states of the Zhou kingdom. Why do you ◀ think they were not accepted? However, after his death, Confucius's thinking became a powerful force in China. In fact, Confucius's ideas became the basis of Chinese law and government. For the next 2,000 years, all education in China also was based on Confucius's teachings. His ideas became the model for people's ways of thinking and behaving. Government officials in China were required to spend years learning Confucius's teachings. Scholars who studied and taught Confucius's ideas were among the most important people in China. In this way Confucius became more important than any ruler in shaping Chinese society.

OUTLOOK

22. The people of ancient China built their civilization in the river valleys of eastern China. Its rulers, the Shang and Zhou dynasties, faced strong nobles who controlled independent city-states. Wars and disorder spread in China, especially during the Zhou Dynasty. About this time a great teacher named Confucius appeared. His teachings about family and government and his rules of conduct came to unite the Chinese people by guiding their thinking and ways of behaving. Why are ideas of ◀ thinkers like Confucius sometimes more powerful and long-lasting than governments or armies? Can you think of some ◀ ideas that have been as important in your own life?

VOCABULARY REVIEW

Write each of the following words on a piece of paper. Then write the definition for each word, using the glossary on pages 728–738.

1. Mandate of Heaven
2. ancestor worship
3. filial piety
4. extended family
5. calligraphy

SKILL BUILDER: READING A MAP

Maps can help you learn much more than where countries or rivers are located. Maps can also be used to trace the development of people and ideas. Look at the map below. It shows the areas of the world's major religions in about 200 B.C. As you can see, there were four major religions at that time in the ancient world. What were they? If you notice, each of the four religions covers certain national boundaries. Some of those boundaries are almost the same today. For example, the religion Zoroastrianism was founded in the sixth century B.C. The basis of Zoroastrianism is that we are involved in a constant battle of good against evil. Members of the religion study fire as a way of helping them pray and worship life. The founder, Zoroaster, was a Persian, and his religion soon became the national religion. Both the rulers and the ruled of Persia (present-day Iran) had a religion in common. This made the nation stronger, because almost everyone shared the same goals and ideas. Islam later replaced Zoroastrianism as Persia's state religion. However, the Persian nation developed a rough outline of its present borders as a nation unified by Zoroastrianism. What does that suggest about religion and national unity in ancient times? Try to answer the questions below by using the information provided in the map.

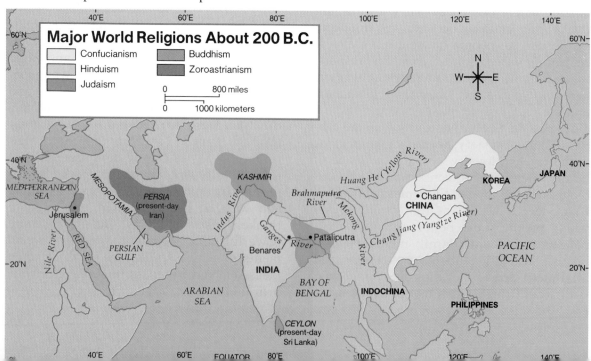

Major World Religions About 200 B.C.

Confucianism
Hinduism
Judaism
Buddhism
Zoroastrianism

0   800 miles
0   1000 kilometers

1. Confucianism was widespread in what country or countries?

2. Where was Zorastrianism popular?

3. What nation or nations practiced Hinduism?

4. Where was Judaism practiced?

5. What water boundaries may have hindered the westward spread of Zoroastrianism?

6. Can you tell where Buddhism originated?

SKILL BUILDER: CRITICAL THINKING AND COMPREHENSION

1. Classifying

A complete history lesson about a group of people usually teaches about their leaders, religion, culture, trade, geography, technology or science, and daily life.

▶ Write the headings below on a piece of paper. Then look through the chapter to find two sentences to write under each head.

Culture of China

Trade of China

Leaders of China

Geography of China

Daily Life of China

Chinese Technology and Science

Religion of China

2. Main Idea

▶ Look at paragraphs 13, 15, and 16. On a piece of paper, write the main idea stated in each paragraph.

3. Summarizing

Sometimes several paragraphs that are grouped together contain parts of one main idea or message. For example, "The Star-Spangled Banner" describes a battle between the British and Americans in 1814. But it uses different stanzas or paragraphs to explain different parts of the battle. The main idea of "The Star-Spangled Banner" is that the United States won a big victory. But the description of that victory is divided into several parts.

▶ Write a summary of paragraphs 2, 3, and 4 in this chapter.

ENRICHMENT

1. China's landscape is dramatically diverse. Use the map on page 50 as a guide in making a relief map of China. You will need a wooden board, plaster of paris, and paint. You may want to do this activity with a small group of students.

2. China's population is so large and diverse that uniting the country has often been a problem. Imagine you were the ruler of China. What steps would you take to bring the various groups of Chinese people together as one nation?

CHAPTER 8

Ancient Africa

▲ Remains of ancient pyramids are reminders of the civilizations that once flourished in Africa's ancient kingdom of Cush.

OBJECTIVE: Where did the early civilizations develop in ancient Africa, and how did they help shape Africa's history?

▶ **1.** How have you learned about your own heritage and ethnic background? Did your relatives tell about their own childhoods? Have you heard your parents or grandparents tell about the "old days"? Do they tell stories about people who died before you were born? Most people learn the histories of their families in this way. They learn by listening to and remembering these stories. Suppose, however, that listening to someone talk was the way you learned everything. For example, suppose it was the only way that you could learn your country's history. In Africa, most early peoples did not have written languages. Instead, the teachers among some of these peoples trained themselves to remember their people's history. These teachers became the main source for passing along the history of their culture. History that is passed along through the spoken word from one generation to the next is called oral history.

Trading region in Cush is founded by Egyptians c. 2000 B.C.

Nok culture is established c. 1000 B.C.

Assyrians invade Egypt and force the Cush out 671 B.C.

2000 B.C.	1500 B.C.	1000 B.C.	500 B.C.

Cush people establish independent kingdom c. 1100 B.C.

King Kashta of Cush invades and conquers Egypt 750 B.C.

Cush rulers found capital city of Meroë 540 B.C.

GEOGRAPHY AND CLIMATE: In what parts of Africa did early peoples find the best land and climate for settlement?

2. Most of North Africa is a hot, dry desert called the **Sahara** (suh-HAR-uh). The Sahara covers nearly all of North Africa except for the Nile River valley in Egypt and the Mediterranean Sea coast in the northwest.

3. South of the Sahara is a hot area of short grasses called the **steppe** (STEP). The steppe gives way to the **savanna**, a warm region with scattered trees, longer grass, and greater rainfall. To the south of the savanna are tropical rain forests. The climate of the rain forests is very warm, and the rainfall is heavy. Much of this rain-forest region lies along the equator. South of the equator is another huge savanna, and still farther south are more steppes. The steppes give way to the large Kalahari and Namib deserts. Africa's rivers, such as the Nile, Zambezi (zam-BEE-zee), and Zaire (ZY-ur) were important water sources, and they served as the main water highways for the early African people.

4. The climate of the Sahara has changed greatly over the thousands of years since its first inhabitants lived there. Archaeologists have found cave paintings in the Sahara that indicate that people were living there as early as 8000 B.C. At that time, the Sahara was covered with forests and grasslands. A long, slow change in climate brought hot, dry winds to the Sahara, changing its fertile land into a desert. This change from fertile land to desert is called **desertification** (dih-zurt-ih-fih-KAY-shun). Today, this change is continuing, and the desert is slowly advancing into the steppe.

THE KINGDOM OF CUSH: How did Cush become a great center of trade and iron making?

5. Cush (KOOSH) was one of the early civilizations of ancient Africa. About 2000 B.C. the Egyptians founded a trading city in the Cush region. At that time, Cush was part of the Egyptian kingdom. Trade in gold and ivory grew between Cush and Egypt and lands in Asia. In 1100 B.C., the people of Cush drove the Egyptians out and established an independent kingdom.

6. About 750 B.C., King Kashta (KAHSH-tah) of Cush invaded and conquered most of Egypt. Kashta's son, King Piankhy (PYAHN-kee) completed the conquest of Egypt and became pharaoh of both Cush and Egypt. For nearly 100 years, Cush rulers controlled this kingdom. Finally, in 671 B.C., the Assyrians invaded Egypt and forced the Cush armies out of Egypt.

7. The kingdom of Cush continued to grow as an important civilization after it was separated from Egypt. About 540 B.C., the rulers of Cush founded their capital city at Meroë (MEHR-uh-way) on the Nile. There Cush culture reached its peak from 250 B.C. to A.D. 150. The people of Cush developed a writing system and built pyramids, a temple, and a royal palace. They also learned how to make iron weapons, because the Assyrian armies had used iron weapons to drive the Cush from Egypt. In addition, there were large deposits of iron ore around Meroë. As a result, Meroë developed into one of the great iron-making centers of the ancient world.

8. Iron weapons gave Cush superiority over enemies that were still using stone or bronze weapons. Although it does not seem that important to us today, the iron-making process was a closely-guarded secret in Cush. It was known only to a select few, such as priests and craftworkers. Why do you think it was important to the Cushites to keep the iron-making process a secret? ◀

9. Although separated from major trade centers by large deserts, the Cushites were anxious to connect with other parts of the world. They traded with Egypt, Arabia, and East Africa, and even with places as far off as India and possibly China. Cush craftworkers were highly skilled in making products from ivory, gold, silver, and copper. Meroë merchants became wealthy from trading these products. They also enriched their country by bringing back food, art, cloth, and ideas from other cultures.

Ask: Why do you think most of what we know about Cush comes from Egyptian chronicles? Is this the best way to learn about a culture? Why or why not?

57

THE KINGDOM OF AKSUM: How was the culture of Aksum different from that of the Cush?

10. Ethopia has its roots in a civilization that arose along the southwest coast of the Red Sea. The civilization began as an area of small settlements. Several groups of people, including southern Arabians, Cushites, and the Habashat, settled here and developed what became the Kingdom of Aksum (AHK-soom). The kingdom was named after its capital city, Aksum.

11. The kingdom of Aksum developed into an important power. Aksum grew to be powerful because it had important trading ports along the Red Sea and was a large supplier of ivory. Besides ivory, Aksum traders traded tortoise shells and rhinoceros horns. Later they traded gold with Greek, Persian, and Indian merchants. Aksum traders were also known for their strong and fast ships. The wealth from trade was seen in the gold and pearl decorated cloth of Aksum kings. The wealth was also seen in the military power that Aksum displayed and in the tall stone needles that decorated the capital city.

12. The people of Aksum brought change to their part of Africa in several ways. Aksum adopted the Greek language and Greek education. Under the leadership of King Ezana and later leaders, Aksum became the African center for the Christian religion. Even after the Arabs and the religion of Islam developed a powerful stronghold in many areas of Africa, Christianity survived in Aksum.

13. In the early 700s A.D. Aksum was weakened by invaders. The Aksumites joined with other groups, including Semites, who crossed to Africa from the Arabian peninsula, in the Ethiopian highlands. Modern Ethiopians are a blend of these groups. When the Portuguese first discovered the kingdom of Ethiopia in the 1400s, it was Christian. Ethiopia was also ruled much like Europe of that time. The

▼ Civilization began in Africa along the Nile river valley and spread out into other parts of the continent. What powerful ancient kingdoms arose south of the ancient Egyptians?

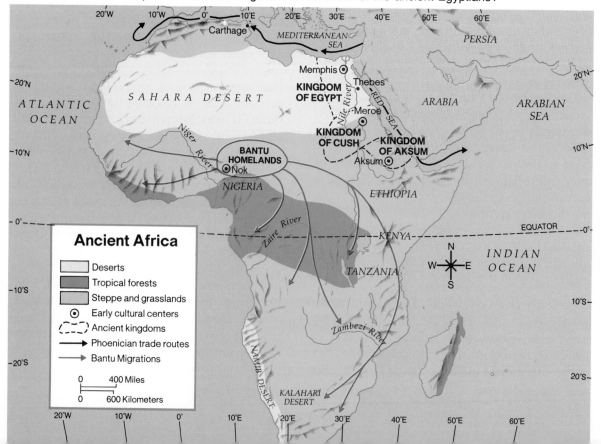

▲ This figure is an example of Nok terra cotta sculpture. Why do you think the Nok believed that the head was the source of life's power?

chaeologists have found that sometime around 300 B.C. iron-making was introduced into the Nok culture. People traveling from either Meroë or Carthage probably were the source of this knowledge. Iron-making changed the Nok culture. With stronger tools, they were able to cut down trees and settle nearby forests. Their crops included yams, palm nuts, peas, okra, and cereal grasses. With stronger iron weapons, the Nok also became better hunters.

16. One of the lasting achievements of the Nok people was their art. Skilled Nok artisans made beautiful sculptures of **terra cotta** (TEH-ruh KAH-tuh), a red and brown baked clay. They also were able to cast sculptures in iron and bronze. The sculptures were mostly of people, although some were of animals. A figure's head on Nok sculpture was always much larger than the body, because the Nok believed the head was the source of life's power. The art of the Nok culture probably influenced the beautiful art of later West African peoples of Yoruba and Benin.

Portuguese admired the Ethiopians' strong moral sense of duty to serve the group. ▶ What do you think are the advantages of having such an attitude?

THE PEOPLE OF NOK: What were the chief contributions of the Nok people to African cultures?

14. In West Africa, another early civilization developed in what is now Nigeria. The civilization takes its name from the village of Nok (NAHK), where the first sculptures from that period were found. Look at the map on page 58 to locate Nok. People first settled here about 1000 B.C. The Nok people were farmers who lived in villages. Their dwellings were huts made with frames of reeds covered with mud and straw.

15. Little is known about the Nok culture, which lasted until about A.D. 200. Ar-

OUTLOOK

17. When the knowledge of iron-making spread from Meroë to other African tribes, many far-reaching changes took place in Africa. Iron tools helped farmers and hunters increase the food supply. More food allowed the population to increase. The expanding population caused the Bantu people to begin one of the greatest **migrations**, or movements of population, around A.D. 1. The Bantu spread out through central, southern, and eastern Africa for more than 1,000 years. As the Bantu moved, they spread their knowledge of iron and crops. Bananas, yams, and taro became the main source of food in the newly settled areas of Africa. The great Bantu migration is responsible for the fact that about one third of Africa today is populated by Bantu. How does knowledge of ancient African societies help you to better understand Africa today?

Background: Bananas, yams, and taros had been imported to Africa from southeast Asia. The Bantu migration would not have been possible without these foods.

59

CHAPTER REVIEW

VOCABULARY REVIEW

On a separate sheet of paper, write each number and word listed below. Then write the letter of the definition next to the word it matches.

1. Sahara
2. steppe
3. savanna
4. desertification
5. terra cotta
6. migration

a. large desert in northern Africa
b. red and brown baked clay
c. a warm region of scattered trees and long grass
d. hot area of short grasses
e. climatic change from fertile land to desert
f. movement of large groups of people

SKILL BUILDER: MAKING A TIME LINE

A time line is a graph that helps us to see the order in which events happened. A time line can help us understand how events relate to each other in time. The history of the world, your neighborhood, or your own life can be better understood through the use of a time line. Copy the time line below, which covers a 20-year period. Using the time line at the beginning of this chapter as a model, fill in events from the history of your life on your time line.

1975	1980	1985	1990

SKILL BUILDER: CRITICAL THINKING AND COMPREHENSION

 1. Classifying

▶ Each of the three ancient African civilizations discussed in Chapter 8 was different. Copy the names of the three ancient African civilizations shown next. Then write at least four special features of each of the three cultures below each heading.

NOK	CUSH	AKSUM
1.	1.	1.
2.	2.	2.
3.	3.	3.
4.	4.	4.

▲ **2. Main Ideas**

▶ Several main ideas in the information presented in Chapter 8 are listed next. Write each main idea. Under each main idea, write the details that support the main idea.

a. The land and climate of Africa are varied.

b. The Kingdom of Cush continued to grow as an important civilization after it was separated from Egypt

c. Nok art has lasted until today.

▲ **3. Summarizing**

▶ Below are listed four paragraph numbers. Following each paragraph number, there are three summary sentences. Re-read each of the paragraphs numbered below. Then match the paragraphs with the summary sentence you think fits.

3-1. Paragraph 4
    a. Africans have a long history.
    b. People lived in the area of the Sahara before it became a desert.
    c. People who lived in the area of the Sahara painted on cave walls.

3-2. Paragraph 8
    a. Iron ore is found in the ground.
    b. Bronze is superior to iron for making tools and weapons.
    c. The ability to make iron gave the people of Cush an advantage over people who did not use iron.

3-3. Paragraph 12
    a. King Ezana was a leader in Aksum.
    b. The Aksumites adopted Christianity and the Greek language.
    c. The Arabs brought Islam to Aksum.

3-4. Paragraph 16
    a. The Noks were skilled artists whose influence can be found in the art of later West African tribes.
    b. The Noks believed the head was the source of life's power.
    c. Nok sculptures were of animals and people.

ENRICHMENT

Much of African history has been passed on orally. Family histories are usually handed down the same way. Talk with your parents and grandparents and find out how far back your family history goes. Or talk with the elderly in your community about your community's history. Be prepared to discuss your oral history findings with your class.

CHAPTER 9

Ancient America

▲ As the Ice Age ended, the earliest Americans crossed into North America over a land bridge now covered by the waters of the Bering Strait.

OBJECTIVE: Who were some of the first peoples who lived in the Americas, and where did they build their ancient civilizations?

1. Did your family come to the United States from some other part of the world? Were any of your friends born in another country? Do you know families who moved to your neighborhood from another nation? Many Americans have come here from other lands. In recent years, many people have come to the mainland United States from Mexico. Others have arrived from Puerto Rico, Cuba, Jamaica, Haiti, and other Caribbean islands. Newcomers have also included people from India, Vietnam, Korea, and other Asian nations. About 400 years ago, people began arriving in America from Africa and Europe. Even earlier than that, people crossed over to America from Asia. The ancestors of all Americans—including Native Americans—came to the United States from somewhere else. You will read about the arrival of the earliest Americans in this chapter.

Pottery is made in
North America
c. 2300 B.C.

La Venta becomes
major Olmec settlement
c. 800 B.C.

| 2000 B.C. | 1500 B.C. | 1000 B.C. | 500 B.C. |

Olmec civilization
begins
c. 1500 B.C.

Oln
civiliza
disappe
c. A.D.

ESL/LEP Strategy: If there are students from Latin America in the class, encourage them to share what they know about the ancient history of their countries.

Background: Until the Cold War began in the 1940s, Eskimos living near the Bering Strait visited across the strait in the USSR. In the winter they could simply walk across on the ice.

EARLY AMERICANS: How did the first people come to the Americas?

2. During the Ice Age, about 30,000 years ago, small groups of people came to North America from Asia. They came by crossing over an **isthmus** (IS-mus) where the Bering (BEH-ring) Strait is today. An isthmus, or land bridge, is land that connects two continents. This land bridge between Asia and North America was formed when the glaciers lowered the sea level there. Find the Bering Strait on the map on page 64.

3. It took many thousands of years for the peoples from Asia and their descendants to spread throughout North and South America. The people who crossed the Bering Strait came only in small hunting groups. Thus, there were few people in an enormous land. Even so, in time, groups of early peoples gradually moved into every part of North America. Other groups moved south along the Pacific coast. From there, they moved into Central America and across the Isthmus of Panama into South America. In time there were people throughout the entire huge continent of South America, and in the Caribbean islands as well. Look at the map on page 64 again to locate Central America, the Isthmus of Panama, and the Caribbean islands.

MIDDLE AMERICA: How and why did the earliest American civilization begin in ancient Mexico?

4. About 5000 B.C., people living in southern Mexico in valleys near the Pacific Ocean learned how to grow corn. Corn became the chief crop of nearly all the early peoples of ancient America. However, for many centuries the people of southern Mexico continued to hunt and fish for most of their food. It was not until about 1500 B.C. that several groups of people in Mexico became settled farmers. They began to live in small farming villages and learned how to grow beans and squash as well as corn. Most important of all, they learned how to irrigate the soil, using ditches to bring water to their fields from nearby rivers or streams. They also learned how to improve their crops by mixing fish into the soil to make it more fertile.

5. The first civilization of ancient America was created in southern Mexico by the Olmecs (ALL-meks). The Olmecs lived in the flat coastal land of southern Mexico. About 1500 B.C., they built several cities along the Gulf of Mexico. These cities were the religious and cultural centers of the Olmec culture. La Venta (luh-VEN-tuh) and Tres Zapotes (trays-suh-POH-tus) were the most important.

6. Most of the Olmec people lived in villages near the cities. There they farmed their crops of corn, beans, and squash. The inland mountains protected the Olmecs and also were the source of several rivers that brought water to Olmec farmlands.

7. Each Olmec city, as an important religious center, was built around a large temple. The temples, made of hardened clay, were in the shape of enormous pyramids but rounded at the bottom. Around each temple was a large courtyard. Nearby were tall altars made of solid blocks of stone. There also were giant stone heads, which are among the most unusual monuments of any civilization. Some of these stone heads weigh as much as 40 tons. There is no stone at all near the places where they are found; the nearest place where stone is found is 80 miles (130 kilometers) away. Can you imagine what it meant for people equipped only with stone tools and muscle power to transport the stones to their sacred temples? The stones must have been cut in the mountains, dragged to the nearest river, loaded on rafts, and floated to the temple. Why would the Olmecs have been willing to make such a tremendous effort?

8. The Olmecs worshiped the **jaguar** (JAG-war), a jungle animal of the cat family, as their chief god. They believed that this god brought water for corn, their chief source of food. The Olmec gods were worshiped in great temples built on top of pyramids. Here, human sacrifices were sometimes offered. The leaders of the Olmecs were the priests, who lived in the cities and ruled from there. These priest-

Background: Ignacio Bernal's *The World of the Olmecs* (Berkeley: University of California Press, 1969) is an excellent source guide for this chapter.

kings held religious ceremonies and made offerings to the god. As rulers, they said that the people who lived in the nearby villages had to offer sacrifices to the god. The people also had to help build the pyramids, altars, and tombs in which the priest-kings were buried.

SPOTLIGHT ON SOURCES

9. Ignacio Bernal is an important Mexican archaeologist who has spent many years studying the Olmec civilization. In his book *The Olmec World*, Bernal describes how important religion was to the Olmec people:

> The vigorous orientation [strict planning] of Olmec cities . . . , the style of the great sculptures, the splendid tomb of La Venta, and the burial offerings of extremely valuable jade [green stone], the attire [clothing] of the priests . . .

on the monuments . . . : all of these indicate the vast importance given to religion.

—*The Olmec World*, Ignacio Bernal

10. The Olmecs made other important contributions to ancient American culture. They developed a calendar to help them plan when to plant corn. What other ancient civilization had developed a calendar? The Olmecs had a system of writing, as well as a way of using numbers to count and measure. However, no one has yet discovered how to read this Olmec writing.

11. The Olmec civilization lasted for nearly 1,500 years, and then, suddenly, it disappeared. Olmec cities fell into ruins. Archaeologists still do not know what happened to the Olmec people. Perhaps they were conquered by some other people. Perhaps they were forced to flee from their cities. Whatever happened, many of the ideas and achievements of the Olmecs survived. Their calendar, counting system,

▼ Olmecs built the earliest Native American civilization beginning about 1500 B.C. In what part of the Americas did the ancient Olmec civilization develop?

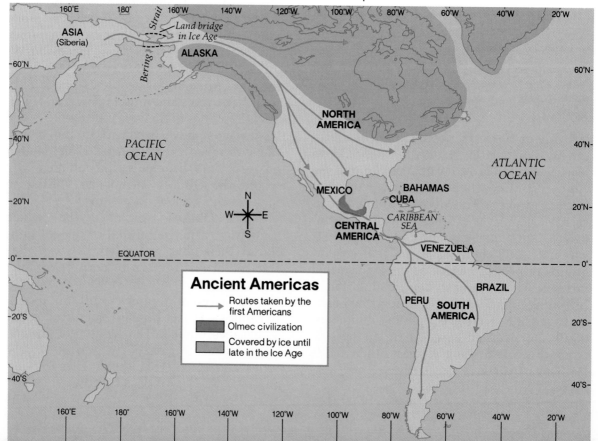

and religion became parts of other civilizations that soon developed in Mexico and South America.

NORTH AMERICA: Where did the early peoples live in North America, and why did they develop many different cultures?

12. In North America, many different groups of early peoples established important cultures. Between 1500 B.C. and 1000 B.C., the early people in California learned to grow corn and settled in villages. During these same years, other early peoples throughout North America learned to farm. However, most of these early people also remained hunters and gatherers. They did not settle in permanent villages until about A.D. 300.

13. The early peoples of North America lived in groups called tribes. These tribes lived in every part of North America. The land was so huge that it was possible for many tribes to develop apart from each other. The tribes in each area developed their own cultures, or ways of living. They practiced their own religions. They developed ways of organizing their tribes and choosing tribal chiefs.

14. The cultures of peoples in ancient America were quite different from the cultures in the early centers of civilization in Asia and Africa. For one thing, civilization developed thousands of years later in the Americas than in Asia and Africa. Farming and cities also took longer to develop in the Americas than in Asia and Africa. This happened partly because early Americans did not know how to make iron and use it for tools. As a result, they did not have iron plows or hoes to break up the soil and make planting easy. Instead, early Americans used tools made of wood, bone, or stone for digging. Such tools made cultivating the land and planting crops difficult and slow. In addition, large parts of early America were covered by thick forests or jungles. With no iron tools to clear the land, many early Americans had to depend mostly on hunting and gathering to supply their food.

▲ Ancient Olmecs carved this massive stone head. The Olmecs created the first civilization in the Americas about 1500 B.C.

OUTLOOK

15. The early peoples who lived in ancient America formed many different cultures. In North America, most of these peoples lived in tribes that developed their own ways of farming, hunting, and gathering food. Some of these tribes later lived in settled villages. However, they did not build civilizations centered in cities. Civilization in the Americas developed independently, as the first Americans learned how to solve the special problems of their land. The most advanced civilization of ancient America was established in Mexico by the Olmecs about 1500 B.C. The Olmecs built several great cities, which soon became centers of the Olmec religion and Olmec society. How ◄ does this show the importance of cities in ancient civilizations? Why are cities still so important today? Can you describe some of the ways that cities affect your life?

Activity: Discuss with students the Native American cultures that developed in your area of the United States. What special climatic or geographic features played a role in the development of those tribes?

65

CHAPTER REVIEW

VOCABULARY REVIEW

Write each of the following words on a sheet of paper. Then write the correct definition for each word. Use the glossary on pages 728–738 to help you.

isthmus

jaguar

SKILL BUILDER: STUDYING FOR A TEST

Most of you may worry somewhat when test-taking time approaches. However, if you study ahead of time and are prepared, it is not difficult to succeed in taking your tests. The first step to studying well is knowing what you need to study. Usually your teacher will tell you ahead of time what subjects will be covered on a test. It is important to begin studying about a week ahead of time. That way you will not be nervous or miss anything, both of which might happen if you left the studying to the last minute. Write an outline of the topics to be tested. This will serve as a guide once you begin. Gather any books, notes, or materials you need. Set aside a certain period each day to study. If possible, make up sample tests on your own or with a friend.

After you have taken your sample test, look up the correct answers to any questions you answered incorrectly. You may need to ask your teacher for an explanation in some cases. This will help you avoid some of the mistakes you might have made in studying for or taking the actual test. Try the following steps to prepare for a test.

1. Imagine you are preparing for a test on this unit. Your first step would be to prepare an outline of the topics. Prepare an outline of Unit 1.

2. Make a list of any books, notes, or other materials you may need for studying.

3. Prepare a study schedule.

4. Prepare a sample test that covers the material in this unit.

5. Working with a classmate, swap your sample tests. After you have taken the sample test, score your results.

6. With your classmate, go back over your sample test. Restudy the text and your notes on subjects where your answers were incorrect.

7. Keep the sample test. Use it as a study aid when you are preparing to take a real test on this unit of your book.

SKILL BUILDER: CRITICAL THINKING AND COMPREHENSION

 1. Classifying

▶ On a separate sheet of paper, write the three headings below. Then classify the information that follows the headings by writing the letter of each description under the correct heading.

Olmec farming　　　　Religion of the Olmecs　　　　Major cities of the Olmecs

a. worshipped the jaguar

b. planted corn, squash and beans

66

c. built large pyramid-shaped temples

d. La Venta

e. used calendar to plan planting season

f. Tres Zapotes

g. learned irrigation

h. offered sacrifices

▲ **2. Main Idea**

▶ Choose the correct main idea for each paragraph identified below:

The main idea of paragraph 3 is that
_____
a. the Americas are a huge land mass.
b. the early people who came to America traveled in small hunting groups.
c. it took many thousands of years for people to settle in the Americas.

The main idea of paragraph 4 is that
_____
a. the climate is warm in Middle America.
b. corn was the main food source that allowed early Americans to settle into farming villages.
c. the earliest and most advanced cultures developed in North America.

The main idea of paragraph 5 is that
_____
a. farmers learned how to grow crops.
b. farmers learned how to irrigate their fields.
c. the Olmecs created the first civilization of ancient America in southern Mexico.

The main idea of paragraph 11 is that
_____
a. the earliest and most advanced American civilization was that of the Olmecs.
b. the Olmecs lived in villages near their cities.
c. the Olmec civilization, which lasted for 1,500 years, suddenly disappeared.

▲ **3. Summarizing**   When you prepare for a test or take notes, it sometimes helps to write a brief summary of the class lesson or the textbook chapter. A summary is an easy way to list the main ideas that you have heard in class or read in your book.

▶ Read paragraphs 2 and 3 in this chapter. Then read the two summaries of the paragraphs below. Which summary is most accurate? Explain why.

3-1. Early Americans walked a long way to get to Asia. They were cold and hungry most of the time. However, they were able to cross the isthmus located where the Bering Strait is today. These early people came into Asia in small hunting groups because they had to move across an enormous land.

3-2. Early Americans traveled across the Bering Strait isthmus from Asia to North America 30,000 years ago. They came in small hunting groups and eventually settled throughout North America, Middle America, and South America and the Caribbean. It took many thousands of years for these peoples from Asia and their descendants to spread through the Western Hemisphere.

ENRICHMENT

1. Using clay or cardboard, make a model of an Olmec pyramid.

2. Find pictures of Olmec artifacts such as cooking supplies, jewelry, or clothing. Bring the pictures to class, and present them as though you are a reporter on the nightly news.

3. Farmers today grow their crops during a certain time each year based on the calendar. Find out what the planting and harvesting seasons are for some fruits and vegetables that your family buys at the store or supermarket. Why do you think few crops are planted in most parts of the United States in the winter?

UNIT REVIEW

SUMMARY

People have lived on earth for hundreds of thousands of years. For most of this time, in what is known as the Old Stone Age, they were wandering hunters and food gatherers. About 10,000 years ago, the New Stone Age brought agriculture and the domestication of animals. These developments made it possible for people to settle in one place in larger numbers.

The development of agriculture led directly to the first civilizations. The ingredients of civilization are specialization of labor, an organized set of laws, a writing system, and a population that can support a culture over a long period of time. The earliest civilizations developed in river valleys: the Tigris-Euphrates valley in Mesopotamia, the Nile valley in Egypt, the Indus valley in India, and the Huang valley in China. In Mesopotamia, the Sumerians were the first people to develop a writing system, called cueneiform, which was later adopted by the Babylonians and other peoples in the Tigris-Euphrates valley. Early Egyptian civilization is remembered for its burial customs, including the huge pyramids in which its early kings, or pharaohs, were buried. Other important early peoples in the regions between Egypt and Mesopotamia were the Hittites, who were the first to make wide use of iron, and the Phoenicians, a seafaring people whose alphabet is the basis of the one we use today. The Hebrews were a small group whose kingdom did not last, but they were tremendously important as the first people to worship a single God.

In India, the development of Hinduism and the caste system established a framework for that civilization. China's civilization was shaped by the teachings of Confucius. New civilizations appeared in Africa south of the Sahara. In Mexico the Olmecs created the first civilization in the Western Hemisphere.

SKILL BUILDER: READING A MAP

When and Where the Civilizations Began

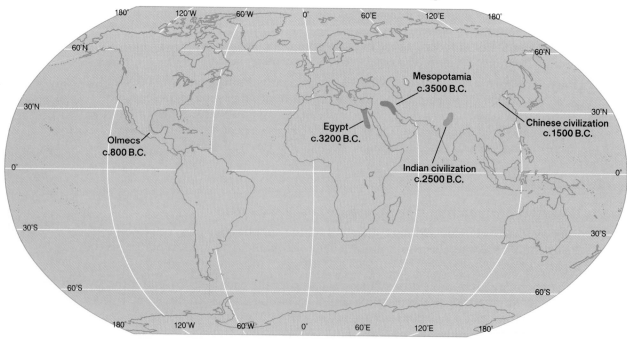

1. Which was the earliest civilization?

2. In what continent did civilization first appear?

3. What other civilizations developed on that same continent?

4. Which civilization developed in Africa?

5. Of the civilizations shown on the map, which was the last to develop?

6. On what continent did this civilization appear?

7. How does the map suggest that all the first civilizations developed in similar climates? What kind of climate was it?

SKILL BUILDER: CRITICAL THINKING AND COMPREHENSION

1. Main Idea

▶ Read the sentences in each group below. Decide which sentence in each group is the main idea and which sentences are details of that idea. Write each group of sentences on your paper with the main idea first and the details below it.

1-1. The sentences in this group are about the contributions of early peoples.
   a. The Hittites were the first people to make wide use of iron.
   b. The belief in only one God was first practiced by the Hebrews.
   c. Smaller nations have introduced many important ideas to the world.
   d. The Phoenicians spread their alphabet to many parts of the ancient world.

1-2. The sentences in this group are about Egypt.
   a. The bodies of dead people were preserved by being made into mummies.
   b. Food and other items were buried with people for their use in the afterlife.
   c. Huge tombs were constructed to protect the bodies of the pharaohs.
   d. The belief in life after death was an important part of Egyptian civilization.

2. Classifying

▶ Classify each of the following items according to whether it has to do with Mesopotamia, Egypt, India, or China.

ziggurat	filial piety	calligraphy
monsoon	cuneiform	pharaoh
papyrus	Hinduism	Code of Hammurabi
caste system	ancestor worship	hieroglyphics
Confucius	rajah	reincarnation
city-state	mummy	

ENRICHMENT

1. Work in groups of three or four students. Each group writes a short radio commercial urging tourists to visit one of the civilizations studied in the unit. The group also prepares a travel poster advertising the civilization.

2. Imagine that you are the ruler of one of the civilizations studied in this unit. Write a letter to the ruler of a different civilization. Offer to sell what your civilization produces, pointing out the advantages of owning it. Suggest what you might be interested in buying from the other civilization in return.

UNIT 2

ESL/LEP Strategy: Divide the class into groups representing each of the four cultural groups in this unit: *India, China, Japan,* and *Australia and Oceania.* Have students work in their groups to prepare an article describing that culture, using vocabulary words from the unit.

CIVILIZATIONS GROW AND SPREAD

OBJECTIVE: Unit 2 will describe the growth of separate cultures and nations among early Eastern and Pacific peoples.

| Buddhism begins 500 B.C. | Early Japanese first cultivate rice 300 B.C. | Shi Huang Di unifies Chinese city-states into an empire 247–221 B.C. | | | Height of Gupta Empire occurs A.D. 320–467 |

| 600 B.C. | 400 B.C. | 200 B.C. | A.D. 1 | A.D. 200 | A.D. 400 |

| | Chandragutpa founds the Maurya Empire of India 321 B.C. | Asoka brings reforms to India 274 B.C. | | Trac sisters lead Vietnamese revolt against Chinese rule A.D. 39 | |

▲ The Great Wall of China was built 2,200 years ago to keep out invaders from the north.

White Huns invade
India; Gupta Empire
ends
c. A.D. 650

Chinese rule of
Vietnam ends
A.D. 939

A.D. 600   A.D. 800   A.D. 1000   A.D. 1200

Japanese begin
missions to
China
A.D. 630

Nara, Japan's first
capital, is built
A.D. 710

Yorimoto becomes
first Japanese
shogun
A.D. 1192

CHAPTER 1

India's Early Empires

▲ Four scowling lions guard the ancient edicts of Asoka, carved on this pillar in India more than 2,200 years ago.

OBJECTIVE: What are the contributions that India's early empires made to the world?

1. As a small child, one of the first things you learned was how to count. Since that time numbers have been a part of your everyday life. Without numbers, how would you know which channel to switch to on your TV to view your favorite program? How would you tell time? The decimal number system that you use is just one example of many useful ideas that spread from the early empires of India to the world today. Arab traders, finding the decimal system easy to use, carried it from India to other places. For that reason, the decimal

system is called the Arabic number system, crediting the people who spread it to other lands. What are some of the other contributions of India's early empires? Scholars in India were the first to understand that the earth moves around the sun. They were the

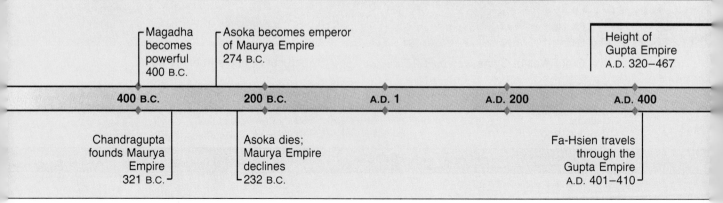

- Magadha becomes powerful 400 B.C.
- Asoka becomes emperor of Maurya Empire 274 B.C.
- Height of Gupta Empire A.D. 320–467

| 400 B.C. | 200 B.C. | A.D. 1 | A.D. 200 | A.D. 400 |

- Chandragupta founds Maurya Empire 321 B.C.
- Asoka dies; Maurya Empire declines 232 B.C.
- Fa-Hsien travels through the Gupta Empire A.D. 401–410

Activity: Ask for examples of foods we eat or customs we have that come from another culture. Point out that traditions evolve over time. Our language, for example, evolved through the centuries from many other languages. (From French: avenue, restaurant; from German; kindergarten; from Spanish; tomato, bronco.)

72

discoverers of many of the stars and planets. Indian healers found ways to make medicines from plants and herbs. When you study math and science today, you are learning about some ideas and systems that were born long ago in India.

THE MAURYA EMPIRE: How did Maurya emperors build their huge empire?

2. By 400 B.C., some kingdoms in northern and eastern India, such as the kingdom of Magadha (MAG-uh-duh) in the east, became especially large and powerful. The kings of Magadha built large armies. The people of Magadha traded products from their farms, forests, and mines with people in other lands, and increased their kingdom's wealth. Soon the Magadha kingdom took over neighboring lands.

3. The first great empire of India was formed about 321 B.C. by a man named Chandragupta Maurya (chun-dray-GOOP-tay MAH-uhr-yah). Chandragupta overthrew the Magadha kingdom in the Ganges River Valley, swept west, and took control of the Indus River Valley. Chandragupta's son and grandson further enlarged the Maurya Empire by conquering lands in central and eastern India.

4. The Maurya Empire was large but it worked well because its government was well organized. The emperor Chandragupta set up a **bureaucracy** (byoo-RAH-kruh-see), to carry out his orders. A bureaucracy is a governmental system of departments run by appointed officials. High officials worked in the capital city. Lower-level officials ran the villages. Spies sent reports to Chandragupta about events in the villages and about plots against the emperor. Chandragupta's huge army of 700,000 men, 9,000 elephants, and 10,000 chariots helped him keep control.

5. Chandragupta improved business and trade for his people. The emperor built canals that brought a steady supply of water to farms. The harvest of wheat, rice, and tea increased as a result. Chandragupta's bureaucracy created government jobs for some of its citizens, similar to jobs some people hold in the United States today. Chandragupta also built a new road system that linked all parts of the empire. The roads made it easier to transport goods to ports. Ships from the Maurya Empire traded goods with the Middle East and with other parts of Asia. Why were the ◀ improved transportation systems key to improving trade between India and other nations?

PEOPLE IN HISTORY

6. Chandragupta's grandson, Asoka (ah-SO-kah), became emperor of Maurya in 274 B.C. Like his grandfather before him, Asoka began his rule by conquering new lands in India. More than 100,000 people died in Asoka's first conquest of Kalinga, a land on India's east coast. Find Kalinga on the map at the bottom of page 74. Asoka, horrified

Daily life in . . .

Early Indian society was based on the extended family system. The extended family was made up of the parents, the unmarried children, and the married sons and their immediate families. Married daughters became members of their husband's families. Sons were favored over daughters. Buddhist women chose their own husbands, whereas Hindu marriages were arranged by the family. Girls were married at a very young age. According to Hindu law and custom, a woman's first duty was to her husband and his family. If widowed, a Hindu woman was not allowed to return to her own family and had to remain with her husband's family. Widows were thought to be unlucky, and were often treated as outcasts.

Ask: What kinds of government jobs do people in the United States hold today? (Examples are President, postal workers, toll taker, tax collector.) Why do governments need bureaucracies? (Each department will do a certain job and become expert at it, keeping the government running smoothly at all levels.)

73

when he learned how many lives had been lost in battle, decided to change his style of rule.

7. Asoka became a Buddhist and set out to win the support of India's people through kindness. Asoka softened the punishment for crimes. He set up hospitals for people and for animals. **Vaccines** (vak-SEENZ) for some diseases were developed in Asoka's hospitals. Vaccines are weakened preparations of organisms that keep people or animals from getting particular diseases. Asoka sent teachers to all parts of the empire. Everyone had the opportunity to learn. Even today in museums, people can read Asoka's **edicts** (EE-dikts), or orders, which were carved on stone pillars. Asoka's edicts asked people to treat one another fairly. He tried to lead his people by his good example, rather than by the use of force.

8. With the death of Asoka in 232 B.C., the Maurya Empire began its decline. The emperors who followed Asoka were weak, and the empire split into smaller kingdoms. But many of Asoka's peaceful ideas were spread to other regions by Buddhist **missionaries** (MISH-uh-nair-eez). A missionary is someone who tries to teach or spread a religion to people in other lands.

THE GUPTA EMPIRE: Why did a Golden Age occur under Gupta rule?

9. About A.D. 320 a strong new power called the Gupta (GOOP-tay) Dynasty arose in northeast India. The Gupta Dynasty lasted from the fourth to the seventh century A.D. The Guptas first took control of Magadha from the Mauryas. Then the Guptas seized northern India, parts of Afghanistan, and part of central India. Look at the map below to locate those areas seized by the Guptas. Then compare the empires of the Mauryas and the Guptas.

10. Ancient India experienced a Golden Age under Gupta rule. Because the Guptas were such strong military leaders, there

▼ Early India's Hindu-Buddhist civilization reached new heights during periods of unity under the Maurya and Gupta emperors. Which early Indian empires ruled the most territory?

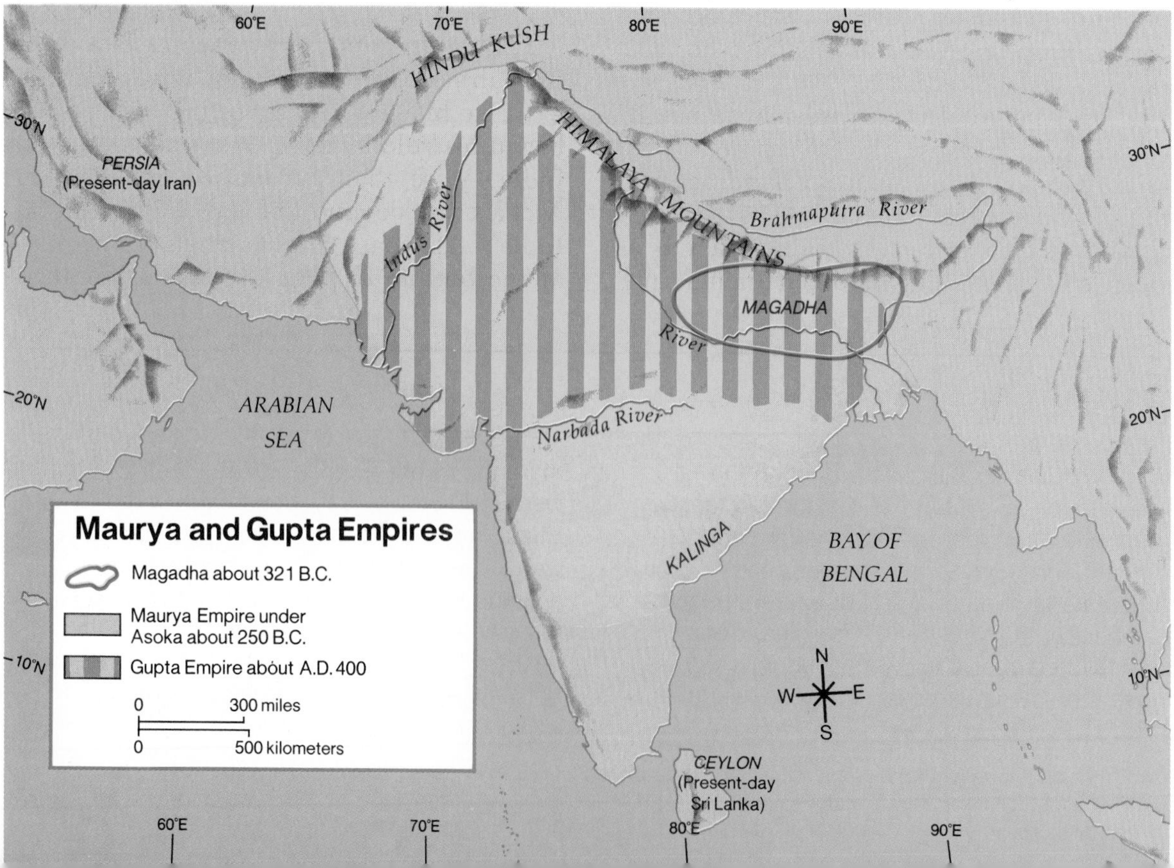

Maurya and Gupta Empires

⬭ Magadha about 321 B.C.

▦ Maurya Empire under Asoka about 250 B.C.

▦ Gupta Empire about A.D. 400

0   300 miles

0   500 kilometers

▲ The murals of the cave temples of Ajanta, painted during A.D. 400–700, illustrate Buddhist legends and gods.

were no threats of invasion for almost 300 years. During those peaceful years, the people of India could concentrate on developing art, music, and writing. Art expressing both Hindu and Buddhist beliefs flourished because the Gupta emperors, who were Hindu, allowed Buddhists to worship freely. Gupta artists made beautiful **murals** (MYOOR-uhlz), or wall paintings. Poets and writers created moving poems and plays in **Sanskrit** (SAN-skrit), the official language of the empire.

11. Science, medicine, and education also flourished. Indian **astronomers** (a-STRON-a-merz)—scientists who study the stars and planets—were among the first peoples to locate the planets. Gupta doctors invented more than 120 surgical instruments. Gupta teachers formed the empire's great **universities** (yew-ni-VUR-si-teez), or centers for learning, which were probably the first of their kind in the world. The university at Nalanda had three libraries, more than 100 classrooms, and a dairy farm for agricultural students. Why do you think students from all parts of Asia traveled to India to study? ◄

SPOTLIGHT ON SOURCES

12. A Chinese Buddhist monk named Fa-Hsien who traveled through India between A.D. 401 and 410 wrote:

> The people were prosperous and happy. . . . The king in his administration used no corporal [bodily] punishments; criminals are merely fined according to the gravity [seriousness] of the offenses [crimes]. Even for a second attempt at rebellion the punishment is only the loss of the right hand. . . . Throughout the country no one kills any living thing, nor drinks wine, nor eats onions or garlic.
>
> —*The Travels of Fa-Hsien or Record of the Buddhist Kingdoms*, translated by H.A. Giles

13. Ancient India's Golden Age ended when White Huns from central Asia invaded India about A.D. 650 and broke up the Gupta Empire. For the next 500 years, small kingdoms were established, fought each other, and died out in India. New invaders, the Muslims, ended Hindu control about A.D. 1200 and ruled India until about 1700. Yet the great accomplishments of the Maurya and Gupta empires survived to present day.

OUTLOOK

14. The music and dance of present-day India have been handed down from the Guptas. What influences from earlier cultures or times can you see in the music and dance of present-day America? What achievements of present-day people would you like to see passed on to future generations? Studying the contributions of past generations can give you a better understanding of how your culture has been affected by people from the past. ◄

Background: Kalidasa has been called ancient India's Shakespeare. His plays are considered to be the best of the period. Indian poets and playwrights were skilled storytellers. Aesop's fables may be traced to ancient India's stories and legends.

75

CHAPTER REVIEW

VOCABULARY REVIEW

Write each number and word on a sheet of paper. Then write the letter of the definition next to the word it defines.

1. bureaucracy
2. vaccines
3. edicts
4. missionaries
5. murals
6. Sanskrit
7. astronomers
8. universities

a. orders that are like laws
b. scientists who study the stars and planets
c. preparations of organisms given to people or animals to keep them from getting a particular disease
d. paintings on walls
e. centers of learning
f. official language of Gupta Empire
g. people who try to teach or spread their religion to people in other lands
h. governmental system of departments run by appointed officials

SKILL BUILDER: READING A TIME LINE

On the first page of every chapter in this book, you will find a special kind of diagram called a time line. A time line tells when certain events took place. It shows the order in which the events occurred.

Look at the time line below. Notice the benchmark dates written between the horizontal lines. Read the dates from left to right. The earliest date is farthest to the left. The earliest date on this time line is 400 B.C. Move your eyes to the right to find the next date. What is it? Events are placed on the time line according to the time that they occurred. For example, Chandragupta started the Maurya Empire about 321 B.C. This date falls between 400 B.C. and 200 B.C. so the event is shown between those two dates. A vertical line goes down from the time line to the words "Chandragupta starts the Maurya Empire, 321 B.C." Name another event that took place between 400 B.C. and 200 B.C.

Use the time line to answer the questions that follow.

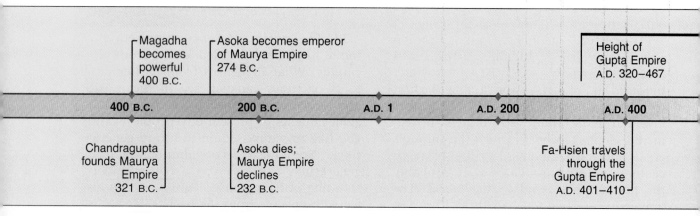

Magadha becomes powerful 400 B.C.

Asoka becomes emperor of Maurya Empire 274 B.C.

Height of Gupta Empire A.D. 320–467

400 B.C.   200 B.C.   A.D. 1   A.D. 200   A.D. 400

Chandragupta founds Maurya Empire 321 B.C.

Asoka dies; Maurya Empire declines 232 B.C.

Fa-Hsien travels through the Gupta Empire A.D. 401–410

STUDY HINT Read the Outlook, paragraph 14, on page 75. What does this Outlook tell you about why people study history? Be sure to think about the closing statement. It will help you see how events in early India affect your life.

1. What is the first event on the time line?

2. What is the most recent event on the time line?

3. Which event took place first: "Asoka becomes emperor of the Maurya Empire" or "The height of the Gupta Empire occurs"?

4. About how long did the golden age of the Gupta Empire last?

SKILL BUILDER: CRITICAL THINKING AND COMPREHENSION

1. Introduction to Generalizing

Read the following statements of fact:

a. To increase crops, Chandragupta built canals that brought a steady supply of water to farms.

b. Under Chandragupta, the Maurya Empire traded goods with other countries.

Are these facts connected in any way? Could you make one statement that links these facts together? A statement that links, or connects, several facts is called a **generalization**. The following generalization links the above facts:

Chandragupta improved farming and trade for his people.

▶ Write a generalization that connects each pair of facts.

a. Asoka set up hospitals. Asoka's edicts asked people to treat one another fairly.

b. Gupta mathematicians invented the decimal system. The Gupta scientists discovered the planets.

c. Hindu marriages were arranged by the family. A Hindu woman's duty was to her husband and his family.

2. Classifying

▶ Listed below are some achievements of the Maurya and Gupta empires. Copy them onto a separate sheet. Beside each item write M if it was a Maurya achievement or G if it was a Gupta achievement.

a. vaccines invented

b. the decimal system invented

c. a government bureaucracy set up

d. canals and roads built

e. astronomers studied the stars and planets

ENRICHMENT

1. Look at examples of the art of the Maurya Empire. Then look for examples of modern Indian art. How are the art styles alike or different? Write a one-page essay that compares the art of the two periods.

2. Read about the Iron Pillar of Delhi that was set up about A.D. 400. Then make a drawing of a pillar or statue that would show something special about your city or state.

CHAPTER 2

China Is Unified

OBJECTIVE: What did the Chinese achieve in the arts, science, and government between 246 B.C. and A.D. 1368?

1. Paris's Eiffel Tower, Egypt's pyramids, New York's Verrazano Narrows Bridge, and the Great Wall of China are some examples of magnificent structures built by people. ► Which of these structures do you think is the only one on earth that astronauts have been able to see from space? It is the Great Wall, which snakes for 1,500 miles (2,400 kilometers) across the center of China. That distance is about as long as from New York City to Omaha. This wall, which is only about 25 feet (7.5 meters) high, is low to the ground in comparison to other great structures. What makes the wall visible from space is its great length. The wall is the longest line of defense ever built. Hundreds

▲ Shi Huang Di made farmers do unpaid labor one month a year. Forced labor made construction of the Great Wall possible.

of thousands of people began building the Great Wall about 2,200 years ago. Thousands of these people died from the hard labor. Imagine how hard it must have been to carry huge loads of bricks or to pull great chunks of granite hour after hour, day after

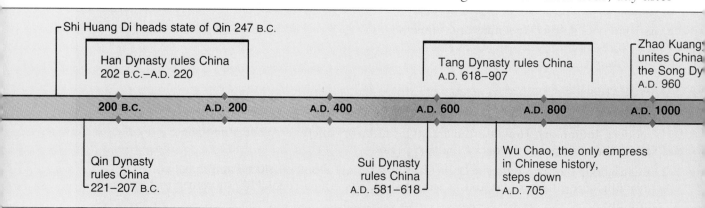

Shi Huang Di heads state of Qin 247 B.C.

Han Dynasty rules China
202 B.C.–A.D. 220

Tang Dynasty rules China
A.D. 618–907

Zhao Kuang
unites China
the Song Dy
A.D. 960

| 200 B.C. | A.D. 200 | A.D. 400 | A.D. 600 | A.D. 800 | A.D. 1000 |

Qin Dynasty
rules China
221–207 B.C.

Sui Dynasty
rules China
A.D. 581–618

Wu Chao, the only empress
in Chinese history,
steps down
A.D. 705

Activity: After students have read paragraph 1, point out that ancient cities had walls to protect the inhabitants. Ask: Why don't we need walls around cities today?

day. The man who ordered all this work to be done called himself China's first emperor. Why do you think he wanted a Great Wall built across the northern border of China?

THE FIRST EMPEROR: What lasting changes did Shi Huang Di bring to China?

2. Shi Huang Di (shee-hwang-dee) was a great warrior who called himself the first emperor. He earned the name by joining China's city-states into an empire. In 247 B.C., Shi Huang Di was the ruler of a city-state in China known as Qin (CHIN). The name China comes from the word Qin. Shi Huang Di saw an opportunity to move in and take control of China's city-states because they were frequently fighting among themselves. Shi Huang Di fought the weakened city-states one by one until he had conquered them all. An ancient Chinese historian said that Shi Huang Di ate the other states "as the silkworm devours the mulberry leaves." What does this quote suggest about Shi Huang Di's style of conquest? In 221 B.C., Shi Huang Di defeated the last of the city-states of the Zhou Dynasty and made himself emperor. During the years of fighting, Shi Huang Di had made many enemies. After taking power, the new emperor, being more of a soldier than a leader, had his enemies killed.

3. Shi Huang Di made many changes that unified China and had lasting effects. The emperor was clever enough to realize that the leaders of China's city-states would try to hold on to their power. So Shi Huang Di invited the ruling families of the city-states to his capital city, and then imprisoned them. Shi Huang Di divided the country into 36 parts. Each part was run by an official who worked directly for the emperor. The emperor made the country operate under only one system of laws. Standards, or common rules, were set for the written language; for weights, measures, and coins; and even for the length of cart axles. The basic government struc-

ture that Shi Huang Di set up lasted in China until A.D. 1911.

4. Shi Huang Di started a series of projects that bound China together. Roads, canals, and bridges were built to connect the towns and states. These thoroughfares allowed the emperor to move soldiers and officials more quickly throughout the empire. Travel increased as it became easier for people to move thoughout the land. Shi Huang Di also gave the order to build the Great Wall. He wanted a wall that would protect China from the fierce tribes to the north. Short sections of a wall had been built earlier, so workers joined those sections together and built watchtowers in the wall. Guards in the watchtowers used smoke or fire to signal the troops at the first threat of invasion. Look at the map at the bottom of page 81. Where does the Great Wall begin and end?

5. Throughout his reign, Shi Huang Di continued to make enemies. By taking power away from the ruling families, Shi Huang Di made a powerful enemy of that class. He angered the peasants by forcing them to pay high taxes and to work on construction projects. Shi Huang Di's order that writings from earlier periods be burned angered the educated class. Books on any subject other than medicine, technology, and agriculture were destroyed, except for those in the imperial library. The emperor wanted the earlier writings burned for several reasons. He feared that people would get ideas from books and try to overthrow him. Being a proud man, he also wanted to wipe out the writings of earlier periods so that the record of his empire would be the first. However, by ordering the destruction of the books of Confucius, Shi Huang Di set the wheels in motion for his own downfall. You have read about how important the ideas of Confucius were to the Chinese people. People who refused to burn the books of Confucius were beheaded by order of Shi Huang Di.

6. Finally, Shi Huang Di's subjects had had enough. In about 210 B.C., the people revolted and Shi Huang Di lost his throne.

Background: Ancient Chinese roads had deep ruts. Unless a cart fit into the ruts of a road, it could not be driven on the road. Before the standardization of axle lengths, a traveler had to change carts whenever he came to a different state, where cart axles were a different length.

▲ Shi Huang Di often traveled throughout the empire, sometimes in disguise, to see whether his orders were being carried out.

Since there was no strong leader to take over, the dynasty of Qin ended in 207 B.C. Obviously, a person who brought warring states together in China had to be strong. Shi Huang Di was both a tyrant with no mercy and a great leader who brought China together.

THE HAN AND SUI DYNASTIES: How did the rise and fall of these dynasties reveal a common pattern in Chinese history?

7. A peasant leader, Gao Zu (KY DZUH), took control of China and started the Han dynasty in 202 B.C. At first the new emperor had no use for the teachings of Confucius—for Gao Zu had no interest in learning. In fact, Gao Zu boasted that he had won the empire on horseback. (At the time, Gao Zu believed, like Shi Huang Di before him, that keeping China together meant being strong and using force.) One adviser to whom Gao Zu had boasted answered, "You won the empire on horseback, but can you rule it from horseback?" What do you think the adviser meant? Gao Zu realized that running an empire was different from running an army. Gao Zu began to study Confucianism, looking for ways to set up a fair system of government.

8. Like Chandragupta in India, Gao Zu soon decided on setting up a bureaucracy. He hired a **civil** (SIV-uhl) **service**, or a group of workers that carries out the government's work. The Han government also followed Confucianism. To become members of the civil service, people had to pass examinations that tested their knowledge of law, math, and the ideas of Confucius.

9. The Han emperor Wu Di (WOO TEE), who came to power in 140 B.C., expanded China's territory and made contact with other peoples. Wu Di took control of lands to the south and southwest. Over the route called the **Silk Road**, the Chinese transported silk and other goods to markets in Central Asia. Some of these goods reached Rome. Find the Silk Road on the map at the bottom of page 81. Why do you think the road divides and then joins together again in western China?

10. Wu Di took several steps to develop China's food supply. The government bought grain during times of plenty when prices were low and sold the grain when food was scarce. Prices were kept stable so that hungry people in one part of China could buy food from other parts. Wu Di also had canals built for irrigating crops and for transporting food. The government built dikes and dams to control the flooding of rivers. Two results of these actions by the government were the growth of the population and greater **prosperity** (pra-SPAIR-uh-tee), or economic well-being.

11. An emperor or a dynasty had to be very strong and clever to keep the empire together. After Wu Di, there were many

forces trying to break the empire apart. The rulers were weak and unpopular. Farmers were angry about high taxes to support the large empire. Finally, the farmers rose up in revolt and China was weakened by civil war. This pattern of strong dynasties followed by a weak government and farm troubles was common in Chinese history. The rise and fall of dynasties is called the **dynastic** (dy-NAS-tik) **cycle**.

12. After the end of the Han Dynasty and a long period with no unity, China was reunited under the Sui (SWIH) Dynasty. During their brief reign, the Sui built lasting symbols of their power. Sui emperors ruled China from A.D. 581 to 618. They improved the city of Changan (CHANG-an) and made it China's capital once again. (The later Han emperors had abandoned Changan for Loyang.) Following a careful plan, the Sui built a city, stone by stone, which spread over 30 square miles (78 square kilometers). Sui emperors made the Grand Canal an important waterway. Find the Grand Canal on the map at the bottom of this page. Parts of the Grand Canal had existed for centuries. The Sui improved and extended the canal between the Yellow River and the Yangtze River. However, these huge building projects were not popular. They were costly, and millions of peasants were forced to do the work. In anger, the people rose up and ended Sui rule in A.D. 618. The Tang Dynasty arose to take the place of the Sui Dynasty.

THE TANG AND SONG DYNASTIES: How did Chinese ideas about religion and foreigners change during this period?

13. Under the early Tangs, China opened its doors to peoples and ideas from many parts of the world. This was an unusual thing for China to do: The Chinese, who had had a great civilization for many centuries, had long looked down on younger cultures as inferior cultures. Under the Tangs, however, this superior attitude softened. People

▼ China's Han emperors ruled during 400 years of peace, prosperity, and expansion. What trade links did Han China have with Central Asia and the Middle East?

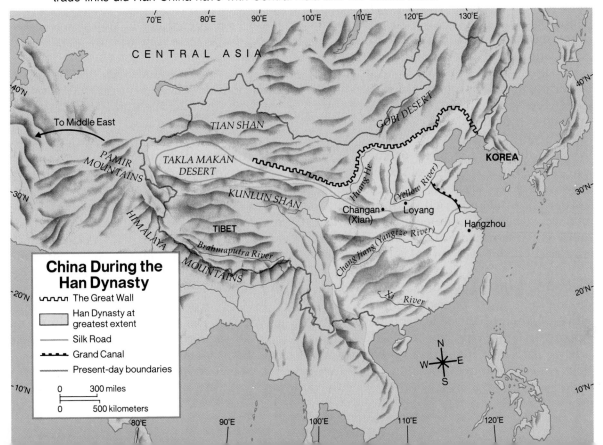

CENTRAL ASIA

To Middle East

TIAN SHAN

PAMIR MOUNTAINS

TAKLA MAKAN DESERT

KUNLUN SHAN

GOBI DESERT

Huang He

Yellow River

KOREA

Changan (Xian)   Loyang

Hangzhou

HIMALAYA MOUNTAINS

TIBET

Brahmaputra River

Chang Jiang (Yangtze River)

Xi River

China During the Han Dynasty

〜〜〜 The Great Wall

☐ Han Dynasty at greatest extent

—— Silk Road

■-■-■ Grand Canal

〜〜〜 Present-day boundaries

0   300 miles
0   500 kilometers

from Syria, Persia, Central Asia, and South Asia freely traded in the two large marketplaces of Changan, Tang China's capital city. Students from Korea, Japan, and other parts of the Chinese empire attended the Chinese university in Changan. Artists, writers, and entertainers from all over the world made life in the capital richer.

14. The city of Changan amazed visitors. A 500-foot-wide avenue led from the main gate to the palace. The rich of the city amused themselves with poetry, art, and sport. Both men and women enjoyed the game of **polo**, which came from Persia. In polo, teams of players on horseback use mallets, or long-handled sticks, to drive a ball across the playing field.

PEOPLE IN HISTORY

15. During the Tang period, a woman became emperor for the only time in Chinese history to date. Wu Chao (WOO CHOU) was born about A.D. 625. As a girl of 13 or 14, she arrived at the emperor's court. The emperor's son fell in love with Wu Chao and married her. When her husband became emperor, Wu Chao's power also increased. Upon her husband's death, Wu Chao became emperor in her own right.

16. During her rule, Wu Chao upgraded government officials and helped Buddhism grow. She used examinations to screen and hire government officials. Too often in the past, people had received government jobs because they were wealthy or knew someone important. The use of examinations, however, gave the best-qualified people, who were often not rich or important, a chance of being appointed to government jobs. Wu Chao made many enemies when she tried to let women take civil service
▶ examinations. Why do you think people of that time might have objected to women taking these tests? Over the centuries, Buddhism, which had begun in India, had spread to China. Wu Chao helped Buddhism to grow in China by having Buddhist writings translated into Chinese. In A.D. 705 Wu

▲ This porcelain figurine of a nobleman playing polo is from the Tang period. From what country did the Chinese borrow this sport?

Chao's son forced her to step down so that he could become emperor and continue the Tang line.

17. In the 700s and 800s the Tangs lost their hold on power. In A.D. 751, Arabs from the west defeated the Chinese in battle and took over Chinese lands in Central Asia. Four years later, a revolt shook the throne. The rulers and many of the people turned against foreigners and all things foreign. Buddhism was attacked as un-Chinese, and many upper-class people gave up Buddhism. Peasants revolted against high taxes and cuts in government services. Bandit gangs roamed the country. By A.D. 907 Tang power was broken. China, which had been one nation, again fell apart into city-states.

18. A strong general called Zhao Kuangyin (KWANG-yin) united China and created the Song (SOONG) Dynasty in A.D. 960. Song leaders brought peace and prosperity once more to China. They promoted a

▲ This hanging silk scroll shows a riderless horse being driven along as tribute to the emperor. It was painted during the height of the Song Dynasty.

lively trade on the rivers within China and across the seas. Chinese ships sailed to India, Southeast Asia, and some Pacific islands. Coal, iron, and steel industries grew larger. China's industries were far ahead of those in other parts of the world. Tea processing and shipbuilding became important businesses in light of the increased trade. The cities of northern China became manufacturing and mining centers. New tools, new farming methods, and water control methods helped farmers. As a result China had plenty of food to feed its growing population. New kinds of rice, which grew faster with less water, were developed.

19. Although times were good, life continued to be vastly different for the rich and the poor of China. For the wealthy, cities like Hangzhou (hang-CHOW) in the south offered a life of pleasure. There were many fine restaurants, bookstores, baths, and places of entertainment. Shops sold jewelry, perfumes, and goods from other lands. At vacation spots outside the city, rich people enjoyed boating and partying. Yet many of the people in the cities were poor and had

a hard life. The cities provided some help for the poor in the form of **alms** (AHMZ), or free food and money. This practice did not greatly improve life for the poor in the cities, however. Why do you think the practice of giving alms did not really help to change things for the poor? In the country, wealthy landowners cared little about the peasants who worked their land. The life of the peasant remained as hard as it always had been.

CENTURIES OF CULTURE: What great ideas and inventions came from China's early dynasties?

20. The Chinese made many scientific advances over the years. When you write on paper, you are writing on a Chinese invention. Around A.D. 105, the Chinese began to make paper from rags, rope, fishing nets, and tree bark. The Tangs printed the first books. An important Han invention was the **seismograph** (SYZ-muh-graf), a machine used to measure the force of earthquakes. In the 600s, the Chinese experimented with

Background: The Song Dynasty is often divided into two periods: The Northern Song (960–1126), when the capital of the Song was in northern China at Kaifeng, and the Southern Song (1127–1279), dating from the loss of northern China to the Mongols. The capital of the Southern Song was Hangzhou.

83

▲ 30,000 clay soldiers were placed in the tomb of Shi Huang Di. It is estimated that 700,000 workers were needed to build this burial site, which spreads over 21 square miles.

The Clay Soldiers of Shi Huang Di

When some Chinese workers were drilling a well in 1974, they unearthed a huge army of clay figures. The workers knew they had found something important. Their accidental discovery turned out to be one of the greatest archaeological finds of this century. The site of the clay army was in the Wei Ho River valley near the ancient capital of Changan. Some 4,000 feet (1,200 meters) away from the army was a tomb mound. The tomb belonged to Shi Huang Di, China's first emperor. The clay figures were created to guard the emperor's tomb. Soldiers, servants, and horses stood in place, ready for battle. These clay figures are incredibly lifelike, and no two are alike. The soldiers once carried swords, crossbows, and spears. The horses stood four across in front of wooden war chariots. There are many thousands of figures. Other objects were also found, including swords, arrowheads, iron farm tools, linen, silks, and gold, jade, and bamboo items. The clay army and other objects found nearby add a great deal to our knowledge of the Qin Dynasty. Until the discovery of the army, little was known about the art of the period. Because the figures are so lifelike, they show that the Qins' concerns lay in the real world. The Qin were different from the earlier people of China, who focused on the supernatural.

1. What do the clay figures tell us about the Qin Dynasty?

2. How do you think historians concluded that the buried army had been created to guard the tomb of Shi Huang Di?

Background: Shortly after Shi Huang Di's death, the buried army was found by rebels. Some figures were smashed and a number of the weapons were stolen. A building that protected the army was set afire, and wooden chariots to which the horses were harnessed were destroyed.

▲ The Song Dynasty was the golden age of Chinese painting. "Summer Mountains" was created then with only shades of a single color.

gunpowder and used it for fireworks. In the Song Dynasty, the army began to use gunpowder for rocket-powered arrows.

21. The Chinese created a rich literature. Si-ma Qian (SOO-MAH chih-YEN), who lived during the reign of Wu Di, wrote a history of China beginning with mythical times. He traveled throughout the country and gathered stories to make his work as complete as possible. Ban Zhao (BAN JOU), a woman author, wrote a history of the early Han Dynasty that offers a look at the role of women in early China. The poet Li Bo (LEE BOH) wrote about daily life. Writers of the Tang Dynasty produced short stories, including the first detective stories.

22. In artwork the brush was used for writing and painting. To the Chinese, calligraphy, or beautiful handwriting, was high art. Calligraphy took years of practice. Chinese painters often used calligraphy in their works. Some beautiful paintings were done in **monochrome** (MON-uh-krome), or only

one color. The Chinese say, "Black is ten colors." In what ways is this saying true? ◄

SPOTLIGHT ON SOURCES

23. Wang Wei (WANG WAY), a popular poet and landscape painter of the A.D. 700s, described the nature of painting:

> Gazing upon the clouds of autumn, my spirit takes wings and soars. Facing the breeze of spring, my thoughts flow like great, powerful currents. Even the music of metal and stone instruments and the treasure of priceless jades cannot match [the pleasure of] this. I unroll pictures and examine documents. I compare and distinguish the mountains and seas. The wind rises from the green forest, and foaming water rushes in the stream. Alas! Such paintings cannot be achieved by the physical movements of the fingers and the hand, but only by the spirit entering into them. This is the nature of painting.
> —from *Sources of Chinese Tradition*, Volume 1, compiled by Wm. Theodore de Bary, et al

24. The Chinese became masters of sculpture and pottery. Chinese sculptors carved huge statues of Buddha in rock cliffs. They made delicate statues of ivory, jade, bronze, and gold. During the Tang period, pottery makers developed **porcelain** (POR-suh-lin), a very hard ceramic ware. Porcelain was called "china" in other parts of the world.

OUTLOOK

25. Over the centuries, Chinese scholars and artists were interrupted by wars, fighting, and lack of unity within China. In spite of these interruptions, however, China managed to produce beautiful art and to give the world outstanding inventions and ideas. During periods of unity and peace in China, great things were done. What have you ◄ learned from periods of uprisings and calm in both early India and China? How do styles of rule contribute to a golden age?

CHAPTER REVIEW

VOCABULARY REVIEW

Write each of the following words on a sheet of paper. Then write the correct definition for each word. Use the Glossary on pages 728–738 to help you.

1. civil service
2. alms
3. Silk Road
4. seismograph
5. prosperity
6. dynastic cycle
7. monochrome
8. polo
9. porcelain

SKILL BUILDER: USING CONTEXT CLUES

Suppose you come across an unfamiliar word or phrase in your reading. Sometimes you can figure out the meaning of the unfamiliar word by thinking about the meanings of the words around it. When you do this, you are using context clues. **Context** means the setting in which the unfamiliar word is placed. Context also means the words around a word or phrase that can throw light on the word or phrase.

▶ In the paragraph below, there is a word in **boldface** type. Three context clues are in *italics*. Read the paragraph. Write the boldface word on a sheet of paper. Then use context clues to write a definition of the word.

　　Early Chinese doctors invented many *medical techniques*. Among these methods were the use of herbs, drugs made from plants, and **acupuncture.** *Other cultures used herbs and drugs, but acupuncture is unique to China.* Even today, doctors in China and many places in the world use *needles inserted in the patient's body during surgery.*

SKILL BUILDER: CRITICAL THINKING AND COMPREHENSION

 1. Classifying

▶ Write the three topics that follow on a sheet of paper. Look through the chapter and find at least three sentences that support each topic. Write the sentences under the topics they support.

Shi Huang Di Unified China

Accomplishments during the Sui Dynasty

China prospered under early Tang rulers

2. Main Idea

▶ The paragraphs listed in the left-hand column are in this chapter. Read each of the paragraphs. Match the paragraph number in the left-hand column with its main idea in the right-hand column. Write your answers on a sheet of paper.

Paragraph Number	Main Idea
3	**a.** Emperor Wu Di made changes that affected China's food supply.
10	**b.** The Sui emperors planned huge building projects that helped China but were unpopular.
12	**c.** Emperor Shi Huang Di was a clever ruler who made changes that lasted a long time.

3. Summarizing:

3-1. Which statement best summarizes paragraphs 9 and 10?

   a. Wu Di expanded China's territory.

   b. Two important contributions made by Emperor Wu Di were expansion of China's trade and improvement of the food supply.

   c. Wu Di stabilized food prices.

3-2. Read paragraphs 17, 18 and 19 in this chapter. Summarize the paragraphs in a few sentences.

4. Generalizing
A generalization is a broad statement that connects several pieces of information.

▶ Read the paragraph below.

During the Song Dynasty in China, industries developed. Tea processing and shipbuilding became important. Cities in northern China became manufacturing and mining centers.

▶ Now choose the lettered statement that makes the best generalization about the information contained in the paragraph above. Write your choice on a sheet of paper.

a. Song emperors encouraged the development of industry.

b. Song emperors favored shipbuilding

c. Song emperors were good traders.

ENRICHMENT

1. Imagine that you are a traveler on the old Silk Road. Describe the land and peoples you might see on a trip from China to the Mediterranean Sea. Use books or other sources to find accurate details for your travel account.

2. Do research and then write a report on the city of Changan (present-day Xian). Tell what the city was like in Sui times and what it was like in Tang times.

3. The Chinese invented many useful things long before the same items were thought of by Europeans. Use an encyclopedia to find out when the following things were invented by the Chinese or by Europeans: paper, movable type, steelmaking methods, seismograph, crossbow, gunpowder. Make a time line comparing the dates of these inventions in China and Europe.

4. Select a poem by Li Bo from a collection of Chinese poetry. Imagine that you are a Chinese calligrapher. Copy the poem in a fancy style of handwriting. Draw or paint a scene described in the poem.

CHAPTER 3

Ideas From India and China Spread

▲ Statue of the Buddha in South Korea. Koreans absorbed Buddhist beliefs and many other traditions from China.

OBJECTIVE: In what ways did India and China influence their neighbors in Asia?

1. Did you ever stop to think how many ideas or products Americans borrow from foreign countries? Opera and pizza from Italy, fashions and perfume from France, folktales from Africa, and hockey from Canada are a few examples of things that have been absorbed into American culture. What Americans have absorbed into their culture has been by choice. The United States has never been overrun by a foreign power. But what happens when a powerful nation influences another nation by conquest or trade? Do you think the culture of the affected nation can survive that kind of shock? The Koreans survived just such a shock. They absorbed many traditions from their Chinese conquerors without surrendering their own culture, and even became enriched by these borrowings. Why are ◄

Trade among Southeast Asians flourishes
A.D. first century

Khmer Empire rules parts of mainland Southeast Asia
A.D. 802 to 1460

| A.D. 100 | A.D. 400 | A.D. 700 | A.D. 1000 | A.D. 1300 | A.D. 1600 |

Funan kingdom rules parts of mainland Southeast Asia
A.D. first century to A.D. 550

Chinese rule of Vietnam ends
A.D. 939

Chams fight Khmers
1100s

Vietnamese revolt against Chinese rule—A.D. 39

Activity: Orient students to this chapter by using a map to identify and locate Burma, Laos, Thailand, Vietnam, Cambodia, and Korea (North and South) on the Asian mainland. Then locate the island nations of Malaysia, Brunei, Singapore, Indonesia, and the Philippines.

some peoples able to accept outside cultures and still maintain their own traditional ways of life?

ASIAN NEIGHBORS: What countries did India and China influence?

2. India's and China's closest neighbors include the countries of Southeast Asia, Korea, and Japan. Look at the atlas map on page 727. Find the present-day nations of Burma, Laos, Thailand, Cambodia, Vietnam, Malaysia, Indonesia, and the Philippines. These are the major nations of Southeast Asia. Find Brunei (BROO-ny) on the island of Borneo. Then look for Singapore, at the tip of the Malay peninsula. Brunei and Singapore are two small nations that are also part of Southeast Asia. You can see that much of Southeast Asia lies between India and China. Look again at the atlas map on page 727 and find Korea and Japan. ▶ How do you think physical land features and location helped Chinese ideas to spread to Korea and even to Japan?

EARLY SOUTHEAST ASIA: What kind of farming methods, arts, and religion developed in early Southeast Asia?

3. Culture in Southeast Asia centered around the region's rivers. Most early peoples lived near the rivers. What other civilizations have you read about that developed in river valleys? On the mainland of Southeast Asia, there are four major rivers. All four flow north to south. In the north the rivers run through high mountains and form deep valleys. Near the sea the rivers grow wider and fan out into huge **deltas** (DEL-tahs). Deltas are low, flat areas made of sand and mud that form at the mouth of a river. Most of the early peoples settled in the valleys or in the delta areas, where the soil was fertile.

4. Before they came in contact with the Indian and Chinese civilizations, the people of Southeast Asia developed their own way of life. They used irrigation to water the fields to grow rice. They also built **terraces**

(TAIR-uh-sehz) so that they could grow rice on hillsides. A terrace is a raised, flat mound of earth with sloping sides. The terraces looked like a flight of steps cut into a hillside. Southeast Asians learned how to grow yams and peas. Some Southeast Asian peoples lived in wooden houses decorated with beautiful carvings. The women created brightly colored clothes of **batik** (bah-TEEK), a specially dyed and printed fabric. Living close to nature, the people practiced **animism** (AN-uh-miz-um), or spirit worship. Animists believed that spirits were everywhere—in trees, rivers, lakes, and mountains. The Southeast Asians also worshipped their ancestors and set up **megaliths** (MEG-uh-liths), or monuments of huge, rough stones, to honor their ancestors.

INDIAN CULTURE IN SOUTHEAST ASIA: What ideas from India were absorbed by Southeast Asians?

5. By the first century A.D., trade flourished among the peoples of Asia. People from India traded with peoples to the east and probably passed Southeast Asian traders on the seas. The Indonesians in particular were expert sailors and are known to have traveled to the eastern ports of India to trade. Through the trading stations, Indians and Southeast Asians began trading ideas.

6. Indian missionaries and scholars first taught Southeast Asians about Hinduism and later about the teachings of Buddha. The map at the bottom of page 90 shows you how Buddhism spread out from India. By the eighth century A.D., Java, in Indonesia, had Buddhist kings.

7. Other cultural influences besides religion spread from India to Southeast Asia. For example, the peoples of Southeast Asia began to use Indian **scripts** (SKRIPTS), or styles of handwriting. The Southeast Asians also took popular Indian story poems and used them to create puppet shows. Indian styles of architecture showed up in many buildings in Southeast Asia. Java's Buddhists built a monument to Buddha at

Background: Spirits were believed to influence all aspects of human life—agriculture, health, and military campaigns. People spent a great deal of time appeasing the spirits and asking for their help in various activities. Animism is still strong in Southeast Asia.

89

The Spread of Buddhism In the days before newspapers and television, news of new ideas moved slowly from one place to another. Sailors, traders, and other travelers on the world's trade routes carried ideas along with trade goods and baggage.

The map on this page shows how Buddhism spread across Asia. Buddhism started in northern India in about 500 B.C. and spread slowly into many parts of Asia. As ancient empires rose and fell, trade routes changed. When trade routes changed, the people carrying Buddhism changed direction, too. For example, one trade route carried Buddhism southward throughout the Indian Peninsula and across a narrow sea into Sri Lanka. A second route carried the religion northwestward across the Indus River into Pakistan and Afghanistan.

Buddhism influenced five main civilizations:

India: In the 200s B.C., Buddhism moved rapidly across India. Emperor Asoka helped spread the religion.

China: Traders and missionaries took Buddhism into western China. These travelers followed trade routes through mountains to the north of India.

Korea and Japan: Chinese traders opened trade routes to Korea and Japan. Buddhist teachers followed these routes.

Southeast Asia: Indian traders and missionaries took Buddhism to nearby countries in Southeast Asia.

Tibet and Mongolia: Buddhism spread to Tibet, where it blended with a native religion of spirit worship. Tibetan Buddhism spread to western China and Mongolia.

Study the map on this page. Then answer the following questions.

1. Where did Buddhism begin?

2. In what century did Buddhism spread to Sri Lanka? In what century did Buddhism spread from China to Korea?

3. Why do you think trade routes changed as empires rose and fell in ancient Asia?

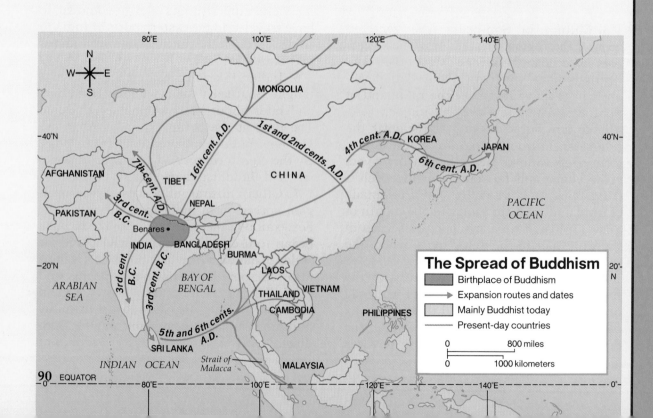

The Spread of Buddhism
- Birthplace of Buddhism
- → Expansion routes and dates
- Mainly Buddhist today
- Present-day countries

0   800 miles
0   1000 kilometers

▲ Scenes from the Buddha's life adorn the carved walls of Borobudur in central Java. The ruins of the Hindu shrine record Java's close ties to India in the ninth century.

Borobudur. The walls of this monument are covered with more than 400 sculptures of Buddha and Buddhist worshippers.

8. The people of Southeast Asia did not accept all of Indian culture, however, which divided people into social groups according to birth and hereditary occupation. They did not adopt the caste system, for example. Also, women had more power and freedom in Southeast Asia than they had in India.

9. An Indian nobleman started the first great kingdom in Southeast Asia in the first century A.D. The nobleman was Kaundinya. His kingdom is known by its Chinese name, Funan, and was located in what is now Cambodia on the delta of the Mekong River. According to an ancient Indian legend, Kaundinya threw a holy **javelin** (JAV-lin), or spear. The site on which the spear fell became the capital of Funan.

10. For more than 500 years, the Funan kings and nobles lived in rich surroundings and expanded the empire. Great palaces dotted the capital. The king and members of his court rode on elephants and watched pig fights as court entertainment. The kingdom

of Funan was a center of industry and trade. The Funanese traded with southern Vietnam, the Malay peninsula, parts of Thailand, and Chenla in Cambodia. At its height, the power of the Funan empire extended over Cambodia along the Menam and into the Malay Peninsula. In about A.D. 550, the power of Funan began to decline. People from Chenla from the north conquered Funan.

11. The Chenla people started what was called the Khmer (kuh-MEHR) Empire. The Khmers set up their empire in A.D. 802. The Khmers probably learned how to run their kingdom from the Indians. Khmer kings used a well-run bureaucracy to manage their lands and people. At the top of the bureaucracy was a god-king, a ruler thought to be part king and part god. The Khmers carried on the Buddhist religion brought in by the Indian missionaries.

12. During their rule the Khmers built Angkor Wat, a temple that has been called one of the great wonders of the world. Temples were often tombs where the god-kings were worshipped. The many stone

▲ The Hindu temple of Angkor Wat was built in the twelfth century—when Indian influences were strong in Southeast Asia.

do you think the stones of Angkor Wat were lifted into place?

SPOTLIGHT ON SOURCES

13. A Chinese traveler to Angkor in the 1200s described its New Year's celebration :

In front of the palace, they set up a grandstand capable of holding more than a thousand people and decorate it with lanterns and flowers. Opposite . . . they make a circle of wood posts about 250 feet [75 meters] around and on them weave the scaffolding at a 250-foot [75 meter] stupa [mound or tower]. On the top they place fireworks and firecrackers. . . . When the night falls they set off the firecrackers and the rockets. The display can be seen for more than 30 miles [48 kilometers]. The firecrackers are the size of swivel guns and their explosion rocks the entire city.

—from *The Great Chinese Travelers: An Anthology*, Jeanette Mirsky, ed.

figures found on the temples represent gods and god-kings. Angkor was the capital of the Khmer Empire. What is known today about the Khmer civilization comes mostly from the large ruins of the city of Angkor. The city had almost one square mile (2.6 square kilometers) of buildings—a large city for its time. The great burial mountain-temple in the capital was gigantic. Visitors to Cambodia today still marvel at the ruins of the temple, which is made completely of stone. Even the roof is stone. Around the shrine are nine towers shaped like the buds of the lotus flower. These towers were once covered with gold. Hundreds of thousands of carved figures that once blazed with bright color ▶ decorate the temple walls. Without the modern equipment of builders today, how

14. In the 1300s and 1400s the Khmer Empire gradually declined. Ongoing wars beginning in the mid 1100s against the Thais and the Chams weakened the empire. The army of the Chams, who were the Indonesian settlers of South Vietnam, invaded Cambodia and destroyed Angkor in 1177. The weakened Khmers moved their capital to Phnom Penh (puh-nom PEN). Find Phnom Penh on the atlas map on page 727. The great days of Khmer power were over by 1460. The Champa Empire lasted until the seventeenth century.

15. Parts of Indian culture as well as early Southeast Asian traditions survive today in Southeast Asia. If you visited Bali, a small island in Indonesia, you would still find some people who are Hindus. In Thailand you would see monasteries where Buddhist monks study. In many countries you would see people wearing clothes with batik designs. Chinese influences also can be seen in Southeast Asia today.

CHINESE CULTURE IN SOUTHEAST ASIA: What ideas from China were absorbed by the Southeast Asians?

16. One group of southeast Asians was strongly influenced by China. That group was the Vietnamese. Ancestors of the Vietnamese originally lived in the Yangtze River valley in southern China. Around 200 B.C. they moved into the Red River valley in what is northern Vietnam today. Soon afterward the Chinese took over this region and made it part of the Chinese empire. For more than 1,000 years, the Vietnamese lived under Chinese rule. They were allowed to hold government posts, but they had to adopt Chinese ways. Chinese scholars taught Chinese script, Confucianism, and the Chinese language to Vietnamese people. All local customs were suppressed.

17. In spite of Chinese rule, the Vietnamese held onto their own culture. They had a strong sense of who they were and how they were different from the Chinese people. Among themselves they continued to speak in their native tongue. When the Chinese government decided to send its own officials to govern Vietnam, the Vietnamese
▶ revolted. Why do you think the Vietnamese were so independent even after 1,000 years of Chinese rule?

PEOPLE IN HISTORY

18. The first uprising against the Chinese was started in A.D. 39 by Lady Trung Trac. Lady Trung Trac was a noblewoman whose husband had been killed by the Chinese. She organized some troops and, with her sister and other nobles, led the troops against the Chinese soldiers who were guarding the new Chinese governor's home. Lady Trung Trac and her supporters defeated the Chinese, and she and her sister became queens in A.D. 40. The sisters ruled for two years, until they were defeated by the Chinese. Rather than be taken captive, Lady Trung and her sister drowned themselves.

19. The Vietnamese did not regain their independence from China until A.D. 939. Later the Vietnamese had to defend themselves against the Mongols when Kublai Khan conquered much land in Asia. The Vietnamese fought off three Mongol invasions in the 1280s, but were again invaded and conquered by China in 1407. In 1427 the Vietnamese expelled the Chinese for good. Over the next 200 years Vietnam expanded southward along the coast, until it occupied most of present-day Vietnam.

20. In many ways the story of the Koreans is like that of the Vietnamese. The Koreans lived in Manchuria, a region in east central Asia. In the first century B.C., they moved south and east as China expanded. Like the Vietnamese, the Koreans developed their own culture. From time to time throughout its history Korea has been ruled by China. Each time Chinese dynasties weakened and lost control of the empire, Korea would become independent for a time.

21. The Chinese people had a strong influence on Korean life because of the many years they ruled Korea. Buddhism from India became a part of Chinese culture that spread to Korea. Paintings, monuments and images of Buddha in Korea were much like those in China. The Koreans changed the Chinese writing system so that it could be used to write Korean words. After the 1200s the government in Korea was based on Confucian ideas from China.

OUTLOOK

22. For about 2,000 years the Indian and the Chinese peoples shared many of their own ideas and achievements with other peoples of the East. These other peoples did not copy Indian and Chinese culture. The Southeast Asians and Koreans borrowed and then changed ideas and traditions from India and China. They made Indian and Chinese culture part of their own cultures. Why might it have been hard for a country ◀ to hold on to its own culture when there were strong influences from other lands?

Background: The Koreans invented a system of writing called Idu, which used Chinese characters as phonetic symbols. Idu was first used to record Korean songs and poems.

93

VOCABULARY REVIEW

Write each of the following sentences on a sheet of paper. Then fill in the blank with the word that best completes each sentence.

deltas   batik   scripts

terraces   animism   javelin

                megaliths

1. _____ is the belief that spirits are everywhere in nature.
2. People in Southeast Asia made a printed fabric called _____ .
3. A _____ is a spear.
4. Monuments built of large, rough stones are _____ .
5. Southeast Asians used Indian _____ , or styles of handwriting.
6. Flat areas of sand and mud where rivers meet the sea are _____ .
7. Farmers use _____ to plant crops on a hill that would otherwise be too steep.

SKILL BUILDER: INTERPRETING A MAP

Study the map on this page and then answer the following questions.
1. What is the region of the world shown on the map?
2. What empires or kingdoms are listed on the map legend?
3. Locate the Irrawaddy River. What country does this river flow through?
4. In which direction would you travel to get from Laos to Thailand?
5. Locate Angkor and Pagan. About how far are they from each other?

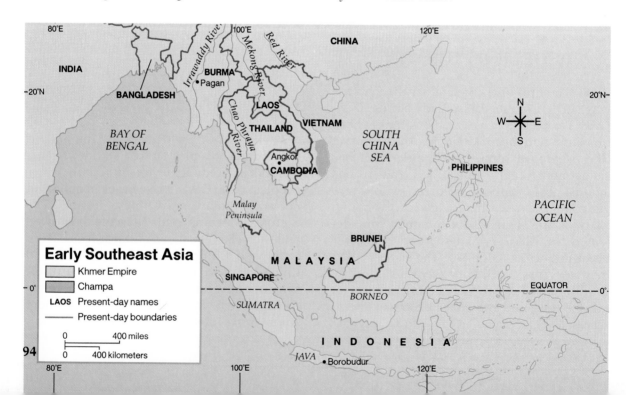

Early Southeast Asia

- Khmer Empire
- Champa
- **LAOS** Present-day names
- Present-day boundaries

0   400 miles
0   400 kilometers

SKILL BUILDER: CRITICAL THINKING AND COMPREHENSION

1. Classifying

▶ Read each statement below. Decide if each one has to do with India or China. Then on a sheet of paper, write the letters a through d. Beside each letter write the name of the country that goes with the statement.

a. Hinduism and Buddhism developed in this country.

b. This country ruled ancient Vietnam for many centuries.

c. Koreans changed this country's writing system so that it could be used for Korean words.

d. Southeast Asians did not borrow the caste system from this country.

2. Main Idea

▶ The sentence below states a main idea from this chapter. Write the letter (*a*, *b*, or *c*) of the statement that supports, or helps to prove, the main idea.

Main Idea: Over the centuries Indian ideas blended with local traditions in Southeast Asia.

a. Hinduism declined in India.

b. In Thailand today monks still study in Buddhist monasteries.

c. Most Indonesians are not Hindu.

3. Summarizing

▶ Which statement below best summarizes paragraph 3 of this chapter?

a. Mainland Southeast Asia has four main rivers running north to south.

b. Early mainland Southeast Asians lived near rivers instead of in the mountains.

c. Early cultures in mainland Southeast Asia grew up around river deltas because these areas were good for farming.

4. Generalizing

▶ The statement below makes a generalization about a paragraph in this chapter. Find the paragraph and write the paragraph number on a sheet of paper.

The Khmers were gifted builders and artists.

ENRICHMENT

1. Find out how the people of Java make batik. Then write a how-to manual that gives a step-by-step explanation of how batik is made. Illustrate your manual.

2. Choose one of the following modern Southeast Asian nations: Burma, Laos, Thailand, or Malaysia. Using encyclopedias and other reference books, identify two examples of either Indian or Chinese influence in the country you have chosen. Take notes on an index card about each example. Use your notes to give a short oral report on your findings to the class.

CHAPTER 4

Emergence of Japan

▲ This silkscreen shows a scene from Lady Murasaki's eleventh-century novel, *The Tale of Genji.*

OBJECTIVE: How did Japan blend its ancient beliefs with ideas from China?

1. Do you like to read a good story? Many good stories are written as novels, or long works of fiction. One of the first great novels ever written in the history of the world was *The Tale of Genji* by Lady Murasaki Shikibu of Japan. Lady Murasaki was a member of the Japaneese royal court in the eleventh century. Her novel described the romances of that way of life. *The Tale of Genji* tells of the many loves of Prince Genji, the fictional son of a fictional Japanese emperor. The book includes colorful descriptions of life in the emperor's court. Lady Murasaki tells her story with a cleverness and light touch that make it a pleasure to read even today. The following passage is from *The Tale of Genji.*

. . . All this while Genji, though he had sometimes joined in the conversation, had in his heart of hearts been thinking of one person only, and the more he thought the less could he find a single trace of those shortcomings and

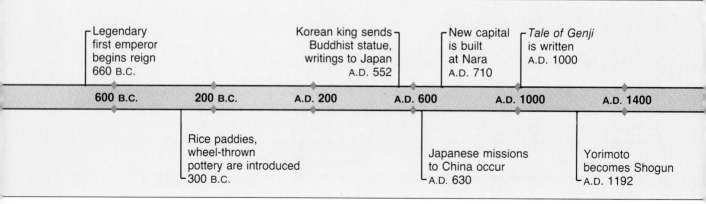

Legendary first emperor begins reign 660 B.C.

Korean king sends Buddhist statue, writings to Japan A.D. 552

New capital is built at Nara A.D. 710

Tale of Genji is written A.D. 1000

| 600 B.C. | 200 B.C. | A.D. 200 | A.D. 600 | A.D. 1000 | A.D. 1400 |

Rice paddies, wheel-thrown pottery are introduced 300 B.C.

Japanese missions to China occur A.D. 630

Yorimoto becomes Shogun A.D. 1192

excesses which, so his friends had declared, were common to all women. 'There is no one like her,' he thought, and his heart was very full. . . .

You will read more about Lady Murasaki on page 99. Her novel was written in the Japanese language of the court ladies, which was unusual. Most other writings in Japan at that time were written in Chinese. Why might this have been so? As you will find out in this chapter, the Japanese way of life was greatly influenced by China. In fact, the literature of Japan is a blend of classic Chinese influences, unique Japanese sources, and Western thought.

EARLY JAPAN: Who were some of the first people to settle in Japan?

2. No one is certain when people first settled on the islands of Japan. Archaeologists think it was at least 200,000 years ago. The Japanese people did not begin to write down their history until they learned Chinese script and adopted Chinese characters for their written language in the early centuries A.D. Why does the lack of a written history make it hard to study about early Japan?

3. Some of the earliest people in the Japanese islands may have been the **Ainu** (EYE-noo). How the Ainu came to Japan is a mystery, but it is believed that they came from mainland Asia. The Ainu lived by fishing and hunting. The Ainu loved and respected the animals they hunted. They believed that kind humans from another world came to earth as animals to be hunted and killed for food. Then, when the animals died, they returned to their human form.

4. Rice farming gradually became part of Japanese culture. Archaeologists know that by 300 B.C. some people had come to Japan who grew rice in **paddies** (PAD-eez), or flooded fields. Rice paddies are a form of irrigation.

ANCIENT RELIGION: What role did religion play in early Japan?

5. The religion of early Japan was based on the worship of **kami** (KA-mee), or anything sacred or special in nature. A high mountain, a shiny stone, the sunset, a rushing waterfall, and an unusual insect are all examples of *kami*. The Japanese people worshipped *kami* in front of simple wooden shrines. They would clap their hands, bow, and give gifts of food, drink, or cloth.

6. The early Japanese people divided themselves into **clans** (KLANZ). A clan is a group of families that are related to each other by blood or by adoption. Each clan had its own god, who was believed to be the founder of the clan. During the fifth century A.D., the head of the Yamato clan declared himself emperor. He believed it was his right because the legend of the

Daily life in . . .

"Hee-AHH!" each of three men cried as they splashed their muscular bodies with icy water from a mountain stream. The men had not made a fire to warm themselves. It had been three days since they had taken food, and they would journey two more before they would eat again. When they did eat, it would be a simple stew of roots and maybe a small animal they snared.

The three were **samurai** (SAM-uh-ry), or members of the hereditary warrior class who served a class of nobles above them. Samurai emerged in Japan in the eleventh century. Samurai lived by a strict, harsh set of rules. They were never without their swords, for they had to be ready for battle at all times. They had to be brave, to put up with pain, and to show neither fear nor joy. If a samurai was captured or was disloyal to his chief, he was expected to commit suicide.

ESL/LEP Strategy: Copy paragraph 2 on a reproducible sheet of paper. Eliminate every seventh word, leaving a blank space in its place. Place the missing words in a word bank on the same page. Have students work in groups to fill in the blanks.

97

sun goddess said that one of her descendents started Yamato.

CHINESE CULTURE: What ideas did Japan borrow from China?

7. Buddhism was one of the first important features of Chinese civilization borrowed by Japan. Buddhism reached Japan through Korea. In A.D. 552 a Korean king sent some gifts to Japan—a bronze statue of Buddha, some Buddhist writings, and a letter. The letter said that Buddhism came from China and was highly respected there. The king urged the Japanese people to accept Buddhism.

8. Over the next 300 years, Japan borrowed much from the Chinese people. The Japanese people combined Buddhism with their own beliefs to form a new religion called **Shinto** (SHIN-toh). They began to use Chinese script to write down their spoken language. They also adopted Chinese ideas

of government. The Chinese government was run from a central capital. Japanese rulers believed that a central government would give the emperor greater power over other clans. Why would a central government give an emperor more power? ◄

9. In A.D. 710 the Japanese rulers chose Nara as the site of their own center of government. The Japanese modeled Nara after the Tang dynasty's capital, Changan, in China. Find Nara on the map on page 99. About how far is Nara from Tokyo, the ◄ modern capital of Japan?

10. The Japanese people grew eager for more ideas from China. Japanese emperors began to send **missions** (MISH-unz), or special representatives, to China. Between A.D. 630 and 838, 13 missions went to China. The missions brought back to Japan new machines, arts, musical instruments, and games. Do you think people are still eager to learn about ideas from other countries? Why or why not?

A NEW AGE IN JAPAN TAKES SHAPE: How did the government of Japan change by the 1100s?

11. In A.D. 794 Japan entered a new age that brought more change. First the capital was moved. A new city, the Capital of Peace and Tranquility, was built on the site of the modern city of Kyoto (Kee-OT-oh). The social center of the capital was the emperor and his court. The emperor no longer had control of the government, however. The powerful Fujiwara clan actually ran the government. The Fujiwara became powerful by arranging marriages between their daughters and the emperor's sons. This practice gave the Fujiwara influence over the emperor. The Fujiwara continued to honor the emperor, according to Japanese custom, but the Fujiwara held the real power. Later, other clans controlled the government.

12. The royal court in the new capital became the center of culture. The Japanese people began to create styles of their own in art, architecture, and literature. Painting,

▼ A samurai warrior was always ready to protect the lord he served. The samurai followed strict codes of honor and behavior.

calligraphy, dance, music, *ikebana* (flower arranging), *chanoyu* (the tea ceremony), and theatrical plays also flourished. Almost all of the best literature of the time was written by women. Women had not been expected to learn the Chinese writing system, which was used for government business and trade. Why do you think women were not expected to learn Chinese writing? Instead women wrote in a Japanese script that was better able to capture the Japanese language and spirit. The most famous of these writer's works was the novel *The Tale of Genji* by Murasaki Shikibu (mur-uh-SAK-ee).

PEOPLE IN HISTORY

13. Lady Murasaki Shikibu had an insider's view of court life. As a lady-in-waiting to Empress Akiko, Murasaki took part in the fancy court ceremonies. She became close friends with the Empress Akiko. The empress had a secret wish to learn Chinese, and Murasaki helped her. As a girl, Murasaki had sat in on her brother's Chinese lessons. Murasaki recorded information and court gossip in her diary. She used this material to write *The Tale of Genji* around the year A.D. 1000. Murasaki died sometime after A.D. 1025.

14. By the twelfth century the central government at the capital began to lose power. In the countryside, clans formed armies and fought each other. In A.D. 1189 Yoritomo, the head of the Minamoto clan, led his forces to a major victory. In A.D. 1192 the emperor gave Yoritomo the title **shogun** (SHOH-gun), or supreme military governor. While the emperor kept his title, the shogun held the real power. Government by shoguns lasted for 700 years.

OUTLOOK

15. Think of some of the traditions that people practice today. One tradition might be going to a family reunion. Another might

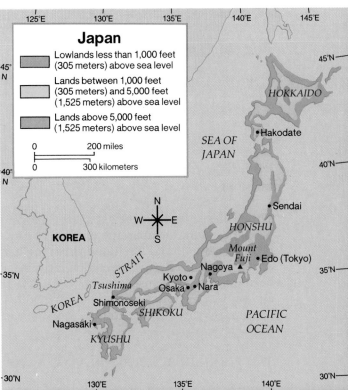

SKILL BUILDER/MAPS
Using Contours

Contours are lines used to show elevations on a map. Elevation is height above sea level. The 1,000 foot (305 meters) contour line on this map joins all places located at 1,000 feet (305 meters) above sea level.

1. What color is used on the map to show lands less than 1,000 feet (305 meters) above sea level?

2. What colors are used on the map to show lands more than 1,000 feet (305 meters) above sea level?

3. Which island of Japan has the most land above 5,000 ft. (1,525 meters)?

be watching a parade on the Fourth of July. Why are traditions important? For centuries in Japan, emperors have not held real power. Today Japan is run by an elected government. Yet Japan still has an emperor. Why do you think Japan keeps this tradition alive? How do traditions help keep alive the culture of a people?

Activity: Divide the class into groups and ask the groups to find out how Yoritomo changed government in Japan as shogun. Then have groups share their findings in a general class discussion.

99

CHAPTER REVIEW

VOCABULARY REVIEW

Write the following paragraph on a sheet of paper. Then fill in the blanks with the words that best complete the paragraph.

shoguns

Shinto

paddies

missions

clans

kami

Ainu

samurai

The earliest people in the Japanese islands may have been the _____ . Early people brought to Japan the method of growing rice in _____ . Early Japanese people also followed a religion that taught that there were sacred things in nature called _____ . Japanese religion later became known as _____ . People in Japan began to divide themselves into _____ . Later, Japanese emperors led the country and sent _____ to China to learn new ideas. Emperors turned over their power to _____ in the twelfth century. A warrior class developed, called _____ .

SKILL BUILDER: INTERPRETING A HISTORICAL TIME LINE

You have learned that a time line shows when events took place and helps you understand how events are connected. The time line below lists some dates from this chapter.

▶ Copy the time line on a sheet of paper. Then follow the directions to interpret the time line.

1. What events are listed on the time line? How do these events show Chinese influence on Japan?

2. What effect did the event in year 552 have on Japan?

3. Write this event in the proper place on your time line: "710—Japanese people build new capital at Nara for a central government." How does the new capital at Nara reflect Chinese influence on Japan?

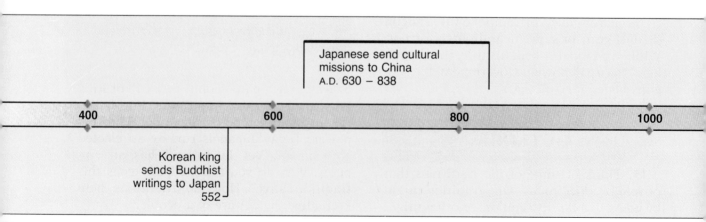

Japanese send cultural
missions to China
A.D. 630 – 838

400   600   800   1000

Korean king
sends Buddhist
writings to Japan
552

SKILL BUILDER: CRITICAL THINKING AND COMPREHENSION

▲ **1. Summarizing**

▶ Read paragraph 11 in this chapter. Then read the statements below. On a sheet of paper, write the statement that best summarizes paragraph 11.

a. The loss of power by the emperor and the rise of clans in the government were part of a new age in Japan that began in A.D. 794.

b. In A.D. 794 Japan moved its capital city.

c. The Fujiwara clan became powerful in A.D. 794 and other clans took power later.

○ **2. Generalizing**

▶ Read the "Daily life in. . ." feature on page 97 of this chapter. Then read the statements below. On a sheet of paper, write the statement that makes the best generalization about the feature.

a. Samurai made themselves exist on very little food.

b. Samurai were never without their swords.

c. Samurai lived by a hard set of rules that kept them prepared for battle.

3. Sequencing Sequencing is the skill of putting pieces of information in their correct time order. When putting events in sequence, ask yourself: Which event came first? Which came second, which came third?

▶ The lettered events below are discussed in this chapter. Decide the correct time order of these events. Then copy them in the correct sequence on a sheet of paper.

a. Early Japanese society divided itself into clans.

b. Shoguns became powerful leaders of Japan.

c. Buddhism was introduced to Japan by Koreans.

d. The Ainu people came to Japan.

ENRICHMENT

1. Some Ainu people still live in Japan today. Find out more about them by using an encyclopedia or other reference book. Write a short paragraph that explains what the Ainu culture is like today.

2. In all countries that adopted Buddhism, artists made statues of Buddha. Find photographs of images of Buddha from India, China, Japan, and other countries. Prepare an oral report explaining how the images of Buddha vary.

3. Make a chart or poster that shows the equipment used by a samurai warrior. Look for facts about samurai in encyclopedias and in books about Japanese history. Your chart or poster might show the steps a samurai followed in putting on his armor.

The Peoples of Australia and Oceania

▲ Outrigger canoes carried Pacific Islanders far across the Pacific Ocean in search of new islands to settle.

OBJECTIVE: How were the southern Pacific islands discovered and settled?

▶ **1.** Have you ever played "Packing for a Trip for Life"? The object is to choose ten items that you would pack if you were going to be stranded on a desert island for the rest of your life. What would you take—clothing, books, a radio, waterproof matches, plants, and seeds? Do you suppose that the early settlers of the Pacific Islands thought about this? Look at the map on page 104. The Pacific is the world's largest ocean. You could sail 10,000 miles (roughly 16,090 kilometers) across the Pacific without seeing land. The Pacific is dotted with many small islands. In spite of the vast size of the ocean and the smallness of the islands, people found the islands and settled on them many centuries ago. Some of the settlers were sailors who were lucky to find the islands after getting lost or being caught in ocean storms.

Polynesian islands of Tonga and Samoa are settled 1000 B.C.

Easter Island and the Hawaiian Islands are settled A.D. 500

| 1000 B.C. | 500 B.C. | A.D. 1 | A.D. 500 |

Micronesia is settled 1000 B.C.

Activity: Have students turn to the map of Oceania on page 104. Have them use the map scale to compute the distance between pairs of Pacific Islands that you name.

OCEANIA: What are the three main island groups in Oceania and how were they settled?

2. Oceania (oh-shee-AN-ee-uh) is the name of a group of more than 10,000 islands in the Pacific Ocean. The islands in Oceania are divided into three regions. Melanesia (mel-uh-NEE-zhuh) is a region north and east of Australia. Micronesia (my-kro-NEE-zhuh) is a region mainly north of the equator and north of Melanesia. Polynesia (pahl-uh-NEE-zhuh) is a region of the central and eastern Pacific. Find Melanesia, Micronesia, and Polynesia on the map on page 104. Australia, also a part of Oceania, is the world's only island continent.

3. Historians believe that people originally came to Oceania from Southeast Asia. These early settlers arrived at the islands of Melanesia about 40,000 years ago during the Ice Age. The sea level was lower then than it is now. People from Southeast Asia may have walked across land bridges between Malaysia, Indonesia, and New Guinea. Later, when the glaciers from the Ice Age melted, these land bridges were covered over by ocean water. People settled first in New Guinea. Find New Guinea in Melanesia on the map on page 104. From New Guinea people **migrated** (MY-grayt-ed), or moved, to other islands.

4. The name Melanesia means "black islands." The name refers to the dark-skinned people of Melanesia, where New Guinea is located. Melanesians are related to the **aborigines** (ab-uh-RIJ-uh-neez) of Australia, who also have dark skin. The aborigines were the first people to live in Australia.

5. Can you guess what Micronesia means? Micro means "small." Micronesia means "small places." The largest island in Micronesia is Guam. Guam is about 209 square miles (543 square kilometers), smaller in size than New York City. Historians believe that people first came to the tiny islands of Micronesia between 3000 and 2000 B.C., from Melanesia, the Philippines, and Indonesia.

6. Polynesia is spread over a larger area of Oceania than either Melanesia or Micronesia. Poly means "many." What do you think the name Polynesia means? The first settlers in Polynesia went to Tonga and Samoa about 3,000 years ago. Find Tonga and Samoa on the map on page 104. Why do you think these islands were settled first? As Tonga and Samoa became crowded, the Polynesians moved to other islands. Polynesians reached Easter Island and the Hawaiian Islands around A.D. 500. Later, Polynesians migrated to the large islands that are now New Zealand.

7. The peoples of Oceania learned to read the signs of nature to **navigate** (NAV-uh-gayt), or steer a course, across the Pacific Ocean. Clouds, stars, winds, and **ocean currents** (OH-shun KUR-unts), or fast-moving streams in the ocean, helped these people move about the Pacific. For example, early sailors learned that the winds in one part of the Pacific blew from east to west. They let

Daily life in . . .

Pacific peoples built special canoes called **outrigger canoes** (OWT-rig-ur kuh-NOOZ) that waves could rarely overturn. Picture a long canoe with a wooden framework that is parallel to one side of the canoe. A log joined to the framework helped to balance the canoe. Another kind of canoe used in the Pacific had two separate hulls, or bodies. People built a platform between the hulls and used these double canoes as ocean-going moving vans. They loaded the platform with their families, chickens, pigs, dogs, and plants—all the things they needed to start a new settlement. With their sails and a strong wind, the canoes almost seemed to fly over the water as they carried Pacific peoples to other islands.

Activity: Geologists believe that Australia and New Guinea were once joined. Have students research the tectonic plates of earth's crust and discuss how continents were once joined in larger land masses.

103

Background: The early peoples of Oceania and their present-day descendants have depended on two staples to sustain them—the breadfruit tree and the palm oil tree. Both trees provide food as well as wood for building. Their inner bark is used for making clothing and floor coverings.

these winds carry them west to Hawaii. Early people sometimes got lost, however, and found new islands by accident.

8. Because the early Pacific islanders left no written records, other clues to their culture have been sought. Some of the clues have led only to more mystery. For example, ancient 50-ton carved stone statues have been found on Easter Island. Historians and archaeologists think the statues ▶ were used as religious symbols. What do you think the statues might have been used for? The statues do let us know that some early people of Oceania knew how to cut and carve stone. People on other islands carved wooden statues and painted magnificent rock murals. The rock murals show

that these early people hunted fish and pythons. There are no clues, however, that islanders had iron or other metals.

AUSTRALIA: How was the island continent of Australia settled?

9. The first people to live in Australia were the aborigines, who came to Australia from Southeast Asia about 40,000 years ago. They did not farm the dry land but hunted and gathered plants for food. These aborigines, like their descendants today, believed that people must never change the land and must always protect all the living things on earth.

10. In the eighteenth century, people in

SKILL BUILDER/MAP Finding Directions

The compass rose on this map of Oceania shows four basic directions—north (N), south (S), east (E), and west (W). Directions halfway between the basic directions are northeast (NE), southeast (SE), southwest (SW), and northwest (NW). Use the compass rose on the map below to find the answers to the following questions.

1. In what direction did Polynesians travel from Raïatéa to the Hawaiian Islands?
2. In what direction did Polynesians travel from Samoa to New Zealand?
3. In what direction did Polynesians travel from Tonga to Easter Island?
4. In what direction did Melanesians travel from New Guinea to Fiji?

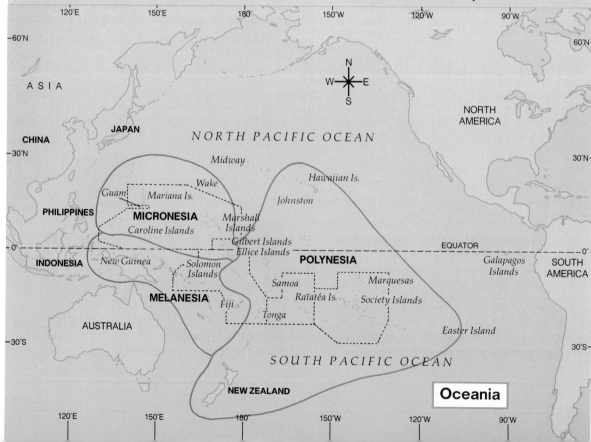

▲ The 600 eyeless stone statues of Easter Island were carved thousands of years ago from hard volcanic rock.

Europe knew very little about the Pacific region. They already knew about South America and Africa, but they still believed that there was another "great southern continent."

PEOPLE IN HISTORY

11. In 1768 the British navy sent Captain James Cook to find the "great southern continent." Cook visited many islands of Oceania. He also sailed up the east coast of Australia, mapping it carefully. Cook found that Australia was a continent, but not the "great southern continent" Europeans had imagined. Australia is, in fact, the smallest of the earth's seven continents. Cook made two more voyages in search of the great southern continent, but never found it. Nevertheless, Cook made great contributions to European's knowledge of the Pacific. He discovered many islands and made maps of
▶ Australia and other places in Oceania. Why

do you think Europeans were interested in maps of the Pacific?

SPOTLIGHT ON SOURCES

12. Captain James Cook met aborigines in Australia in the late 1700s. This is how he described the aborigines' life:

> They covet [want] not magnificent houses, household stuff, etc.; they live in a warm and fine climate, and enjoy every wholesome air, so that they have very little need of clothing; . . . many to whom we gave cloth, etc., left it carelessly upon the sea beach and in the woods, as a thing they had no manner of use for; in short they seemed to set no value upon anything we gave them . . . This, in my opinion, argues that they think themselves provided with all the necessaries of life.
> —from *The Voyages of Captain James Cook Round the World*, Christopher Lloyd, ed.

13. Other Europeans arrived in Australia in the late 1700s, but they were not explorers. They were British convicts who had been released from prison to start new lives for themselves in Australia. In fact, one of the first of these convicts was 14-year-old Matthew Everingham, whose crime was stealing two law books. Some British women arrived, and the early settlers and their families founded new towns along Australia's southern coast.

OUTLOOK

14. People everywhere develop skills to help them get along in their environment. People of the Pacific Islands learned to use what nature provided. They also learned to travel over the ocean. Today people still travel from island to island in outrigger canoes. However, most of the old ways of life in Oceania are gone. When Europeans came to Oceania in the 1700s, they brought new skills to the region. What changes do ◀ you think took place in the culture of Australia and Oceania as a result.?

CHAPTER REVIEW

VOCABULARY REVIEW

Write each of the following words on a sheet of paper. Then write the correct definition for each word. Use the Glossary on pages 728-737 to help you.

1. migrated
2. navigate
3. outrigger canoes
4. ocean currents
5. aborigines

SKILL BUILDER: MAKING AN OUTLINE

An outline is a method of organizing information in order to help you remember the important ideas. Making an outline can help you organize your ideas before studying for a test or writing a report. Outlines are made up of main topics, subtopics, and supporting details. Here is a sample outline:

I. Oceania (Main topic: Use a Roman numeral.)
  A. Melanesia (Subtopic: Use a capital letter.)
    1. First islands settled (Supporting detail: Use an ordinary numeral.)
    2. New Guinea largest island (Supporting detail.)
  B. Micronesia
    1. Early people came from Melanesia, the Philippines, Indonesia
    2. Guam largest island
  C. Polynesia
    1. Spread over largest area of Oceania
    2. First settlers on Tonga and Samoa

II. (More main topics can be added; use Roman numerals.)

As you can see, an outline uses short terms or phrases which are the important ideas of the chapter. Later, when you study for a test, you can use the phrases as a guide.

Read paragraphs 9 and 13 of this chapter. To practice making an outline, copy the outline started below and complete it using information from paragraphs 9 and 13.

I. Australia
  A. The First Inhabitants
    1. Aborigines came from Southeast Asia about 40,000 years ago
    2. Hunted and gathered plants for food
    3. Did not change the land
  B. European settlers
    1. (Add at least three details.)
    2.
    3.

SKILL BUILDER: CRITICAL THINKING AND COMPREHENSION

1. Main Idea

▶ Read paragraphs 3 and 7 of this chapter. Then write a sentence about each paragraph that gives the main idea of the paragraph.

2. Summarizing

▶ Write the number of the paragraph that these three sentences summarize.

Polynesia is an area of many islands in the Pacific. Tonga and Samoa were first settled about 3,000 years ago. As these two islands became crowded, Polynesians moved to other islands, including New Zealand and the Hawaiian Islands.

3. Generalizing

▶ Read paragraph 10. On a sheet of paper, write why you think the following generalization is a either a good or poor generalization about the paragraph.

Europeans in the eighteenth century were foolish to think there was a great southern continent.

4. Sequencing Sequencing means putting events in the correct order.

▶ Read the sentences below. Then rewrite the sentences in the order in which they happened.

Captain James Cook mapped the east coast of Australia.

Aborigines came to Australia.

Polynesians reached the Hawaiian Islands around A.D. 500.

The first people came to Micronesia.

ENRICHMENT

1. Some scientists think that people from South America might have sailed west to the islands of Oceania. To find out more about this idea, read *Kon Tiki* by Thor Heyerdahl. This book tells how Heyerdahl and his crew sailed in a reed boat across part of the Pacific Ocean in the late 1940s. Prepare an oral book report for your class.

2. Make a chart titled "The Aborigines' Way of Life." The chart should have the following headings: "Food," "Clothing," "Shelter," "Tools and Weapons," "Religion," and "Government." Using encyclopedias and books about Australia, record information under each heading listed on your chart.

3. Read more about the stone statues of Easter Island. Report on when they were discovered by archaeologists and why historians believe the statues were used as religious symbols. Make a drawing of one of the statues to illustrate your report.

4. Do library research on Matthew Everingham (see paragraph 14 of this chapter). Write a brief biographical sketch of Everingham to share with the class. Include information on his early life in England, his imprisonment, and his experiences in Australia.

UNIT REVIEW

SUMMARY

The ebb and flow of empires in the East from the 200s B.C. to the A.D. 1200s marked a time of great creativity and change. Missionaries and traders spread Buddhism from India to Southeast Asia, Tibet, Mongolia, and China, and from China to Vietnam, Korea, and Japan. The Japanese borrowed many ideas from the Chinese, ranging from structures of government to styles of writing to forms of religious worship. Peoples of northern Vietnam and Korea absorbed many ideas and traditions from their Chinese conquerors while managing to hold on to their own strong cultures. During this long period, artists from India and China created art that is some of the most distinguished the world has ever seen. During the same period, the Chinese achieved economic and technological advances that were unmatched in other parts of the world. What role do you think increased travel and trade played in the development and advancement of these countries? Meanwhile, many Pacific islands were developing unique cultures without benefit of an exchange of ideas with other countries.

SKILL BUILDER: FINDING LONGITUDE ON A MAP

Meridians of longitude are the north–south lines on a globe or map. These lines measure degrees of longitude east and west, or 0° degrees at the Prime Meridian.

▶ Study the map below and then answer the questions that follow.

The World About 500 B.C.

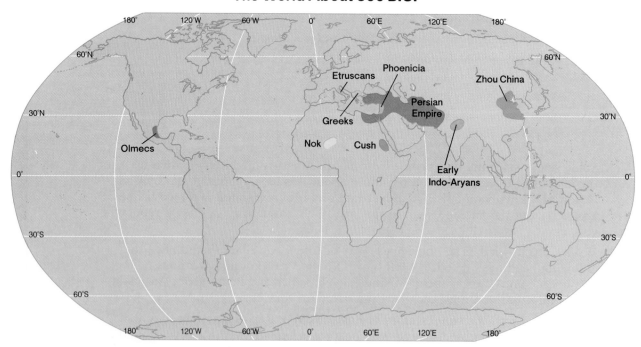

1. Between what two meridians did the Nok and Cush civilizations develop?
2. What other civilizations existed between these two longitudes about 500 B.C.?
3. What civilizations developed between the Prime Meridian and 179° W longitude?

108

SKILL BUILDER: CRITICAL THINKING AND COMPREHENSION

1. Compare and Contrast

▶ How did Chandragupta Maurya of India and Shi Huang Di of China build huge empires? Create a chart that compares and contrasts their methods.

2. Fact versus Opinion

▶ Label each of the following statements *fact* or *opinion*.

a. The religion of early Japan was based on the worship of kami.

b. The ancient 50-ton carved stone statues found on Easter Island were used as religious symbols by the early Pacific Islanders.

c. The Vietnamese held on to their own culture in spite of Chinese rule.

d. Shi Huang Di was both a tyrant with no mercy and a great leader who brought China together.

3. Classifying

▶ Write the name of the country studied in this unit that describes each statement below.

a. The seismograph, a machine used to measure the force of earthquakes, was invented in this country.

b. Scholars in this country invented the decimal number system.

c. A pattern of strong dynasties followed by a weak government and farm troubles was common in this country's history.

d. Kaundinya started the Funan kingdom in this country.

e. Some of the earliest people to settle these islands may have been the Ainu.

f. Lady Trung Trac started an uprising in this country in A.D. 39.

g. This country sent 13 missions to China between A.D. 630 and 838.

ENRICHMENT

1. Women played an important role in the history of early Eastern peoples. During the Tang period a woman, Wu Chao, became ruling emperor for the only time in Chinese history to date. The first uprising in northern Vietnam against the Chinese was started in A.D. 39 by a noblewoman, Lady Trung Trac. In the eleventh century, a Japanese lady of the court named Lady Murasaki Shikibu wrote one of the first great novels ever written.

▶ Do research on the lives of these women and write brief character sketches outlining their personal histories and contributions.

2. Form a group with 2 to 3 other students. Present a radio play to the class in which great figures of early Chinese, Japanese, and Indian history are interviewed. Select and identify your cast of characters from the historical figures discussed in this unit. Prepare questions that will reveal their important contributions to their country's history.

UNIT 3

CLASSICAL CIVILIZATIONS

OBJECTIVE: Unit 3 will focus on the growth of Ancient Greece and Rome and on the lasting contributions these cultures made to the Western World.

First Olympic Games take place 776 B.C.

Persian Wars begin 499 B.C.

Age of Pericles begins 460 B.C.

Alexander the Great dies; the Hellenistic Age begins 323 B.C.

700 B.C.   **600 B.C.**   **500 B.C.**   **400 B.C.**   **300 B.C.**

Roman Republic is founded 509 B.C.

The Golden Age of Greece begins 480 B.C.

Plato founds the Academy c. 387 B.C.

Punic Wars begin 264 B.C.

▲ The Parthenon's simple, balanced style was the model for the Lincoln Memorial in Washington, D.C.

Senate names
Julius Caesar
dictator for life
44 B.C.

Pliny writes
Historia Naturalis
A.D. 77

Pax Romana
ends
A.D. 180

Constantinople is
made capital of
Roman Empire
A.D. 330

| 200 B.C. | 100 B.C. | A.D. 100 | A.D. 200 | A.D. 300 | A.D. 400 |

Augustus becomes the
first Roman emperor;
Pax Romana begins
31 B.C.

Jesus
is born
A.D. 1

Diocletian partitions
Roman Empire into
eastern and western half
A.D. 286

The Heruli dethrone
Romulus Augustus; Western
Roman Empire ends
A.D. 476

CHAPTER 1

Governments of Ancient Greece

▲ The statue *Contemplating Athena* stands in the Acropolis Museum in Athens. Athena is the Greek goddess of wisdom and warfare.

OBJECTIVE: What kinds of government developed in the city-states of ancient Greece?

1. One of the ancient Greeks' most famous myths was about a sculptor named Pygmalion. He created an ivory statue of a woman that was so beautiful he fell in love with it. A goddess heard his prayer, brought the statue to life, and Pygmalion married his own work of art. This story tells two important things about the Greeks. First, they had a strong belief in their gods. Second they had great skill in creating statues that looked real. Unlike ancient Egyptian statues that are stiff and straight, ancient Greek statues are full of life. What separated the Greeks from the other peoples of the ancient world was their belief in the importance of the individual. "Wonders are many," wrote one Greek, "but none is more wonderful than [a person]." Because the Greeks took human beings seriously, they

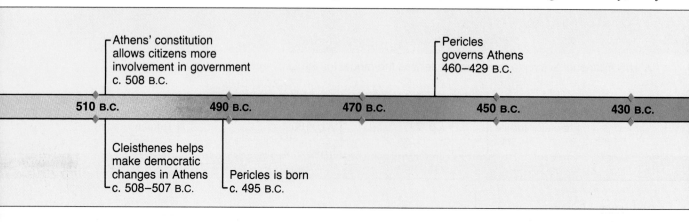

Athens' constitution allows citizens more involvement in government c. 508 B.C.

Pericles governs Athens 460–429 B.C.

| 510 B.C. | 490 B.C. | 470 B.C. | 450 B.C. | 430 B.C. |

Cleisthenes helps make democratic changes in Athens c. 508–507 B.C.

Pericles is born c. 495 B.C.

thought hard about human rights. As a result, they were the first people in history to suggest that ordinary people had the right to choose their own government.

CITY-STATES: How did the city-states of ancient Greece first develop?

2. The people of ancient Greece developed independent communities with their own unique forms of government. The *polis*, or Greek **city-state** as these communities were called, became the center of life in ancient Greece. Look at the Atlas map of Europe on page 726. Greece is a country with many mountains and a deeply indented coastline. While you might think that it was the mountains that kept the city-states separate, that is not so. Each Greek *polis* developed separately for several reasons. First, although Greece is mountainous, there were fertile plains for growing crops within each city-state. Abundant food allowed for economic independence. Second, the center of the *polis* was usually built on the highest part of the mountain for protection from invaders. The mountain city also became the central market and meeting place. Since Greeks enjoyed gathering and talking together, the Greek city-states became tight-knit communities. There was no need for a large centralized government over all of Greece.

3. The governments of the city-states varied. Around 800 B.C., most city-states were ruled by a **monarchy** (MON-ar-kee), the kind of government in which a king or a queen has complete power. Often, the monarch would be aided by **nobles**, or people of high rank or birth. As the noble families gained more power over time, the city-state became an **oligarchy** (OL-uh-gar-kee), a kind of government in which a few people rule.

4. In many city-states, however, government by oligarchy did not last. People of the trading class wanted a voice in government. Poor farmers saw their lives getting worse—many were forced into debt because of high taxes, and subsequently be-

came slaves of the rich. Some citizens who wanted power took advantage of the unrest. They promised the people a greater voice in government if the people would help them overthrow the ruling nobles. Once these new leaders took control, they went back on their promise. These new leaders were known as **tyrants** (TY-ruhnts), or rulers who take complete power and use it in a brutal or harsh way. Around 600 B.C., the brutal rule of most tyrants was replaced by a **democracy** (duh-MAHK-ruh-see), or government by the people. Why do you think this ◄ occurred?

ATHENS: What characteristics made Athens a democracy?

5. Athens was one of the most well-known of the Greek city-states. By 508 B.C., Athens had adopted a constitution that allowed citizens more involvement in the government. It was the duty of all male citizens over the age of 18 to take part in the passing of laws. Laws were made and voted on in the General Assembly, where meetings were very lively. Anyone had the right to stand up and express a viewpoint. There was always a lot of discussion before a new law was passed. In addition to making the laws, members of the Assembly had the final word on spending tax money. They also decided on who was to fill important government posts. Even the declaration of war had to be voted on by the Assembly.

6. Over time, new systems were developed to insure the smooth running of the government. As Athens grew, this meant that several thousand men might vote on such matters as spending money or declaring war. This was much too large a number of people to gather in the Assembly at one time. Therefore, a Council of Five Hundred was chosen among the citizens. Any Athenian male citizen over the age of 30 could become a member. No member was allowed to serve on the Council more than twice. The Council chose its own officers and decided which laws would be presented to the General Assembly for discussion. The

Ask: What similarities do you see between our democratic government and that of Athens? What are some of the differences?

113

▲ Pericles led Athens from 460 to 429 B.C. He believed strongly in the people's right to rule and helped make democracy work in Athens.

Council also worked with the Board of Ten Generals, which led the Athenian army and held a great deal of power. One of the most famous of these generals was Pericles (PAIR-uh-kleez), who was the leader of Athens from 460 to 429 B.C.

PEOPLE IN HISTORY

7. Pericles had a strong need to make democracy work in Athens. Pericles was born around 495 B.C. to famous Athenian parents. Pericles' father was a member of a powerful ruling family and a strong supporter of democracy in Athens. Pericles' mother was the niece of Cleisthenes (KLYS-thuh-neez). Cleisthenes was a government leader who helped make many democratic changes in Athens about 508–507 B.C.

8. By the age of 33, Pericles had become the spokesperson for democracy in the gov-

ernment. He believed strongly in the people's right to rule. Pericles told the General Assembly that more powers should be taken away from the nobles and given to the people. The Assembly agreed and opened most government offices to male citizens, rich or poor. Later, Pericles supported the idea that the state should pay the jurors when they served on the popular courts. A juror is a member of a group of people sworn to hear evidence and decide a law case. State pay allowed poor people to take time off from work to be jurors. Why do you ◄ think women were not allowed to have a voice in this "democracy"?

9. Pericles worked hard to keep Athens strong and peaceful. He used his skill as a statesman and leader to prevent war between Athens and Sparta, another city-state and an Athenian enemy. Pericles spread democracy in the lands he conquered and established good relations with neighboring countries such as Egypt and Sicily.

10. To honor the city-state's goddess Athena, Pericles used the riches of Athens to build beautiful temples on the **acropolis** (uh-KROP-uh-lis). The acropolis was the fortified area of each city-state. It was also the home of the ruler, the place of assembly, and the religious center. The goddess Athena was said to watch over Athens. The largest and most important temple honoring her was the Parthenon. That white marble building with its evenly spaced columns rests on a hill overlooking the city.

SPARTA: How was the government of Sparta different from that of Athens?

11. Unlike other Greek city-states, Sparta never developed a democratic government. The government remained an **aristocracy** (ar-is-TAHK-ruh-see), a government ruled by a small group of people from the upper class. However, some citizens were allowed a voice in some matters. For example, all male citizens of Sparta over the age of 30 belonged to the Assembly. The Assembly elected government workers and voted on laws that were introduced by the Council of

Background: Pericles was elected by the people as their chosen general for 14 consecutive years. He died during the time of the Peloponnesian War in 429 B.C.

Elders. The Council of Elders was made up of two kings and 28 men. Its members had to be citizens of Sparta who were also over 60 years of age.

12. The real power in Sparta, however, belonged to the five **ephors** (EF-orz), or overseers, who were elected by the Assembly. The ephors had the power to carry on business with foreign countries, disagree with the kings, and control the slaves. For any change in the government of Sparta to take place, the Assembly, the Council, and the ephors each had to agree to that change.

▶ Would you have preferred the government of Athens or that of Sparta? Why?

SPOTLIGHT ON SOURCES

13. There was no formal education in Sparta. While some Spartans could read and write, it was considered more important for Spartans to develop physical

---

▼ Spartan warriors underwent a rigorous military training. This bronze sculpture of a Spartan warrior dates to the sixth century B.C.

strength and defend the city-state. Spartan girls were more athletic than other Greek girls. As women they were in charge of the household and could even run their own businesses. All male Spartan citizens belonged to the city-state from birth. Spartan boys were cared for by their mothers until the age of seven. Then they were taken from home and trained for the military until the age of 30, when they became citizens. Sparta's army was its pride and joy. In the passage that follows, an ancient Greek historian describes some of the military training a Spartan would undergo.

> Instead of softening [the boys'] feet with shoe or sandal, [the] rule was to make them [the boys] hardy through going barefoot.
>
> . . . [the] rule was [to get them used to] a single garment the whole year through, thinking that so they would be better prepared to withstand the [changes] of heat and cold. . . .
>
> In the streets they were to keep their hands within the folds of the cloak; they were to walk in silence and without turning their heads to gaze, but rather to keep their eyes fixed upon the ground before them . . . .
>
> from *Readings in the History of the Ancient World,* William C. McDermott and Wallace Caldwell, eds.

How would you feel about that kind of training?

OUTLOOK

14. Many of the freedoms Americans enjoy today began in ancient Greece. For example, the right to speak freely and the right to vote were practiced first by the Greeks. The idea that citizens should have a say in government also began in ancient Greece. The ancient Greeks took their roles as citizens seriously and regarded government as the center of their lives. To what ◀ extent is this true for Americans today?

Background: Every male citizen between 20 and 60 years old was subject to military service in Sparta. This explains why the Council of Elders was made up of men older than 60. Also note that true Spartans were in the minority. Most people who lived in Sparta were the helots or enslaved Greeks.

CHAPTER REVIEW

VOCABULARY REVIEW

Write each number and word on a sheet of paper. Then write the letter of the definition next to the word it defines.

1. city-state
2. monarchy
3. nobles
4. oligarchy
5. tyrants
6. democracy
7. acropolis
8. ephors
9. aristocracy

a. leaders who seize absolute power for themselves and use it brutally
b. the fort in the city of Athens
c. a government ruled by a small privileged class that is usually made up of nobles
d. government by the people
e. a Greek community made up of a city and its surrounding territory
f. government by the few
g. rule by one person, often a king, who had absolute authority
h. Spartan overseers
i. people of high rank of birth

SKILL BUILDER: USING CONTEXT CLUES

There are several ways you can determine the meaning of an unfamiliar word. You can sound the word out to see if it's a word you've heard but haven't yet read. You can see if the word contains smaller word parts whose meanings you do know. Or you can examine the word's context to see if the words or sentences surrounding the unfamiliar word give clues to its meaning.

For example, you might not know the meaning of the word *context*. But in the last sentence of the paragraph above, you can figure out from the clues in the sentence that *context* means the setting or surroundings of an unfamiliar word.

Use context clues to choose the best definition for the underlined word in each sentence below.

1. The people of ancient Greece developed independent communities with their own unique forms of government.
   a. unusual or distinct
   b. similar but unequal
   c. peculiar or odd

2. Since Greeks enjoyed gathering and talking together, the Greek city-states became tight-knit communities. There was no need for a large centralized government.
   a. circular
   b. in, at, or near the center of
   c. organized under one control

3. Any Athenian male citizen over the age of 30 was eligible to become a member of the Council of Five Hundred. No member could serve more than two terms.
   a. allowed by the rules
   b. fit or suitable
   c. forbidden

4. Throughout the city-states, abundant food allowed for economic independence.
   a. thrifty or cheap
   b. financial, material, or monetary
   c. excessive or extreme

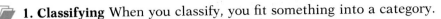

STUDY HINT Read the People in History on page 114. This brief biography of Pericles tells about a person who has had an important part in early history. Think about what he accomplished. How is Pericles an example of an important subject discussed in the chapter?

SKILL BUILDER: CRITICAL THINKING AND COMPREHENSION

1. Classifying When you classify, you fit something into a category.

▶ Read each of the statements below. Decide whether the statement describes Sparta or Athens. Copy the letter of each statement on a sheet of paper and write Sparta or Athens after the letter.

a. The acropolis was where beautiful temples were built.

b. These women had greater freedoms than other Greek women.

c. The five ephors had a lot of power in the government.

d. All boys had to leave home at the age of seven and go to a training camp for the military.

e. The government was known as an aristocracy.

f. Pericles was a strong leader who wanted democracy to work.

g. Education was not as important as physical strength.

h. Laws were made by and voted on in the General Assembly.

i. Jurors were paid by the state.

j. The Parthenon was built as a temple to honor the goddess Athena.

2. Drawing Conclusions

▶ A direct democracy is a type of government in which decisions are made by the people. A representative democracy is a government ruled by representatives chosen by the people. Which kind of democracy do you think was at work in the government of Athens before the Council of Five Hundred? Support your answer with two statements from the chapter.

3. Generalizing

▶ Reread paragraphs 7, 8, 9, and 10. Then read each generalization below. Write the letter of the statement that makes the best generalization about these paragraphs.

a. By the age of thirty-three, Pericles had become the spokesperson for democracy in the Athenian government.

b. Pericles' mother and father were supporters of democracy in Athens.

c. Pericles was one of the most influential statesmen in the history of Greece.

ENRICHMENT

1. Find out how the court system worked in Athens during ancient times. Use an encyclopedia or other reference book to research this topic. Then invent a short tale about an ancient Athenian who was accused of a crime. Write a short story that describes how this person was treated by the court system in Athens during ancient times.

2. Research and write a description of at least three Greek gods or goddesses. Report your findings to the class.

117

CHAPTER 2

Life in Ancient Greece

▲ The *Charioteer* is one of the earliest bronze statues in Greek art. The winner of a race had it made as an offering to Apollo.

OBJECTIVE: What was daily life like in ancient Greece?

1. Imagine it is several thousand years from now. Scientists who study the past are exploring what was once your neighborhood. By digging up your yard, they hope to find evidence that someone once lived there. They want to find out what life was like in the distant past of the 1990s. What would these scientists find buried under the street where you lived? They might find a television, a microwave oven, a skateboard, a VCR, soda cans, or fast food wrappers. What would these things tell them about how you lived? Scientists would be able to get an idea of what twentieth century Amer-icans did for entertainment. They also would learn about American eating habits. They would see how advanced American technology was by examining the kinds of goods people of your time produced. Much of what we know about ancient Greece has

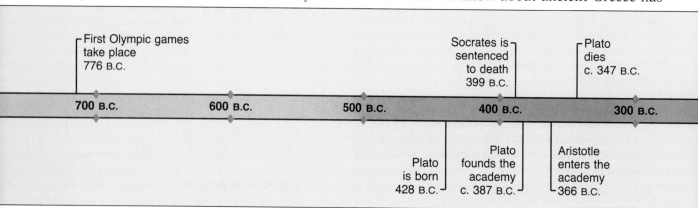

First Olympic games take place 776 B.C.

Socrates is sentenced to death 399 B.C.

Plato dies c. 347 B.C.

| 700 B.C. | 600 B.C. | 500 B.C. | 400 B.C. | 300 B.C. |

Plato is born 428 B.C.

Plato founds the academy c. 387 B.C.

Aristotle enters the academy 366 B.C.

been unearthed in the same way. By studying the items the Greeks left behind, scientists who study the past can tell us how the ancient Greeks lived.

WORK: What kinds of work did the ancient Greeks do for a living?

2. Many ancient Greeks were farmers and shopkeepers. They sold their crops and products at the **agora** (AG-uh-ruh), a marketplace and meeting place in the center of town. Early each morning people would gather to sell their goods. There was much shouting and bargaining over prices for fish, cheese, wine, pottery, goats, and sheep. There were also political discussions. By the 400s B.C., many of the goods sold in the agoras were shipped to other parts of the world. Greek ships carried wine, oil, wool, minerals, marble, and works of art to foreign ports. Greek merchants would bring back nuts, metals, luxury goods, and, of most importance, grain.

3. Not all of the work in ancient Greece was done by Greek citizens. Some of it was done by **metics** (MEH-tiks), or foreigners who settled in Greece. Metics were not allowed to become citizens. Many shopkeepers were metics, as were traders, bankers, and artists. Most of the hard labor in ancient Greece was done by slaves. Many slaves were prisoners of war from places such as Persia or Egypt. They worked in homes as servants and in shops as craftsworkers. Some were even teachers and business managers. A small number worked in slave gangs at state-owned mines and quarries. During the Golden Age of Athens more than one-third of the 300,000 people in Athens were slaves. A slave could become free by saving enough money to buy his freedom or by service in war. But once free, a slave still could never become a Greek citizen.

4. Greeks believed that a truly free people would be able to devote all of their time to government, war, reading, and thinking about life. If possible, free Greek citizens should spend none of their time working. Slaves and metics were there to take care of the everyday worries of making a living. Why do you think the Greek people had this ◄ outlook on life?

AT HOME: What were the homes of the ancient Greeks like?

5. Most citizens in ancient Greece owned their own homes. In town, the houses were built close together on narrow streets. These homes built of sun-dried bricks often had an open-air courtyard. All the rooms of the house looked out onto this courtyard. In

Daily life in . . .

Dinner time in ancient Greece was an event in itself. All of the family members would gather in the evening for the main meal of the day. They generally sat at one table unless there were guests. If there were guests, the women and children sat at separate tables. Before guests could be seated, slaves would remove the guests' sandals. After the slaves had washed the guests' feet, the guests would be given water with which to wash their hands. Often, perfumed oils were dabbed on their foreheads.

The typical main course was fish, but if the family was rich, meat would be served instead. Along with the meat or fish, vegetables cooked with onions, garlic, and olive oil were served. Dessert was usually a platter of honey, nuts, and cheese. Cheesecake was a special favorite.

Food was served on clay or metal plates and was often eaten with the fingers. After the meal was over, fingers were cleaned with scraps of bread and water. Perfumes and wine were then passed around. The rest of the evening was spent dancing, playing games, and talking.

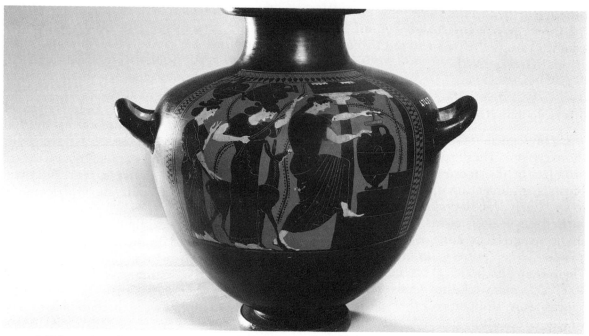

▲ This ancient Greek vase is from the sixth century B.C. During the Golden Age of Athens, women managed the household but could not become Greek citizens.

the center of the courtyard there was usually an altar set up to honor the family god.

6. For the most part, the inside of a Greek home was very simple. The house might have had a porch with columns. The porch would have looked out onto the street. Windows were rare and found only in the upper floor of the house. Windows had no glass panes but they did have shutters to keep out the sun. The house was sparsely furnished with a few chairs and tables, some chests, and a bed. Chairs and beds were often carved and decorated with silver or ivory.

THE FAMILY: What was family life like in ancient Greece?

7. The family was the most important unit in ancient Greece. It was usually made up of a father and a mother, their unmarried daughters, their sons, and their slaves. The sons' wives, children, and slaves were also part of the family. The men of the house spent most of their time away from home. They left the house early in the morning to

work, to meet with other Greek citizens at the agora, or to exercise at the gymnasium.

SPOTLIGHT ON SOURCES

8. Unlike the men, women of Athens spent their entire day at home. They did not leave the house even to go shopping. The men did the shopping. Athenian women were not citizens, nor could they own property. The main job of the Athenian woman was to manage the household. This included managing the family's money, the children, and the slaves. Here a Greek citizen tells his new wife her duties.

. . . Over those whose appointed tasks are wrought [carried out] indoors, it will be your duty to preside [supervise]; yours to receive the stuffs brought in; yours to [divide] part for daily use, and yours to [handle] the rest, to guard and garner [store] it so that the outgoings destined for a year may not be [spent] in a month. It will

Background: Greek women could leave the home, if veiled and accompanied by someone, to visit relatives, to take part in a religious festival, or to see a play. Otherwise, women had to stay at home.

be your duty, when the wools are introduced, to see that clothing is made for those who need; your duty also to see that the dried corn is rendered fit and serviceable for food . . .

Should any of our household fall sick, it will be your care to see and tend them to the recovery of their health . . .

[But] there are other cares . . . to take some maiden who knows naught of carding [weaving] wool and to make her [good] in the art . . . you have it in your power to [return] by kindness the well-behaved whose presence is a blessing to your house; or maybe to [make pure] the bad character, should such a one appear. But the greatest joy of all will be to prove yourself my better . . . as you come to be a better helpmate to myself and to the children, a better guardian of our home, so will your honour increase throughout the household as mistress, wife, and mother, daily more dearly prized . . .

—from *Readings in the History of the Ancient World*, William C. McDermott and Wallace Caldwell, eds.

In Sparta women were honored as the mothers of Spartan soldiers. They worked in the fields as well as in the home. Why do you think women were treated differently in Athens and Sparta?

LEARNING: What were young people taught in ancient Greece?

9. Children stayed at home until the age of six. Boys were then sent to school, while girls remained at home. Girls were taught reading, writing, and arithmetic by their mothers or by slaves. The girls also learned how to spin and weave, and to dance, sing, and play an instrument. Few women in ancient Greece learned any more than what they were taught at home.

10. Athenian boys went to private schools from age six to sixteen. Each day they would be taken to school by a family slave. At school, the boys would sit on benches and use their knees as a table for the wax tablets on which they wrote. Reading, writing, arithmetic, music, and gymnastics made up the course of study. Gymnastics, which included learning how to wrestle, swim, and use the bow and sling, was taught in the town's gymnasium. Why do you think the ancient Greeks believed gymnastics to be the most important part of a boy's education?

11. After a boy turned 16, he was expected to concentrate on making his body strong for war. At 18, the Greek youth became a soldier. For two years, he was drilled in the art of war and taught the duties of citizenship. Greek soldiers also learned literature, music, geometry, and **rhetoric** (RET-uh-rik). Rhetoric is the art of speaking or writing effectively. At 21, the young Greek male became a full citizen of the city and was free to leave his parents.

12. Only young men from well-to-do families could afford a higher education. These young men paid a lot of money to traveling teachers called **Sophists** (SAF-ists). The Sophists were a class of Greek teachers who were specially trained in the art of teaching rhetoric, grammar, logic, and **philosophy** (fi-LAHS-uh-fee). Philosophy is a subject that tries to answer questions about people, society, and nature. For example, philosophers might seek the answer to the question, "What is love?" Some young Athenians worked night jobs just to be able to go to a class held by a Sophist. Among the most famous of these philosopher-teachers was Plato (PLAY-toh).

PEOPLE IN HISTORY

13. Plato was born in Athens in 428 B.C. to a very old and important Athenian family. As a young boy, Plato was good in nearly every subject he studied. One of his favorites was poetry. When he got older, Plato could not decide whether to follow a career in poetry or politics. Then he met Socrates (SOK-rah-teez). Socrates was a close friend of Plato's family. More important, he was a

Ask: To reinforce the students' understanding of what a philosopher of ancient Greece would do, ask students their views on love, beauty, good government, and why people should obey the laws.

121

▲ Greek vases were often painted with scenes from daily life. This vase shows school lessons in reciting and writing.

famous Greek **philosopher**. A philosopher searches for knowledge, truth and wisdom. Socrates tried to teach the people around him to think and understand. One of Socrates's famous sayings is "Know thyself."
▶ What do you think Socrates meant by that statement?

14. From the time he met Socrates, Plato's life work became the writing of philosophy in the form of **dialogues** (DY-uh-lawgz). Dialogues are written compositions in which two or more people are engaging in a discussion. In his dialogues, Plato would have the character of Socrates pose questions to a group of students. The students would provide answers and discuss them. Then Socrates would ask another question.

15. Some Athenians regarded Socrates' questions as a threat to their way of life. In 399 B.C., Socrates was tried for teaching the young to think for themselves and to question the government. After he was sen-

tenced to death, Socrates gathered his friends and drank a poison made from a hemlock plant. Plato fled Athens in despair. Around 387 B.C., he visited the court of Dionysius I, a tyrant of the city of Syracuse in Sicily. The visit ended with Plato being thrown out of Syracuse and nearly sold as a slave. However, a friend appeared just in time to rescue Plato, who finally returned to Athens.

16. Plato dreamed of starting a school in which all fields of knowledge could be studied. Plato's friends bought him a grove in Athens named after the god Academus. Here Plato founded the Academy. Plato taught his students by using dialogues and by presenting them with problems to solve. One of Plato's greatest dialogues is *The Republic*, about the ideal state and how it would be governed. Plato's ideas are still studied today. Besides philosophy, the chief subject studied at the Academy was mathematics. In fact, above the door of the Academy was the saying, "Let no one without geometry enter here." The Academy became the center of learning in Greece for the next 900 years.

17. As a major thinker of his day, Plato was called upon by many for his knowledge. One of Plato's students was Aristotle, who became another great Greek philosopher and thinker. Aristotle developed **logic,** or the science of reasoning. Plato was asked to teach Dionysius II, who was the son of the Syracuse leader, and to draw up a set of laws for a Greek colonial city. Plato was still finishing the laws when he died in Athens at age 80. In his writings, Plato created a system of ideas to explain the universe and human life. These ideas have had a huge influence on western philosophy ever since.

RELIGION: What role did the gods play in the everyday life of ancient Greece?

18. The people of ancient Greece believed in many gods. Some of these gods were gods of love, of war, of art and music, and of the harvest. Although the gods were considered to be superhuman, they were not without

Background: In *The Republic*, Plato suggests that the ruling class be those citizens with the most intelligence, i.e., the philosophers. **Ask:** What do you think Plato thought of democracy?

weaknesses. Every city had its own god to honor, as did every family. As a result, towns were filled with temples and shrines. Each god had a **myth** (MITH), or fictitious story explaining historical events, attached to him or her. For example, Athena (uh-THEE-nuh), the goddess of wisdom, was said to be the founder of Athens.

19. Once a year the people held festivals to honor their town god. There would be parades, feasting, and games. One of the most important festivals was an athletic competition held in honor of Zeus, the father of all the gods. This festival was held at Olympia. Athletes from all Greek city-states attended the games. They competed in discus- and javelin-throwing contests, chariot racing, and running events. Winners were looked up to as heroes and received special honors. The Olympic games of today ▶ are based on the early Greek games. What purpose do these games serve today?

20. Myths of the gods were the basis of much of the cultural life of ancient Greece. For example, many songs were written in praise of Apollo, the god of music and art. Adorning the temples of the towns were beautiful sculptures of the gods. Vases were painted with scenes from the myths, as well as from daily life. Many of the plays written for the theater were based on the ceremonies of Dionysus (dy-uh-NY-sus), the god of song and merriment. The performance of plays of ancient Greeks such as Aeschylus (ESS-kuh-luss), Sophocles (SOF-uh-kleez), and Euripides (yoo-RIP-uh-deez) are still enjoyed by many today. Euripides' plays reflect his concerns about human nature and the human environment. In one of his plays, *The Women of Troy*, he expresses his feelings against slavery through a group of women. The women have been captured in war and are waiting in anguish to be taken away as slaves.

OUTLOOK

21. In some ways, the daily life of the ancient Greeks was not very different from

▲ The statue of the Greek discus thrower is a beautiful sculpture that celebrates the athletic ability of the Greeks. Discus throwing continues to be a key event in the Olympics today.

daily life in America today. People worked, shopped, raised children, went to school, joined the military, and learned the duties of good citizenship. They enjoyed music, art, the theater, and athletics. The ancient Greeks were also great thinkers and creators. However, Greek society was not a free society. Slaves, metics, and women were denied important rights given to Greek male citizens. This seems to go against Greek beliefs in democracy. Imagine that you are in the audience listening to Plato and his students engage in a dialogue. Plato has just asked his students, "Why should we deny slaves, metics, and women the rights of citizenship?" What are some answers ◀ that you might hear? How would you answer Plato's question?

Background: Since women were not allowed to act, men played the female parts in plays. The whistling and stamping of feet meant audience approval of the performance.

123

CHAPTER REVIEW

VOCABULARY REVIEW

▶ Write each of the following words on a sheet of paper. Then write the correct definition for each word. Use the Glossary on pages 728-737 to help you.

1. agora
2. metics
3. rhetoric
4. Sophists
5. philosophy
6. dialogues
7. myth
8. philosopher
9. logic

SKILL BUILDER: OUTLINING

Studying for a test or writing a report can seem hard to do when you have mounds of material to read. One way you can make your tasks easier is to prepare an outline. An outline organizes and condenses the material you have read into main ideas and supporting details. Outlines follow a standard format. The information that appears after each Roman numeral in an outline is always a main idea, or main topic. The information that appears under each main idea is a subtopic. Supporting details are listed under the subtopics.

The outline below is based on the information presented in this chapter. Part of the outline has been completed for you.

▶ Copy the outline on a sheet of paper. Fill in the blanks by referring to the chapter text.

I. Work in ancient Greece
  A. _____
    1. They sold their goods in the agoras
    2. They traded with foreign peoples
    3. Their goods included _____
  B. Metics and slaves
    1. _____
    2. _____

II. _____
  A. Most Greeks owned their own homes
    1. _____
    2. _____
    3. _____
  B. Greek homes were simple inside
    1. Houses were sparsely furnished
    2. _____

III. The family in ancient Greece
  A. The family was the most important unit in ancient Greece
    1. It was made up of _____
    2. The men _____
  B. Women of ancient Greece worked at home
    1. _____
    2. _____
    3. _____

IV. _____
  A. Girls were taught at home
    1. _____
    2. _____
  B. _____
    1. At school they were taught reading, writing, arithmetic, music and gymnastics
    2. Gymnastics was the most important part of the boy's education
    3. At 18 _____
    4. At 21 _____

V. Religion in ancient Greece
  A. _____
    1. There were gods of love, art, music, and harvest.
    2. _____
  B. Festivals were held once a year to honor the gods
    1. _____
    2. _____

Form a research group with three students and assign each person one of these chapter topics: kinds of work, family life, education, or religion in ancient Greece. Use reference materials to gather more information about your topic.

SKILL BUILDER: CRITICAL THINKING AND COMPREHENSION

1. Drawing Conclusions

▶ Many of the goods sold in the agoras of ancient Greece were shipped to other parts of the world. Based on your reading in earlier units of your book, what other empires might the Greeks have shipped their goods to? Write your conclusion on a sheet of paper.

2. Generalizing

▶ Explain why you agree or disagree with the following generalization:
The gods formed the center of life in ancient Greece.

3. Classifying

▶ Answer each of the following questions on a sheet of paper.

3-1. A good title for paragraph 18 is
 a. Athena, the Founder of Athens
 b. The Importance of Greek Myths
 c. Religion in Ancient Greece

3-2. Label the following statements *true* or *false*.
 a. Few ancient Greeks were farmers and shopkeepers.
 b. Metics were not allowed to become Greek citizens.
 c. Most citizens in ancient Greece owned their own homes.

3-3. According to the social structure in Ancient Greece, whose role was it to
 a. perform most of the hard labor?
 b. think about government, war, reading, and life?
 c. manage the household?

4. Fact *versus* Opinion

▶ Write the following statements on a sheet of paper. Then label each statement *fact* or *opinion*.

 a. Ancient Greek farmers sold their crops and products at the agora.
 b. All Greek males spoke and wrote effectively.
 c. One of Plato's greatest dialogues is *The Republic*.
 d. The people of ancient Greece believed in many gods.
 e. Slaves, metics, and women were denied important rights given to Greek male citizens.

ENRICHMENT

1. Prepare a floor plan of a typical house in ancient Greece. Use this plan to build a model of the house from clay, plaster, or paper and cardboard.

2. Find out more about what the Olympic games of ancient Greece and the games of today have in common. Reference books in your school or local library may contain helpful information. For example: Why is the laurel wreath used as a symbol in the Olympics today? What current Olympic events were also a part of the original games?

CHAPTER 3

The Spread of Greek Culture

▲ This ancient vase shows Alexander the Great in battle with the Persians. Why do you think he was called "the Great"?

OBJECTIVE: How did Greek civilization spread to other parts of the Mediterranean and Asia?

1. Chances are that you are closer to some relatives in your family than to others. You may feel that you have everything in common with a cousin your own age. With an aunt or uncle, you may feel that your interests or views are not quite the same. Nevertheless, when it comes to helping you in times of trouble, you expect all of your relatives to be helpful. Family members can give you courage and support. In the fifth century, the Greek city-states were very much like a group of relatives. Although they were separated from each other, they had the common bond of being Greek. They shared a pride in being Greek. They worshipped the same gods. Some city-states had closer relationships than others. Some did not always agree or share the same concerns. However, when the well-being of

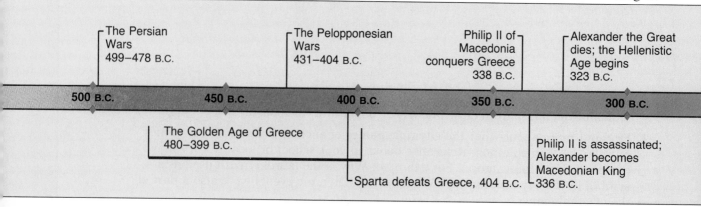

The Persian Wars
499–478 B.C.

The Pelopponesian Wars
431–404 B.C.

Philip II of Macedonia conquers Greece
338 B.C.

Alexander the Great dies; the Hellenistic Age begins
323 B.C.

500 B.C.　　450 B.C.　　400 B.C.　　350 B.C.　　300 B.C.

The Golden Age of Greece
480–399 B.C.

Sparta defeats Greece, 404 B.C.

Philip II is assassinated; Alexander becomes Macedonian King
336 B.C.

any one of them was threatened, they joined forces and posed a mighty challenge for any power.

THE PERSIAN WARS: How did the Persian Wars unite the Greek city-states and make Athens a leading power?

2. In the fifth century B.C., the Greek city-states faced a serious threat from the Persian Empire. Persian influence had grown so successfully that Greece was the only important power left for Persians to conquer. Persian kings had, in fact, already taken over some Greek city-states along the Ionian Sea. In 499 B.C., with help from Athens, those city-states rebelled against the Persians. The rebellion was put down quickly. With the easy victory, the Persians decided it was time to take over more Greek lands. The Persians planned to do this by striking at Athens, the very heart of Greek civilization.

3. Persia tried to invade Athens in 492 B.C., but a storm destroyed the Persian fleet. With such a strong power almost at their doorstep, the Greek city-states moved into action. In 490 B.C., while waiting for aid from Sparta, an Athenian army of 20,000 attacked a much larger Persian force at Marathon. Surprised by the strength and force of the Greek attack, the Persians were crushed. According to legend, the news of the victory was brought to Athens from Marathon by a runner who raced the entire way, more than 25 miles (40 kilometers). The modern marathon race gets its name from that event.

4. Ten years later, when the Persians again tried to take Athens, messengers were sent to all the city-states asking for troops and supplies. Athens joined other Greek city-states under the leadership of Sparta. The Persians moved by land from the north and successfully defeated a small Spartan army in the northern mountains of Greece. Once again, the Athenians came to the rescue when their powerful navy defeated the Persians in the **straits** of Salamis. (A strait is a narrow passageway of water connecting two large bodies of water.)

5. The Persians were dealt the final blow the following year. In 479 B.C., a combined army of men from all the Greek city-states and the Athenian navy defeated the Persian land force. Thus, the threat of Persian power was ended.

THE GOLDEN AGE: How did the Persian Wars lead to the spread of Greek culture?

6. With the Persian defeat, ancient Greece became the leading power of the Mediterranean. The Greek navy helped open ports in the Mediterranean Sea to Greek trade. As the money made from trade poured in, the Greeks could spend more money and time developing the culture of

Daily life in . . .

Some kings of the Hellenistic Age were so rich, they spent huge sums on all kinds of luxuries. Hiero (HY-uh-roh) II, king of Syracuse, hired Archimedes, the mathematician and inventor, to design a pleasure boat for him. Hiero's boat would outdo some of the fanciest yachts of today. His boat was 407 feet (123 meters) long, weighed 1,000 tons, and could carry 3,900 tons of goods. It had a sport deck with a gym, a large marble bath, and a garden deck with many types of plants. If the king chose to have a party, there was room for 300 guests. On board were 60 cabins, should anyone want to stay overnight. Some of those cabins had tile floors and doors made of ivory and fancy wood. Moving the ship in the water required the muscle power of 600 men in 20 groups of oars. Eventually Hiero found the ship too costly to maintain. He filled it with corn and fish from Sicily and sent it as a gift to Egypt.

Athens. Historians call this period the **Golden Age of Greece**.

7. What a golden age it was! Great temples were built. Statues of breathtaking beauty were carved. Greek works of art were so highly prized that they were shipped to lands throughout the Mediterranean. Writers glorified Greek history in plays about Greek cities and heroic wars. Greek scientists used science to understand the causes of disease rather than blaming the gods. Greek philosophers suggested ways to have a more perfect life. The Golden Age started around 480 B.C. and lasted until 399 B.C. ► What might have happened to Greek culture if the Greeks had lost the Persian Wars?

PELOPONNESIAN WARS: How did the Peloponnesian Wars bring an end to the power of ancient Greece?

8. After the Persian Wars, Athens became the cultural center of Greece and the most powerful city-state, too. To keep the Persians from ever thinking about attacking Greece again, the Greek city-states formed a group called the Delian (DEE-lee-un) League. Athens gave the most money and troops to the group, and, as a result, became the league's leader. Soon Athens was ruling the league as though it were an empire. Some city-states began to resent the way Athens was taking over government and trade. The city-state that disliked Athens the most was Sparta. The two city-states were like opposite sides of the same coin—different in almost every way. Spartans feared that the Athenian empire would soon include them as well.

SPOTLIGHT ON SOURCES

9. In 431 B.C., Sparta and Athens went to war. Sparta's strength lay in its army, while Athens had the advantage of a strong navy. The Spartans attacked by burning the farms and homes around Athens. They wanted to force the Athenians inside the city's walls to come out and fight. But Pericles, the famous general and statesman, advised the Athenians not to fight. (He had plans to attack the Spartans by sea.) At the end of the first year of the war, Pericles gave a speech to honor Athenians who had died in battle. Here is part of what he said:

> . . . in the hour of trial Athens alone among her contemporaries [the other powers of the time] is superior to [better than] the report of her. No enemy who comes against her is [angered] at the reverses which he [must deal with] at the hands of such a city; no subject complains that his masters are unworthy of him . . . there are mighty monuments of our power which will make us the wonder of this and succeeding ages . . . For we have [forced] every land and every sea to open a path for our valor [bravery], and have everywhere planted eternal memorials of our friendship and our [hatred]. Such is the city for whose sake these men nobly fought and died; they could not bear the thought that she might be taken from them; and every one of us who survive should gladly toil [work] on her behalf. . . .
>
> —*Readings in European History,* Leon Barnard and Theodore B. Hodges

10. The Peloponnesian (pel-uh-puh-NEE-zhun) Wars, as these wars between Sparta and Athens were called, split ancient Greece apart. Some city-states sided with Athens, while others sided with Sparta. The wars ended in 404 B.C. with the surrender of Athens. Sparta demanded that the Athenian empire be broken up. With the fall of the Athenian empire, the Golden Age of Greece came to an end. For many years after the Peloponnesian Wars, the Greek city-states remained divided. Sparta and Persia fought over who would rule parts of the empire. City-states fought among each other, and this constant fighting weakened them. In the middle of the fourth century B.C., a rising power called Macedonia (mas-uh-DOH-nya) became a threat to the Greek

cities. The kingdom of Macedonia lay to the north of Greece.

THE MACEDONIAN EMPIRE: How did the Macedonians build an empire?

11. The leader of Macedonia in the second half of the fourth century B.C. was Philip II. While a young man, Philip was imprisoned in Greece. There Philip learned a great deal about the Greek way of life and about the differences that divided the Greek city-states. When Philip returned to Macedonia, he trained his army to fight using a **phalanx** (FAY-lanks). A phalanx is a body of foot soldiers formed close and deep, bearing shields and spears. The Macedonian army soon became the best in the ancient world. Philip conquered Greece, but he did it slowly, playing city against city. By 338 B.C. Philip was master of Greece—including Athens. His power spread as far north as the ▶ Danube River. Which city-state do you think was the only one that Philip did not conquer? Philip soon decided to declare war

on Persia. Before he could carry out his plan, however, Philip was assassinated.

PEOPLE IN HISTORY

12. Philip's 20-year-old son, **Alexander**, inherited the throne. Alexander was a short man, but what he lacked in height he made up for in ambition. He fulfilled his father's dream of enlarging the Macedonian empire. But winning battles and conquering lands were not his only successes. Wherever he went, he brought Greek customs and learning. He founded cities that became centers of culture for hundreds of years.

13. Although not a Greek by birth, Alexander was greatly influenced by Greek culture. When Alexander was about 13, his father invited Aristotle (AR-uh-stot-ul) to come to Macedonia to be his son's teacher. Aristotle was the most famous Greek philosopher of Alexander's time. As a result of Aristotle's teaching, Alexander grew to admire Greek art, drama, and philosophy.

▼ War between Athens and Sparta brought an end to Greece's Golden Age in 432 B.C. The war lasted for thirty years. Was Byzantium allied with Athens or Sparta in the war?

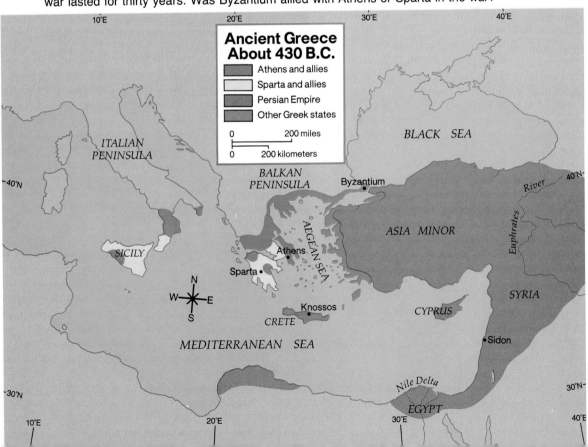

14. After Philip's death, Alexander proved how great a military leader he was. He put down a revolt in the Greek city of Thebes. Then, in 334 B.C., Alexander led his army into Asia Minor, where he defeated the Persians. Then he moved south and took Egypt from the Persians as well. Marching east with his army, he finally crushed the Persians in Mesopotamia. By 331 B.C. Alexander was King of Persia, Pharaoh of Egypt, King of Babylon, and King of Macedonia.

15. Alexander was responsible for bringing together the cultures of East and West. During his conquest of the Persians, Alexander came to admire their culture. He admired the manners of the Persian aristocracy. In fact, Alexander asked some Persian nobles to help him run the empire. Alexander married a Persian princess and began to wear Oriental clothing. He thought of himself not as a Macedonian king but as a Greco-Persian emperor. He molded an empire in which eastern and western cultures mixed in harmony. Trade increased between Greece and Persia. People moved from Greece to Asia Minor.

16. In 327 B.C., Alexander headed east once again, this time to India. Despite the battles won on this march eastward to the Indus River, Alexander's army refused to go any farther east. They feared that their leader had come to love Persian culture too much and had forgotten that he was Macedonian. In 323 B.C., Alexander returned to Persia with his homesick troops. Weary from battle, he died suddenly in Babylon

SKILL BUILDER/MAPS Using map scale and compass directions to follow a route.

The map on this page shows the journeys of Alexander the Great. Use the map scale and compass rose to answer these questions.

1. What was the westernmost city conquered by Alexander the Great?

2. What was the easternmost city conquered by Alexander the Great?

3. How many miles apart are the easternmost and westernmost conquests?

4. What city lies about 1,200 miles (1,920 km) to the southeast of Sparta?

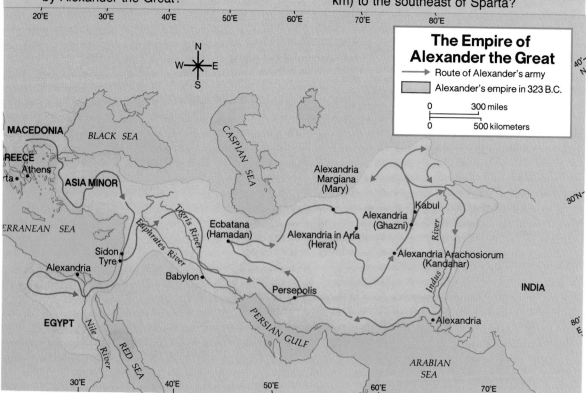

ESL/LEP Strategy: Review with students the above map showing the lands conquered by Alexander the Great. Then, show them a present-day map of the region. Ask students to compare the place names on the two maps.

▲ This famous painting shows Alexander the Great in battle with the Persians. Why do you think he was called "the Great?"

after a short illness. Alexander was only 33.

17. The huge empire that Alexander the Great left behind grew and prospered under his Macedonian generals. These generals began dynasties that ruled Egypt, Syria, Macedonia, and many smaller kingdoms. From the death of Alexander until around 31 B.C., Greek and Persian cultures continued to mix. During this **Hellenistic Age,** Athens no longer was the center of trade, science, and learning. Alexandria, in Egypt, a city built by Alexander, became the center of the Hellenistic world. Trade during this time spread to distant Asia. Spices and perfumes came from India. Silks came from China. Ivory and gold came from Africa. ▶ What do these goods tell you about how the people of the Hellenistic world lived?

HELLENISTIC CULTURE: How did Alexander help to spread Greek culture?

18. As Alexander conquered more lands, Greek culture and influence spread. Alexander's love of Greek ideas influenced every city he founded. Many Greeks **emigrated** to these cities seeking a better life. To emigrate means to move from one country to another. Hellenistic cities became centers of Greek culture for hundreds of years. Greek became the language of the learned people.

19. Greek interest in science, the arts, and learning grew under Hellenistic rule. The system of geometry you study today was written by Euclid (YOO-klid), a Greek mathematician who lived in the third century B.C. Students of physics still study the teachings of the Greek mathematician, Archimedes (ar-kuh-MEE-deez). He was the first to explain how a lever moves heavy objects. Greek scientists learned how certain organs of the body work. Libraries were founded in every Hellenistic city.

OUTLOOK

20. Although the power of the Greek city-states had faded by the 350s B.C., Greek culture continued to spread. However, Greek culture was changing. It was taking in ideas from cultures of the east. In many ways, the changes that Greek culture experienced are like the changes American culture has experienced over the past 200 years. Each ethnic group that has come to America has made contributions to the shaping of American culture. Jazz, for example, is an American form of music that owes its beginnings to African Americans. Many foods that we think of as being "American," such as hamburgers, were introduced to America by people from other nations. The greatness of American art, music, literature, and science is due to the influence the nation's ethnic groups have had on the culture. Which ethnic groups are having an important influence on American culture today?

Activity: Show students examples of Hellenistic sculpture. Then have them compare these examples to sculptures of the Golden Age of Greece.

VOCABULARY REVIEW

Write each of the sentences below on a sheet of paper. Then fill in the blank with the word that best completes each sentence.

Golden Age of Greece   emigrate   Hellenistic Age

phalanx   strait

1. A _____ is a narrow passageway of water connecting two bodies of water.

2. The _____ was the time when ancient Greece produced the finest works in art, literature, science, and philosophy.

3. A body of foot soldiers formed close and deep, bearing shields and spears, is called a _____ .

4. The period after the death of Alexander, when Greek and eastern cultures blended, is known as the _____ .

5. To _____ means to move from one country to settle in another.

SKILL BUILDER: USING THE CARD CATALOG

The easiest way to look for a nonfiction book in the library is to use the card catalog. The card catalog is a set of drawers filled with cards that tell where books can be found in the library. The cards are filed in alphabetical order. For each nonfiction book in the library there are three kinds of cards filed in the card catalog. The *title card* lists the book according to its title. The *author card* lists the book according to the author's last name. Finally, the *subject card* lists the book according to what it is about. In the upper left-hand corner of each card is the call number. The call number tells you where the book can be found in the library. All the cards that relate to a particular book carry the same call number.

▶ Use the sample cards to answer the questions that follow.

```
I.  930    The mask of Jove
    B      Barr, Stringfellow, 1897–
             The mask of Jove; a history of Graeco-Roman
           civilization from the death of Alexander to the death
           of Constantine. Philadelphia, Lippincott /c 1966/
           598 p. plates, map. 24 cm.
```

```
II. 930    Barr, Stringfellow, 1897–
    B        The mask of Jove; a history of Graeco-Roman
           civilization from the death of Alexander to the death
           of Constantine. Philadelphia, Lippincott /c 1966/
           598 p. plates, map. 24 cm.
```

```
III. 930   Hiistory, Ancient
     B       Barr, Stringfellow, 1897–
               The mask of Jove; a history of Graeco-Roman
             civilization from the death of Alexander to the death
             of Constantine. Philadelphia, Lippincott /c 1966/
             598 p. plates, map. 24 cm.
```

1. Which card is the title card?

2. Which card is the author card?

3. What is the title and who is the author of this book?

4. Under what general subject matter could this book be found? From which card did you get this information?

5. What is the call number of this book?

6. What is this book about?

7. When was this book published?

8. How many pages does this book have?

9. In what year was this author born?

SKILL BUILDER: CRITICAL THINKING AND COMPREHENSION

1. Spatial Relationships   One way to understand the order of events in history is to understand when the events took place in relation to one another.

▶ Answer the questions below about the timing of events in relation to one another. Refer to the timelines on pages 118 and 126 to help you.

a. The Persian Wars ended _____ years before Plato was born.

b. Plato founded the Academy during Greece's _____ .

c. The Peloponnesian Wars began _____ years after the Persian Wars ended.

d. Alexander the Great became king of the Macedonian empire _____ years after the death of Plato.

e. Alexander the great ruled for _____ years.

2. Summarizing

▶ Write a summary explaining why the period between 480 B.C. and 399 B.C. is called the "Golden Age" of Greece.

3. Generalizing

▶ Write a generalization that tells about Ancient Greece after the Peloponnesian Wars.

4. Sequencing

▶ List the areas Alexander the Great conquered in the order in which he conquered them.

5. Drawing Conclusions

▶ What effect do you think the Peloponnesian Wars had on Greek culture?

ENRICHMENT

1. Research the battles of either the Persian or Peloponnesian Wars. In a booklet, write a brief description of each battle. Include a map of ancient Greece in the booklet showing the location of each battle.

2. Women were active in government during the Hellenistic Age. Two famous Egyptian queens during this period were Arsinoe and Cleopatra. Read about the lives of one of these women. Then write a newspaper article for the *Egyptian Times* that describes how the queen handled a government matter.

CHAPTER 4

Rome: From City to Empire

▲ Hannibal, the great general of Carthage, made one of the most remarkable marches of all time. Why was his march "incredible"?

OBJECTIVE: How did Rome grow from a small city into a huge empire?

1. There were many legends about Rome's beginnings, but the story most Romans accepted was the one that told about a Trojan hero named Aeneas. Aeneas fled from the fallen city of Troy in Asia Minor and journeyed to Italy. There he built a city near the present site of Rome, and there Aeneas's descendants ruled. Then the time came when two brothers quarreled over who should be king. The brother who won ordered his brother's grandsons, twins named Romulus and Remus, to be thrown into the Tiber River. In the legend, the twins were rescued by a wolf. Romulus became the first king of the new city he and his twin brother founded along the Tiber in 753 B.C. Every year on April 21 the Romans proudly celebrated their city's birthday. They had good reason for their pride. Rome was to rule one of history's greatest empires.

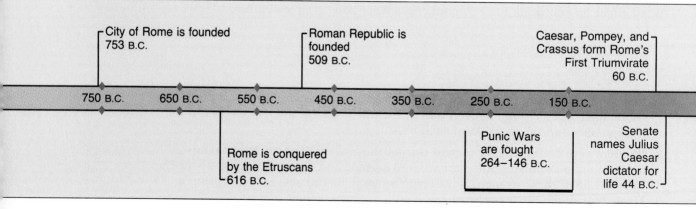

City of Rome is founded
753 B.C.

Roman Republic is founded
509 B.C.

Caesar, Pompey, and Crassus form Rome's First Triumvirate
60 B.C.

750 B.C.	650 B.C.	550 B.C.	450 B.C.	350 B.C.	250 B.C.	150 B.C.

Rome is conquered by the Etruscans
616 B.C.

Punic Wars are fought
264–146 B.C.

Senate names Julius Caesar dictator for life 44 B.C.

Activity: Review the geography of Italy using the map on page 136. Locate the Apennine Mountains and the Alps. Point out that Italy is a peninsula. Discuss how geography might have affected Rome's history.

THE ROMAN REPUBLIC: How was the early Roman Republic formed and what was this representative government like?

2. Before the seventh century B.C., the area around Rome was settled by a number of different Italian peoples. These people lived separately from one another until they were conquered by the Etruscans (ih-TRUS-kanz) in 616 B.C. For about the next 100 years, Etruscan kings ruled Rome. The Etruscans built roads, bridges, tunnels, and walls to protect Rome from invasion. What had once been a swampland dotted with wooden huts was changed into a city of wood, brick, and stone.

3. In about 509 B.C., the Romans drove the Etruscans out of Rome and set up a **republic** (ree-PUHB-lic). (At this time, the Greeks were defeating the Persians at Marathon.) In a republic power rests in the hands of the citizens who elect a group of people to represent them in government. The Republic was headed by two **consuls** (CAHN-sulz), or elected officials who enforced the laws of Rome. The consuls were advised by the **Senate**, a body of 300 men who served a life term. Senators were the most powerful lawmakers in the Roman Republic. The early Roman Republic was not truly democratic, however. All Senate seats and government offices were held by **patricians** (pah-TRISH-unz). Patricians were the wealthy landowners descended from the original settlers of ancient Rome. The poorer people were called **plebeians** (plih-BEE-yunz). The plebeians had few rights and could not vote. They were allowed to become members only of the Roman assembly. Since the Senate could overrule the assembly, the poorer classes had little power in the Roman Republic. Neither patrician nor plebian women could vote, nor could slaves.

ROME CONQUERS ITALY: How did the Romans expand their power and take over all of Italy?

4. Rome expanded its power in the first 250 years of the Republic. When Rome first became a republic, it was made up of an area that was only about 19 miles (31 kilometers) square. Rome was surrounded by many tribes, each with its own government. In the process of protecting their lands, the Romans conquered all their northern neighbors. By 270 B.C., the Romans had taken over Greek lands to the south as well. Although the Romans let the people they conquered govern themselves, the Romans kept complete control of the army.

5. The strong Roman army was the main reason why Rome was able to take over all of Italy. The Roman army was divided into **legions** (LEE-junz), or groups of 6,000 foot soldiers. Consuls usually led the army. In times of emergency, a **dictator** (DIK-tay-tor) was appointed by the Senate. This dictator would have absolute power over the army, but he could not rule for longer than six

Daily life in . . .

Everyday life for a Roman soldier was not all honor and glory. It was hard work. Soldiers marched day and night. They carried their helmets around their necks and their tools, food, and bedding on their backs. Sometimes they would march as much as 30 miles (48 kilometers) a day. Their meals consisted of bread or porridge, vegetables, and sour wine. Each soldier was given four bushels of corn each month. If that corn ran out, the soldier was responsible for finding more food. No one ate meat. Not only were Roman soldiers required to be brave fighters, but they also had to be woodcutters, carpenters, engineers, and stonemasons. Work in a Roman military camp was hard. Some soldiers might have preferred to fight in a bloody battle than go through the daily camp life.

▶ months. Why do you think the Senate set that time limit?

6. The Roman army was equipped with the latest war weapons. The army had machines that could throw huge stones against city walls or hurl flaming missiles against wooden gates. The most successful weapon of all was the siege tower. The siege tower was a high wooden tower on wheels. It could be pushed forward until it was right up against the walls of an enemy's city. The Romans would let down a drawbridge, and soldiers who were waiting inside the tower would charge over the city's walls.

ROMAN POWER SPREADS: What new lands did the Romans conquer beyond the borders of Italy as a result of the Punic Wars?

7. The Romans' desire to control the Mediterranean trade led to war in 264 B.C. with the Carthaginians (kar-thuh-JIN-ee-yuhnz). Carthage was a city on the north coast of Africa. It had been founded as a Phoenician colony but had become independent and powerful. The Carthaginians controlled colonies in North Africa, Spain, Sicily, Sardinia, and Corsica. They were the masters of trade in the western Mediterranean. The Romans fought three wars with Carthage over control of trade in the Mediterranean. These wars were called the Punic (PYOO-nik) Wars. The Punic Wars lasted from 264 B.C. to 146 B.C. For the first war, the Romans built a strong navy. As a result, the First Punic War gave Rome control of the islands of Sicily, Corsica, and Sardinia.

8. The Second Punic War began in 218 B.C. when Hannibal, a Carthaginian general, decided to march with his army from Spain into Italy to attack Rome. To do this, the army had to cross two mountain ranges, including the mighty and rugged Alps. Making Hannibal's march even more difficult were the animals he brought with the army, including many horses and 38 elephants. Although few of the elephants survived, the fact that Hannibal was able to lead ele-

▼ Rome and Carthage fought each other for control of Mediterranean trade in three Punic Wars. What land did Rome capture from Carthage by 239 B.C.?

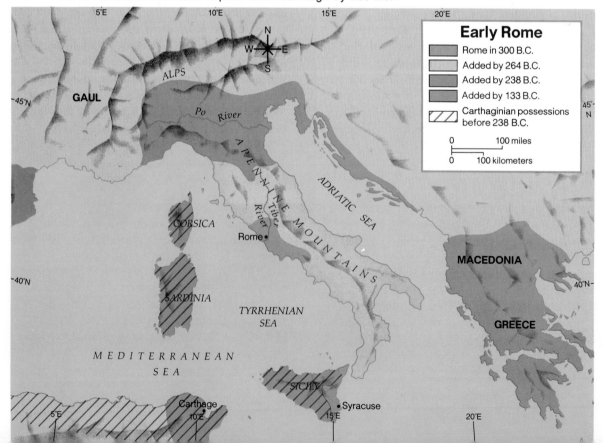

▲ Julius Caesar used his popularity and military success to become the all-powerful ruler of the Roman Republic.

phants over the Alps has made his march famous.

9. Once in Italy, Hannibal's army defeated the Roman armies in several battles. However, other parts of Italy did not join Carthage against Rome as Hannibal had hoped. Then the Romans sent an army to attack Carthage, and the Second Punic War ended with a Roman victory. In the Third Punic War, the Romans completely destroyed Carthage and gained control of all the Carthaginian colonies.

10. While the Roman army was fighting Carthage, Roman influence was spreading to other areas of the ancient world. Several Greek states appealed to Rome for help against the Macedonians. As a result, Roman armies soon had a tight hold on many Greek states. All newly conquered areas became **provinces** (PRAHV-uhn-suz), or districts, of the Roman Republic ruled by Roman governors. One of the most famous and

popular of these Roman governors was Julius Caesar (SEE-zar).

PEOPLE IN HISTORY

11. Julius Caesar was born in Rome about 100 B.C. As he grew older, his interest in political office grew. His brilliant career as a general in the army brought him much acclaim. In 60 B.C., Caesar joined with two other Roman leaders, Pompey (POM-pee) and Crassus, to form the First Triumvirate (try-UM-vuh-rut). The Triumvirate was a ruling committee of three. A year later, Caesar became consul of Rome and later was made governor of Gaul.

12. Caesar increased his power in Gaul by building a loyal army and winning military fame. Under Caesar's leadership, the Roman army drove the German peoples out of Gaul. Then Caesar and his army invaded Britain in 55 B.C. Fearing Caesar's growing power, Pompey and other Senate leaders demanded that Caesar give up his army and return home. Civil war began when Caesar refused, and Caesar finally, in 48 B.C., defeated Pompey and his army in Greece.

13. When he returned to Rome, Caesar was hailed as a hero by the Romans and made dictator for life. However, some Senators felt it was a mistake to give one person so much power. Why might people have ◀ feared Caesar's growing popularity and power? In 44 B.C., on the Ides of March (March 15), Caesar was stabbed to death in the Senate. With the death of Julius Caesar, the Roman Republic came to an end.

OUTLOOK

14. In less than 500 years, the small settlement of Rome grew into a great empire. In less than 200 years, the United States expanded from thirteen small colonies into the world's most powerful nation. Both nations had great military power. But they also had other strengths. What are some ◀ qualities that superpowers share?

Background: As dictator, Caesar introduced many reforms. He ended corruption in government. He allowed people in the provinces to become citizens. He tried to make peace with his enemies by appointing them to public office.

137

CHAPTER REVIEW

VOCABULARY REVIEW

Write each number and word on a sheet of paper. Then write the letter of the definition next to the word it defines.

1. republic
2. consul
3. patricians
4. plebeian
5. legions
6. dictator
7. provinces
8. Senate

a. wealthy families descended from the original settlers of ancient Rome

b. districts of the Roman empire

c. Romans who had few rights and could not vote

d. officials who enforced the laws of Rome

e. a form of government in which power rests in the hands of the citizens, who elect representatives

f. groups of 6,000 foot soldiers

g. a Roman leader given absolute power in times of emergency

h. a body of 300 men who were the most powerful lawmakers in the Roman Republic

SKILL BUILDER: MAKING A TIME LINE

A time line is a chart that shows the dates that events took place in history. Time lines put these events in chronological order, which is the order in which they happened. The earliest event is listed first, followed by the next earliest event, and so on. Some time lines cover time periods of hundreds or even thousands of years. Others cover much shorter spans of time. Whatever the time span, time lines are always divided into equal time periods. For example, they can be divided into 10-year periods, or decades, or they can be divided into 100-year periods, or centuries.

To make a time line, first list your events and their dates in chronological order. Then look at the first and last dates and figure out how long a period the time line will cover. On a piece of paper, draw a horizontal line. Put in the first and last dates at each end of the line. Divide the line between those dates into evenly spaced sections. Each section stands for an equal number of years. Then write in the name of each event, with an arrow showing its place on the time line. The earliest date should be at the left, while the most recent date should be at the right.

Using the dates that follow, make a horizontal time line.

55 B.C.—Julius Caesar invades Britain

44 B.C.—Senate names Caesar dictator for life

60 B.C.—Caesar, Pompey, and Crassus form Rome's First Triumvirate

59 B.C.—Julius Caesar is elected consul of Rome

100 B.C.—Julius Caesar is born

49 B.C.—Senate orders Julius Caesar to disband his army

48 B.C.—Caesar defeats Pompey in Greece

SKILL BUILDER: CRITICAL THINKING AND COMPREHENSION

▲ 1. Summarizing

▶ Read paragraph 3. On a sheet of paper write the letter of the statement below that best summarizes paragraph 3.

  a. The early Roman Republic was a democracy.

  b. The early Romans set up a representative form of government called a republic.

  c. Neither Roman women nor plebeians nor slaves could vote in the Roman Republic.

◯ 2. Generalizing

▶ On a sheet of paper, write a generalization that can be drawn from the following facts.

  a. In about 509 B.C. the Romans drove the Etruscans out of Rome and set up a republic.

  b. In the Punic Wars Rome conquered lands belonging to Carthage.

  c. While Rome was fighting Carthage, several Greek states appealed to Rome for help and were taken over by the Romans.

◣ 3. Compare and Contrast

▶ Compare the Roman leader, Julius Caesar, with the Macedonian king, Alexander the Great. Read the desciptions below. Decide which descriptions apply to Caesar, which apply to Alexander, and which apply to both men. Write the descriptions on a sheet of paper and label them *Caesar, Alexander,* or *Both*.

  a. This man was a military leader.

  b. This leader took a keen interest in culture and made great efforts to spread the growth of culture in the lands he conquered.

  c. This man spent most of his career leading armies and planning to gain power as ruler of the empire.

ENRICHMENT

1. Imagine you are a Roman soldier writing an entry in your diary. In the entry, describe what your typical day is like. Your diary entry should include information about how you feel about the meals, the long hours, and the hard work. You should also include a description of a recent battle. End the entry by describing why you like or dislike being a part of the Roman army.

2. Locate a biography of Julius Caesar in your school or local library. Read those sections of the biography that describe the events that led to Caesar's murder. Using this information, write the script for a made-for-television movie about Caesar's death.

CHAPTER 5

The Height of the Roman Empire

▲ The mighty Augustus defeated Marc Antony and, as emperor, led Rome into 200 years of glory.

OBJECTIVE: What enabled the Roman empire to prosper in peace for almost 200 years?

1. Which soap opera is this plot from? A powerful businessman dies, leaving his company to his best friend and his adopted son. For some time they get along well and share control of the business. Soon, however, the best friend marries a powerful woman who wants total control of the business. Rumors circulate in the company that the best friend and his wife are plotting to take control. The adopted son launches a corporate takeover attempt first. Some employees side with him, and others side with the best friend. After a few years of in-fighting, the adopted son takes sole control of the business. The best friend and his wife leave the company in disgrace. Sound familiar? This may be a standard soap opera plot, but a similar situation actually occurred in 44 B.C. when Julius Caesar died.

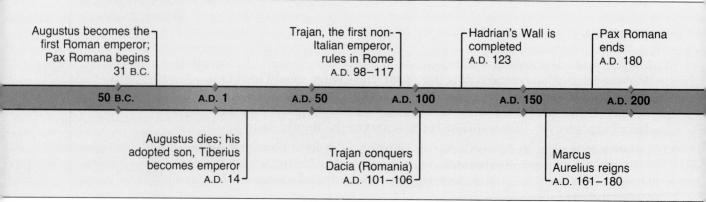

Augustus becomes the first Roman emperor; Pax Romana begins 31 B.C.

Trajan, the first non-Italian emperor, rules in Rome A.D. 98–117

Hadrian's Wall is completed A.D. 123

Pax Romana ends A.D. 180

| 50 B.C. | A.D. 1 | A.D. 50 | A.D. 100 | A.D. 150 | A.D. 200 |

Augustus dies; his adopted son, Tiberius becomes emperor A.D. 14

Trajan conquers Dacia (Romania) A.D. 101–106

Marcus Aurelius reigns A.D. 161–180

Background: After Caesar's death, Rome was ruled by a triumvirate made up of Mark Antony, Lepidus, and Octavian. When Lepidus retired, Octavian and Antony divided the empire between themselves.

ANCIENT ROME: How and when did the Roman Republic end and the Roman Empire begin?

2. After Caesar's death, a power struggle temporarily weakened the government of Rome. Marc Antony (Caesar's close friend) and Octavian (Caesar's grandnephew and adopted son) co-ruled—Octavian from Rome, Antony from Egypt. When Octavian learned that Antony and his Egyptian queen, Cleopatra, were plotting a **coup** (KUU), or political takeover, civil war broke out. Octavian won an important victory at sea at Actium, and Antony and Cleopatra, admitting defeat, retreated to Egypt, where they committed suicide. The Roman people and the Senate proclaimed Octavian **emperor** (EM-puhr-uhr), or chief ruler, of Rome. The Senate also gave this first emperor of Rome the title *Augustus*, meaning "great one."

3. Under Augustus, the dictatorship already begun by Julius Caesar took a firm hold. It permanently replaced the form of self-government that Rome had enjoyed under the Republic. With this change the Roman Republic officially came to an end, and the Roman Empire took its place.

4. Augustus took complete control and power—more power than Caesar ever had. The Senate now believed that the only hope for domestic peace rested in a single strong ruler and gave many powers to Augustus. The Senate continued to meet, but all final decisions were made by the emperor. Augustus became chief priest of the Romans. He—not the Senate—appointed the governors of the provinces. Even when it had the power, the Senate exercised no strict control over the provincial governors. As long as Rome received the provincial taxes, the Senate allowed the governors to keep supreme military and civil authority in the provinces. But under Augustus the generals were to report to the new chief ruler of the provinces—Augustus himself.

5. By making the provincial governors answerable to him, Augustus effectively curbed their growing power. For years Roman soldiers had supported the governors over the government because the governors paid the salaries of the army. (As provincial governor of Gaul, Caesar had used the support of his armies to defeat his political enemies and become consul, and then dictator, of Rome.) Augustus set out to gain the backing of the troops. He appointed himself commander of the Roman army and navy, promising Roman citizenship to all men from the provinces who enlisted. How ◄ would this action have encouraged the army's loyalty to the emperor?

6. Augustus proved a strong and popular military leader, and under his rule the legions of the Roman army almost doubled. More than ever before the Roman leadership needed the backing of the army in order to maintain power. The Empire now reached from the Atlantic Ocean and Britain in the west to the Rhine and Danube Rivers in the north. It went as far as Mesopotamia in the east, and to North Africa, including Egypt, in the south.

7. Why did the Roman people, with their rich history of self-government, let go of their political rights and power? Part of the answer lies in the actions and character of Augustus, who was careful to cloak his increasing power under the wraps of republican reforms. Augustus was a powerful speaker. His **orations** (o-RAY-shunz), or speeches, convinced the people that he was sincere in his promise to restore Rome to the greatness and glory of earlier times. He vowed to do this by: reforming the administrative structure of the Empire; increasing the Empire's territories, especially in Europe; bringing stability and prosperity to Rome; and establishing peace in the Empire. Most Romans were also overjoyed to see an end of the civil wars that had long plagued Rome. They hardly noticed that with the end of the civil wars came the end of the Republic.

8. The powerful Augustus continued to soften his image as dictator. By allowing the people to elect the consuls, Augustus created the illusion that free elections still existed under his reign. But in reality only

The Boundaries of the Roman Empire

Boundaries are important to nations and empires. Some are drawn by imaginary lines, while others are determined by physical land features such as rivers or mountains. The most effective boundary lies far from the center of the nation or empire.

The map below shows the boundaries of the Roman Empire. Those boundaries, with minor changes, protected Rome from hostile attacks for more than 400 years. Read the facts that follow, which are about the boundaries of the Roman Empire. Then study the map and answer the questions.

Facts

Rome's boundaries grew from encircling a small village in western Italy to the edges of a vast empire.

Much of the Roman Empire had coastal boundaries.

Some Roman borders lay in desert areas.

In northern Europe, rivers and forests made up most of the Empire's boundaries.

Rome's other European boundary was in the British Isles.

1. What parts of the Roman Empire had coastal boundaries?

2. How did these coastal boundaries provide protection for Rome?

3. What parts of the Roman Empire had desert boundaries?

4. How did these desert boundaries help protect the Roman empire?

5. What rivers served as boundaries of the Roman Empire?

6. Why were river boundaries protection for the Empire?

7. Describe the boundaries of the Roman Empire in Asia. Why do you think they were more of a problem for Rome than were the boundaries in Africa?

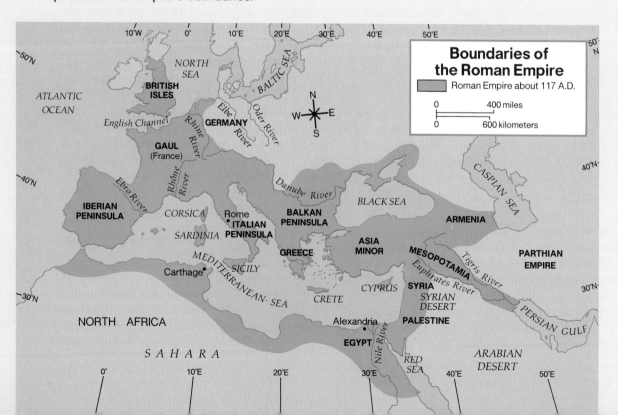

Boundaries of the Roman Empire

Roman Empire about 117 A.D.

0   400 miles

0   600 kilometers

Augustus's friends were allowed to run for these offices.

SPOTLIGHT ON SOURCES

9. According to one Roman historian, Augustus felt justified in continuing the dictatorship that Caesar had begun.

> He twice entertained thoughts of restoring the republic . . . . But [thinking] at the same time that it would be both [harmful] to himself to return to the condition of a private person, and might be dangerous to the public to have the government placed again under the control of the people, he [decided] to keep it in his own hands . . . . His good intentions he . . . declared . . . in the following terms: "May it be permitted me to have the happiness of establishing the [state] on a safe and sound basis, and thus enjoy the reward of which I am ambitious, that of being celebrated for [shaping] it into the form best adapted to present circumstances; so that, on my leaving the world, I may carry with me the hope that the foundations which I have laid for its future government, will stand firm and stable."
>
> —from *Readings in the History of the Ancient World,* William C. McDermott and Wallace E. Caldwell, eds.

▶ How would you describe Augustus's motives for continuing the dictatorship?

THE AUGUSTAN AGE: How did Rome prosper under Augustus's rule?

10. Augustus, with his ability to handle the army and stabilize the government, brought such prosperity to the Empire that his reign became known as the Augustan Age. Trade and business increased, and the standard of living rose dramatically. Writers produced the greatest Latin works during this age. Architecture thrived. As Roman power spread, Augustus continued Caesar's practice of writing down Roman

▲ Trajan's Column in Rome, built in A.D. 113, illustrates the emperor's victory over the peoples of Romania.

laws. The founding of schools for the study of law was one of Augustus's greatest contributions.

11. Augustus's rule ushered in a period of peace for the Roman Empire that lasted for 200 years. These years are known as the **Pax Romana**, or Roman Peace. No nation was more powerful than the mighty Roman Empire. That any nation or tribe would invade the Empire during this period was unthinkable to Romans. For the Roman people, the Pax Romana was a time of stability, prosperity, and growth.

AFTER AUGUSTUS: How did the quality of life in the Roman Empire continue to improve under the later emperors?

12. With the exception of Nero and Caligula, the rulers who followed Augustus over the next 200 years were very capable rulers. In fact, the emperors who ruled from

Activity: Have students research Nerva and Antoninus Pius in the library. Ask them to give a brief oral report on the contributions of these emperors.

143

▲ Hadrian's Wall, built across northern England in the A.D. 120s, linked 70 forts that stood about 1 mile apart.

A.D. 96-180 were known as the Five Good Emperors. They were named Nerva, Trajan, Hadrian, Antoninus Pius, and Marcus Aurelius.

13. Nero was an unjust ruler who murdered his mother and his wife. One day a devastating fire spread through a section of Rome. By then Nero was so disliked that he was blamed for starting the fire. Some Romans even started the rumor that the cruel, uncaring Nero had fiddled while Rome burned. The story wasn't true, but so many Romans believed it that Nero felt compelled to end the rumor. So he made up his own story, also false, that the Christians had started the fire.

14. Caligula was a favorite of the army who began his reign with good works. He issued a general pardon to all state prisoners and proposed many just and liberal measures to the Senate. But midway through his short reign, Caligula began to show signs of madness. He wasted the state treasures on luxuries and resorted to increased taxation and bribes to restore the monies. He forced the Senate to decree his dead sister a goddess. Executions and exiles became frequent. Caligula proclaimed himself a god, ordering his statue to be placed for worship in Roman and Jewish temples throughout the Empire. He dressed as Hercules, Apollo, and Venus and pretended to imitate the thunder and lightening of Jove, the supreme Roman god. The mad Caligula was killed in the fourth year of his reign by a soldier he had insulted.

15. Nero was succeeded by Nerva, a fair and kind ruler who diminished taxes and distributed Roman land to the poor. Nerva was succeeded by Trajan, another fair ruler who expanded the empire's territory in an important area. He took land along the lower Danube from the **barbarians** (bar-BAIR-ee-enz), the primitive, uncivilized tribes of central Europe. Roman civilization took a strong hold there, and to this day the land is called Romania.

16. Hadrian was the first emperor to become seriously concerned with the military defenses of the Empire. The Empire had nearly stopped acquiring new territories by the time Hadrian came to power. The empire had grown so large that it was becoming harder to defend the borders against raiding tribes. One of Hadrian's solutions was to have a great wall built at the Roman border in Britain to keep out the Picts, a raiding Scots tribe.

17. Hadrian believed that the whole empire, not just Rome, was important. He was one of the first emperors to travel throughout the Empire. He ordered construction of buildings and cities as he went, and promoted Roman customs and culture throughout the territories. By the end of his reign, Gaul, Britain, Rome, and all other territories of the Empire had adopted Roman customs.

18. Under Antoninus Pius, the well-constructed Roman roads that helped the empire to operate efficiently were kept in such good shape that Romans actually trav-

 Background: The first emperor to come from outside of Italy was Trajan, who was born near Seville, Spain. He ruled from A.D. 98 to A.D. 117.

eled to the provinces for pleasure as well as for business. Travel became so pleasant that one emperor had a revolving chair built in his carriage. (He wanted to be able to take in all the scenery!) Antoninus Pius founded schools, repaired harbors, and encouraged trade. The last watchword he gave to the Roman soldiers before his death was *equanimitas*, meaning purity, contentment, and serenity of mind. This one word embodied the whole character of his life.

19. The good Roman roads also fueled the growth of trade. By the A.D. 100s, carts of **raw materials**, such as grains, timber, metal, and wool that could be made or **manufactured** into other products, often traveled the roads of the Empire. Woolen goods and fine pottery from Gaul were traded freely throughout the empire. Ships sailed across the Mediterranean bringing linen and paper from Egypt to Rome. Camels carrying silks and other luxuries from China were not uncommon sights in the eastern part of the Empire. Furs and slaves were imported into the Empire from Germany and Russia.

20. Marcus Aurelius, the last emperor of the Pax Romana, was one of the Empire's strongest and best rulers. He was known as the philosopher king. He adopted a popular philosophy of the time called **Stoicism** (STO-uh-siz-um), which stressed the importance of a strict regard for duty and the need to be self-reliant. According to Stoicism, virtue is obtained through reason, and reason is obtained by remaining indifferent to the external world and to passion, emotion, or pain.

21. Life in the Empire continued smoothly under much of Marcus Aurelius's rule. But the end of Pax Romana was foreshadowed by several key events of the 160s. A plague broke out that lasted many years. A food shortage arose. In A.D. 167, for the first time in the Empire's history, a full-scale invasion of the Empire was attempted by barbarian tribes from the north and east. Thousands of barbarians were killed, taken hostage, or enslaved by the Roman army in the ensuing battle. When the smoke cleared,

▲ The Via Appia was the first of the great highways of Rome. Built in 312 B.C., it linked Rome with its southeastern provinces.

Marcus Aurelius had put a stop to this latest threat of invasion. But soon the threat of invasion would again become reality.

OUTLOOK

22. Cradled by the security of a powerful emperor and a mighty army, the Roman Empire flourished for over 200 years. No matter where Roman citizens traveled in the Empire, the laws, currency, and political systems were identical. At the height of the Empire, peace and prosperity were commonplace. What direction does a nation ◀ take once it has achieved such peace and prosperity? It can either continue to grow—or start to decay. What do you think happened to the Roman Empire next?

CHAPTER REVIEW

VOCABULARY REVIEW

Write each of the following words on a sheet of paper. Then write the correct definition for each word. Use the glossary on pages 728-738 to help you.

barbarians   orations

coup   Pax Romana

emperor   raw materials

manufactured   Stoicism

SKILL BUILDER: INTERPRETING A DIAGRAM

The purpose of a diagram is to take complex information and present it in a simple and understandable way. The following diagram illustrates how the Roman government worked. Study the diagram and then answer the following questions on a sheet of paper.

STRUCTURE OF THE ROMAN GOVERNMENT DURING THE REPUBLIC

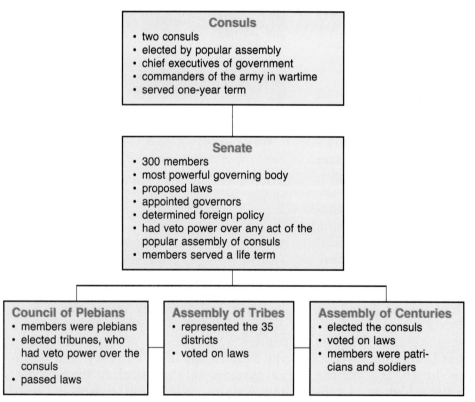

Consuls
- two consuls
- elected by popular assembly
- chief executives of government
- commanders of the army in wartime
- served one-year term

Senate
- 300 members
- most powerful governing body
- proposed laws
- appointed governors
- determined foreign policy
- had veto power over any act of the popular assembly of consuls
- members served a life term

Council of Plebians
- members were plebians
- elected tribunes, who had veto power over the consuls
- passed laws

Assembly of Tribes
- represented the 35 districts
- voted on laws

Assembly of Centuries
- elected the consuls
- voted on laws
- members were patricians and soldiers

1. What is the title of the diagram?

2. Which government members were chosen for life?

3. Which parts of the government determined who became Rome's consuls?

4. Who had more power, the Senate or the assemblies? Give examples.

SKILL BUILDER: CRITICAL THINKING AND COMPREHENSION

1. Cause and Effect   A cause is the action or event that makes something happen. An effect is what happens as a result of that action or event. For example, because soldiers needed to move quickly throughout the Empire for reasons of defense (the cause), the Roman roads were kept in good shape (the effect).

▶ On a sheet of paper, write the cause or causes for each of the following effects.

a. Civil war broke out in Rome in 31 B.C.

b. Nero blamed the Christians for starting a tragic fire in Rome.

c. The Republic officially came to an end, and the Roman Empire took its place.

2. Generalizing

▶ On a sheet of paper, write a generalization from the following facts.

Roman law held that a person was innocent until proven guilty.

According to Roman law, a contract, or written agreement, was binding.

In the United States, a person is innocent until proven guilty.

Written contracts are binding in the United States.

3. Spatial Relationships   Direction words such as *north, south, east,* and *west* tell where an object or place is in relation to another object or place.

▶ Use the map on page 142 to answer the following questions.

a. In which direction did Antony have to sail from Egypt in order to reach Rome?

b. In which direction did Octavian have to travel from Rome to reach Actium in northwestern Greece?

c. Where was Hadrian's Wall in relation to the British Isles?

d. In which direction did Trajan have to travel to reach Romania, the land along the lower Danube River?

ENRICHMENT

1. The Romans were great builders and engineers. Some of the roads they built are still used today. Find out how these roads were built. What steps were involved in building the Roman roads? What materials did the Roman engineers use? On the basis of the information you find, draw a diagram or make a model that shows how the Romans built the roads.

2. The history of the Roman Empire has been the source for some of the greatest movies Hollywood ever made. *Spartacus, Cleopatra,* and *Ben Hur* are a few examples. Rent one of these movies on video cassette. View the movie and write a summary of its plot. Explain why you would or would not recommend that others see it.

3. The emperors chosen by military leaders after the reign of Marcus Aurelius were known as "soldier emperors." Sculptures of these men were made at the time. Look for pictures of some of these sculptures in art books in your library. After studying one or two, describe what you think these emperors were like. Find pictures of sculptures of Augustus and Marcus Aurelius. How do their sculptures compare in feeling to the ones of the soldier emperors? What was happening in Rome that might explain the difference in the sculptures of these men?

CHAPTER 6

Life in Ancient Rome

▲ This relief shows a chariot race from the *Circus Maximus*, where games and festivals were held in honor of the Roman gods.

OBJECTIVE: What was everyday life like in the Roman Empire?

1. How did Romans keep on top of what was happening in the far corners of the empire? In the days when no newspapers existed, letters were almost the sole means of conveying information. Governors, before departing to their provinces, arranged to have news sent regularly to them by appointed correspondents, or letter-writers. Letters were written with a pointed writing instrument called a stylus. They were written on thin slips of wood pulp, covered with wax, and folded together with the writing inward. The slips were held together by a thread, which was fastened with a seal of wax stamped with a ring. Letters were usually sent by special messenger. Officials could employ public messengers. Sometimes important messages were sent by carrier pigeon. After roads were constructed from Rome to the provinces, messengers

Cicero, the greatest writer of Roman prose, is born
106 B.C.

Vespasian orders the construction of the Colosseum
A.D. 72

Colosseum is completed
A.D. 80

| 100 B.C. | 50 B.C. | A.D. 1 | A.D. 50 | A.D. 100 |

Virgil, the most important Roman poet, is born
70 B.C.

Pliny writes *Historia Naturalis*
A.D. 77

and letters moved quickly and regularly over long distances.

THE CAPITAL CITY: Why did all roads lead to Rome?

2. The saying "All roads lead to Rome" describes the position Rome held at the height of its glory. Rome was the center of the civilized world. It was also the capital and largest city of the Roman empire. Roads for public and military transport fanned out from the capital to all corners of the empire. The roads were so well built that some have lasted into modern times.

3. The beauty of Rome's monuments and the splendor of its public buildings and temples was unsurpassed by those of any other city in the empire. Marketplaces and shops in Rome were cleaner and had more goods to choose from than did the markets and shops of any other Roman city. Properties were protected by a public fire department and a police department. Other public service workers collected garbage, cleaned the streets, and repaired and maintained buildings. **Aqueducts** (AK-wuh-duhKts)—channels built to carry water over long distances—brought fresh water to the city.

4. Wealth and goods flowed into Rome from all parts of the empire. Tourists and merchants flocked to the city. Well over one million people lived in Rome when Hadrian ruled, at the height of the Roman Empire. While this number may seem small by today's standards, Rome had the largest population—and the highest standard of living—of any city in the Western world up to that time. About 200,000 of the population of Rome were poor, but more than 800,000 of its population were rich. Never before in the history of the world had a larger number of people living in one place enjoyed so much comfort.

ROMAN SOCIETY: What was the class system like?

5. Like many other cultures of that time, the ancient Romans had a definite and strict class system. At the top of the ladder was the aristocracy. Members of this class held offices in the emperor's government or the army. Rome's senators came from the aristocracy. The working class included merchants, shopkeepers, artisans, and laborers. Slaves and unemployed people were at the bottom of the class ladder.

6. Military victories may bring glory, but in Rome's case they also brought enslavement to many conquered peoples. Slaves worked in the homes and shops of Rome, in the mines, and on the farms that lay outside the city's borders. Many educated people—even doctors and lawyers—were forced into slavery by their Roman conquerors. Slaves could buy their freedom, but even when they had the money to do so, freedom usually meant joining the ranks of the unemployed. A few slaves and their children were fortunate enough to be adopted by aristocratic families. Adoption was a status symbol of the times, meant to show a family's wealth and patronage. To be adopted meant that you were held in great esteem.

7. Unemployed Romans led miserable, hungry, and restless lives in the midst of Rome's splendor. Romans who had been forced out of work by the use of slaves in the countryside flocked to Rome looking for work. Most of Rome's unemployed people lived in crowded neighborhoods along the edges of the **Forum** (FOR-um). The Forum was a former marketplace that had been built up under Augustus into the main business section of the city. The Roman government often provided food and free medical care for unemployed people.

ROMAN LIFE: How and where did Romans live and work?

8. The typical one-story Roman house was built around the **atrium** (AY-tree-um), a large central room with an opening in the middle of the roof that let in the sun and air. Bedrooms, offices, and a kitchen often surrounded the atrium. In homes that contained shops, illustrated signs hung outside

▲ Many Roman aqueducts still stand today. Tunnels and aqueducts from the mountains brought fresh water to ancient Rome.

indicating the nature of the articles to be sold within. Homes of the very rich had a glorified atrium called a **peristylum** (pair-ih-STY-lum), an open courtyard lined with columns and filled with plants, statues, and a bathing pool. Romans didn't have much furniture, but their furniture was beautifully carved and inlaid with bronze, ivory or precious stones.

9. Aristocrats considered all manual labor beneath them. Aristocrats usually derived their income from the crops their properties yielded through the labor of the slaves. If they worked at all, aristocrats worked in the Senate or other government office. Their afternoons were normally spent at the public baths. The homes of the aristocrats often had central heating.

10. Afternoons may have been a time of leisure for the rich, but merchants, laborers, and shopkeepers often worked until sunset. Workers took a lunch break at noon and another break at three or four in the after-

noon, when dinner was served. Meat was generally a luxury for the working class, although rich families consumed great quantities of it.

11. Romans entertained at lavish dinner parties, which often started at four in the afternoon and lasted through the night. Guests brought their own linen napkins, but the eating utensils—two pointed spoons that functioned as knives and forks—were provided by the host. When eating, Romans reclined on couches set along three sides of the room. The fourth side was left open to give the slaves access to the table. Unusual foods such as peacocks and wild boars were often served at parties given by rich Romans. Servants fanned the foods with peacock feathers throughout the meal to keep flies away.

12. Men in Rome controlled the government, the military, and the economy. Women held important roles both in the family and in Roman society. At home Roman women managed the household, taking charge of their children's education and giving instructions to the slaves. Outside the home women who had to work held a variety of jobs. Poorer women often worked as spinners and clothing makers. Some worked alongside their husbands making perfumes or crafting silver. A few educated Roman women became doctors or lawyers. Other educated Roman women became writers or artists. Wealthier Roman women managed their own land and businesses. How was the role of women in ancient ◄ Rome different from that of the women in ancient Greece?

FORMS OF RECREATION: What kinds of inexpensive or free entertainments did the Roman government provide for the people of Rome?

13. Public baths, or **thermae** (THUR-may), were built by the Roman government as places where Romans could go to relax. A small admission fee was charged. The baths included hot, warm, and cold pools; and also libraries, gardens, race courses, and

Background: Lead pipes carried water from the aqueducts to the indoor bathtubs of the rich. The very rich kept a villa in the country in addition to their permanent residence in town.

exercise rooms where Romans could indulge in wrestling, boxing, or the ball games of the time. The *thermae* were the favorite meeting places of Rome and the center of socializing.

14. Roman emperors often set aside certain days as holidays. On these holidays free grain was handed out to the poor people. Free entertainment often lasting from 6 to 15 days was held in large **amphitheaters** (AM-fih-thee-turz), oval arenas surrounded by rising rows of seats.

15. Chariot racing and gladiator fighting were probably the favorite contests of the Romans. As many as ten two-wheeled, horse-drawn chariots sped around a narrow track in a typical chariot race. The speed and danger thrilled the crowd. Winning drivers not only became famous; they also received prize money. A typical gladiator fight pitted slaves or criminals or prisoners of war against each other in armed or hand combat. These **gladiators** (GLAD-ee-ay-turz) had been highly trained in the art of fighting. Chariot races and gladiator contests were very costly. They were paid for by the Roman government and by the emperors or consuls who had arranged for the entertainment.

CULTURAL CONTRIBUTIONS: What did the Romans achieve in architecture, science, medicine, and literature?

16. Much of Roman culture was built on ideas borrowed from the Greeks and Etruscans. For example, the Etruscan **arch** (ARCH), a curved structure that spans an opening and supports the weight above it, was preserved and passed down by the Romans. In science and medicine, the Romans preserved and added to knowledge already possessed by the Greeks. Pliny (PLIN-ee), a Roman naturalist and writer, collected all that was known about natural science at that time into a book called *Historia Naturalis*. Published in A.D. 77, this book remained the most important reference source on natural science for hundreds of years. The Romans also built hospitals that were models of good medical care for the rest of the world.

17. Writing flourished at the height of the Roman Empire. Roman literature, which was patterned on the style of Greek literature, was written in Latin, the language of the empire. Even after the fall of Rome, the Latin language remained the language of educated people in Western Europe for over a thousand years. The Romance languages—French, Spanish, Italian, Portuguese, and Romanian—have their roots in the Latin of the Roman Empire.

18. The Latin writer Cicero is considered the greatest writer of Latin **prose**, the form of speech or writing that is not poetry. Cicero was a master at finding the right words to catch the attention of his audience. The speeches and letters of Cicero on politics and human behavior are still read and loved today. Another Latin writer, Virgil (VUR-jul), is considered the greatest writer of Latin poetry.

▼ This mosaic from the second century shows gladiators in combat. How do Roman sports compare with sports events today?

ESL/LEP Strategy: Write the word *amphitheater* on the chalkboard, pronounce the word, and ask if students see a familiar word part (*theater*). Discuss the meaning of *theater* and explain that the prefix *amphi* means *around; on both sides*.

151

The Arts and Artifacts

▲ The Colosseum as it looks today. It was shaped like a football stadium and could seat 45,000. The building was completed in A.D. 80.

The Colosseum   (kal-uh-SEE-um) was the largest and most important amphitheater in Rome. Construction on it began in A.D. 72 by order of the emperor Vespasian (veh-SPAY-zhun). Eight years and two emperors later, the work was finally completed.

The Colosseum was about 620 feet by 513 feet (998 kilometers by 825 kilometers) and covered 6 acres (3 hectares). It had eighty entrances and enough room for 45,000 spectators. Stone sewers kept the site dry. The building itself was made of concrete and bricks, with miles of staircases and **vaults** (VAWLTS), or arched stone roofs.

No costs were spared to make the amphitheater pleasing. Inside walls were decorated with precious marbles and paintings embedded with sparkling gems. The arena was open to the sky, but an awning shielded spectators from the sun and **porticos,** or doorways, offered shelter in case of rain. Cooling streams of water cascaded down the aisles on particularly hot days. Seats in the

arena were entwined with gold cords. Senators and other leaders had seats on a marble terrace overlooking the arena. Above them, on thrones of gold and ivory, sat the emperor and his wife. Often, at the conclusion of events, little slips of wood were thrown down from the upper story to the poor, who were seated in the lowest level. Each slip won for whoever caught it a present from the sponsor of the event—a sum of money, a slave, a horse, a robe, or some other object of more or less value.

Sections of wooden floor in the center of the arena could be lowered or raised according to entertainment needs. Beneath the floor were cages of wild beasts and holding areas where gladiators awaited their turn to show their skill in the arena.

1. What were the favorite entertainments of the Romans?

2. How does the Colosseum compare to modern stadiums?

152

Background: The Colosseum was built on the site of a lake and palace that had belonged to the emperor Nero. The Flavian amphitheater was even more elaborately designed. Statues emitted showers of perfume that descended upon the crowd. The nets designed as a defense against the beasts were made of gold.

SPOTLIGHT ON SOURCES

19. Fifty-seven of Cicero's speeches and about 900 of his letters to friends have survived to modern times. These works paint a vivid portrait of Rome at the time of Caesar's rise to power. Cicero held many important political offices in Rome and had very definite ideas on how to run an orderly government. He believed that a republic, with its system of checks and balances, was the best form of government. Here he writes of the consequences of a people having unlimited political freedom.

> Plato says that from the exaggerated license [that] people call liberty, tyrants spring up as from a root . . . and that at last such liberty reduces a nation to slavery. Everything in excess is changed into its opposite . . . . For out of such an ungoverned populace one is usually chosen as leader . . . someone bold and unscrupulous . . . who curries favor with the people by giving them other [people's] property. To such a man, because he has much reason for fear if he remains a private citizen, the protection of public office is given and continually renewed. He surrounds himself with an armed guard and emerges as a tyrant over the very people who raised him to power.
>
> —*De Re Publica*, Cicero

▶ How do checks and balances keep a democracy from becoming a dictatorship?

PEOPLE IN HISTORY

20. In many of his poems, Virgil drew on early memories of the Italian countryside where he grew up. He was born in a small farming community in northern Italy in B.C. 70. The life evidently suited him. Two of his best poems, the *Eclogues* and the *Georgics*, idealized, or glorified, farm life.

21. In 29 B.C., Virgil was introduced to Octavian, the future emperor Augustus. During their meeting, which lasted four days, Virgil recited over 2,000 lines of his poetry. If this meeting had not taken place, the *Aeneid* (ih-NEE-id), Virgil's greatest work, might never have been written.

22. Augustus encouraged Virgil to write a poem that would glorify the empire. Virgil wrote the *Aeneid*, which is modeled on the Greek poet Homer's *Iliad* and *Odyssey*. The *Aeneid* tells the fictional story of Aeneas (ih-NEE-us), the Trojan founder of the first settlement at Rome. The poem also promises a golden age during Augustus's reign.

23. The greatest mark the Romans left on the world was probably in the field of government and law. Their efficiency in ruling such an enormous empire has been unmatched in history. They were among the first to hold that a person accused of a crime was innocent until proven guilty, a written contract was binding, and anyone had the right to appeal a conviction. Roman laws were written, fair, and flexible. Why do you ◀ think a country ought to have a body of written laws?

OUTLOOK

24. At the height of the Roman Empire, Romans made great achievements in art, architecture, literature, science, and the law. The high standard of living in ancient Rome was unsurpassed by any other city of the time. In many respects the United States today resembles the ancient Roman Empire at the height of its glory. Americans seem to achieve breakthroughs in medicine and science almost weekly. American literature and art attract worldwide audiences. The standard of living in the United States is generally high. But over the last decade the United States has faced a growing poverty problem. In 1985, 33 million Americans, or 14 percent of the United States population, were living below the poverty level. The Romans helped their poor people by handing out grain and providing them with free medical care. What measures can a country take today to reduce poverty levels among its people?

Activity: Have students look up the Latin origin of legal terms such as *habeas corpus*, *ex post facto*, *litigant*, and *prosecutor* to underscore the influence the Romans have had on law.

153

CHAPTER REVIEW

VOCABULARY REVIEW

Write each of the following sentences on a sheet of paper. Then fill in the blank with the word that best completes each sentence.

thermae   atrium   Forum
arch   amphitheater gladiator
prose   vault   peristylum

1. The central room of a typical Roman home was the _____ .

2. The main business center of Rome was called the _____ .

3. The Roman government built _____ to provide citizens with an inexpensive place to exercise and relax.

4. The Romans watched chariot races in an oval or circular building with rising rows of seats called an _____ .

5. A _____ was an armed man highly trained in the art of fighting who fought another man before a crowd of people in armed or hand combat.

6. A curved part of a building that spans an opening and serves to support the weight above it is called an _____ .

7. The writing in this book is an example of _____ .

8. An arched stone ceiling or roof is called a _____ .

9. A light-filled court open to the sky, lined with columns and filled with plants, statues, and a bathing pool, is called a _____ .

SKILL BUILDER: INTERPRETING A TIME LINE

Time lines usually present a series of related events in a sequence of earliest to latest. For example, the time line below lists events having to do with the cultural contributions of the Romans. People study time lines to see how events are related.

Use the time line below to determine if the statements that follow it are true or false. Write the numbers of the statements on a sheet of paper. Then write (T) if the statement is true and (F) if the statement is false. If the statement is false, explain why.

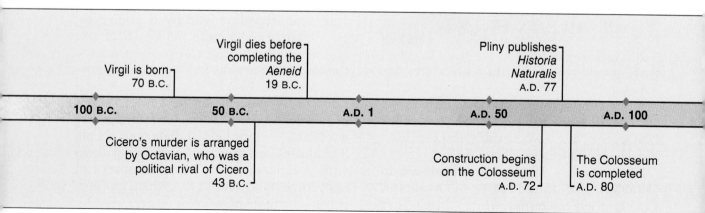

1. It is likely that Virgil and Cicero knew each other.
2. It took nine years to build the Colosseum.
3. Virgil was 61 years old when he died.
4. Pliny completed his book before the Colosseum was open to the public.
5. Virgil was born 80 years before the Colosseum was completed.

SKILL BUILDER: CRITICAL THINKING AND COMPREHENSION

 1. Cause and Effect   A cause is an action or event that makes something happen. An effect is what happens as a result of that action or event.

▶ On a sheet of paper write the cause or causes of each of the following effects.

a. Few Roman slaves bought their freedom.

b. At the height of the empire, messengers and letters moved quickly and regularly over long distances.

c. At the height of the empire, Rome was the center of the civilized world.

2. Generalizing

▶ On a sheet of paper write a generalization that connects each pair of facts:

a. After roads were constructed from Rome to the provinces, messengers and letters moved quickly and regularly over long distances.
Some Roman roads have lasted into modern times.

b. Roman aristocrats generally derived their income from the crops their properties yielded through the labor of slaves.
Afternoons were a time of leisure for the rich, but merchants, laborers, and shopkeepers often worked until sunset.

3. Sequencing

▶ Write the following events in the order in which they occurred.

a. *Historia Naturalis* is published.

b. The building of the Colosseum is completed.

c. Virgil writes the *Aeneid*.

d. Cicero is born.

ENRICHMENT

1. Livia, the wife of Augustus, had great influence on her husband and the emperors who ruled after his death. Research the life of Livia and the role she played in Roman history. Use the information you find to write a brief report on her life. Explain how her life provides a good example of the roles women played in Roman society.

2. Caesar dedicated one of his books, *On Analogy,* to Cicero, whom he greatly admired. Caesar claimed that by discovering the treasures of oratory (the art of giving effective speeches), Cicero had gained a greater triumph than had the greatest Roman generals. According to Caesar, ". . . it is a nobler thing to enlarge the boundaries of human intelligence than those of the Roman Empire." State whether you agree with Caesar's opinion. Support your opinion with facts.

The Decline of the Roman Empire

▲ Marcus Aurelius, the last emperor of the Pax Romana, rides victorious after battling the barbarians.

OBJECTIVE: What caused the decline of the Roman Empire?

1. The imperial Roman court in Milan was in panic. News had just arrived that a barbarian army had dared to set foot on the soil of Italy. An entire tribe—old, young, women, and children—was packed onto the ox carts that trailed lazily behind these warriors. It was about the year 400, and the Visigoths had come to Italy to live—permanently. Within ten years, the Visigoths attacked Rome itself. Houses were burned, treasures were taken, and many proud Roman citizens were sold into slavery. The shock was felt throughout the ancient world. One Roman writer said about the invaders, "They increase daily; we decrease daily. They prosper; we are humbled. They flourish; we are drying up." The Visigoths were but one of the strange new tribes pressing upon the Roman Empire. Vandals, Alans, Lombards, Franks,

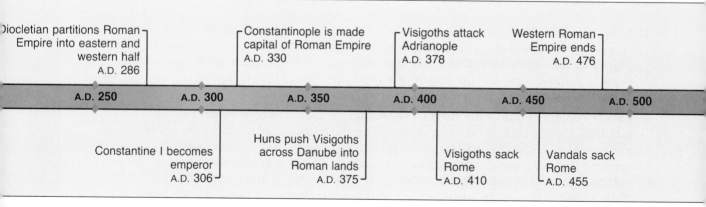

Diocletian partitions Roman Empire into eastern and western half A.D. 286

Constantinople is made capital of Roman Empire A.D. 330

Visigoths attack Adrianople A.D. 378

Western Roman Empire ends A.D. 476

A.D. 250 — A.D. 300 — A.D. 350 — A.D. 400 — A.D. 450 — A.D. 500

Constantine I becomes emperor A.D. 306

Huns push Visigoths across Danube into Roman lands A.D. 375

Visigoths sack Rome A.D. 410

Vandals sack Rome A.D. 455

and Saxons crossed the empire's boundaries, and their leaders had mysterious, frightening names: Gaiseric, Ataulf, Theodoric. Rome's power was giving way to other peoples and a new age of history was beginning.

THE WEAKENING OF THE CENTRAL GOVERNMENT: Why did the great Roman Empire begin to falter?

2. The Roman Empire began its decline after the rule of Marcus Aurelius, whose death in A.D. 180 had marked the end of the Pax Romana. Most of the emperors who followed Marcus Aurelius were more concerned with increasing their personal wealth and power than with the well-being of the Roman people. These emperors grew rich at the expense of the Roman people, many of whom were reduced to poverty by the unfair taxes imposed. Economic problems and civil strife began to plague the empire.

3. As a result of Roman conquests of bordering lands during Marcus Aurelius's rule, the character of the Roman army changed. Some Germanic peoples joined the Roman army as **mercenaries** (MUR-suh-nair-eez)—soldiers serving for pay in a foreign army. Unlike the citizen-soldiers of old, these men fought because of their love for money and not because of their love for country. How might a nation that uses mercenaries for defense be more vulnerable to invasion?

4. The emperors following the Pax Romana lacked the knack for controlling and using the army effectively. The Roman generals had been quietly increasing their power since the death of Augustus. By the third century A.D., the Roman army was the master and not the servant of the state. Military leaders made government policy and chose emperors from their own ranks. Instead of the leadership in Rome, Roman soldiers again supported the commanders who paid them. Bloody civil wars were constantly being fought. In one period of fifty years, twenty-five emperors were murdered while in office.

5. By the close of the third century, the great Roman Empire was in decline. Trade with other nations had seriously decreased. Barbarians periodically attacked the Roman borders. Local leaders within the Roman provinces attacked other Roman territories in a bid for more power. One such leader was a woman named Zenobia (zuh-NOH-bee-uh), queen of the Syrian city of Palmyra (pal-MY-ruh).

PEOPLE IN HISTORY

6. Because she treated her people fairly, Queen Zenobia was one of the few popular rulers of her time. She brought scholars, poets, and artists to her court and beautified Palmyra with magnificent palaces. Zenobia was a highly educated woman who could speak Greek, Latin, Egyptian, and Syriac. She had studied Greek literature and philosophy and had written a history of the East.

7. But she was not content to rule a small city. In A.D. 270 her armies took over most of Asia Minor and then invaded Egypt. Zenobia rode at the head of her troops. At first the Roman emperor Aurelian believed the queen was simply protecting Roman lands from advancing barbarian tribes. But when Zenobia and her son, Wahballat, declared themselves emperors of the Roman Empire, Aurelian flew into action.

8. Roman troops soon recaptured Egypt and conquered Palmyra. Zenobia was captured in A.D. 273 while trying to flee to Persia. She was paraded through Rome, her hands and feet bound in gold chains. But Romans admired this spirited woman who had challenged the power of the emperor. Her life was spared—once she convinced Aurelian that it was really her advisers who had led the revolt. In return for her life, Zenobia agreed to retire from politics. She married a Roman senator and spent her remaining years living quietly in Rome.

▲ A Roman tax collector at work. Heavy taxes in the A.D. 300s contributed to the falling productivity of Roman farms.

9. By the late 200s, it had become impossible to adequately defend the Roman frontiers, or borders, which were almost 10,000 miles (16,000 kilometers) long. Money was being spent on building up the army at the expense of the upkeep of the great Roman roads, which fell into disrepair. The troops could no longer move quickly and efficiently throughout the empire. Barbarian tribes again threatened its northern and eastern borders.

SPOTLIGHT ON SOURCES

10. Writing in the mid A.D. 200s, the Roman bishop Cyprian describes a Roman Empire very different from that of the Pax Romana.

The world has aged and lost its former strength. It bears witness to its own decline. The sky no longer gives rain enough to nurture the seed, nor the sun light enough to warm the crops. . . . The supply of silver and gold from the mines is nearly exhausted. . . . Farmers are deserting their fields . . . there is a growing lack of justice in judgments, skill in trades, discipline in daily life. . . .

—from *Caesar and Christ*, Will Durant

GOVERNMENT REORGANIZATION: What did Diocletian and Constantine do to strengthen the faltering Roman government?

11. In A.D. 286 the emperor Diocletian (dy-uh-KLEE-shun) took steps to make sure that the empire stayed in Roman hands. He partitioned the faltering empire into an eastern and western half. He chose a peasant's son, Maximian, to be responsible for military defense and for the western half of the empire. From a base in Anatolia close to the Persian frontier, Diocletian—who retained the title of senior emperor—controlled the eastern half. Diocletian later partitioned the eastern and western halves into twelve smaller districts, called **dioceses** (DY-ah-suh-suz). He and Maximian appointed two assistants, or deputy emperors, to run these dioceses.

12. As a result of this reorganization, the Roman government was strengthened for a time. Some of Rome's more serious problems were eased. Many unemployed persons got jobs in the public works department revamped by Diocletian. Despite rising prices, the government distributed food to poor people at half the market price. The tax collection system was improved and the army strengthened to 500,000 men. Barbarian attacks at the borders diminished during Diocletian's reign.

13. After the retirement of Diocletian and Maximian in A.D. 305, the two deputy emperors who succeeded them were challenged by several ambitious men who wanted to rule the empire. By A.D. 306, Constantine I had defeated all the contenders, proclaiming himself sole emperor.

14. Constantine I kept many traditions of

Background: Diocletian was an avid persecutor of Christians. Ironically, many of the organizational changes (e.g., dioceses) and titles (e.g., vicar) created by Diocletian were subsequently adopted by the very Christians he persecuted.

the Roman Empire, but is best remembered for making two important changes. He moved the capital from Rome to Constantinople in the eastern half of the empire. The move was meant to strengthen the empire. But the transfer of the capital only strengthened the eastern half and actually caused the two regions of East and West to pull further apart. Constantine's second important change was outlined in the Edict of Milan, issued in A.D. 313. The edict allowed Christians to worship freely for the first time in the history of the Roman Empire without fear of **persecution** (pur-sih-KYOO-shun), or ill treatment for reasons of religion, politics, or race.

15. By about A.D. 400, Christianity had become the official religion of the Roman Empire. By then, conditions had so worsened in the empire that most Romans were ready to embrace a religion that held a promise of a better life. What had happened after Constantine's death to so dishearten the Roman people?

ECONOMIC AND SOCIAL DECLINE: What were the long-term effects of splitting the Empire between East and West?

16. After Constantine's death, more divisions of the empire and bloody civil wars followed. By A.D. 395, a formal—and permanent—division of the Empire into East and West took place. By then the eastern and western halves of the empire had grown different in character. The East was urban and commercial. The West was the agricultural center of the empire.

17. But agriculture, the cornerstone of the Roman economy, was in decline. For too many years, rich landowners had been buying up land and forcing small farmers out of business. As Roman farms grew large and self-sufficient, trade with other nations fell off, causing food to become less plentiful but more expensive. Most of the available foods farmed in the West were consumed by the people who could afford them—the Romans in the East. Many people in the West began to starve.

18. Heavy taxes contributed to the falling productivity of the farms and drained and impoverished the Romans. To finance the cost of building Constantinople, Constantine had heavily taxed the farmers, many of whom fled to the cities to hide from the tax collectors. The empire soon faced serious food shortages. Constantine ordered farmers bound to their lands for life. But this action only slowed the food shortages for a time.

19. Further damage was inflicted to the economy by an unfavorable balance of trade that sent all gold to the new capital in the East. The West, hard pressed for gold, became increasingly unable to pay its debts, which caused a devaluation of Roman coins. As the value of Roman coins fell, the prices of Roman products and services rose rapidly, creating an economic condition known as **inflation** (in-FLAY-shun). What countries today suffer from inflation? With the rising costs, it became harder for the average Roman to make a living.

20. As economic conditions worsened, Romans became disheartened. By the 300s the empire was in both a spiritual and economic decline. Taxpayers helplessly watched from the sidelines as all their tax monies were channeled to the military. None of these monies were put back into public services or works. How loyal do you think the taxpayers felt toward a government that was so indifferent to their economic problems?

BARBARIAN INVASIONS: How did the fall of Rome come about?

21. Droughts, famines, and floods in their own lands pushed some Germanic tribes across Roman borders in search of food. By A.D. 375, the Huns, an invading warrior tribe from central Asia, were pushing many Germanic tribes out of their homelands. The German tribes were pushed further and further south. Eventually German tribes had nowhere to go but across the Danube into Roman territory.

22. One Germanic tribe, the Visigoths

Background: Roman officials in Constantinople used some of the gold to buy off many of the barbarian tribes. As a result, many barbarians turned their attention to the West.

159

(VIZ-uh-goths), tried to resolve this situation peacefully. They negotiated with Roman officials to buy Roman land instead of taking it by force. Roman officials accepted the offer but then took Visigoth women and children hostage to ensure the peace. Additionally, until the new fields yielded crops, the Visigoths were dependent on the Romans for food. The Romans charged them such high prices for food that the Visigoths nearly starved.

23. By A.D. 378 the Visigoths had had enough of the Romans' ill treatment. As part of their original negotiations with the Romans, the Visigoths had been allowed to keep their weapons. Now they turned these weapons against the Romans, attacking the city of Adrianople and killing two-thirds of the Roman population there. For the first time in the history of the Roman Empire, barbarians had won a major victory inside the Roman borders. After the battle of Adri-anople, the Romans forged a shaky peace with the Visigoths, giving them tenant farms and paid positions in the Roman army. But the Visigoths no longer trusted the Romans and were now determined to govern themselves. More than ever they wanted land and homes of their own.

24. After only twenty years the Visigoths uprooted themselves and traveled west in search of land. They took Athens, sacked Corinth, and invaded Italy in the process. Alaric was the first barbarian invader to stand before Rome's gates. His army surrounded the city, cutting off the food supply to the soldiers within. Alaric offered to spare the city in exchange for two things: the rank of commander-in-chief in the Roman army and a homeland for his people between the Gulf of Venice and the Danube. The Western emperor Honorius agreed to these terms, but when Alaric and his troops retreated, Honorius went back on his word.

Daily life in . . .

The chief invaders of the Roman Empire were the Germanic tribes who lived closest to the northern and eastern borders. A love of combat colored everything they did. They carried spear and shield to all tribal meetings. According to tribal law, cowards, traitors, and deserters were executed but murderers paid a fine—usually of cattle or sheep—to the family of the murder victim. Germanic women served as priestesses and warriors, and in one tribe, the Sitones, they even ruled. About 100 warriors and their families made up a typical Germanic village, and several hundred villages made up a tribe.

Oaths were very important in tribal life. A person who lied under oath risked angering the gods. Physical evidence was inadmissible at a trial, where oaths determined guilt or innocence. The accused person swore that he or she was telling the truth. Friends and relatives could also take an oath swearing that the accused person was innocent. If there was doubt, the accused person was made to undergo an ordeal. A typical ordeal was to pour boiling water on the accused person's hand. If the burn healed within three days, the people considered this a sign from the gods that the accused person was innocent. If the burn failed to heal, the accused person was found guilty.

The fear Germanic warriors inspired in battle was often sufficient to defeat their enemies. Because Germanic horses were short and stocky, they didn't turn well or fast, so Germanic warriors preferred to attack on foot. Germanic warriors often attacked by night, in wedge formation. They blackened their bodies and weapons with coal or oil and chanted as they marched, usually about the bravery of their heroes. The chants, which were meant to stir the courage of the Germanic warriors, often unnerved the enemy. "Defeat in battle often begins with the sight [of the Germanic warriors]," said Tacitus, a Roman historian writing in A.D. 98. About three hundred years later, Romans would find out firsthand what it was like to face Germanic warriors in battle.

25. In A.D. 410 the great city of Rome itself fell to the Visigoths. Alaric's troops stormed Rome three times over the course of several months of siege. One night a great thunderstorm arose without warning. The Roman guards, not expecting an attack in such harsh weather, left their posts on the walls seeking dry cover below. But the Visigoths quietly placed ladders against the outside walls. A few Visigoth warriors crept stealthily inside and forced the city gate from within. For three days the Visigoths sacked Rome. Warriors rode through the Forum and across the marble floors of wealthy homes, carrying away riches. What they couldn't carry, they burned. Rome, long the center of western civilization, was almost completely destroyed. After their victory the Visigoths traveled across Gaul and by A.D. 485 had settled in Spain.

26. About twelve years later the Vandals, another Germanic barbarian tribe, invaded the provinces of Roman North Africa from Spain. The arrival of the Visigoths in Spain had caused the Vandals to look for other lands. The Vandals captured Carthage in North Africa in A.D. 439, using it as a pirate base from which to control the Mediterranean. In A.D. 455 the Vandals sacked Rome. Pope Leo I intervened, and the Vandals agreed not to burn buildings or murder Romans as long as Romans offered no resistance to the looting. For fourteen days the Vandals cleaned the city of its remaining wealth and treasures. Then they returned to Carthage, their ships laden with Rome's riches. One ship sank in the Mediterranean, and its cargo of Roman art still lies hidden somewhere at the bottom of the sea.

27. By the mid-fifth century, the end of the Roman Empire was close at hand. The Huns, who had pushed the Visigoths south into Roman lands, were united under one rule by Attila in A.D. 445. In A.D. 451 the Huns marched westward into Gaul and then turned toward Italy, burning all townships in the invasion path. But upon Attila's natural death in A.D. 453, the Huns returned north of the Danube and mixed with other tribes living there. In A.D. 476 the last Ro-

▲ Alaric and his Visigoth warriors sacking Rome in A.D. 410. The Visigoths spared Rome's churches at the Pope's request.

man emperor of the West, Romulus Augustus, was dethroned by one of these tribes, the Heruli. Another tribe, the Franks, conquered Gaul by A.D. 486.

28. The rule of Rome came to an end with the dethroning of Romulus Augustus. The eastern half of the Roman Empire, however, continued to live on for another thousand years as the Byzantine Empire.

OUTLOOK

29. The political, social, and economic declines after the Pax Romana had made the Romans weak. They were no match for the fierce Germanic tribes. Romans had been growing more self-centered and undisciplined since the reign of Augustus, who had limited their voice in government. Why would lacking a voice in government make a people more selfish?

161

CHAPTER REVIEW

VOCABULARY REVIEW

Write each of the following sentences on a sheet of paper. Then fill in the blanks with the word that best completes each sentence.

dioceses

inflation

mercenaries

persecution

1. The Roman army was weakened when it began to use _____ instead of patriotic citizen-soldiers.
2. The Edict of Milan put an end to the _____ of Christians in the Roman Empire.
3. Diocletian subdivided the empire into twelve districts, or _____ .
4. When the value of money falls and the prices of goods and services rise, an economic condition known as _____ results.

SKILL BUILDER: READING A MAP THAT HAS ARROWS

Historical maps provide information about people and places in history. Symbols are often used to represent information that might otherwise take up too much space on the map. One symbol often seen on historical maps is the arrow. The arrow is used to show direction. On this map, the directions are shown on a compass rose. Find the arrow that shows the route taken by the Jutes to invade the British Isles. Using the compass rose, you can see that the Jutes headed in a southwestern direction to invade this land.

Use the map below to answer the questions that follow.

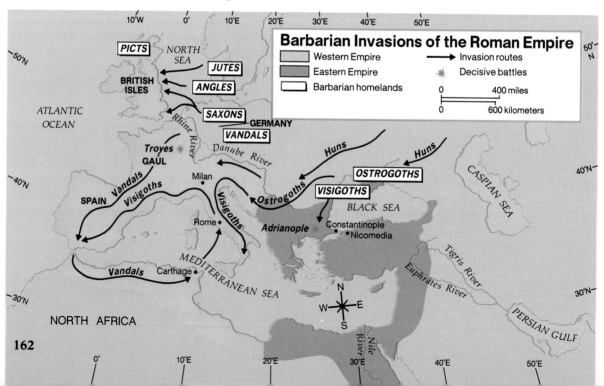

1. Through which Roman provinces did the Vandals pass before invading Carthage?

2. Find Rome on the map. Which barbarian group invaded Rome from the southwest?

3. In which direction did the Huns travel to invade the Roman Empire?

SKILL BUILDER: CRITICAL THINKING AND COMPREHENSION

1. Generalizing

▶ Make a generalization about the division of the Roman Empire from the following facts. Write your generalization on a sheet of paper.

a. The East was richer, urban, and commercial.

b. The West was poorer and agricultural.

c. The East had the superior defenses.

d. Gold was siphoned off to the East.

2. Sequencing

▶ Place the following events in the order in which they occurred.

a. Rome was sacked by the Vandals.

b. The Roman army began using mercenaries.

c. The Roman Empire was subdivided into dioceses.

d. The capital was moved from Rome to Constantinople.

e. Queen Zenobia captured Egypt.

f. Christianity became the official religion of the Roman Empire.

3. Spatial Relationships

▶ Refer to the map on page 162 to answer the following questions.

a. Where is Spain in relation to the British Isles?

b. On which sides—north, south, east, or west—is Constantinople bordered by water?

c. Where is the city of Adrianople in relation to the capital city of Constantinople?

d. Where is the Tigris River in relation to the Euphrates River?

4. Cause and Effect   A cause is an action or event that makes something happen. An effect is what happens as a result of the action or event.

▶ On a sheet of paper, write the effect of the following causes.

Germanic lands had suffered severe droughts, famines, and floods; tribes were in search of food.

By A.D. 375, the Huns were seizing land from many of the Germanic tribes.

ENRICHMENT

1. Research the tribal customs of the Visigoths, Vandals, or Huns and prepare a brief oral report to give to the class.

2. Research the life of the slaves in ancient Rome. Then imagine that you are a newspaper reporter living in the fourth century. Write an editorial on why slavery should be stopped in the Roman Empire.

UNIT REVIEW

SUMMARY

During the thousand years between the Golden Age of Greece and the fall of the Roman Empire (about 470 B.C. to A.D. 470), the basic ideas of western civilization were formed. In Greece, scattered communities moved toward greater democracy. The *polis*, or city-state, became a center of culture. Athens, under Pericles, developed a government in which all adult male citizens could vote. Sparta had a military government offering fewer freedoms. However, all Greeks practiced slavery and excluded slaves, foreigners, and women from voting. Threat of invasion by Persia temporarily united the Greek city-states. The defeat of Persia encouraged the Greeks to develop philosophy, science, and the arts. With the Peloponnesian War between Athens and Sparta, Greek civilization began to change. Philip of Macedonia became monarch of Greece. Alexander, his son, ruled Greece and conquered Egypt, Persia, and Babylon. Meanwhile, the Romans were gaining strength and territory in Italy. The Roman Republic absorbed Greek ideas about government and the arts, but added ideas of military rule and civil engineering. Rome defeated Carthage in wars over Mediterranean trade. Julius Caesar gained power by leading Roman legions in conquests of Gaul and Britain, but was murdered by rivals. After a power struggle, Augustus became emperor of Rome. For two hundred years the Roman Empire expanded and prospered. After the "five good emperors," Rome declined. The splitting of the empire and barbarian invasions finally caused Rome to fall.

SKILL BUILDER: READING A MAP

▶ The map below shows the major areas of unified rule around the world at the height of the Roman Empire. Use the map to answer the following questions.

The World About A.D. 1

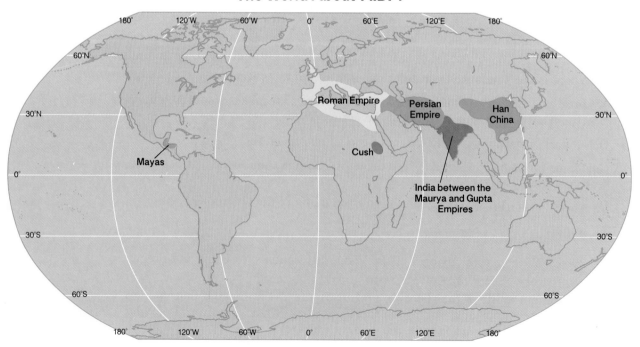

1. Which area is shown in yellow?

2. Which area is shown in red?

3. Which area is shown in purple?

4. Which area included Greece and much of Alexander the Great's Empire?

5. Which area was once invaded but never conquered by Alexander?

6. Which area was completely unknown to Rome in A.D. 1?

SKILL BUILDER: CRITICAL THINKING AND COMPREHENSION

1. Sequencing

▶ Place the following events from Unit 3 in the order in which they took place.

Augustus is made the first Roman emperor.

Sparta defeats Athens in the Peloponnesian War.

Rome conquers all of Italy.

Julius Caesar is made dictator for life.

Germanic tribes invade the Roman Empire.

Alexander rules the Hellenistic World

Pax Romana comes to an end

The Greek city-states join to defeat the Persians

Rome becomes a Republic

Rome defeats Carthage for the last time

2. Classifying

▶ Identify the historical figures from Unit 3 who made the following contributions.

a. This writer philosopher wrote *The Republic*.

b. This emperor issued the edict of Milan.

c. This philosopher taught Alexander the Great.

d. This famous Roman poet wrote *The Aeneid*.

e. This leader strengthened democracy in Greece.

3. Making Judgments

a. How did the Greeks and Romans spread their ideas about government, science, and the arts to other parts of the world?

b. What causes rich and powerful nations like those of Greece and Rome to fall apart?

ENRICHMENT

1. Imagine that you have received a letter from the Roman emperor Constantine. He is trying to convince you that his plan to move the capital of the empire to Constantinople is a good one. Write a letter to Constantine explaining why you think his plan is a mistake that will only weaken the empire.

2. The ancient Greeks thought of the peoples living to the north, including the Macedonians, as "barbarians." Use an encyclopedia or other library resources to make a map showing who these people were and where they lived. Instead, you may wish to write a brief report about how being a "barbarian" might have influenced the career of Alexander the Great.

UNIT 4

ESL/LEP Strategy: Have students categorize vocabulary words. Help them to create headings such as *Christianity and the Church, Government,* and *Contributions of Major Rulers.* Then, tell students to write vocabulary words under the appropriate headings.

EUROPE'S EARLY DEVELOPMENT

OBJECTIVE: Unit 4 begins by exploring the impact of Christianity as a major religion and ends with Western Europe surviving important changes. You will be able to recognize and describe the contributions of the church, of kings and queens, and of people in the towns.

Jesus is put to death A.D. 30

Christianity becomes a major religion C. A.D. 400

Justinian I becomes emperor of Byzantine Empire A.D. 527

| A.D. 100 | A.D. 200 | A.D. 300 | A.D. 400 | A.D. 500 | A.D. 600 | A.D. 700 |

Christianity becomes official religion of Roman Empire A.D. 395

Clovis becomes King of the Franks A.D. 481

Charlemagne becomes king of the Franks A.D. 768

▲ In the Middle Ages, teams of knights fought for fun as their ladies looked on.

Charlemagne dies
and his empire begins
to fall apart
A.D. 814

Trade guilds
begin in
England in
A.D. 1093

First
Crusade
begins
A.D. 1096

Franciscan
Order
begins
A.D. 1210

Black Death
appears in
Western Europe
A.D. 1347

A.D. 800   A.D. 900   A.D. 1000   A.D. 1100   A.D. 1200   A.D. 1300   A.D. 1400

William, the Conqueror,
leads Norman Invasion
of England
A.D. 1066

Middle Class
begins to
appear
c. A.D. 1100

Conflict between
King Philip IV and
Pope Boniface
weakens papacy
A.D. 1301

Great Schism
splits Roman
Catholic Church
A.D. 1378

CHAPTER 1

Christianity Spreads New Ideas

▲ No one knows how Jesus actually looked, though he has often been pictured. This is how an Italian painter of the 1300s imagined him.

OBJECTIVE: How did Christianity spread in the Roman Empire and become a major world religion?

1. In 1981, researchers who were counting the number of people in each of the world's religions discovered a remarkable fact. For the first time since ancient times, more than half of the Christians in the world lived outside Europe and North America. Christianity had truly become a world religion. For example, in 1900, there were few Christians in Nigeria, Africa's largest nation. Today, one half of Nigeria's population is Christian. Today, so many people in South Korea have become Christians that they are soon expected to make up nearly one half of that country's population. From the beginning, Christians have always tried to spread their religion to other people throughout the world. This desire to share the faith with others is an important part of Christianity.

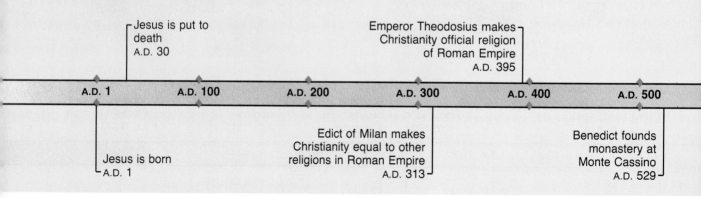

Jesus is put to death
A.D. 30

Emperor Theodosius makes
Christianity official religion
of Roman Empire
A.D. 395

A.D. 1 — A.D. 100 — A.D. 200 — A.D. 300 — A.D. 400 — A.D. 500

Jesus is born
A.D. 1

Edict of Milan makes
Christianity equal to other
religions in Roman Empire
A.D. 313

Benedict founds
monastery at
Monte Cassino
A.D. 529

ESL/LEP Strategy: Write the words *Christianity* and *crucifixion* on the chalkboard. Have students identify a familiar word part or the base or root words (*Christian, crucifix*). Explain that looking for root words can help to understand new words.

CHRISTIANITY BEGINS: How did Christianity develop as a religion?

2. Christian beliefs began almost 2,000 years ago with the life and teachings of Jesus. Jesus was born in the Roman province of Judea, a part of Palestine. Jesus was raised in Judaism, the Jewish religion. Judaism, with its belief in one God, was the foundation for Christianity.

PEOPLE IN HISTORY

3. From the age of about 30 to the age of 33, Jesus traveled around his homeland teaching about the kingdom of God. The most revolutionary idea in Jesus's preaching was his claim that God loved sinners as well as the good. Jesus told his listeners that God also loved the poor, the suffering, and the social outcasts. Jesus told his followers that there was a better life to come after death. He encouraged people to follow the teachings of God as he explained them. This would ensure life after death and would provide a better life on earth, too.

4. Jesus's influence on the people of Judea alarmed some Jewish leaders. Many of his followers believed that Jesus was the **Messiah** (meh-SY-uh), or deliverer, who was supposed to come and free the Jews. The Romans were also concerned about the influence Jesus was gaining. They arrested him and turned him over to Pontius Pilate, the Roman governor, for sentencing. Under Roman law, political rebels were sentenced to death by **crucifixion** (kroo-sih-FIK-shun). In crucifixion a person is nailed or tied to a cross and left there to die of exposure.

5. According to Christian belief, Jesus rose from the dead on the third day after his crucifixion. This event is called the **Resurrection** (reh-sur-REK-shun) and Christians celebrate it each year at Easter. Christians believe that God sacrificed his only son in order to show all people that there is life after death.

CHRISTIANITY SPREADS: How did Christianity spread quickly through the Roman Empire?

6. After the death of Jesus, the Christian religion spread gradually throughout the Roman Empire. Christianity did not, however, find many believers among the Jews themselves. Jesus's teachings attracted others for two main reasons. The most important reason was the promise of life after death. The second reason had to do with the nature of Jesus's message: Do unto others as you would have them do unto you. As Christians traveled, they shared the teachings of Christianity with the people they met. In addition, some of Jesus's followers became the first Christian missionaries. A missionary is a person sent out by the church to win new people to the religion. One of the most successful of all the Christian missionaries was Paul, whose letters are now part of the New Testament of the Bible.

7. Many Roman officials were alarmed by the spread of Christianity. They believed that Christians were disloyal to the emperor. Christians would not worship the Roman gods and did not acknowledge the emperor to be a god. The Romans also thought that Christians might be plotting against the empire because of their strong network of communication. As a result, some emperors **persecuted** (PUR-seh-kyoo-tud) Christians by having them put to death. To persecute means to harass or injure people because of their religion, race, or political ideas. The persecutions forced many Christians to worship secretly in Rome's **catacombs** (KAT-uh-kohmz). The catacombs were a series of underground vaults that were used for burying the dead. Why do you think Christianity continued to grow and spread despite persecution? ◄

SPOTLIGHT ON SOURCES

8. The persecutions of Christians by Roman officials took place from shortly after Jesus's death until A.D. 313. Some Roman emperors persecuted Christians severely, while others did not bother to persecute them. Christians were usually given the chance to save themselves by disowning their faith and affirming their belief in the Roman gods.

In A.D. 156, in Smyrna, a Christian leader named Polycarp was brought into the arena where other Christians had been killed. The Roman governor called to Polycarp from his seat and said, "Swear by Caesar's fortune; change your attitude; say, 'Away with the godless.' "

Polycarp looked at all the crowd in the stadium, sighed, looked up to heaven and cried, "Away with the godless!"

The governor pressed him further: "Swear, and I will set you free: execrate [curse] Christ."

"For eighty-six years," replied Polycarp, "I have been His servant, and He has never done me wrong: how can I blaspheme my King who saved me!" Although the governor tried several more times to get Polycarp to save himself, Polycarp refused. The governor ordered Polycarp to be put to death.

—*The Genuine Epistles of the Apostolic Fathers,* translated by William, Archbishop of Canterbury

9. In A.D. 313, Christianity was made equal to other religions in the Roman Empire by the Edict of Milan. The Edict of Milan was issued by the Roman emperor Constantine I. In A.D. 395, Emperor Theodosius made Christianity the official religion of the empire. From that time on, Christian church leaders became more and more powerful in the empire.

THE CHURCH: What were the roles of the different leaders in the Christian church?

10. The organization of the Christian church grew from small group meetings to

▼ Emperor Theodosius made Christianity the official religion of the Roman Empire in A.D. 395. What parts of the empire practiced the new religion in A.D. 476?

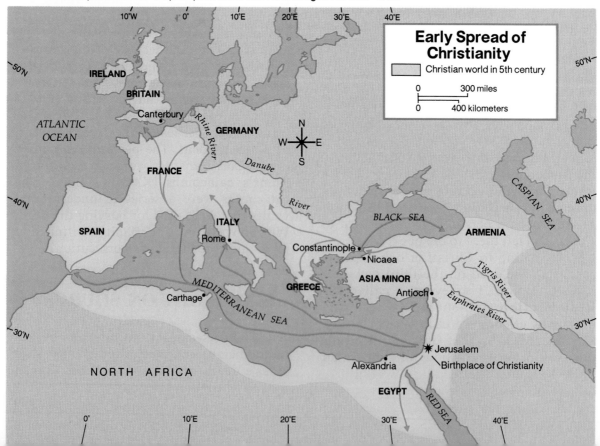

Early Spread of Christianity

Christian world in 5th century

0   300 miles
0   400 kilometers

▲ These catacombs are near Rome. Early Christians worshiped secretly in these underground vaults in order to escape persecution.

a large **hierarchy** (HY-rar-kee), or system of church government. At the top of the hierarchy was the **pope**, who was bishop of Rome. The pope appointed other **bishops** to head all the churches throughout a large area. The bishops supervised the priests in local churches. At the bottom were deacons and other clergy who helped the priests.

11. Some Christians chose to live their lives totally devoted to Christian thought and prayer. They wanted to live apart from the world and its temptations. Such people are called **monks**. A place where a number of monks live together is a **monastery** (MAHN-uh-steh-ree). As early Christianity spread, the number and size of monasteries grew. A Greek monk named Basil and an Italian monk named Benedict took important steps to set up monasteries. To make the monks self-supporting, Basil established rules requiring monks to build their own monasteries and grow their own food.

The monks were to worship together, eat together, and work together. They also were to do works of charity in nearby towns.

SPOTLIGHT ON SOURCES

12. In A.D. 529, Benedict set up a monastery in Italy at Monte Cassino, where he wrote the Benedictine Rule. The Benedictine Rule required that monks take vows of poverty, chastity, and obedience. It organized every hour of the day for them:

> Idleness is the enemy of the soul. The brethren [brothers], therefore, must be occupied at stated hours in manual labor [labor by hand], and again at the other hours in sacred reading . . . . From Easter until September 14, the brethren [brothers] shall work in the morning from the first hour until the fourth to do the tasks that have to be done. From the fourth hour until about the sixth, let them apply themselves to reading. After the sixth hour, having left the table, let them rest on their beds in perfect silence, or if anyone wishes to read by himself, let him read so as not to disturb others.
>
> —from *Rule of St. Benedict*

OUTLOOK

13. In the beginning, Christians were disliked and often persecuted by many Roman leaders. However, people who believed in Christianity were strong enough to overcome persecution. In A.D. 395, Christianity became the official religion of the Roman Empire. As a result, when the Roman Empire weakened in western Europe, the Christian church provided both political and religious leadership. In this way Christianity became more powerful. In fact, Christianity helped to unite many different groups of people. By the fifth century, Christianity had become a well-established religion. What appeal do you think Christianity ◄ had that gave Christians the courage to stand fast to their beliefs?

Activity: Have students, working in small groups, devise a set of rules for a monastery. Each group should make up one or two rules and be prepared to explain the reasons for the rule.

171

CHAPTER REVIEW

VOCABULARY REVIEW

Copy each word from the list, then find its definition and write the definition after the word.

1. Messiah
2. crucifixion
3. Resurrection
4. persecute

5. missionary
6. hierarchy
7. pope
8. bishop

9. monk
10. monastery
11. catacombs

a. Underground vaults for burying the dead

b. Church leader who supervised the priests

c. To harass or injure people because of their religion, race, or political ideas

d. System of church government

e. A place where a number of monks live together, separate from the world, under religious vows

f. Execution by being nailed or tied to a cross

g. Christian who lives apart from the world and its temptations

h. A religious deliverer who was supposed to come and free the Jews

i. The bishop of Rome and head of the Church

j. Jesus's rise from the dead after his crucifixion

SKILL BUILDER: USING AN ENCYCLOPEDIA

One of the reference books that is used to find facts on any subject quickly and easily is the **general encyclopedia**. The general encyclopedia is a set of books that give general information about important people, places, and events. **Special encyclopedias** give facts about one subject, such as music, history, or science. Most special encyclopedias are in one or two volumes. However, general encyclopedias have many volumes. On the spine, or back, of each volume is a number. The volumes of an encyclopedia are arranged in alphabetical order according to the first letters of the topics found in each volume. Look at the **guide words** on the sample spines given below. These words help you find the topic you want in alphabetical order. The first topic in Volume 18 is *plastics*. The last topic in Volume 18 is *raisin*. If you wanted to find information on Poland, you would look in this volume since *po* follows *pl* alphabetically. But if you wanted to find facts about Rome, you would not look in Volume 18. Words beginning with *ro* come after those starting with *ra* when arranged in alphabetical order.

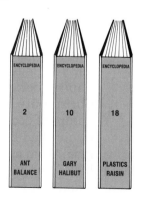

Use the paragraph and the drawing of the encyclopedias to answer the following questions.

1. How is a special encyclopedia different from a general one?

2. What is the word used to describe the part of an encyclopedia pictured here?

3. What is the first and last topic covered in Volume 10?

4. In which volume would you find facts about Benedict?

SKILL BUILDER: CRITICAL THINKING AND COMPREHENSION

1. Introducing Comparing and Contrasting

▶ When you compare and contrast objects, you not only are searching for ways in which they are different. You are also searching for ways in which they are the same.

From what you learned in this chapter, compare and contrast the Christian beliefs with the beliefs of Buddhism explained in Unit 1, Chapter 6.

2. Sequencing

▶ Arrange the following events in the order in which they happened. Place a number from 1-4 in the blank, indicating earliest to most recent.

Christianity is made an equal with other religions of the Roman Empire.

Jesus is crucified.

Christianity becomes the official religion of the Roman Empire.

Jesus travels his homeland of Judea teaching about the kingdom of God.

3. Cause and Effect

▶ Below are a list of causes and a list of effects. Write the effect that matches the cause in the second column.

Cause

3-1. Christians would not worship the Roman gods.

3-2. Edict of Milan

3-3. The Roman Empire weakens.

3-4. Christians wanted to live apart from the world and its temptations.

Effect

a. Ended persecutions of the Christians.

b. Monasteries were established.

c. Christians were persecuted.

d. Christian church leaders become more powerful.

ENRICHMENT

1. Imagine you are a Roman citizen trying to understand why Christians will not worship Roman gods. Write a paragraph from the point of view of a wealthy Roman. Write another paragraph from the point of view of a poor Roman.

2. Use an encyclopedia or other library source to study about the hierarchy of the Roman Catholic Church. Draw a diagram of the church hierarchy. Then write a short paragraph describing the duties of each church leader.

CHAPTER 2

The Rise and Fall of Carolingian Europe

es fire lame reim
tout maintenant

▲ The baptism of the Frankish king, Clovis, brought the most important Germanic kingdom into the Christian church.

OBJECTIVE: How did Charlemagne create the first great empire after the fall of Rome, and why did the empire not last?

1. Germanic youth were trained to be warriors. Above all things, the Germanic people prized their weapons and armor. They were proud of their daggers, axes, and swords, and they took great care of their helmets and shields. As these warriors took over the lands of the Western Roman empire, formal education almost disappeared. It took the courage and wisdom of a great leader named Charlemagne to recognize the importance of education. Through Charlemagne's support of education, many of the writings of ancient Greece and Rome were saved. Without Charlemagne's schools, these works might have been lost.

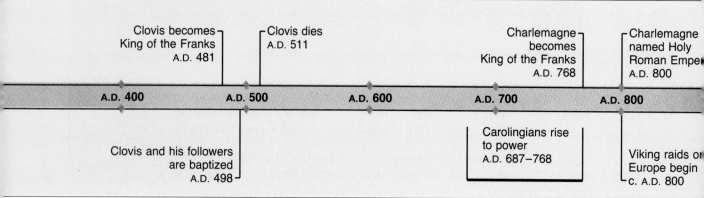

Clovis becomes King of the Franks A.D. 481

Clovis dies A.D. 511

Charlemagne becomes King of the Franks A.D. 768

Charlemagne named Holy Roman Emperor A.D. 800

A.D. 400 — A.D. 500 — A.D. 600 — A.D. 700 — A.D. 800

Clovis and his followers are baptized A.D. 498

Carolingians rise to power A.D. 687–768

Viking raids on Europe begin c. A.D. 800

174

THE KINGDOM OF THE FRANKS: How did a Germanic tribe called the Franks become the rulers of a great empire?

2. When the Germanic tribes took over the weakened Western Roman Empire, government as the Romans knew it disappeared. At first, some of the Germans tried to keep peace and maintain the power and greatness of Rome. Before long, however, Europe was divided into many small kingdoms. These kingdoms often fought each other, and some of their leaders were more like gang leaders than kings. Travel became dangerous, so that trade almost ended. Cities became empty and decayed. Schools disappeared, so that hardly anyone knew how to read. Why do you think this era is sometimes called the Dark Ages?

3. About A.D. 500, one of these little kingdoms, the kingdom of the Franks, conquered much of Gaul and part of Germany. The Franks owed their power to Clovis, the first great leader of the Merovingian (mehr-oh-VIN-jee-un) dynasty. Clovis became king in A.D. 481, and in A.D. 496 he announced that he was becoming a Christian. Two years later he and 3,000 of his warriors were baptized by a leading bishop. Christian **baptism** (BAP-tiz-um) is a ceremony in which a person becomes a member of the church. Clovis's baptism won him the support of the church in his wars with other, non-Christian Germanic leaders. More important, it established Christianity in all the lands that the Franks controlled.

4. After Clovis died in A.D. 511, Frankish rule weakened. This was true mainly because when a Germanic king died, his kingdom was divided among all his sons. The sons often then went to war with each other to enlarge their kingdoms. However, in about A.D. 750 a new dynasty, the Carolingian (kahr-uh-LIN-jee-un), reunited the Frankish kingdom. Under this dynasty, the Franks also conquered new lands, and by A.D. 800 they ruled more of western Europe than anyone since the Romans. The most powerful Carolingian king was Charlemagne (SHAR-luh-mayn).

PEOPLE IN HISTORY

5. Charlemagne, whose name means Charles the Great, is one of the mighty figures of history. He became king of the Franks in A.D. 768, and when he died in A.D. 814, he ruled much of Europe. Charlemagne returned law and order to lands that had once been ruled by the Roman Empire—and, in the case of Germany, to lands that Rome had never ruled.

6. Charlemagne believed that education and learning were important. He invited scholars to his court at Aachen (AH-kun). The greatest scholar of the age was Alcuin (AL-kwin) from England. In Charlemagne's palace, Alcuin taught religion, astronomy, and Latin. Charlemagne also founded other schools and monasteries. Scholars made copies of ancient writings and helped keep Greek and Roman learning alive. What do ◄ you think the Romans might have thought of Charlemagne?

7. Charlemagne was also a good Christian and a loyal supporter of the pope. He hurried to Rome in A.D. 799 to rescue Pope Leo III, who had been driven from the city by rioters. On Christmas Day in A.D. 800, the grateful pope placed a crown on Charlemagne's head and named him Roman Emperor. Of course, Charlemagne's empire was very different from the Roman Empire of old. However, the title was important, for it showed that Charlemagne had the support of the pope. Why was this important for ◄ Charlemagne?

8. Charlemagne brought a centralized system of government to lands that had not known one since the fall of Rome. Every year representatives called *missi dominici* (MIS-see doh-MIH-nih-kee) went around the empire to see that Charlemagne's orders were obeyed. What government agency in the United States today might be similar to the *missi dominici*? Local communities were run by nobles called **counts**. The counts kept law and order.

9. After Charlemagne's death in A.D. 814, his empire began to crumble. Charle-

ESL/LEP Strategy: Have students describe the accomplishments of Charlemagne. Ask them to select a great ruler from their countries of origin and to compare his or her accomplishments to those of Charlemagne.

175

magne's son, Louis, proved to be a weak ruler. After Louis's death, his three sons fought over who would get what parts of the empire. Look at the map on page 178. How was the empire finally divided?

THE VIKINGS: How did the Viking invasions change western Europe?

10. The breakup of Charlemagne's empire was hastened by a new wave of invasions that began in the early 800s. Arabs, who controlled North Africa and much of Spain, attacked Europe from the south. From the east, Europe was invaded by a group of people from Asia, the Magyars (MAHG-yarz). After attacking Germany, the Magyars settled permanently in Hungary. By far the most feared of all the new invaders, however, came from the north. These were the Vikings, or Northmen.

11. The Vikings came from Scandinavia—present-day Sweden, Norway, and Denmark. They entered western Europe in

the early 800s for several reasons. First, they were fighting among themselves for power. Second, their homeland was not able to support a growing population. Finally, many Vikings were driven by a desire for adventure. How do these reasons for invading compare with those of the groups who invaded the Roman Empire?

12. The Viking raids were heaviest on the northern and western coasts of Europe. The Vikings sailed in fast, strong ships, called **long ships**, that were decorated with the shapes of snakes and dragons. Sailing up rivers in these ships, the Vikings attacked many inland cities and monasteries. They usually attacked at night. They stole what they could and destroyed what they could not take with them.

SPOTLIGHT ON SOURCES

13. The Vikings destroyed many monasteries, which had been the centers of learn-

▼ Vikings sailed from their homeland in the ninth and tenth centuries and attacked cities throughout Europe. What rivers did the Vikings follow to reach Constantinople?

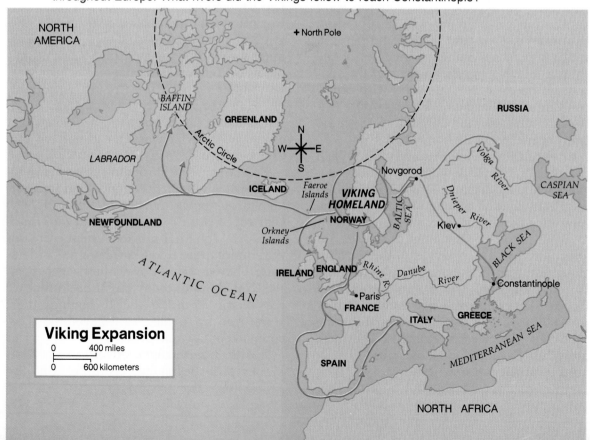

▲ This decoration from a long ship captures some of the Vikings' fierce spirit. Such decorations were intended to frighten their opponents.

ing in Charlemagne's empire. Some of the monks wrote about what they saw the Vikings and other invaders do. Here are three descriptions. Why do you think the Viking attacks could not be stopped?

> . . . [A] party of invaders devastated Gaul [France]; of these more than six hundred men perished [died] . . . Charles [Charlemagne's grandson] agreed to give them many thousand pounds of gold and silver if they would leave Gaul, and this they did. Nevertheless the cloisters of most of the saints were destroyed and many of the Christians were led away captive . . .

According to their customs the North-men plundered [robbed] . . . and burned the town of Dordrecht, with two other villages, before the eyes of Lothair [Charlemagne's grandson], who was then in the castle of Nimwegen, but could not punish the crime. The Northmen, with their boats filled with immense booty, including both men and goods, returned to their own country . . . .

> At this time . . . the basilica of the apostle Peter [in Rome] was taken and plundered by the Moors [Muslims] . . . [They] slaughtered [killed] all the Christians whom they found outside the walls of Rome, either within or without the church. They also carried men and women away prisoners. They tore down, among many others, the altar of the blessed Peter, and their crimes from day to day bring sorrow to Christians . . . .
>
> —*Readings in European History*, Leon Bernard and Theodore B. Hodges

14. Viking raids spread the greatest fear and destruction in Ireland, England, and France. Other raids took them as far east as Russia and as far south as the Mediterranean Sea. The raids by Vikings in the north and by Arabs in the south destroyed much of what Charlemagne had built.

OUTLOOK

15. Viking raids continued in Europe until about A.D. 1000. Then they gradually died down, partly because the Vikings adopted Christianity and changed some of their ways. The raids had some lasting results. One was the opening of a new trade route linking the Baltic Sea to the rivers of Russia and to Constantinople. Another result was that the Vikings established stronger governments in places where there had been none before. One of these places was Normandy, on the coast of France, which would play an important part in the histories of both France and England.

Ask: In what ways did the destructive Viking raids lead to important changes in Europe?

CHAPTER REVIEW

VOCABULARY REVIEW

Look up the following vocabulary words in the glossary and write out their definitions. Then fill in the blank with the word that best completes each sentence.

baptism   counts

missi dominici   longships

1. The _____ traveled throughout the empire of Charlemagne to make sure his orders were obeyed.

2. The Vikings in their _____ reached the coasts of northern and western Europe.

3. During the time of Charlemagne, the _____ were responsible for law and order in local communities.

4. Clovis and 3,000 of his warriors took part in a _____ ceremony performed by a leading bishop in A.D. 498.

SKILL BUILDER: READING A MAP

Sometimes the course of history can be influenced by geography. Historians use the term "spatial relationship" to refer to the geographic connections between land, bodies of water, and history.

The following questions are about the three kingdoms set up by Charlemagne's grandsons.

▶ Use the map below to help you answer the questions on the next page.

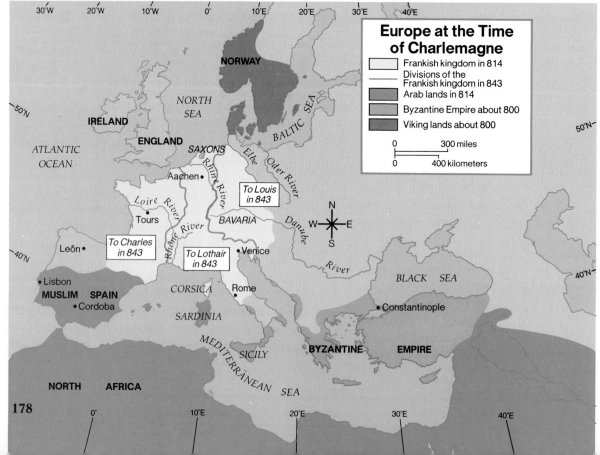

1. Charlemagne's empire was divided among his three grandsons, Lothair, Charles, and Louis. Which grandson inherited the westernmost kingdom?

2. The Vikings repeatedly raided the north and west coasts of Europe. Which of the three brothers's kingdoms probably suffered most from Viking raids?

3. Which brother's kingdom shared a land border with the Arabs?

4. Look at a map of present-day Europe. Name two countries that cover land that once was part of Louis's kingdom.

5. Modern-day Italy's northern area was once part of which brother's kingdom?

SKILL BUILDER: CRITICAL THINKING AND COMPREHENSION

1. Sequencing

▶ On a separate piece of paper, rewrite the following events in the order in which they happened.

a. The Vikings raid the coasts of northern and western Europe.

b. Clovis becomes the first king in the Merovingian dynasty.

c. Charlemagne rescues Pope Leo III in Rome from the rioters, who were threatening his power.

d. The Dark Ages begin in Europe.

e. The Carolingian kings reunite the Frankish kingdom under one rule.

f. The Western Roman Empire is gradually taken over by the Germanic tribes.

2. Compare and Contrast

Charlemagne earned his title of Charles the Great because he made a big difference in the lives of Europeans. What was life like during his reign?

▶ Make a copy of the chart below. Then fill in the blanks with facts about Europe before and during Charlemagne's reign. Some of the chart has been filled in for you.

	Before Charlemagne	**During Charlemagne's Reign**
Education		Education was encouraged Schools were set up Old writings were copied
Government		
Christianity	The Christian church had little support during the years before Charlemagne's rule	

ENRICHMENT

1. Pretend that you are Charlemagne's press secretary. Write three news releases that highlight major accomplishments under his leadership. One should concern the military, another religion, and the last, education and culture.

2. Do some research in the library on the Vikings and their ships. Then make a diagram of a Viking longship and label each part of the ship.

CHAPTER 3

The Byzantine Empire

▲ Inside Hagia Sophia today. The great church was built in Constantinople by the Byzantine emperor Justinian in A.D. 527.

OBJECTIVE: How did the Byzantine Empire carry on the culture and traditions of Rome?

1. He was the greatest ruler in the western world. He had driven back his enemies on all fronts and had built new cities, churches, and 700 forts. Now he wanted the capital city of the empire to have a glorious church that would be the finest building in the world. He was the emperor Justinian, and his church was indeed one of the greatest ever built. It was called Hagia Sophia, which means Holy Wisdom, but the people called it simply the Great Church. Its walls were covered with golden pictures, which sparkled in the light that streamed from

countless windows. Splendid works of art were everywhere. High above it all was a great dome 100 feet (31 meters) across. The dome was built in such a clever way that, as one ancient writer described it, it seemed "suspended from heaven by a golden

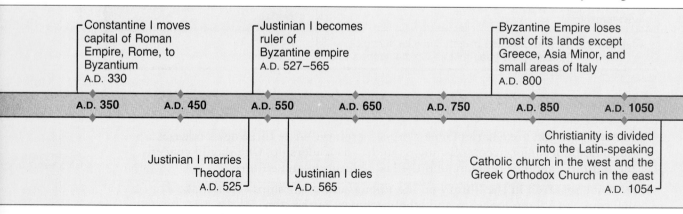

┌Constantine I moves capital of Roman Empire, Rome, to Byzantium A.D. 330	┌Justinian I becomes ruler of Byzantine empire A.D. 527–565	┌Byzantine Empire loses most of its lands except Greece, Asia Minor, and small areas of Italy A.D. 800

A.D. 350	A.D. 450	A.D. 550	A.D. 650	A.D. 750	A.D. 850	A.D. 1050

Justinian I marries Theodora A.D. 525┘	Justinian I dies └A.D. 565	Christianity is divided into the Latin-speaking Catholic church in the west and the Greek Orthodox Church in the east A.D. 1054┘

chain." This church was Justinian's way of showing the world that a new Christian empire had replaced the old pagan empire of Rome.

THE BYZANTINE EMPIRE: How did the Byzantine Empire come into existence?

2. In A.D. 330, the emperor Constantine I had moved the capital of the Roman Empire from Rome to Byzantium (bih-ZANT-ee-um). Byzantium was a Greek city in southeastern Europe. Constantine renamed the city Constantinople (kahn-stan-tih-NOH-pul), in honor of himself. After Constantine's death, the Roman Empire was divided into two parts, with Constantinople the capital of the eastern half. While the Germanic invasions gradually caused the Western Roman Empire to fall apart, the Eastern Roman Empire remained strong and united. In fact, the Eastern Roman Empire lasted for almost 1,000 years after the fall of Rome. This Eastern Roman Empire is also called the Byzantine (BIZ-un-teen) Empire, or sometimes just Byzantium, after the original name of its capital city.

3. For many centuries, Constantinople was the economic and cultural center of the Mediterranean world. On the map on page 182, find Constantinople. How would you describe its location? You should discover that the city is on the Bosporus (BAHS-pur-us), a strait that separates Europe and Asia. A strait is a narrow waterway connecting two larger bodies of water. What two bodies of water does the Bosporus connect? What trade routes do you think met at Constantinople? Traders from all over Europe came to Constantinople. They not only traded goods but they also exchanged art and ideas.

4. The heavy flow of trade brought great riches to Constantinople. **Profits** from trading silk cloth, fine woolens, jewelry, grain, and many other items poured into Constantinople. Profits are money earned from trade and business. Byzantine gold coins became the most valued form of money among European and Asian traders. The economic strength of the Byzantine Empire helped make the empire powerful. How might the wealth of Constantinople have helped the Byzantine Empire last for almost a thousand years?

SPOTLIGHT ON SOURCES

5. Byzantine emperors enjoyed showing off their power and wealth to visitors. Here a visitor from western Europe describes what he saw in the court of a Byzantine emperor in A.D. 949:

> Before the emperor's seat stood a tree, made of bronze gilded [painted with gold] over, whose branches were filled with birds, also made of gilded bronze, which uttered different cries. . . . The throne itself was of immense size and was guarded by lions, made either of bronze or of wood covered over with gold, who beat the ground with their tails and gave a dreadful roar. . . . At my approach the lions began to roar and the birds to cry out. . . . So after I had three times bowed to the emperor with my face upon the ground, I lifted my head and behold! the man who just before had been sitting on a slightly raised seat. . . . was sitting on the level of the ceiling. How it was done I could not imagine . . .
>
> —from *Antapodosis*, Liudprand of Cremona

JUSTINIAN I: How did Justinian's rule strengthen the Byzantine Empire?

6. One of the greatest Byzantine emperors was Justinian I (juss-TIN-ee-un), who ruled from A.D. 527 to A.D. 565. Justinian's goal was to bring together again the eastern and western parts of the old Roman Empire. That goal led to many costly wars in Italy and other lands around the Mediterranean Sea. Justinian did not completely reach his goal. However, his armies were able to add Italy, northern Africa, and parts of Spain to the Byzantine Empire. Look at

Background: The city of Byzantium was founded about 657 B.C. It was always important because of its location. Conflict had weakened it until Constantine moved the Roman Empire's capital there.

181

the map below. Compare it with the map on page 142. Which parts of the old Roman Empire were included in Justinian's Byzantine Empire? Which parts were not included in the Byzantine Empire?

7. In Constantinople, Justinian began a building program that added to the city's greatness and beauty. The most famous of his buildings is the great church of Hagia Sophia (HAH-ghee-ah Soh-FEE-ah). Hagia Sophia is an immense church, topped by a huge dome that seems to float on top of a ring of windows. Although it no longer contains the rich decorations that were in it during the Byzantine Empire, the church still stands as a monument to Byzantine faith and genius.

8. The most lasting achievement of Justinian's reign was his reform of the laws of the Roman Empire. Justinian ordered a group of scholars to collect all the existing laws. These scholars then studied these laws very carefully. Finally, they wrote down a summary of all these laws and organized them according to subject. This law code was called the Justinian Code. A **law code** is a group of laws arranged for easy use. The Justinian Code was one of the last important Byzantine documents to be written in Latin, the language of Rome. The code lives on today in the legal systems of every country in Europe except England, and in many countries outside Europe as well.

PEOPLE IN HISTORY

9. Theodora was one of the most powerful women in history. The wife of Justinian I, she fully shared in ruling the Byzantine Empire. Theodora was not born a princess, nor was her family even wealthy. Her father trained bears to perform at the Constantinople circus, and Theodora herself had been a child actress. When Justinian met her, she was a beautiful and intelligent young

▼ Roman traditions lived on in the Byzantine or Eastern Roman Empire long after the fall of Rome. What lands once ruled by Rome did the emperor Justinian add to the Byzantine Empire?

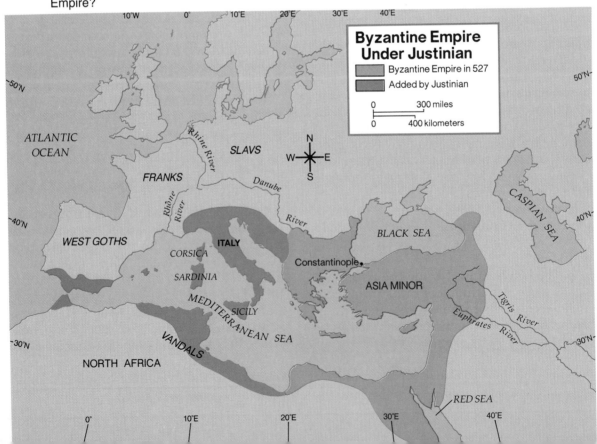

Byzantine Empire Under Justinian
- Byzantine Empire in 527
- Added by Justinian

0 — 300 miles
0 — 400 kilometers

woman in her early 20s. They were married in A.D. 525, when Theodora was about 25. Two years later, Justinian became emperor, and Theodora was crowned empress.

10. Theodora was a very strong-willed woman. Only five years after Justinian's rule began, a group of important people tried to overthrow his government. Most of Justinian's advisors told him that he should leave Constantinople. Theodora, however, told him that he should stay and fight his enemies. He followed Theodora's advice—and won. After that, Theodora's influence on the government grew. Because of her, the Byzantine Empire was one of the first governments to pass laws recognizing the rights of women. She often met with foreign ambassadors, and she had a voice in almost all the new laws that were passed.

11. For two centuries after Justinian's death in A.D. 565, the Byzantine Empire was at war much of the time. Enemies attacked from every direction. As a result, the empire lost many of its lands, including almost all of those that Justinian had conquered. By A.D. 800, the empire's land included only Greece, Asia Minor, and small areas of Italy.

RELIGION: How did religion affect the lives of people in the Byzantine Empire?

12. By the time of Justinian, Christianity had grown to become a major world religion. In the Byzantine Empire, the emperor was the supreme head of the church. The emperor chose the top church leaders. His right to rule was believed to come from God. In return for being God's ruler, the emperor had the duty to protect the people and guide them in Christian ways.

13. Christianity had a strong impact on the beautiful art of the Byzantine Empire. This art became famous for its wonderful use of **mosaics** (moh-ZAY-iks). Mosaics are pictures made of small pieces of colored stone, glass, and tile. Byzantine mosaics also included gold. The mosaics of Rome had shown hunts and banquets. What do you think the mosaics of the Byzantine Empire showed? The walls and ceilings of Byzantine churches were covered with glittering mosaics of religious figures. Byzantine artists also painted **icons** (EYE-kahnz), or pictures of religious figures like Christ and the saints. Icons were found in Byzantine homes as well as in churches.

14. As the Christian religion grew in numbers and importance, it also began to divide into two parts. In Italy and the Germanic kingdoms of western Europe, Christians looked to the bishop of Rome, now called the pope, as their leader. Here Latin, the language of the Western Roman Empire, was the language of the church. In the Byzantine Empire, where Greek was the language of the church, emperors and church leaders at first accepted the pope's authority. Gradually, however, the two parts of the church came to disagree on a number of important religious matters. In A.D. 1054 the split between eastern and western Christianity was made official. Christianity was now divided into the Latin-speaking Catholic church in the west and the Greek-speaking Orthodox church in the east.

OUTLOOK

15. The Byzantine Empire provided a great service to the modern world. For more than 1,000 years, the Byzantine Empire kept alive the cultures and laws of Greece and Rome. To this day, Byzantine art ranks among the world's most beautiful. After becoming the official religion of the Roman Empire, Christianity grew and spread. The Greek Orthodox church developed in Byzantium, while the Catholic church took shape in western Europe. At the same time, missionaries were bringing Christianity to parts of Europe where it had not been known before. Some of these countries were converted by Catholic missionaries, who looked to Rome for leadership. Others were converted by Orthodox missionaries, who looked to Constantinople. How do you think religious differences might affect relations between these two parts of Europe?

183

CHAPTER REVIEW

VOCABULARY REVIEW

Write each of the following sentences on a sheet of paper. Then fill in the blank with the word that best completes each sentence.

law codes   icons

mosaics   profits

1. _____ are pictures made with small pieces of colored stone, glass, and tile.
2. _____ are pictures of religious figures.
3. _____ are groups of laws arranged for easy use.
4. _____ are money earned from trade and business.

SKILL BUILDER: INTERPRETING A PHOTOGRAPH

Look at this photograph of a mosaic of Empress Theodora and her court. Then answer the questions about it on a separate piece of paper.

1. Empress Theodora is the figure just to the right of center. What clues in the mosaic tell you that she is the most important figure shown?
2. Look at the women at the left in the photo. They are women from Theodora's court. As a historian, what conclusions might you draw from observing their clothing?
3. The man standing beside Theodora is a priest. What is Theodora doing? What does her action tell you about her relationship with the church?

SKILL BUILDER: CRITICAL THINKING AND COMPREHENSION

1. Sequencing

▶ Write the letters of the following events in the correct sequence in which they happened.

a. Justinian becomes emperor of the Byzantine Empire.

b. The Byzantine Empire loses much of its land.

c. Constantine I moves the capital of the Roman Empire to Byzantium.

d. Justinian I dies.

e. Christianity is split between an eastern church and a western church.

f. Justinian I married Theodora.

2. Spatial Relationships

▶ How did the location of the Byzantine Empire help it become an important center of trade between Europe and Asia?

3. Cause and Effect

▶ For each pair of sentences, label the cause (C) and the effect (E).

3-1. a. Constantinople was located on an important trade route.
b. Constantinople became the economic and cultural center of the Mediterranean world.

3-2. a. The Eastern Roman Empire became strong and united.
b. Germanic invasions caused the Western Roman Empire to fall apart.

3-3. a. Hagia Sophia was a great church built in Constantinople.
b. Justinian wanted to add to Constantinople's greatness.

3-4. a. Justinian ordered a group of scholars to gather and reorganize the old Roman laws.
b. The Justinian Code of laws was written.

3-5. a. The Greek Orthodox Church and the Roman Catholic Church each had its own leader.
b. The Christian religion became divided into two parts.

4. Compare and Contrast

▶ Compare the achievements of the Byzantine Empire during Justinian's rule with the Byzantine Empire in A.D. 800.

ENRICHMENT

1. Reread the description of the Byzantine court in Spotlight on Sources. Imagine that you are the visitor in the story about life at court. Consider the description as the beginning of a story. Write an ending of the story.

2. Look again at the mosaic picture of Theodora from the Byzantine Empire. Then design a mosaic showing one of the persons or an event described in this chapter.

185

CHAPTER 4

Government in the Middle Ages

▲ Louis IX of France, known since his death as Saint Louis, was one of the greatest kings of the Middle Ages. One of America's greatest cities is named for him.

OBJECTIVE: How was western Europe governed during the Middle Ages?

1. In the 1960s, when John F. Kennedy was President, there were some people who called Washington, D.C., "Camelot." Camelot (KAM-ul-ot) was the home of King Arthur, the legendary superhero of the **Middle Ages**. The Middle Ages is the name given to the period of time covering about 1,000 years after the fall of Rome. Camelot was an ideal place, and Arthur was the ideal ruler. He was the hero of an age that was far from ideal, however. Arthur and his knights were too noble and good. They would never have survived the hardships and the reality of the **medieval** (mee-dee-EE-vul) period. The me-dieval period is another name for the middle ages. In this age, kings struggled for land and power, and ordinary people struggled just to stay alive. Camelot never existed, and Arthur lived only in people's imagination.

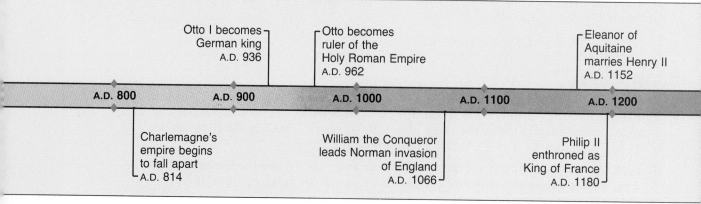

Otto I becomes German king
A.D. 936

Otto becomes ruler of the Holy Roman Empire
A.D. 962

Eleanor of Aquitaine marries Henry II
A.D. 1152

A.D. 800 — A.D. 900 — A.D. 1000 — A.D. 1100 — A.D. 1200

Charlemagne's empire begins to fall apart
A.D. 814

William the Conqueror leads Norman invasion of England
A.D. 1066

Philip II enthroned as King of France
A.D. 1180

Background: Tell students that the term feudalism is derived from the Latin *feodum*, which means fief, the land given by a lord to his vassals.

FEUDALISM: How did feudalism work? Why did it develop as a form of government?

2. After the break-up of Charlemagne's empire, a new system of government gradually took form in western Europe. This system is called **feudalism** (FYOO-dul-iz-um). Feudalism was different from modern governments, which usually are strong and **centralized** (SEN-trul-yzd). A centralized government is one in which the power comes from one central place or person. In the Middle Ages, however, feudalism was a **decentralized** (dee-SEN-trul-yzd) government. This meant that the power to govern was spread out among many local places and people.

3. Feudalism was based on ties of loyalty among the people. In feudalism a powerful person, called a **lord**, gave the right to rule part of his land to a less powerful person, called a **vassal** (VAS-ul). The land the lord gave to his vassal was called a **fief** (FEEF). The lord also promised to protect the vassal. In return, the vassal owed military service and other duties to the lord. Both lords and vassals were fighting men.

4. There were several levels of lords and vassals. The most powerful lord was the king. Next most powerful were the greater lords, who were vassals of the king and usually had the title of duke or count. Under the greater lords were lesser lords, who often had vassals of their own. In feudalism, the least powerful were the knights, who had no vassals. However, to be a knight in armor was a great honor in medieval times. The kings and their vassals made up the **ruling class** of medieval Europe. This ruling class was the small group of people in Europe who held all the power. Members of the ruling class were called nobles or, as a group, the nobility. Which person in the feudal system was a lord but not a vassal?

5. Feudalism developed gradually as a way of bringing order to western Europe. It did not appear in every country at the same time, nor did it develop in the same way in every place. Feudalism depended on lords and vassals sharing power. However, each feudal group tried to increase its power at the expense of other groups. Kings continually tried to gain greater, more centralized power. Vassals wanted to keep as much power as possible for themselves. This struggle for power had different outcomes in different countries.

FEUDALISM IN FRANCE: How did the medieval kings of France gain power over the nobles?

6. In the early Middle Ages, France was ruled by weak kings who were kings in name only. They ruled only small areas and had trouble ruling even there. The rest of France was divided among the nobles. Why was the French king unable to control the nobles? Only some of the nobles were the king's vassals, and only these men had to obey the king. Many other nobles were vassals of other lords, and they obeyed those lords.

7. Within his own fief, every noble had full power to govern. Medieval kings were not strong enough to put down the many wars between their own vassals. Nobles loved to fight. Fights over boundaries, family quarrels, and disputes between lords and vassals were some of the many reasons why nobles fought.

8. In the twelfth century, the kings of France took steps to gain more power over the nobles. French kings in the early part of the century improved their prestige by using all the royal power and feudal rights they had. However, it was a series of great kings beginning in the late twelfth century who finally gained the greatest success. Philip II was one of these kings. Philip was a bold feudal warrior. He also was clear-headed and very shrewd. Philip used his power to put down rebellions by some of his vassals. By the end of these wars, Philip II had doubled the size of his land. Philip used people who were not feudal lords to help him rule France. How would this move weaken the power of the nobles? As a result of Philip's rule, France was on its way to becoming Europe's leading monarchy.

Activity: On the chalkboard, draw a triangle to represent the pyramid of feudal power. Ask students to determine where on the pyramid each level of power would fall. Write these levels on the triangle where indicated by students.

187

▲ In a feudal system of government, lords gave their vassals land to rule in exchange for military service and other duties. Here a king is shown with some of his vassals.

SPOTLIGHT ON SOURCES

9. Philip II's grandson, Louis IX, was thought by most people to be the ideal medieval king. Louis IX was a just and peace-loving ruler who was best known for the order and justice he brought to the French kingdom. Here a friend and servant describes Louis IX as a judge.

> . . . Often in the summer [Louis IX] went after Mass to the wood of Vincennes and sat down with his back against an oak tree, and made us sit all around him. Everyone who had [a case] to settle could come and speak to him . . . The King would speak himself and ask, "Is there any one here who has a case to settle?" All those who had would then stand up and he would say, "Quiet, all of you, and your cases shall be dealt with in turn." . . . Once in the summer I saw him as he went to the gardens in Paris to give judgment for his people. He wore a tunic of natural wool, a sleeveless surcoat of cotton, and a black satin cloak around his shoulders; he wore no cap, but his hair was well combed, and on his head he wore a hat of white peacocks' feathers. He had carpets spread so that we could sit about him, and all who had business with him would stand around. . . .

> —*Western Awakening: Sources of Medieval History*, Charles T. Davis, ed. (New York: Irvington Publishers, 1967)

FEUDALISM IN ENGLAND: How did the medieval kings of England make the feudal system more centralized?

10. Until the end of the eleventh century, England was made up of small Anglo-Saxon kingdoms. The Angles, Saxons, and other Germanic groups had moved into Britain after the Romans left in A.D. 410. The Anglo-Saxon period ended with the takeover of England by the Normans. The Normans were Vikings who had settled in northern France. In A.D. 1066, William, the duke of Normandy, crossed the English Channel

▲ William the Conqueror gives orders to his soldiers in this scene on the Bayeux Tapestry. William led the Norman conquest of England in A.D. 1066.

from France with about 5,000 knights and defeated the Anglo-Saxons at the Battle of Hastings. William the Conqueror, as he has since been called, became king of England.

11. William the Conqueror brought feudalism to England. He used feudalism in such a way that the nobles did not become more powerful than himself. William took the largest amount of land for himself. He broke up the rest into small fiefs. William then gave these fiefs to his Norman followers. He also demanded that all vassals, whether they were the king's vassals or not, ▶ must be loyal to him. What problem of the French kings was William trying to avoid?

12. William set up a centralized government in England. He counted on local officials, called sheriffs, to collect taxes and find soldiers for his army. William also sent officials out to gather information about all the land in the kingdom. Which officials under Charlemagne traveled to different parts of his kingdom? William's officials recorded information in two huge volumes called the *Domesday Book*. These records helped the king decide what taxes people should pay. The information in this survey also has helped historians learn about England under the Normans.

13. England's greatest king in the twelfth century was Henry II. Henry had tremendous energy and worked so hard that he tired out his own officials. Under him, government in England ran very smoothly. Henry II is best remembered for the changes he made in English law. Henry had judges travel to different parts of England to try criminal cases. By hearing local cases in royal courts, Henry took power away from the courts of the nobles. Why might the royal judges be fairer to the people than feudal lords? In each town, the traveling judges would find citizens to report on criminals in their neighborhoods. These people swore an oath that they would tell the truth. This group of people was known as a **jury**. Henry II was the first ruler to make regular use of juries. Henry also used juries to hear evidence as well as to decide whether a person was guilty of a crime. In this way, the king's law slowly replaced feudal law. How are juries used today? ◀

189

▲ Eleanor of Aquitaine and Henry II of England were played by Katharine Hepburn and Peter O'Toole in the *The Lion in Winter*, a popular film for which Hepburn won an Academy Award.

14. Henry II was married to a strong-willed woman named Eleanor of Aquitaine. Aquitaine (AK-wuh-tayn) was one of the largest fiefs in medieval France, and its duke was one of France's most powerful nobles. The land over which a duke ruled was called a **duchy** (DUCH-ee). Eleanor, the daughter of a duke of Aquitaine, played a key role in governing first France and then England.

PEOPLE IN HISTORY

15. Eleanor of Aquitaine was born about 1122. She grew up to be a bright young woman, full of life. After her father's death, Eleanor became ruler of the vast duchy of Aquitaine, in southern France. The French nobles thought her to be a great marriage prize, since she ruled more land than the king of France himself. The king was happy when he was able to arrange the marriage of 15-year-old Eleanor to his 17-year-old son. The marriage added most of southern France to the land directly controlled by the king.

16. Soon Eleanor would prove to be a powerful leader with a mind of her own. In 1137 her young husband was crowned King Louis VII. As his wife, Eleanor advised him on political and military matters. However, Louis ended their marriage because there was no male heir. Shortly thereafter, Eleanor married Henry, duke of Normandy and heir to the English throne. This marriage brought a large part of France into English hands. After their marriage, Eleanor's husband became King Henry II. Together, Eleanor and Henry ruled over England, Normandy in northern France, and Aquitaine in southern France. Together they controlled a larger part of France than the French king did.

17. Eleanor's marriage to Henry II proved to be a troubled one. For one thing, Eleanor sided with her sons against their father. In 1185 Eleanor returned to Aquitaine, where she set up her own court. Eleanor's court became a center for poets, singers, and scholars from all over Europe.

Background: Eleanor of Aquitaine had three daughters and five sons with Henry II, who was 11 years younger than she. Only two of their sons survived their father, Richard I ("the Lionhearted") and John. Eleanor sided with her two sons in their rebellion against Henry in 1173.

Singers and poets proclaimed the beauty of life, love, and women. Their works, which showed great respect for women, spread to the other courts of Europe. Until her death at the age of 82, Eleanor was active in government. During her long life, she had married kings, fought battles, ruled kingdoms, and inspired poets.

THE HOLY ROMAN EMPIRE: How did Otto I gain power as a ruler?

18. The Holy Roman Empire began in the land that earlier had been the eastern part of Charlemagne's empire. Look at the map on page 178. As in medieval France, the German rulers in this part of Charlemagne's empire held little power during the ninth century. The rulers of the large duchies held the real power. However, things began to change when the duke of Saxony, Otto I, was chosen king of Germany in A.D. 936.

19. Soon after he became king, Otto the Great, as he has been called, gained more control over the German dukes. He kept the largest duchies in his own hands. However, Otto also asked the church to help him govern. He chose his advisors from among church leaders. Otto gave land to bishops of the church. The bishops became Otto's vassals and used their armies to aid him in his struggle with the German dukes. In return, Otto helped protect the church. When the pope asked Otto for help against the Roman nobles, Otto invaded Italy. In return, in A.D. 962 the pope declared Otto Emperor of the Romans. The lands Otto ruled became known as the Holy Roman Empire. This huge empire included all of Germany and the northern part of Italy.

20. The emperors who followed Otto I made the Holy Roman Empire even more powerful by adding more land and becoming closer allies of the pope. The empire reached the peak of its power in the eleventh century. Thereafter, the emperors' desire to control Italy weakened the Holy Roman Empire. While the emperors fought in Italy, the nobles in Germany regained their power. They ruled their little areas

▲ The German king Otto I receives several dukes at his court. Otto used the church's support to create the Holy Roman Empire in 962.

independently, largely free from control by the emperor, whose position became mainly honorary. As a result, Germany did not become a unified country like France or England. Instead, It remained divided into many small feudal states until the 1800s.

OUTLOOK

21. What might have happened to western Europe without feudalism? Western Europe would not have become what it is today. The loyalties of lords and vassals brought better order and organization to a world of warring barbarians. This order was the first step toward the development of powerful monarchies in western Europe. As a result, medieval rulers were able to establish strong centralized governments in England and France. Why do you think the ◄ system of feudalism could not continue into today's world?

Background: Saxony was one of the five duchies which comprised Germany in the ninth and tenth centuries. The others were Bavaria, Franconia, Swabia, and Lorraine.

CHAPTER REVIEW

VOCABULARY REVIEW

On a separate piece of paper, write each number and word listed below. Then write the letter of the definition next to the word it matches.

1. Middle Ages
2. feudalism
3. vassal
4. fief
5. duchy
6. decentralized
7. jury
8. medieval
9. centralized
10. lord
11. ruling class

a. a word that means Middle Ages in Latin

b. a group of people who helped the judge decide cases in England

c. the name given to the period between the fall of Rome and the beginning of modern times

d. a lesser lord who was given the right to rule his land by a greater lord

e. a system of government in which power is spread out among many local places and people

f. the land the greater lord gave to his vassal

g. government in which the power comes from one central place or person

h. a powerful person who gave the right to rule part of his land to a less powerful person

i. system of government in which lords gave land to their vassals in return for military service and other duties

j. the land ruled by a duke

k. the group of people in Europe who held all the power

SKILL BUILDER: READING A TIME LINE

Use the time line below to answer the questions about the life of Eleanor of Aquitaine.

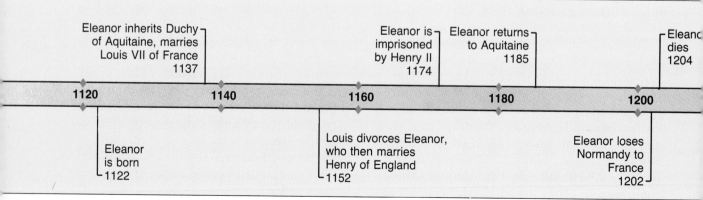

Eleanor inherits Duchy of Aquitaine, marries Louis VII of France 1137

Eleanor is imprisoned by Henry II 1174

Eleanor returns to Aquitaine 1185

Eleanor dies 1204

1120   1140   1160   1180   1200

Eleanor is born 1122

Louis divorces Eleanor, who then marries Henry of England 1152

Eleanor loses Normandy to France 1202

1. When did Eleanor marry Louis VII of France?
2. How old was Eleanor when she married Henry II?
3. What key event in Eleanor's life took place in 1174?
4. How long did Eleanor live?

SKILL BUILDER: CRITICAL THINKING AND COMPREHENSION

1. Cause and Effect

▶ Below are listed four causes and four effects. Write the effect statement next to the number of the cause it matches.

Cause

1-1. Europeans needed a way of bringing order and government to their lands.

1-2. King Philip used royal officials instead of nobles to help him govern.

1-3. Otto I saved the pope.

1-4. The nobles gained control in Germany.

Effect

a. The power of the nobles in France declined.

b. Otto I was named Holy Roman Emperor.

c. Feudalism developed.

d. Germany did not become a unified country.

2. Introduction to Drawing Conclusions

Detectives often solve mysteries by using clues. This process is called deductive reasoning because people try to decide what has happened by examining clues. Historians often must act like detectives. For example, when historians study a past civilization, they have to put together many pieces of information to help them learn about that civilization.

▶ Below are three statements and possible conclusions about those statements. Write the number of each statement, and after it write the conclusion that best fits.

2-1. A picture of a medieval battle shows two groups of armored warriors fighting.

2-2. Women of medieval times wore layers of clothing.

2-3. There are many pictures of castles in books about the Middle Ages.

Possible Conclusions

Everyone lived in castles in the Middle Ages

It was the fashion for women of the Middle Ages to often change their clothing.

Most medieval battles were fought to defend church lands.

Castles helped protect lords from attacks by their enemies.

Warriors of the Middle Ages protected themselves by wearing metal armor.

Women of the Middle Ages wore layers of clothing because houses and castles often were cold and damp.

ENRICHMENT

1. Research and report on the steps a young man had to go through to become a knight. Use an encyclopedia or a book on knights as the source for your report.

2. Imagine you are a poet at the French court of Eleanor of Aquitaine. Write a poem about the queen in which you praise her for one of her special qualities.

CHAPTER 5

Manor and Town Life

▲ Villagers harvest hay in this idealized picture of life on a medieval manor. A moat and wall surround the lord's castle.

OBJECTIVE: How did people live on medieval manors and in medieval towns?

1. Suppose you saw an advertisement like this in the housing section of the newspaper: "Large home available. Located on hilltop with views for miles. Woodburning fireplaces. No glass in windows, so fresh air comes in all year long. Stone floors and walls guarantee that all rooms stay cold, dark, and damp. Almost no furniture. No heating except for fireplaces. No ▶ plumbing." Would you move into such a house? If you had a choice, you probably would not. However, most people of the Middle Ages would have jumped at the chance to live in this kind of castle. This is what the best housing was like then, and only the feudal lords and their families enjoyed such luxury. Most families had to settle for one-room huts with dirt floors. Life in the growing towns was usually crowded, noisy, and smelly. Whether rich or poor, in the village of a manor or in one of the growing towns, life in the Middle Ages had few comforts.

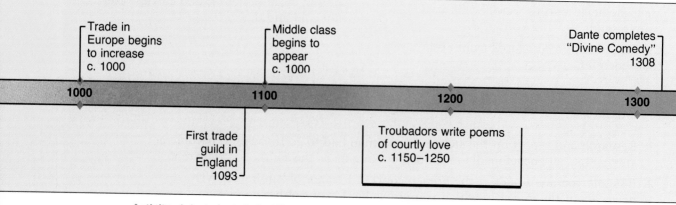

Trade in
Europe begins
to increase
c. 1000

Middle class
begins to
appear
c. 1000

Dante completes
"Divine Comedy"
1308

1000	1100	1200	1300

First trade
guild in
England
1093

Troubadors write poems
of courtly love
c. 1150–1250

Activity: Ask students to find the parts of the castle in the opening photograph of the chapter as they read paragraph 2.

MANOR LIFE: What was life like in a lord's castle and in a peasant's hut?

2. Village life in the Middle Ages centered around the manor. The manor was the land owned by the lord. The most important building on a manor was the lord's castle. Since the lord of the manor spent most of his time fighting wars or getting ready to fight, his castle was built to be a lookout and a fortress as well as a home. The castle was built with stone and had at least one thick wall surrounding its yard. The walls were topped by small towers. From these towers, arrows could be shot at the enemy and stones dropped on them. Surrounding the castle wall on the outside was a deep trench filled with water. This was the **moat** (MOHT). A drawbridge across the moat could be raised to keep people out.

3. Life in a castle was not always pleasant and comfortable. The castle was built entirely of stone. Since cement and mortar were unknown, there were many cracks in the walls. Glass was rare and expensive, so animal skins usually covered the windows. The windows themselves were often just slits in the wall from which arrows could be shot. Straw, reeds, and other grasses were scattered on the floors to help keep the floors dry. Sweet-smelling herbs and flowers were mixed with the grasses as a room freshener. Bad smells were a problem in castles, because food scraps and other gar-

bage were often just left on the floor. Before there were fireplaces, a large cooking fire was built in the middle of the floor. The smoke was let out through a hole in the ceiling.

4. The peasants lived outside the walls of the lord's castle, in villages of 200 to 500 people. Peasant families lived in small huts made of mud or wood with straw roofs. These huts had only one room. As in the castle, there were no glass windows, only holes in the walls. There were no chimneys either. What do you think happened in the ◀ huts when a fire was lit in winter?

5. Nearly all of the peasants' time was spent farming. Peasants had to farm both the lord's land and the land they were allowed to use for themselves. In return for the use of this land, the peasants had to pay the lord in goods or services. If peasants fished in a stream of the manor, they had to give the lord a part of what they caught. If their pigs fed in the woods of the manor, the peasants had to pay the lord in pork. What ◀ did the lord provide the peasants in return for their work besides the use of the land?

6. Peasants usually belonged to one of three groups. Some were slaves, who could be bought or sold by the lords. Others were **serfs**, who were tied to the land. A serf was considered as much a part of a manor as its trees or buildings. Serfs were not free to leave the manor, nor could they be forced to

Daily life in . . .

Imagine a woman of the Middle Ages walking past the makeup counters of a department store today. Believe it or not, she probably would feel right at home. Beauty aids were very popular in the Middle Ages. Medieval women used oils and creams to improve the complexion. Herbs also were popular. Rosemary mixed with white wine was believed to be an aid to facial beauty. Red lily was used for blushing the cheeks, and the root of the madonna lily was used to make the face whiter.

To cover gray hair, people applied a mixture of iron, gall nuts, and alum boiled in vinegar. Perfumes from sweet-smelling flowers, such as lavender and roses, were used by many. Noblewomen and peasant women alike would buy combs, mirrors, hair frizzers or curlers, powder, and toothbrushes from the town peddler. By the end of the Middle Ages, makeup and beauty aids had become so widespread that reformers tried to put an end to their use.

Background: Some of the games people would play in the Middle Ages were blindman's bluff, checkers, backgammon, chess, and other board games.

195

leave. The third class were the **freemen**, who owned or rented their land and could come and go as they pleased. The numbers in these three groups changed somewhat as the times changed. The greatest number of peasants were serfs. The number of slaves became smaller and the number of freemen grew larger as the Middle Ages progressed.

TRADE AND TOWNS: How did trade cause the growth of towns in the Middle Ages?

7. After the year 1000, there was a gradual increase in trade in western Europe. Earlier, during the Germanic invasions, trade in western Europe had nearly stopped. With no trade to keep them going, towns shrank in size, and some even disappeared. But after A.D. 1000, as western Europe grew stronger, trade began to revive. Old Roman towns were resettled. New towns sprang up along overland trade routes, along rivers, and near harbors. Why did towns appear in such places?

8. Medieval towns often were crowded and dirty. Streets were narrow and twisting, dark and foul-smelling. Houses were jammed together, allowing little light to reach the streets. People had no other place to throw their garbage and waste but into the streets. There were no sewers or plumbing, and water often was polluted. Why was disease a problem in medieval towns?

9. Growing trade also led to the growth of trade fairs. A trade fair was a gathering of people to buy and sell goods and to do business with one another. Trade fairs attracted people not only from nearby villages. They also brought traders from faraway cities and countries. At trade fairs you would have found woolen cloth from Flanders and furs from northern Europe. You also might have found silks, spices, and rugs from faraway Asia.

10. Many people came to these fairs just to have a good time. Imagine how crowded and noisy the narrow streets of medieval towns would be on a busy shopping day during a trade fair! People would take part in dancing, wrestling, and games of chance. Acrobats and jugglers also would put on a good show for the crowds. People would marvel at the strange languages and customs of visitors from faraway places.

▼ The walled city of Siena in Italy prospered as trade and city life revived throughout Europe during the Middle Ages.

ESL/LEP Strategy: Have students review the meanings of the words *moat, serfs, castle, manor, lord,* and *peasants* on pages 194–195. Then, ask them to choose three of these words to illustrate on flashcards. Have students use the cards to test one another.

THE RISE OF THE MIDDLE CLASS: What was the middle class, and what changes did it bring to Europe?

11. The most important result of the growth of towns in the Middle Ages was the rise of the **middle class**. It was called "middle" because its status was higher than the peasants but lower than the lords. This middle class was made up of merchants and other townspeople. A merchant was a business person who bought and sold goods for profit. Members of the middle class were different from both lords and peasants in medieval society. They were not lords, nor did they work on the manor for a lord. Unlike the lords, the power and wealth of the middle class was measured in money, not by the land it owned.

12. As trade increased, merchants and other townspeople organized themselves into guilds. A **guild** (GILD) was an organization to protect the interests of people who worked in the same trade or business. Only merchant guild members could open shops and sell goods. The guilds also set rules for their members to follow in doing business. Guilds also were able to buy large amounts of goods for their members at lower prices than a single merchant would have paid.

13. Merchants also found new ways to increase profits by borrowing money on credit. **Credit** (KREH-dit) is the trust that a person will pay back the money he or she borrows. The medieval merchants used credit to buy businesses that would make more money for them. In the late Middle Ages, merchants joined with other merchants to form corporations to do business in money-lending, banking, and international trade. A **corporation** (kor-por-AY-shun) is an organization in which many people own shares in a business. The merchants of the Middle Ages began many of today's business practices.

14. Another change brought by the new middle class was in education. Before middle class children could join the family business, they had to learn how to read, write, and work with numbers. Schools

▲ A banker deals with a customer. Bankers grew wealthy in the Middle Ages lending money to merchants and traders.

were started by guilds and the church to teach children what they needed to know. In this way, towns became centers of learning. Students also paid wandering scholars to teach them. By the twelfth century these students and teachers had also formed guilds to protect their interests. Out of these teaching guilds grew Europe's first universities.

LITERATURE: How did literature develop in the Middle Ages?

15. People of the Middle Ages greatly enjoyed stories and poems of love and romance. Much of this interest had to do with the knight's code of behavior called **chivalry** (SHIH-vul-ree). Chivalry taught knights to be gentlemen as well as heroes. Knights pledged their loyalty not only to their lords but to the leading women of the court as well.

Background: Books were expensive during the Middle Ages. Not until after Johann Gutenberg's invention of the printing press in the 1450s did books gradually become more available to students.

A Geographic View of History

Strategic Straits   In the Middle Ages, trade moved mainly by sea. The ships were small wooden sailing vessels. They had only primitive navigational tools, and captains found their way by following familiar landmarks along the coast.

The map on this page shows some of the major trade routes in Europe during the Middle Ages. Only a few of the trade routes went overland. Most hugged the coast and passed from sea to sea through narrow straits. Study these facts about straits and trade routes.

Straits are important because they are narrow and easy to fortify. Traffic through them can be controlled by forts built on one or both shorelines.

Straits funnel traffic to the advantage of trading cities built alongside them.

Some straits are so narrow that people on one shore can see across to the other shore. The Strait of Gibraltar, for example, is only about 8 miles (13 kilometers) wide at its narrowest point.

The English Channel ends in a narrow strait guarding the main entrance to the North Sea.

Bruges, Antwerp, and London were protected when a friendly power ruled the English Channel.

The Strait of Gibraltar guards the western entrance to the Mediterranean Sea. Tangiers grew rich trading with ships that passed through the narrow strait.

The island of Sicily guards two straits linking the eastern and western ends of the Mediterranean Sea.

The Bosporus and the Dardanelles guard the entrance to the Black Sea. Constantinople prospered selling Asian luxury goods to traders from Venice and Genoa.

Answer the following questions, using the above information and the map below.

1. What symbol and color are used on the map to show straits? How many are indicated in this way?

2. List the straits a merchant from Genoa would use to reach Novgorod entirely by sea.

3. What is the special importance of the Bosporus and Dardanelles and the Skaggerak and Kattegat?

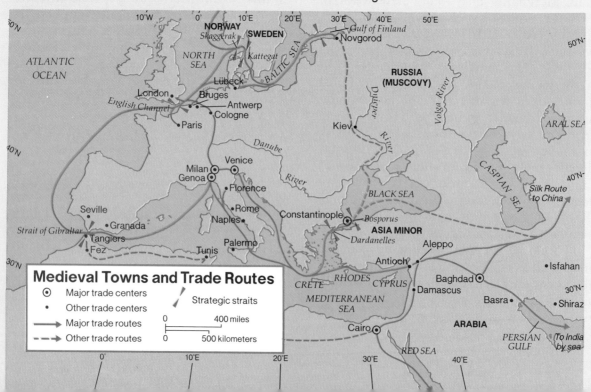

Medieval Towns and Trade Routes
- ⊙ Major trade centers
- • Other trade centers
- → Major trade routes
- --→ Other trade routes
- / Strategic straits

0   400 miles
0   500 kilometers

SPOTLIGHT ON SOURCES

16. Most of the poems of courtly love were written by wandering poets called **troubadours** (TROO-buh-dorz). Most troubadours were men. They sang verses in praise of the beauty and charm of the women of the court. In these songs, they always said that they were hopelessly in love and that they would do anything the lady ordered. A few troubadours, however, were women, who wrote poems about their love for handsome knights. Castelloza was one of these women troubadours. Here is part of one of her poems.

> All other love's worth naught,
> and every joy is meaningless to me
> but yours, which gladdens and restores
>   me,
> in which there's not a trace of pain or
>   of distress;
> and I think I'll be glad always and
>   rejoice
> always in you, friend . . .
>
> I don't know why you're always on
>   my mind,
> for I've searched and searched from
>   good to evil
> your hard heart, and yet my own's
>   unswerving . . .
>
> —Castelloza, *Whoever Blames My*
> *Love*, translated by Meg Bogin

▶ What kind of music today might have been influenced by the love poems of the Middle Ages?

17. The work of the troubadours had an effect on more serious writers of the late Middle Ages. One of the greatest of these writers was Dante Alighieri (DAHN-tee al-ih-GYEH-ree). Dante, an Italian poet, wrote his masterpiece, a long poem called the *Divine Comedy*, in the 1300s. As a young man, Dante had loved a woman named Beatrice. She is the key figure in the *Divine Comedy*, which tells of a journey from earth to hell and then to paradise.

▲ A troubadour sings to his lady in the garden of a medieval castle. This illustration depicts a scene from a popular poem of the Middle Ages.

OUTLOOK

18. As strange as life in the Middle Ages might seem to you, what happened then has changed our lives for the better. The idea that people can move up in the world because of the work they do was started by the merchants of the Middle Ages. Workers today who depend on unions to protect their rights owe thanks to the medieval guilds. Today's accountants and bankers profit from the ideas of medieval merchants, who brought order and system to the business world. The school that you attend has its origin in the medieval schools. The whole idea of a college education and the way it helps people's chances in life had its roots in the Middle Ages. In your daily life, too, every time you are touched by the sweet chords of a love song, think of the troubadours.

Ask: What role do you think education played in the rise in power of the middle class and the fall of the feudal lords?

CHAPTER REVIEW

Write each of the following words on a piece of paper. After it, write the correct definition for each.

1. moat   **4.** corporation   **7.** freemen

2. guilds   **5.** chivalry   **8.** middle class

3. credit   **6.** troubadours   **9.** serfs

a. merchants and other townspeople thought of as a group

b. wandering poets

c. an organization in which many owners share in a business

d. a peasant who could move from place to place

e. an organization for people in the same trade or business

f. trust that a person will repay borrowed money

g. a deep trench filled with water as part of a castle's defenses

h. the code of behavior of a medieval knight

i. a peasant who was considered part of a manor

SKILL BUILDER: COMPLETING A TABLE

Copy the following table on a sheet of paper. Use information from the chapter to fill in the table.

CHANGES IN THE MIDDLE AGES

	Reasons for Change	Description of Change
Middle Class		
Guilds		
Credit		
Corporations		
Education		

SKILL BUILDER: CRITICAL THINKING AND COMPREHENSION

☐ **1. Spatial Relationships**

▶ How did trade fairs affect people from other parts of the world?

STUDY HINT To show how events relate to each other as causes and effects, make a flow chart. Start by drawing two squares, with an arrow pointing from the left one to the right one. Continue until you have a full picture of the relationship of causes and effects in the chapter.

2. Cause and Effect

▶ Read the following statements, and fill in the blanks.

a. *Cause:* Merchants and townspeople wanted to ______ .
Effect: They organized themselves into guilds.

b. *Cause:* Medieval people liked songs about love and romance.
Effect: ______ .

c. *Cause:* ______ .
Effect: Trade fairs grew up in many places.

d. *Cause:* ______
Effect: In a castle, the windows usually were covered with animal skins.

e. *Cause:* Trade began to revive after A.D. 1000.
Effect: New towns ______ .

3. Compare and Contrast

▶ Copy the following chart. Use the chart to compare and contrast the living conditions of a lord and a peasant. Note that you should compare their lives in at least three ways.

Peasant	Lord

4. Drawing Conclusions

4-1. Read the *Daily Life in . . .* section. Then answer this question: After reading about the use of beauty aids, what can you conclude about the importance or unimportance of a woman's appearance in the Middle Ages?

4-2. Reread paragraphs 3, 4, and 8. Then answer this question: From the information in these paragraphs, what can you conclude about sanitation in the Middle Ages and the effects on people's health?

ENRICHMENT

1. Using encyclopedias or other reference books in the library, research the architecture of a castle of the Middle Ages. List the elements in the castle's design. Then make a diagram of a castle, showing the purpose or use of each feature on your list.
2. Imagine you live in a medieval town. Write a letter to a friend who lives on a manor. Give several reasons why you think your friend would like living in a town.
3. Research the steps by which a crafts guild member learned a trade in the Middle Ages. Then prepare a biographical sketch of the crafts worker. Explain the time and training needed to go from apprenticeship to journeymen to master.

CHAPTER 6

The Role of the Church in the Middle Ages

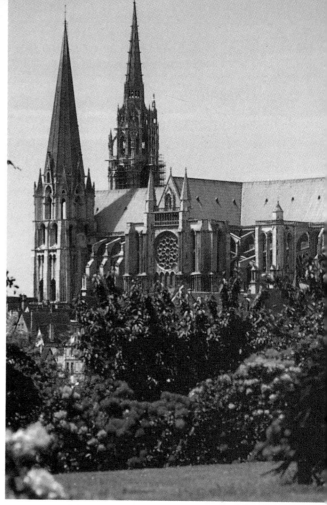

▲ The spires of Chartres cathedral were not built at the same time, and each shows the style of a different century.

OBJECTIVE: Why was the church powerful in the Middle Ages?

1. Suppose you are flying in an airplane over the city or town where you live. You can see every building and street in town, and you can see them all at the same time. What one thing would stand out above everything else when looking at your city or town from above? Now suppose that instead of your own town, you were flying above a medieval town or village. What would you expect to stand out most? What probably would have stood out above everything else was the spire of a church reaching upward toward the sky. Whether plain or richly decorated, it would soar over houses and fields, making everything else look smaller. What would this tell you about ◄ what was important in the Middle Ages?

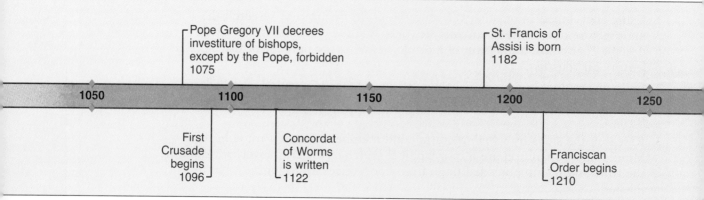

Pope Gregory VII decrees investiture of bishops, except by the Pope, forbidden 1075

St. Francis of Assisi is born 1182

| 1050 | 1100 | 1150 | 1200 | 1250 |

First Crusade begins 1096

Concordat of Worms is written 1122

Franciscan Order begins 1210

ESL/LEP Strategy: As students read about each event on the timeline, ask them to write a sentence that explains the effect on the Middle Ages and on the role of the church.

Background: The Roman Catholic church recognizes seven sacraments. Most Protestant churches recognize only two.

THE SPIRITUAL CHURCH: How did the church influence the everyday lives of people in the Middle Ages?

2. The center of all medieval life was the church. Why did the church play such an important role in the lives of medieval people? Medieval people believed that their souls could be saved only through the church. The people of the church whose job was to make salvation possible for everyone were the **clergy**. The clergy were the priests and bishops who performed certain important ceremonies of the church called **sacraments** (SAK-ruh-munts). Members of the church believe that sacraments are an outward sign of God's mercy toward sinning human beings. Most priests and bishops lived among the people in towns and villages.

3. Other members of the clergy lived apart from the outside world. These were the monks who lived in monasteries. The monks had little or no contact with people in the outside world. However, in the 1200s, some groups of monks decided to leave the monastery and preach among the people. These monks were called **friars** (FRY-urz). The friars wandered freely among the people, teaching about Christ and depending on the people for their own food and shelter. One order of friars, called Franciscans, was started in 1210. Its founder was a remarkable man named Francis of Assisi.

PEOPLE IN HISTORY

4. Francis was born in Assisi, Italy, in 1182. His father was a rich merchant, but Francis had little interest in participating in the family business. He just wanted to enjoy life. Francis was a generous, charming young man who had a sense of humor and a love of poetry, music, and nature. When Francis was about twenty, he fought for Assisi in a war with another Italian city. Francis was captured by the enemy and taken prisoner for about a year. In prison, Francis spent many hours thinking about the meaning of life.

5. After seeing a vision of Jesus, Francis decided to give up his money and his worldly pleasures to serve God. He dedicated his life to teaching the importance of loving people and trying to live his life as Jesus had lived. Like Jesus, he walked from town to town, spreading the gospel and preaching love for all creatures. Soon his message and his way of life attracted many followers. Francis founded an order called the Friars Minor (FRY-urz MY-nur), or "Little Brothers." These friars in gray cloaks, also called "Franciscans," were soon a familiar sight in towns throughout Europe. Through their simple lives and good works, Franciscans helped the church's influence grow.

Daily life in . . .

One of the most important Christian sacraments is baptism. Baptism is a rite by which a person becomes a member of the church. For rich and poor alike, the ceremony of baptism was a reason to celebrate in the Middle Ages. A new Christian life had begun! After the ceremony, parties for guests followed. Gifts were given. The lord of a manor sometimes gave a peasant woman some fish from his stream, or perhaps he gave her some firewood. In German villages, peasant women received a gift of wine and white bread at their children's baptism. A finer gift, especially in England, was a set of silver spoons. They were given in sets of two or four, or even twelve or fourteen. Most people of the Middle Ages received the sacraments from the priest of the **parish** (PAIR-ish), or local church. Only members of the clergy could give the sacraments to the people. How does this fact explain why the clergy had so much power in medieval society?

Background: Orders of friars, such as Franciscans and Dominicans, were formed to fight heresy. The orders later became devoted to learning and education.

▲ Francis of Assisi loved all living creatures. Once he preached a sermon about God's love to a flock of birds.

THE WORLDLY CHURCH: What powers did the church have in ruling medieval society?

▶ **6.** The church played an important part in the government of the Middle Ages. Can you guess why? How was power measured in the medieval period? The church owned a large amount of land. Much of this land had been received as gifts from dying kings or lords. This land made powerful feudal lords of many archbishops, bishops, and other church leaders. Since members of the clergy were not allowed to fight, they had people from the feudal class as vassals. These vassals would give military service in return for these fiefs. Church leaders themselves thus became great feudal lords. Why would the support of these church nobles be more important to a king than would be the support of other lords?

7. The church also became rich in other ways. Each parish church was given land and a share of the crops of the manor to which it belonged. The parish priest lived off this land as well as from the money he received from the **tithe** (TYTH). The tithe was a tax on the earnings of all people of the parish, usually one tenth of their income. Part of the money from this tax was given to the bishop. The rest was divided between the parish and the lord. Who would get most of the tithe money on the manors where the lord was a bishop?

8. The church also had its own system of courts. In **ecclesiastical** (ek-klee-zee-AS-tih-kul), or church, courts, bishops would decide whether someone had broken church laws. One kind of case that the ecclesiastical courts handled was **heresy** (HAIR-uh-see). Christians were charged with heresy if they held beliefs different from church doctrine. Payment of a fine was the usual way people were punished for their crimes against church law, but people who committed serious offenses could be **excommunicated** (eks-kuh-MYOO-nih-kay-tid). To excommunicate someone is to cut the person off from receiving the sacraments. The pope and the bishops had the power to excommunicate. Church members were not allowed to have anything to do with an excommunicated person. How could excommunication give ◄ the church and its leaders great power over kings and nobles?

INVESTITURE: How does the investiture crisis show how powerful the church was in medieval Europe?

9. The popes and the Holy Roman emperors did not agree on who should have the power of **investiture** (in-VES-tih-choor). Investiture was giving a bishop the power to carry out the duties of his office. In 1075, Pope Gregory VII decreed that the investiture of bishops by anyone but the pope was forbidden. Soon after, Holy Roman Emperor Henry IV pressured the bishops of the empire into declaring that Gregory was no longer pope. Not surprisingly, Gregory excommunicated Henry. German nobles began to turn against Henry. When the nobles met to choose a new emperor, Henry hurried to Italy to beg the pope to forgive him. For three days, Henry stood barefoot in the snow in front of the pope's castle waiting for an answer. Finally, Pope Gregory had to forgive Henry and let him back into the church. Who do you think was the winner in this confrontation?

10. The fight between popes and emperors over investiture went on until 1122. In that year a compromise was reached, known as the **Concordat of Worms**. A concordat (kun-KOR-dat) is a formal agreement. Worms (VORMSS) is the German city where the concordat was signed. It was agreed that the emperor would be allowed to give land and political power to the bishops of the empire. However, the church won the right to decide who the bishops would be. Who really won the battle over investiture?

THE CRUSADES: Why did the people of the Middle Ages join the crusades?

11. The church proved how real its power was in the eleventh century when it called on Christians to join the **crusades** (kroo-SAYDZ). The crusades were military missions to save the Holy Land from possession by the Turks. The Holy Land was in Palestine, the place where Jesus had lived and died. The Christians called the Turks the **infidel** (IN-fih-del), or faithless, because the Turks were Muslims—not Christians. In the eleventh century, the Seljuk (SEL-juk) Turks, a warlike Muslim people, had taken over the Holy Land. The Seljuk Turks then threatened the Christian Byzantine Empire as they swept northward. In 1095, the Byzantine emperor asked Pope Urban II to send some knights to help fight the Turks. At a church council at Clermont in France, Pope Urban called for a crusade to drive the Turks out of the Holy Land. Thousands of people in Europe answered his call.

12. Many people who joined the crusades did so because they really wanted to fight the enemies of their faith. However, some people had other reasons for going. Some dreamed that Palestine was a land of wonderful riches and great adventure. Criminals and debtors went to escape their punishment. Even runaway children joined a crusade. What else about a crusade would attract medieval people?

SPOTLIGHT ON SOURCES

13. The First Crusade began in 1096. Many of the members of this crusade were peasants. A large number of them died on the way to the Holy Land or were killed by the Turks. Others gave up and returned home. But an army of nobles and knights from France, Italy, and Germany went on to fight bravely in Asia Minor and Syria. On

▼ This bronze sculpture depicts Henry IV, the Holy Roman Emperor who challenged Pope Gregory VII in the investiture controversy.

Background: The pope promised Christians who joined the crusades "imperishable glory in the kingdom of heaven." He also guaranteed that their families and property would be protected while they were away.

205

The Arts and Artifacts

▲ The interior of a Gothic church shows the pointed arches and beautiful stained glass of this style. In contrast, the Romanesque church at the right has only one window.

Styles of Architecture   In the Middle Ages, there were two major styles of **architecture** (AR-kih-tek-choor) in Europe. Architecture is the way a building is built and the way it looks. From 1100 to 1150, churches and other religious buildings were built in a style called **Romanesque** (roh-muh-NESK). Romanesque buildings looked like huge fortresses. The buildings were of stone and had rounded arches and domed roofs. Inside, they were dark and gloomy, because they had only a few narrow slits for windows.

Then, in the late 1100s, a new style of architecture was developed. This style was called **Gothic** (GAH-thik). Gothic buildings, especially churches, were tall, airy, and light. These Gothic churches seemed to soar into the heavens. They looked this way because of a new invention called a **flying buttress**. A flying buttress was a long stone arm that leaned against the outside wall of the church. This arm helped support the weight of the roof. With the use of flying buttresses, churches could be built thinner and taller. Thin walls made larger windows possible. Larger windows made of colorful stained glass meant a lighter, brighter interior. Pictured on the stained-glass windows were scenes from the Old Testament, the life of Jesus, and the lives of the saints. These windows are one of the glories of the Middle Ages. They also were a kind of picture book for the medieval people, most of whom could not read.

1. What is the difference between Romanesque and Gothic-style buildings?

2. What do Gothic churches tell us about the skill and faith of medieval people?

Activity: Show students examples of both Romanesque and Gothic church architecture. Have them identify the style of each example you show.

▲ The capture of Jerusalem by crusaders. The painter has made Jerusalem look like a city in Europe. What does the painting tell you about how wars were fought in the Middle Ages?

July 15, 1099, they reached the Holy Land and captured Jerusalem. Here is a description of what happened during the taking of the city.

> . . . The work again began at the sound of the trumpet, and to such purpose that the rams, by continual pounding, made a hole through one part of the wall [of the city of Jerusalem] . . . . At the noon hour on Friday, with trumpets sounding amid great commotion and shouting "God help us," the Franks entered the city . . . . Those who were already in rapid flight began to flee more rapidly . . . .
>
> [This] over, the crusaders entered the houses and took whatever they found in them . . . . Whatever he found there was his property. Thus many poor men became rich.
>
> Afterward, all . . . repeated prayers and made their offering at the holy places that they had long desired to visit . . . .
> —*Readings in European History,* Leon Bernard and Theodore B. Hodges.

14. By the end of the thirteenth century, people of Europe began to lose interest in the crusades. One reason was that the later crusades were driven more by a hunger for wealth or power than by faith. But more than any other reason, Europeans were getting involved in newer and more exciting things. So, by the 1290s, the Holy Land was back in Turkish hands.

OUTLOOK

15. In the Middle Ages, the church was the center of everyone's life. From birth to death, people devoted their lives and thoughts to it as never before or since. Gradually, however, other things began to compete for people's attention. People remained loyal to their religion, but it no longer played so big a part in their lives. When the pope moved away from Rome, many people lost confidence in the papacy. When the church's influence began to lessen, the Middle Ages, too, were beginning to give way to a new age.

Activity: Have different students report on the various crusades, especially the Third and the Fourth. Have these reports presented to the class.

CHAPTER REVIEW

VOCABULARY REVIEW

Select a word from the list that best completes each sentence.

a. clergy
b. Concordat of Worms
c. crusades
d. ecclesiastical
e. excommunicated
f. friar
g. heresy
h. infidel
i. investiture
j. parish
k. sacraments
l. tithe

1. The _____ are the people in the church who performed its ceremonies.
2. The _____ were special ceremonies of the church.
3. Another word for a local church is a _____ .
4. A member of the clergy who promised to live a life of poverty and devotion to God was a _____ .
5. The _____ was a tax on earnings of all people of the parish.
6. Another name for a church court was an _____ court.
7. A person holding beliefs against church doctrine was charged with _____ .
8. If you were _____ from the church, this meant that you were cut off from receiving the sacraments.
9. Giving a bishop the power to carry out the duties of his office was known as _____ .
10. The church won the right to choose its own bishops as result of the _____ .
11. Missions to save the Holy Land from the Turks were called _____ .
12. The Christians called the Turks _____ , which meant faithless.

SKILL BUILDER: READING A MAP

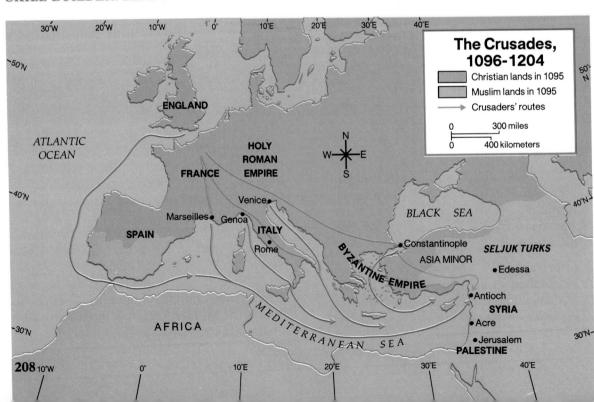

The Crusades, 1096-1204

- Christian lands in 1095
- Muslim lands in 1095
- Crusaders' routes

0   300 miles
0   400 kilometers

If you were asked to draw a map showing how to get to your home, what would the map look like? Probably it would have lines on it showing the direction of the streets leading to your house. The map on page 208 shows the routes taken by crusaders to get to the Holy Land. The course of each route is shown with arrows. To find the direction of each route, follow each line in the direction its arrow is pointing. If the pope went from Rome on a crusade, which route would he have taken? Place your finger on the land route going through Rome to the southeastern tip of Italy. Notice how, from this point, the route becomes a sea route. It goes through the Mediterranean Sea eastward toward the Islamic lands.

▶ Use the map on page 208 to answer the following questions.

1. Through what body of water did all but one of the water routes to the Holy Land have to pass? Which route did not pass through this body of water?

2. Through which bodies of water did the route from England pass?

3. Describe the route from northern France to the Holy Land that was almost all by land.

4. If you lived in Venice, which route to the Holy Land would you have taken—the land route, the water route, or both? Why?

SKILL BUILDER: CRITICAL THINKING AND COMPREHENSION

1. Cause and Effect

▶ Write the sentence from each pair that is the cause.

1-1. a. The center of all medieval life was the church.
b. People believed that their souls could be saved only through the church.

1-2. a. The church owned a great deal of land.
b. Church leaders were often powerful feudal lords.

1-3. a. A crusade was organized to push the Seljuk Turks out of the Holy Land.
b. The Seljuk Turks had taken over Palestine and were threatening the Byzantine Empire.

2. Compare and Contrast

▶ Compare the lives of monks in monasteries to those of the friars. How were they different? How were they similar?

ENRICHMENT

1. Write a scene for a play about Henry IV and Gregory VII. The scene should focus on Henry's standing outside the castle and what he and Gregory said to each other. Pick another student to help you present this scene for the class.

2. Imagine you are a knight who is leading a crusade to save the Holy Land. Write a letter to your family explaining why you went and telling how your group is dealing with the hardships of the trip. Describe the route you are taking. Trace the route on an outline map of Europe and the Holy Land.

The Closing of the Middle Ages

▲ As trade increased, some merchants became very wealthy. Measuring wealth in money instead of in land was an important change.

OBJECTIVE: What changes in the late Middle Ages brought an end to the medieval way of life?

1. Do you have an after-school job? If so, why did you want to get your job? You probably work for money to buy clothes, a car, or to pay for a college education. For many people in the late Middle Ages, the return of money and trade held out hope for a better life. The old system of loyalty to feudal overlords was slowly breaking down. New relationships based on money and trade were changing medieval Europe. Peasants could escape from serfdom by going to one of the growing towns and working for money. Merchants and others in the towns could acquire a great deal of money. More and more, power depended less on land and titles and more on money and possessions. Feudalism was being replaced by political and economic trends that were much more like today's trends.

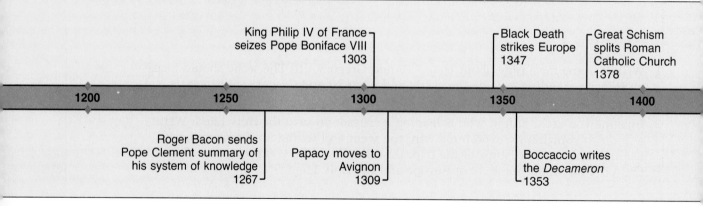

King Philip IV of France seizes Pope Boniface VIII 1303

Black Death strikes Europe 1347

Great Schism splits Roman Catholic Church 1378

1200　1250　1300　1350　1400

Roger Bacon sends Pope Clement summary of his system of knowledge 1267

Papacy moves to Avignon 1309

Boccaccio writes the *Decameron* 1353

THE CRUSADES: How did economic life in western Europe change as a result of the crusades?

2. Although the crusades failed to free the Holy Land, they had a lasting effect on the way Europeans lived. When the crusaders returned to Europe, they brought back such things as spices, sugar, and silk. Spices were used to keep food from spoiling. Silk replaced wool in the clothing of many lords and ladies. Nobles and merchants enjoyed the new luxuries and wanted more of them.

▶ How did the desire for more products from the East change the medieval system of trade?

3. Trade in Eastern goods made the Mediterranean Sea a busy highway of commerce. Cities such as Venice and Genoa became trading links between Europe and the East. Look at the map of western Europe on page 726, and locate Venice and Genoa. Why did these cities become so important? Italian traders made contact with Islamic traders and sold their goods all over Europe. The flood of commerce led to an economy based on money. In the Italian cities, merchants started the first banks in western Europe. They lent money to crusaders and other merchants and made huge profits for themselves.

NOBLES AND PEASANTS: What events and changes led to the end of feudalism in western Europe?

4. The eleventh and twelfth centuries had introduced improvements in farming. Food was cheap and plentiful. But from 1300 to 1320, bad weather caused a **famine** (FAM-in). A famine is a crisis in which food is scarce or unavailable for a long time and over a large area. Driven by famine, people moved from the farms and manors to towns looking for work. This caused the towns to grow. It also marked the beginning of exchange based on money.

5. The famine introduced serious malnutrition, exposing the European people to several diseases, such as tuberculosis, scurvy, and rickets. However, the worst disease ever to strike Europe was not caused by the famine. It was caused by **bubonic plague** (boo-BAH-nik PLAYG). A plague is a disease that kills large numbers of people in a short time. Medieval people called this plague the **Black Death**. People in the Middle Ages did not know the disease's cause, but it now is known that it was carried by rats. People were infected when they were bitten by fleas that had already bitten an infected rat. Infected rats were often found on ships from China, and these ships traveled through the Middle East and into Italy. The plague swept across Europe from 1347 to 1351, killing between a third and a half of Europe's population and wiping out whole towns and villages. As towns and farms were abandoned, food production dropped. Those serfs who did not move to cities began to seek wages from their lords in return for work. Why would the ◀ shortage of labor and the payment of wages take power away from the lord of a manor?

SPOTLIGHT ON SOURCES

6. Giovanni Boccaccio (1313-1375) described the Black Death in his book *The Decameron.* Boccaccio (boh-KOTCH-ee-oh) lived in Florence during the worst stages of the plague and could make an accurate report.

> The violence of this disease was such that the sick communicated [gave] it to the healthy who came near them, just as a fire catches anything dry or oily near it. And it even went further. To speak to or go near the sick brought infection and a common death to the living; and moreover, to touch the clothes or anything else the sick had touched or worn gave the disease to the person touching. Such was the multitude of corpses brought to the churches every day and almost every hour that there was not enough consecrated [holy] ground to give them burial, especially since they wanted to bury

Background: To this day, many rodents carry bubonic plague, including some in the western United States. There still are a few cases of bubonic plague each year, but it is now easily cured by antibiotics.

211

Ginger

India, China,
West Indies,
Nigeria

Cinnamon

Sri Lanka

Pepper

Indonesia
Brazil

Clove

Indonesia,
China,
Tanzania

Cardamon

India,
Guatemala,
Sri Lanka

Nutmeg

Indonesia

▲ These are some of the spices that Europeans imported from India and places farther east. Spices were a basic part of Europe's trade.

each person in the the family grave, according to the old custom. Although the cemeteries were full, they were forced to dig huge trenches, where they buried the bodies by hundreds . . ."

7. The change to an economy based on money weakened the power of many lords and strengthened a growing middle class. Owning land was no longer an important power symbol. Instead, money gave a person power. Nobles had lots of land but not much money. They wanted money to buy luxurious Eastern goods to keep up a rich way of life. The nobles looked to the king for help. The king helped the nobles by giving ▶ them paid jobs in the royal army. How would paying for army service affect the idea of feudalism? In addition, those who had become wealthy through trade were often given noble status by the monarchs of Europe.

8. Feudalism was also weakened by new inventions in weapons of war. In the early 1300s the use of gunpowder changed war in many ways. Metal balls could go through heavy armor. Cannon fire could drill holes through the thickest castle walls. In the 1340s, the English invaded France and defeated the French by the use of the longbow and cannon.

PEOPLE IN HISTORY

9. Roger Bacon, an English philosopher and scientist, was the founder of experimental science in Europe. Born about 1214, Bacon did extensive research in **optics** (AHP-tiks). Optics is the branch of physics that deals with the study of light. He was able to describe the parts of the eye and the optic nerves, a remarkable achievement for a thirteenth-century scientist.

10. Bacon was deeply concerned about educational reform. He was particularly in favor of teaching mathematics. In 1266, Bacon wrote to Pope Clement IV about a great project describing his system of knowledge. Thinking that the book already was written, the pope asked to see it. Bacon responded with a summary of his system. In his work, the *Opus Maius*, Bacon told scholars to study languages. He believed that this would allow them to learn more about Greek and Arabic scientific knowledge. Clement died before he was able to read Bacon's great work, but the work itself stands as one of the greatest monuments of medieval scholarship.

THE CHURCH: Why did the Church's power decline in the late Middle Ages?

11. During the late Middle Ages, the **papacy** (PAY-puh-see), or the office of the pope, suffered several blows to its power and prestige. Trouble started in 1301 when

Activity: Have students skim Chapter 5 on medieval town life to find other factors in the weakening of feudal lords. List their findings on the chalkboard along with the factors given in this chapter.

a conflict arose between France's King Philip IV and Pope Boniface VIII. Philip wanted to tax the clergy. He also wanted to try a bishop in court because the bishop had criticized him [Philip]. The pope refused to allow the trial. Philip then sent a letter to Boniface that accused the pope of being a false pope. Boniface said he was ready to excommunicate Philip from the church. Before the pope could carry out this threat, Philip sent soldiers to Italy to capture the pope. They held him for two days. Boniface died about a month later, and the next popes gave in to Philip.

12. Under pressure from Philip, in 1309 the papacy moved to Avignon (ah-veen-YAWN), a city on the Rhone River. Today Avignon is in France. In 1309, because of different national boundaries, it was just outside France, but it was close enough that Philip could control what went on there. The papacy stayed in Avignon for almost seventy years. During this time, the popes depended on the kings of France in ▶ important ways. What does this move tell you about the power of the papacy?

13. An even worse disaster for the church happened in 1378. One year earlier Pope Gregory XI had moved the papacy back to Rome. After Gregory's death, French and Italian cardinals elected an Italian to be pope. **Cardinals** (KAR-dih-nulz) are a special group of bishops who elect the pope. Thirteen French cardinals then claimed that they had voted for the Italian out of fear of the Italian crowds. They named a French cardinal to be pope at Avignon. Europe now had two popes, one in Rome and one in Avignon. This **schism** (SIZ-um), or split, in the church lasted until 1417.

14. During the schism, the church suffered terrible damage. Both popes abused their powers. The selling of church offices was practiced more openly than it ever had been before. People did not know which pope to honor. Many lost respect for the church. By the late 1400s, many people felt more loyalty to their ruler and their nation than to the church. This had never happened before.

▲ Philip IV of France, shown here with one of his vassals, was one of the most powerful and successful rulers of the Middle Ages.

OUTLOOK

15. With the Middle Ages coming to an end, Western Europe survived major changes and crises. The nations of Europe slowly recovered from the plague. However, once social changes had taken place, there was no going back to old ways. The manorial system began to give way to the growth of cities. A middle class appeared in the cities, supported by trade and the new money system. Finally, the last major element of feudalism, the influence of the church, was badly shaken, as popes lost the power they had enjoyed in the Middle Ages.

Background: Councils held in the 1400s failed to reform the church. From the 1500s on, papal powers would be limited by strong monarchs and by the growth of Protestantism.

213

CHAPTER REVIEW

VOCABULARY REVIEW

Select the word that best completes each sentence. Number your paper and write the correct word by each number.

bubonic plague

Black Death

optics

papacy

cardinals

schism

simony

1. In 1309, the _____ was moved from Rome to Avignon.

2. The dispute that split the Church and ended in 1417 was called the _____ .

3. A _____ is a disease that kills many people.

4. The plague that killed about one third of the population in the Middle Ages was called the _____ .

5. After a pope dies, _____ meet to elect a new pope.

6. Selling church offices for money is called _____ .

7. The study of light is called _____ .

SKILL BUILDER: MAKING A TIME LINE

In Chapter 4 of this unit, you learned about time lines that show the events in a person's life. Time lines also can show the events in the history of a group. This group may be a government, a class of people, or a religious group. The time line below shows events in the Roman Catholic Church. The period it covers is the late Middle Ages. It is a horizontal time line, which means you read it from left to right. You can make a time line yourself. To add an event, find the number on the line that is closest to the date of the event. If you were adding an event in 1319, you would find 1320 and put your mark a little to the left of it. Remember, moving to the left on a time line is going back in time. Moving to the right is going forward in time.

▶ On your paper, copy the time line that follows. Then read the dates and events that follow. Add these to your time line in the places where they belong.

1300	1320	1340	1360	1380	1400	1420

1309—The papacy moves from Rome to Avignon.

1301—Conflict begins between King Philip IV and Pope Boniface VIII.

1417—The schism ends.

1378—The schism begins with the election of two popes.

1377—Pope Gregory XI moves the papacy back to Rome.

214

STUDY HINT Fold a piece of paper in half down the middle. On the right side, write one-sentence summaries of the conditions described in this chapter. On the left side, tell in a sentence or two what the conditions had been earlier in the Middle Ages, as described in earlier chapters.

SKILL BUILDER: CRITICAL THINKING AND COMPREHENSION

1. Hypothesizing

▶ Gunpowder was first used by the ancient Chinese. It was not widely used in Europe until the 1300s. How can you explain the difference in time between when Asians used gunpowder and when Europeans began to use it?

2. Cause and Effect

▶ The Black Death helped cause many changes in Europe. What happened to feudalism as a result of the Black Death?

3. Compare and Contrast

▶ Compare the power and importance of medieval lords before and after the crusades.

4. Classifying

▶ The following chart gives lists of the popes between 1378 and 1430. What can you tell about the leadership of the church during this time by studying this chart? List facts from Chapter 7 that support your findings.

Years	Roman Popes	French Popes	Popes chosen by Councils of Pisa and Bologna
1378-1389	Urban VI		
1378-1394		Clement VII	
1389-1404			
1394-1423		Benedict XIII	
1404-1406	Innocent VII		
1406-1415	Gregory XII		
1409-1410			Alexander V
1410-1415			John XXIII
1417-1431	Martin V		

ENRICHMENT

1. Unfair work laws, low wages, and heavy taxes caused English peasants to revolt in 1381. Find out how the revolt started, how it was stopped, and what the peasants gained or lost from it. Write a newspaper story about the revolt as though you saw it happen. Remember that a newspaper story should answer these questions: Who? What? When? Where? Why? and How?
2. Reread the section in this chapter about Roger Bacon. Write a short piece about the life of another medieval scientist. You might choose Thomas Aquinas, Albertus Magnus, or Peter Abelard.
3. Design a mural for a museum of medieval history. For the mural, draw scenes that show how feudalism slowly died.

UNIT REVIEW

SUMMARY

After the collapse of the western Roman Empire, the Christian church survived as the only institution holding western Europe together. The church's influence spread to an important new area when Clovis, king of the Franks, accepted Christianity. The Frankish kingdom grew into an empire under Charlemagne, who ruled over much of western Europe. However, after Charlemagne's death his empire fell apart, partly because of fighting among his descendants and partly because of many years of destructive raids by the Vikings.

While western Europe went through difficult times, the eastern Roman Empire survived and grew rich. For centuries the eastern, or Byzantine, empire's capital at Constantinople was one of the world's great cities.

About A.D. 1000, western Europe began to revive. The church, under the leadership of a series of strong popes, widened its influence. At the same time, the feudal system brought some order to government. Greater safety caused trade to increase, leading to the growth of towns and the beginning of a town-dwelling middle class. When this class increased its power at the expense of the church and the feudal lords, the Middle Ages were near their end.

SKILL BUILDER: READING A MAP

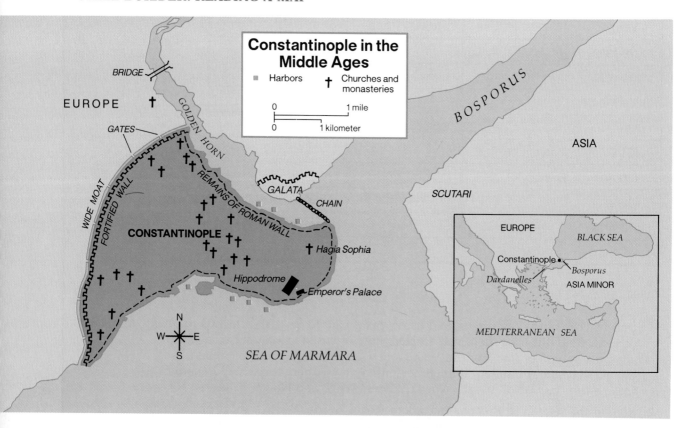

Constantinople in the Middle Ages

■ Harbors   † Churches and monasteries

216

SKILL BUILDER: CRITICAL THINKING AND COMPREHENSION

1. Main idea

▶ Read the sentences in each group below. Decide which sentence in each group is a main idea and which sentences are details of that idea. Write each group of sentences on your paper with the main idea first and the details below it.

1-1. Each sentence in this group is about the church in the Middle Ages.
   a. Some bishops were also powerful feudal lords.
   b. The church played a leading role in every aspect of life.
   c. Churches were the tallest buildings in many towns.
   d. The church could discipline people by excommunicating them.

1-2. Each sentence in this group is about the rise of the middle class.
   a. Money became as important a form of wealth as land.
   b. As trade revived, towns grew in size and importance.
   c. By the end of the Middle Ages, the middle class was an important part of society.
   d. Guilds controlled many aspects of trade.

2. Classifying

▶ Classify each of the following items according to whether it had to do with the church, the feudal system, or life in medieval towns.

guild	fief	university
manor	excommunication	vassal
monastery	investiture	sacrament

3. Cause and Effect

▶ Rewrite each cause statement. Next to each cause write the correct effect.

Causes

3-1. Trade revives in Europe.

3-2. The Black Death strikes Europe.

3-3. Clovis is baptized.

3-4. The pope moves from Rome to Avignon.

3-5. William of Normandy wins the battle of Hastings.

3-6. Viking raids strike Europe.

Effects

a. The Franks accept Christianity.

b. Collapse of Charlemagne's empire is hastened.

c. Many serfs escape to freedom.

d. The prestige of the church suffers.

e. Feudalism is introduced to England.

f. Towns grow in size and number.

ENRICHMENT

1. Medieval churches were built with stained-glass windows that told stories from the Bible. List as many events from Unit 4 as there are members of the class. Each class member then chooses one event and illustrates it in the style of a stained-glass window. Display these pictures in the correct sequence.

2. Write a paragraph that describes a person discussed in Unit 4. Do not name the person. Have classmates use the information to identify the person.

UNIT 5

ESL/LEP Strategy: As students read the chapters in this unit, have them compile a list of the people who contributed to building great civilizations in Asia, Africa, and the Americas. When they have completed the unit, ask students to describe these people and their contributions.

THE RISE OF ASIA, AFRICA AND THE AMERICAS

OBJECTIVE: Unit 5 will describe how the peoples of Asia, Africa, and the Americas built great civilizations and developed unique cultures during the years before European influence was felt on their societies.

Incas rise in Peru
A.D. 600

Muhammad conquers Mecca
A.D. 630

Ummayads are destroyed
A.D. 750

Berbers convert to Islam
A.D. 800

Ghana rises as trade empire
A.D. 1000

A.D. 600   **A.D. 700**   **A.D. 800**   **A.D. 900**   **A.D. 1000**

Muhammad flees Mecca for Medina
A.D. 622

Moslems conquer Syria, Iraq
C. A.D. 633

Northpeople invade Russia
A.D. 800

Vladimir I converts to Greek Orthodoxy
A.D. 988

▲ Machu Picchu, a great fortress city of the Incas, lay undiscovered for centuries high in the Andes Mountains of Peru.

Alp Arslan leads
Seljuks to victory
in Anatolia
A.D. 1071

Mali displaces
Ghana as trade
empire
A.D. 1230

Turks take
Constantinople,
Eastern Empire falls
A.D. 1453

Ieyasu Tokugawa
becomes shogun,
unites Japan
A.D. 1600

| A.D. 1100 | A.D. 1200 | A.D. 1300 | A.D. 1400 | A.D. 1500 | A.D. 1600 |

Mongols begin
attacks on Russia
A.D. 1223

Mongols overthrown;
Ming dynasty begins
A.D. 1368

Incans establish
empire
A.D. 1400

Babur invades India,
begins Mogul dynasty
A.D. 1526

CHAPTER 1

The Rise of Early Russia

▲ St. Basil's Cathedral, now a museum, was built in 1554 by order of Ivan IV. Its ornate domes overlook Moscow's Red Square.

OBJECTIVE: How did Russia lose its close ties with the Western world and become isolated?

1. The Russians call their country *Rossiya*. But when they write the name of their country, Russians write Россия, using the Russian or Cyrillic alphabet. The Russian writing system is based on an alphabet composed mainly of Greek and Latin characters. In the Russian alphabet the letter Р is pronounced like the English letter R, С is pronounced like S, И represents an "EE" sound, and Я is a "YAH" sound. A different alphabet is one of the differences between Russia and the nations of Western Europe. Russia occupies parts of both the European and Asian continents. Because of its location, Russian civilization and history have been influenced by Asian cultures as well as by Western European cultures. But in the early 1200s, Mongols from Asia invaded and conquered Russia. The Mongol occupation cut Russia off from outside influences for more than 200 years.

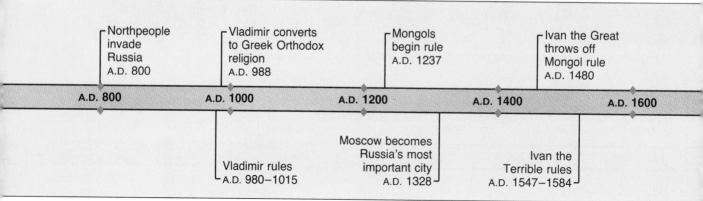

┌Northpeople invade Russia A.D. 800	┌Vladimir converts to Greek Orthodox religion A.D. 988	┌Mongols begin rule A.D. 1237	┌Ivan the Great throws off Mongol rule A.D. 1480
A.D. 800	**A.D. 1000**	**A.D. 1200**	**A.D. 1400** **A.D. 1600**
	Vladimir rules └A.D. 980–1015	Moscow becomes Russia's most important city A.D. 1328┘	Ivan the Terrible rules A.D. 1547–1584┘

KIEVAN RUSSIA: What was early Russia like?

2. The Northpeople, Swedish peoples related to the Vikings, helped form the first Russian state. Around A.D. 800 these northern adventurers traveled into Russia along the Volga (VOL-ga) and Dnieper (NEE-pur) rivers to trade and raid. Establishing trading posts throughout the region, these people gained control of trade with the Byzantine Empire and made themselves rulers of the Slavs—the original settlers of the area. One group of Northpeople set up a kingdom around the town of Kiev. Kiev soon became the most important trading town in the developing Russian state. The area became known as *Russia* after the Northpeople who called themselves Rus.

3. Kievan Russia was a **federation** (fed-uh-RAY-shun), or loosely organized political group, of about 200 towns. Each town was led by a ruler and a group of **boyars** (BOH-yarz), or nobles. Some towns had a democratic body known as the *veche*, which held different powers in different towns. Townspeople lived by a generous code of laws. At the time there was no death penalty. Women had many guaranteed rights, and peasants were free to buy and sell land.

4. In this early period Russia maintained strong contacts with Europe and with the Byzantine Empire. Look at the map on page ▶ 222. How did the Dnieper and Volga rivers provide a natural trade route between Russia and Constantinople? Via river boats, the Russians carried honey, wax, fur, and slaves to Constantinople. The boats returned to Russia with cloth, wine, spices, and gold.

PEOPLE IN HISTORY

5. About a thousand years ago Vladimir (VLAD-uh-meer), the grand prince of Kiev, sought a new religion for Russia. After rejecting Islam, Judaism, and Roman Catholicism, he became interested in the Greek Orthodox religion. He sent messengers to Constantinople to find out about the Greek Orthodox Church. The messengers returned excited, reporting, "There is no such . . . beauty anywhere on earth . . . . We know that God dwells there among [the people], and that their [the Greek Orthodox] service surpasses [is better than] the worship of all other places." On the basis of this report, Vladimir ordered his subjects to become Greek Orthodox Christians. To reinforce this order he had the statues of the old Russian gods thrown into the Dnieper River.

6. The Russians adopted other aspects of Byzantine culture as well. Byzantine influences could soon be seen in Russian art, architecture, education, and law. The picture of St. Basil's Cathedral on page 220 is an example of Byzantine architecture. A standard practice in the Byzantine Empire was to set up monasteries, schools, and houses for the poor people. The Russians adopted this practice. In the new schools many Russians learned to read and write using an alphabet created by two Greek monks, Cyril and Methodius. The Cyrillic alphabet is still used in Russia today.

MONGOL RULE: What changes did Mongol rule bring to Russia?

7. Between 1237 and 1242, Kievan Russia fell to Mongol rule. Fierce Mongols from Asia pushed across the vast Russian **steppe** (STEP), or plain. Bloodthirsty warriors and excellent horseback riders, the Mongols easily overran every important city in their path except Novgorod. Kiev had been the cultural, political, and economic center of the Russian state for about 400 years. Six years after the Mongols destroyed Kiev, a Westerner reported a grim sight. Only 200 houses remained standing. Bones were scattered everywhere.

8. The Mongols were able to control Russia for over 200 years. Imposing harsh rule, these Asian invaders demanded heavy taxes from the Russians as well as **allegiance** (uh-LEE-jans), or loyalty. However, the Mongols allowed the Russians to keep their

Activity: Have students use the map on page 224 to locate Kiev and other sites in early Russia. Have students note the correspondence of these sites to major rivers. Discuss how rivers served as highways for exploration and settlement.

▶ own laws, customs, and religion. Why might an invader allow a conquered people to keep their own laws and customs?

9. Although their culture continued to develop, the Russians were now cut off from the West. Since the Mongols handled all foreign affairs for the country, the Russians missed out on the European Renaissance. Russia's close ties with the Western world were severed.

MUSCOVITE RUSSIA: What was life like in Russia under the Moscow rulers?

10. Over the 200 years of Mongol rule, a strong new power slowly developed in the region lying to the east of Kiev. This region was called Muscovy. Moscow, its city, had replaced Kiev as the political center of Mongol Russia. Moscow princes quietly gained power by earning the Mongols' trust. By 1480 the princes had grown strong enough to push the Mongols out of Muscovy. Led by

Ivan the Great, Muscovy expanded westward. Within 100 years, nearly all of Russia was under Muscovy's rule.

11. Life in Russia under Ivan the Great was little better than it had been under Mongol rule. Harsh and ambitious, Ivan III was one of the more ruthless of the Moscow princes. He had earned the title "the Great" because he had been the first to defeat the Mongols in Russia. After that conquest, he seized **absolute power** (AB-suh-loot POW-er), or total power, in running the country. When he took over Novgorod, he removed the bell of Novgorod that had called the *veche* to their democratic meetings. He **banished** (BAN-isht), or sent away, many of Novgorod's people. He also established a strict code of law.

12. Ivan IV, the grandson of Ivan the Great, took the title *czar* (ZAR), or emperor. He ruled Russia even more cruelly than his grandfather did. He hated the boyars, who had been trying to gain more power, and

▼ The Russian state began along the Dneiper and Volga rivers. Kiev and Novgorod were early trade centers until Moscow began to expand westward in the 1400s. What cities did Moscow rule in 1505?

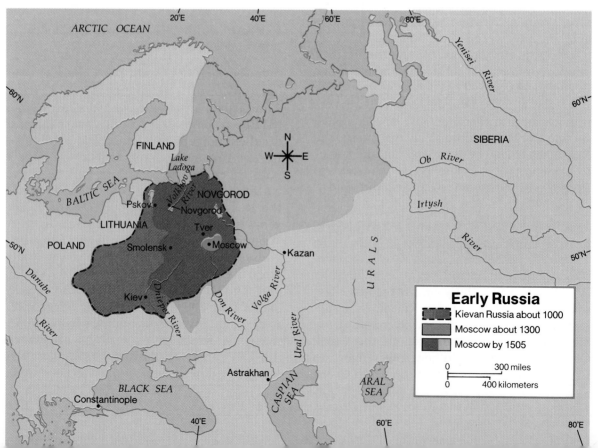

▲ Ivan IV was crowned the first czar of Russia at the age of 16. It was Ivan IV who gave Russia its first secret police force.

created a special police force to deal with them. Dressed in black and riding black horses, the police drove the boyars off their land, killing many of them and burning their properties.

13. After putting down the boyars, Ivan IV created a new class system in Russia. At the top of the class system he created a new class of landowners called the **dvoryane** (dvor-YAH-nuh) to serve the czar. At the bottom were Russia's peasants, who became tied to the land and their masters by ▶ law. Why do you think Ivan IV became known as Ivan the Terrible?

14. Ivan IV's negative acts outweighed his positive ones. By the end of his reign, Russia's eastern frontier reached to the Ural Mountains. Yet Ivan IV's attack on the boyars and his creation of a new class system set Russia far behind the rest of Europe. At a time when other countries were giving peasants more rights, Russia was taking rights away. How might such acts have further isolated Russia from the rest of Europe?

SPOTLIGHT ON SOURCES

15. The harshness of Ivan the Terrible's rule was felt in all areas of life. The following is from the *Domostroy* (doh-mo-STROY), or household code, of the time.

> If you love your son, punish him frequently, that you may rejoice later....
> Do not smile at him or play with him, for though that will diminish [lessen] your grief while he is a child, it will increase [your grief] when he is older .... Give him no power in his youth, but crush his ribs while he is growing ... lest there be ... a loss to your house, destruction to your property, scorn from your neighbors and ridicule from your enemies, and cost and worriment from the authorities.

—from *Readings in Russian History,* vol. 1, edited by Warren B. Walsh

OUTLOOK

16. Moscow, one of the great cities of today's world, was born in the midst of the rise of early Russia. The first **Kremlin** (KREM-lin), or stockade wall, was built in Moscow in 1147 to protect the settlement from invaders. Ivan III expanded the Kremlin to its present size and shape—a triangle almost one half mile long enclosing 70 acres of a hill. The triangle was formed with brick walls that were in places up to 60 feet (18m) high. From 1554 to 1560 Ivan IV had St. Basil's Cathedral built within the Kremlin walls to celebrate the defeat of the Mongols. If you were to visit Moscow today, you would be able to visit the Kremlin, which forms the center of the city. There you would see the imprint left by those powerful early rulers of Russia.

Background: The special police used by Ivan IV were called *oprichniks* and numbered around 6,000. From the saddle of each *oprichnik's* horse hung a dog's head, meant to frighten people, and a broom, meant to symbolize the *oprichniks'* job of sweeping away enemies of the state.

223

CHAPTER REVIEW

VOCABULARY REVIEW

Write each of the following words on a sheet of paper. Then write the correct definition for each word. Use the glossary on pages 728–737 to help you.

1. federation
2. boyars
3. steppe
4. allegiance
5. absolute power
6. dvoryane
7. banished
8. kremlin

SKILL BUILDER: INTERPRETING A TIME LINE

Study the time line below and answer the questions that follow it.

1. Who lived first?
   a. Vladimir
   b. Ivan the Great
   c. Ivan the Terrible

2. How many years separated the Northpeople's invasion of Russia from the Mongol invasion of Russia?
   a. about 500 years
   b. about 700 years
   c. about 400 years

3. About how many years did the Mongol rule of Russia last?
   a. 250 years
   b. 150 years
   c. 350 years

4. About what year did Moscow become Russia's most important city?
   a. 1320
   b. 1350
   c. 1300

5. Who defeated the Mongols?
   a. Ivan III
   b. Vladimir
   c. Ivan the Terrible

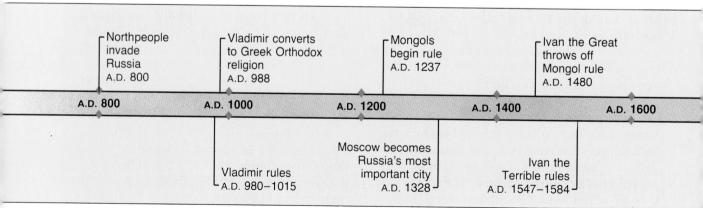

Northpeople invade Russia A.D. 800 — Vladimir converts to Greek Orthodox religion A.D. 988 — Mongols begin rule A.D. 1237 — Ivan the Great throws off Mongol rule A.D. 1480

A.D. 800   A.D. 1000   A.D. 1200   A.D. 1400   A.D. 1600

Vladimir rules A.D. 980–1015 — Moscow becomes Russia's most important city A.D. 1328 — Ivan the Terrible rules A.D. 1547–1584

SKILL BUILDER: CRITICAL THINKING AND COMPREHENSION

1. Cause and Effect

▶ Match each cause with its effect.

Cause

1-1. Russian messengers to Constantinople reported to Vladimir about the Greek Orthodox Church.

1-2. Moscow princes quietly gained power over the years.

1-3. Around A.D. 800 the Northpeople traveled into Russia and set up a kingdom around the town of Kiev.

Effect

a. The first Russian state was formed.

b. The Mongols were pushed out of Muscovy in 1480.

c. Vladimir ordered his subjects to become Greek Orthodox Christians.

d. Vladimir sought a new religion for Russia.

2. Compare and Contrast

▶ Make a chart of three similarities and three differences between Ivan the Great and his grandson, Ivan IV.

3. Drawing Conclusions

▶ Reread paragraphs 7, 8, and 9 carefully. Which of the following conclusions is supported by the information in those paragraphs? On a sheet of paper, write the letter of the conclusion that is best drawn from the facts contained in paragraphs 7, 8, and 9.

a. Mongol rule was tolerable because the Russian people could keep their laws, customs, and religion.

b. The Mongols caused the Russians to become isolated from Byzantine and Western influences.

c. The Russian people wanted to be governed by the Mongols.

4. Predicting   Have you looked up at the sky on a gray, cloudy day? The first thought that may have crossed your mind was that it was going to rain. What you were doing was **predicting,** or guessing about what might happen next. Predicting is the skill of guessing what will happen next on the basis of clues and facts. For example, the fact that it was gray *and* cloudy helped you to predict rain.

▶ Reread paragraphs 2, 3, and 4 carefully. Then make a prediction about the future importance of Kiev. Write your prediction on a sheet of paper.

ENRICHMENT

1. Imagine that you are Vladimir, the grand prince of Kiev. Write a letter to send to representatives of different religions to find out whether their religion is right for the Russian people. Supply information about what you are looking for in a religion and ask specific questions about religious practices and beliefs.

2. Create an outline map of European Russia showing the Baltic, Black, and Caspian seas and the major rivers and cities mentioned in the chapter. Use the map to show the route the Northpeople used to travel from Scandinavia to Kiev and from Kiev to Constantinople. Also indicate the route the early Moscow princes might have followed to get to the Byzantine city.

CHAPTER 2

The Rise of Islam

▲ Rules about wearing the veil and other aspects of Islamic behavior are strictly enforced by religious leaders in present-day Iran.

OBJECTIVE: How did Islam become one of the world's great religions?

1. In Saudi Arabia a young woman prepares to leave her home for the day. Before going into the street, she covers her face with a veil. The veil is a sign of modesty. Far away in Indonesia a woman dons a veil for the same reason. Meanwhile a woman of Nigeria puts on a robe before going out in ▶ public. Why are all these women concerned with modesty? They are **Muslims** (MUZ-lums), followers of the religion of Islam. Dressing modestly is only one of the many customs shared by Muslim women around the world. Customs widespread among both Muslim men and women include not eating pork, not drinking alcoholic beverages, and praying five times each day. There are more than 800 million Muslims in the world today who follow the Islamic religion. They live mainly in Asia, the Middle East, and Africa. In this chapter, you will learn about the beginnings of Islam and about how it became one of the world's great religions.

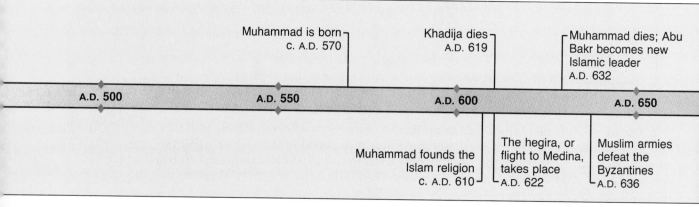

Muhammad is born
C. A.D. 570

Khadija dies
A.D. 619

Muhammad dies; Abu Bakr becomes new Islamic leader
A.D. 632

A.D. 500   A.D. 550   A.D. 600   A.D. 650

Muhammad founds the Islam religion
C. A.D. 610

The hegira, or flight to Medina, takes place
A.D. 622

Muslim armies defeat the Byzantines
A.D. 636

226

ESL/LEP Strategy: Have students paraphrase the caption of the above photograph. Then, ask them to discuss customs relating to dress in the United States or in their countries of origin.

ORIGINS OF ISLAM: Where, when, and how did Islam begin?

2. The people of Arabia were herders and traders who lived on a dry, rugged peninsula between the Red Sea and the Persian Gulf. They carried on an active trade with peoples in Asia and Africa. Arabian products such as incense and hides were exchanged for spices, gold, ivory, and silk. These goods were sold in the fairs and markets around Mecca. Mecca was Arabia's busiest trading center and an important center for religion.

3. Each year Arabs from all over the peninsula would make pilgrimages to Mecca's temples. A **pilgrimage** (PIL-gruh-mij) is a religious journey to a shrine or other sacred place of worship.

PEOPLE IN HISTORY

4. Islam was born nearly 1,400 years ago in Mecca. Islam officially began with the teachings of a man named Muhammad (moh-HAM-ud), who was born in Mecca about the year A.D. 570. His name means "chosen one" in Arabic. Muhammad spent his early life as a camel driver on the trade routes to northern parts of Arabia. At 25, Muhammad married Khadija, a rich widow. Following the marriage, Muhammad made his fortune in the caravan trade.

5. Over the years Muhammad grew increasingly dissatisfied with the religious and social practices of the times. He worried about the condition of the poor people and thought that fathers and husbands had too much control over wives and daughters. He thought the rich and powerful needed more spiritual guidance. He also thought there were too many gods. While he admired the Jewish and Christian religions, because of their belief in one God, Muhammad saw weaknesses in those religions.

6. At the age of 40, Muhammad had a vision of the angel Gabriel—the first of many dreams that would change his life. During this vision, a voice told Muhammad to preach the word of God. At first, Muhammad was unsure how to begin. But more dreams and visions followed, and Muhammad began to discuss his religious views with his family and friends. Soon he was preaching to large crowds at the market in Mecca. Muhammad's wife was the first to **convert** (kahn-VURT) to, or join, the new faith he preached.

7. Muhammad preached a religion in which all people were equal before God. He taught that there is but one Allah. "Allah" is the Arabic word for God. He also said that for Muslims to gain Allah's grace, they must **submit**, or give in, to Allah's will. In fact, the word "Islam" means "submission to Allah." Muhammad taught that people owed their lives to Allah and should praise

Daily life in . . .

Although women did not achieve equal status with men under Islam, there was some improvement in their treatment. In pre-Islamic days an Arab could marry as many women as he wanted, a practice called polygamy. He could treat his wives in whatever way he chose and he could divorce them and remarry them the next day. A bride never received a bridal gift.

The Koran of Islam said that a man could have no more than four wives. The wives had to be treated kindly and equally with equal private living space, household slaves and cooking equipment. A bride still had no say in marriage arrangements, but she did receive the bridal payment as her own property. A husband still could divorce his wife by saying "Thou art dismissed" three times, but he could not remarry her for at least three months. Muhammad also said that all true believers in Islam would be rewarded after death. How is this belief similar to Christianity?

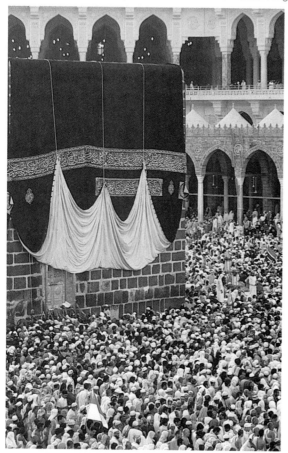

▲ Muslims gather in the courtyard of the Great Mosque in Mecca. The black-veiled *kaaba* [center] is Islam's holiest shrine.

and obey Allah as a sign of worship. In Muhammad's eyes, Adam, Abraham, Moses, and Jesus were all **prophets** (PRAHF-uts), or spokespersons for the word of Allah. Muhammad claimed to be "the last of the prophets."

8. The middle years of Muhammad's life were full of sorrow. In A.D. 619, Khadija died. Three years later, Muhammad discovered that people who feared the power of Islam were plotting to kill him. Muhammad and a handful of followers escaped to Medina, a city about 200 miles north of Mecca, where Muhammad started a Muslim community. Muslims call Muhammad's move to Medina the *hegira*, or flight.

9. Muhammad's followers collected Muhammad's teachings into one book of rules

and laws called the **Koran**—the holy book of Islam. Medina became the center of Islam, and Muhammad served as Medina's religious and political leader.

10. Soon Muhammad felt powerful enough to return to Mecca. There he and his followers defeated Islam's enemies in several battles. Muhammad smashed the idols, or statues of the gods, that stood in the temples of Mecca. Even today Muslims are not allowed to make statues or holy pictures. How is this practice different from ◄ many Christian faiths? Many of the people of Mecca began to convert to Islam after witnessing Muhammad's power. Today Mecca remains the holiest Islamic place.

ISLAMIC PRACTICES: How is Islam a whole way of life as well as a religion?

11. To be a good Muslim, a person must follow Islamic daily rules of living. Islam is, therefore, a way of life as well as a religion. A Muslim must carry out the five major duties known as the Five Pillars of Islam. First, a Muslim must publicly declare that there is only one god, who is called Allah and that Muhammad is Allah's prophet. Second, a Muslim must pray five times a day between dawn and dusk. Each time Muslims pray, they are to kneel and face the holy city of Mecca. A Muslim's third duty is to give alms. Alms include money, food, and clothing, which are given to the poor. Fourth, a Muslim must fast, or not eat, from dawn to sundown each day of the holy month of Ramadan. For the fifth duty, Muslims must make a *hajj*, or pilgrimage, to Mecca once in their lives.

12. Prayer is an important part of a Muslim's daily life. Muslims can pray anywhere, but prayers said in a **mosque** (MOSK), or Islamic house of worship, are held to be most powerful. Each mosque has a **minaret** (min-uh-RET), or tower. From the tower Muslims are called to prayer daily. The walls of the mosques are decorated with flower and lace designs and Arabic calligraphy, usually of words from the Koran. Calligraphy, a kind of decorative

Background: Every able-bodied Muslim is expected to make at least one *hajj*, or pilgrimage, to Mecca. However, those who are disabled or very poor are released from this duty.

writing, is a special art form for the Islamic world. Because Muhammad taught that all Muslims are equal before Allah, Islam has no priests. Any Muslim can lead other Muslims in prayer.

ISLAM SPREADS: How did leaders after Muhammad spread Islam?

13. Muhammad had told his followers to "spread the word." They did just that. After his death in A.D. 632, Abu Bakr, Muhammad's closest follower, became the new leader of Islam. He was called the **caliph** (KAY-luf), or successor. Abu Bakr finished the job Muhammed had started of uniting the Arabian peninsula under Islam. After Abu Bakr came a caliph named Omar. Under Omar, Muslim armies began to carry Islam to the lands outside Arabia. The first important Muslim victory was in A.D. 635 near Damascus, a Byzantine city. The Muslims told the pagans of the area to convert to Islam or be killed. Christians and Jews

were allowed to practice their own religion as long as they paid a tax to Islamic leaders. Why do you think Christians and Jews were ◄ allowed religious freedom?

14. Muslim armies were tough to beat. Muslim soldiers were both good horseback riders and fearless fighters. Muslims believed that if they died while fighting for the cause of Islam, they would enter paradise. With their long, curved swords, they conquered neighboring peoples easily. Muslims called their holy war a *jihad*, which meant "struggle in the path of God."

15. Before long the rest of the Middle East fell to Muslim rule. By the year A.D. 636, Muslim armies defeated the Byzantines at the Battle of Yarmak. One year later Jerusalem was taken. The Muslims attacked Egypt and then attacked the Persians. By A.D. 645 the Muslims controlled Persia, Syria, Iraq, Palestine, and Egypt.

16. The Muslim faith also spread south and west. The power of Rome had long

▼ The religion of Islam began in the holy cities of Mecca and Medina and spread outward across Arabia to other lands. To what parts of the world had Islam spread by A.D. 656? Where did Islam spread between A.D. 656 and A.D. 750?

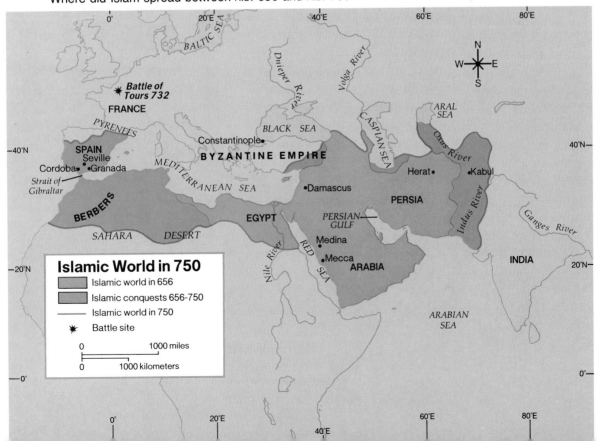

The Spread of Islam   Today, the total Muslim population of the world is about 800 million. Muslims are followers of Islam, a religion that began among Arabs but has since spread to much of Asia and Africa. Most Arabs are still Muslims, but many of today's Muslims are non-Arabs. Saudi Arabia remains the center of the Islamic world because it contains the holy cities of Mecca and Medina. The map on this page shows how Islam has spread to where it is today. Read these facts about the Islamic world. Look at the map. Then answer the questions that follow.

Facts

Indonesia in Southeast Asia has the largest Muslim population in the world. More than 160 million Indonesians are now followers of Islam.

Pakistan and Bangladesh each have large Muslim populations. About 103 million Pakistanis and 90 million Bangladeshis are now followers of Islam.

More than 89 million Muslims live in India, even though Muslims make up only 11 percent of India's total population of more than 800 million.

Nigeria has the most Muslims in Africa. Some 62 million Nigerians now follow the faith of Islam.

Egypt and Iran each have more than 50 million Muslims. Egyptians are Arabs but Iranians are not. Egyptians are mainly Sunni Muslims. Iranians are mainly Shiite Muslims.

Saudi Arabia, where Islam began, has only 15 million people today. Ninety percent of them are Arabs. All of them are Muslims.

1. Did the Islamic world in A.D. 750 cover more or less land area than the Islamic world today?

2. What countries in Africa are mainly Islamic today?

3. What city was a part of the Islamic world in 750 but is not Islamic today?

4. Where was Islam spread by mainly overland routes? By mainly oceanic routes?

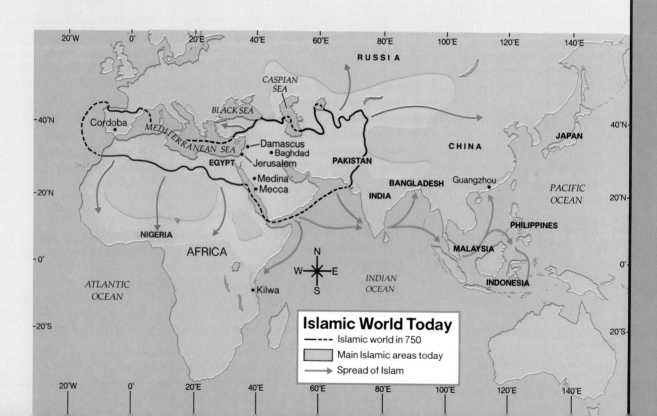

Islamic World Today
- - - - Islamic world in 750
☐ Main Islamic areas today
→ Spread of Islam

since gone. All of North Africa fell to Muslim forces. North African Muslims, called Moors, crossed into Spain and conquered it by A.D. 719. The Muslims next moved into France but were defeated and turned back to Spain in A.D. 732.

17. Even as the Muslims fought their holy war, divisions developed among them. After Muhammad died, conflicts arose over who would succeed him. From these conflicts grew two distinct Muslim groups—the Sunnis and the Shiites (SHEE-ite). These two groups exist among Muslims even today.

18. The differences between the Sunnis and Shiites were both political and religious. The Sunnis, the larger group, supported the leadership of the early caliphs. They believed that the Koran was the only go-between needed between Allah and his followers. The Shiites disagreed. They believed a person had to act as go-between. They felt, further, that the correct person had to be a direct descendent of Muhammad. They called this person the imam. According to Shiites the imam should act as both religious and government leader.

MUSLIM RULE: What were some of the accomplishments of the early Muslims?

19. A little over a century after Muhammad's death, the Islamic empire stretched from Spain in the west to India in the east. Because Muslims were asked to memorize parts of the Koran, they learned Arabic and developed a taste for literature. Reading and writing were greatly valued in the Islamic world. Poems and stories were eagerly read by early Muslims. The most famous Islamic poetry is found in the *Rubaiyat* by Omar Khayyam. Another work called *The Arabian Nights* is a popular group of stories set in ancient Baghdad.

SPOTLIGHT ON SOURCES

20. Mu'awiyah (mu-A-wiyah), who was caliph in A.D. 661, was a great supporter of literature. He gave rewards to poets whose works praised Muslim unity and encouraged patriotism. One of his wives, Maysun, wrote poetry. Maysun grew up among nomads in the Syrian desert. After she married Mu'awiyah, she wrote about her life in the capital city of Damascus. Read this excerpt from a poem by Maysun to learn how she felt about her settled city life.

> Breeze-flowing tents I prefer
> to ponderous [thick] halls
> And desert dress
> to diaphanous [sheer] veils . . .
> I'd sleep to the wind's tune,
> not to the tambourine.
> —*A Literary History of the Arabs*,
> Reynold A. Nicolson

21. Muslims developed centers of learning throughout the empire where Arab, Asian, and Western scholars could share ideas. In A.D. 830, the House of Wisdom was founded in Baghdad. Muslim scholars copied the great works of literature by the Greeks and Romans into their own language, Arabic. Muslims studied mathematics, chemistry, and medicine from India and China. Avicenna, an eleventh-century Muslim doctor, wrote a book on medicine that was used in Europe for over 600 years. Muslim architects studied the skills and ideas of the Greeks and Romans. They changed those ideas for their own needs. For example, they changed the Roman arch into the horseshoe dome of a mosque.

OUTLOOK

22. Muslims live in many countries. They live in a wide variety of environments. They make their livings in a host of different ways. Muslims are of a wide range of ethnic groups and speak a wide range of languages. Yet Muslims the world over think of themselves as brothers and sisters. They all know Arabic from their study of the Koran and follow the same rules of conduct. What would a Muslim in Saudi Arabia have in common with a Muslim from Nigeria, Indonesia, or Pakistan?

Activity: Have students bring in newspaper articles about Muslim peoples today. Share and discuss the content of the articles.

231

CHAPTER REVIEW

VOCABULARY REVIEW

Write each of the following words on a sheet of paper. Then write the correct definition for each word. Use the glossary at the back of the book to help you.

Muslims

pilgrimage

convert

submit

prophet

Koran

mosque

minaret

caliph

SKILL BUILDER: OUTLINING

Read the passage on page 227 titled "People in History." Then, on a sheet of paper, create an outline of the section. First arrange the following phrases into main headings. Then list two or more supporting facts under each heading. Title your outline "The Life of Muhammad."

I. Grew up in Mecca

II. Religious and Social Concerns

III. Develops Religious Leadership

IV. Escapes from and Returns to Mecca

SKILL BUILDER: CRITICAL THINKING AND COMPREHENSION

 1. Cause and Effect

▶ Match the cause in column 1 to its effect in column 2. Write your answers on a sheet of paper.

Cause

1. A voice spoke to Muhammad.

2. People feared Islam.

3. People threatened to kill Muhammad.

4. Muhammad taught that all Muslims are equal.

5. Muhammad told his followers to "spread the word."

6. Muhammad claimed to be "the last of the prophets."

Effect

a. Muslims carried Islam outside Arabia.

b. People threatened Muhammad.

c. Any Muslim can lead other Muslims in prayer.

d. Muhammad fled to Medina.

e. Muhammad founded a new religion.

f. Adam, Abraham, Moses, Jesus, and other figures important to Judaism and Christianity are also important to Islam.

2. Drawing Conclusions

▶ Write your conclusion to the following question on a sheet of paper. Use information in the chapter to form your conclusion.

Why might Muhammad's message of equality have appealed more to poor Arabs than to rich ones?

3. Predicting When you predict, you make a guess about an outcome on the basis of details or supporting facts.

▶ Read the following statement of fact.

In Islamic republics where Islam is the major religion, Islamic law is also the law of the state.

▶ Predict how your life would change if you lived under Islamic religion and law. Write your prediction on a sheet of paper.

4. Contrast and Compare

▶ Compare and contrast a religious holiday or practice of your choice with the five pillars of Islam. Write the similarities and differences on a sheet of paper.

Five Pillars of Islam

Pillar	Description
1	Repetition of Shahada: "There is no God but the one God and Mohammed is His prophet."
2	Salat: The daily ritual prayer at dawn, mid-day, mid-afternoon, sunset and after dark.
3	Zakat: Giving alms to the poor.
4	Fasting during the month of Ramadan
5	Hajj: The pilgrimage to the holy shrine in Mecca.

ENRICHMENT

1. Research and then draw a diagram of the interior and exterior of a typical Islamic mosque. Label the diagram.
2. Read a story from *The Arabian Nights* and write a short report on it.

CHAPTER 3

The Ottoman Empire

OBJECTIVE: How did the Turks capture a huge empire in the Middle East?

1. "I know of no State which is happier than this one," reported a traveler in 1525. "It is furnished with all God's gifts. It controls war and peace with all; it is rich in gold, in people, in ships, and in obedience; no State can be compared with it." The land the traveler was praising so highly was not the England of Henry VIII, the Spain of Charles V, the France of Francis I, the Russia of Ivan the Terrible, nor any other Christian kingdom of the sixteenth century. It was Turkey, a Muslim sultanate ruled by the great Muslim leader and Ottoman Turk, Suleiman the Magnificent. If you looked for

▲ Attacks by the Mongol warrior Genghis Khan contributed to the downfall of the Seljuks and the rise of the Ottoman Turks.

Turkey on a map of Europe, you might have trouble finding it, because only a tiny corner of Turkey is still part of Europe. Most of Turkey lies outside Europe in the area called Asia Minor. Events in Turkey rarely make headlines today. But a century ago,

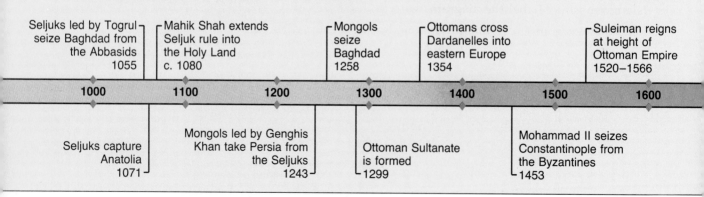

Seljuks led by Togrul seize Baghdad from the Abbasids 1055	Mahik Shah extends Seljuk rule into the Holy Land c. 1080	Mongols seize Baghdad 1258	Ottomans cross Dardanelles into eastern Europe 1354		Suleiman reigns at height of Ottoman Empire 1520–1566
1000	**1100** **1200**	**1300**	**1400**	**1500**	**1600**
Seljuks capture Anatolia 1071	Mongols led by Genghis Khan take Persia from the Seljuks 1243	Ottoman Sultanate is formed 1299		Mohammad II seizes Constantinople from the Byzantines 1453	

234

Turkey was one of the most important nations in the world.

TURKIC EXPANSION: Who were the Seljuk Turks and how did they create an empire?

2. Throughout the eighth, ninth, and tenth centuries, groups of nomadic **Turkic** (TUR-kik) people began invading the Middle East. As they came into contact with the Muslims who controlled the region, these Turks gradually converted to Islam and adopted other aspects of Muslim culture, including the Arabic alphabet.

3. During the eleventh century, one group of Turks, the Seljuks (sel-JOOKS), seized power over much of the Middle East. By this time, war and civil unrest had greatly weakened the Abbasid caliphate, the reigning Islamic government centered in Baghdad. The caliph, who had only a weak hold over the sprawling empire, began using Seljuks as mercenaries to help guard the caliphate against rebellion. But in 1055, under the command of their great leader, Togrul (TOH-gruhl), the Seljuks seized Baghdad for themselves. Togrul took the title of **sultan,** meaning prince or ruler of Muslims. He led his people on a campaign to conquer new lands in the name of Allah. Persia, which today is called Iran, came under Seljuk control.

4. The ambitious sultans who succeeded Togrul further expanded Seljuk rule. Seljuk warriors of Sultan Alp Arslan captured most of Asia Minor, then called **Anatolia,** (an-uh-TOH-lee-uh) from the Byzantines. Mahik Shah, Arslan's successor, extended Seljuk rule into the Holy Land, or Palestine. By 1092, Persia, Palestine, and most of Anatolia lay inside Seljuk borders.

SELJUK DOWNFALL: What brought about the downfall of the Seljuk Turks?

5. Over the next 200 years the Seljuk Turks, like the Abbasids before them, were weakened by war and civil unrest. In response to Seljuk expansion into the Holy Land, European Christians started the Crusades against the Turks in 1095. In addition to fighting outside invaders, Seljuk leaders fought among themselves. By the time Mongol warriors from Asia crossed Russia and invaded Persia in 1243, the Seljuks were in a state of disunity. In short order, Mongols under the leadership of Genghis Khan conquered Persia. By 1258 the Mongols owned Baghdad as well.

THE OTTOMAN TURKS: Who were the Ottoman Turks and how did they end the Byzantine Empire?

6. In the wake of the Mongol invasions, Asia Minor was overrun by several Turkic tribes from Central Asia. Chiefly, these nomadic herders were looking for lands on which to settle. As Seljuk power declined, one of these tribes, the Ottomans, formed an independent community in central Anatolia. The tribe united under the rule of Osman to form the Ottoman Sultanate in 1299.

7. The Ottoman Sultanate replaced the remaining Seljuk empire in Anatolia. The Ottomans soon expanded beyond former Seljuk borders, and conquered Byzantine territories bordering the Bosporus and the Sea of Marmara. By Osman's death in 1326 the western coast of Anatolia was part of the Ottoman empire. The Ottomans then pushed into Europe. In 1354 Ottoman troops led by Murad I crossed the Dardanelles into eastern Europe, seizing the European part of modern-day Turkey. Over the next hundred years, the Ottomans conquered the Balkan kingdoms one by one, including Greece. By about 1450, all that remained under Byzantine control was Constantinople and the area surrounding it.

8. Finally in 1453 the Ottoman sultan Mohammad I conquered Constantinople. The city had been considered invulnerable to a sea attack because of a great iron chain that shut out ships from the harbor. But Mohammad had 70 warships disassembled, moved overland from the Bosporus to the city's harbor, and then reassembled and launched. As Byzantine soldiers marched

Activity: Togrul retained the Caliph of Baghdad in the government as a figurehead. Explain that a figurehead is a person holding a leadership position but having no real power, authority, or responsibility.

235

north to defend the city, troops of nearly 200,000 Ottoman soldiers marched to the city's landward side on the west. After two months of siege, Islam triumphed inside the walls of this Christian stronghold and the city fell to Turkic rule. The last Byzantine emperor, Constantine XI, was killed in the battle.

9. The fall of Constantinople marked the end of the thousand–year history of the Byzantine Empire and shook the Christian world. For about the next 400 years Ottoman sultans controlled most of the former Byzantine territories. After taking Constantinople, one of the Turks' first acts was to turn St. Sophia, a symbol of Christian ▶ piety, into a mosque. What do you think this act symbolized for devout Muslims?

SPOTLIGHT ON SOURCES

10. Ashikpashazade, a Turkic writer who was present at the fall of Constantinople, describes the scene:

> For fifty days the battle went on by day and night. On the fifty-first day the [Ottoman] Sultan ordered free plunder. They attacked. On the fifty-first day, a Tuesday, the fortress was captured. There was good booty and plunder. Gold and silver and jewels and fine stuffs were brought and stacked in the camp market . . . . They made the people of the city slaves and killed their emperor [Constantine XI] . . . . On the first Friday after the conquest they recited the communal prayer in Aya Sofya, and the Islamic invocation was read in the name of Sultan Mohammad Khan Gazi . . . .''
>
> —From *Istanbul and the Civilization of the Ottoman Empire*, by Bernard Lewis. Copyright © 1963 by the University of Oklahoma Press.

11. Ottoman expansion did not stop with the fall of Constantinople. Future sultans continued to push deeper into Europe and into North Africa. By the early 1500s, the Ottomans had made important technologi-

▲ For two months Turkic soldiers bombarded Constantinople's city walls with cannon fire. On May 29, 1453 the city fell to Turkic rule.

cal gains in warfare. Ottoman troops under the leadership of the sultan Selim I used artillery, or guns and cannons, to conquer rival Islamic states. Under Selim's leadership. Ottoman troops functioned as a war machine. They ground down lands and peoples with their superior military equipment. The size of the Ottoman holdings doubled. Why do you think Selim I was ◀ called Selim the Grim?

GOLDEN AGE: Why is the reign of Suleiman I called the Golden Age of the Ottoman empire?

12. Suleiman (SOO-lay-mahn) I, son of Selim I, led the Ottomans into their Golden Age. Like his father, Suleiman was an effec-

Background: Today St. Sophia is once again a cathedral although Constantinople, which was renamed Istanbul as the capital of the Ottoman Empire, remains Turkic.

tive general. He pushed even deeper into Europe, extending Turkic rule west through much of Hungary to the very borders of Austria. The Ottoman empire now covered all of the Middle East and parts of Hungary, northern Africa, and Russia. But Suleiman was also a **visionary** (VIZH-uhn-er-ee)— someone who sees beyond the immediate task to the result and who knows how to act now to make things better later. Suleiman expanded trade and brought about many reforms that made life better for his people. Because of his accomplishments, he became known as Suleiman the Magnificent.

PEOPLE IN HISTORY

13. Suleiman the Magnificent was loved and respected by his people. He repaid merchants for goods unlawfully seized by his father and released 1,500 of his father's captives. He also punished corrupt government officials who had committed crimes ▶ while in office. Why would this act earn him the respect of his people?

14. Suleiman led the Ottomans into a golden age. During his reign, mosques, schools, baths, hospitals, bridges, and covered markets were built throughout the empire. Aqueducts carried water into most homes. Turkic laws were rewritten to make them more fair. Turkic markets sold goods such as silks, ivory, spices, and fruits and vegetables from all over the world. With the improvement of mining techniques, great lodes of silver were unearthed and traded freely with other nations for raw materials and goods. Suleiman encouraged artists, craftspeople, and writers in their work.

▶ **15.** But how long could the Ottoman Empire last? It showed the first signs of weakness in the late 1700s, when it lost the Crimea, a peninsula in the Black Sea, to Russia after a six-year war. In the 1800s Greece won its independence. The Ottoman Empire also lost territories to Russia, France, and Great Britain. And with the opening up of the Americas, and the flooding of the European market with cheap

silver, the Ottoman economy began to suffer. By 1914, the empire had lost almost all of its European territory.

OUTLOOK

16. During the last centuries of the first thousand years A.D., the Arabs spread Islam throughout North Africa and the Middle East, at first by force and later by example. Dreaming of a single world united under the control of Islam, Ottoman Turks fought to conquer Constantinople in the 1400s and carried Islam deep into Europe. Religion can be a strong motivating force in the history of the development of an empire. In ◀ what ways were the Byzantine and the Ottoman empires alike?

▼ Suleiman I, known as Suleiman the Magnificent, led the Ottoman Empire to its Golden Age in the sixteenth century.

Activity: Discuss religion as a motivating force in world politics. Cite the Crusades as an example of religious wars. Discuss wars fought among opposing Muslim groups in present-day Lebanon.

237

CHAPTER REVIEW

VOCABULARY REVIEW

Write each of the following sentences on a sheet of paper. Then fill in the blank with the word that best completes each sentence.

Anatolia

sultan

Turkic

visionary

1. A _____ in the Ottoman Empire held great power.

2. _____ is the Asian part of Turkey.

3. A _____ is someone who sees how to act now in order to make things better later.

4. The Seljuks and Ottomans were _____ people who moved into the Middle East from central Asia.

SKILL BUILDER: USING AN INDEX

When you want to find information in a book about a particular person, place, subject, or event, turn to the index. An index is an alphabetical list of names, places, subjects, and events together with the page numbers where they appear in the text. An index usually is placed at the end of the book or publication.

Look at the example from an index below. On what page would you find information on Bach? How many pages mention Roger Bacon?

B

Baader-Meinhof Gang, 622
Baber, 165
Babylon, 25; Hanging Gardens, 24
Bach, Johann Sebastian, 264
Bacon, Roger, 182, 193, 194
Baghdad, 132, 451 456
Baikal, Lake, 622
Bakewell, Robert, 382
Balance of power, 241–242
Balboa, Vascó de, 213
Baldwin, James, 606
Balkans: and Turkish Empire, 367–370;
    and World War I, 456–457
Balkan Wars, 457
Baltic Sea, 247
Balzac, Honoré de, 414
Bangladesh, 35, 532
Banks and colonization, 220
Bantu, 539, 543
Barbarians, 110, 111, 137–138

Use the index at the back of this book to answer the following questions. Write your answers on a sheet of paper.

1. On what pages will you find information about Suleiman?

2. If you wanted to find information about the downfall of the Seljuks, where would you look—under *Seljuks, Turks,* or *Abbasid caliphate*?

3. Under which heading in the index will you find information about the fall of Constantinople?

SKILL BUILDER: CRITICAL THINKING AND COMPREHENSION

 1. Cause and Effect

▶ On a sheet of paper, write three causes of the downfall of the Seljuk empire.

▶ **2. Drawing Conclusions**

▶ Why was it so important to the Ottomans that they capture Constantinople? Choose the letter of the statement that best explains the Ottomans' motives. Write your choice on a sheet of paper.

a. The capture would symbolize a religious victory of Islam over Christianity.

b. The population of the Ottomans had doubled and they needed to expand their lands.

c. The Ottomans wanted to topple the Byzantine Empire and become sole rulers of Europe.

▶ **3. Predicting**   When you predict, you guess about the outcome of a situation or event on the basis of clues or facts.

▶ A crusade was organized against Murad I to stop him from crossing the Dardanelles. What do you think the outcome of this crusade was? Write your prediction on a sheet of paper. On what evidence from the chapter did you base your answer? Write down the clues or facts that helped you make your prediction.

 4. Compare and Contrast

▶ How was Suleiman the Magnificent different from his father, Selim the Grim? List three differences between them on a sheet of paper.

ENRICHMENT

1. Make a chart comparing the Byzantine, and Ottoman empires. Consult the text and study the maps on pages 182 and 574 to make the chart. Headings for the chart might include: Territories, Capital City, Important Rulers.

2. Find out more about Suleiman the Magnificent by consulting an encyclopedia, a book about Turkey, a biography, or the November 1987 issue of *National Geographic* magazine. Give an oral report to the class on your findings.

3. Find out more about the battle of Constantinople. Draw a battle map showing how the battle was won.

CHAPTER 4

African Empires

OBJECTIVE: What kinds of societies did Africans build below the Sahara between A.D. 800 and 1500?

► **1.** When you think of a desert, what comes to mind? Blistering, hot temperatures? Endless miles of barren, sandy wasteland? Skin blasting sand storms? Not all deserts would fit this description, but the great Sahara in northern Africa does. It would be hard to imagine a place more desolate and hostile than the Sahara. Yet as early as 350 B.C.—perhaps even before—the Sahara served as a highway of trade. **Berbers** (BUR-burz), North African nomads from what are now Mauritania and Morocco, wanted to expand their trade. They began traveling south across the vast scorching desert to exchange goods with the people of the **Sudan** (soo-DAN), the part of

▲ Trade carried by camels across the Sahara enriched Africa's early empires in the Sudan during the 1400s and 1500s.

Africa just south of the Sahara. Many peoples north and south of the Sahara grew rich from this trade. Trade with the Middle East also developed along the coast of East Africa. Other African peoples benefited from trade across the Indian Ocean.

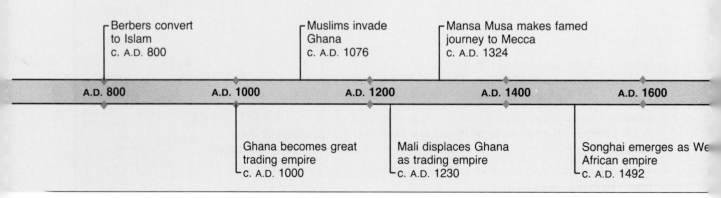

Berbers convert to Islam
C. A.D. 800

Muslims invade Ghana
C. A.D. 1076

Mansa Musa makes famed journey to Mecca
C. A.D. 1324

A.D. 800   A.D. 1000   A.D. 1200   A.D. 1400   A.D. 1600

Ghana becomes great trading empire
C. A.D. 1000

Mali displaces Ghana as trading empire
C. A.D. 1230

Songhai emerges as We African empire
C. A.D. 1492

TRADING EMPIRES: How did great trading empires develop in West Africa?

2. The main items in the trans-Saharan trade were salt and gold. People in hot climates need salt for their health. Salt also is used to flavor foods and to keep foods from spoiling. Great quantities of salt were available to be mined in the northwest Sahara. There was so much salt in Taghaza, for example, that people used blocks of it to build their houses. People in the Sudan had large amounts of gold, but no salt. A brisk trade grew between the two regions. In addition to salt the northerners traded tools and other goods. The southerners traded kola nuts, rhinoceros horns, and hides, as well as gold.

3. Around 100 B.C., the Berbers began using camels to transport goods across the desert. Unlike horses and donkeys, camels could walk a long distance before needing water. Camels also traveled faster than did horses and donkeys. Their large hoofs kept them from sinking into the desert sand. Caravans of hump-backed beasts, each carrying a heavy load, soon became a common sight in the market towns of the Sudan.

4. The trans-Saharan trade in gold and salt slowly changed life for the people of the western Sudan. For centuries these people had lived as farmers, trading only among themselves and with neighboring groups. As the salt-gold trade increased, some towns in the Sudan grew and prospered. Eventually some of these towns became well-developed centers of great trading empires.

5. The towns that grew and changed the most were those located along trading routes. Find the town of Kumbi on the map on page 246. Founded in the A.D. 200s, Kumbi lay about halfway between the salt mines of the Sahara and the forests of West Africa where gold was mined. From this central position, the kings of Kumbi were able to control trade between the Berbers and the peoples of the forests. The kings prevented robbers from attacking the rich caravans as they made their way north and south. The kings also collected a tax on all the goods going and coming.

6. Kumbi grew into the prosperous Kingdom of Ghana (GAH-nuh). From the profits and taxes gained through trade, the kings of Ghana were able to build up huge armies. They used their armies to gain control over their neighbors. In time, the kings of Ghana ruled a sprawling empire, which spread over a large part of the Western Sudan. Look at the map on page 246 to see how far Ghana extended. The lands that were conquered by Ghana sent tribute and soldiers to the king. In exchange the king provided protection. The conquered lands usually continued to be ruled by their own leaders.

7. The wealth of the Kingdom of Ghana was clearly seen in the king's court. The king sat on a throne surrounded by horses that wore gold-embroidered blankets. Behind him stood pages, or court servants, carrying gold-mounted swords. He was guarded by fine dogs, who wore collars of silver and gold. The people of Ghana thought their king was a god.

8. The Berbers and other Arab traders in West Africa brought their religion—Islam—to Ghana along with salt. The Berbers had become Muslims in the eighth century A.D. as Islam spread across North Africa. The Berbers carried their new faith wherever they went. The kings of Ghana did not convert to Islam, but they tolerated the new religion. Eventually, they allowed the Muslims to build mosques in Ghana. In addition, they hired Muslims to work as **civil servants,** or government employees. A few, but not many, city people converted to Islam. How did Islam's entry into the western Sudan differ from its entry into northern Africa centuries before? ◄

9. Meanwhile, the common people outside the central city continued to live as they always had. Most farmed and traded. Some worked gold, wove cloth, or made pottery. They took these goods to the local market town to trade. In time, the fine cotton cloth of Ghana was prized as far away as Baghdad. Gold from Ghana was minted into coins in France and England.

Background: Present-day Ghana was the first European colony in Africa to win its independence, on March 6, 1957.

241

MALI AND SONGHAI: What empires came after Ghana?

10. After the mid-1000s Ghana experienced revolts from within and invasions from outside. The most serious invasion came in A.D. 1076. In that year an army of devout Muslims from the north attacked Ghana. They were angered by the refusal of Ghana's king to become a Muslim. Although Ghana fought off the invasion, its power was shaken. Territories broke away and Ghana steadily lost power.

11. Over the next several hundred years, two other great empires rose up to replace Ghana. The first of these, Mali (MAH-lee), flourished from about 1230 to 1337. Mali was larger than Ghana and far richer. In the 1300s, a visitor to Mali said the kingdom was so big that it would take months to cross it on a horse. The cities of Timbuktu (tim-buk-TOO) and Gao, both on the Niger River, became Mali's chief trading centers. Look at the map on page 246. How far did

▶ Ghana extend east to west? How much farther did Mali stretch?

12. For government purposes Mali was divided into several regions. The king ruled the central region directly. He appointed a governor to rule each of the other regions. Conquered lands usually kept their local rulers, but the ruler had to swear loyalty to the empire of Mali.

PEOPLE IN HISTORY

13. Perhaps Mali's greatest **mansa**, or king, was Mansa Musa. Word about the wealth of his court spread throughout the Arab world. Mansa Musa himself helped to spread that word. A devout Muslim, Mansa Musa made a pilgrimage across Africa to Mecca in A.D. 1324. The size and wealth of his caravan dazzled people along the way. It was said that 60,000 men traveled with Musa on his pilgrimage. Each of his 80 camels carried 300 pounds (135 kilograms) of gold. The generous king gave each town he stayed in enough money to build a

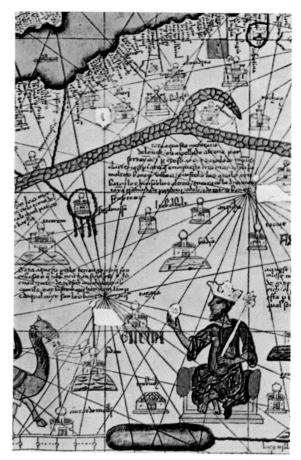

▲ Mansa Musa ruled Mali from 1312 to 1337. Mali became a great center of trade and Islamic culture during his reign.

mosque. He also gave gifts of copper wares, precious gems, and fine cotton cloth to the local rulers.

14. Mansa Musa was a forward-thinking man. He was described by a North African scholar of the day as "the most powerful, the richest, the most fortunate, the most feared by his enemies and the most able to do good to those around him." When he returned to Mali after his pilgrimage, the great king brought an Arab **architect** (AR-kuh-tekt), or building designer, with him. The architect built new mosques and a magnificent palace in Mali. He built them of brick, the first time this material was used in Mali for such large buildings. Mansa Musa also cared about learning. He hired Arab scholars to come to Timbuktu. Timbuktu soon attracted many students from other areas.

15. After Mansa Musa died in 1337, the Empire of Mali declined. Songhai, the western part of the empire, grew in power. Led by their king, Sonni Ali, the Songhai people conquered their neighbors. By the time Sonni Ali died in 1492, Songhai was the greatest empire that had ever been built in West Africa. Look at the map on page 246. ▶ How did the size and shape of Songhai compare to the size and shape of Mali?

16. Askia the Great ruled Songhai at the height of its power, from 1494 to 1538. Askia tried to make the empire run without his direct control. He divided his kingdom into provinces, each with its own governor. This way, Askia did not have to make every decision himself. Of course, the king kept a close watch on the governors. If they were unjust or dishonest, Askia punished them.

17. Timbuktu reached its golden age during Askia's reign. The city had a university, as well as about 150 other schools. Students from all over Africa went there to study law, religion, poetry, and medicine. Many students were wealthy, but poorer ones some-

times got scholarships from the merchants of Timbuktu. Other students worked as tailors or potters and went to school part-time. Classes were given in Arabic, but students and teachers spoke many African languages as well. "Here at Timbuktu there are a great many doctors, priests, judges, and other learned men," wrote a visitor from North Africa. "Many books and manuscripts are brought here, which sell at higher prices than any other merchandise."

OTHER EMPIRES: Where else in Africa did great empires develop?

18. After Songhai fell, no large empire took its place in the western Sudan. Elsewhere, however, empires were thriving. Kanem-Bornu developed in the Sudan around Lake Chad. It was an important center in the trans-Saharan trade. Kanem-Bornu also traded with the Egyptians and Nubians to the east. In 1086 the king of Kanem-Bornu converted to Islam. This further strengthened the kingdom's ties to Muslims in the north and east. By the late sixteenth century Kanem-Bornu controlled

▼ Timbuktu was one of the world's greatest cities in the 1400s and 1500s. The city was the leading center of trade and Islamic culture for the West African kingdoms of Mali and Songhai.

Background: The Sultan of Egypt wanted Musa to bow down to him, or kiss his hands. Mansa Musa refused, then agreed to bow to Allah, in front of the sultan. Then everyone was satisfied.

243

a huge portion of the trans-Saharan trade. Kanem-Bornu gained fame for having an effective cavalry. This armored cavalry helped strengthen and expand the empire. Kanem-Bornu lasted until the mid-1800s, making it one of the most enduring empires of the Sudan.

19. To the south a huge kingdom, the Congo, developed in the Congo River Valley. The Congolese prided themselves on their work with iron. They made hoes and other tools for growing crops, as well as fine swords. Portuguese sailors visited the Congo in the late 1400s. They described it as "great and powerful, full of people, having many vassals."

20. In southern Africa, several great kingdoms developed and faded in the years between A.D. 1000 and 1500. The people of one of these kingdoms built a stone city surrounded by a giant stone wall. These stone structures are known as *Zimbabwe* (zim-BAH-bwee), which means houses of stone. The people who built the *Zimbabwe* fit the stones together, using no mortar. Ruins of the *Zimbabwe* still stand today.

AFRICAN CITY-STATES: How did the city-states of West and East Africa differ from the great African empires?

21. Smaller states, or nations, grew up in West and East Africa at the same time that the great African empires developed. Most of these smaller states, like the great empires, prospered as a result of trade. In general, a city served as a center of government, trade, and religion. Farming communities surrounded the central city. A king or sultan usually ruled the state. People from the outlying communities paid tribute to the ruler. In exchange, the ruler provided them with protection from outside enemies.

22. Along the Atlantic coast, south of Songhai, several smaller nations of this type grew up in the African rain forests. Ife (EE-fee) and Benin (beh-NEEN) were the most important. Miners in these states often supplied gold to Songhai and the earlier empires. The people of Benin were skilled metal workers, famous for their bronze sculptures. The people of Ife are best remembered for their beautiful bronze and **terra-cotta** (TER-uh CAHT-uh), or clay, statues. In the Sudan, the Hausa (HOU-suh) people formed a number of states. Loosely, these states were called Hausaland, but they were not united under one leader.

23. On the other side of Africa, along the east coast, several city-states grew rich from a busy trade across the Indian Ocean. Kilwa and Mombasa (mahm-BAH-suh), in present-day Tanzania (tan-zuh-NEE-uh) and Kenya (KEN-yuh), were among the richest of these seaports. An Arab traveler in the 1300s called Kilwa "one of the most beautiful and well-constructed towns in the world." The people of Kilwa lived in stone houses built into the sides of the hills. Merchants in Kilwa bought gold, ivory, copper,

Daily life in . . .

Religion was important in the daily lives of early Africans. Across the vast continent, there was a wide variety of beliefs. The kings of Mali and Songhai were Muslims, as were many people in the busy trading towns throughout the Sudan and East Africa. But in the country and to the south, people still held on to older African beliefs.

Most Africans thought that a supreme spirit ruled the world. This spirit was too important to worry about individuals. There were, however, lesser spirits that lived on earth. The spirits of dead relatives, for example, came back to watch over the living. Many Africans believed that natural things, like trees and rivers, also had spirits. Africans honored their ancestors and nature because they did not want to make these spirits angry.

and iron from towns far inland. They traded these goods for products from other lands, including porcelain from China and cotton from India. The traders of Kilwa were extremely prosperous. Most of their homes were filled with many luxury items paid for by trade.

SPOTLIGHT ON SOURCES

24. East African cities were built on small islands or along the coast of the mainland. Narrow streets fanned out from the city square, which was situated on the waterfront. Stone houses rose above the streets. A famous scholar on Africa described the houses.

> . . . Many of the larger houses enclosed a pillared courtyard, usually shaped as a rectangle, off which there opened a series of small rooms kept dark and cool against the brilliant light and fierce heat of the glittering coastland. Skilled craftsmen decorated these houses with painted pottery and plates from Persia and China, arranging them in decorative niches [hollow places] carved in the coral walls. Much attention was given to the supply of fresh water for washing and sanitary purposes. . . .
>
> —*Discovering Our African Heritage*,
> Basil Davidson

25. The city-states of East Africa were a melting pot of Arabic and Bantu cultures. Many Muslim Arabs lived there. Some of the native African people also became Muslims and knew Arabic. The majority, however, spoke Bantu. **Swahili** (swah-HEE-lee), which today is spoken throughout East Africa, blends Bantu and Arabic. The word "Swahili" comes from the Arabic word for coastal plain. Like many Africans, East Africans composed poems and folktales, which storytellers repeated from one generation to the next. In the 1600s, after Swahili had grown in use, many of these works were written down, in Swahili, for the first time.

▲ The African city of Zimbabwe flourished as a trading center in about A.D. 1200. The ruins are in present-day Zimbabwe.

26. The coming of the Europeans in the fifteenth century halted the growth of the trading cities. Portuguese troops attacked the cities, one by one, and destroyed them. You will read more about African contact with Europeans in Unit 6.

OUTLOOK

27. Merchants in Timbuktu grew rich selling gold, cotton, and ivory. From about A.D. 800 African traders in Timbuktu and elsewhere played an important part in the world economy. Goods from Africa were prized as far away as Europe, India, and China. But in the fifteenth century, something would happen to upset the natural growth of African trade and culture. How would the European demand for slaves undermine the rich societies that Africans had built over the centuries?

Background: African traditions were passed from generation to generation by *griots,* or oral historians.
Ask: What values or traditions are passed down orally today? Give examples.

245

CHAPTER REVIEW

VOCABULARY REVIEW

Write each number and word on a sheet of paper. Then write the letter of the definition next to the word it defines.

1. Sudan
2. civil servant
3. mansa
4. Berbers
5. Swahili
6. architect
7. terra-cotta

a. the area just south of the Sahara
b. someone who plans buildings
c. king or emperor in Mali
d. the main language of East Africa
e. North African nomads
f. clay
g. government employee

SKILL BUILDER: COMPARING MAPS

Compare the two maps below. Then answer the questions on a sheet of paper.

1. What is the subject of the map at left? at right?
2. What was Ghana's central city?
3. What two cities were important both to Mali and Songhai?
4. In what vegetation zone did the cities of Kumbi, Timbuktu, and Gao lie? On the basis of this information, what could you say about this region as a place for people to live in?
5. Through what kind of vegetation would you travel on your way from Timbuktu to Benin?
6. On what river might you travel to get from Ife to Gao?

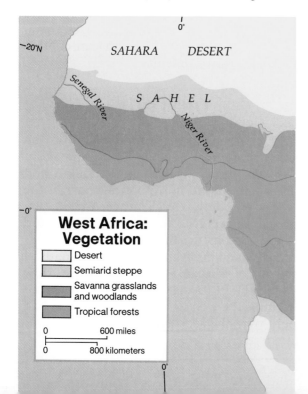

West Africa: Vegetation
- Desert
- Semiarid steppe
- Savanna grasslands and woodlands
- Tropical forests

0   600 miles
0   800 kilometers

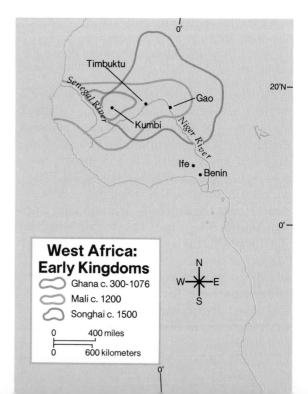

West Africa: Early Kingdoms
- Ghana c. 300-1076
- Mali c. 1200
- Songhai c. 1500

0   400 miles
0   600 kilometers

SKILL BUILDER: CRITICAL THINKING AND COMPREHENSION

1. Compare and Contrast

▶ On a sheet of paper, make a chart about Timbuktu and an East African city such as Kilwa. The chart should show at least three ways that the cities are the same or different. For example, Timbuktu was located in West Africa; Kilwa was located in East Africa.

2. Drawing Conclusions

▶ Read the three facts below. Then, on a sheet of paper, write a conclusion you can draw from these facts.

Fact: Mansa Musa traveled to Egypt with a huge caravan carrying much gold.

Fact: It took several months to cross Mali by horse.

Fact: Timbuktu and Gao were important cities in Mali.

3. Predicting

▶ The coastal cities of East Africa carried on trade with other parts of Africa and with India. The traders from these different lands did not always speak the same language. How do you think they could understand each other? How might the languages of each group have changed because of this contact? Write your prediction on a sheet of paper.

4. Fact *versus* Opinion
A fact is something that can be proved. You can check in other sources to see if the fact is true. An example of a fact would be: Askia ruled Songhai from 1494 to 1538. An opinion is a statement telling what someone believes about something. An opinion cannot be proved. An example of an opinion would be: Askia was the greatest ruler of Songhai. Why do you think it is important to know the difference between a fact and an opinion?

▶ Now read the statements below and decide whether each one is a fact or an opinion. Write the letter of each statement on a sheet of paper. Label each statement **F** for fact or **O** for opinion.

a. People in hot climates need salt for their health.

b. Camels can walk a long distance before needing water.

c. The Ghana empire reached its height before the rise of Mali.

d. By 1494 Songhai was the greatest empire ever built in West Africa.

e. Kilwa was one of the most beautiful towns in the world.

ENRICHMENT

1. Find out more about Mansa Musa. Then write a diary entry that Mansa Musa might have made during his trip to Mecca. You might describe how North Africa was different from Mali or how people reacted to the king's generosity.

2. At its height Timbuktu had about one million residents. Today it is a town of less than 10,000. Yet Timbuktu is still an important West Africa city. Find out in what present-day country Timbuktu is located and what life is like there today. Also try to find out why the number of people in Timbuktu shrank.

CHAPTER 5

Mogul India

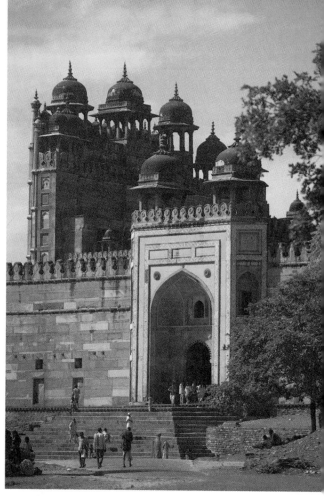

OBJECTIVE: How did the Muslim invasion affect India?

1. Akbar, the emperor of India, had everything he wanted—except a son to inherit his throne. Then he visited a holy man who, it was said, would bless anyone who came to see him. Shortly afterward Akbar's wife gave birth to a boy. Akbar was so happy that he ordered a new capital city to be built overlooking the holy man's village. This city was called Fatehpur Sikri, and it was built in the incredibly short time of six years. Akbar was a Muslim who respected all religions, and the city's design combined Muslim and Hindu styles. It was a fabulous place of red sandstone palaces, mosques, and towers, all inlaid with marble. Three bands of walls ran for seven miles around the city. The stones of one courtyard were laid out in the pattern of the board used in the Indian game of parcheesi. Akbar would roll dice, and persons acting as playing

▲ Akbar founded the city of Fatehpur Sikri as the capital of the Mogul Empire in 1570. The Moguls conquered India in 1530.

pieces would move around the stones in the moonlight. Unfortunately the local water supply was too small to supply Fatehpur Sikri, and Akbar abandoned the city after 15 years. But the city remains in nearly perfect condition. It is one of the finest relics

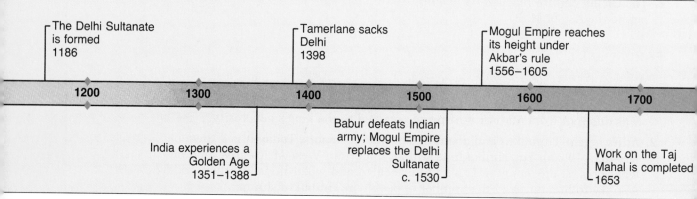

The Delhi Sultanate is formed 1186

Tamerlane sacks Delhi 1398

Mogul Empire reaches its height under Akbar's rule 1556–1605

| 1200 | 1300 | 1400 | 1500 | 1600 | 1700 |

India experiences a Golden Age 1351–1388

Babur defeats Indian army; Mogul Empire replaces the Delhi Sultanate c. 1530

Work on the Taj Mahal is completed 1653

of the age when Muslim conquerers invaded India. These invaders created what was known as the Mogul Empire.

TROUBLES IN INDIA: How did the Muslims gain control in northern India?

2. After the collapse of the Gupta Empire in the sixth century, India entered a long period of political upheaval. The empire broke up into small kingdoms, each under the control of a separate leader. For about 600 years these princes fought for control of India. However, none was strong enough to unite India into one country. Tribes from central Asia added to the chaos. They crossed the northern mountains to raid and pillage Indian cities.

3. Among the fiercest of the outside invaders were Muslims from Afghanistan and its northern neighbor, Turkestan. From time to time these excellent horseback riders would swoop down from the mountains into the plains of Northern India. Find ► Afghanistan on the map on page 729. What direction is it from India?

4. The Muslim invaders carried off Hindu art, jewels, gold, silver, and slaves. One of the most ruthless of these raiders was an Afghan ruler, or **sultan** (SULT-un), named Mahmud of Ghazni (GAZ-nee). At least 17 times this cruel warrior invaded India. In 1024 Mahmud led his forces into the town of Somnath. He robbed the Hindu temple of its treasures and even carried off the gates of the town. During the raid 50,000 Hindus were killed.

DELHI SULTANATE: What changes did the Delhi sultanate bring to India?

5. Until the twelfth century, few Turkic invaders from Afghanistan settled in India. They took what they wanted and returned to their own kingdoms in central Asia. All this changed in 1186 when a Muslim Turk, Qutb ud-Din Aibak (KOOT-bood-deen EYE-bak), started a Muslim state in northern India. After conquering the city of Delhi and the kingdoms around it, he took control of the whole area. This large kingdom became known as the Delhi sultanate.

6. The Delhi sultanate soon became famous as a center of Islam. One of Qutb's first acts as sultan was to destroy the Hindu temples in northern India. Then he set out to force the Hindus to convert to Islam. Hindus who would not accept Islam had to pay additional taxes. Others were imprisoned or sold as slaves.

Daily life in . . .

When a child was born in India, everyone knew what its whole life would be like. The caste system (KAST SIS-tum) spelled out each person's place in society. It also defined a person's occupation. If a man's father was a farmer, the man would be a farmer. If a man's father was a tailor, the man would be a tailor. People belonged for life to the caste into which they were born.

Socializing with people of another caste was forbidden. People also had to marry within their caste. It was believed that only in another life might a person move up in the caste system.

There were four main castes in India. The highest caste was the Brahman caste. Kings and warriors came from the Kshatriya caste. People of the Vaisya caste were the merchants. Workers and servants were the Sudras, the lowest caste. Beneath the Sudras were the **untouchables** (un-TUCH-uh-bulz), who did not belong to any caste.

Untouchables were considered unclean. They could not enter temples. No one who was part of a caste would eat food cooked by untouchables. Untouchables could not take water from village wells. They did jobs people in castes would not do, like sweeping streets.

ESL/LEP Strategy: Have students summarize the caste system in two or three sentences. Then, ask if there are social divisions in the students' countries of origin. Lead a class discussion about whether there are social divisions in the United States.

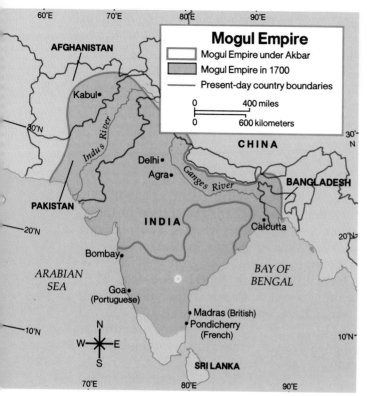

Mogul Empire

☐ Mogul Empire under Akbar
▨ Mogul Empire in 1700
— Present-day country boundaries

0   400 miles
0   600 kilometers

AFGHANISTAN

Kabul•

Indus River

PAKISTAN

Delhi•
Agra•

Ganges River

CHINA

BANGLADESH

INDIA

Calcutta

Bombay•

ARABIAN
SEA

Goa•
(Portuguese)

BAY OF
BENGAL

• Madras (British)
• Pondicherry
  (French)

N
W—E
S

SRI LANKA

▲ Mogul rule brought a new golden age to India in the sixteenth century. What present-day countries were once part of the Mogul Empire?

7. With the wealth gained from trade and taxes, Qutb and later sultans maintained lavish courts. They built beautiful mosques throughout the northern kingdom. One sultan, Firuz Shah Tughlak, built hospitals, schools, and irrigation systems. While he ruled, from 1351 to 1388, India was peaceful and prosperous. By the late fourteenth century Delhi had become a great center of civilization.

8. Muslims and Hindus were uneasy neighbors in India. Conflicts developed many of India's Hindus had to choose between converting to Islam or be killed or taken into slavery. The beliefs of the two groups were so different that their cultures did not blend easily. For example, a basic Muslim belief was the idea of one God. Muslims were shocked by the Hindus' belief in many gods and goddesses. In addition, music played an important part in Hindu religious ceremonies. Muslims, however, thought music offended God. Also, Muslims believed in following strictly the laws of the Koran. Hindus, on the other hand, were willing to accept many different beliefs and ways of behaving.

9. Muslim and Hindu differences caused conflicts, yet the two peoples shared some ideas. For instance, a new language called Urdu developed. It combined the languages of the Indians and Muslims and was written with Arabic letters. Also, *purdah*, the Hindu practice of secluding women from society spread to other parts of the Muslim world.

ATTACKS ON DELHI: How was the Delhi sultanate destroyed?

10. Delhi's success soon attracted the envy of rulers from other lands. In 1398 the great Mongol prince, Tamerlane, set his sights on the Delhi sultanate. He had already established an empire that included Persia, the Tigris-Euphrates Valley, and Afghanistan. (Find these places on the map on page 44.) Now he wanted more.

11. With a large force, Tamerlane swept into India, seizing everything in his path. Stories of Tamerlane's cruelty spread terror throughout the region. Tamerlane nearly destroyed the city of Delhi. It was said that "for two whole months not a bird moved a wing in the city." However, after collecting his booty, Tamerlane left nearly as quickly as he had come. He and his army were off to conquer other lands.

MOGUL EMPIRE: How did Babur and Akbar rule the Mogul Empire?

12. The Delhi sultanate never fully recovered from Tamerlane's assault. The sultanate continued its decline and was finally destroyed by a new wave of Muslim invaders. In 1526 one of Tamerlane's descendants, Babur, marched into northern India. With only 12,000 men, this Mongol known as "the lion" defeated an Indian army of 100,000. Babur's forces used gunpowder, which the Indians did not have. Why was ◄ this an advantage for Babur's army? By the time of his death in 1530, Babur controlled

Background: In accordance with *purdah*, women could have only their male relatives visit them. In the presence of other men, they had to cover their faces with veils.

most of northern India. Because Babur was from Mongolia, the area became known as the Mongol, or **Mogul** (MOH-gul), Empire.

SPOTLIGHT ON SOURCES

13. Babur did not respect the Hindus. Like many Muslims, he thought Muslim life was best. Babur kept daily notes about his life and the people he met. These notes were put together into a book of **memoirs** (MEM-warz). A memoir is a highly personal account of events. This part of his memoirs tells how Babur felt about the Hindus.

> Hindustan [northern India] is a country of few charms. Its people have no good looks; of . . . paying visits and receiving visitors there is none; of genius and capacity [ability] none; of manners none, in handicraft and work there is no form of symmetry [balance], method, or quality; there are no good horses, no good dogs, no grapes, muskmelons, or first rate fruits, no ice or cold water, no good bread or cooked food in the bazaars [markets], no hot baths, . . . no candles, torches, or candlesticks . . . there are no running waters in their gardens or residences . . . . Its towns are all of one sort; there are no walls to the orchards and most places are in the dead, level plain. . . .
>
> —*Memoirs of Babur*,
> translated by Annette S. Beveridge

14. Babur's grandson, Akbar, became emperor of the Mogul Empire in 1556. Akbar fought many wars to increase his empire. Eventually the empire extended south to include much of Central India.

PEOPLE IN HISTORY

15. The Mogul Empire reached its golden age under Akbar, who ruled from 1556 to 1605. Akbar felt it would be impossible to keep his empire united if he tried to make all the people live as Muslims. So he allowed people of all religions to worship as they pleased. Besides Islam and Hindu, religions practiced at this time were Buddhism, Christianity, and Sikhism, a form of Islam. Akbar himself developed a religion

▼ The Mongol conqueror Tamerlane attacked and weakened the Delhi sultanate in 1398. His descendant Babur overthrew the sultanate in 1530 and founded the Mogul Empire.

Background: Guns were something unknown in India. The Muslim Turks had guns because they were the descendants of Mongols, who had captured China where gunpowder was invented.

251

▲ Shah Jahan built the famous Muslim temple, Taj Mahal, as a tomb for his wife. It took about 20,000 workers over 20 years to craft this memorial out of marble and precious stones.

The Taj Mahal   In 1607 Shah Jahan asked his father, the emperor Jahangir, for permission to marry Arjumand. The two young people had fallen in love. Many Indians were shocked by Shah Jahan's request. It was the custom for parents to pick wives for their sons. However, because Jahangir was deeply in love with his own wife, he agreed to his son's marriage. Jahangir gave Arjumand the name Mumtaz Mahal, "Chosen One of the Palace."

Shah Jahan built the beautiful Taj Mahal for Mumtaz Mahal. They had been married for 19 years when Mumtaz Mahal died giving birth to their fourteenth child. The Taj Mahal became her tomb. It took 21 years to build. White marble was brought from 250 miles (400 kilometers) away. Jewels were set into the walls. A blanket of pearls was placed over Mumtaz Mahal's coffin.

In 1650 Shah Jahan was taken prisoner by his son Aurangzeb. Shah Jahan was kept in a palace called the Red Fort. For nine years Shah Jahan spent his time looking at the Taj Mahal from the windows of the Red Fort. During his last illness, Shah Jahan had a mirror hung on the wall beside his bed. In the mirror he could see the Taj Mahal. He died alone one afternoon, his head turned toward the mirror and its view of his wife's tomb. Shah Jahan was buried next to his beloved wife Mumtaz Mahal.

Over the past 300 years, the Taj Mahal has been visited by millions of people. Its white marble walls sparkle in the sun. At night, the Taj Mahal glows softly in the light of the moon. At all times, its reflection fills the pools of water in the gardens around the Taj Mahal.

1. How did Shah Jahan show his love for Mumtaz Mahal?

2. Today, how do we honor people who have died?

252

Background: Shah Jahan had planned to build his tomb at the other end of the reflecting pool, facing the Taj Mahal. The two tombs were to be connected by a bridge of solid silver.

that was a mix of Islam and Hinduism. Akbar ended the tax on non-Muslims. He also gave some important government jobs to Hindus. He even married a Hindu princess. How do you think Akbar's actions helped keep the empire united?

16. Akbar reformed the economy and the tax system, which enriched the empire. With these riches Akbar began to make great changes in the lives of his people. He sponsored writers, artists, and architects. In honor of the birth of his son, Akbar ordered his people to build an entire city, Fatehpur Sikri, on a mountainside. Akbar's city had a fine palace and many other beautiful buildings. To this day tourists can visit Fatehpur Sikri's beautiful buildings, almost all of which are still in perfect condition.

THE END OF THE EMPIRE: Why did the Mogul Empire decline?

17. Akbar was succeeded by his son Jahangir (Ja-HAHN-ger), who ruled from 1605 to 1627. Control of the empire then passed to Akbar's grandson Shah Jahan, who ruled from 1628 to 1658. Both rulers continued Akbar's tolerant policies toward Hindus and expanded Mogul rule in the South

18. Akbar's great-grandson Aurangzeb (AW-ruhng-zehb), who became emperor in 1658, had few of his grandfather's good qualities. He became emperor by imprisoning his own father, Shah Jahan. Then he ruled harshly over his subjects. Aurangzeb required all citizens to practice Islam. No other religions were allowed. Aurangzeb's actions led to revolts throughout India. However, Aurangzeb was too powerful for his enemies.

19. Aurangzeb extended Mogul rule over all but a small part of southern India. However, later emperors had trouble keeping the empire together. Within a few years of Aurangzeb's death, the Mogul Empire collapsed. India again became a land of small kingdoms, each ruled by a local leader.

20. Other events were taking place in India. The first 150 years of Mogul rule brought peace and prosperity to India. In-

▲ These three rulers—Akbar (seated right), his son Jahangir (center), and grandson Shah Jahan (left)—brought the Mogul Empire in India to its height.

dia was then one of the world's richest countries. European traders began arriving in India anxious to profit from India's rich trade. As the Mogul Empire collapsed, the foreigners began to gain more and more power over troubled India's affairs.

OUTLOOK

21. Much of India's history tells of conflict between peoples of different religions. The Muslims conquered the Hindus. The Moguls destroyed Hindu temples. The Sikhs and others fought to throw out the Moguls. However, every now and then a ruler came along who tried to do things differently. Akbar, for example, ended unfair treatment of Hindus. He was tolerant of Hindus and other religious groups, and India flourished under his rule. What lessons do you think rulers of today might learn from Akbar?

CHAPTER REVIEW

254

VOCABULARY REVIEW

Write each of the following sentences on a sheet of paper. Then fill in the blank with the word that best completes each sentence.

sultan

memoirs

untouchables

Mogul

1. Babur wrote his _____ , in which he described daily events and his ideas about life and the empire he ruled.

2. In Afghanistan a ruler was called a _____ .

3. People in India who belonged to no caste are called _____ .

4. Babur invaded India and started the _____ Empire.

SKILL BUILDER: INTERPRETING A TIME LINE

A time line is a line that shows the sequence of events during a period in history. By studying time lines, you can review the dates certain events occurred, as well as the order in which the events took place. The time line below highlights the important events in the life of Shah Jahan. Study the time line, and then answer the questions that follow.

1. Into what time periods do the tick marks divide the time line?

2. What is the first event listed on the time line? What is the last event?

3. In what year did Shah Jahan begin work on the Taj Mahal? When was the work finished?

4. What happened to Shah Jahan in 1657?

5. Suppose you wanted to add the following event to the time line. Between what two dates would you enter the event?
   1607–Shah Jahan asks his father for permission to marry Mumtaz Mahal.

6. When did Mumtaz Mahal die?

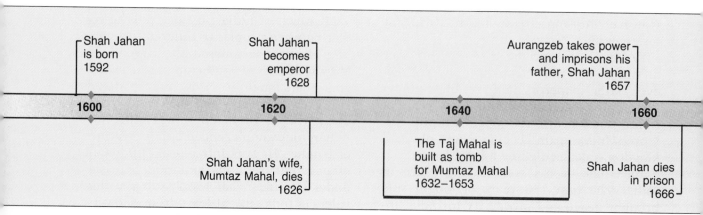

Shah Jahan is born 1592

Shah Jahan becomes emperor 1628

Aurangzeb takes power and imprisons his father, Shah Jahan 1657

1600   1620   1640   1660

Shah Jahan's wife, Mumtaz Mahal, dies 1626

The Taj Mahal is built as tomb for Mumtaz Mahal 1632–1653

Shah Jahan dies in prison 1666

SKILL BUILDER: CRITICAL THINKING AND COMPREHENSION

1. Fact *versus* Opinion   A fact is information that can be proved. An opinion is a belief or judgment. In reading about history it is important to be able to tell the difference between facts and opinions.

▶ Reread the excerpt from Babur's memoirs on page 251. Then, on a sheet of paper, list three facts and three opinions stated in the excerpt.

2. Compare and Contrast

▶ Look closely at the picture of the Taj Mahal on page 252. Then find in the book another picture of a building. How are the buildings the same? How are they different? On a sheet of paper, write a paragraph comparing and contrasting the two buildings.

3. Drawing Conclusions

▶ What conclusion do you draw from the following facts? Write your answer on a sheet of paper.

Fact: Akbar was a Muslim.

Fact: Akbar ended the tax on non-Muslims.

Fact: Akbar gave some important jobs to Hindus.

Fact: Akbar married a Hindu princess.

Fact: India prospered under Akbar's rule.

4. Predicting

▶ As centuries passed and new conquerors took over India, what probably happened to the jewels in the Taj Mahal? Write your prediction on a sheet of paper. How can you find out if your prediction is true?

ENRICHMENT

1. Imagine that you are a non-Muslim living in northern India during the reign of Aurangzeb. Write a diary entry about a time when his troops came to your city to collect the special tax that non-Muslims must pay. Describe what happened and your reactions.

2. Find out more about the layout and design of the Taj Mahal. Look in an encyclopedia or other reference book. Draw a detailed picture of the Taj Mahal or create a model or blueprint of it.

3. Pakistan, a mostly Muslim country, was once part of India. In 1947 Pakistan became a separate nation. Find out why Pakistan broke off from India and what the relationship among the three nations of Bangladesh, Pakistan, and India is today. Report your findings to the class.

4. In 1984 Prime Minister Indira Gandhi of India was shot and killed by two members of her own guard. They were both Sikhs, members of one of India's many minority religions. Find out why from time to time fighting breaks out between Sikhs and other religious groups in India. Make a short oral report to share your findings with the rest of the class.

Isolationism in China and Japan

▲ Portuguese traders first visited Japan in 1543. Why did the Togugawa shoguns decide to end all contact with the West in 1640?

OBJECTIVE: How did China and Japan deal with foreigners from the 1200s to the 1600s?

1. Suppose someone told you she had traveled to a distant planet and discovered life there. Suppose she told you that the people there ate exotic foods, practiced fascinating customs, and had invented some ▶ amazing machines. Would you believe the report? Probably not. Then you can imagine how Europeans of the Middle Ages reacted to a story about a fabulous city in the center of a remarkable civilization in China, thousands of miles to the east. To Europeans of that day, China was as distant and unknown as outer space is to us today. And

what did the Chinese think of Europeans and other foreigners who came there? For a time the Chinese welcomed foreign visitors and traders. As a result, outsiders became acquainted with Chinese silk, porcelain, and other products. But a time came when

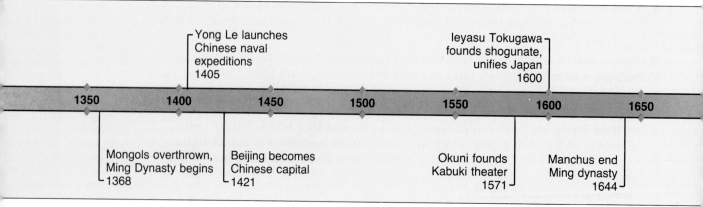

Yong Le launches
Chinese naval
expeditions
1405

Ieyasu Tokugawa
founds shogunate,
unifies Japan
1600

| 1350 | 1400 | 1450 | 1500 | 1550 | 1600 | 1650 |

Mongols overthrown,
Ming Dynasty begins
1368

Beijing becomes
Chinese capital
1421

Okuni founds
Kabuki theater
1571

Manchus end
Ming dynasty
1644

China no longer opened its doors to foreigners. This decision brought both costs and benefits to the Chinese.

THE MONGOLS: How well did these non-Chinese rulers govern China?

2. The Song Dynasty was ended by the Mongols, a fierce tribe from Central Asia. The Mongols were probably the world's finest horse back riders. They lived on horseback and could ride for days without sleep or food. Genghis Khan (gen-guhs-KAHN) was the great Mongol conqueror who drove the Song in northern China farther south. Genghis Khan's grandson, Kublai Khan (koo-bla KAHN), started the Yuan (WAN) Dynasty in northern China in 1260. Kublai Khan established his capital on a site near present-day Beijing (bay-JING). By 1279 Kublai Khan had taken the rest of China, but only after a hard fight with the Song in the south. Find Beijing on the atlas map on page 729. Why is Beijing important today? China became part of the huge Mongol Empire that extended from the Pacific Ocean across Asia into eastern Europe.

3. There was constant tension between the Mongols and the Chinese. The Chinese never accepted the fact that their country was being ruled by non-Chinese rulers. The Chinese were further angered because the Mongols did not share the Chinese view that Chinese culture was remarkable and special. The Mongols, for their part, did not trust the Chinese. They filled many of their government posts with Mongols and other foreigners.

PEOPLE IN HISTORY

4. Marco Polo, a merchant from Italy, was one foreigner hired by the Mongols. He arrived in China in 1275, and stayed for nearly 20 years as the guest of the emperor, Kublai Khan.

5. Both China and Europe benefited from the exchange of ideas between Marco Polo and the Chinese people. For example, Marco Polo taught the Chinese how to build a war machine called a catapult. This weapon could hurl a stone weighing 300 pounds (135 kilograms). The Chinese taught Marco Polo how silk was made and showed him a new material, called asbestos, that did not burn and another called coal, that did.

6. When Marco Polo returned to Europe, he wrote a book about China. In it he told of Chinese tea and spices, a Chinese food called spaghetti, and remarkable marriage and religious customs of the Chinese. Why did trade between China and Europe increase as a result of these stories?

7. Under Mongol rule, China's trade with the West reached new heights. The tales of Marco Polo alerted Europeans to the value of trade with the Chinese people. Goods weighed down camels as traders from east and west traveled the Silk Road. Great amounts of Chinese tea and silk went west. Kublai Khan built new highways and improved ports and canals. Better highways helped the postal service, which used 200,000 horses, to carry mail. Yet great distances and cultural differences separated the many peoples in the Mongol Empire, making it hard for the Mongols to hold the empire together.

8. After Kublai Khan's death in 1294, the Mongol Empire began to decline. Weak rulers could not solve the problems caused by floods and other disasters. Prices rose and Chinese resentment of the foreign rulers grew. As a result, revolts sprang up around the country.

MING DYNASTY: How did China gain new pride in its past and faith in its future?

9. Soon the Chinese began to push for a return to native rule. In 1356 Zhu Yuanzhang (choo yoo-wan-JONG), the son of a poor Chinese peasant family, formed an army of rebellion. After 12 years of fighting, he finally drove out the Mongols and proclaimed himself emperor of China. The dynasty he founded, called Ming (which

means "bright" in Chinese), lasted almost
▶ three hundred years. Why was "bright" a good choice of adjectives?

10. As the first native emperor of China in almost a hundred years, Zhu was determined to keep power. No one was permitted to question his laws or his actions. He also was concerned about enemies outside the country's borders. One precaution he took was to build a strong army and navy to protect China from foreign invasion.

11. Zhu was determined to end all reminders of foreign rule. He reorganized the government to make it more like the government of the past. Zhu reestablished the requirement that all government employees pass a civil service test based on Confucian teachings. Confucian writings again became the guideline for the government. Zhu divided the large empire into more manageable units. Each of these provinces, or states, had its own leader. Zhu kept control of the central army for himself, to make

sure none of the local lords grew more powerful than he.

12. As the new emperor grew stronger, China grew stronger. During the Mongols' rule, dikes and canals in China had fallen into disrepair. Zhu had them repaired. The floods ended and the lands again began to yield crops. Zhu created a standard form of money. How might a standard form of ◀ money help unify a country? The Chinese regained their pride in their country and its accomplishments. More and more they thought of outsiders as inferior barbarians.

13. The next strong leader of the Ming Dynasty was Yong Le (yong LEE), Zhu's son. Yong had a deep interest in the lands and treasures outside China. Yong sought to establish trade with other nations. He assembled seven fleets of ships to travel to other lands. The ships traveled to Southeast Asia, to India, and as far away as Africa. The captains of these "treasure boats," as they were called, were instructed to demand

▼ The Ming Dynasty ruled China from 1368 to 1644. It was a time of great prosperity, trade, and cultural achievements. What other parts of Asia traded with China during the Ming era?

East Asia During the Ming Dynasty

Ming Empire in 1415
Great Wall
Trade routes

0 300 miles
0 400 kilometers

MONGOLIA
GOBI DESERT
MANCHUS
SEA OF JAPAN
JAPAN
Overland route to Europe
XINJIANG
Huang He (Yellow River)
Beijing
KOREA
Edo
Kyoto
YELLOW SEA
Nagasaki
Xian
TIBET
(Yangtze River)
Nanjing
Chang Jiang
INDIA
PACIFIC OCEAN
Xi River
Guangzhou
TAIWAN
BAY OF BENGAL
PEGU
Hanoi
ANNAM
HAINAN
SOUTH CHINA SEA
PHILIPPINES
SIAM
Manila

payments wherever they went. Foreign rulers who would not pay were threatened with the ships' cannons and their goods seized. Among the treasures Yong collected in this way were money, horses, metals, and spices. Unusual gifts, like a giraffe from Africa, were especially prized.

14. In 1421 Yong moved China's capital from Nanjing to Beijing. Look at the map on ▶ page 258. How far is Nanjing from Beijing? Ming rulers still feared invasion from the north—the direction from which the Mongols had swept into China. By moving the capital farther north, leaders felt China could more easily defend its northern borders against invasion.

15. Yong had the Forbidden City built within Beijing. This splendid city within a city was built for China's emperor, his family, and their servants. Violet walls separated the emperor's court from the rest of the city. Many of the treasures Yong collected decorated the halls of his palace within the Forbidden City. Only high officials were allowed inside the city. Anybody trying to enter without permission was put to death.

16. In the mid-1400s Chinese sea expeditions stopped abruptly. Historians are not sure why this happened. Maybe the Chinese, with their advanced civilization, felt they had no more need for the ideas and products of other lands. At any rate, China turned inward until the 1800s, when foreign countries forced new contact.

CLOSED GATES: How did China's isolation affect its development as a nation?

17. When China ended its overseas expeditions, it also placed restrictions on foreigners trading in China. In the early 1500s Portuguese traders came to China, but they were not allowed to come to shore. Instead, Chinese merchants sailed out to the anchored Portuguese ships. When the trading was completed, the Portuguese were told to sail away.

18. In the 1600s other European countries also wanted to trade in China. They were allowed to settle only in Guangzhou (Canton), on the southern coast of China. They were not allowed to bring their wives, to carry firearms, or to learn Chinese. What ◀ do you think was the purpose of each of these restrictions, which China maintained for over 200 years?

19. At the same time that Ming rulers cut off most outside contact, China's own culture flourished. In fact, China reached a golden age under the Ming emperors. Artists and scholars became as important as army officers. Pupils studied China's past. Schools encouraged study of classical Chinese writing and culture.

20. The best Ming artists and writers created many works of high quality. Artists began to paint portraits as well as landscapes and to use color in their paintings. Large numbers of books were printed. Many were stories and poems written in the **vernacular** (ver-NAK-ya-ler), or everyday language. Crowds enjoyed new plays. Plays called the "telling of the strange" had music and singing and used stories from daily life. People of the lower classes sang folk songs that told stories in rhyme.

21. One of the great cultural achievements of this period in Chinese history was Ming porcelain. This fine "china" and other ceramics made in China during the Ming dynasty are still prized today. People of all classes used pots, jars, and vases of exquisite painted porcelain. Artists made beautiful works in copper and silver. Most tried to please the tastes of the people. Ming rulers supported new styles of architecture. Beijing, with its Forbidden City, became known for its beautiful palaces and other buildings.

22. The Ming managed to keep China secure until the Manchurian invasion in 1644. In that year, the Manchus from Manchuria (to the north) overthrew the Ming Dynasty and conquered China. They set up the Qing Dynasty. The Manchus, like the Ming before them, kept China isolated. This policy would cause serious problems for China when it had to deal with foreign countries in later years.

259

TOKUGAWA: How did Japan benefit from the Tokugawa Shoguns?

23. In the last years of the Ming Dynasty, China's neighbor Japan was also undergoing changes. Toward the end of the sixteenth century, Japan's 66 provinces were brought together under one government. Hideyoshi (hye-de-YOH-shee), Japan's military leader at this time, built a strong group of **alliances** (a-LIE-enz-ez). An alliance is an agreement among groups to work together. These alliances helped establish peace throughout the land.

24. After Hideyoshi's death in 1598, however, the alliances broke apart. Several generals fought for control of Japan. Finally, in 1600, Tokugawa Ieyasu (toh-koo-GAH-wah eye-ee-YAH-zoo) became the new shogun, or supreme military governor. Ieyasu started a line of Tokugawa shoguns that ruled for more than 250 years. The emperor, who had little military power, continued his role as figurehead, or symbolic ruler.

25. As leader of Japan, Ieyasu built a strong government. He moved the center of government to Edo, which is now Tokyo. He also formed a secret police to keep watch for any plans against the government. The samurai, or warrior class, defended Ieyasu from his enemies. The **daimyos** (DYE-mee-ohz), or great lords, kept their lands in the countryside. However, Ieyasu restricted their power. Daimyos now needed permission from the shogun to sign a contract or arrange a daughter's marriage. Also, the daimyos had to live in Edo every other year. Their families had to live in Edo year-round. Why do you think the shogun imposed these restrictions on the daimyos?

26. Ieyasu's government brought peace and prosperity to Japan. Farmers were no longer called away to fight wars. Taxes were lowered. Gold and silver coins replaced rice as a form of money. People used the coins to buy luxuries such as fancy clothes and new foods. One trading family opened shops that were like today's department stores, with goods that had fixed prices. As trade grew, cities such as Kyoto, Edo, and Osaka became large business centers.

27. Peace-time also gave the Japanese more time to enjoy art and culture. Even the samurai turned their attention to other arts. The fifth Tokugawa shogun set up schools that taught Japanese philosophy along with samurai skills. Many samurai learned to write as well as they fought. These schools began to hold games that trained the body and the mind. The study of judo and karate mixed fighting skills with ideas about simple living and discipline.

28. Under the Tokugawa shoguns, two new kinds of theater appeared. One was the

Daily life in . . .

In the large cities of Edo, Kyoto, and Osaka a new type of entertainment arose. It began as an outdoor performance of song and dance. Eventually it grew into a type of theater called kabuki.

At a kabuki play, the audience sat on two sides of the stage. A narrow passageway to the back of the theater allowed actors to pass among the viewers during a play. The plays called for elaborate costumes, colorful face make-up, and larger-than-life gestures by the actors. The word kabuki comes from a Japanese word meaning strange or unusual. All roles in a kabuki play are acted by men.

Kabuki grew in popularity during the Tokugawa shogunate. During this time people had become more educated. This era of peace also left them with more money to spend. Every day hundreds of people attended performances in kabuki theaters. They watched love stories or plays about real events of the times. Other plays featured adventure, martial arts, and violence. What do you think is the "people's theater" of today?

puppet theater. Large, life-like puppets would act out adventure or love stories. Another new form of theater was the **kabuki** (kuh-BOO-kee). Started in 1571 by a woman named Okuni, kabuki theater combined music, dance, and acting. Kabuki was the first theater for common people in Japan.

29. During this time, poets began writing **haiku** (HYE-koo), a kind of short poem. A haiku has only 17 syllables. It tries to capture a scene or mood in a few words. Haiku began as comic poems that were easy to write. Bashō Matsuo (bah-shon ma-tsu-o) made haiku into a serious form of writing in the late 1600s.

SPOTLIGHT ON SOURCES

30. Here are three of Bashō's haiku translated, or rewritten, into English. What scene or mood does each poem suggest?

These summer grasses,
of all the dead warriors' dreams,
Are all that remains.
—from *Full Moon Rising*

A withered tree branch
On which a crow has settled—
The autumn night falls.
—from *The Narrow Road to the Deep North*

Can it be springtime?
A mountain without a name
Lies in morning mist.
—from *Full Moon Rising*

31. For most of its history under the Tokugawa shoguns, Japan remained isolated from the West. For a brief time, Ieyasu allowed Christian missionaries from Portugal and Spain to teach their religion in Japan. In exchange, the Japanese traded with Portuguese and Spanish merchant ships. However, Iemitsu (eye-ee-MIT-zoo), Ieyasu's grandson, feared that the Europeans would change his people. In 1640 he ended the Portuguese and Spanish visits to Japan and kept the Japanese from sailing to Europe. He expelled the missionaries and

▲ Japanese kabuki plays feature elaborate face makeup and costumes. The traditional plays combine music, dance, and acting.

treated Japanese Christians harshly. He distrusted the Christians' loyalty to the Pope and feared they would grow strong enough to overthrow him. Following these actions by the shogun, Japan had little contact with the West for the next 200 years.

OUTLOOK

32. China and Japan each lived isolated from the West for hundreds of years. They both gained and lost from this isolation. Each built rich, strong cultures. Each promoted traditions that made people feel safe and proud of their country. However, both China and Japan also fell behind the West in some ways. In the 1500s, China and Japan were equal or superior to the Europeans in science and technology. By the 1900s when contact started again, however, China and Japan had fallen far behind.

Activity: Another popular new art form of the time was wood-block printing. Many were beautiful paintings with flowing lines. Have students research wood-block printing and bring examples into class.

261

CHAPTER REVIEW

VOCABULARY REVIEW

Write each of the following sentences on a sheet of paper. Then fill in the blank with the word that best completes each sentence.

haiku

vernacular

translated

kabuki

daimyos

alliances

1. Something written in everyday language is in the _____ .

2. Hideyoshi created peace in Japan by building strong _____ .

3. "Great lords," or _____ , had to live in Edo every other year.

4. The first theater for the common people in Japan was the _____ .

5. A poet writing a _____ can express an idea or image in just a few words.

6. Many Japanese poems have been _____ into English.

SKILL BUILDER: INTERPRETING A TABLE

The following table gives some information about the status of women in Japan before and during the rule of the Tokugawa shoguns. Study the table. Then, on a sheet of paper, answer the questions that follow.

Before Tokugawa	During Tokugawa Shoguns
1. A husband often went to live in the home of his wife's family.	**1.** A wife went to live in the home of her husband's family.
2. Women could inherit property.	**2.** Women's right to inherit property was restricted.
3. Women had some divorce rights.	**3.** A man could divorce his wife whenever he chose; a woman could not divorce her husband.
4. Women could control some property in marriage.	**4.** Women could not travel freely.
5. The ideal woman was educated and witty.	**5.** Women were not thought to need education equal to that of men.
	6. One of the wife's duties was to give birth to a son.

1. What can you conclude from the facts presented in item **1** on each side of the table?

2. How would you describe the standing of women before the Tokugawa shoguns?

3. How would you describe their standing during the Tokugawa shoguns?

4. At which time did women have more rights? Give two examples to support your answer.

SKILL BUILDER: CRITICAL THINKING AND COMPREHENSION

1. Compare and Contrast

▶ Compare the Mongol attitude toward foreign trade with the Ming attitude toward foreign trade. On a sheet of paper, write a paragraph telling how their attitudes were the same or different.

2. Drawing Conclusions

▶ What conclusion can you draw from these facts about the rule of China's Zhu Yuan-Zhang? Write your conclusion on a sheet of paper.

Fact: He restored Confucian teachings as a guideline for government.

Fact: He strengthened the army and navy.

Fact: He created a standard form of money for all of China.

3. Predicting

▶ You have read about Chinese reaction to Mongol rule. In 1644 China was again conquered by foreigners—the Manchus. How do you think the Chinese would react to this new rule by foreigners? Why? Write your prediction on a sheet of paper and support it with at least two facts.

4. Fact versus Opinion

▶ On a sheet of paper, write three statements of fact based on information you have read in this chapter. Then write a statement of opinion about each of the facts. For example:

Fact: Tokugawa Ieyasu, who came to power in Japan in the year 1600, built a strong government.

Opinion: It was good for Japan that Ieyasu came to power.

ENRICHMENT

1. Find out more about China's Forbidden City. Do research about its layout, how it was decorated, and so on. Draw a diagram or make a model of the city based on your research.

2. Study the three haiku in this chapter. Then use these as a model to write a haiku of your own. Remember, a haiku has three lines and only 17 syllables. The first line has 5 syllables, the second has 7 syllables, and the third has 5 syllables. A haiku is often about something in nature.

3. Learn about Japanese wood blocking. Create a wood block of your own to decorate stationery or notecards.

CHAPTER 7

Civilization of the Americas

▲ This Aztec calendar stone is modeled on the Mayan calendar of 365 days. The Aztecs adopted many Mayan inventions.

OBJECTIVE: What are the similarities and differences of the Maya, Aztec and Inca civilizations of the Americas?

1. Three great Indian civilizations—the Maya, the Aztecs, and the Incas—developed in the early history of Latin America. These cultures were isolated from each other and from the rest of the world. They were isolated from each other by thick rain forests and high mountains. They were isolated from the rest of the world because neither Europeans nor any other "Old World" cultures knew that the land of the Americas existed. Despite their isolation from one another, the three civilizations had some things in common: corn, the sun, and great cities. Corn was the main source of food for the Maya, the Aztecs, and the Incas. An early visitor to Mexico reported that the Indians "almost regarded corn as a god." The Maya filled the mouths of their dead with ground corn for the afterlife. They also

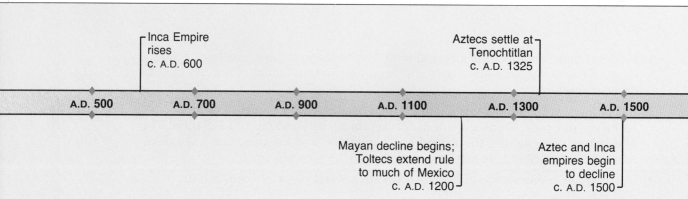

Inca Empire rises
C. A.D. 600

Aztecs settle at Tenochtitlan
C. A.D. 1325

A.D. 500 — A.D. 700 — A.D. 900 — A.D. 1100 — A.D. 1300 — A.D. 1500

Mayan decline begins; Toltecs extend rule to much of Mexico
C. A.D. 1200

Aztec and Inca empires begin to decline
C. A.D. 1500

believed the stars were kernels of corn helping people to find their way in the dark. While each of these civilizations worshipped many gods, they all had a sun god.
▶ Why do you think the sun would be so important to them? The Maya, Aztecs, and Incas also were great builders. They built cities with splendid temples and squares. Many of their works—such as the pyramids of Mexico and the fortresses of Peru—have survived to today.

MAYA CITY-STATES: How was religion important to the Maya?

2. The Maya (MYE-ah) were an ancient people who lived in the rain forests of what is today known as Guatemala, Belize, and the Yucatan Peninsula. Their civilization lasted from about 2400 B.C. to A.D. 1200. The Maya built great stone cities. While most Maya were farmers living outside the cities, many Maya did live in these centers of religion, government, and trade.

3. The city of Tikal was the largest Mayan city. At the center of Tikal was a tall stone pyramid. Other pyramids were nearby. Steps rose all the way to the top of each pyramid where a holy temple was located. Around the pyramid in the center of Tikal was a huge square and buildings for the king, ruling classes, and priests. Standing in front of the pyramids and temples were tall stone shafts called **steles** (STEE-leez). There were more than 115 steles in Tikal. Some of them were blank, but most were carved. Some carvings showed images of the Mayan gods or of important priests or rulers. Oth-

ers contained writing, telling when and why the stele had been put up. The pictoral style of writing was far ahead of other peoples then living in the New World.

4. Mayan farmers lived in farming villages outside the center city. To work the land the farmers first had to clear an area of rain forest. Then they planted corn and other crops such as sweet potatoes, beans, onions, and squash. From time to time the villagers took their produce and home-made goods to markets in the city.

5. Mayan religion included the worship of many gods. There were gods of corn, earth, rain, sun, and other natural elements. All these gods had to do with protecting the corn crop. A good corn harvest meant the people would live. A poor harvest meant they would starve. The Maya performed many rituals and held large celebrations to honor their gods. During these religious events, villagers would crowd into the city square. They came with crops and animals to sacrifice to the gods.

6. The people were ruled by priests, but no one leader ruled all the Maya. The city-states were only loosely united by their common religion and languages. Within each city-state the villagers helped to build and keep up the center city. Skilled stone masons carved beautiful decorations into the steles and the walls of the buildings. Talented artists painted scenes and messages on the walls.

7. Building the pyramids and erecting the steles was an amazing accomplishment. The Maya had only stone tools with which to cut and shape the building stones. Some

Daily life in . . .

The Maya played a ball game to worship their gods. The game was like basketball, with a raw rubber ball that was thrown through a basket hanging from the wall. The game was also like soccer. No player's hands could touch the ball. Imagine trying to shoot a basket using only your head, elbows, and feet! On game days, the Maya filled rows of seats to watch the games. The games had a religious significance to the Maya. They believed the outcome of the game was a message from the gods. Priests explained what the message was to the people.

Background: Some people apply the term Native Americans to early peoples of the Americas—other people use the term Amerindian.

265

of these stones weighed as much as 65 tons (58.5 metric tons). Yet the Maya did not have wheeled carts or draft animals to haul the stones. How do you think the Maya lifted or moved the stones to build the pyramids?

8. Not only were the Maya talented builders, they were great artists and craftspeople as well. Some of the world's finest jade and gold jewelry was fashioned by Mayan jewelers. The Maya developed a system of mathematics that included the idea of zero. They also created a system of writing and a calendar. What special knowledge did the Maya need in order to design a calendar?

9. About A.D. 900 the Mayan civilization began to decline. No one really knows why. Perhaps the Maya had worn out their soil and needed new farmland. Perhaps they were struck by disease. Or maybe the farmers revolted against the priests. Whatever the case, the Maya were finally taken over by another Indian group, the Toltecs. The Mayan culture did not end at that time, however. It mixed with Toltec culture and flourished in its new form for another 400 years. At the end of the tenth century the Maya moved to what is called the Yucatan Peninsula in present-day Mexico. Locate the Yucatan Peninsula on the map on page 268. The major city there was Chichen Itza (cha-CHEN its-AH). The ruins of Chichen Itza can still be seen today.

THE FIERCE AZTECS: How did the Aztecs rule their empire?

10. Another important group of early Americans to found a great civilization was the Aztecs. At first the Aztecs were nomads, wandering through the hills and deserts of Mexico. About 1200 they settled on an island in Lake Texcoco.

11. The Aztecs built a great city, Tenochtitlan (tay-NAWCH-tee-TLAHN), on their island in Lake Texcoco and developed unusual farming methods. Today Mexico City, the capital of Mexico, is located on the place where Tenochtitlan once stood. How did

▲ The Pyramid of the Sun rises from the ruins of an ancient city in central Mexico. Why did early Indian civilizations worship the sun?

Tenochtitlan's island setting protect the city from attack? The island's soil was swampy and not very good for farming. The Aztecs found a way to grow food anyway. They built floating gardens, made of rafts covered with roots, weeds, and mud. These floating gardens were called **chinampas**. Here they planted crops to feed the people of the city. The chinampas were exceptionally fertile and the Aztec kingdom grew and flourished.

12. In time Tenochtitlan became the largest Indian city in America. Over 100,000 people lived there. The Aztecs even increased the size of the island. They loaded soil into canoes and dumped it in the water at the edge of the island. Imagine how many loads of soil it would take to build up just a

Activity: Some students might want to create a diagram of the magnificent city of Tenochtitlan.

266

one foot ring around the island! Canals were dug throughout the city to be used like streets. People traveled through the city in canoes. The Aztecs loved flowers, so gardens were planted everywhere. There were also zoos, orchards, and open-air theaters. Three moveable bridges joined the city to land. The bridges could be removed to keep enemies away. But most of the time traders with goods from Mexico, Central America, and even the southwest deserts of today's United States came across these bridges. In the city's central marketplace, thousands of people gathered to buy and sell their goods. When people first saw Tenochtitlán, they marveled at its splendor.

13. The Aztec civilization was quite advanced. Engineers found ways to build stone buildings on soft, swampy land by driving piles into the ground for support. Priests developed a type of writing that used pictures and symbols. They also made detailed observations of the stars and planets and developed a calendar. No animals were used as beasts of burden in Central America during Aztec times. Most items of trade were carried on men's backs or in canoes. There were no carts in Aztec times either, since the Aztecs knew nothing about the advantages of wheeled transportation.

14. The Aztecs, like the Maya, worshipped many gods. The main god was Huitzilopochtli, which means "hummingbird of the south." Despite his pleasant name, he was the cause of much death. Huitzilopochtli was the god of the sun and of war. The Aztecs believed they had to make human sacrifices in order to keep Huitzilopochtli happy. The warlike Aztecs often conquered new lands and used their captured prisoners as sacrifices to the god of war. In 1500, after building a great temple at Tenochtitlán, the Aztecs sacrificed at least 20,000 people to Huitzilopochtli. Such sacrifices were founded on an ancient Aztec belief about the sun or Sun-god. Every night, it was believed, the Sun god descended into the land of the dead and lost his flesh. Only by the Aztecs sacrificing human flesh was the sun able to rise every

day and make his journey across the sky.

15. At the height of the empire, there were as many as five million people being ruled by Aztec leaders. The government was made up of a council and a ruler, chosen by the council. The ruler lived in a huge palace and ate from gold dishes. The priests were powerful in government as well as in religion. The priests collected taxes from the people for the gods and the ruler. For example, in one year they might collect 14 million pounds of corn, 8 million pounds of beans, and 2 million cotton cloaks. To keep control over the empire, the government sent out spies who sent information back to the leaders.

16. By the 1500s, the Aztecs had conquered almost all of Mexico. The Aztecs did not rule all of Mexico directly, however. Local kings were allowed to rule their own kingdoms as long as they paid **tribute**, a type of tax. Among the items sent in tribute

▼ American Indian civilizations flourished until the 1500s. What present-day countries lie within the Mayan and Aztec empires?

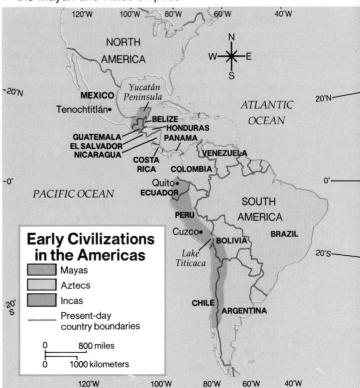

Early Civilizations in the Americas
- Mayas
- Aztecs
- Incas
- Present-day country boundaries

0   800 miles
0   1000 kilometers

were gold, silver, food, cloth, feathers, and captives. Some captives were made slaves. The best fighters among them were freed.

INCA EMPIRE: What did the Incas achieve in building, farming, and government?

17. Even before the Aztecs built their empire, the Incas had begun an empire about A.D. 600 in the Andes Mountains of South America. Like the Aztecs, the Incas were great warriors. By 1400, the Incas had reached their golden age and ruled about 15 million people. Their empire, larger than the Aztec empire, stretched over almost the entire western coast of South America.

18. The Inca empire was the only empire in the New World to have a **hereditary** dynasty. Hereditary means passed down from an ancestor. The emperor, called the Inca, ruled the empire directly. In time, the people also came to be called Incas. The emperor owned all of the land in the Inca empire, and had total power. Most of the people thought that the emperor was a descendant of the Sun god, and did not question his authority.

19. The Inca took good care of the people, who all worked for the empire. Food was stored in huge buildings. When crops were poor, the Inca gave food to the people from the stores. The Inca also made sure that every family had a place to live and enough clothing to wear. In turn the people worked for the empire. They were farmers, gold- and silversmiths, potters, stonecrafters, weavers and toolmakers. Everything the people made was for the improvement of the empire. No system of money was needed. Instead the gold and silver were used to craft beautiful jewelry and statues and decorations for the temples. The Incas thought gold was holy. They called it the "tears of the sun."

20. Most Incas worked as farmers and herders. Before the New World was discovered by Europeans, the Incas were the only American Indians to use animals to do work. Incas used llamas, a wooly mountain animal, for meat, wool, and to carry heavy loads. The farmers were highly skilled at building terraces into the steep hillsides for their crops, such as corn and potatoes. They used irrigation ditches to water the crops.

SPOTLIGHT ON SOURCES

21. The father of the great Peruvian historian, Garcilaso de la Vega, was Spanish. His mother was an Inca. De la Vega wrote down many Incan legends. In one, he tells how the people came to think of the Inca and the Inca's relatives as gods.

Among the famous temples of Peru dedicated to the sun there was one . . . on an island known as Titicaca, which means ridge of lead . . . . The Incas say that the Sun put his son and daughter there when he sent them to earth to enlighten [teach] the wild and barbarous people who inhabited the land at that time, and to teach them a better way of living . . . . The first Inca, Manco Capac, . . . seeing that the Indians believed [this old fable] and held the lake and the island to be a holy place, made up the second fable, saying that he and his wife were the offspring of the Sun, and that their father had placed them on that island that they might go forth throughout the world teaching the people . . . . With these and other made-up stories, the Incas made the other Indians believe they were the children of the Sun, and with the many good works they carried out they confirmed them in this idea.

—*Royal Commentaries of the Incas,*
Garcilaso de la Vega

22. Cuzco, the capital city of the Inca empire, was located high in the Andes Mountains. Only the wealthy lords had homes in Cuzco. The emperor's palace had walls of silver and gold. Other buildings were made of large stones, so carefully cut and fitted that not even the blade of a knife could slide in between them. Many of the walls, temples and palaces they built still

Ask: Many Inca buildings and walls still stand in Peru, an area of many earthquakes. What might have happened to the empire if earthquakes had destroyed the road system?

▲ These Inca walls in the Andes Mountains near Cuzco have survived many earthquakes. Stones were so carefully cut and tightly fitted that many Inca walls still stand.

stand today. Important religious ceremonies took place in the Temple of the Sun. The temple garden was full of plants and animal statues made of gold.

23. The Inca civilization was probably more advanced than the Maya and Aztec civilizations. The Incas used **Quipu** (KEE-poo), or knotted pieces of string, to keep government records. Message runners would carry information across an amazing network of roads built thousands of miles through the mountains. Where rivers and canyons blocked the way, the Incas built bridges made of vine ropes with wooden walkways. The Incas also learned how to use **anesthetics**, or drugs to numb pain, and they even performed brain surgery.

OUTLOOK

24. An American explorer named Hiram Bingham went to Peru in 1911 to look for the ruins of ancient Inca cities. He searched where no explorer had gone before. At the top of a nearby mountain, "We were confronted with an unexpected sight," Bingham wrote, "a great flight of beautifully constructed terraces, perhaps a hundred of them, each hundreds of feet long and ten feet high . . . . It seemed like an unbelievable dream." Bingham had found the lost Inca city known as Machu Picchu. It is one of the greatest ancient cities ever found. It had fine stone houses, squares, altars, and a temple made of shining white stone. Machu Picchu had once been a leading city of the Inca empire. Like the empires of the Maya, Aztecs, and Incas, Machu Picchu had become overgrown with plants and forgotten. How had these great empires been destroyed? No one knows what caused the decline of the Maya empire. Historians believe that the late Aztec and Inca empires were destroyed by something they had in common—a lot of gold. It was not their own desire for gold that destroyed these empires. It was the discovery of the gold by outsiders with different religious beliefs and more advanced technologies that brought down the Aztecs and Incas.

CHAPTER REVIEW

VOCABULARY REVIEW

Write each of the following sentences on a sheet of paper. Then fill in the blank with the word that best completes each sentence.

chinampas

quipu

steles

tribute

hereditary

anesthetics

1. The Maya erected stone slabs called _____ in front of their pyramids and temples.
2. The position of emperor was a _____ position.
3. Local kings in the Aztec Empire had to pay _____ to the Aztec ruler.
4. The Aztecs had floating gardens called _____ .
5. The Incas used a knotted string called a _____ to record words, ideas, and numbers.
6. _____ were used by the Incas to numb pain during surgery.

SKILL BUILDER: CREATING A TABLE

Make a table that compares the Maya, Aztecs, and Incas.

1. Write the three headings "Maya," "Aztecs," and "Incas" across the top of the table.
2. List the three categories "Gods," "Cities," and "Farming Methods" down the side of the table.
3. On a sheet of paper, set up the table with those headings and categories.
4. Add information from the text to fill in the table.

SKILL BUILDER: CRITICAL THINKING AND COMPREHENSION

► 1. Drawing Conclusions

▶ Read the list of facts in column 1. Then choose the statement (a, b, or c) that draws the most logical conclusion from those facts. Write the letter of your choice on a sheet of paper.

1-1. **Fact:** The Aztecs knew how to build heavy stone buildings atop piles driven into soft swampy land.

1-2. **Fact:** Aztec priests used a type of writing.

1-3. **Fact:** Aztec priests developed a calendar.

a. Most Aztecs knew how to write.

b. The Aztecs developed an advanced civilization.

c. Most Aztecs were priests.

> ## 2. Predicting

You have read about the Incas and their empire. In the 1500s people from Spain came to America and met the Incas. The Spanish who came were soldiers hoping to conquer America.

▶ Which of the events listed below do you think would have happened when the Spanish met the Incas? Why? Write the letter of your answer—and your reason for choosing it—on a sheet of paper.

a. The Spanish and Incas fought a war.

b. The Spanish settled in America and lived under Inca rule.

c. The Incas decided to become part of the Spanish empire.

3. Fact *versus* Opinion

▶ Decide whether each of the following statements is a fact or an opinion. Write each statement on a sheet of paper. Next to each statement, write (F) for a fact or (O) for an opinion.

a. Tikal was the largest Mayan city.

b. Tikal was a beautiful city.

c. The Maya worshiped many gods.

d. The Maya devised an accurate calendar.

e. The Mayan ball game was even more exciting than today's basketball.

4. Main Idea

▶ Reread paragraph 19 on page 268. Which of these sentences states the main idea of the paragraph? Copy the sentence on a sheet of paper.

a. The Incas worked for the empire because the emperor took good care of them.

b. The Inca gave his people food.

c. The Inca empire was young in the 1500s.

5. Sequencing

▶ On a sheet of paper, write the following events in the order in which they happened.

a. The Mayan built great pyramids of stone.

b. The Mayan civilization begins to decline.

c. Toltec and Mayan cultures mix.

d. Aztec civilization arises.

e. Incan civilization arises.

ENRICHMENT

1. Find out more about the *quipu*. Then make one out of colored strings and threads.

2. Make up a crossword puzzle using words that have to do with the Maya, Aztecs, and Incas. Write the clues for all the *across* words and all the *down* words. Have a classmate try to complete your puzzle.

271

SUMMARY

People in Africa, Asia, Eastern Europe, and the Americas developed unique societies as Western Europe recovered from the fall of Rome. The rapid growth of Islam unified the nomadic tribes of the Middle East, North Africa, and Saudi Arabia. Trade enriched early African empires, and provided interaction with the peoples of the Middle East and Asia. Religion played a major unifying role in the lives of the early American nations of the Aztecs, Incas, and Maya. Strong military leaders in the nations of Asia created central governments which brought both order to society and isolation. Russia, once a small society of traders and farmers, suffered Mongol domination for years. By throwing off Mongol control, the Russians began the process of centralizing their government and becoming a modern nation.

In all the major areas of world settlement during this time, people were forming centralized nations based on religious unity or overwhelming military power. The pursuit of unity led some Eastern nations such as China to isolate themselves from the rest of the world. But in the Middle East, Africa, and the Americas, trade and expansion often led to cultural interchanges and sometimes war. Some of these nations were weakened or destroyed by war, which paved the way for eventual invasion from Europe.

SKILL BUILDER: READING A MAP

▶ Use the map of "The World About A.D. 1000" to answer the following questions.

The World About 1000

1. On what continents was Islam established by A.D. 1000?
2. What empire lay between southeastern Europe and the Muslim empires?

3. What natural feature of Japan made it easier for Japan to practice isolationism?

4. What empire separated Western Europe from Kievan Russia?

5. The Mongols conquered China, parts of the Muslim world, India, and Kievan Russia. Based on the map and what you have read, do you think they made their conquests by land or by sea?

SKILL BUILDER: CRITICAL THINKING AND COMPREHENSION

1. Drawing Conclusions

▶ What conclusion can you draw from the following facts?

a. People in subSaharan Africa needed salt.

b. People in North Africa wanted gold.

c. The quickest route between sub-Saharan Africa and North Africa was through the Sahara Desert.

2. Compare and Contrast

a. Priests led all religious ceremonies in the Mayan society. Who led the followers of Islam in prayer?

b. The main trading partners of the West African kingdoms were the North Africans. Who were the major trading partners of the East Africans?

c. China, India, Russia, and parts of the Muslim world were all invaded by what fierce tribe of nomads?

d. What was the foreign policy of Manchu China and of Japan under the Shoguns?

e. What positive accomplishments did Suleiman, Akbar, and Mansa Musa make toward education?

f. The Maya raised crops on rich soil in Central America. How did Aztec farmers develop land upon which to farm?

3. Point of View

▶ Copy the following statements that express a point of view. After each statement, write the name of the person who probably would have expressed that point of view.

a. Hindustan is a nation of few charms.

b. I must divide Songhai into provinces in order to improve the government.

c. I must end our contact with the West and expel all Portugese and Spanish from our island nation.

ENRICHMENT

Form a group with two or three other members of your class. Research the art of a nation or empire discussed in the unit. Then create artwork representing the culture you have selected. The artwork can range from drawings and poems to paper or clay three-dimensional objects, depending on materials available. Share your creation with the class.

ESL/LEP Strategy: Have students select a person, an event, or an achievement that is significant to them and write a paragraph describing how this person, event, or achievement might have affected their lives had they lived during this era.

THE BIRTH OF MODERN EUROPE

OBJECTIVE: Unit 6 will describe the changes that took place in Europe during the period known as the Renaissance. During that time, a vigorous interest in learning sparked new achievements in art and literature. Improvements in sailing and mapping led to the discovery of North and South America. Powerful leaders in Western Europe and in Russia gave many European countries stronger central governments.

Dante begins writing
Divine Comedy
1300

Leonardo da Vinci
paints the
Mona Lisa
1503

The Council
of Trent
meets in Italy
1545

| 1300 | 1350 | 1400 | 1450 | 1500 | 1550 |

Columbus lands at San Salvador
1492

John Calvin publishe
*Institutes of the
Christian Religion*
1536

▲ What can you tell about life in Venice from the painting "Miracle of the Relic of the Cross"?

Thirty Years War
begins
1618

Frederick William I
is named king of
Prussia
1713

1600   1650   1700   1750

England defeats
Spanish Armada
1588

Louis XIV is crowned
king of France
1643

CHAPTER 1

The Renaissance

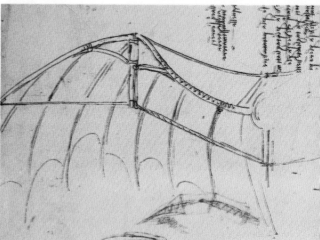

▲ Da Vinci designed several flying machines. Where do you think he got his ideas for the one shown above?

OBJECTIVE: In what ways was the Renaissance a turning point in European civilization?

1. Picture yourself traveling across the Atlantic Ocean in the flying machine shown at the right. It was designed by an artist named Leonardo da Vinci (lee-uh-NARD-o ▶ duh VIN-chee) about 500 years ago. In what ways does it look like a modern airplane? No one knows if da Vinci ever built this machine. However, he and other Europeans of his time created many great works of art, including poems, plays, paintings, and statues. Da Vinci lived during the **Renaissance** (REN-a-sans). The word "renaissance" means "rebirth." The Renaissance began in the early 1300s and lasted until about 1600. It started in Italy but quickly spread through Europe. During this time, people became more interested in the world around them. Individual achievement was valued as never before. Although da Vinci's flying machine probably never got off the ground, European civilization reached new heights during the Renaissance.

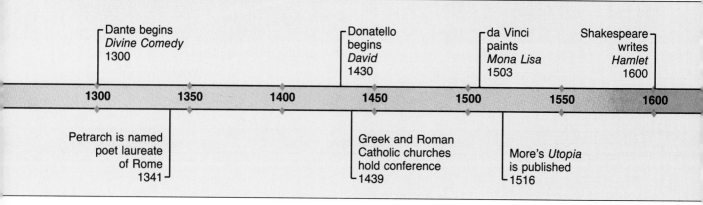

Dante begins *Divine Comedy* 1300

Donatello begins *David* 1430

da Vinci paints *Mona Lisa* 1503

Shakespeare writes *Hamlet* 1600

| 1300 | 1350 | 1400 | 1450 | 1500 | 1550 | 1600 |

Petrarch is named poet laureate of Rome 1341

Greek and Roman Catholic churches hold conference 1439

More's *Utopia* is published 1516

2. The rebirth that took place in the Renaissance was a renewed interest in learning for its own sake. **Scholars** (SKAHL-urz), or specialists in learning, became very interested in the writings of the ancient Greeks and Romans. These writings, called **classical** (KLAS-ih-kul) writings, had been preserved during the Middle Ages. They were considered important only as they related to Christianity. Thoughts about classical writings changed in the early 1300s. Scholars in Florence and other Italian cities studied, discussed, and wrote about the ideas of ancient Greece and Rome. These scholars began to call themselves **humanists** (HYOO-meh-nists).

3. The humanists of the early Renaissance did not, for the most part, reject the ideas of the Middle Ages. Through their studies, however, they gained a new excitement about learning and a new confidence in people's abilities. Scholars now spent less time studying religion and became more interested in people and their activities here on earth.

4. One writer who combined ideas from both the Middle Ages and the Renaissance was Dante Alighieri. Dante was an Italian poet who lived in Florence. He had mastered much of the learning of his time. This included both Christian and classical writings. In addition, Dante was active in the politics of his day. He served in the army and held several government posts.

5. Dante's great knowledge is shown in his most famous work, a long poem called *The Divine Comedy*, written in the early 1300s. *The Divine Comedy* was not meant to be entertainment. Instead it is a tour of life after death. The guide on this journey is Virgil, the great classical Latin poet. The poem is populated with persons from classical Greece and Rome, from Christian history, and from Dante's time. The reader can tell what Dante thought of a person's actions by his placement of the person in the poem—in heaven or in hell.

6. Many of the Renaissance scholars became important figures in the royal courts of European rulers. In fact, these scholars often added to the popularity of many royal courts. Francesco Petrarch (fran-CHES-koh PE-trark) was a poet who became so famous that the kings of two cities—Paris and Rome—invited him to become a **poet laureate** (LOR-ee-it), or chief poet. Petrarch accepted the invitation from Rome, and the king of Naples crowned him poet laureate in Rome in 1341.

SPOTLIGHT ON SOURCES

7. Petrarch was a scholar and poet. He wrote poems both in Latin and in Italian. Today Petrarch is remembered mainly for his excellent Italian poems, especially those dedicated to Laura. Did Laura exist only in Petrarch's mind, or was she real? Many experts think that Laura was a real person. However, because she was probably already married, Petrarch could only admire her from afar. Laura inspired some of Petrarch's best poems. Read these lines from one of Petrarch's "Laura" poems and decide for yourself whether she was real or not.

While I was hiding the fair thoughts I bore,
That have undone my mind in this desire,
I saw compassion shine upon your face;
But when Love made you conscious of my fire,
The blond hair became veiled and was no more,
The loving look closed in itself its grace.
What I loved most longed for its hiding place
In you; the veil rules me,
Which to my death, hot or cold though it be,
Covers your eyes' sure light as with a shade.

—from *Sonnets and Songs by Petrarch*, translated by Anna Maria Armi

Background: The interest in ancient manuscripts was so great that they often brought huge prices. Some scholars even produced forgeries of classical manuscripts to enchance their careers.

277

ART: How did the Renaissance spirit encourage the development of painting and sculpture?

8. The Renaissance spirit influenced all branches of knowledge. Its effect can be seen very clearly in painting and sculpture. Just as the humanist scholars admired the writings of the ancient Greeks and Romans, Renaissance artists studied ancient Greek and Roman sculpture. The artists admired the **realism** (REEL-iz-um), or lifelike appearance, of the ancient statues. A Renaissance sculptor, Donatello (don-uh-TEL-oh), made a bronze statue of King David of ancient Israel. While most statues in the Middle Ages were part of a building to which they were attached, Donatello's statue was large and free-standing. Soon other sculptors were creating similar large and heroic statues.

▶ **9.** How did Renaissance painting benefit from realism? Painters now studied nature carefully. Their paintings became more lifelike than those of the Middle Ages. One way that paintings became more realistic was the development of **perspective** (per-SPEK-tiv). Perspective is a way of showing distance realistically. Compare the painting of Mona Lisa on this page with the picture of

▶ Clovis on page 174. Which shows more perspective? What kinds of paintings would benefit most from improvements in perspective? Why?

▲ The *Mona Lisa* is one of the world's best-known paintings. Why do you think art lovers find the woman's smile fascinating?

PEOPLE IN HISTORY

10. Leonardo da Vinci was a man of many talents. He was an artist, a writer, a historian, and a scientist. His statues were beautiful, but he became even better known for his paintings. Da Vinci's *Mona Lisa* and *The Last Supper* are among the most famous paintings in the world today.

11. Da Vinci was also one of the first people to study the human body in a scientific way. In order to paint people realistically, he studied the way human bodies are formed. Da Vinci was interested in every-

thing he saw in nature. He studied the flight patterns of birds and how animals moved. He developed plans for buildings, bridges, and many kinds of machines. During his life he filled over 4,000 pages with his notes. Da Vinci's notebooks are works of art in themselves.

12. Artists such as Leonardo da Vinci and Michelangelo were sought out by wealthy and powerful church and government leaders. These leaders gave money to support the artists and were called **patrons** (PAY-trunz). The artists in turn decorated the rooms, halls, and chapels of their patrons with wonderful paintings and statues. This system of support for the arts continued for many centuries. Artists had to learn how to please people who had power in the courts

Background: Although the themes of many Renaissance paintings were religious, attention to textures of fabrics, skin, and hair gave a more secular look than those of the Middle Ages.

in order to gain support. While most artists of the Middle Ages were unknown, Renaissance artists had the chance to gain personal fame and honor. Do you think that this made an artist's life easier?

SOCIETY: How did the Renaissance affect other aspects of life?

13. The excitement about accomplishment that artists, writers, and scholars felt soon was shared by people in other fields. By the 1400s the world was ready for change. Better trade routes had opened new lands for exploration. Schools set up by men such as Prince Henry of Portugal led to improvements in ships and methods of navigation. Ships were made larger and stronger for longer journeys. The development of more exact sailing charts and maps made travel by sea much safer. Improved travel also meant improved trade. As trade grew, banking grew as well. The traders needed bankers to handle the exchange of money over long distances.

14. In Italy a few families who took part in the growth of trade and banking became extremely rich and powerful. One of the most famous of these was the Medici (MED-i-chee) family, who controlled Florence for about 300 years. How did the Medicis become so powerful? In the 1300s, Giovanni de' Medici gained a huge fortune through banking. His son, Cosimo de' Medici, never held public office, but he controlled the most important political offices in Florence.

15. Cosimo de' Medici was involved in many of the important events of his time. In 1439 a meeting was held between groups representing the Roman Catholic and Greek Orthodox churches. The meeting began in the city of Ferrara, but a plague broke out there. Cosimo then invited the members to Florence to continue their talks. Although the members of the council did not reach a final agreement, their exchange of views helped spread Renaissance ideas.

16. Cosimo de' Medici was a great patron of the arts. He assembled a huge library of classical writings. He hired many of the greatest artists of the day to create works of art for his court. Donatello, who carved the famous statue of King David, had Cosimo as his patron for many years.

▼ Renaissance life was colorful. Today, the games, plays, dancing, and music from Renaissance peasant and court life is reconstructed at Renaissance fairs.

Activity: Students might compare the plight of the Renaissance artists dealing with the politics of royal courts with a present-day actor or rock star encountering press interviews, agents, and difficult directors.

17. Cosimo's son Lorenzo kept up the family tradition by exercising very great influence in Florence. Like his father, he controlled the city through his wealth and family power. Lorenzo spent large sums of money on public pageants and celebrations. He supported artists and scholars, and he became known as Lorenzo the Magnificent because of his generous aid. When Florence was losing a bitter war with Naples, Lorenzo went to Naples to try to bring peace. As a result, the king of Naples finally agreed to end the war. When Lorenzo returned to Florence, he received a hero's
▶ welcome. Why do you think the people were so glad to see Lorenzo return?

18. Lorenzo did many things that would not be accepted today. He hired spies to check into the lives of ordinary citizens. In fact, he has often been called a **tyrant** (TY-rent), or leader with no controls on his power. At the same time Lorenzo was quite popular with many people in Florence. Life

in Florence under Lorenzo's rule was better than in many other cities of that time.

THE RENAISSANCE SPREADS: What Renaissance achievements took place throughout Europe?

19. Although the Renaissance began in Italy, it quickly spread throughout Europe. Many of the Italian artists traveled to other countries to work and teach. Leonardo da Vinci, for example, went to France, where King Francis I became his patron. In northern Europe painters such as Albrecht Durer (AL-brekt DUR-ur) and Pieter Brueghel (PAY-tur BROO-gul) produced realistic and imaginative paintings.

20. Movable type, which made printing much faster, was developed in Germany. The first book printed in this way appeared in 1455. It was a Bible printed by Johann Gutenberg. The improved method of printing helped to spread Renaissance ideas

---

▼ Merchants from Florence, Venice, and Genoa grew rich from trade during the Renaissance. How did geographic location help these cities? What advantages might Venice have had over the other cities?

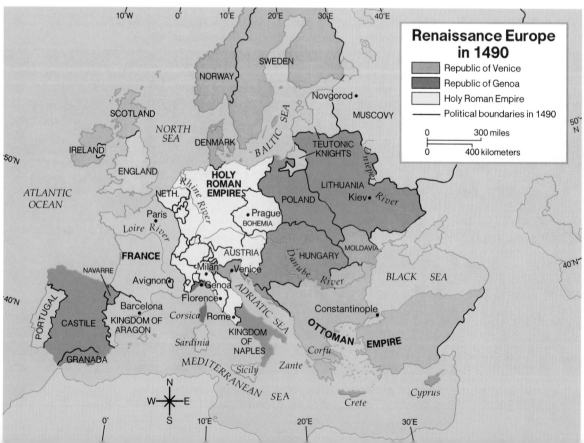

▲ Many of Shakespeare's plays were first performed in the Globe Theatre, shown above. The Globe was an open-air theater. Performances were held only in the daytime.

throughout Europe. Books were affordable to many more people. New ideas in all fields of knowledge could be shared quickly.

21. As Renaissance ideas spread, writers and scholars in many northern European countries added to those ideas. Erasmus (ih-RAZ-mus), a writer called the Prince of Humanists because of his brilliant work, was Dutch. Erasmus became well known throughout Europe. He traveled widely and lived in England, France, and Italy at various times in his life. One of his major contributions was a new edition of the New Testament translated from Greek texts. In England, Sir Thomas More, a leading scholar, was also a statesman in the royal court. He wrote a book called *Utopia* (yoo-TOH-pee-uh), which describes an ideal society. ▶ Why would a book on this topic be especially appealing to people in the Renaissance?

22. The most famous writer of the Renaissance was William Shakespeare of England. Shakespeare lived late in the Renaissance. He was both a poet and a playwright. Such Shakespearean plays as *Hamlet*, *King Lear*, and *Macbeth* are among the greatest works of English literature. The reason for their lasting fame is the beauty of Shakespeare's language and his deep understanding of human nature. Shakespeare's plays are still read, studied, and performed today.

OUTLOOK

23. Why is the Renaissance sometimes ◀ thought of as the beginning of "modern" times? Renaissance artists created works that were far more realistic than the works of the Middle Ages. Travel by sea became safer because of improved navigation. Ideas could be spread more rapidly because of the invention of the printing press. These developments caused life in Europe to change. The most dramatic change that took place during the Renaissance, however, was a change in the way people thought. A new self-confidence was born that led to the exploration of unknown lands and challenges to the authority of the church.

Activity: Students might prepare brief oral reports on the Harlem Renaissance or some other recent revival of interest in a culture of the past.

281

CHAPTER REVIEW

VOCABULARY REVIEW

Write each of the following sentences on a sheet of paper. Then fill in each blank with the word that best completes each sentence.

patrons   perspective   humanists

tyrant   classical   Renaissance

realism   poet laureate   scholars

1. People who are specialists in learning are called _____ .

2. The term "_____" means "rebirth."

3. Writings from ancient Greece and Rome are called _____ .

4. The Renaissance scholars who studied ancient Greek and Roman writings called themselves _____ .

5. The lifelike appearance of people and animals in Renaissance statues and paintings is called _____ .

6. Persons who give financial support to artists are called _____ .

7. If an artist's work shows distance in a realistic way, he or she has mastered the technique of _____ .

8. The chief poet of a court or city was called the _____ .

9. A ruler who has no controls to limit his or her power is called a _____ .

SKILL BUILDER: OUTLINING

An outline is a way of organizing information. Outlines contain the main ideas and supporting details of a paper or other written work.

Write the answer to each question below on a separate sheet of paper.

1. Which paragraph of Chapter 1 is outlined below?
   I. Cosimo de' Medici as a patron of the arts
      A. Library of classical writings
      B. Artists at his court

2. Which statement is the main idea of paragraph 2?
   a. Scholars are people of learning.
   b. The rebirth in the Renaissance was a rebirth of learning.
   c. Classical writings were preserved during the Middle Ages.
   d. Italian scholars translated classical works.

3. Which details from paragraphs 19–22 would complete the outline below?
   I. The spread of the Renaissance
      A. Contributions of northern Europe
         1. Painters
            a. _____
            b. _____
         2. Invention of printing
         3. English writers
            a. _____
            b. _____

SKILL BUILDER: CRITICAL THINKING AND COMPREHENSION

Follow the directions below. Write your answers on a separate sheet of paper.

▶ 1. Drawing Conclusions

▶ Choose a conclusion for the following statement from the list of sentences given below: The Renaissance grew out of a new interest in Greek and Roman writings.
   a. Scholars used only Latin to write about Roman times.
   b. Artists began to study Greek and Roman statues.
   c. The Renaissance took place only in Italy.
   d. Interest in trade declined because people were interested only in the past.

2. Predicting

▶ Reread paragraphs 13 and 17. Which one of the statements below best predicts what might happen later in the Renaissance?
   a. Europeans will become tired of learning and turn to trade.
   b. European rulers will establish colonies in newly discovered lands.

3. Fact *versus* Opinion

▶ Which of the following statements are *fact* and which are *opinion*?
   a. Rich Italians became patrons of the arts.
   b. Italian patrons should have given more money to painters and less to writers.
   c. It was a waste of time for Renaissance poets to keep up with politics.
   d. Paintings became more realistic during the Renaissance.
   e. The Renaissance rulers should have spent less time collecting manuscripts and more time improving living conditions in their cities.
   f. Realistic art is more beautiful than art that is not realistic.
   g. Many countries in Europe made contributions to the Renaissance.

4. Point of View

▶ A point of view is an attitude or way of thinking about something. Choose the points of view that might be held by a person in the Renaissance. Write the letters of these points of view on a sheet of paper.
   a. The study of mathematics should form the basis of all education.
   b. Ideas of the past, especially ideas of ancient Greece and Rome, are important to the present.
   c. An important goal for artists is to make their paintings more lifelike.
   d. A scholar must be an expert in classical Latin to be up-to-date.
   e. The most important goal of the Renaissance is to improve education for all people.

ENRICHMENT

1. Write a short description of a piece of Renaissance art. Use a picture from the chapter or find one in a book from the library. Describe what you see and write about these questions: Do you think this work of art is an example of realism? Does it show people and objects as they really are?

2. Imagine that you are a ruler who needs more people to help you run your royal court. You want someone who is a true Renaissance person. Make a list of the skills and qualifications that are needed.

283

CHAPTER 2

Protestant Reformation

▲ The ruler of Saxony is shown with several reformers. Martin Luther, the leader of the reformation, stands at the far left.

OBJECTIVE: How did the Reformation cause important changes in Christianity in Europe?

1. "CITY OFFICIAL URGES REFORM"

▶ Have you ever seen a newspaper headline like this? Powerful people in government and business sometimes become more interested in getting rich than in doing a good job. They may take money for doing favors or break the law in other ways. Eventually someone notices what they are doing and calls for reform. By the late 1400s the Catholic Church had become the most powerful institution in Europe. Church officials often had great political power. Many had great wealth and lived in luxury. People began to question this behavior. In Germany and elsewhere, reformers began to speak out against some church officials and the church itself. In the early 1500s these reformers finally broke with the Catholic Church. In a few years, many new churches were formed. The unity of religious belief that had lasted in Europe for 1,000 years came to an end, and an age of reform began.

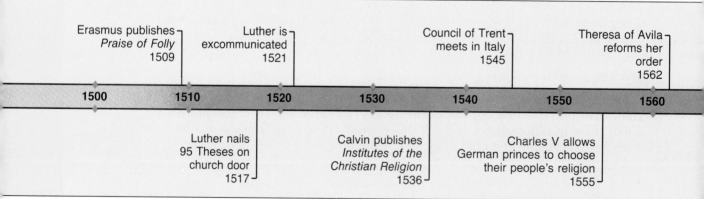

Erasmus publishes *Praise of Folly* 1509

Luther is excommunicated 1521

Council of Trent meets in Italy 1545

Theresa of Avila reforms her order 1562

| 1500 | 1510 | 1520 | 1530 | 1540 | 1550 | 1560 |

Luther nails 95 Theses on church door 1517

Calvin publishes *Institutes of the Christian Religion* 1536

Charles V allows German princes to choose their people's religion 1555

284

ESL/LEP Strategy: Have students use a dictionary to define the word *reform*. Ask if they know about any attempts at reform in their countries of origin. Then, ask students if they think that reforms are needed in the communities they live in now.

THE CHURCH AND REFORM: What problems did the Catholic Church in Europe face?

2. The church was deeply in debt by the late 1400s. The popes owed money for their armies and for rebuilding Saint Peter's Basilica in Rome. The church owned huge amounts of land, and many church officials had become used to a life of luxury. These wealthy clergy often forgot that they had promised to obey the laws of God and the laws of the church. Many were willing to use dishonest methods to raise money. Bribery became common. Church offices were sold to the highest bidder. The church also raised money through the sale of **indulgences** (in-DUL-junts-sez). An indulgence is a release from all or part of the punishment for committing a sin. The sale of indulgences led to other problems. Members of the clergy eager to sell indulgences often distorted church teachings. For example, they invented benefits that people who bought indulgences would receive. Yet, these promised benefits were not part of actual Church **doctrines** (DAHK-truns). Doctrines are the teachings and beliefs of a church. As a result, many people believed such practices were doing great harm to the church.

SPOTLIGHT ON SOURCES

3. In the early 1500s new critics of the church appeared. The Dutch humanist Erasmus was one of the best known of these critics. In the following passage from *The Praise of Folly* (1509), Erasmus makes fun of priests who worried more about making money than saving people's souls.

Now the general run of priests . . . how stoutly [boldly] they fight for their tithes [taxes], with sword, spear, stones, with every imaginable sort of armed force [weapon]. In this point how sharp-sighted they are in ferreting [finding] out . . . anything they can use to intimidate [bully] the simple people and make them think they owe even more [money]. . . . They do not even consider . . . that a priest is supposed to be free from all worldly desires and ought to meditate on [think about] nothing but heavenly matters.

The Praise of Folly, by Desiderius Erasmus, translated by Clarence Miller. Copyright © 1979 Yale University Press

MARTIN LUTHER: How did Luther's ideas lead to the formation of new Christian churches?

4. Although many people had talked about reforming the church, the ideas of one person were so influential that actual reform took place. This person was Martin Luther.

PEOPLE IN HISTORY

5. Martin Luther was born in Germany in 1483. In his early twenties he became a monk and devoted himself to a life of study and work. After several years of deep thought, he began to form his new ideas. For some time Luther had been troubled by the question of how a person could be saved. The church taught that good works such as prayer and fasting are needed for salvation. However, Luther came to believe that a person is saved not by good works, but only by faith in God.

6. In 1517 Luther made his ideas public. He did this because he was outraged by the sale of indulgences in his own town of Wittenberg. Luther expressed his point of view in the 95 **Theses** (THEE-seez), or statements of ideas, which he wrote down and then nailed to the door of the Wittenberg church. In these theses Luther argued against the indulgence system. Luther did not intend to break with the church when he took this action. However, his writings were soon printed, read, and discussed throughout Germany. Before long others began to agree with him. When Pope Leo X learned of the theses, he ordered Luther to take back his words. However, instead of

Background: In the three centuries prior to the Reformation, nine world councils were held by the church. Reform was an important goal of each of these councils, but none was able to bring about a lasting effect.

285

▲ Members of the clergy sold indulgences throughout Europe in the early I500s. Religious reformers protested this abuse of church doctrine.

backing down, Luther developed his ideas even further. He now denied the authority of the pope. The gap between Luther's ideas and Catholic doctrine was becoming wider and wider.

7. The church and the emperor soon took action against Luther. In January 1521 the pope excommunicated Luther. Excommunication was the most serious punishment the church could make because it denied a person the right to receive the sacraments. Three months later Charles V, the Holy Roman emperor, called Luther to the German town of Worms. Luther was asked to deny his teachings at a **diet** (DY-ut), or formal meeting of church leaders and nobles. Luther again defended his ideas. The diet of Worms declared Luther an outlaw whose writings were illegal. As a result Luther went into hiding for a while but he continued to develop his religious ideas and write about them.

8. Luther's ideas now spread quickly. People supported them for different reasons. Some German princes wanted to free themselves from the control of the Holy Roman emperor. They were eager to take over church land and stop paying taxes to Rome. For similar reasons many peasants also accepted Luther's ideas. Other people, however, were attracted to Luther's ideas because they were sincerely convinced that he was right.

9. Many people in Europe worried that breaking with the church would bring new problems. An event in 1524 seemed to confirm their fears. That year many German peasants rebelled in an outbreak that came to be known as the Peasants' War. The peasants wanted more liberties and less harsh hunting and tax laws. Many were inspired by Luther's stand against the church and the Holy Roman Empire. Luther was in favor of some of the peasants' goals, but he was against their use of violence. Finally, the local authorities brutally crushed the revolt in 1525.

10. For years Emperor Charles V tried to force the German princes who followed Luther to stay in the Catholic Church. These princes and others who supported Luther became known as **Protestants** (PROT-us-

tunts), because they protested, or spoke out against, Catholic doctrine. The Protestant princes stood firm, however. Finally, in 1555, Charles V agreed to let each German prince choose the religion of his kingdom.

THE REFORMATION SPREADS: What lasting effects did the Reformation have?

11. All across Europe Protestants started their own churches in a movement called the **Reformation** (ref-ur-MAY-shun). One of the most influential Protestant leaders was John Calvin. In 1536 his book *Institutes of the Christian Religion* was published. The book was a summary of many Protestant beliefs. In it Calvin emphasized the doctrine of **predestination** (pree-des-tuh-NAY-shun). This is the idea that God knows in advance who will be saved. Calvin believed that a newborn baby was already either saved or condemned. However, those who led good lives also might be showing they had been chosen to be saved.

12. The spread of the Reformation changed religion in many parts of Europe. Calvin's ideas took hold in Scotland, the Netherlands, and parts of Germany. Many Protestants in northern Europe followed Luther's beliefs. Why might Protestantism have been more popular in the north of Europe then in the South?

13. Catholics reacted to the Reformation by making reforms within the church. In 1545 Pope Paul III called a meeting of church leaders at Trent, in Italy. The purpose of the Council of Trent was to re-affirm church doctrine and to correct abuses in the Church that still existed. The Council of Trent ended the sale of indulgences and set strict rules of behavior for the clergy. In addition to the work of the Council of Trent, many individuals also worked for other church reforms. For example, Theresa of Avila, a Spanish Carmelite nun, became concerned that her religious order had become too worldly and lacking in discipline. She traveled throughout Spain and reformed many monasteries and convents there during the last 15 years of her life.

▲ John Calvin's ideas formed the basis of the Presbyterian religion. Protestants throughout Europe read his writings.

These reforms in the Catholic church were called the **Counter-Reformation** (COWNT-ur-re-fur-MAY-shun).

OUTLOOK

14. The Reformation was a turning point in world history. In 1500 there was only one Christian church in Europe. Within the next 50 years, many new churches came into existence. Many of the churches you see in your town or city—Baptist, Methodist, Presbyterian, and others—grew out of changes that started in the Reformation. The idea that each person has the right to worship as he or she wishes was still a long way off, however. For many years after the Reformation, the people were supposed to follow the religion of their ruler. Many people died for the right to worship as they wished. Do people today hold beliefs that they would undergo hardships to defend?

CHAPTER REVIEW

VOCABULARY REVIEW

Write each number and word on a sheet of paper. Then write the letter of the definition next to the word it defines.

1. Protestants
2. Reformation
3. predestination
4. diet
5. theses
6. indulgences
7. doctrines
8. Counter-Reformation

a. statements of ideas

b. release from all or part of the punishment for committing a sin

c. a movement of reforms within the Catholic Church

d. the idea that God knows in advance who will be saved.

e. persons who protested, or spoke out against, the Catholic church

f. a formal meeting of church leaders and nobles

g. a movement in which Protestants split with the Catholic church

h. the teachings and beliefs of a church

SKILL BUILDER: INTERPRETING PRIMARY SOURCES

Primary sources are an important tool for learning history. A primary source is a book, letter, essay, or other writing that comes from the period you are studying. A secondary source is something that was written later about the events of the period. Your textbook is a secondary source. Encyclopedias and biographies are other secondary sources. What features of your textbook contain primary sources?

Reading a primary source is a good way to learn about a person in history. You can find out how the person felt about the topics of the day. Many of the primary sources from the time of the Reformation were written in languages other than English. What language was used for Church writings of the time?

Include quotes from primary sources in your history reports to make them more interesting and to support your point of view. For example, in a report on Luther, you might include quotes from his books or from the writings of people who knew him.

▶ Read the quotes from primary sources below. Then answer the questions.

a. "The gospel [Bible] demands no works to make us holy and to redeem [save] us. Indeed, it condemns such works, and demands only faith in Christ, because He has overcome sin, death, and hell for us."

Martin Luther

b. "We are subject to the men who rule over us, but subject only in the Lord. If they command anything against Him, let us not pay the least regard to it."

John Calvin

1. Which primary source would you use in a report about the Protestant doctrine that faith alone is necessary for salvation? Why?

2. Would the second quote fit better in a report on the idea of predestination or in a report on church and government in the Reformation?

SKILL BUILDER: CRITICAL THINKING AND COMPREHENSION

1. Drawing Conclusions

Read the following sentences. Then answer the question on a sheet of paper.

In the Peasants War of 1524, many of the war's leaders were inspired by Luther's protests against the church and the Holy Roman emperor.

Luther favored some of the peasants' goals but was against their use of violence.

Luther wrote a letter in which he said that the rebellion should be crushed with brute force. This letter was not published until after the end of the uprising.

How do you think the peasants felt about Luther when his letter was published?

2. Predicting

Reread paragraph 13 about the Counter-Reformation. What effects might the Counter-Reformation have had on artists and writers of the next one hundred years?

3. Fact *versus* Opinon

Read the following sentences. Decide whether each sentence is a fact or an opinion. Then write letters a. through d. on your paper. Write *fact* or *opinion* beside each letter.

a. The Bible can be understood only by religious leaders.

b. Pope Leo X excommunicated Martin Luther from the Catholic Church.

c. Luther was right to oppose peasants who were taking land by force.

d. Luther's ideas spread quickly after he made them public.

4. Point of View

Read the following paragraphs. Then answer the questions that follow.

a. "Martin Luther is a dangerous man. He is chipping away at the foundations of the Church. He has no respect for the pope or his bishops. If he is not stopped, he will cause terrible trouble for religious life in Europe."

b. "I have nothing but respect for Martin Luther. Without his voice calling for reform, the people of Europe would be left to worship in a church that cares more for money than for spiritual life. His ideas begin a great new age."

4-1. Which paragraph was written by a loyal Catholic monk?

4-2. Write two short paragraphs telling how each writer would react to the news that Martin Luther has been excommunicated.

ENRICHMENT

1. Make a list of the Protestant churches in your town or city. Using an encyclopedia, find out when and where each church was formed. Write one-paragraph summaries about the histories of these churches.

2. Martin Luther's 95 Theses listed his ideas and criticisms of the Catholic Church. Think of ways your school could be improved. Write a list of "theses" describing your ideas and encouraging your classmates to support your reforms. Try to include possible reforms that would affect everyone at school, not just you.

CHAPTER 3

Western Monarchies and City-States

▲ King Louis XIV gave France a strong central government. The reign of this powerful king lasted from 1643 to 1715.

OBJECTIVE: How did governments change in western Europe as feudalism declined?

1. Today, a mistake in manners is usually quickly forgiven. For a French noble of the 1600s, however, such a mistake was a serious matter. The rules of conduct were very complicated at the court of King Louis XIV at Versailles. For example, if you entered the room of a person of higher rank, your servant must open only one, but not both, of a set of double doors. You would be considered rude if you knocked on a door at the palace. Instead, you should scratch the door with your little finger. These rules resulted from extreme concern with people's rank at court. Louis XIV's court reflected his great wealth and power. Between 1400 and 1600, in France, England, and Spain, the feudal

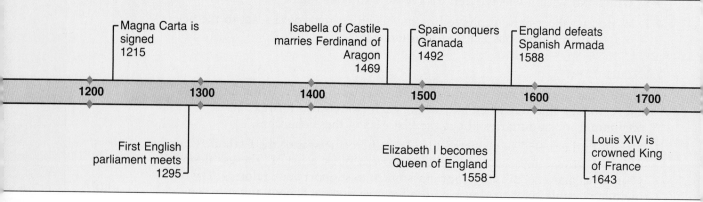

Magna Carta is signed
1215

Isabella of Castile marries Ferdinand of Aragon
1469

Spain conquers Granada
1492

England defeats Spanish Armada
1588

| 1200 | 1300 | 1400 | 1500 | 1600 | 1700 |

First English parliament meets
1295

Elizabeth I becomes Queen of England
1558

Louis XIV is crowned King of France
1643

ties between rulers and nobles were re-placed with strong royal governments.

GOVERNMENT IN EUROPE: What two kinds of government developed in Europe?

2. During the Renaissance in Europe, new nations were formed, led by rulers who were **monarchs** (MAHN-urks). A monarch is a queen or king who rules a nation. When a monarch dies, the power to rule passes to another member of the same family. Nations led by monarchs are called monarchies. During this time, England, Spain, and France became monarchies.

3. At the same time, another form of government developed in Italy. Italy was a country of city-states. Each Italian city-state was like a separate nation. Leaders of some city-states were called princes. Other city-states were led by small groups of people who controlled the city-state's trade. The de' Medici family of Florence was an example of such a group.

4. Europe's monarchies and city-states were alike in some ways. Both had strong governments that controlled the land and people within their borders. Both monarchies and city-states had armies to protect them from attack. Often, monarchies and city-states tried to gain more land and power by waging war with one another.

ITALY: How did Italy's city-states gain power in Italy and govern the people?

5. After the fall of the Roman Empire, Italy was divided into several states. From A.D. 476 to A.D. 800, most of Italy was ruled by Germanic tribes. The popes ruled the lands around Rome in central Italy. They raised armies to keep the Germanic tribes from capturing Rome. With the help of Charlemagne, the popes defeated the Germanic invaders. The Catholic Church kept control of the areas around Rome. These areas were known as the Papal States.

6. About the year 1000, city-states began to gain power in Italy. Although the city-states were part of the Holy Roman Empire, they were ruled almost as independent states. The Italian city-states included Florence, Pisa, Genoa, Milan, and Venice. Many of these cities had walls around them that had been built by the Romans. People gathered in the cities because they were safer there. Landowners and farmers often lived within the city walls even though they had to travel several miles to reach their farmlands. Because Italy was a gateway to the eastern Mediterranean and Asia, the Italian city-states became important centers of trade, banking, and culture. The city-states served as channels through which the cultures of Asia passed before spreading to the rest of Europe. How did the location of Italy help to explain why the Renaissance began there?

7. By the 1400s, some city-states were governed by a **commune** (KAHM-yoon), or a group of the city-state's leading citizens.

Daily life in . . .

The monarchs of Europe entertained each other with lavish feasts. The number of guests was often several thousand, and the meal would last a full day. The menu for such a celebration might include roast oxen, sheep, goats, pigs, swans, hens, larks, and pigeons. Rabbits in syrup, sweet custards, and elaborate pastries also would be served. Vegetables were considered too ordinary to be part of a feast, but fruits cooked in syrup sometimes were served. The dinner usually was served in three courses, but both meat and sweet dishes were included in each course. Forks were not yet in use, nor were china plates. The guests brought their own knives. Loaves of bread, called trenchers, were split in half and used as plates. The trenchers were given to the poor after the feast.

Background: Conquest was the main method used to gain territory. As France and Spain each grew in power, they fought to gain control of various Italian city-states.

291

▲ This painting shows Siena as it looked during the 1300s. Siena prospered early in the Renaissance, but in the 1500s came under the control of Florence.

For example, the merchants were in control in Genoa and Pisa. Other city-states were ruled by groups of nobles and landowners. These leaders helped pay for armies to defend the city-states. They set the standards for weights and measures, and they organized markets and fairs. However, disputes among the city-states led to conflicts that eventually weakened them.

SPAIN: How did Spain become a unified nation under a strong monarchy?

8. Spain was attacked by invading tribes for hundreds of years. By A.D. 600, the Visigoths, Germanic tribes that had invaded Italy, had taken over Spain and Portugal and set up a monarchy there. Both the Romans and the Visigoths established Christianity in Spain. However, in the early 700s, the **Moors** (MOORZ), or Muslims from North Africa, conquered most of Spain. Different groups of Moors fought among themselves, and Spain became divided into small Moorish states. Because the Moors were divided, the Visigoths and other Christian groups

were slowly able to reconquer areas of northern Spain. Castile and Aragon became two of the largest Christian kingdoms in Spain.

9. The first step toward unifying Spain began with the marriage of Isabella of Castile and Ferdinand of Aragon in 1469. In 1474 Isabella became queen of Castile, and five years later Ferdinand became king of Aragon. Isabella and Ferdinand ruled together but neither was the monarch of the other's kingdom. Each kingdom had its own laws and government. Isabella and Ferdinand began to strengthen the monarchy by taking back property that the nobles had seized from the crown. The king and queen changed laws so that the nobles would have fewer rights. At times the monarchs used force to take property and money from the nobles.

10. Isabella felt that the people of Spain should all belong to the Catholic church. In the late 1400s a church court called the Spanish **Inquisition** (in-kwuh-ZISH-un) was set up. The purpose of this court was to bring to trial **heretics** (HER-uh-tiks), or per-

Background: Under Muslim rule, Spain achieved the highest level of learning and culture in western Europe. The Moors established libraries to preserve the knowledge of many cultures of the world.

▲ Spain's strength enabled its monarchs to support exploration in the New World. This painting shows Queen Isabella and King Ferdinand greeting Christopher Columbus.

sons who did not agree with the doctrine of the Catholic church. During the Inquisition, thousands of Moors and Jewish people were tried as heretics and sentenced to imprisonment or death. Thousands more were driven out of Spain.

11. Isabella and Ferdinand also led their kingdoms in battle to conquer more of Spain. In 1492 they captured Granada, the last of the Moorish states in Spain. Isabella died in 1504 and left the throne of Castile to her son-in-law, Philip of Habsburg. When Philip died in 1506, Ferdinand became the king of Castile. After Ferdinand's conquest of the kingdom of Navarre in 1512, all of Spain became united under one monarch. During the 1500s, Spain became the most powerful nation in Europe.

ENGLAND: How did the monarchy in England change during the years from 1066 to 1660?

12. In 1066 William of Normandy, a powerful noble of northwestern France, invaded England and defeated King Harold of England at the Battle of Hastings. William was crowned King William I of England. William I, who came to be known as William the Conquerer, required all the nobles to take oaths of allegiance to the king. By securing the loyalty of his nobles, William was able to build a strong monarchy in England.

13. Struggles between the English kings and the nobles for land and power went on almost constantly. Kings at that time could send any person to prison without a trial. When nobles were arrested for crimes, the king often took their land and estates for his own. The nobles began to feel that the English monarchs were abusing the power of government.

14. In 1215 the **barons** (BAR-unz), or nobles who were wealthy landowners, forced King John of England to sign an agreement that would guarantee them certain rights. This agreement came to be known as the **Magna Carta** (MAG-na KAR-ta), or great charter. Under its terms, the king agreed to discuss new laws and taxes with the barons. The Magna Carta also stated that a person

Background: For many years after the Norman Conquest, French was the language of the ruling classes and Anglo-Saxon the language of the common people. Eventually, the two languages blended together.

293

A Geographic View of History

The Changing Political Geography of the Iberian Peninsula   The political geography of Europe's Iberian Peninsula is different today from what it was in the past. Only two countries are now found on the Iberian Peninsula: Spain and Portugal. The map on this page shows that six medieval kingdoms ruled the Iberian Peninsula in 1150. Those six kingdoms are the lands from which present-day countries of Portugal and Spain later developed.

Read these facts about the changing political geography of the Iberian Peninsula. Think about them when you study the map. Then answer the questions that follow.

Facts

In 1150, five Christian kingdoms ruled the northern half of the Iberian Peninsula. They were Portugal, Leon, Castile, Navarre, and Aragon.

In 1150, Moors, who were Muslims, ruled the southern half of the Iberian Peninsula and several islands in the Mediterranean Sea. Their capital city was Granada.

Portugal expanded southward and conquered Moorish Portugal by 1250. The conquest gave Portugal a long Atlantic coastline that later helped its trade and exploration overseas.

The conquest of Granada in 1492 ended nearly 800 years of Moorish rule in the Iberian Peninsula.

Christian kings called their conquest of Moorish land the reconquest because it restored Christian rule to lands the Moors had ruled since 711.

1. Name three Christian kingdoms on the Iberian Peninsula in 1150.

2. Name the cities on the map that were ruled by the Moors in 1150.

3. What Moorish city did the Christian kings capture in 1492?

4. What island did the Christian Kings capture? In what sea is this island found?

5. How do you think the Christian Reconquest of the Iberian Peninsula prepared for Spain and Portugal to expand overseas?

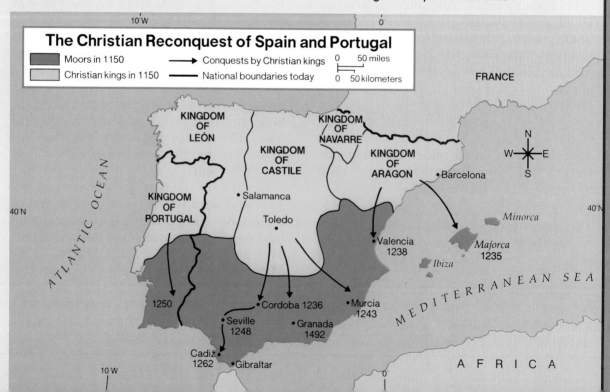

The Christian Reconquest of Spain and Portugal

Moors in 1150
Christian kings in 1150
→ Conquests by Christian kings
— National boundaries today
0   50 miles
0   50 kilometers

FRANCE

KINGDOM OF LEÓN

KINGDOM OF NAVARRE

KINGDOM OF CASTILE

KINGDOM OF ARAGON
• Barcelona

KINGDOM OF PORTUGAL

• Salamanca

Toledo

• Valencia 1238

Minorca

Majorca 1235

Ibiza

1250

• Cordoba 1236

• Murcia 1243

ATLANTIC OCEAN

MEDITERRANEAN SEA

• Seville 1248

• Granada 1492

Cadiz 1262
• Gibraltar

AFRICA

10°W   0
40°N   40°N
10 W   0

could not be sent to prison without first having a trial by a jury. After the Magna Carta, the monarchy no longer had unlimited rights. For this reason, the signing of the Magna Carta was an important step forward toward a more just government in England.

15. In 1295 the first **parliament** (PAR-li-ment) met. A parliament is a lawmaking body. The English parliament was made up of four groups of people. These groups were the nobles, the clergy, the knights, and the townspeople. Parliament had the power to decide how much money the king could spend. Parliament also could decide what
▶ taxes people would pay. Why do you think the English people wanted to have Parliament set these rules rather than the king?

16. During the early part of the Reformation, England remained Catholic. Then, King Henry VIII broke with the Catholic church because he wanted a divorce. When the pope refused to end Henry's marriage, the king fought back. He refused to pay taxes to the pope and took over all the church's lands in England. In time he separated the church in England from the church in Rome. Henry VIII declared himself the head of the Church of England. The wealth and power Henry gained as head of the Church of England made the English crown stronger. Henry's younger daughter became one of England's greatest monarchs, Queen Elizabeth I.

▲ Elizabeth I of England was respected throughout Europe. What characteristics of her face show that she would be a strong ruler?

PEOPLE IN HISTORY

17. Elizabeth I, who ruled from 1558 to 1603, prided herself on her strength as a leader. "I know," she said, "I have the body of a weak and feeble woman, but I have the heart and stomach [strength] of a king. . ."
▶ Do you think Elizabeth was serious or joking when she said this? Elizabeth spoke several languages and knew how to deal with foreign rulers. Elizabeth claimed that she never married because she did not want to share her power with a husband.

18. Queen Elizabeth was one of England's strongest rulers. She spent tax money to build up the navy as a way of protecting the country and its shipping. England's strong and stable government under Elizabeth helped increase its trade with other countries. This trade made England a wealthy nation.

19. During the mid-1500s, Spain was the most powerful country in Europe. It was also the greatest threat to England's safety. Elizabeth worked hard to keep Spain from becoming even more powerful. She and her ambassadors gave aid to France and the Netherlands so that those countries would not be conquered by Spain. Elizabeth herself secretly allowed English pirates, called seadogs, to raid Spanish ships. In 1588

Background: Henry VIII's daughter Mary Tudor, who ruled England from 1553 to 1558, married Philip II of Spain and tried unsuccessfully to reunite the English church with Rome.

295

Spain sent an **armada** (ahr-MAHD-uh), or an armed fleet, to invade England. England's smaller, faster navy defeated the Spanish Armada. England's victory was an important one. It proved that England was now one of the great powers of Europe.

20. The English monarchs who followed Elizabeth had trouble with Parliament because they tried to collect taxes without ► Parliament's approval. Why would Parliament object to this? King Charles I then tried to govern without Parliament's approval. This led to a **civil war** or a war between groups within the same country, in l642. Supporters of Parliament went to war against supporters of King Charles. Parliament's army, led by Oliver Cromwell, won the war, and in 1649 King Charles I was executed.

21. After the war ended, England was without a monarch for eleven years. A **commonwealth** (KOM-un-welth), or a government founded on law and united by the agreement of the people, was set up. Cromwell became lord protector of England. He was supposed to share his power with Parliament. Cromwell had to dissolve Parliament twice, however, because of serious disagreements over how much authority he should have. Until his death in 1658, Cromwell ruled England as a dictator with the help of the army.

22. After Cromwell's death, the monarchy was brought back, or restored. This period is known as the **Restoration** (res-tor-AY-shun). In 1660 Parliament asked Charles II, the son of Charles I, to become a **limited monarch**, or a monarch who shared power with Parliament. England would never again have a king or queen with absolute power. The English people, through Parliament, now had a share of the power.

FRANCE: How did a strong monarchy gain power in France?

23. Because feudalism remained strong in France during the Middle Ages, the French monarchy did not gain power quickly. Gradually, during the 350 years between 987 and 1328, a series of monarchs known as the Capetian (kuh-PEE-shun) kings began to increase the territory and power of the French monarchy. Then in 1337, the English invaded Normandy. England and France fought until 1453 to determine who would rule western France. These battles are known as the Hundred Years' War.

24. Joan of Arc became famous during the Hundred Years' War. In 1428 it seemed that England would take over all of France. Joan, a seventeen-year-old girl from Orleans, persuaded French leaders to let her lead an army. She believed that voices from heaven had told her to help France. Joan led the French armies to several victories. By 1429 she had freed the French city of Orleans. In November 1430, Joan was captured by her enemies and turned over to the English. The English tried her as a witch, found her guilty, and burned her at the

▼ In the 1400s, it was unusual for a woman to be a prominent leader. How might this have influenced opinions about Joan of Arc?

ESL/LEP Strategy: Discuss the meanings of the terms *civil war* and *commonwealth*. Ask students if their countries of origin ever experienced a civil war or were are part of a commonwealth.

▲ Louis XIV had the huge palace of Versailles built near Paris. To keep an eye on the nobles, he had them live at Versailles rather than on their own estates.

stake. Today, Joan is honored as a hero in France for her brave actions and brilliant military activity.

25. The victories of the French armies gradually forced the English out of France. Louis XI, who ruled France from 1461 to 1483, greatly increased the power of the French monarchy. During his reign, Louis added Burgundy, a large area southeast of Paris, to his kingdom. By the end of his life, he controlled an area almost as large as France is today.

26. Louis XIV, who was king of France from 1643 to 1715, was an **absolute monarch**. An absolute monarch is a ruler who has absolute, or complete, power of government. Louis XIV spent huge sums of money, but he made France the strongest nation in Europe. He taxed the people heavily to pay for four wars and the luxuries of his royal court. At the same time, the king built up France's trade and industries. Roads and canals were built to help merchants send their goods all over France and to other countries as well. With Louis XIV in charge of the government and the economy, France became a nation with a strong central government. By the end of Louis XIV's reign, however, France was in debt from the wars. The gap between the luxury of Versailles, the King's residence, and the poverty of many French citizens was becoming wider. How might this lead to problems for the ◄ monarchy in later years?

OUTLOOK

27. During the years from the 1400s to the 1600s, Spain, England, and France became unified nations ruled by strong monarchs. Italy, on the other hand, remained divided into small city-states. As strong central governments were established over much of Europe, trade and commerce grew. Merchants and tradespeople, as well as monarchs, began to grow wealthy. Why ◄ might the merchants have wanted to keep the power of the monarchs under control? In what ways does the struggle between government support and government control continue today?

Background: Louis XIV used the court at Versailles as a showplace for the nobles to come under his scrutiny. In this way, he consolidated his position as absolute monarch.

297

CHAPTER REVIEW

VOCABULARY REVIEW

Write each word on a sheet of paper. Then write the letter of the definition next to the word it defines.

1. parliament
2. armada
3. Magna Carta
4. absolute monarch
5. monarchs
6. civil war
7. Moors
8. Restoration
9. Inquisition
10. heretics
11. commonwealth
12. limited monarch
13. barons
14. commune

a. kings or queens who rule nations

b. Muslims from North Africa who took over Spain

c. people who do not agree with church doctrine

d. church court that rid Spain of Jews and Moors

e. nobles who were wealthy landowners

f. charter that gave specific rights to the barons

g. law-making body made up of nobles, clergy, knights, and townspeople

h. an armed fleet

i. war between groups within the same country

j. government founded on law and united by agreement of the people

k. period of time when the English monarch was brought back to power after Cromwell's death

l. ruler who shares power with parliament

m. ruler who has complete control of government

n. a governing group made up of a city-state's leading citizens

SKILL BUILDER: INTERPRETING TIME LINES

A time line can show a summary of a person's life or a time or age of history. Copy the blank time line below on a sheet of paper. Use information from the chapter to write statements 1 through 5 in the correct places on the time line. Look at the time line on page 290 for an example of how to set up your time line.

1400	1450	1500	1550	1600	1650

1. England defeats the Spanish Armada.
2. Ferdinand takes over the kingdom of Navarre.
3. Civil war breaks out in England.
4. Isabella and Ferdinand marry and begin unification of Spain.
5. Elizabeth I becomes queen of England.

SKILL BUILDER: CRITICAL THINKING AND COMPREHENSION

1. Drawing Conclusions   Each set of sentences below contains a statement and possible conclusions.

▶ Read each statement, then choose the sentence that states the logical conclusion of that statement. Write the number of the conclusion on a sheet of paper.

Set 1: Parliament had the power to decide how much the king could spend. It also decided what taxes would be collected and how much these taxes should be.

a. Parliament's members were thrifty.

b. Parliament had little power in government matters.

c. Parliament, not the king, controlled taxes.

d. Parliament met in the king's palace at Westminster.

Set 2: As a youth, Oliver Cromwell felt everyone should believe as he did. In his later years, he was more tolerant of other religions.

a. Cromwell was very religious.

b. Cromwell sent Parliament home and made himself lord protector of England.

c. Cromwell set up the commonwealth.

d. Cromwell changed his ideas about religion as he grew older.

2. Predicting

What do you think might happen in France if absolute monarchs began to abuse their powers?

3. Fact *vs.* Opinion

▶ Which of the following sentences are facts and which are opinions?

a. Henry VIII separated the church in England from the church in Rome.

b. England's monarchs were the finest in the world.

c. England's government under Elizabeth I encouraged trade and shipping.

d. Joan of Arc was more important than Elizabeth I to the history of Europe.

4. Points of View

▶ Which of the following points of view would most likely have been held by Isabella and Ferdinand?

a. Spain should be united as a Catholic country.

b. A wide variety of cultures and religions in a country is a healthy sign.

c. An inquisition should be set up to rid Spain of Jews and Muslims.

d. The power and wealth of Italy's city-states should be encouraged.

ENRICHMENT

1. King Louis XIV of France was known as the Sun King. He chose the sun as his symbol. Imagine you are a ruler. What symbol would you use to express who you are? Draw this symbol and explain what it means.

2. Many monarchs built magnificent castles. Do research on castles in an encyclopedia or other reference book and present your findings in a short oral report.

CHAPTER 4

Discovery of Overseas Empires

▲ This map, made in 1585, shows the southeast coast of the United States. What do you see that tells you travel was still considered risky?

OBJECTIVE: How did European exploration affect the world?

1. "Beyond this place there are monsters." Can you imagine finding these words on a map of our modern world? Such warnings, with pictures of the monsters, were common on maps in the Middle Ages. To medieval sailors, the oceans were terrifying and mysterious. It was commonly thought that sea monsters lurked in the ocean depths, waiting to devour ships. Ignorance of the lands beyond the oceans kept Europeans close to their own shores until the fifteenth century. Then, in the 1400s, a few brave explorers ventured beyond the familiar trade routes. Instead of monsters, they found new continents full of great riches. Before long, European monarchs were competing with each other to set up colonies in the newly discovered lands. Within two centuries, the world had become a less frightening place.

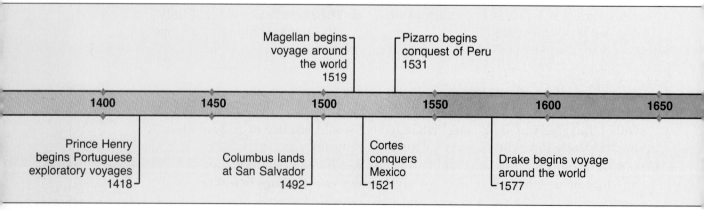

Magellan begins voyage around the world 1519

Pizarro begins conquest of Peru 1531

1400	1450	1500	1550	1600	1650

Prince Henry begins Portuguese exploratory voyages 1418

Columbus lands at San Salvador 1492

Cortes conquers Mexico 1521

Drake begins voyage around the world 1577

THE UNKNOWN: What led the Portuguese to find out more about the world?

2. By the early 1400s Portugal had become a leader in trade. Because of limited land for farming, much of the food Portugal needed had to be imported. The shipping trade was the lifeline of the Portuguese people. As a result, Portugal's King John I began to look toward northern Africa as a possible area of expansion. He hoped to find a route to the spice trade of the **Indies**, or Asia. He also wanted to spread Christianity to Muslim lands. In 1415 John's army conquered the city of Ceuta (SAY-oo-tuh) on the northern coast of Africa. A series of African explorations followed. King John's third son, Prince Henry, was governor of a province in the southern tip of Portugal. From there he sent a series of ships to explore along the northwest coast of Africa. By 1460, when Henry died, Portuguese sailors had gone as far south as Sierra Leone.

3. Prince Henry started a navigation school that brought together the best sailors and geographers in Europe. Maps made at the school were more exact and had more ▶ detail than others of the time. Why might Portugal's government have tried to keep the mapmakers' work secret? Another important result of Henry's school was the designing and building of new ships called **caravels** (KAR-a-vel). Caravels were lighter and faster than other ships. They had smaller sails that could be shifted more easily to take advantage of changing winds. Because of the work at his school, Henry has an important place in the history of exploration. He is often called "the Navigator," even though he only led one voyage himself.

4. Portuguese explorers hoped to find a route around Africa to Asia. Most scholars in the 1400s believed that there were three routes to Asia. One route was by sea to Constantinople and beyond. Venice had total control of this route and the trade with Asia. Since scholars knew the world is round, they suspected there was also a second route that went west across the Atlantic Ocean. No one, however, had tried such a route. Sailors were reluctant to sail in strange waters out of the sight of land. The route the Portuguese explored was thought to be the safest because it followed the west coast of Africa. Look at the map on page 306. How might Portugal's location have ◀ led its sailors to choose the African route?

5. In the late 1400s and early 1500s, Portugal's explorers discovered the route around Africa. In 1488, three Portuguese ships led by Bartolomeu Dias (bahr-too-loo-MAY-uh DEE-ahsh) were caught in a storm off the southern coast of Africa. When Dias sailed back north to reach land again, he discovered that he had rounded the tip of Africa. However, a lack of food and a need

Daily life in . . .

Long voyages to unknown areas made sailors' lives very difficult. Magellan's crew ran out of food during their three-year voyage. They were so hungry that they ate leather used on the ship. Water was also a problem for crews, who often did not know where land, let alone fresh water, could be found. Since fruit and vegetables were not available on long voyages, sailors often developed **scurvy** (SKUR-vee), a disease caused by a lack of vitamin C. Scurvy causes weakness and makes people's gums bleed. A sailor's life was dangerous. The possibility of shipwreck from a storm or an attack by pirates was always present. In addition, sailors often had accidents on board. Just climbing the ropes, or rigging, to set sails in place could result in a fatal fall. On shipboard, the captain's word was law, but crews often became restless and rebelled. Weapons were kept under lock and key to avoid trouble. Sailors who returned home alive and well were lucky indeed.

Activity: Ask students to use atlas maps to trace Vasco Da Gama's voyage around Africa to India. When Da Gama reached the eastern coast of Africa, merchants from India told him how to reach India.

for ship repairs forced Dias to return to Porgal. In 1497–1498 Vasco Da Gama (VASH-koo deh GAH-mah), another Portuguese explorer, and his crew became the first Europeans to sail around Africa to India.

EXPLORATION: How did European explorers find their way to North and South America?

6. The discovery of the Americas was an accident. Navigators had little idea of what lands they would find if they sailed west. Although many thought it would be possible to reach Asia by this route, it took an explorer of exceptional daring to try. In the late 1400s, such an explorer appeared, an experienced Italian sailor named Christopher Columbus.

PEOPLE IN HISTORY

7. Born in Italy about 1451, Christopher Columbus spent his early years at sea. He

▼ When Columbus landed at the tropical island of San Salvador, he claimed the land for Ferdinand and Isabella.

settled for a time in Portugal, where he began to form a plan of sailing west to find Asia. Using reports from other explorations, Columbus estimated the distance of this voyage. Although Columbus's ideas were correct, he made a mistake figuring out the distance to Asia. He thought that the earth was much smaller than it actually is.

8. Once Columbus had made his plans, he had to find money for his trip. He asked the king of Portugal to pay for his voyage, but the king denied his request. In 1486 Columbus proposed his plan to Isabella and Ferdinand of Spain. For several years the plan was studied, rejected, and then finally accepted. In August 1492 Columbus and his crew sailed west in three small ships.

9. Many of Columbus's sailors were fearful of setting out in unmapped waters. Columbus tried many ways of keeping up their spirits. For example, he would tell the crew they had traveled a much shorter distance than they actually had. Columbus never failed to point out birds and floating pieces of grass as signs that they were approaching land. However, by early October the crew was very restless.

10. Early in the morning of October 12, a crew member sighted land. Columbus's ships arrived at one of the islands in the Bahamas. Columbus believed that he had reached Asia. He thought the gold jewelry the island people were wearing was proof that he was close to Asian trading cities. When Columbus returned to Spain, the royal court honored him as a hero. News of his discovery spread rapidly throughout Europe.

11. In the following years several **explorations**, or voyages to search for new land, were conducted by Spain and Portugal. A major goal of the explorations was to find new sources of wealth. Portuguese officials were convinced that Columbus had discovered a "New World" and wanted to explore it themselves. Isabella and Ferdinand wanted to keep any riches discovered in the new lands for Spain. Both countries went to the pope for his help. In 1493 the pope drew a line on the map of the world. The line ran

Background: Spain is now building replicas of Columbus's three ships. These will sail to America in 1992 in honor of the anniversary of America's discovery.

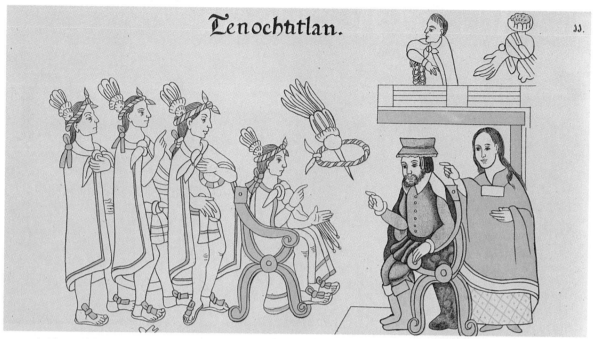

𝕿enochtitlan.

▲ Montezuma met Cortés in the royal Aztec city of Tenochtitlán. Montezuma's palace contained 300 rooms, including libraries, accountants' offices, and meeting halls.

north and south, about 350 miles (580 km) west of the Azores and Cape Verde Islands. Spain was to have the land to the west of the line, and Portugal the land to the east of the line. This line put all of North and South America under Spanish control. In 1494, the line was moved to about 1,295 miles (2,150 km) west of the Cape Verde Islands. When the line was moved, Portugal gained what is ▶ now Brazil. Why would this agreement have angered the other nations of Europe?

12. Early in the 1500s, Spain continued to search for a route to China through the new lands. The purpose of Columbus's last voyage in 1502 was to find this route. Columbus thought that the islands he had discovered bordered China. However, Columbus and other explorers discovered new lands instead. Vasco de Balboa (VAHS-koh deh bal-BOH-uh), a Spanish explorer, discovered Panama. In 1513 he saw the Pacific Ocean from a mountain in Panama. He was the first European to see the Pacific. Juan Ponce de Leon (wan pahnts-uh day LEE-ohn) discovered Florida. The explorers heard stories of still richer lands to the

south of Florida in what is now Mexico.

13. Stories of a great empire rich in gold encouraged Spanish officials to explore Mexico. Hernando Cortés (er-NAHN-doh KOR-tez) sailed from Spain in 1518. He discovered a land ruled by a great people called the Aztecs. Aztec legends told of a god who would come from the east, returning from a voyage. Cortés had arrived from the east and also fit the description of the god. He had pale skin and black hair and beard. The Aztecs believed Cortés was this god. With great rejoicing, they brought him into the capital, Tenochtitlán (tay-nawch-tee-TLAN) to meet Montezuma, their ruler.

14. When the Aztecs realized that the Spanish wanted to rule them, war between the two groups broke out. The Spanish took Montezuma prisoner. The Aztecs surrounded the palace where Montezuma was kept. When he appeared on a balcony to ask for peace and for safety for the Spanish, the Aztecs threw stones and shot arrows at him. Montezuma was killed, and the Spanish were driven from the city.

15. Seeking help in their war, the Span-

303

The Arts and Artifacts

▲ The ruins of the city of Tikal are found in Guatemala. The Mayans worshipped several gods. The small statue of the Mayan corn god is typical of their art.

Mayan Art The Mayans created great cities and beautiful art when their culture developed about 800 B.C. to A.D. 950. Other people in Mexico and Central and South America were influenced by the Mayans to build their own beautiful cities. Mayan buildings were made of stone and intricately carved with pictures of gods, animals, and people. Walls were painted with scenes of religious events that were important to the Mayans. Cities like Chichén Itzá were used only for religious ceremonies. Priests and other officials lived in the cities. Other people came to the cities only on important holidays. Chichén Itzá still stands in the jungles of Mexico's Yucatan Peninsula. It is a city of pyramids topped with temples. The largest is the Pyramid of the Sun. The Mayans sacrificed animals and even humans to the gods. At Chichén Itzá people who were going to be sacrificed were weighted with golden chains and drowned in a deep pool. Since there are few written records of the Mayans, most of our knowledge of them comes from their buildings.

1. How did the Mayans use their cities?

2. Which people were probably shown in the paintings and carvings that decorated buildings and walls?

ish found neighboring Indians who were enemies of the Aztecs. These Indians had been conquered by the Aztecs. Indian captives had been sacrificed to the Aztec gods. With the neighboring Indians as allies, Cortés attacked and conquered the Aztec empire. Cortés and his soldiers gained great wealth for themselves and for Spain. The stories of all the Aztec gold had been true.

▶ Why did this experience encourage other people to explore these lands?

16. Spanish explorers also heard stories from natives of another wealthy empire to the south. Francisco Pizarro (fran-SIS-koh pih-ZAHR-oh), one of Cortés's soldiers, finally found the empire in the area that is now Peru. The ruler, or **Inca**, of the empire was carried on a litter to meet Pizarro. Pizarro sent a priest to talk to the Inca about Spain and about Christianity. When the priest handed the Inca a Bible to encourage him to become a Christian, the Inca threw it to the ground. Pizarro ordered an attack on the Inca people, and their leader was taken prisoner.

17. Pizarro demanded payment for the Inca's freedom. The people of the empire filled a large room once with gold and then twice with silver to buy back their ruler. The Spanish took the money, but they never released the Inca. During the Inca's imprisonment, he had been plotting to overthrow the Spanish. When Pizarro learned of the plot, the Spanish tried and executed the Inca. The Inca's people were captured and made into slaves. Many were taken back to Europe and sold. Most of the Inca people were sent to work mining gold and silver. Many died working in the mines that had supplied their ruler with his wealth. The land and wealth of the Incas helped Spain gain an empire in the New World.

COLONIZATION: Why did Europe found colonies in the Americas?

18. Another voyage of exploration proved without a doubt that Columbus's discovery was not the Indies. In 1519 Ferdinand Magellan (muh-JEL-un) sailed from Spain. Magellan was a Portuguese sailor who, like Columbus, had been unable to persuade the Portuguese to support his plans. Magellan wanted to find a route through the new lands and sail west to the Indies. He planned to continue west until he found his way around Africa and then follow the Portuguese route back to Europe. With five Spanish ships and 234 men, Magellan sailed along the eastern coast of South America looking for a strait, or a passageway connecting the two oceans. He found a strait at the southern tip of the continent. Magellan expected to sail 600 miles across the Pacific to reach the Spice Islands. However, his journey was really 11,000 miles, and he discovered the Philippine Islands instead. There Magellan met Chinese and other Asian traders who told him that the Moluccas, or Spice Islands, were about 500 miles to the south. Magellan was killed in a local war between two Philippine groups. Magellan's lieutenant Juan del Cano (wan del KAH-noh) sailed the last ship back safely to Spain in 1522, and thus became the first person to **circumnavigate** (ser-kem-NAV-ih-gayte), or circle, the world.

19. When Spain realized that the western lands were not the Indies, they set up colonies in the new lands. These colonies were first managed like estates for the people who settled them. Columbus was made the **viceroy** (VYSE-roy), or governor, of the territories to be discovered. Columbus, who was such a fearless explorer, proved to be a weak ruler, and was removed from his post in disgrace. Cortes, Pizarro, and others established new colonies and cities. Gold and silver were mined and shipped back to Spain. The colonies grew crops, which they sent back to Spain, together with lumber, furs, and exotic feathers. Soon this new empire made Spain far richer than Portugal or Venice had become through trade with Asia.

20. Other European nations envied Spain's wealth. Soon France, the Netherlands, and England began explorations in North America. France took the northern part. England and the Netherlands claimed the eastern coast.

21. Sir Francis Drake helped extend English claims to the west coast of North America. In 1570 Drake began voyages for Elizabeth I of England. He raided ships and colonies in the West Indies and Panama and brought great wealth to the queen. On December 13, 1577, Drake sailed from Plymouth, England, to explore the Pacific Ocean. Since only the Spanish sailed in the Pacific, their western colonies in Mexico and Central and South America were not guarded against attack from the sea. Drake raided these Spanish settlements and collected a huge treasure. Then he sailed north and landed on the west coast of North America in September 1578. He called this place New Albion, which some historians believe is the spot where San Francisco was later founded. From there Drake sailed west to the Spice Islands and then around Africa. He returned to England in September 1580 and became the second European explorer to circumnavigate the world. Even with explorations and voyages like Drake's, England, France, and the Netherlands failed to find gold and silver in North America. To gain wealth they founded colonies. The colonies sent crops, lumber, and other goods back to Europe. Why would the Spanish have felt that these nations were stealing Spanish lands?

22. By the 1600s, towns had been built along the eastern coast of North America. Some of these towns became prosperous cities that were important centers of transportation and trade. People in Europe began to look to the New World as a place to escape religious persecution. Some came because they would have a chance to own land and create a better life for themselves and their families. Others came to grow rich from trade.

RESULTS: How did life change around the world as a result of exploration?

23. American gold and silver increased trade with Asia. Asians had little need for

▼ The nations of Western Europe competed for colonies in the New World after 1500. What European nation claimed the most land in North America?

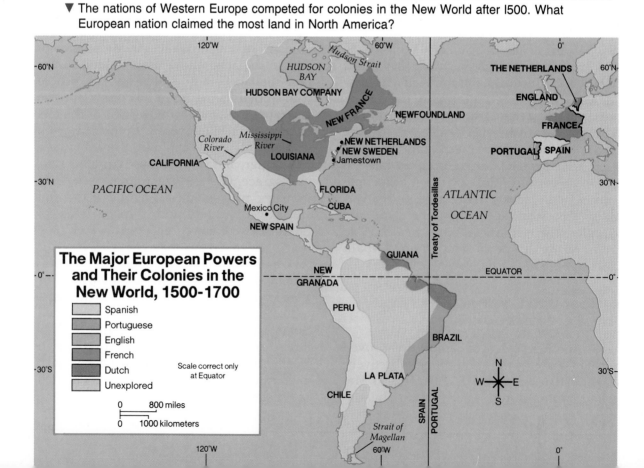

The Major European Powers and Their Colonies in the New World, 1500–1700

- Spanish
- Portuguese
- English
- French
- Dutch
- Unexplored

Scale correct only at Equator

0   800 miles
0   1000 kilometers

European goods since they produced much finer goods themselves. However, the Asians were eager to trade for gold and silver. European trading companies were founded to handle the increased trade with Asia. Spanish coins made from American gold and silver were accepted all over the world. Goods from the East, such as spices, tea, and silk, became more widely available to the people of Europe.

24. New colonies in the Americas also provided more food and other supplies for Europe. Settlers found rich lands and grew large crops of sugar, coffee, cotton, and tobacco. These crops were shipped to Europe. In exchange, the colonies received manufactured goods such as cloth, glass, and books. Europeans found new foods in the Americas that helped Europe's farmers. Native American crops such as potatoes, corn, tobacco, bananas, coffee, and cacao for chocolate were introduced to Europe and became important foods in most nations. Corn was even sent to China. It became an important crop in areas of China where rice could not be grown.

25. A development of colonial life that would have tragic results was the growth of the African slave trade. From the early 1500s, slaves were brought from Africa to work in the Spanish colonies. A profitable slave trade grew between Africa and the Americas. Beginning in the early 1600s, African slaves were brought to English, French, and Dutch colonies in the West Indies. They were also brought to the English colonies in North America. These Africans were captured and brought to the New World against their will. They worked on plantations and mines under conditions that were hard and often cruel. Many Europeans objected to slavery for moral reasons. However, slave labor was profitable. As the years went by, the large plantation owners of North and South America began to rely more and more on slave labor, and thousands of Africans were brought to the New World. It was not until the late 1800s that slavery finally ended in the Western Hemisphere.

▲ Slaves were sold on the coast of Africa, then crowded into ships for the long voyage overseas. Many did not survive the trip.

OUTLOOK

26. Not only did Europe gain wealth from western exploration, it also gained knowledge. Exploration brought new and more accurate information about the shape and size of the earth, and the people who live on it. Europeans were fascinated by the many kinds of plants, birds, and animals that they had never seen before. The Pacific islands such as Tahiti, Hawaii, and Australia, became known for the first time to the people of Europe. When this knowledge was put to use, people's lives changed. How ◄ would your life be different if the Americas were still unknown to Europe?

307

CHAPTER REVIEW

VOCABULARY REVIEW

Write each number and word on a sheet of paper. Then write the letter of the definition next to the word it defines.

1. caravel
2. Indies
3. explorations
4. Inca
5. circumnavigate
6. viceroy
7. scurvy

a. Asia
b. ruler of the empire conquered by Pizzaro
c. lightweight, fast sailing ship
d. searches for new lands
e. governor
f. circle
g. bleeding of the gums caused by a lack of fruits and vegetables in the diet

SKILL BUILDER: READING A MAP

Mapmakers use a special language to describe what a map contains. This language uses lines and other symbols. There are symbols for cities, countries' borders, oceans, and mountains. Sometimes a circle shows a city. Two wavy lines can stand for a river. Colors are other symbols mapmakers use. A map key tells you how to read this language.

Look at the map carefully. Study the map key. On a sheet of paper, write answers to these questions.

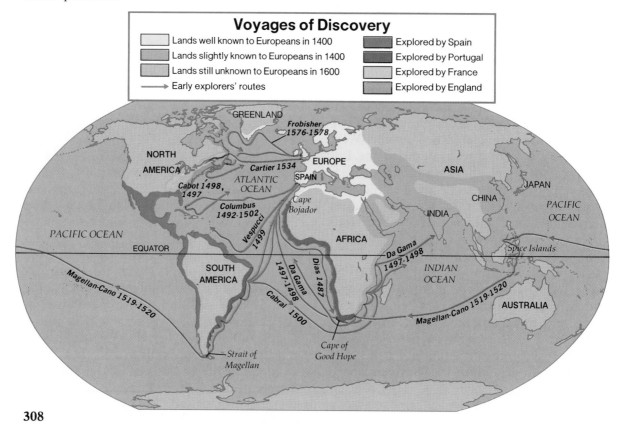

Voyages of Discovery

- Lands well known to Europeans in 1400
- Lands slightly known to Europeans in 1400
- Lands still unknown to Europeans in 1600
- → Early explorers' routes
- Explored by Spain
- Explored by Portugal
- Explored by France
- Explored by England

STUDY HINT Using the map on page 308, review the voyages of Columbus, Magellan, Dias, and Da Gama. Then write as many facts as you can remember about each voyage. Re-read paragraphs 5–10, and 18 to check your work.

1. Which lands were well known to Europeans in 1400?

2. What were the early explorers' routes?

3. Which lands were unknown to Europeans in 1600?

4. Which lands were explored by Portugal?

5. Which lands did Spain explore?

6. Which lands did France explore?

7. Which country explored most of the world?

SKILL BUILDER: CRITICAL THINKING AND COMPREHENSION

Answer the questions or follow the directions below. Write your answers on a sheet of paper.

1. Predicting

a. What would encourage Europeans to explore all areas of the western lands?

b. How will the Indians probably be treated by the Europeans?

2. Fact *versus* Opinion

On a piece of paper, write the letters **a.** to **h.** Then write **fact** or **opinion** for each of these statements.

a. The Spanish were wrong to conquer the Aztecs and Incas.

b. Venice had total control of one of the trade routes to Asia.

c. It would have taken hundreds of years longer for the Americas to be discovered if Prince Henry had not encouraged exploration.

d. Other countries became angry when Portugal and Spain claimed the western lands for themselves.

e. England, the Netherlands, and France settled the eastern coast of North America.

f. The Spanish and Portuguese forced people they conquered to work for them.

3. Point of View

Which of these statements is a point of view that was held by Prince Henry?

a. The best mines produce gold.

b. Portuguese control should be spread to other lands.

c. The Spanish had the right to establish colonies in the Americas.

d. The Aztec wealth belonged to the Europeans.

4. Making Judgments

What good came from European exploration of the Americas?

ENRICHMENT

1. Imagine that you are a European explorer making a trip across the Atlantic Ocean during the 1500s. You are keeping a diary of what happens on your ship. Write an entry for your diary. Describe what happened today. Try to give as many details as possible, including your thoughts or feelings.

2. Choose two European nations that had colonies in the Americas. Then find out how they ruled their colonies. Write a report that compares how the colonies were ruled.

The Holy Roman Empire

▲ Maximilian I, shown with his family, expanded the power of the Holy Roman Empire through marriage and through military strength.

OBJECTIVE: Why was the Holy Roman Empire unable to unify under a strong monarch?

1. Have you ever had the job of getting people in a group to do a specific task? Imagine that you are the new president of a school club. One of your jobs is to try to get the club to work as a unit. Last year's club president was not a strong leader. The club members are not used to looking to the president for advice. Every time you make a suggestion, people in the club start talking among themselves. No one pays any attention to you. How would you feel? In the 1300s, the emperor of the Holy Roman Empire must have felt about the same way. The

nobles had more power than the emperors. Some of their subjects refused to accept the emperors as rulers. When the emperor would try to exercise more power, the nobles would rebel. The situation finally grew worse until it led to a war that spread

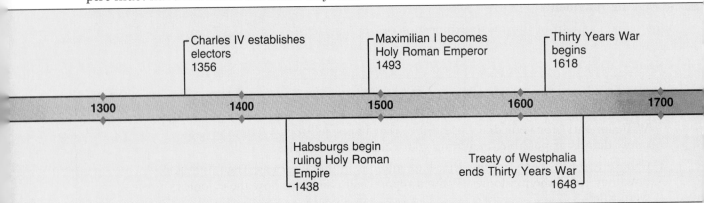

Charles IV establishes electors
1356

Maximilian I becomes Holy Roman Emperor
1493

Thirty Years War begins
1618

1300   1400   1500   1600   1700

Habsburgs begin ruling Holy Roman Empire
1438

Treaty of Westphalia ends Thirty Years War
1648

through all of Europe. When this war was over, the Holy Roman Empire was weakened beyond repair.

THE BOUNDARIES OF THE EMPIRE: Which lands were part of the Holy Roman Empire?

2. By the 1300s, the Holy Roman Empire covered most of eastern and central Europe. It stretched from Poland and Hungary in the east to France in the west. Most of the empire was made up of Germany, Austria, and the Papal States, but borders changed often. The French made advances into the empire from the west. In the east, Slavic rulers would not accept the emperor as their leader. Even German nobles challenged the emperor's authority.

THE EMPEROR: What weakened the power of the Holy Roman Emperor?

3. Loss of church support decreased the power of the emperors. As you learned in Unit 4, in 1075 a struggle began between Henry IV, Holy Roman Emperor, and Pope Gregory VII. The trouble was mostly over the issue of who had the right to appoint German bishops. In 1122, a concordat was established. This agreement, known as the Concordat of Worms, stated that the elections for bishops would still be controlled by the church. The emperor would attend the election and could make a final decision if there was a disagreement. However, rivalry between emperors and the popes continued.

4. The emperors also had difficulty governing because they were absent from the empire much of the time. Some emperors fought wars to gain more land or to keep the land they already controlled. Others joined the crusades. While the emperors were away, German nobles got used to doing as they pleased.

5. In 1356, Emperor Charles IV set up a new way to choose the emperor. No longer would an emperor gain this title by hereditary right. When an emperor died, seven German princes and archbishops, called **electors** (ih-LEK-terz), would choose the new emperor. This new system prevented election disputes, but it resulted in a further loss of power for the emperor. The electors could select an emperor who would not interfere with their authority. Do you think that electors would choose a person who was a strong leader or a weak one?

6. With political power in the hands of the princes, the lands they ruled became **petty monarchies**, or small independent states. Each petty monarchy was ruled by a different noble. In Germany the nobles and emperor were always in conflict for power. To gain favor, both the nobles and the emperor gave privileges to the cities. Some cities made their own laws and treaties and even minted their own money. In what ways were the German petty monarchies similar to the Italian city-states?

THE HABSBURG DYNASTY: Why were the Habsburgs able to rule the empire for such a long time?

7. After 1438, the electors chose Habsburgs to rule the empire. The Habsburgs were an Austrian family. Through marriages, inheritance, and war, they became one of the largest and most influential families of Europe. They ruled the Holy Roman Empire almost continuously until 1806.

PEOPLE IN HISTORY

8. Maximilian I, who was Holy Roman Emperor from 1493 to 1519, was a Habsburg born in Austria in 1459. He succeeded in greatly expanding his power through marriage. When Maximilian was in his late teens, he married Mary, daughter of Charles the Bold of Burgundy. Mary inherited Burgundy and the Netherlands. After his wife's death, Maximilian had great difficulty holding on to these areas, but he finally won.

9. Maximilian's reign as Holy Roman Emperor began in 1493. He tried to introduce reforms that would strengthen the

Background: The brilliant marriages that the Habsburgs were able to arrange led to a popular saying: "Let others wage wars; you fortunate Austria, marry."

311

central government of the empire, but the princes resisted any changes that would make the emperor more powerful. The princes set up a council of their own that took over some of Maximilian's powers. Maximilian increased the territory ruled by the house of Habsburg. He was unsuccessful, however, in uniting Germany and other parts of the Holy Roman Empire under a strong central government.

THE THIRTY YEARS WAR: What were the causes of the Thirty Years War?

10. The Protestant Reformation caused further divisions in the empire. Some German states remained Catholic, while others became Protestant. Conflict between the religions grew. In 1618, fighting broke out in Bohemia when a group of Protestant nobles revolted. They refused to acknowledge Fer-

dinand II, a Habsburg Catholic, as emperor and elected Frederick V as their king. Ferdinand II sent an army to defeat the rebelling nobles. This was the beginning of the Thirty Years War.

11. The Thirty Years War was really a series of wars. It began with a small conflict in Bohemia and grew into a war that included much of Europe. As the war progressed, political rivalries became mixed in with the religious disputes. After the initial fighting in Bohemia died down, the Protestant princes struck again, this time with the help of King Christian IV of Denmark. Other European monarchs such as King Gustavus Adolphus of Sweden joined the battle against Ferdinand. Some fought to decide who would control the Baltic towns and their trade. Why might other European ◀ leaders have wanted to challenge the power of the Habsburgs?

▼ Judging from its location, why might Sweden have been interested in joining the Protestant forces against the Holy Roman Emperor?

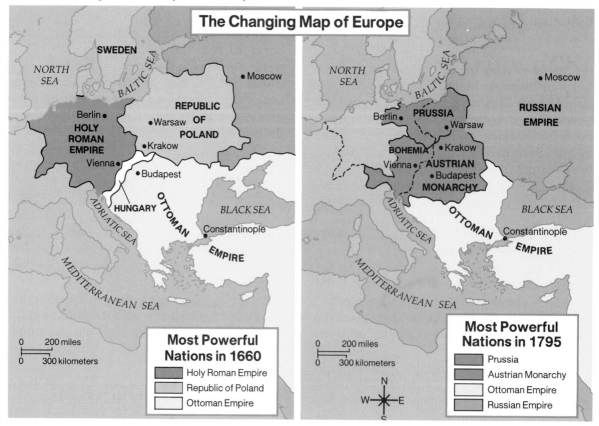

The Changing Map of Europe

Most Powerful Nations in 1660
- Holy Roman Empire
- Republic of Poland
- Ottoman Empire

Most Powerful Nations in 1795
- Prussia
- Austrian Monarchy
- Ottoman Empire
- Russian Empire

Ask: If a war started today that lasted thirty years, how would it affect your own future? What plans might you have to change?

END OF THE THIRTY YEARS WAR: What were the effects of the Thirty Years War?

12. The war took its toll on the Habsburg forces. In 1648, both sides ended the fighting and signed the Treaty of Westphalia. This treaty had a major effect on the power structure in Europe. The Treaty of Westphalia made the German states independent governments. The empire needed the consent of the German states before it could make laws, raise taxes, or declare war. The Netherlands and Switzerland were recognized as independent countries.

13. People became concerned with the horrors of war. The Thirty Years War left Germany in a terrible state. Many of the armies travelling through Germany were not paid. They stole from farmers to eat, and took whatever valuables they found. It has been estimated that as many as 10 million people, one–third of Germany's population, died during the war. Those who were not killed in battle starved or died from disease. Many Europeans felt that international laws should be made to keep peace and to set limits on conduct in war.

SPOTLIGHT ON SOURCES

14. Hugo Grotius (GROH-shee-us) was a Dutch lawyer and scholar who wrote on legal, moral, and religious issues. Some of his best known work deals with the lawfulness of war. Grotius felt that civilian lives should not be sacrificed in war. Grotius said,

> ". . . forbearance [self-control] in war is not only a tribute to justice, it is a tribute to humanity, it is a tribute to moderation, it is a tribute to greatness of soul. . . . Though there may be circumstances in which absolute justice will not condemn the sacrifice of lives in war, yet humanity will require that the greatest precaution should be used against involving the innocent in danger . . . .

> *The Rights of War and Peace,*
> translated by A. C. Campbell

▲ The Count of Tilly was a general who served the Habsburgs during the Thirty Years War. This picture shows an attack by his army.

OUTLOOK

15. The Holy Roman Empire was troubled by rebellions throughout much of its history. Conflicts following the Reformation erupted into the Thirty Years War. During the 1500s and 1600s, as countries got stronger, they often joined together to equalize each side's power. This helped to prevent any one country or group of countries from dominating other countries. Many nations follow the same strategy today. For example, the United States belongs to NATO, an association of countries in Europe and North America. In what parts of ◄ the world might the United States have similar arrangements in the future?

313

CHAPTER REVIEW

VOCABULARY REVIEW

Write each of the following sentences on a sheet of paper. Then fill in the blank with the word that best completes each sentence. Choose from the list below.

elector   petty monarchies   concordat

1. Small kingdoms could also be called _____ .

2. A German prince or archbishop who had the authority to choose the emperor was known as a(n) _____ .

3. A formal agreement is called a(n) _____ .

SKILL BUILDER: INTERPRETING A TABLE

	Holy Roman Empire	Ottoman Empire	Republic of Poland
Religion	Roman Catholicism, Protestantism	Muslim	Roman Catholicism, Judaism
Central Government	weak—had emperor, but power was held by local rulers	weak—had central leader, but power was not central	weak—had central leader, but power was not central
Ethnic Groups	varied	varied	varied
Military Power	none	some, but losing power	none
Expansion into Colonies	none	none	none

The table above gives characteristics of three empires after the signing of the Treaty of Westphalia. Compare the three empires. Then answer the questions.

1. Why would a weak central government have made the empires hard to rule?

2. What had happened to the military power of all three empires?

3. Look at the information on ethnic groups. What problems in government might have resulted from the variety of ethnic groups in each empire?

4. What colonies belonged to these empires?

5. By looking at the table, what is the main conclusion you can draw about the empires and their futures?

SKILL BUILDER: CRITICAL THINKING AND COMPREHENSION

▶ **1. Predicting**

▶ Which of the outcomes would be reasonable to predict for the situation described on the following page? Write the correct outcomes on a separate piece of paper.

The Thirty Years War brought death and destruction to all the people of Germany. Civilians were killed and their towns were destroyed, leaving nothing. People starved because their food had been taken by the armies. Disease killed even more people. By the time the war was over, few people had anything left of their possessions, and land had been destroyed so that few crops could be grown. Those who survived the war had nothing to look forward to.

a. International laws would be made to govern the conduct of armies in war.

b. No nation would ever go to war again because of the sufferings of war.

c. No laws would be made because no one can really help what happens in war.

d. Treaties made at the end of future wars would provide help to damaged nations.

2. Fact *versus* Opinion

▶ Read each of the following statements. Decide whether each statement is a fact or an opinion. On a separate piece of paper, write F if the statement is a fact and O if it is an opinion next to the letter of each statement.

a. Grotius was the wisest man to live during the seventeenth century.

b. The Thirty Years War was partly a religious conflict.

c. Gustavus Adolphus's army joined the war against the Habsburgs.

d. The Thirty Years War was a very destructive war.

3. Point of View

▶ Choose the statement that best describes Grotius's point of view about war.

a. People who serve as soldiers in war are made stronger by the experience.

b. Church and state leaders should speak out against war.

c. Care should be taken during war to avoid the killing of innocent people.

d. Nations should develop better weapons so that wars can be fought more quickly.

4. Making Judgments

▶ When you make a judgment, you weigh evidence to decide whether a statement is accurate, whether it is supported, or whether it is logical. On a separate piece of paper, write the statement that is NOT supported by the evidence in the chapter.

a. The Holy Roman Emperor was weakened by political and religious developments in the 1600s.

b. Life in the Holy Roman Empire was similar to life elsewhere in Europe.

c. The effects of the Thirty Years War were felt mainly in Germany.

d. Electors of the Holy Roman Empire chose emperors to serve their own purposes instead of for the good of the empire.

ENRICHMENT

1. Imagine that you are a soldier from Sweden fighting in Germany at the end of the Thirty Years War. Write a letter home describing what you see around you.

2. There are many famous paintings and photographs of peace treaties being signed. What do you imagine the scene looked like when the Treaty of Westphalia, ending the Thirty Years War, was signed? Do you imagine some people looking like winners and others like losers? Why or why not? Sketch the scene as you imagine it.

CHAPTER 6

The Rise of Russia and Prussia

▲ When Peter the Great introduced European customs to Russia, the long beards then popular were forbidden.

OBJECTIVE: How did strong leadership change Russia and Prussia into important powers in Europe?

1. Have you ever read "The Bronze Horseman"? In this poem, a young clerk named Eugene is wandering through the streets of Saint Petersburg in old Russia. A heavy rainstorm has flooded the city and the girl Eugene loves has drowned. As he comes near a large statue of Czar Peter the Great, Eugene begins to curse the statue. He blames Peter for having built the city that caused his beloved's death. Suddenly the statue, angry at being cursed, comes to life and chases Eugene through the city. This poem by Alexander Pushkin shows the mixed feelings Russians had about their rulers. The czars were honored, but they also were feared because of their great power. In both Russia and Prussia, powerful rulers brought about change by commanding it to happen.

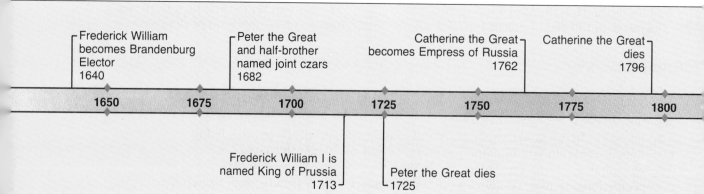

Frederick William
becomes Brandenburg
Elector
1640

Peter the Great
and half-brother
named joint czars
1682

Catherine the Great
becomes Empress of Russia
1762

Catherine the Great
dies
1796

| 1650 | 1675 | 1700 | 1725 | 1750 | 1775 | 1800 |

Frederick William I is
named King of Prussia
1713

Peter the Great dies
1725

PETER THE GREAT: How did Peter the Great spread European influences in Russia?

2. Until the 1600s, the culture of Russia was influenced more by Byzantine and Asian customs than by those of western Europe. Russian rulers followed in the tradition of the ancient emperors and adopted the title **czar** (ZAR) from the Caesars of ancient Rome. Life in Russia was very different from life in other European countries. While England, France, and Spain were exploring the New World and establishing colonies in America, Russia was still a feudal society. In Russia most of the people were serfs, or peasants. They worked on lands owned by a small class of wealthy nobles. The middle class, consisting of merchants and artists, was very small in Russia. How might the location of Russia have contributed to a lack of contact with countries farther west?

3. The first czar to introduce many western ways of life into Russia was Peter the Great. Peter was a member of the Romanov family. The Romanovs came into power in 1613 and ruled Russia until 1917. Peter was only 10 years old when he became czar in 1682. He shared the title with his half-brother Ivan until Ivan's death in 1696. The following year, Peter set off on a trip through western Europe. He wanted to learn about the ideas and tools that the other nations had developed. In England, he worked as a carpenter in a shipyard and attended a session of Parliament. When Peter returned to Moscow, his first act as czar was to crush a revolt by the Russian royal guards. Then he began to change Russia into a modern nation, able to compete with the other countries of Europe.

4. During the next 25 years, Peter introduced many changes from the West. He forced Russians to adopt European clothes and manners, and ordered all nobles to cut off their beards. Members of the royal court had to wear European clothing instead of long-skirted Russian coats.

SPOTLIGHT ON SOURCES

5. Many Russians did not welcome Peter's changes. The following lines are the observations of an Englishman working in Russia in the early 1700s.

". . . It had been the manner of the Russes [Russians] . . . to wear long beards . . . which they comb'd out with pride, and kept smooth and fine . . . . The Czar, therefore, to reform this foolish custom, and to make them look like other Europeans, ordered a tax to be laid, on all gentlemen, merchants, and others of his subjects (excepting the priests and common peasants, or slaves) that they should each of them pay a hundred rubles per annum, for the wearing of their beards . . . .This

Daily life in . . .

In eighteenth century Russia, riches and poverty often were found side by side. Peasants lived under terrible conditions while nobles enjoyed the finest things of Russian life. Though in principle serfs were not slaves, in practice they were. Serfs belonged to the land. When the czar gave land to the nobles, the serfs were part of the gift. Rich nobles kept huge staffs of serfs as servants, sometimes numbering several hundred or more. Nobles' estates were far from large cities. Most of them were set up like small towns, with serfs serving as dishwashers, carpenters, and stable keepers. Serfs could not own property or move to another place. Their children were sure to become serfs as well. When serfs escaped from an estate, they were hunted down and punished. Some were sent to Siberia, a cold and isolated region in the north, to do hard labor as punishment.

Activity: Have students do research to find how serfdom in Russia was different from slavery in the United States.

was look'd upon to be little less than a sin in the Czar, a breach of their religion, and held to be a great grievance for sometime, as more particularly by [because of] being brought in by the strangers. But the women liking their husbands and sweethearts the better, they are now for the most part, pretty well reconciled to [accepting of] the practice."

—from *Seven Britons in Imperial Russia, 1698–1812*, Peter Putnam, ed.

6. Peter also built up Russia's military forces and industries. A series of reforms brought the nobles and the leaders of the Russian Orthodox Church under Peter's control. All who opposed Peter were dealt with brutally. Peasants were taxed heavily

▼ Catherine the Great became a powerful empress, but her early years as a German princess at the Russian court were lonely.

and their revolts were put down with force. During his reign, Peter was able to greatly increase the size of his empire through military victories.

7. Early in the 1700s Peter built a city on the swampy banks of the Neva River, in the northern part of Russia. This city, named St. Petersburg, became the new capital of Russia. Peter faced great difficulties in building this city. The climate in that part of Russia is cruelly cold, and the river was frozen much of the year, making transportation difficult. Thousands of workers were brought in to do the back-breaking labor, and many died from the harsh conditions. In spite of all these difficulties, St. Petersburg was built in about seven years. When Peter died at the age of 52, he left Russia greatly changed because of his rule.

CATHERINE THE GREAT: How did Catherine the Great strengthen ties between Russia and western Europe?

8. The rulers who followed Peter continued to be open to European culture. Life at the imperial court became brilliant and fashionable, and the performing arts such as dance and music were supported. Peter's work of increasing Russia's position as a European power was continued by Catherine II, known as Catherine the Great.

PEOPLE IN HISTORY

9. Catherine the Great, the daughter of a German prince, was born in 1729. Her first name at birth was not Catherine but Sophia. At the age of 15, she was brought to Russia to marry the heir to the Russian throne. She took the name Catherine to avoid confusion with Peter the Great's sister Sophia. Catherine learned the Russian language, joined the Russian Orthodox Church, and worked hard to win the affection of the people. In 1762, her husband, Peter, became czar. However, he proved to be a poor leader. Several months later he was overthrown by a group loyal to Catherine. Catherine ruled as empress of Russia for 34 years.

10. Under Catherine's rule, Russia became even more of a European nation than it had been under Peter the Great. French became the language of her court, and French foods were served at court dinners. Under Catherine's rule, nobles and merchants enjoyed greater freedom than ever before. Manufacturing and trade grew. Catherine supported education for women, and many schools and hospitals were built during her reign. Catherine also supported the arts. She established a museum to hold the collection of famous paintings that she had purchased from all over Europe.

11. Catherine thought of herself as an **enlightened despot** (in-LYT-nd DES-pet), or an absolute ruler who uses his or her power to help the people. However, her early attempts at reform came to nothing. During her reign, Catherine exercised great power without any real understanding of the needs of the people. Conditions for serfs became

worse than ever. In 1773, thousands of serfs joined in one of the largest protests ever recorded in Russian history. Catherine's army used brutality to stop the revolt. Entire villages were destroyed, and their inhabitants hanged on gallows that lined the roads. The leader of the peasants, a man named Pugachev (poo-guh-CHOF), was captured and beheaded. After this revolt, the government took severe measures to control the farm areas. The serfs lost all hope of freedom. Why might it have been difficult ◄ for Catherine to improve life for the serfs?

12. Catherine's greatest successes were in foreign affairs. She wanted to add as much land as possible to the Russian empire. Peter the Great had fought to expand Russia to the north to gain land on the Baltic coast. Catherine concentrated on gaining territory that would expand Russian control south to the Black Sea and west into Europe. The western European nations feared Russian expansion and made a settlement with the Russians for the disputed land. In 1772,

▼ Did most of the expansion of Russian territory shown on the map take place to the east or to the west of Russia? Why?

Expansion of Russia
- Russia in 1589
- Lands added 1589-1796

Empress Marie Therese of Austria, Frederick the Great of Prussia, and Catherine the Great agreed to the first of what would be three partitions of the land called Poland. By 1795, the country of Poland would no longer exist on the map of Europe. Poland would not regain its independence until 1918. By the time of her death in 1796, Catherine had added more than 200,000 square miles (520,000 square km) of land to the Russian Empire.

THE GREAT ELECTOR: How did Prussia become a strong, independent state under the rule of Frederick William?

13. While the Romanovs were changing the face of Russia, members of the Hohenzollern (HOE-en-tzoll-ern) family were turning Prussia into a great power. Prussia was a country in northern Europe. Today the land that was once Prussia's is divided up between Germany, Russia, and Poland. The Hohenzollerns were a family of German nobles. In the 1400s a Hohenzollern was chosen by the Holy Roman Emperor to be the elector of Brandenburg, a province in
▶ northeast Germany. How would this appointment have increased the influence of the Hohenzollerns? Over the years, the family extended its territory and power. By 1640, when Frederick William succeeded his father as elector, the Hohenzollerns were the leading power in northern Germany. Frederick William's success in making Prussia a strong state earned him the title of the "Great Elector."

14. The Great Elector's first task was to rebuild Prussia after its defeat in the Thirty Years War. He began by using tax money to build a larger, better organized military force. He united the armies of the German states of Prussia, Cleves, and Brandenburg.

15. Frederick William believed that it was the duty of a ruler to serve the people. Agriculture, commerce, and industry were all encouraged by his government. Frederick William welcomed foreigners with special skills to settle in Brandenburg. He was a Protestant who followed the teachings of

John Calvin. The **Huguenots** (HYOO-geh-nahts), a Protestant group who were driven out of France, were welcomed in Prussia by the edict of Potsdam in 1685. The Huguenots' skills in weaving, glass making, and other trades helped make Prussia a commercial center. The capital at Berlin grew from a village of about 8,000 people to a thriving city of more than 20,000. Up to the time of his death in 1688, the Great Elector worked to build a backward area of Europe into a powerful, centralized, and progressive nation.

FREDERICK WILLIAM I: How did Frederick William I use his absolute power to improve Prussia?

16. The next important ruler of Prussia was Frederick William I, the Great Elector's grandson, who became king of Prussia in 1713. He was determined to follow his grandfather's ideas of building a strong nation. He wanted Prussia to be powerful and wealthy enough to act independently of other European countries.

17. As an "enlightened despot," Frederick William I worked to improve his government and his army. He enlarged the army from 38,000 to more than 80,000 soldiers. Dependent on his army as basic to his power, he wore military uniforms and organized his government along military lines. Officers were drawn only from the families of Prussian nobles, called **Junkers** (YUNG-kerz). However, officers were promoted only on merit rather than on wealth or social standing.

18. Under Frederick William I, almost everything was measured by how much it helped the army. Certain industries received government support if they were important to the military. For example, the wool industry was protected because it made cloth for uniforms. Frederick William I freed his army from the need for foreign money. He also built up a huge "war chest" of money for future military needs. Under his rule, Prussia built one of the finest armies in Europe. Today the word

"Prussianism" means the practice of strict rules and military discipline.

19. Frederick William I improved on his grandfather's efforts to centralize power in Prussia. Royal lands that had been rented to noble families were taken back by the crown. Workers on these lands were given new freedoms to encourage them to produce more. Areas that had been barren were saved by moving serfs onto the lands for farming. East Prussia, which had been devastated by the plague of 1709, was improved in this way. Frederick William I played an active part in the daily government of his country. His ministers answered only to him on questions of state. All over Prussia the laws of the land were strictly enforced by an army of government officials.

20. Some people claimed that Frederick William I's government gained efficiency at the cost of art and culture. Why might the arts suffer in a state like Prussia? The king himself had simple tastes and did not enjoy art, music, or philosophy. The only sciences that interested him were those that might help his armies. When his son Frederick showed an interest in these subjects, Frederick William I was deeply troubled. Little did he know that his son, Frederick the Great, would one day make Prussia even stronger.

OUTLOOK

21. The great Romanov and Hohenzollern rulers of Russia and Prussia were successful in changing weak and backward nations into European powers. Peter the Great, Catherine the Great, the Great Elector, and Frederick William I all used absolute power to achieve their goals. They crushed any opposition by military force. In a democracy no single person has the kind of power that those European rulers had. Today the President of the United States works in cooperation with the Congress to bring about reform. Do you think an enlightened despot would be a more efficient ruler than an elected president?

▼ Frederick William I is shown selecting recruits for the "Potsdam Giants Guard." This regiment was made up of very tall men from all over Europe.

Background: Frederick William I loved the army and battles more than anything else. He often called a battle he fought as a 21-year-old soldier the greatest day of his life.

CHAPTER REVIEW

VOCABULARY REVIEW

Write each of the following sentences on your paper. Then fill in the blank with the word that best completes each sentence.

enlightened despot   czar

Huguenots   Junkers

1. Catherine the Great was an _____ because she used absolute power to help her people.

2. The class of nobles from which Prussian officers were drawn was called the _____ .

3. The title of the Russian _____ came from the name of a line of ancient Roman rulers.

4. The French Protestants that were welcomed by Frederick William were called the _____ .

SKILL BUILDER: READING A BIOGRAPHICAL TIME LINE

As you have learned, a biographical time line shows the major events in the life of a person in history. Biographical time lines also can show events in the lives of two or more historical figures. In this way, a time line gives you an idea of what events were going on at or about the same time. You can also tell how much time passed between events. For example, in the time line below, which two people were ruling before 1700?

Look at the time line below. Then answer the questions that follow.

1. Which of the four leaders you studied in this chapter was the first to rule?
2. Was Peter the Great alive when Frederick William I became king of Prussia?
3. How many years after Peter the Great died did Catherine become empress of Russia?
4. Who was the czar of Russia when Frederick William issued the edict of Potsdam?
5. Could Catherine the Great have ever met Peter the Great?

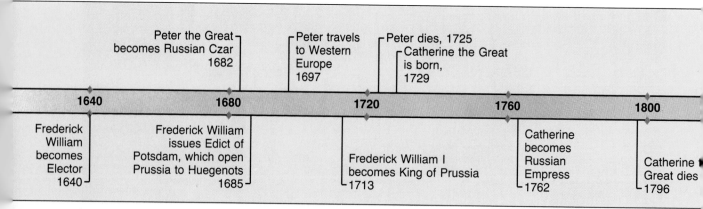

Peter the Great becomes Russian Czar 1682

Peter travels to Western Europe 1697

Peter dies, 1725
Catherine the Great is born, 1729

1640   1680   1720   1760   1800

Frederick William becomes Elector 1640

Frederick William issues Edict of Potsdam, which open Prussia to Huegenots 1685

Frederick William I becomes King of Prussia 1713

Catherine becomes Russian Empress 1762

Catherine Great dies 1796

SKILL BUILDER: CRITICAL THINKING AND COMPREHENSION

1. Hypothesizing

Frederick William I reorganized and strengthened the Prussian army. He built up a "war chest" of military funds for the next king to use. Form a hypothesis about what might happen during the reign of the next king of Prussia. A hypothesis is a statement that is not proved but is accepted in order to form the basis of further study. Write your hypothesis on a separate sheet of paper.

2. Fact *versus* Opinon

On your paper write the letters **a** to **f**. Then write *fact* or *opinion* for each of these statements.

a. Under Peter the Great, peasants were taxed heavily and treated badly.

b. No one other than Peter could have changed Russia into a modern nation.

c. Catherine worked hard to win the love of the Russian people.

d. Life for the peasants did not improve much under Catherine's rule.

e. The Great Elector wanted foreigners with special skills to come to Prussia.

f. The Prussian government services were organized like military groups.

3. Point of View

▶ Read the statements below. Decide if each statement was made by a noble in Catherine's court or by a peasant during Catherine's reign. Number your paper and write *noble* or *peasant* after each number.

a. I never knew how beautiful the French language was until I began hearing it every day.

b. Because of Catherine, our daughter will get a better education.

c. Catherine was cruel in the way she used her army to stop the Pugachev revolt.

d. Today I have more freedom to conduct my business and I am more wealthy than ever.

e. We had hopes that Catherine would bring changes in our lives but things only have gotten worse.

4. Making Judgments

To make a judgment is to come to a decision based on facts and evidence. Make a judgment about the following question: Do you think Prussia would have grown as quickly if Frederick William I had placed more importance on economics and culture and less on the military?

ENRICHMENT

1. Imagine that you are a noble at the court of Peter the Great. Write a letter to a friend describing the changes that took place after the czar's return from Europe. Also in your letter describe an imaginary meeting with Peter the Great.

2. Use encyclopedias or other books to write a report on the Hohenzollern family. How did they first gain power? What did they accomplish? How did they change the history of Prussia?

UNIT REVIEW

SUMMARY

The three hundred years between 1300 and 1600 were a time of great change for Europe. A renewed interest in learning called the Renaissance began in Italy and spread throughout Europe. A German priest, Martin Luther, began to question the doctrines of the Roman Catholic Church. He broke away from the Catholic Church and began a movement known as the Protestant Reformation. The political life in Europe also changed. During this era, strong monarchs in Spain, England, and France made these the most powerful countries in Europe. They spread their influence further through exploring and colonizing areas in the New World. Italy remained divided into smaller city-states. Some of these city-states became rich from trade, but by the end of the Renaissance, their influence had declined. In northern Europe, the Habsburgs, a powerful Austrian family, increased the power of the Holy Roman Empire. The empire was weakened by the Thirty Years' War in the early 1600s. In Russia, Peter the Great, an influential czar, introduced many western ideas to Russia. In Prussia, King Frederick William I built up strong and efficient government.

SKILL BUILDER: READING A MAP

▶ Study the map below. Then answer the questions that follow the map.

The World About 1763

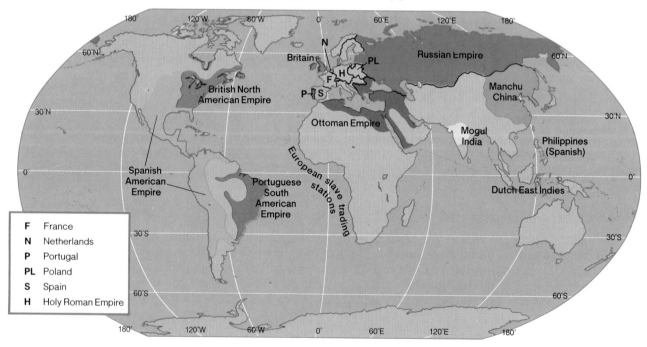

F	France
N	Netherlands
P	Portugal
PL	Poland
S	Spain
H	Holy Roman Empire

1. What three European nations had empires in the Americas?
   a. the Netherlands, Spain, and Portugal
   b. England, Spain, and Portugal
   c. England, Spain, and the Netherlands

2. How were the Asian empires different from the European empires?
   a. They controlled one large area.
   b. They controlled several small areas.
   c. They were spread throughout the world.

3. What were three Asian empires?
   a. Russian, Chinese, and Mogul empires
   b. Russian, Chinese, and Spanish empires
   c. Russian, Spanish, and Mogul empires

4. Which empire held northern Africa?
   a. the Spanish Empire
   b. the Ottoman Empire
   c. the Holy Roman Empire

SKILL BUILDER: CRITICAL THINKING AND COMPREHENSION

 1. Point of View

▶ Write the letters **a** to **d** on a sheet of paper. Read each statement and choose the person who would be the most likely to hold that opinion. Write the name of that person next to the letter.

Leonardo da Vinci   Martin Luther   Peter the Great
Isabella of Castile   Elizabeth I   Maximilian I

a. Art would improve if we studied nature more carefully.

b. My country would be better off if it were united under one religion.

c. I should travel to other parts of Europe to see how to bring my country up to date.

d. Salvation is gained by faith alone.

 2. Fact versus Opinion

▶ Write the letters **a** to **d**. Then write *fact* or *opinion* for each of these statements.

a. The Renaissance was a change in Europe's culture that began in Italy.

b. Monarchies had better governments than city-states.

c. Without Henry the Navigator, America would never have been discovered.

d. Prussian and Russian rulers strengthened their nations by taking complete power.

3. Predicting

▶ Read the paragraph below. Then select the statement that is the best prediction for this statements.

3-1. Spain and Portugal established colonies in the New World. They shipped slaves from Africa to work on large farms and in mines. The owners of these farms and mines became very wealthy, but the lives of the slaves did not improve.
   a. The owners will train European workers to do the work of the slaves.
   b. The slaves will rebel.
   c. The owners will shut down the farms and mines and move back to Europe.
   d. African farming methods will become popular.

ENRICHMENT

1. Choose a person discussed in this unit. Find out more information by checking library sources. Write a report that tells what the person was like: greedy, wise, stubborn, or brave. Give examples or quotations to support your views.

2. Make an illustrated poster showing examples of Renaissance life. Choose a topic such as the following: (1) games and sports; (2) castles (3) renaissance dress.

ESL/LEP Strategy: Have students work together to formulate definitions of the vocabulary words for each chapter prior to reading. After they read the chapter, ask students to write sentences for the words using context clues. Students should check their definitions against the definition provided in the chapter or in the glossary.

UNIT 7

NATURAL RIGHTS AND REVOLUTION

OBJECTIVE: In Unit 7 you will learn how new methods of scientific research led to important discoveries in science in Europe. Philosophers began to apply scientific reasoning to social problems. This new way of thinking encouraged people to revolt against unjust governments.

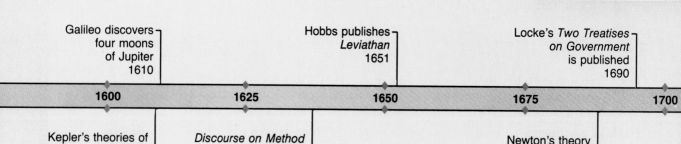

Galileo discovers four moons of Jupiter 1610

Hobbs publishes *Leviathan* 1651

Locke's *Two Treatises on Government* is published 1690

| 1600 | 1625 | 1650 | 1675 | 1700 |

Kepler's theories of planets' movements is published 1609

Discourse on Method published by Descartes 1637

Newton's theory of gravity is published 1687

▲ Napoleon accepts praise after leading his army against Prussian and Russian forces.

Rousseau publishes
The Social Contract
1762

French mob
storms the
Bastille
1789

Haiti gains
independence
1804

Iturbide leads
Mexico to
freedom
1821

1725	1750	1775	1800	1825

Americans adopt
Declaration of
Independence
1776

Treaty of Paris
recognizes United
States
independence
1783

Napoleon
becomes
emperor of
France
1804

Brazil declares
freedom from
Portugal
1822

CHAPTER 1

Scientific Revolution

▲ According to some accounts, Galileo tested the speed of falling bodies by dropping them from the leaning tower of Pisa.

OBJECTIVE: How did new discoveries beginning in the 1500s change the world of science?

1. In 1971, an American astronaut landed on the moon. As television cameras sent pictures back to Earth, the astronaut held a feather in one hand and a hammer in the other. He dropped them at the same time. ▶ Which landed first? Do you know why? On earth, the hammer would land before the feather. On the moon, however, there is no air and no air friction. Therefore, both objects landed at the same time. When he saw this, the astronaut exclaimed, "How about that! Mr. Galileo was correct!" The astronaut was talking about one of Europe's greatest scientists, Galileo Galilei (gah-lee-LAY-oh gah-lee-LAY-ee). Nearly 400 years ago, Galileo had discovered that objects of different weights fall at the same speed in a **vacuum** (VAK-yoo-um), or completely empty space. Galileo was a leader of one of the greatest revolutions in history. This revolution was not a war, but a revolution of the mind, the Scientific Revolution.

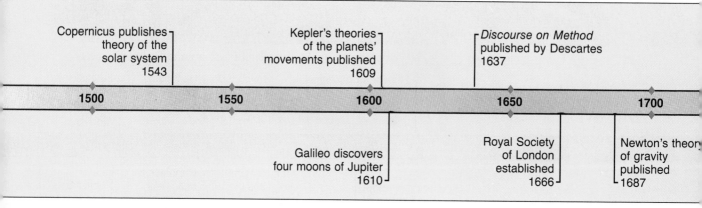

Copernicus publishes theory of the solar system 1543

Kepler's theories of the planets' movements published 1609

Discourse on Method published by Descartes 1637

1500	1550	1600	1650	1700

Galileo discovers four moons of Jupiter 1610

Royal Society of London established 1666

Newton's theory of gravity published 1687

NEW IDEAS IN SCIENCE: Why did scientists' views begin to change?

2. In the 1500s and 1600s a scientific revolution took place in Europe. During this time, **scientists** (SY-un-tists), or scholars who study the physical world and nature, began to approach their work in a new way. They began to test their ideas and conduct experiments to see if their ideas were correct. The result was a great change, or revolution, in how people thought about the world. In the Middle Ages, most European thinkers accepted the ideas of Aristotle and other early writers. These people were not scientists, however, but philosophers . They explained nature by observing it and using logic to reason about its causes. When the philosophers of the Middle Ages studied nature, they accepted things as they seemed. They observed the world around them and formed ideas about what they saw. They used logic in forming their conclusions, but they did not test their ideas to see if they were accurate. In the 1500s and 1600s scientists began to question the conclusions of the early philosophers. Scientists began to test their ideas through measurement and through experiments to support their observations and ideas.

3. The early Greek astronomer Ptolemy (TAHL-uh-mee) studied the universe and concluded that the earth was the center of the universe and that all other heavenly ▶ bodies moved around it. Why might Ptolemy have drawn this conclusion from observation? In the 1500s, Nicolaus Copernicus (nik-uh-LAY-uhs koh-PUR-ni-kus), a Polish astronomer, questioned Ptolemy's ideas. Copernicus believed that the sun was the center of the universe. His observations convinced him that the Earth and other planets moved around the sun.

4. Johannes Kepler (yoh-HAN-us KEP-lur), a German scientist, observed the movement of the planets with a telescope. His findings confirmed that the planets move around the sun. Kepler also found that planets move in oval paths, not in perfect circles as Copernicus had believed. Kepler used math to test his observations. He learned that planets move faster as they approach the sun. They move more slowly as they move away from it. Kepler showed that a planet's distance from the sun determines the time it takes for the planet to travel around the sun.

PEOPLE IN HISTORY

5. Copernicus' idea of the solar system was supported strongly by Galileo Galilei, who was born in 1564. As a young man, Galileo entered the University of Pisa to study medicine. He never received a degree because he ran out of money and had to withdraw from the University. While he was still there, he became very interested in math and science. When Galileo learned of the invention of the telescope, he developed a new telescope more powerful than any other then in use.

6. Using this powerful telescope, Galileo studied planets and stars closely and gathered valuable new information about the universe. Since early times, people had believed that heavenly bodies never changed. However, the universe as seen through Galileo's telescope was different. He saw that the moon's surface was rough. The sun had dark, changing spots. Galileo also found that four moons circled Jupiter. This showed that not all heavenly bodies moved around the earth. Galileo now had evidence that Copernicus' ideas were correct.

7. When Galileo wrote about his findings in the early 1600s, he made many people angry. Authorities of the Catholic Church warned that such ideas were dangerous to religion. Why would the Catholic Church ◀ have been especially sensitive to new ideas in the early 1600s? Galileo was told by church leaders not to defend or teach his ideas. In spite of the opposition, Galileo quietly continued his work. Finally, he was tried by the church and found guilty of heresy. Galileo was forced to deny that the ideas of Copernicus were true. He was placed under house arrest for the rest of his

Background: While a student, Galileo watched a swinging lamp and used his observations to suggest that a pendulum might be used to help clocks keep regular hours.

329

life. However, Galileo never changed his views, and he continued to study and write until his death. His discoveries were a giant step forward in the field of **astronomy** (uh-STRAHN-uh-mee), or the scientific study of the universe.

A NEW SCIENTIFIC METHOD: Why were the new ways of thinking about science important?

8. Scientists and philosophers began to develop other ways of studying nature that would lead to a rapid increase in scientific knowledge. The English philosopher Francis Bacon, who lived about the same time as Galileo, proposed a new way of working for scientists. Bacon believed scientists should first observe nature and then test their observations. In the Middle Ages, scientists had used the **deductive** (dee-DUK-tiv) **method**. This meant that a scientist would begin with a conclusion, then make studies and search for facts to support that conclusion. Bacon believed that a better way to study science was to use the **inductive** (in-DUK-tiv) **method**. This meant scientists should gather facts first and then study and test them. Scientists could then use the tested facts to form a conclusion.

9. The scientific method Bacon proposed was helped by the use of math in experiments. In France, another mathematician, René Descartes (ruh-NAY day-KAHRT) believed that nature and philosophy should be studied by mathematical analysis. As a result of this approach, he believed that everything except God and the human soul could be viewed as mechanical. Complex ideas should be broken down into smaller, simpler parts to arrive at the truth. Descartes thought that a person should begin any study by doubting everything. This idea, known as the universal doubt, paved ▶ the way for modern philosophy. How was the idea of the universal doubt different from the approach of most philosophers before Descartes? Descartes made known his ideas through his writings. His most famous work, *Discourse on Method*, was published in 1637.

LAWS OF GRAVITY: Why were Newton's discoveries important?

10. Isaac Newton, an English mathematician, was the first person to explain the laws of force and motion that operate in the universe. Newton was acquainted with the ideas of Galileo and Kepler. He was very influenced by Descartes's mathematical approach to science. Newton developed an advanced branch of mathematics, called **calculus** (KAL-kyuh-lus) to help investigate his ideas.

11. Newton's greatest discovery was the law of **gravity** (GRAV-uh-tee). According to Newton, gravity is a force that pulls objects toward each other. The force of gravity between two objects depends on the mass, or amount of matter, in each object. This force also depends on the distance between the objects. The heavenly bodies, like all other objects, have gravity. The sun's gravity is the strongest of all because it has the most mass of any body in the solar system. The sun's gravity holds the planets in their orbits as they move around the sun. In 1687, Newton published his theory of gravity in his famous book, *Mathematical Principles of Natural Philosophy*.

12. Newton continued his work in science all his life. He explained why planets travel in ovals, as Kepler had found. He investigated the nature of light and was the first to explain why objects appear to have color. Newton used science to show that the universe was orderly and worked by natural laws that science could describe and explain. Why was Newton's work so important to science? ◀

SCIENCE SPREADS: How did new fields of science develop because of the Scientific Revolution?

13. Once scientists began to use accurate observation and measurement as the basis for their work, they made great progress.

Chemists began to study the gases that make up the air. During the 1700s, hydrogen, oxygen, and carbon dioxide were discovered. Antoine Lavoisier (ahn-TWAN luh vwah-ZEE-ay), a French scientist, discovered the true nature of fire. He demonstrated that fire is caused by the burning material uniting with oxygen. He was also the first to prove that matter cannot be created or destroyed, only changed chemically. Lavoisier's work formed the foundation of modern chemistry.

14. Life sciences and medicine also benefited from the new scientific methods of observation and measurement. Just as the telescope revealed the heavens, the microscope revealed living things too small for the naked eye to see. A Dutch scientist, Anton van Leeuwenhoek (AN-tahn van LAY-vun-hook), used a microscope to examine red blood cells, bacteria, and some of the smallest forms of life. He was the first to prove that fleas were hatched from eggs instead of being produced from sand. At that time, the idea that living things could be produced from nonliving things was a common error. Leeuwenhoek recorded his findings in careful notes and drawings. An English doctor, William Harvey, discovered how blood circulates in the human body.

15. As scientists made more discoveries, European monarchs helped support scientific research. King Charles II of England founded the Royal Society of London. King Louis XV of France helped the new French Academy of Science. These societies brought together teams of scientists and paid for their research. The societies also gathered information from scientists and published their findings.

OUTLOOK

16. Galileo, Newton and other members of the Scientific Revolution were pioneers in changing the way people saw the world. These scientists found ways to arrive at a more accurate knowledge of nature. They learned about the movements of the stars

▲ Lavoisier touches a spark to a mixture of hydrogen and oxygen to determine the elements that water is made of.

and planets and the laws of nature on earth. Some of the ideas of Newton and others were later modified or disproved. However, these early scientists established methods of careful experimentation and testing. These methods and the discoveries that resulted from their use made possible a rapid increase in all branches of scientific knowledge. Modern science owes a great deal to these early thinkers. How could we explore ◄ outer space without being able to measure the distance between planets? How would it be possible to perform open heart surgery without understanding the circulation of the blood? What other recent developments in science and medicine can you trace back to the work of Galileo, Newton, and other early scientists?

331

CHAPTER REVIEW

VOCABULARY REVIEW

Write each number and word on a sheet of paper. Then write the letter of the definition next to the word it defines.

1. calculus
2. vacuum
3. scientist
4. deductive method
5. inductive method
6. gravity
7. astronomy

a. the force that pulls objects toward each other
b. an advanced branch of math
c. studying facts in order to form an idea
d. a completely empty space
e. a scholar who studies the physical world and nature
f. the scientific study of the universe
g. forming an idea and then searching for facts to prove it

SKILL BUILDER: USING A DICTIONARY

When using a dictionary to find a definition, you sometimes must determine which definition of a word fits what you are reading. The following are words from Chapter 1. Two definitions for each word are shown. Both the definitions are correct.

According to the content of Chapter 1, determine which definition you would use. Write the letter of the correct definition next to the number of the word.

1. planet
   a. a very important person or thing
   b. one of the bodies that move around the sun in the solar system

2. nature
   a. the controlling force in the universe
   b. temperament of a person

3. telescope
   a. a tube-like instrument for seeing distant objects
   b. to decrease size by sliding half an object into the other half

4. orbit
   a. a range of activity
   b. an oval path taken by one heavenly body around another

5. universe
   a. a great number
   b. the whole heavenly cosmos

SKILL BUILDER: CRITICAL THINKING AND COMPREHENSION

1. Fact *versus* Opinion

▶ Write the word *fact* by the letter of the statement if the statement is a fact. Write the word *opinion* if it is an opinion.

a. In the 1700s, scientists began to rely on observations and experiments.

b. The work of astronomers is more important that the work of biologists.

c. The telescope is more important than the microscope.

d. Isaac Newton used math to help him form his scientific ideas.

2. Point of View

▶ The following are points of view held by people mentioned in Chapter 1. If the point of view belongs to Newton, write N by the letter of the statement. If it belongs to Copernicus, write C. If it belongs to Descartes, write D.

a. A person should begin any study by doubting everything.

b. The best way to study science is through mathematics.

c. Although Ptolemy thought the earth was the center of the universe, the sun is the center of the solar system.

d. The gravity of the sun is the strongest force in the solar system.

3. Making Judgments

▶ Using your ability to make a judgment, write the answer to these questions on a separate sheet of paper.

3-1. Do you think Galileo's work really was important to modern science? Why or why not?

3-2. In your judgment, which of the events listed below contributed most to the development of science?

a. Newton discovered the law of gravity.

b. Johannes Kepler proved the planets move around the sun.

c. Francis Bacon developed the inductive method to study science.

d. Anton van Leeuwenhoek used the microscope to study bacteria.

4. Hypothesizing

▶ Write the statement that makes a hypothesis.

a. Kepler observed the movements of the planets with a telescope.

b. The planets move around the sun at different speeds.

c. Newton supposed that an apple fell straight down to the ground because it was being pulled by the earth's power.

d. Lavoisier established chemistry as a science.

ENRICHMENT

1. It is the time of Galileo's trial. Imagine that you are his lawyer. You have been asked by the judge to tell the jury why Galileo should be found innocent of the charges against him. As Galileo's lawyer, try to make a good case for him. Prepare a statement that will tell the jury about all of Galileo's accomplishments. Also, explain why his ideas are worthwhile. Use an encyclopedia or a biography of Galileo from the library to help you.

2. Work together with your classmates in two groups. Do research on ideas about the structure of the solar system that were held by scholars before Copernicus. Then find out what Copernicus said about the structure of the solar system. One group should build a mobile of what people before Copernicus thought the solar system looked like. The second group should build a mobile of what the solar system really looks like.

CHAPTER 2

The Age of Reason

▲ Voltaire, one of the leading thinkers of the Age of Reason, was admired throughout Europe for his brilliance and wit.

OBJECTIVE: How did the thinkers of the Age of Reason prepare the way for democracy in Europe and the United States?

1. Imagine a society in which the heavyweight boxing champion is the president. The middleweight boxing champion is the vice president. In this society, leadership would be determined by physical strength. If you lived in such a society, you would probably protest that this system of government is not reasonable. Today, people are used to the idea that a society has a right to choose qualified leaders. In Europe during the 1700s, however, many countries were still ruled by monarchs. If the monarch was industrious and fair, the country was well governed. If the ruler was greedy or lazy, however, the people would suffer. The progress that was made in science during the 1600s led European thinkers to apply scientific reasoning to problems of government. They hoped to discover laws of government similar to the laws of nature. What ◄ groups might have resisted these ideas?

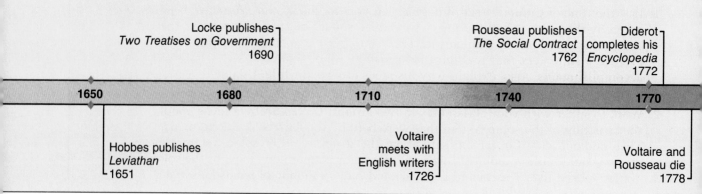

Locke publishes
Two Treatises on Government
1690

Rousseau publishes
The Social Contract
1762

Diderot
completes his
Encyclopedia
1772

| 1650 | 1680 | 1710 | 1740 | 1770 |

Hobbes publishes
Leviathan
1651

Voltaire
meets with
English writers
1726

Voltaire and
Rousseau die
1778

334

ENLIGHTENMENT THINKERS: What did the Enlightenment thinkers believe were the basic laws of society?

▶ **2.** The late 1600s and the 1700s in Europe are called the period of the **Enlightenment** (en-LITE-en-ment). During that time, ideas from the Scientific Revolution spread to other areas of thought. Scientists such as Isaac Newton had discovered the laws of the universe through mathematical reasoning. Might there not also be laws of society and human behavior? Enlightenment thinkers were certain they could use the power of reason to solve all human problems and improve people's lives. Because of this growing belief in the power of reason, the Enlightenment is also called the **Age of Reason**.

3. One of the first philosophers to search for the natural laws of government was England's Thomas Hobbes. Hobbes believed that people were by nature evil and needed a strong government. The English civil war that took place in the 1640s caused great unrest and suffering for the people. The war had a lasting effect of Hobbes's thinking. In his book *Leviathan* (luh-VYE-uh-thun), Hobbes described people as being naturally cruel and interested only in themselves. Their desire to protect their own lives must always lead to conflict. Without laws and government, Hobbes wrote, people's lives would be "solitary, poor, nasty, brutish, and short." People could escape this natural state of disorder in only one way. They must come to the conclusion that survival and protection from each other could only be achieved by establishing a strong government. They had to agree to obey some ruling power or monarch. Only the monarch would provide peace and order, and the agreement of the people gave

▶ the monarch absolute power. What groups of people might have been attracted to Hobbes's ideas?

4. Later, another English philosopher, John Locke, proposed new theories on people and government. His ideas, which he explained in his book *Two Treatises on Government*, did not agree with those of Hobbes. Locke argued that government was based on a cooperative agreement between the people and the government of their choice. Locke had a more optimistic view of human nature than Hobbes. How might ◀ this have affected Locke's thinking? Locke thought that people in a state of nature are guided by reason and good will. Individuals possess the natural rights of life, liberty, and property. The power to govern is a trust given to a ruler by the people. This idea is known as the consent of the governed. If a ruler does not work for the public good, Locke wrote, the people have the right to change that government. The duty of the government to protect the rights of the governed became important to democracy in Europe and North America.

THE PHILOSOPHES: What ideas made the philosophes important to the Enlightenment?

5. In France, the thinkers of the Enlightenment were known as **philosophes** (FEE-luh-ZOFS). The philosophes believed that science and reason could work together to improve the lives of the people. These philosophers believed strongly in progress through education. For this reason, they were interested in preserving knowledge from the past as well as spreading their own ideas. The philosophes spoke out strongly for individual rights such as freedom of speech and freedom of worship.

PEOPLE IN HISTORY

6. One of the leading philosophes was the great French writer Voltaire (vohl-TAYR). Voltaire came from a middle-class background. He was raised by his godfather, a freethinking church officer. As a young man, Voltaire became well known in Paris for his plays and poetry. He also became very popular because of his razor-sharp wit. His quick temper and wit often got him into trouble, however. As a result of a quarrel, he was imprisoned in the Bastille, then fled to to England in 1726.

Background: The purpose of the first of Locke's *Two Treatises* was to refute the idea of the divine right of kings, which said that kings derived their authority to rule from God.

335

7. Voltaire stayed two years in England and met the great English writers of the time. He eagerly studied the ideas of Newton and Locke. Voltaire was delighted by the freedom of speech he found in England. When he returned to Paris, he began to write about the natural laws of government and the rights of all people as a model for the citizens of France. In 1734, Voltaire published *Philosophical Letters.* He wrote that the purpose of life should be to bring greater happiness to people through progress in science and art. Until his death in 1788, Voltaire wrote many essays, letters, and plays in which he urged reform of French society. He argued for freedom of speech and criticized the Catholic Church for the role it played in the class system.

SPOTLIGHT ON SOURCES

8. Voltaire knew how to criticize the government and the Catholic Church without stepping over certain lines. Here, in a section from his *Portable Dictionary of Philosophy*, he gives his views on "equality."

What does one dog owe to another or one horse to some other horse? Nothing. No animal depends on his fellow. But man, having received from God the light we call reason, has with it made himself—what? A slave nearly everywhere . . . . All men would necessarily be equal if they were free from needs. It is want that subjects one man to another—not that inequality is in itself an evil, but dependency is. It does not matter if someone is called Your Highness and somebody else His Holiness, but it is grievous [very sad] to slave for the one or the other.

—from *The Columbia History of the World*,
John A. Garraty and Peter Gay, eds.

9. Jean Jacques Rousseau was another French philosopher whose ideas had great influence. Rousseau was born in Switzerland in 1712. His mother died when he was a baby, and his father abandoned him when he was 10. Rousseau's early life was spent wandering from place to place working at various jobs. In Paris, he met the famous philosophes and learned about their faith in reason and progress. Rousseau disagreed

▼ Many nobles were very interested in the ideas of the philosophes. The group pictured below is listening to a reading of a new work of Voltaire.

336

Background: Voltaire's most popular book was *Candide* (1758), a short novel about a young adventurer whose chain of misfortunes spoil his belief that this is "the best of all possible worlds." The book was a satire of many Enlightenment ideas.

with the philosophes, however, on the value of pure reason. He realized that people were not just thinking machines. Rousseau believed that people should also be guided by their emotions.

10. Rousseau's own hard life led him to believe that human beings were born good but were spoiled by society. Society set people against each other and made them unequal and unhappy. Rousseau urged people to return to simpler ways of living. His book *The New Heloise* showed the goodness of nature and the life of country people.

11. In Rousseau's most famous book, *The Social Contract*, he spoke out strongly against the government and society of his day. Like Locke, Rousseau believed that government was based on an agreement made by the people. He called this agreement the **social contract**. "Man was born free, and everywhere he is in chains," Rousseau wrote. By this he meant that people in society lose the freedom they have in nature. Therefore, when the social contract is written, it should provide protection for the liberties that people had in the state of nature. Things achieved by means of strength in nature, such as holding property, are achieved by law in society. Rousseau also believed that rulers have no part in making the social contract. Rulers serve only by the "general will" of the people. If the people choose, they have the right to ▶ bring down any ruler. Why might Rousseau's ideas be important to people living in democracies today?

THE *ENCYCLOPEDIA:* How did the ideas of the Enlightenment spread?

12. The philosophe Denis Diderot (de-NEE dee-DROH) did more to spread the ideas of the Enlightenment than anyone else. Through travel and letters, the philosophes of the Enlightenment exchanged ideas with rulers and thinkers in other countries. As these ideas became more widely known and accepted, Diderot decided to bring them together in one collection. He asked Voltaire, Rousseau, and the

others to write about different subjects for a new set of books that he was planning. The subjects included science, religion, government, philosophy, and the arts. All the writings were put together in an **encyclopedia** (in-SY-kluh-PEED-ee-uh). This work filled 35 volumes and took 20 years to compile. The *Encyclopedia*, which was finished in 1772, was one of the great achievements of the Enlightenment.

13. Authorities of the French government and of the Catholic Church were alarmed at the ideas presented in Diderot's *Encyclopedia*. Church authorities thought that the writings of the philosophes would weaken people's faith in God. The ideas about justice and progress were thought to be a threat to the authority of the crown. Opposition to the *Encyclopedia* was so great that Voltaire offered to arrange for its publication outside of France. The project stayed in Paris. Diderot later discovered, however, that his publisher had removed some of the more controversial material without his knowledge.

THE ENLIGHTENMENT AND SOCIETY: How did the ideas of the Enlightenment influence society?

14. In the early part of the 1700s, when the philosophes were beginning their work, freedom of expression was limited in France. The country was controlled by an absolute monarch, and criticism of the crown or the nobility was discouraged. The religion of France was Catholicism, and there was little toleration of other religions. In spite of this, the philosophes were able to write and spread their ideas. Many of the philosophes were popular among the fashionable nobility. They were frequently honored guests in the nobles' homes. The new ideas of equality did not change French society much in the earlier part of the eighteenth century. However, these same ideas provided the basis for the revolutions that took place in the late 1700s and early 1800s.

15. Rulers of European countries other than France became interested in the writ-

Background: Wealthy French women such as Emile du Chatelet helped several of the philosophes. Emile gave Voltaire refuge from the authorities when the outspoken writer had disputes that threatened to get him thrown in jail.

337

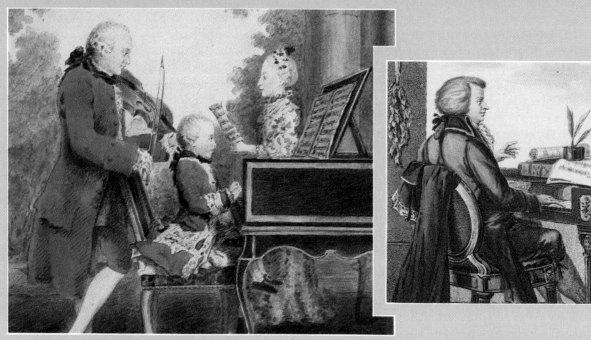

▲ At left, the young Mozart is performing with Nannerl, his sister, and Leopold, his father. Mozart composed quickly and could improvise music as he played.

The Music of Mozart

Wolfgang Amadeus Mozart of Austria was one of the greatest composers of all time. Mozart was born in 1756. He learned to play both piano and violin at age four, and began to compose when he was five. Mozart's older sister, known as Nannerl, was also talented. When Wolfgang was seven, he went with Nannerl on the first of several performance tours. The two children played for rulers throughout Europe. They were received with wild enthusiasm.

In spite of his early fame, Mozart had a difficult time earning a living. At that time musicians still depended on patrons for financial support. For a time, Mozart was in the service of the Archbishop of Salzburg. Mozart became dissatisfied with the way he was treated and resigned. He did not receive his next official appointment for six years. The Emperor of Austria, Joseph II, hired him as court composer in 1787. His salary was not large, and to supplement his income he gave public concerts. At these concerts, Mozart played his own piano concertos and would often improvise, or make up, parts of the music during the performance.

Mozart lived to be only 35. He died of an unknown illness in 1791, deeply in debt. Although Mozart's life was short, he left an enormous amount of music. He composed 41 symphonies, 21 piano concertos, 11 masses, 16 operas, and many other works. His operas, such as *The Marriage of Figaro*, were the first to present realistic characters from all classes in society. Mozart's music reflects the ideals of the Age of Reason because of its balanced forms, clarity, and beauty.

1. What types of music did Mozart write?

2. Which Austrian monarch hired Mozart as court composer?

3. In Mozart's time, musicians were regarded as servants. Why might Mozart have had difficulty holding an official position when he was an adult?

ings of the philosophes. Catherine the Great of Russia exchanged letters with Voltaire and invited Diderot to Russia, where he was received with honors. Catherine understood and agreed with the need to improve rights for the lower classes. She tried to make some reforms during her reign, but her program was not effective. Why would reform have been difficult in Europe during the 1700s?

16. Frederick II of Prussia, who became known as Frederick the Great, was able to put some of the ideas of the Enlightenment into practice. Frederick became king of Prussia in 1740, when his father died. He was a capable leader who strengthened and improved his kingdom. Through letter-writing, Frederick kept up a long friendship with Voltaire. Early in his reign, Frederick wrote "the prince is not the absolute master but only the first servant of his people." Why would it have been unusual for a monarch of the 1700s to make a statement such as this? Frederick promoted freedom of the press and religious toleration in his kingdom.

17. Maria Theresa, who was Empress of Austria from 1740 to 1780, made many reforms. She made sure that all her own children were well educated, and she began plans for required early education for all Austrian children. Maria Theresa also did away with enforced labor for the peasants of Austria. Although her reforms were made mainly for practical reasons, they brought about greater equality in Austrian society.

18. Maria Theresa's son Joseph, who followed her as ruler of Austria, continued her work of reform. He improved education by seeking top scholars and scientists for the University of Vienna. He saw that health care was improved, and supported freedom of the press and freedom of religion. However, his enthusiasm for change brought him into conflict with the Roman Catholic Church and with many of the people of Austria who wanted to keep their older ways of life. What other European monarch had similar problems when he tried to modernize his country?

▲ Maria Theresa had a large family. One of her daughters was Marie–Antoinette, who was executed in the French Revolution.

OUTLOOK

19. The thinkers of the Enlightenment believed reason and knowledge were the keys to a better and more just society. They believed that people were born with natural rights and freedoms. If a government did not protect these rights, Rousseau said, people had the right to change the government. Why would these ideas have encouraged ◄ revolution? Today, we often take for granted rights such as freedom of speech and freedom of religion. Why might it be ◄ dangerous to take these rights for granted? What should be done to protect those rights?

339

CHAPTER REVIEW

VOCABULARY REVIEW

Write each of the following words on a sheet of paper. Then write the correct definition for each word. Use the glossary on pages 728–740 to help you.

Age of Reason   Enlightenment

philosophes   social contract

encyclopedia   equality

Write the following paragraph on your paper. Then fill in the blanks with the words that best complete the paragraph.

The _____ was a period when ideas from the Scientific Revolution spread to theories about government and society. Because people of the time thought that reason would lead them to the truth, the period is also called the _____ . The French thinkers of the Enlightenment were called _____ . Jean–Jacques Rousseau was interested in the agreement between the people and their ruler, or the _____ . Another philosophe, Denis Diderot, brought together the ideas of the Enlightenment in a large _____ .

SKILL BUILDER: MAKING A TABLE

A good way to write and compare information on a subject is to make a table. Tables are often used to show statistics about nations in numbers. Such tables may list the wealth of certain nations, their populations, or other facts. Tables can also be used to list and compare ideas. They can show what ideas came first, where they came from, and how they affected later ideas.

Look at the table below. What would be a good title for this table? Read the words at the top of the columns. The information in this table is taken from Chapter 2. When you complete the table, you will have an overview of the main points about the thinkers of the Enlightenment.

Read the table below and copy it on your paper. Use facts from the chapter to fill in the blanks. Then write a title for the table that describes it.

Writer	Country	Important Ideas
Hobbes	England	**1.** People by nature are cruel and interested only in themselves. **2.**
Locke		**1.** Every person has natural rights to life, liberty, and property. **2.**
	France	**1.** The purpose of life is to bring greater happiness to people through progress in science and art. **2.**
Rousseau		**1.** **2.**

SKILL BUILDER: CRITICAL THINKING AND COMPREHENSION

1. Main Idea

▶ Read each paragraph listed below. Then read the sentences that follow. Choose the sentence that gives the main idea for each paragraph and write its letter on your paper.

1.1 Paragraph 2

a. Reason is important in the lives of human beings.

b. Enlightenment thinkers discovered natural laws.

c. Reason can solve all the problems of government.

d. The Enlightenment was a time when thinkers believed reason could help solve human problems.

1.2 Paragraph 4

a. Locke started democracy in North America.

b. Locke wrote a book called *Two Treatises of Government*.

c. Locke's ideas of natural law and government protection of rights were important to the start of democracy.

d. Locke had a more positive view of human nature than Hobbes, which led Locke to believe that democracy could work.

2. Classifying

▶ Classify the people and things listed here into three groups. On your paper, label the groups and write the names of the people or things that belong to each group.

John Locke	Denis Diderot
The Social Contract	Voltaire
Jean Jacques Rousseau	*Encyclopedia*
Thomas Hobbes	*Philosophical Letters*

3. Summarizing

▶ Reread paragraphs 5–13 about the philosophes. Write a paragraph that gives a summary of the main points in these paragraphs.

4. Making Judgments

▶ Read the following statement about the influence of the Enlightenment. Write why you think the statement is valid or invalid according to the facts in the chapter.

The ideas of the Enlightenment had little influence on society because the nobles did not take these ideas seriously.

ENRICHMENT

1. Research a person from this chapter. Describe work that person did in areas other than philosophy. For example, what works of history did Voltaire write?

2. Write short definitions in your own words for terms from this chapter, such as government, consent of the governed, and toleration. Use Voltaire's paragraph on "equality" as a model for your definitions.

CHAPTER 3

American and French Revolutions

▲ A Bastille Day parade passes in front of the Triumphal Arch in Paris. The French celebrate July 14 as their Independence Day.

OBJECTIVE: How did revolutions in America and France change how those countries are governed?

1. On July 14, 1789, the people of Paris attacked the grim prison known as the **Bastille** (bah-STEEL). Three months later, in an impressive ceremony, the key to the Bastille was given to an American, Thomas Paine. Paine had been one of America's leading spokespersons when his country had fought off English rule ten years before. The French revolutionaries hailed Paine as a "friend of the people, enemy of kings and royalty, and zealous defender of republican liberty." The success of the American revolution encouraged French people who were dissatisfied with French rule. Today, visitors to Mount Vernon, the former home of George Washington, can see the key from the Bastille hanging on a wall. Why is ◄ Mount Vernon a suitable place to keep this key?

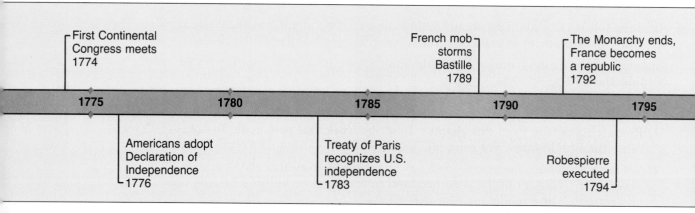

First Continental
Congress meets
1774

French mob
storms
Bastille
1789

The Monarchy ends,
France becomes
a republic
1792

1775   1780   1785   1790   1795

Americans adopt
Declaration of
Independence
1776

Treaty of Paris
recognizes U.S.
independence
1783

Robespierre
executed
1794

ESL/LEP Strategy: Discuss the importance of Bastille Day, or French Independence Day. Ask students how Independence Day is celebrated in their country or culture. Encourage students to bring to class pictures, flags, or other examples of patriotism.

COLONIALISM: What events led the American colonies to revolt?

2. By the 1770s, the British had established a powerful empire in the New World. Thirteen colonies had been settled along the eastern coast of North America. In 1763, a long struggle with France for territory, known as the French and Indian Wars, had ended in an English victory. The expense of maintaining this new territory and of paying for the war was enormous. The British parliament decided that taxing the American colonies would be an effective way to raise the necessary money. The colonists, however, felt that these taxes were unfair because the colonies were not represented in Parliament.

3. In the ten years following the English victory of 1763, new laws and taxes were passed that were irritating to the colonists. For example, in 1764, Parliament passed a Sugar Act that increased taxes on many goods. The Stamp Act of 1765 created a tax in the form of special stamps required for newspapers and other printed items.

4. Increased dissatisfaction caused the colonies to unite against the British. In September 1774, twelve colonies sent representatives to the First Continental Congress in Philadelphia. The delegates pledged to stop trade with Britain until the colonies were represented in Parliament.

SPOTLIGHT ON SOURCES

5. Although most colonists only wanted full rights under Britain, some began to call for total independence from Britain. Thomas Paine, a colonial writer and editor, published a pamphlet, *Common Sense*, in early 1776. In lines such as the following, Paine urged the colonists to break from Britain and form their own government.

> . . . "Tis not in the power of Britain to do this continent justice; the business of it will soon be too weighty and intricate to be managed with any tolerable [reasonable] degree of conven-

ience, by a power so distant from us, and so very ignorant of us; for if they cannot conquer us, they cannot govern us . . . .

> America is only a secondary object in the system of British politics. England consults the good of this country no further than it answers her own purpose . . ."

—from *The Road to Independence*, John Braeman

6. Members of the Second Continental Congress, which first met in 1775, chose Thomas Jefferson to write the Declaration of Independence. The Declaration of Independence was a document that stated the colonists' intention of breaking away from Britain. The Declaration of Independence was signed on July 4, 1776.

7. Jefferson was influenced by the ideas of John Locke, and many ideas in the Declaration of Independence came from Locke's writings. Locke felt all people had certain rights. These rights included the right to "life, liberty, and pursuit of happiness." He felt that government should provide these three basic rights. If a government failed its citizens, the citizens should have the right to do away with the government. How might Jefferson have used these ◀ ideas as reasons for the colonies to declare independence?

WAR OF INDEPENDENCE: How did the colonists win the war?

8. By the time the Declaration of Independence was written, the colonies were already at war with Britain. On April 19, 1775, fighting broke out in Lexington, Massachusetts. News of the fighting spread, and the colonists rushed to join the armies against the British.

PEOPLE IN HISTORY

9. In June 1775, the Second Continental Congress chose George Washington to lead the Continental Army. Washington was a

Activity: Students interested in architecture and technology might do research on Thomas Jefferson's home in Monticello, Virginia, and the technical innovations he introduced there.

343

▲ To march on Princeton, Washington had to move his army across the icy Delaware River. In the 1800s, the artist Emanuel Leutze painted this trip in a dramatic style.

43-year-old landowner who had distinguished himself as a military leader during the French and Indian Wars. Washington had excellent qualifications to lead the Continental Armies. He was level-headed and able to command respect and loyalty from his troops. These qualities became increasingly important as the war progressed, because the odds were often heavily in favor of the British.

10. Experience in the French and Indian Wars had given the colonists the ability to fight successful battles. Britain had a powerful navy, and gained control of Boston and many coastal areas. Washington's troops retreated inland. In December 1776, Washington led a surprise attack in New Jersey. By early January, 1777, the Patriot army had captured both Trenton and Princeton. News of this victory encouraged the Patroits and made them more determined than ever to continue the war. Another turning point came when a British army led by General Burgoyne (bur-GOIN) was defeated by American troops at Saratoga, New York, on October 17, 1777.

11. America's victory at Saratoga changed the revolution into a global war. France was convinced that America could defeat the British and declared war on Britain in 1778. France hoped to weaken Britain and build up its colonial empire. Other European nations entered the conflict as well. Spain declared war on Great Britain in 1779. The Netherlands loaned money to the American colonies to help pay for the war. In 1780, Great Britain declared war on the Netherlands. As these nations entered the war, fighting spread to places as distant as India and the coast of Africa.

12. After losing an important battle in Yorktown, Virginia, the British decided to end the war. Final peace terms were agreed on in the Treaty of Paris, signed on September 3, 1783. Britain recognized the independence of the United States. The States was granted all British land west of the Appalachian Mountains and east of the Mississippi River. Britain also returned Florida to Spain. Only Canada remained a British colony. Look at the map on page 345. Which 13 ◄ states made up the first United States?

A Geographic View of History

Rivers and the Early Territorial Growth of the United States Rivers played an important role in the early history of the United States. They formed clear boundaries between the young United States and its neighbors. They also served as a way to transport goods and people before roads were built.

The map on this page shows how rivers influenced the early growth of the United States. Read the facts below and study the map. Then answer the following questions.

In 1763, Britain drew a Proclamation Line along the Appalachian Mountains and forbade settlement west of that line. The Proclamation Line followed the division of rivers flowing east to the Atlantic Ocean and south to the Gulf of Mexico.

Colonial Americans resented Britain's ban on settlements west of the Proclamation Line. They had helped Britain win the western lands from France and wanted to settle on them.

The Mississippi River became the first western boundary of the United States in 1783. West of the river was Louisiana, which was controlled by France. New Orleans and the mouth of the Mississippi River lay in Louisiana.

Americans wanted control of New Orleans, the only outlet for trade moving down the Ohio, Tennessee, and Mississippi Rivers.

In 1803, the United States purchased Louisiana from France. The purchase doubled the size of the United States.

1. Name two rivers flowing westward from the Proclamation Line of 1763.

2. What city is the natural outlet for rivers emptying into the Mississippi River?

3. How different would the United States be today if the Mississippi had remained the nation's western border?

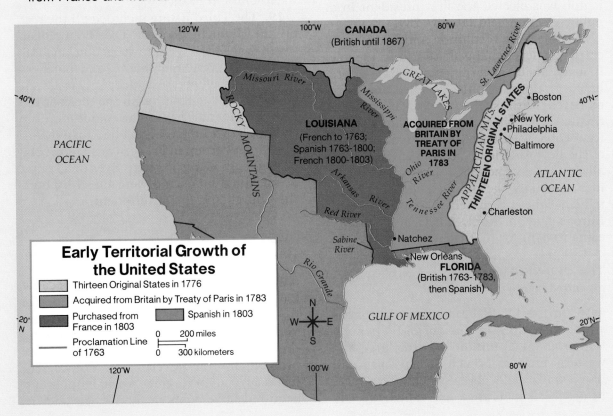

Early Territorial Growth of the United States

- Thirteen Original States in 1776
- Acquired from Britain by Treaty of Paris in 1783
- Purchased from France in 1803
- Spanish in 1803
- Proclamation Line of 1763

0   200 miles
0   300 kilometers

345

13. After the revolution a permanent government was set up for the new American nation. The Articles of Confederation, adopted in 1781, became the first constitution for the United States. Under these Articles, the national government was not given enough power to collect taxes or settle disputes between states. In 1789, a convention was called in Philadelphia to revise the Articles. Instead, the delegates wrote a new constitution that provided for a stronger central government.

14. The new United States government would consist of three branches. Congress, the legislative branch, would make the laws. The chief executive, the President, would see that the laws were enforced. A system of courts was set up to interpret the laws. The delegates also devised a system to prevent any one of the branches of the government from taking complete power. All of the states had approved the new Constitution by early 1789. George Washington was elected the first president in a public election held late in 1789.

15. America's revolution and new democratic society changed the way people thought about governments. Never before had a group of colonies rebelled against a monarch with such success. In France, Spain, the German states, and Latin America, people were encouraged by the success of the new American government. They realized that they no longer had to accept the idea that only the nobility had a right to influence the government. People in parts of Europe and in South America eventually came to fight for that right.

THE OLD REGIME: How was French society organized before the Revolution?

16. In the 1770s, France was one of the strongest nations in the world. Its population of about 25 million was the largest in western Europe. French society was still based on a rigid class system. The years before 1789 in France are called the **Old Regime** (old ray-ZHEEM), which means the old form of government. In the Old Regime the French people were divided into three estates.

17. The First Estate was made up of the clergy of the Roman Catholic Church. The First Estate was also the smallest estate, with about 100,000 people. The church owned about ten percent of all the land in France. High-ranking church officials often were themselves wealthy nobles. The church in France collected taxes such as the tithe, a tax of one-tenth of the common people's income. The church itself did not have to pay most taxes.

18. The Second Estate was the aristocracy, which numbered about 400,000. These nobles owned almost 20 percent of the land. Nobles also had many special rights and privileges. Only nobles could reach the highest positions in the government, Church, and army. Nobles did not have to pay many taxes that the peasants paid. The lower classes were jealous of the nobles' privileges. The Second Estate was the most hated class in France.

19. The Third Estate included all the rest of the French people. The **bourgeoisie** (buzh-wah-ZEE) were town people such as doctors, lawyers, merchants, and business people. Many of these people were well educated and familiar with the ideas of the Enlightenment. They began to question the existing government and called for reform. The largest group in France consisted of the peasants. Peasants led hard lives of farming or unskilled labor and were taxed by both the Church and the government.

THE ESTATES-GENERAL: How did the Third Estate gain new political power?

20. In 1774, when Louis XVI became king, the French monarchy had lost much of its authority and respect. Food shortages and rising prices led to local revolts among the peasants. Foreign affairs were another problem for the government. France had lost nearly all of its New World empire and acquired huge debts in the French and In-

Background: In the late 1700s, more than 80 percent of the French were farmers. Few had more than 20 acres and fewer still knew scientific methods of farming. As a result the yield was very poor.

dian Wars. When Louis XVI spent more money in helping the colonists fight the American Revolutionary War, his government came close to financial collapse. Why would Louis XVI have been interested in helping the American colonists?

▶ **21.** The monarchy tried to solve the financial crisis by raising new tax money. When a plan was announced to tax the nobles, an assembly of nobles and clergy rejected it. Instead, the assembly asked for a meeting of the Estates-General, a governing group that had not met since 1614. The king granted their request, and early in 1789 elections were held for representatives from all three estates. The nobles and clergy each elected 300 deputies, while the Third Estate elected 600.

22. In May 1789, the Estates-General met to discuss the king's tax proposals. For their meeting place they chose Versailles, a city near Paris that was also the king's residence. From the beginning of the meeting there was a dispute over whether votes would be counted by number of deputies or by estate. If votes were counted by estate, the clergy and nobles could unite to outvote the Third Estate two to one. The king favored the nobles and clergy in the matter. On June 20, members of the Third Estate found their meeting hall occupied by the king's troops. These members moved to another large building, the royal tennis court. There the Third Estate voted on its own plan. It declared that it would serve as the National Assembly and that it would write a constitution for the country. This declaration became known as the **Tennis Court Oath**.

23. Louis XVI's next order angered the people so much that they reacted with violence. The king sent soldiers to Versailles. Many people believed he was preparing to break up the Assembly. On July 14 an angry mob broke into the **Bastille** (ba-STEEL), a fortress that served as a prison. The mob murdered the guards and freed the prisoners. News of the Bastille's fall set off uprisings in other parts of France. Peasants turned against their feudal lords. They de-

▲ After the Tennis Court Oath was declared, it was only a short time before revolution was sweeping through France.

stroyed the nobles homes and burned records of taxes they owed the nobles.

THE NATIONAL ASSEMBLY: What changes in French government did the Assembly make?

24. Members of the Assembly acted quickly to pass new laws that would end the special privileges of the nobles and clergy. On August 4, the Assembly voted to end feudalism, the tithe, and special rights of nobles. On August 26, it adopted the *Declaration of the Rights of Man and Citizen*. This statement set forth the ideals of the Revolution. It stated that people were free and equal in rights, and that all political power came from the nation, or the people. It also stated that all offices and positions should

▲ This painting of the capture of the Bastille was done from the description of a lieutenant present during the fighting.

be filled according to talent and skill, not social rank. The declaration affirmed such rights as freedom of speech, freedom of religion, and freedom to own property.

25. Louis XVI turned down the Assembly's reforms, saying he would not agree to "robbing my clergy and nobility." In October 1789, an angry crowd marched from Paris to Versailles. The group included thousands of women who had gathered in the streets of Paris to demand bread. Reaching Versailles, the marchers spent the night outside the king's palace. The next day the crowd forced Louis XVI and his family to return with them to Paris.

26. The National Assembly also went to Paris. It spent two years writing the new constitution that made France a **constitu-**

tional monarchy. This meant that the king still ruled but his power was limited by an elected lawmaking body. The Assembly also declared that international law allowed all people to change their governments. Other European rulers, who until now had been indifferent to the revolution, became alarmed. Rulers of Austria and Prussia proclaimed their support for Louis XVI, although they actually were not planning to use armed force. The leaders of the revolution, however, believed that the rulers' threat was real and decided to attack first. In April 1792, France went to war with Austria and Prussia.

27. In August 1792, **radicals** (RAD-a-kulz), people who favored far-reaching changes in society and government, took over Paris. A young lawyer named Maximilien Robespierre (max-a-MIL-yon rohbz-pee-AIR) became the leader of one of the radical groups. Robespierre was a bold and ruthless leader who believed that enemies of the revolution should be destroyed.

28. In the first months of war with Austria and Prussia, France suffered many defeats. Some of the radicals believed that Louis XVI had betrayed his country to foreign armies to keep his power. They spread stories that the king wanted the invading armies to crush the revolution so that he could have complete power again. The radicals finally took the king prisoner. Early in September crowds in Paris exploded in anger against the Old Regime. They broke into prisons and killed over 1,000 people, mostly nobles and clergy.

29. On September 21, 1792, the National Convention, a new radical assembly, ended the monarchy and made France a republic. A strong spirit of enthusiasm had led many to join the army. By late September, French forces began to conquer invading armies.

30. Urged on by Robespierre, the National Convention tried Louis XVI as an enemy of the state. The members found the king guilty and voted to execute him. In January 1793, Louis XVI was sent to the **guillotine** (GIL-uh-teen), a machine that dropped a huge blade to chop off a person's head. News of the king's death shocked other countries, and caused them to join the war against France. Many French people feared that the radicals were harming the revolution by their violence. Uprisings against the National Convention began all over France.

THE REIGN OF TERROR: What did the Committee of Public Safety do for France?

31. The National Convention set up an emergency government led by a Committee of Public Safety. The Committee was run by Robespierre and other radicals. The Committee directed the French armies in war and took harsh action against any "enemies of the revolution." The Committee's rule was called the Reign of Terror. A large army of ordinary citizens was raised to uphold order and to join the fight against the other European nations. Robespierre ordered his forces to seek out anyone who supported the king or spoke out against Committee policy. More than 17,000 people were guillotined, while thousands of others died in prisons or in massacres. Most of the victims were innocent peasants. As the Revolution progressed, many of the former leaders of the Revolution were also killed. Finally the radicals turned against each other, and Robespierre himself was captured and put on trial. He was found guilty of crimes against France and was sentenced to death by guillotine.

32. The revolutionaries succeeded in reaching some their objectives. They replaced the monarchy with a republican government. The new government was able to begin the work of putting the ideas of the revolution into practice. Workers and peasants were given new political rights. Free schools for children were started. Price controls and laws creating taxes based on income were passed. The French citizens' army of more than one million soldiers began to be successful against other European forces. In spite of these gains, the work of restoring peace and order in France took many years.

▲ Robespierre was an admirer of Rousseau. Would Rousseau have admired Robespierre if he had known him?

OUTLOOK

33. A desire for independence led the British colonies in North America to break with Britain. The success of the American revolution encouraged other countries to fight for their rights. Late in the 1780s, problems of injustice and hunger led to revolution in France. The French Revolution gave the country a new constitution and a republican form of government. These revolutions caused lasting changes in the way government was thought of throughout Europe and the Americas. What ◀ ideals did both revolutions share? How does the United States constitution protect these ideals? Are these ideals still alive today?

CHAPTER REVIEW

VOCABULARY REVIEW

Write each of the following words on a sheet of paper. Then write the correct definition for each. Use the glossary in the back of the book.

Old Regime

Tennis Court Oath

constitutional monarchy

radicals

guillotine

bourgeoisie

Bastille

SKILL BUILDER: INTERPRETING A CARTOON

Do you read the cartoon section in the newspaper? Most cartoons are meant only to be entertaining. However, some cartoons, called political cartoons, have another purpose. They are intended to express a point of view about politics or current events. These cartoons are found on the editorial page of the newspaper. The following cartoon is from the time of the French Revolution. Look at it carefully and then answer the questions on your paper.

1. Who or what does the man in the blindfold and chains represent?

2. Who or what do the other figures represent? How do you know?

3. What point was the cartoonist trying to make by showing the three people riding on top of the chained man?

4. What facts and events from Chapter 3 does this cartoon bring to mind?

5. What is the message of the cartoon?

6. Why do you think someone would decide to express such a message in a cartoon instead of in words?

SKILL BUILDER: CRITICAL THINKING AND COMPREHENSION

▲ **1. Main Idea**

▶ Read each sentence. Then number your paper. For each sentence that gives a main idea from the chapter, write M. For each sentence that gives a detail, write D.

1-1. A series of taxes and unpopular laws led the American people to revolt against the British government.

1-2. High taxes and a lack of food were major problems for the French government in the late 1700s.

1-3. The deputies of the Third Estate met in the royal tennis court.

1-4. The last decisive battle of the American revolution was fought at Yorktown, Virginia.

1-5. The storming of the Bastille was one of the first revolutionary acts of the people in the French Revolution.

1-6. The Declaration of Independence was the American colonists' statement that they intended to break away from the British government.

📁 **2. Classifying**

▶ Read the headings below and write them on your paper. Find one fact from the chapter that belongs with each heading. Write the facts under the headings on your paper.

Act of the First Continental Congress   Act of the National Assembly

Act of the Second Continental Congress   Act of the National Convention

▲ **3. Summarizing**

▶ Write an article on the American Revolutionary War as if you were a newspaper reporter. Imagine that the war has just ended and you are writing a summary of it.

◯ **4. Generalizing**

▶ Find sentences from the chapter that support the following two generalizations.

a. Unfair taxation was the main problem that led the American colonists to revolt against the British government.

b. The Reign of Terror was a time of great violence and cruelty in France.

ENRICHMENT

1. Find books that tell about the American army's experiences at Valley Forge during the winter of 1777. Work with your classmates to write and perform a short play about this period of the Revolutionary War.

2. Do research and write a brief report about the French painter Jacques Louis David (1748-1825) and his relationship to the French Revolution. Find reproductions of his paintings in library books or encyclopedias and pass them around during your report.

3. Look up information about these items and sketch one or all of them.

a. American flintlock musket   **c.** French liberty cap

b. old North Church of Boston   **d.** guillotine

CHAPTER 4

Napoleon's Empire

▲ When Napoleon declared himself Emperor of France, he also crowned his wife Josephine Empress.

OBJECTIVE: How did Napoleon build a great French empire in Europe?

1. At age 33, Ludwig van Beethoven was already considered one of Europe's leading composers. When Beethoven was working on his Third Symphony, he planned to dedicate it to Napoleon Bonaparte, the military leader of France. Beethoven admired Napoleon as a heroic leader who would carry out the ideals of the French Revolution. The music was barely finished when Beethoven heard shocking news. Napoleon had just declared himself Emperor of France! Beethoven exploded in anger. "Now he will crush the rights of people," the composer cried out. "He will become a tyrant!" Beethoven grabbed the first page of his new symphony and tore it in two. Napoleon was supposed to be the person who would put an end to the rule of tyrants. Instead, he had become one! Ever since Beethoven's time, people have argued about Napoleon's place in history. Did he fulfill the ideals of the ◄ French Revolution or did he betray them? Was he a hero or a tyrant?

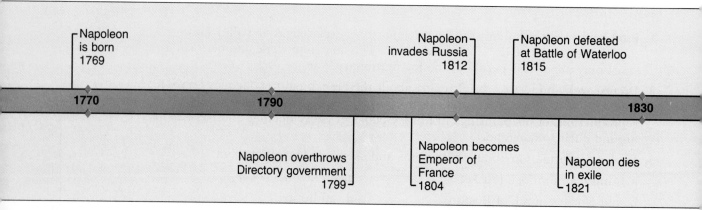

Napoleon is born 1769

Napoleon invades Russia 1812

Napoleon defeated at Battle of Waterloo 1815

1770   1790   1830

Napoleon overthrows Directory government 1799

Napoleon becomes Emperor of France 1804

Napoleon dies in exile 1821

THE DIRECTORY: What troubles faced the new government of France after the Revolution?

2. After the Reign of Terror ended in 1794, a new government called the **Directory** was established in France. The Directory was controlled by a group of five. This new government proved to be too weak to deal with the problems that faced France after the Revolution. French families were not able to pay the high prices for food, housing, and clothing. The government itself needed money. Many people wanted to bring the monarchy back as a way of restoring law and order.

3. In addition to the problems that existed within France, the country had been engaged in a war with Austria and Prussia since 1792. In 1793, England and Spain joined the conflict against the French. The Directory strongly supported the French armies in the ongoing war in Europe. The leader who would bring new military glory to France was a brilliant young officer named Napoleon Bonaparte (na-PO-lay-on BO-na-part).

PEOPLE IN HISTORY

4. Napoleon Bonaparte was born on the Mediterranean island of Corsica (KOR-sih-kuh) in 1769. Napoleon studied at military schools in France and fought on the side of the revolutionaries in the French revolution. Napoleon distinguished himself early in his career and was made a general at the age of 24.

5. In 1796, Napoleon was sent to drive the Austrians out of Italy. He defeated the Austrians, and two years later he invaded Egypt with the intention of weakening British influence in the Middle East. When Napoleon returned to France, he was hailed as a national hero. He then showed the boldness that made him famous. He quickly moved to overturn the weak and unpopular Directory government in a **coup d'état** (kood-ay-TAH), or sudden revolution, in the fall of 1799.

6. Napoleon had a new government called the **Consulate** (KAHN-suh-lut) set up. In this government, the power was given to three Consuls. Napoleon as First Consul was the only ruler with any real authority. In 1804, he had himself crowned emperor of the French people. These actions made Napoleon a dictator in France. Each time, the French people approved his actions by a **plebiscite** (PLEB-ih-syt), or a vote on a change in government. How did Napoleon's government differ from a monarchy? ◄

NAPOLEON'S POLICIES: What changes did Napoleon make in France?

7. Napoleon lost no time in restoring order to the government of France. He reor-

Daily life in . . .

During the Revolution, French theaters presented mostly dull political plays expressing the ideals of the Revolution. Napoleon loved the theater, however. Under his rule, the quality of the theater improved greatly. Napoleon supported a law providing a large subsidy to the Théâtre Français (tay-AH-truh frahn-SAY). He even found time during the disastrous months in Moscow to draw up a set of rules for this theater.

Inexpensive tickets and frequent new productions led all classes of society to attend the theater. The greatest actors were treated like modern rock stars. Their fans would cheer wildly whenever they appeared on stage. Talma (TAHL-mah), one of the most celebrated actors of the French theater, was often invited to visit with Napoleon. They would discuss the theater for hours, and sometimes Napoleon would give Talma advice on improving a role.

Background: Napoleon also was a novelist. In 1794, he wrote a novel in which the main character, Clisson, gives up a wife and child and dies gloriously in battle.

ganized the Bank of France and placed it partly under government control. He made improvements in the canals and roads. Napoleon was influenced by ideas from the Enlightenment. He encouraged freedom of religion in France and set up secondary schools and universities.

8. Napoleon established a new system of laws for France. This system became known as the **Napoleonic** (nuh-pole-YON-ik) **Code.** The code made into law many of the revolution's ideals. The basic idea of the code was that all people are equal before the law. The code supported individual liberty. However, the Napoleonic Code put the interests of the country above the rights of citizens. Freedom of speech and of the press were limited. The Napoleonic Code is still the basis of French law today.

NAPOLEON'S EMPIRE: How did Napoleon win an empire for France?

9. Napoleon's goal was to rule the entire world, and for a while it seemed that he would succeed. He was a military genius. His basic technique was to find a weak spot in the enemy lines, then attack with great speed and force. In addition, he inspired great admiration and loyalty in his soldiers. During the first 15 years of the 1800s, much of Europe was caught up in a series of conflicts known as the Napoleonic Wars. Other European countries joined forces to protect themselves from France. In spite of this, Napoleon was able to conquer Austria, Prussia, and Spain. England remained Napoleon's greatest threat because of its superior navy.

10. Within a few years, Napoleon had taken over most of Europe. Look at the map. What parts of Europe did Napoleon control? From 1807 to 1812, Napoleon's empire stretched from Spain to the borders of Russia. Napoleon also forced Austria, Prussia, and Russia to become France's **allies** (AL-lyz). Allies are nations that agree to support each other in war. Napoleon sent his own relatives and friends to rule many of the

▼ By 1812, Napoleon controlled most of Europe. What European states were controlled by Napoleon? Which states were his allies?

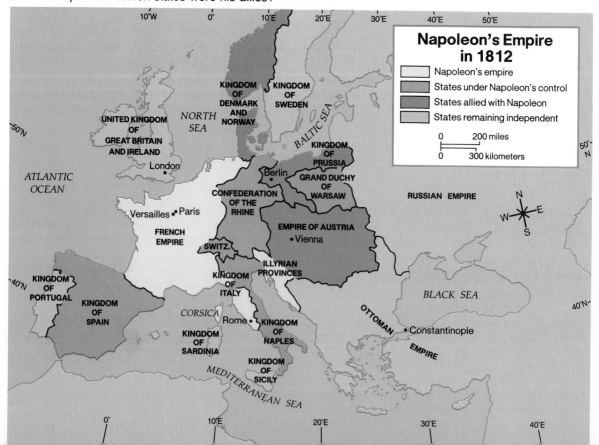

► countries he conquered. Why do you think he chose people that he knew well for these jobs? Napoleon spread the ideas of the French Revolution across his huge empire. He ended serfdom in countries that he conquered and encouraged freedom of religion. He also made the Napoleonic Code the basis of law in many European countries.

SPOTLIGHT ON SOURCES

11. When Napoleon's armies conquered Spain, Napoleon set up a new constitution for that country. An excerpt from this constitution is given below. What ideas from the French Revolution are expressed in these lines?

> To date from the publication of this decree, feudal rights are abolished in Spain. All personal obligations, all exclusive rights, . . . are suppressed [put down]. Everyone who shall conform to the laws shall be free to develop his industry without restraint.
>
> The tribunal [court] of the Inquisition is abolished [done away with], as inconsistent with the civil . . . authority. Its property shall be sequestered [seized] and fall to the Spanish state . . . .
>
> —from *The Age of Napoleon*, Will and Ariel Durant

EUROPEAN ALLIANCES: How did the nations of Europe overthrow Napoleon?

12. Napoleon's huge empire soon began to cause problems for France. Since England's navy controlled the seas, it cut off most of Europe's trade. The French and other Europeans now lacked many of the products and supplies they needed. As life became more difficult, the conquered people of Europe disliked more than ever paying taxes to France. A feeling of **nationalism**, or pride in one's country, began to grow among the nations under Napoleon's rule. In 1808, the Spanish and the Portuguese people rose in revolt. By 1813, both

nations had won their independence from France.

13. Even though Russia was France's ally, Czar Alexander I of Russia no longer trusted Napoleon. When Alexander resumed trade with England, Napoleon declared war on Russia. In 1812, Napoleon invaded Russia with an army of 500,000. Alexander's army drew back into Russia and refused to fight any major battles. The Russians moved back toward Moscow instead. They burned crops and destroyed villages, leaving no food or shelter for the French. When Napoleon's army arrived in Moscow, the city was almost deserted. The French soldiers captured an empty and burning city, then had to turn back because of the severe Russian winter. About 400,000 of France's army starved or froze to death during the retreat from Russia.

14. The nations of Europe bonded together against France once again. This time they met with greater success. In 1813, an army composed of soldiers from England, Austria, Prussia, Russia, and Sweden defeated Napoleon at the Battle of Leipzig (LYP-sig). Napoleon was sent to prison on the island of Elba. He escaped in 1815, however, and returned to France. For 100 days he ruled as emperor. He worked quickly to rebuild the army. England, Austria, Prussia, and Russia sent their troops against him. In June, the European army led by England's Duke of Wellington met Napoleon at Waterloo in Belgium. Napoleon's army was defeated, and Napoleon was sent to the far-off island of St. Helena in the Atlantic Ocean. He died there in 1821.

OUTLOOK

15. Napoleon was one of the greatest military leaders in history. He was also able to establish a strong central government in France when this was badly needed. Through military victories, he gained control of much of Europe for France. Do you think it would be possible for one ruler to conquer much of the world today? ◄

Activity: Have students read short biographies of Napoleon and his rival, Czar Alexander I of Russia. Lead the class in a discussion of their early lives.

355

CHAPTER REVIEW

VOCABULARY REVIEW

Write each number and word on a sheet of paper. Then write the letter of the definition next to the word it defines.

1. Consulate
2. coup d'etat
3. Directory
4. Napoleonic Code
5. nationalism
6. plebiscite
7. allies

a. set of laws developed by Napoleon
b. French government formed after the Reign of Terror
c. pride in one's country
d. vote to approve or turn down a change in government
e. nations that agree to support each other in war
f. French government under the rule of three consuls
g. a government takeover

SKILL BUILDER: READING A MAP

Use the map below to answer the following questions. Write your answers on a sheet of paper.

1. Which is farther north, Paris or London?
2. What three kingdoms or empires border the Baltic Sea?
3. In which direction is the Ottoman Empire from the Russian Empire?
4. What body of water surrounds the Kingdom of Sicily?
5. What nations were under France's control in 1815?

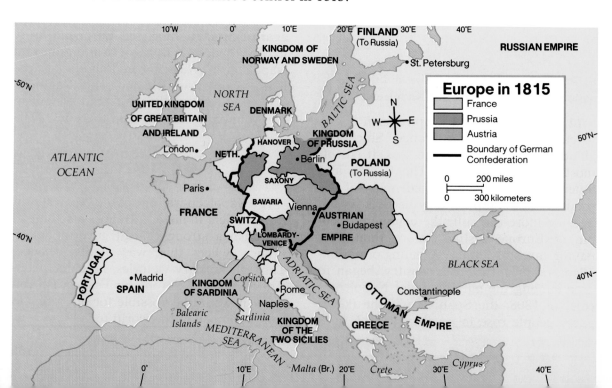

SKILL BUILDER: CRITICAL THINKING AND COMPREHENSION

1. Sequencing

▶ Write the letters of the following events in the sequence in which they happened. Use information in the chapter to help you.

a. Napoleon led a coup d'etat against the Directory.

b. Napoleon was sent to St. Helena.

c. Napoleon was born.

d. Napoleon crowned himself emperor.

e. The Reign of Terror ended.

2. Spatial Relationships

▶ Look at the map on p. 354 and the map in the atlas on page 728. Answer these questions about spatial relationships.

a. Did Napoleon control much of the eastern or western territory in Europe?

b. How does the size of Napoleon's empire relate to the size of France today?

3. Cause and Effect

▶ Each pair of statements below has a cause and effect. Write the statement that is the effect for each pair.

a. Napoleon set up secondary schools in France.
Napoleon wanted to carry out the work begun during the French Revolution.

b. The Napoleonic Code favored the interests of the country over the rights of its citizens.
Freedom of French citizens was limited.

c. The people of Europe disliked paying taxes to France and sending their sons to fight in Napoleon's army.
The nations of Europe allied themselves against France.

4. Contrasting and Comparing

▶ Compare and contrast the methods used by Napoleon and Alexander I in the war between France and Russia. Which leader believed in destroying enemy armies by attacking them?

ENRICHMENT

1. Find an English translation of a play by either Corneille or Racine. Bring it to class and encourage your classmates to take parts. Practice reading the play together. Then read part or all of it for the class.

2. Find information about the Empress Josephine, who was Napoleon's first wife. Write a short biography about her and share it with the class.

3. How successful would Napoleon be if he tried to conquer Europe today? Write a short paragraph giving your opinion.

CHAPTER 5

Freedom for Latin America

▲ Many native–born persons of Spanish descent enjoyed comfortable lives but resented the privileges held by the Spanish-born.

OBJECTIVE: How did the nations of Latin America achieve their independence?

1. The Avenue of the Americas, a street over sixty blocks long in New York City, is named in honor of all the countries of the Americas. At the northern end of this avenue is a large statue of José de San Martín (hoh-ZAY duh sahn mahr-TEEN), a South American revolutionary leader. The statue stands as a tribute to the independence movements that took place all over Latin America in the early 1800s. During his lifetime, San Martín was hailed as a liberator of his region. However, many of the other leaders in the cause for independence were executed before they saw the results of their struggle. These leaders came from many groups of people in Latin America—native-born people of Spanish descent, Indians, African slaves, and persons of mixed blood. What events in the late 1700s might have ◄

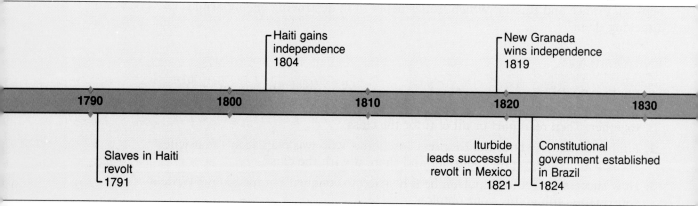

Haiti gains independence 1804

New Granada wins independence 1819

1790 · 1800 · 1810 · 1820 · 1830

Slaves in Haiti revolt 1791

Iturbide leads successful revolt in Mexico 1821

Constitutional government established in Brazil 1824

358

encouraged the Spanish colonists to seek independence from Spain?

COLONIAL LATIN AMERICA: Why were the people of Latin America interested in seeking independence?

2. For 300 years before the start of the 1800s, Spain and Portugal ruled large empires in the Americas. The colonies in Spain's empire reached from what is now the southwestern United States to the southern tip of South America. Portugal's colony of Brazil also covered a large area of South America. These colonies brought great wealth to both Spain and Portugal. Gold and silver were mined there, and sugar, coffee, and cotton were grown on large plantations. These products were shipped back to Europe in exchange for the manufactured goods used in the colonies.

3. Because the colonial empires were so valuable to Spain and Portugal, they kept tight control over the colonies. In the Spanish colonies, the highest positions in the government, church, and army could be held only by people born in Spain. These people were known as **peninsulares** (pay-nin-syoo-LAR-ays). The wealth and prestige that the peninsulares enjoyed were bitterly resented by other groups in the colonies.

4. In addition to the peninsulares, there were much larger numbers of people who were born in America as descendants of Spanish settlers. These people were known as **creoles** (KREE-ohls). Creoles often became wealthy landowners and traders, and were often well educated and well traveled. Many of the creoles had military experience from serving in the War for Independence or in the French Revolution. Others had fought in Spain's armies against Napoleon. They were well acquainted with the philosphical ideals that inspired the French and American revolutions.

5. Many persons of mixed race lived in the Latin American colonies. People who were both Spanish and Indian were known as **mestizos** (mes-TEE-zos). Some mestizos lived in the towns and made a living as craftspeople or skilled workers. Others were farmers on plantations.

6. The native Indians of Latin America, the largest group of people living in the colonies, were mostly farmers. Many of the Indians were forced to work for Spanish landowners on plantations and in mines. Living conditions for most Indians were terrible. They lived in extreme poverty with almost no rights. They were ready to fight for their independence when the chance came.

Daily life in . . .

Peru's Spanish conquerer, Francisco Pizarro, ruled the Inca Empire by taking the Indian emperor's place. When Spain took control of Peru, some of the Indian leaders were allowed to continue as local rulers of the Indians. Many became wealthy landowners.

Incas who were members of the emperor's family were proud of it. Some people even faked family histories so that they could claim to be descendants of the emperors. Many were members of the ruling class in the Indian empire, and they became wealthy landowners under Spanish rule. In the 1700s, pride in Inca heritage led many of these landowners to have their portraits done in Indian clothing.

At times, however, it was a disadvantage to be a member of the emperor's family. One descendant of the emperor's brother was Tupac Amaru II. He led an Indian revolt against the Spanish in 1780. The revolt failed, and he was killed in 1781. The Spanish feared that another member of Tupac's family would start a new revolt. The Spanish rounded up everyone they could find from the emperor's family. They sent the entire group to Spain, where they were imprisoned for the rest of their lives.

ESL/LEP Strategy: Write the words *peninsulares, creoles,* and *mestizos* on the chalkboard. Discuss the word meanings and derivations and explain that the English language contains many words from other languages. Ask students to make a list of other foreign words that are now part of English.

359

7. Large numbers of Africans had been imported as slaves in the years following the Spanish conquests. Like the Indians, the slaves worked on plantations and in mines. Their lives were very hard, and they had no rights. In some of the colonies, the slave population was larger than the population ▶ of Spaniards. How might this have encouraged the slaves to revolt?

8. Napoleon's victories in Europe led to favorable conditions for revolution in the colonies. Napoleon invaded Spain and Portugal in 1808. He forced King Ferdinand of Spain to step down from the throne. In his place, Napoleon made his own brother Joseph King of Spain. The Latin American colonists realized that while the crown was under French control, revolutions would have a better chance of succeeding. The Spanish government was badly weakened.

EARLY ATTEMPTS: How did the fight for freedom begin in South America?

9. During the late 1700s, a number of uprisings took place in Latin America. In 1780, a large group of Indians and mestizos revolted in Peru. However, they were poorly equipped with weapons and were easily defeated. Another major protest occured in Bogotá (bo-guh-TA), Colombia, around the same time. Mestizos and Indians marched in the city to protest unfair taxes. Similar revolts occurred in Venezuela and Ecuador. All of these revolts were put down, and the leaders were usually executed. The harsh treatment of these revolutionaries only increased the desire for independence.

HAITI: How did Haiti become the first nation in Latin America to achieve its freedom?

10. The first successful uprising in Latin America took place in the small French colony of Haiti. Haiti, called at that time Saint Domingue, was the western portion of the island of Hispaniola. Haiti was a prosperous colony inhabited mostly by French landowners, slaves, and former slaves. The number of slaves in Haiti was over 10 times the number of people of European descent. There was also a sizable population of **mulattoes** (muh-LAT-ohs), or people of both European and African ancestry. During the French revolution, the mulattoes and slaves in Haiti were inspired by the ideals of liberty, equality, and fraternity. They revolted against the French government in Haiti in 1791. The revolt was crushed, but in 1794, slavery was abolished in Haiti.

11. One of the leaders of the Haitian revolt was Toussaint L'Ouverture (too-SAN loo-vair-TOOR), a former slave. He joined the slave revolt of 1791 and soon established himself as a military leader. At that time, the eastern two-thirds of the island was a Spanish colony called Santo Dom-

▼ Toussaint L'Ouverture had the ability to inspire loyalty in his followers. What other qualities does a successful military leader need?

Background: Toussaint L'Ouverture had little education, but could read and write. He corresponded with Napoleon and tried to convince the emperor that he was a loyal French citizen.

ingo. When Spain and France went to war in Europe, fighting broke out on the island. Toussaint at first fought for the Spanish. When the slaves were freed in Haiti, Toussaint went over to the French side.

12. Toussaint was made lieutenant governor of Haiti and instituted many reforms there. As time went on, the European governors were eased out, and Toussaint took control of the entire French portion of the island. Next, he overran the Spanish part of the island, Santo Domingo, and freed the slaves there. By 1801, Toussaint had become dictator of the entire island.

13. Meanwhile, Napoleon had taken over the government of France. Napoleon was in favor of slavery, and was not pleased about a former slave governing a French colony. He sent Charles Leclerc to replace Toussaint. Leclerc succeeded in winning back the island for Napoleon, and Toussaint was deported to France. Another black general, Jean Jacques Dessalines (das-uh-LEEN) finished the work Toussaint had begun. He began a new campaign against the French and was victorious. On January 1, 1804, Dessalines declared Haiti independent.

MEXICO AND CENTRAL AMERICA: How did Mexico and the countries of Central America gain their independence?

14. Spain had divided its empire into **viceroyalties** (vyse-ROY-ul-teez), or royal colonies, each governed by a viceroy. The largest of the viceroyalties was New Spain. New Spain included Mexico, much of Central America, and a part of what is now the southwestern United States. By 1800, the number of people of European descent in Mexico was less than one million. Only 15,000 of these were Spanish-born peninsulares. The remainder were mostly creoles, many of whom were wealthy but had few privileges. There were about 2,000,000 mestizos and other people of mixed blood. Most of the slaves in Mexico had been freed or had been absorbed into the general population. About 3,000,000 Native American Indians formed the largest group in Mexico.

15. When Napoleon replaced the king of Spain in 1810, creoles began to demand a greater voice in the colonial government. While the peninsulares and creoles were debating this, a call to organized revolt came from a parish priest in Dolores, a town in Mexico. The priest, Miguel Hidalgo (mih-GHEL ee-DAHL-goh), wanted to gain rights for the mestizos and Indians. On September 16, 1810, Hidalgo declared Mexico's independence from Spain. Hidalgo led a band of Indians and mestizos against both the creoles and the peninsulares. The revolt at first seemed successful but was soon crushed. Hidalgo was shot as a rebel in 1811. The revolution was taken up by another priest, Morelos, who drafted a republican constitution. He too was executed, but fighting continued for many years.

16. In 1821, the viceroy of New Spain sent Augustín Iturbide (ah-goo-STEN ee-toor-BEE-thay), an ex-officer in the Mexican army, to battle with the rebels. Without the viceroy's knowledge, Iturbide signed a compromise measure with the rebel leaders. This agreement included equal rights for the creoles. Most of the people of Mexico supported this plan. Spain was forced to recognize the independence of Mexico. A new government was set up with Iturbide as its temporary head.

17. The independence movement quickly spread south. Central America declared independence from Spain in 1821. At first, this area came under the rule of Iturbide. When Iturbide stepped down from power in 1823, the Central American Union was set up. The Union was troubled from the start by internal rivalries. By 1840, it no longer existed, and Central America was divided into Guatemala, El Salvador, Honduras, Nicaragua, and Costa Rica.

NEW GRENADA: How did Bolivar and Miranda free Venezuela, Colombia, Panama, and Ecuador from Spanish rule?

18. In the northern part of South America was Spain's viceroyalty of New Granada. This area included Venezuela, Colombia,

Ask: Support for the crown was stronger in the Latin American colonies than it had been in the British colonies. Which groups in the Spanish colonies were interested in keeping things as they were?

361

Panama, and Ecuador. One of the first fighters for independence was Francisco de Miranda (fran-THEE-sko duh mee-RAHN-dah), a creole. Miranda was an experienced soldier who had fought in the American Revolution and in Europe with the French army. Miranda returned from Europe in 1810 to defeat the Spanish army in Venezuela. The Spanish won back Venezuela in 1812 and a long struggle followed. Miranda was sent to Spain, where he spent the rest of his life in prison. Look at the map below.

▶ When did Venezuela gain its independence?

PEOPLE IN HISTORY

19. Another leader, Simón Bolívar (see-MOHN boh-LEE-vahr) took up the struggle that Miranda had begun and helped New Granada finally win its freedom in 1819.

Bolívar was the son of a Venezuelan family. He was well educated and had traveled in Europe and the United States. In 1819, Bolívar led an army from Venezuela over the Andes Mountains and into Colombia. The army was exhausted by the difficult trip over the freezing mountains. Against great odds, they defeated a large Spanish army. Bolívar was elected president of Greater Colombia, which included the countries of Colombia, Ecuador, Panama, and Venezuela.

20. Bolívar was unsuccessful in uniting Greater Colombia. The war for independence continued for about five years after the 1819 victory, with terrible losses on both sides. To make the government stronger, Bolívar declared himself dictator. But many of his followers turned against him. What kinds of rivalries and problems might ◀ have caused this? Bolívar resigned from the government in 1830. Disappointed and in bad health, he died that same year.

▼ Long and bitter struggles won independence for Latin Americans in the early 1800s. What present-day countries remained colonies after 1825?

SPOTLIGHT ON SOURCES

21. Bolivar's greatest wish was to have Greater Colombia become strong and united. He was urged by some of his followers to become emperor to achieve this goal. Although he eventually became a dictator, he rejected the idea of naming himself an emperor. In the words that follow, he explains why.

"Colombia is not France, and I am not Napoleon . . . nor do I wish to be. Neither shall I emulate [copy] Caesar, even less Iturbide. Such examples seem unworthy of my glory. The title of Liberator is beyond any reward ever offered to human pride . . . . A throne would produce terror . . . . Equality would be obliterated [destroyed] and I wanted freedom and fame. I have achieved both. What else can I wish?"

—*Bolívar*, Donald E. Worchester

ARGENTINA, CHILE, AND PERU: How did these Spanish colonies become independent nations?

22. Spain's viceroyalty of La Plata was located in the southern part of South America. La Plata included Argentina and Peru. The creoles seized power from a weak local government in 1810. They formed their own government in the city of Buenos Aires.

23. One of La Plata's greatest leaders was Jose de San Martín. He led the successful revolution in Buenos Aires. Next, he spent several years raising an army and training the soldiers to fight for Peru's independence. San Martín's soldiers were joined by the force of Bernardo O'Higgins, a military leader from Chile. San Martín and O'Higgins led their army of 5,000 soldiers on a difficult journey across the Andes and into Chile in early 1817. The rebel soldiers defeated the Spanish near Santiago later that year. O'Higgins declared Chile an independent country in 1818 and became its first president.

24. San Martín next turned his attention to Peru. His army sailed north and landed in Peru in 1820. They fought their way north to the city of Lima. San Martín declared the independence of Peru and called on Bolívar's help in defeating the rest of the Spanish army. In 1822, the two great liberators met in Ecuador. They were not able to agree on a plan, and San Martín turned his army over to Bolívar. Two years later, the Spanish army was finally defeated. In 1825, one of Bolívar's generals won control of the northern part of La Plata, and the new nation of Bolivia was formed. For whom ◀ was Bolivia named?

BRAZIL: Why did Brazil become an independent empire?

25. Portugal's colony of Brazil won independence without a revolution. In 1808, Napoleon invaded Portugal and the monarchy with its court fled to Brazil. After Napoleon's defeat, the king returned home to Portugal. He left his son Pedro as the ruler of Brazil. In 1822 the creoles demanded that Pedro declare Brazil's independence from Portugal. Pedro agreed, and declared himself emperor of the new nation. A constitution was drawn up in 1824 to set up a new government for Brazil.

OUTLOOK

26. Spain and Portugal ruled rich empires in the Americas for nearly 300 years. In most parts of Latin America, the creoles were the group that led the fight for freedom. The Indians, the mestizos, and the African slaves did much of the fighting. They all joined the struggle to improve their own lives. When the struggle for independence was over, however, the great differences in living conditions and privileges among these groups did not disappear. Why ◀ might this have caused difficulties in the years following the revolutions? Does the struggle for equality of rights and privileges still exist in parts of South America today?

Ask: The terrain of much of South America is rugged and mountainous. How might this setting have been an advantage to rebels fighting soldiers from Europe?

363

CHAPTER REVIEW

VOCABULARY REVIEW

Write each of the following sentences on a sheet of paper. Then fill in the blank with the word below that best completes each sentence.

creoles

mestizos

peninsulares

viceroyalties

mulattoes

1. Descendants of Spanish settlers who were born in the American colonies were called _____ .
2. Spain's royal colonies were known as _____ .
3. The government officials who ruled Spain's colonies were born in Spain and belonged to the group of people called _____ .
4. _____ were people of both Indian and European descent.
5. _____ were people of both African and European descent.

SKILL BUILDER: TIME LINE

Time lines are diagrams that show events in history. Look at the time line below. Use it to answer the questions that follow. Write your answers on a sheet of paper.

1. How long is the period covered in this time line?
2. What is the first date shown?
3. What happened on this date?
4. When did Haiti's first revolt break out?
5. Why did France send General Leclerc to Haiti?
6. When did Haiti win independence?
7. How long did the first revolt last?
8. How long did General Leclerc hold Haiti?
9. Who helped Haiti achieve its independence?

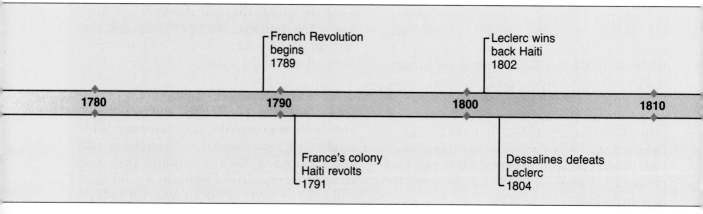

French Revolution begins 1789

Leclerc wins back Haiti 1802

1780   1790   1800   1810

France's colony Haiti revolts 1791

Dessalines defeats Leclerc 1804

SKILL BUILDER: CRITICAL THINKING AND COMPREHENSION

Follow the directions below. Write your answers on a separate sheet of paper.

1. Sequencing

▶ Write these statements in the correct order.

a. Napoleon conquered Spain, and this gave the Spanish colonies a good opportunity to revolt.

b. Augustín de Iturbide declared himself the emperor of Mexico.

c. Guatemala, El Salvador, Honduras, Nicaragua, and Costa Rica became independent nations.

d. The Central American Union was founded.

2. Spatial Relationships

▶ Copy and fill in the table below. Not all spaces can be filled. Locate the countries on the map, page 362. What relationship might there be between the dates of independence and the location of the countries?

Nation	Viceroyalty	Year of Independence	Liberator
Mexico			
Guatemala			
El Salvador			
Costa Rica			
Venezuela			
Colombia			

3. Compare and Contrast

How did Brazil's revolution compare with those of the Spanish colonies?

4. Cause and Effect

Re-read paragraphs 14 through 17. Write two sentences about the Mexican independence movement. One statement should give a cause of the revolts and the other statement should give an effect.

ENRICHMENT

1. Make a list of Latin American nations that did not achieve independence in the early 1800s. Research these nations and write a report on them. Explain why they achieved independence later.

2. Draw a large map of Latin American independence like the one on page 362. Hang it on the bulletin board. Have a volunteer point to a nation on the map. The volunteer must answer another player's question about that nation to have another turn. When the player cannot answer a question, the next player takes a turn. The questions must be on material covered in the chapter.

UNIT REVIEW

SUMMARY

In the 1600s and 1700s, Galileo, Newton, and other European scientists made important discoveries about nature and the universe. These discoveries changed the way people thought about the world around them. During the late 1600s and 1700s, philosophers in England and France began to apply the rules of reasoning to government. They thought that if laws of government were based on reason, people would have more rights and freedom. The ideas of the Enlightenment, as this thinking was called, influenced political leaders. In America, the English colonies revolted against the King of England. The colonists fought and won a War for Independence and formed a new nation, the United States of America. France was inspired by the ideals of the Enlightenment and the success of the American Revolution. The French people revolted against their monarchy and set up a republic. France's new government was too weak to handle the problems that came as a result of the revolution. Napoleon took over the French government, then conquered most of Europe. In Latin America, freedom fighters were successful in winning independence from Europe.

SKILL BUILDER: READING A MAP

▶ Study the map below. Then answer the questions that follow the map.

The World About 1812

1. Which of the following areas was largest?
   a. Russian Empire
   b. Ottoman Empire
   c. Napoleon's Empire

2. What took place on the coast of Africa?
   a. The Spanish started colonies.
   b. Slaves were traded.
   c. Napoleon's armies invaded this area.

3. Where did the Spanish have colonies?
  a. North America and Africa
  b. South America and Asia
  c. North America and South America

4. What bordered Napoleon's Empire on the east?
  a. the Russian Empire
  b. the Ottoman Empire
  c. the Spanish colonies

SKILL BUILDER: CRITICAL THINKING AND COMPREHENSION

1. Main Idea

▶ Read the sentences below. They are all about France in the 1700s. Decide which sentence is a main idea and which are details. Write the sentences on your paper and write **M** or **D** beside each one.

a. The French philosophes included Voltaire, Rousseau, and Diderot.

b. Robespierre was executed during the Reign of Terror.

c. Ideas from the French philosophes and other Enlightenment thinkers inspired the leaders of the French Revolution.

d. The statement that the National Assembly adopted in 1789 was called the *Declaration of the Rights of Man and Citizen*.

2. Classifying

▶ Classify the following people according to whether they were scientists, political leaders, or philosophers.

King Louis XVI	Johannes Kepler	Toussaint L'Overture	Voltaire
Galileo Galilei	Robespierre	Thomas Hobbes	Isaac Newton

3. Sequencing

▶ Use the information in the unit to put the following events in order. Write them on your paper in the correct sequence.

a. Paris citizens storm the Bastille.

b. Napoleon invades Russia.

c. Constitutional government is started in Brazil.

d. The British surrender to revolutionary troops at Yorktown.

4. Compare and Contrast

▶ Write a short essay in which you compare the French Revolution to the American Revolution. Compare the reasons they began, their leaders, their goals, and results.

ENRICHMENT

1. Imagine you are producing a television series about trends in history. Prepare a script on revolutions in the 1700s and 1800s. Define revolution and tell how they began in the late 1700s. Suggest scenes to illustrate your ideas.

2. Draw a political cartoon showing an event from this unit. For example, you could show Napoleon being trapped by a Russian bear.

UNIT 8

ESL/LEP Strategy: Divide students into seven groups representing the following republics: *Great Britain, France, Russia, Germany, Italy, Austria-Hungary,* and the *Ottoman Empire.* Have each group create dialogue for a scene portraying the effect of nationalism on their republic. Ask volunteers to perform their scenes for the class.

NATIONALISM AND UNIFICATION

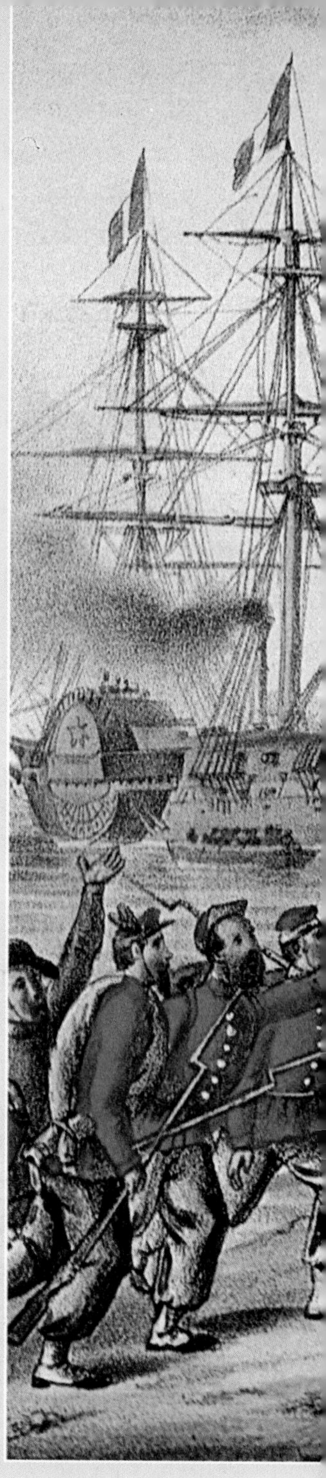

Chapter

OBJECTIVE: You will learn how the desire for self-determination and democracy caused men and women to build nations at the expense of the traditional empires.

Congress of Vienna meets 1814–1815

1815

Greek revolt begins 1821

1825

Decembrist revolt in Russia 1825

Greeks gain independence 1829

Uprisings sweep Belgium, Italy, France and Poland 1830

Reform Bill passes in Great Britain 1832

1835

1845

Uprisings occur in France, Austria, Prussia and Italy 1848

1855

Crimean Wa
1853–1856

▲ Giuseppe Garibaldi rallies his troops as his army lands on the Italian island of Sicily.

Bismarck becomes
Prussian
Chancellor
1861

Franco-Prussian
War ends in
French defeat
1870–1871

First Russian
Duma formed
1905

Austria annexes
Bosnia-Herzegovinia
1908

1865   1875   1885   1895   1905   1915

Russo-Turkish
War
1877

Congress of
Berlin
1878

Russo-Japanese war
ends in Russian
defeat, revolution
1905

Balkan Wars
1912–1913

CHAPTER 1

Restoration of Europe

OBJECTIVE: How did the Congress of Vienna bring both order and rebellion to Europe?

1. In the game of Monopoly, the object is to acquire the most property and avoid bankruptcy. Suppose that you are playing Monopoly with five other players. One of your opponents has won control over almost everything. His name is Napoleon. You and the other players decide to band together to defeat Napoleon. Your efforts are successful. Napoleon is bankrupted, and, as a result, he is out of the game. You and the other players then divide the properties that were won from Napoleon. In 1814, when the real Napoleon was defeated, the situation in Europe was much like this Monopoly game. The countries of Europe had united to defeat Napoleon. Then their

▲ The years after 1815 are called the "Age of Metternich" after Klemens von Metternich, the leading European statesman of the time.

leaders met in Vienna, the capital of Austria, to plan the peace. They also tried to undo many of the changes that the era of the French Revolution and Napoleon had brought to Europe. This meeting was called the Congress of Vienna.

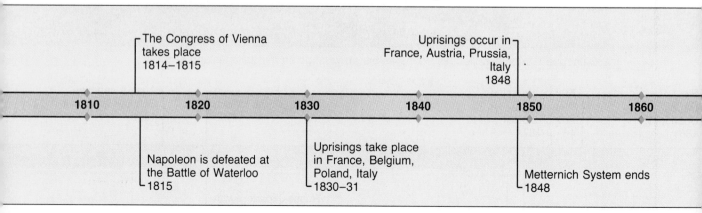

The Congress of Vienna takes place 1814–1815

Uprisings occur in France, Austria, Prussia, Italy 1848

| 1810 | 1820 | 1830 | 1840 | 1850 | 1860 |

Napoleon is defeated at the Battle of Waterloo 1815

Uprisings take place in France, Belgium, Poland, Italy 1830–31

Metternich System ends 1848

THE CONGRESS OF VIENNA: What countries took part in the Congress of Vienna, and what changes did the congress make in Europe?

2. Many countries in Europe sent their officials to the peace meeting of 1814 and 1815 known as the Congress of Vienna. The most powerful countries represented were Great Britain, Russia, Prussia, and Austria. In the later months of the congress, defeated ▶ France also took an important part. Why would Europe's leaders allow the country they had just defeated to take part in the congress? The leading role throughout the congress was taken by an Austrian statesman named Klemens von Metternich (KLEM-munz fawn MET-ur-nik).

PEOPLE IN HISTORY

3. Metternich was born into a noble German family in 1773. As a young man, Metternich had come to hate the French Revolution. When he was studying in Strasbourg, in northeastern France, he was shaken by an uprising that took place there. The fighting and disorder convinced Metternich that rule by the people brought only lawlessness. He concluded that law and order could be maintained only by strong monarchs. Then, in 1794, he had to move to Vienna after French soldiers took over his family's estate in Germany.

4. Metternich entered the service of the emperor of Austria and in time became a powerful figure in the government. After serving as an ambassador, Metternich became head of foreign affairs. This position was much like being Secretary of State in the United States today. Metternich was a brilliant statesman, and the Austrian emperor gave him full control of Austria's relations with other countries. The Congress of Vienna was Metternich's idea, and he played an important part in all its decisions. His influence was so great that the years between 1814 and 1848 are often known as the Age of Metternich.

5. A main goal of the Congress of Vienna was to bring back the **balance of power** among the nations of Europe. The balance of power was a means of keeping peace by making sure that no nation or group of nations became so powerful that it could take over another nation. During the years of Napoleon, France had upset the balance of power by becoming much stronger than any other country. Between 1799 and 1814, most of Europe had come under Napoleon's control. Large areas, including entire countries, had been added to France. Napoleon also had conquered other countries and set up new governments controlled by France. Still other nations were forced to become allies of France. Study the map on page 354. What important countries had Napoleon controlled? Which countries were ◀ his allies?

6. The Congress of Vienna redrew the map of Europe. The congress's main aim was to restore the balance of power. At the same time, the congress also brought back many of Europe's royal governments. In France, the monarchy that had existed before the French Revolution was returned to power. The new king of France was a brother of the executed Louis XVI. The Congress also brought back monarchies in Spain, Portugal, and many Italian states. But members of the Congress of Vienna knew that they could not turn the clock back completely. Therefore, in some countries they made different kinds of changes. In order to keep France from again becoming too powerful, they set up stronger nations along its borders. The Dutch and the Austrian Netherlands were made into one country, the Netherlands. Many small German states were joined to larger ones. Switzerland once again became a free nation. The congress also rewarded nations that had helped defeat Napoleon. Great Britain received South Africa and the islands of Malta in the Mediterranean Sea and Ceylon in the Indian Ocean. Russia was given Finland and a large part of Poland. Austria, which lost land in Poland, was repaid with parts of northern Italy.

Activity: Have some students find out more about the remarkable assemblage of outstanding leaders at the Congress of Vienna.

371

7. While the Congress of Vienna was meeting, Napoleon escaped from Elba. Elba is a small Italian island in the Mediterranean where the defeated Napoleon had been sent in exile. As soon as he returned to France, Napoleon raised a new army. However, British and Prussian armies defeated him for the final time at the battle of Waterloo in June 1815. To be sure that he did not escape again, Napoleon now was sent to the faraway island of St. Helena in the South Atlantic.

THE METTERNICH SYSTEM: What was Metternich's plan for controlling nationalism and liberalism in Europe?

8. For Metternich and most other leaders at the Congress of Vienna, the nationalism and liberalism spread by the French Revolution and Napoleon were dangerous forces. Nationalism is a people's feeling of pride in their history and culture. Nationalism made many of the peoples of Europe want to achieve independence and self-government.) **Liberalism** (LIB-er-ul-iz-um) is a belief in changes and reforms that guarantee people's rights and freedom.

9. The leaders of the congress were **conservatives** (kun-SER-vuh-tivz). Conservatives are people who want to keep things the way they are and prevent unnecessary change. Many of the choices made at the Congress of Vienna showed conservative feelings in action. For example, the congress decided not to let the people of Poland come together and rule themselves. The congress also took steps to prevent future uprisings in Europe. Together, these plans are known as the Metternich System.

10. One part of the Metternich System was the formation of the Quadruple Alliance (kwah-DROOP-ul uh-LY-uns). What does the word "quadruple" mean? The members of the Quadruple Alliance were Great Britain, Russia, Prussia, and Austria. The governments of these countries promised to meet regularly and to help each

▼ Delegates to the Congress of Vienna redrew the map of Europe. They hoped to preserve peace by achieving a balance of power among the major European countries.

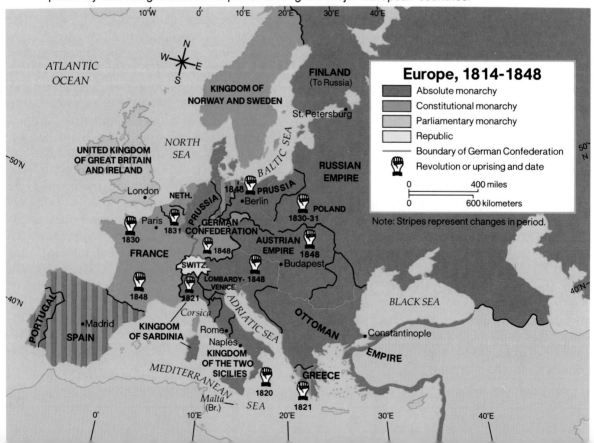

▲ A large number of important European statesman attended the Congress of Vienna than had ever before been gathered in one place.

other stop uprisings when trouble broke out. The name of the alliance changed over the years, but its goal stayed the same. Until the late 1840s, the members of the alliance worked successfully together to keep order in Europe.

11. Another part of the Metternich System was a plan to stop the spread of "dangerous" ideas like nationalism and liberalism. To whom would such ideas be dangerous? In Austria, Metternich sent out spies to search for and arrest people who might be plotting against the government. Censors carefully checked all books and other materials to make sure that they contained no "harmful" ideas. The Russian government followed these same policies. In the German states, where universities were centers of nationalist and liberal ideas, student organizations were not allowed. What does this tell you about the importance of students in the political life of their time?

EUROPEAN REVOLTS: How did the uprisings of 1830 and 1848 end the Metternich system?

12. In spite of the Metternich System, the ideals of nationalism and liberalism continued to grow. They gathered strength underground, and from time to time they broke out into the open. In 1830 and 1831, serious uprisings broke out in France, Belgium, Poland, and Italy. In France, the king fled the country, and a new, more liberal king came to the throne. Belgium succeeded in gaining its independence from the Netherlands. But in Poland and Italy, when nationalists tried to win freedom from foreign rule, Russian and Austrian troops put an end to the uprisings.

13. In 1848, a wave of uprisings spread across Europe like a great forest fire. In France, the people overthrew the king and established a republic. Austrians in Vienna rose up and forced Metternich to leave the country. Metternich's downfall led to uprisings against Austrian rule by Czechs and Hungarians. Revolts broke out in several German and Italian states. However, except in France, these uprisings were quickly crushed. Even so, the Metternich System now was ended.

OUTLOOK

14. By slicing the European pie so evenly among themselves, the leaders at the Congress of Vienna were able to keep peace. However, they overlooked the nationalist feelings of the peoples whose lands they were dividing. When the people tried to voice their views, their leaders responded with force. The uprisings of 1830 and 1848 failed. But throughout Europe, the people supported the ideals of nationalism and liberalism more than ever. Soon these forces would lead to the creation of several new European nations. Ideals have been a powerful force all through history. In fact, they often have been more powerful than the strongest armies. What are some of these ideals that Americans hold today?

ESL/LEP Strategy: Copy each sentence from paragraph 7 onto a separate index card. With books closed, have students work in small groups to arrange the sentences in the order that makes the most sense. Ask students to explain the order they chose.

373

CHAPTER REVIEW

VOCABULARY REVIEW

Write each of the following sentences on a sheet of paper. Then fill in the blank with the word that best completes each sentence.

liberalism   balance of power

nationalism   conservatives

1. _____ is a state or condition where no one nation has more power than another.

2. _____ favors reforms that would recognize the rights of the individual.

3. People who want to avoid unnecessary changes in government and society are called _____.

SKILL BUILDER: INTRODUCTORY PARAGRAPHS

The first sentence in a newspaper story is called the lead, or introductory paragraph. In this paragraph, the writer usually tries to include the "five W's"—who, what, when, where, and why. Sometimes the first paragraph in a textbook may cover the five W's. However, in some cases those five questions may be answered in the first and second paragraphs. They are important guides to what you will be studying in the chapter. Reread paragraphs 1 and 2 on pages 370 and 371 of your textbook. Then answer the questions about these two introductory paragraphs below.

a. In what sentences in paragraph 2 do you find who attended the Congress of Vienna?

b. In what sentence in paragraph 1 do you find out what the Congress of Vienna was?

c. In what sentence in paragraph 1 do you find out when the congress was held?

d. In what sentence in paragraph 1 do you learn where the congress was held.

e. In what sentences in paragraph 1 do you learn why the congress was held?

SKILL BUILDER: CRITICAL THINKING AND COMPREHENSION

1. Sequencing

▶ Look at the time line on page 370. How soon after the Congress of Vienna ended did uprisings take place in several European countries?

2. Spatial Relationships

▶ Look at the map of Europe on page 372. Use the information on the map to answer the following questions.

a. What country in the Quadruple Alliance was best situated to help keep the balance of power in western Europe?

STUDY HINT As you read paragraph 6, follow the changes on the map on page 372. Compare the boundaries on this map to those on the map on page 354.

b. Which three countries were best located to help keep the balance of power in eastern Europe?

c. What country was created to serve as a middle state along the border between France and Prussia?

3. Compare and Contrast

Look at the map of Europe in 1810 on page 354 and the map of Europe after the Congress of Vienna on page 372. Use the information on these maps to answer the following questions.

a. Did France increase or decrease in size after the Congress of Vienna?

b. What new nation was created after the Congress of Vienna?

c. What countries gained territory after the Congress of Vienna?

d. Did England gain territory in Europe after Napoleon was defeated?

4. Cause and Effect

▶ Copy the following flow chart. Complete the flow chart by inserting two *causes* of the Metternich System in the top boxes and two *effects* of the Metternich System in the lower boxes.

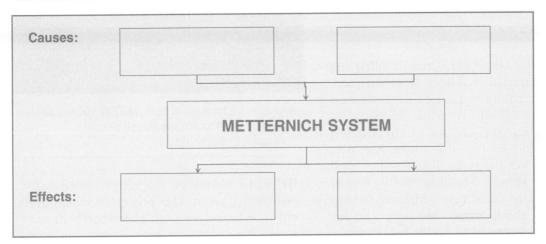

ENRICHMENT

1. Imagine that you are an American journalist sent to cover the Congress of Vienna. Prepare an article for your newspaper in which you report on an important event at the congress.

2. Prepare a class report on the French leader Talleyrand and his role at the Congress of Vienna.

3. Draw two maps, one showing Europe in 1789, before the French Revolution, and one showing Europe in 1815, after the Congress of Vienna. Make a list of the important European countries. Discuss the important boundary changes that took place in each of these countries during these years.

CHAPTER 2

The Growth of Democracy in Britain

▲ Queen Victoria ruled from 1837 to 1901. She worked hard to win the British people's respect and admiration.

OBJECTIVE: How did the British people gain a greater voice in their government?

1. The year was 1897. Crowds filled the streets of London. Soldiers marched past. Politicians made speeches and offered toasts. The ceremony and celebration honored Victoria, Queen of the United Kingdom and Empress of India. She was celebrating her Diamond Jubilee—her 60th year on the throne. The time during which Victoria reigned is remembered for its strict rules about proper behavior and for the worldwide power of the British Empire. It was also a time during which the monarchy lost some of its political power. Today,

Britain's monarch no longer holds any political power. The power to make and enforce laws lies with the British Parliament. The story of how British citizens gained the right to vote for Parliament is the story of democracy's growth in Britain.

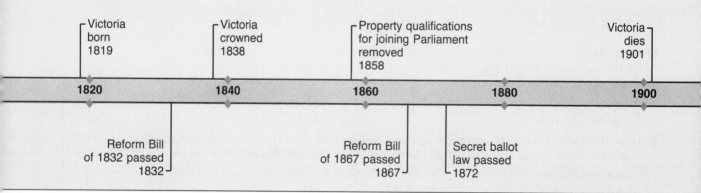

Victoria born 1819	Victoria crowned 1838	Property qualifications for joining Parliament removed 1858		Victoria dies 1901
1820	**1840**	**1860**	**1880**	**1900**
Reform Bill of 1832 passed 1832		Reform Bill of 1867 passed 1867	Secret ballot law passed 1872	

Activity: Show students headlines about the British royal family from newspapers and magazines. Have a discussion about why the public is so fascinated by the royal family.

REPRESENTATION AND VOTING: Why did the British people in the 1800s want changes in their system of government?

2. While most Europeans were fighting to free themselves of absolute rule, the British people were enjoying some freedom. Since the 1600s, British monarchs had been required to share their power with Parliament. They were not above the law. They could not interfere in elections to Parliament, and they needed Parliament's approval to raise taxes. Parliament's duty was to check the monarchs and protect the rights of the people. Still, the British government was far from democratic, and many people felt that it was in need of **reform**. Reform is change for the purpose of correcting faults or defects.

3. An important problem with the British government in the 1800s was that not all the people were represented in Parliament. The number of representatives from each **borough** (BUR-oh), or voting area, was supposed to be based on population. But the number of representatives in each borough had not been changed as the population rose or fell. Large, underpopulated farming areas, owned mostly by aristocratic families, had the greatest representation. On the other hand, new factory cities, where the population was growing the fastest, had no one representing them in Parliament. In boroughs where the population had fallen, seats in Parliament could easily be bought by wealthy people. Boroughs of this kind were called **rotten boroughs**.

4. The number of voters was another problem. In the early 1800s, there were only 245,000 eligible voters in Britain out of a population of 9,000,000. Only men who owned a certain amount of land had the right to vote. This left farm workers, businesspeople, factory workers, and women without a vote.

5. Even those who could vote were not treated fairly. A rich property owner often told the people living in his borough how they should vote. These were called **pocket boroughs** because they were in the pocket of one man. He could be sure that people voted as he wished, because voting was not done in secret. Does voting in Britain in the 1800s ◄ compare in any way with voting in the United States today?

GOVERNMENT REFORMS: What government reforms increased the political rights of the British people in the nineteenth century?

6. By 1830, many British people were demanding the right to vote and a greater voice in the government. Many members of Parliament recognized that reform was necessary. Why do you think other members of ◄

Daily life in . . .

Members of Parliament spent their mornings working in their offices. A member would begin each day by reading his mail, answering letters, meeting people, and working on special committees. Each member shared a small office with another member. At exactly 2:30 in the afternoon of most days or at 9:30 on Friday morning, Parliament met as a body. Business always followed in the same order. An hour of questions about the previous day's business was first. Then any announcements by the government party were made. Finally, debates between the parties over bills would begin. Debates could go on for hours and last far into the night. Members often grew tired and hungry during a single meeting. It was not unusual to see a member stretched out asleep on one of the benches. Members also ate in the meeting chambers and were often seen cracking nuts or peeling whatever fruit was in season. When business was finished for the day, men bearing torches would call out, "Who goes home?" Members would then gather in groups and be led safely to their houses.

Background: Some seventeenth-century legislative acts that limited the power of the British monarch were the Petition of Right (1628), and the Bill of Rights (1689). See also Unit 6, Chapter 3.

377

Parliament thought that reform would destroy the government? After months of talk in Parliament and fighting in the streets, the Reform Bill of 1832 was passed.

7. The Reform Bill of 1832 was the first important reform in nineteenth-century Great Britain. The bill helped businesspeople and merchants by lowering the amount of property they needed to be allowed to vote. The bill also got rid of many rotten and pocket boroughs. It made representation in Parliament more equal by including the new factory cities. Still, only about five percent of the total British population could vote. Which people did the bill leave out?

▶ 8. Workers kept on pressing for equal voting rights and democratic reform. They finally reached their goal in the later half of the 1800s. In 1858, it was decided that a person no longer needed to own property to become a member of Parliament. In 1867, a new reform bill gave the right to vote to all men living in cities, whether they owned property or not. In 1872, the secret ballot
▶ became law. How would the secret ballot make voting in Britain more democratic? The 1880s brought the vote to farmers and other rural people. However, women would not be given the right to vote for another 40 years.

POLITICAL LEADERS: How did some of Britain's leaders help democracy to grow?

9. Two government leaders had a great deal to do with making Great Britain a more democratic country in the nineteenth century. They were Benjamin Disraeli (diz-RAY-lee) and William Gladstone (GLAD-stun). Though they were bitter enemies, both leaders worked for reform. As a liberal in the Conservative party, Disraeli was able to convince his party's members that reforms were needed. It was Disraeli who first brought the Reform Bill of 1867 before Parliament. Gladstone then worked to make the bill stronger by doubling the number of new voters. Since the new voters were mostly urban workers, they voted for the Liberals. It was therefore to Gladstone's

advantage to support Disraeli's reform bill. The era of Disraeli and Gladstone has come to be called the **Victorian** (vik-TOH-ree-un) Age, after the queen of the time, Victoria.

PEOPLE IN HISTORY

10. Alexandrina Victoria became queen of Great Britain in 1837 at the age of 18. Her reign of 64 years was the longest in British history. Victoria was honest and serious about carrying out her duties as she saw them. In this she was greatly helped by her husband, Prince Albert, a hard worker with a no-nonsense attitude. Victoria and Albert were devoted to each other, and she was deeply grieved by his premature death in 1861.

▼ Although Gladstone (left) and Disraeli were the greatest British statesmen of their time, they did not get along well together.

" CRITICS."

(WHO HAVE *NOT EXACTLY* " FAILED IN LITERATURE AND ART.")—*See Mr. D.'s New Work.*

Mr. G-d-s-t-ne. "HM!—FLIPPANT!"   Mr. D-s-r-li. "HA!—PROSY!"

Activity: Have students read biographies of Disraeli and Gladstone to compare the background and styles of the two leaders.

378

▲ Victoria maintained her popularity with the British people throughout her 64 years on the throne. Here she is shown at a military ceremony early in her long reign.

11. The reign of Queen Victoria strengthened the idea of government by the people and not the monarch. She spoke often with government leaders, such as Disraeli and Gladstone, but she felt it was her duty not to take sides. However, the queen was a great help in settling fights between parties in Parliament. Although she disliked the idea of a "democratic monarchy," she supported bills like the Reform Bill of 1867.

12. Queen Victoria was a popular monarch throughout her long reign. Her quiet, dignified way of life and her strong beliefs about proper behavior set the tone for an age. Victoria brought greater dignity to the throne than had the kings who came before her. She related well with her subjects, even though she made no public appearances for many years after the death of her husband in 1861. The people loved her in return. By making the monarchy both respectable and loved, Victoria guaranteed that it would continue for long after her. It is no wonder that the Victorian Age was conservative in some ways and yet was also an age of important reforms.

OUTLOOK

13. The reforms made in England's government in the 1800s have stood as a model for other countries. In many places, particularly in Europe, kings or queens still occupy their thrones, but the power is held by a parliament elected by the people. It is no longer the rule, as it once was, for a government to have only leaders who are members of rich or powerful families. People from every background and walk of life now take part in government, both as voters and as government leaders. In democratic countries today, every citizen can run for office or work in government. In August 1963, hundreds of thousands of Americans traveled to Washington, D.C., to march in a rally in support of civil rights for all Americans. Dr. Martin Luther King, Jr., spoke eloquently about the still unmet need for full freedom for everyone in the United States. How did King's powerful words echo those of reform leaders in nineteenth-century Victorian England?

Activity: Many of the values and tastes of the Victorian Age were affected by the middle class. With more political power, industrialists and merchants were able to influence the social and cultural life as well.

CHAPTER REVIEW

VOCABULARY REVIEW

Write each of the following sentences on a sheet of paper. Then fill in the blank with the word that best completes each sentence.

reform

borough

rotten borough

pocket borough

Victorian

1. _____ refers to a period in history when Queen Victoria ruled England.

2. A _____ was a voting district that could usually be controlled by only one person.

3. Some English people worked to _____ the voting laws so that more people could participate in the election process.

4. A _____ was a voting district that could be bought by wealthy people.

5. A _____ was any voting district.

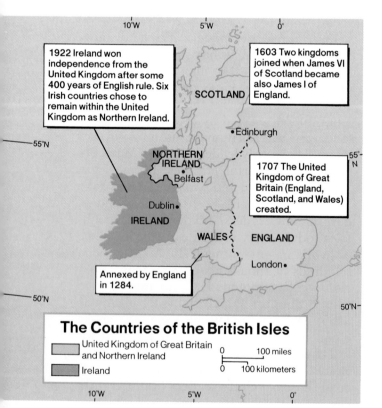

The Countries of the British Isles

- United Kingdom of Great Britain and Northern Ireland
- Ireland

1922 Ireland won independence from the United Kingdom after some 400 years of English rule. Six Irish countries chose to remain within the United Kingdom as Northern Ireland.

1603 Two kingdoms joined when James VI of Scotland became also James I of England.

1707 The United Kingdom of Great Britain (England, Scotland, and Wales) created.

Annexed by England in 1284.

SKILL BUILDER: READING A MAP

Look at the map on this page. Answer the questions below using the information on the map.

1. What part of Britain was annexed by England in 1284?

2. In what year was the United Kingdom created?

3. Name the four capital cities shown on the map.

4. Name the four countries of the United Kingdom today.

5. Using the map key at the bottom of the map, estimate the distance between London and Edinburgh.

SKILL BUILDER: CRITICAL THINKING AND COMPREHENSION

1. Drawing Conclusions

▶ Write the letter of the conclusion you think matches the statement.

1-1. Before the Reform Bill of 1832, less than 300,000 people in England were allowed to vote.
  a. England had a small population.
  b. Many people did not have the right to vote.

1-2. Queen Victoria helped restore the respect people had for the crown.
  a. Victoria was a good queen.
  b. People liked her crown.

1-3. Rich property owners told people how to vote.
  a. No one knew how to vote without being told for whom they should vote.
  b. People worried that a rich property owner would treat them unfairly if they did not vote the way he wanted them to vote.

1-4. Large farming areas had more representatives than urban areas did.
  a. Few people lived in the cities.
  b. The system of representation was unfair.

2. Predicting

▶ Reread the chapter. Then answer the following questions.

  a. Based on the English tradition of expanding the role of Parliament while reducing the power of monarchs, do you think future kings and queens will have more power or less? Why?

  b. As more people went to work in factories and gained the right to vote, unions became more powerful. Do you think this trend continued? Why or why not?

  c. The reform bills made it possible for a wider variety of English people to vote. At one time, only property owners could vote. After reform, poor people, factory workers, and people who did not own property could vote. As a result, different kinds of people with different ideas about how government should work began voting. Do you think this made the English government and political system stronger or weaker? Why?

ENRICHMENT

1. Have a class debate between two teams on the subject of abolishing the House of Lords and the monarchy. Prepare a team report so that each member understands the information to be discussed during the debate.

2. Imagine that you are a tourist visiting Parliament while it is in session. Write a letter home describing what you have seen.

3. Research and prepare a report on one of the well-known features of the Victorian Age. Possibilities include (a) Victorian taste in furniture and clothing, (b) family life in the Victorian Age, (c) education in the Victorian Age, (d) Victorian literature, especially the novels of Charles Dickens, or (e) the light operas of Gilbert and Sullivan

CHAPTER 3

France, A Republic

▲ In an impressive ceremony, Emperor Napoleon III and Empress Eugenie receive ambassadors from the Asian Kingdom of Siam (now Thailand).

OBJECTIVE: Why were there so many changes in government in nineteenth-century France?

1. Imagine what it would be like if your social studies class were given a new teacher every few weeks. One month, you might have a teacher who encouraged class discussion. Another month, you might have a teacher who preferred to lecture and to make all the decisions herself. The next month, yet another teacher might require you to spend the entire period reading and writing about history. Each time your class was given a new teacher, you would have to get used to a new way of doing things. Getting used to new ways would take time. It could also make you resent the constant changes. A similar situation existed in France in the nineteenth century. The gov-

ernment changed often. How might these ◄ changes affect the French people? French citizens saw themselves gain new rights, only to lose them again a short while later. It was difficult for France to progress because governments changed often.

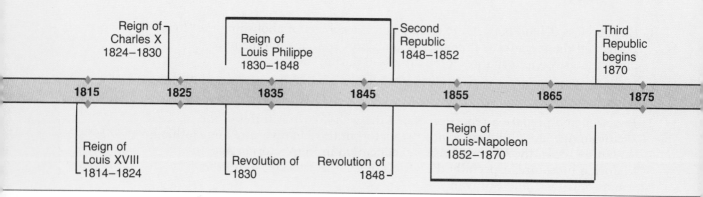

Reign of Charles X 1824–1830

Reign of Louis Philippe 1830–1848

Second Republic 1848–1852

Third Republic begins 1870

| 1815 | 1825 | 1835 | 1845 | 1855 | 1865 | 1875 |

Reign of Louis XVIII 1814–1824

Revolution of 1830

Revolution of 1848

Reign of Louis-Napoleon 1852–1870

ESL/LEP Strategy: Ask students to choose one key person from Chapter 3. Then, have them form small groups to determine the identity of the historical figure through a series of *yes* or *no* questions.

SHIFTS IN GOVERNMENT: Why did a revolution take place in France in 1830?

2. At the Congress of Vienna, France was restored to the monarchy that had existed before the French Revolution. Louis XVIII came to the throne. Although he claimed to rule by "divine right," Louis was willing to accept the new constitution of France that was written in 1814. This constitution recognized the right of the people to elect a lawmaking body, and it included a bill of rights to protect the individual citizen.

3. When Louis XVIII died in 1824, the throne of France was inherited by his brother, Charles X. Unlike Louis, Charles believed that the king should hold all the power of government in his own hands. He believed that the constitution of France had no authority over his actions.

4. In July 1830, new elections were held. Opponents of the king won more seats in the legislature than they had held before. Charles ordered the newly elected legislature to go home. He also ended freedom of the press and limited the people's right to vote in future elections. In reaction, there were protest marches and riots in the streets of Paris. When Charles X ordered the army to stop the riots, the soldiers joined the people in rebellion. With the army against him, the king realized he had no chance of winning. He gave up the throne and fled to England.

THE "CITIZEN KING": Why did the reign of Louis Philippe also end in revolution?

5. The new king was Louis Philippe, a cousin of the deposed King Charles X. Louis Philippe, known as the Citizen King, agreed to accept the Constitution of 1814. The right to vote was given to more people in the middle class. This satisfied some people who had taken part in the Revolution of 1830. However, it disappointed those who had fought for the right of all adult men to vote.

6. As a ruler, Louis Philippe was more successful than Charles X. Some of Louis Philippe's policies, however, were no better than those of Charles X. He allowed **tariffs** (TAIR-ufs), or taxes on imported goods, to remain high. High tariffs helped French manufacturers by making imports more expensive than goods produced at home. However, high tariffs hurt consumers. Goods produced at home were too expensive for them to afford. Louis Philippe lost popularity. What effect could this have in a ◄ country like France?

7. In February 1848, thousands of workers demonstrated in the streets of Paris as they had in 1830. This time, however, the troops fired on the people, and some demonstrators were killed. This bloodshed led to a revolution. Crowds marched to the king's palace and forced him to abdicate. Once again the people of France had deposed a king.

Daily life in . . .

Many people's lives were unchanged by the revolutions in France. During the 1800s, most French people still worked on small farms, ran small shops, or worked in crafts. Many farmers did not own their land. As they had for centuries, farmers gave part of their crops to their landlords as rent.

Only rich people could afford to send their children to school. Even after Napoleon III gave recognition to church schools, poor people got little benefit. Most French voters could not read or write.

Napoleon III and his court led the wealthy people in a grand lifestyle. People in Europe and the Americas looked to Paris for styles in clothes, food, art, music, literature, and many other areas. Napoleon III's great public ceremonies, such as his marriage to Countess Eugénie Montijo of Spain, became popular entertainments for the people.

Ask: Why did many people in Europe react fearfully to this new revolution?

THE SECOND REPUBLIC: Why did the Second Republic soon become the Second Empire?

8. As a result of the Revolution of 1848, a new government was established. For six months, groups argued whether another monarchy should rule France. Finally the temporary government wrote a new constitution. This constitution provided for a republican form of government with a National Assembly elected by universal male suffrage and a president elected by the people. The new government was called the Second Republic, the first republic having been the republic during the French Revolution in the 1790s.

9. In December 1848, the people of France went to the polls to vote for their new representatives and president. By a large majority, they elected Prince Louis Napoleon to the office of president. Louis Napoleon was the nephew of the Napoleon who had led France to its peak of power before 1814, and the people hoped that he could restore the glory of France.

10. In the years that followed his election, Louis Napoleon increased his hold on power in France. In 1852 he became Emperor Napoleon III, based on a vote of the people. His government became known as the Second Empire, the first empire having been that of his uncle Napoleon. Once installed in power, Napoleon III formed a secret police to spy on those groups that still wanted a republican form of government. He also limited freedom of speech and of the press. The Revolution of 1848 was undone, and France was once again under the rule of one man.

11. To regain glory for France, Napoleon III went looking for foreign conquests. In 1854 he involved France in a bloody war between Russia and Turkey called the Crimean War. In the 1859 he sent armies to Italy to aid the fight for Italian unity. Later, in 1870, his government made the mistake of going to war against Prussia. Napoleon III's army was no match for Prussia's. In less than two months, the French army was forced to surrender, and Napoleon III was taken prisoner. He soon abdicated, and the Second French Empire had ended.

A STABLE GOVERNMENT: How was France's government organized under the Third Republic?

12. In 1870 France again became a republic. Its first leaders could not settle peace terms with Prussia's leader Otto von Bismarck. The Prussians surrounded Paris on September 19. Paris held out until the end of January 1871, when it fell to the Prussians.

13. New **delegates** (DEL-ih-gets), or representatives, were elected to discuss peace terms. They agreed to pay Germany 5 billion francs. France was to pay the German soldiers who would stay in France until the debt was paid. France also lost its province of Alsace and a large part of the province of Lorraine. Finally, the German army was allowed to parade through Paris.

14. The election of a new government was supervised by the victorious Germans. Some groups in France wanted to return to a monarchy, but they were divided over who the monarch should be. Others fought for a republican form of government. This division led, once again, to bloodshed in the streets of the city of Paris. In 1871 a bloody clash between the troops of the National Assembly of France and the protesters ended in a week-long battle, with more than 20,000 men and women killed.

15. Finally, in 1875, a new set of laws was adopted for the Third Republic. According to these laws, the National Assembly would elect the president, but the president would have little power. Instead, the party or group of parties with the most delegates would choose the prime minister and other ministers. These officials would actually run the government. The Third Republic became France's first stable government in almost 100 years. It established a republican form of government that endured until World War II.

SPOTLIGHT ON SOURCES

16. During its early years, scandals plagued the Third Republic. A **scandal** (SKAN-dul) is something that shocks people's sense of right and wrong and disgraces those associated with it. One of the most serious scandals involved a Jewish captain in the army named Alfred Dreyfus. Dreyfus was charged with selling military secrets to Germany. He was found guilty and sentenced to life imprisonment in the notorious prison of Devil's Island, off the coast of South America. Three years later, it was discovered that false evidence had been used against Dreyfus. The army, supported by **anti-Semites** (AN-ty SEH-myts), or people who are hostile toward Jews, refused to reopen Dreyfus's case. One person who knew that the army was covering up the truth was the writer Emile Zola (zoh-LAH). Zola at this time was one of the best-known writers in France. He had first won attention as a young man for his novels about the less attractive aspects of the French way of life under Napoleon III. Now he attacked officials of a different government, writing a letter to the president of France to expose the army's behavior. Zola also saw to it that the letter was published in a number of French newspapers.

"I accuse General Mercier of injustice of the century! . . . I accuse General Gense of sharing in the same crime! I accuse three handwriting experts hired by the army of making false reports! I accuse the War Office of a plot with the newspapers to fool the public and cover up their own crimes! Finally I accuse the War Office of injustice for calling a man guilty on the basis of secret papers! . . . I accuse them of protecting the guilty! I accuse them of a crime against justice and the people of France!"

—from *Readings in European History Since 1814*, Alexander Baltzly and Jonathan F. Scott, eds.

The letter rocked the country. The French eople wanted to know the truth. In 1899 Dreyfus was pardoned by the president of France, and in 1906 he was cleared of all charges. The government reformed the army and won back the people's trust.

▼ A French army officer breaks Dreyfus's sword after his conviction for treason, indicating that Dreyfus is no longer an officer.

OUTLOOK

17. France's government changed many times in the 1800s. Even under the Third Republic, prime ministers never held power long. There were so many political parties that several had to join together to choose ministers. When these parties fought among themselves, they lost power. However, all the parties had learned one important lesson that kept the Third Republic stable. They knew that they had to keep the trust and support of the people. What could happen to make the people turn against the government as they had done so many times before?

Background: Prime ministers and their coalitions of parties held power for very short times during the Third Republic. By 1900, the Third Republic had already had 39 different sets of ministers.

CHAPTER REVIEW

Write each of the following sentences on a sheet of paper. Then fill in the blank with the word that best completes each sentence.

Second Republic

Second Empire

scandals

tariffs

anti-Semites

delegates

1. _____ are favored by manufacturers because they make imports more expensive than goods produced at home.

2. The government established after the Revolution of 1848 was called the _____ .

3. Under the constitution drafted during the Second Republic, citizens elected _____ , or representatives, to serve in the government.

4. The Dreyfus Affair was one of the most serious _____ of the Third Republic.

5. _____ are people who are hostile toward Jews.

6. The _____ of Napoleon III lasted from 1852 to 1870.

SKILL BUILDER: USING A TABLE

The table below presents information about the types of work people did in France between 1856 and 1896. Study the table and then answer the questions that follow.

WORKING POPULATION OF FRANCE
1856–1896

	1856		1876		1896	
	Number of workers (millions)	% of population	Number of workers (millions)	% of population	Number of workers (millions)	% of population
Agriculture, forestry, fishing	7.305	51.4%	7.995	49.3%	8.463	45.3%
Manufacturing and industry	4.418	31.1%	4.469	27.6%	5.452	29.2%
Services	2.493	17.5%	3.754	23.1%	4.749	25.5%

Source: Eugen Weber, *Peasants into Frenchmen*, Stanford, CA: Stanford University Press, 1976. p. 116.

Make a chart showing the various governments of France from 1815 to 1900. Divide a sheet of paper into four columns. Label the columns (1) "Dates"; (2) "Kind of Government"; (3) "Important People"; and (4) "Reason for Ending."

1. How many workers had jobs in manufacturing and industry in 1876? What percentage of the working population was this?

2. In what year were there more than 8 million people in agricultural jobs?

3. When did the percentage of workers in service jobs first exceed 20%?

4. What happened to the *number* of workers engaged in agricultural, forestry, and fishing jobs between 1856 and 1898? What happened to the *percentage* of workers in these fields between 1856 and 1896? What would explain this difference?

5. Which category of work nearly doubled its number of workers between 1856 and 1896?

6. What would you expect the percentage of workers engaged in agricultural jobs to be in 1906? Why?

7. What would you expect the percentage of workers engaged in service jobs to be in 1906? Why?

SKILL BUILDER: CRITICAL THINKING AND COMPREHENSION

1. Drawing Conclusions

a. Based on your reading of this chapter, what conclusions can you draw about the rights of individual citizens?

b. Based on your reading of this chapter, what can you conclude about the political rights of women in France during the nineteenth century?

2. Predicting

a. During the Third Republic, various political groups competed with each other to control the legislature. Predict what kind of ministers were chosen to lead France in light of the fact that no party had a majority in the legislature.

b. Predict what might have happened had the people lost trust in the government of the Third Republic.

ENRICHMENT

1. The Revolution of 1830 was a violent uprising. Paris was a battleground as civilians from all walks of life fought the army. Locate books in the library that describe the revolution. Then write a newspaper article that might have appeared in July 1830 describing what the streets of Paris were like.

2. Draw a political cartoon that illustrates why consumers are generally opposed to high tariffs.

3. Write an essay explaining which French government you would have wanted to live under during the nineteenth century. Be sure to include the reasons why you have chosen that particular government.

4. Prepare a report on one of the French Impressionist painters (Manet, Monet, Degas, or Renoir) or on the American Impressionist Mary Cassatt. Give an outline of the painter's life, describe the main characteristics of the paintings, and tell what were the main subjects of the artist's paintings. Bring books to class that show examples of the painter's work.

CHAPTER 4

Czarist Russia

▲ Parades and other military ceremonies were important in the Russia of Czar Nicholas I, shown here at the head of a troop of cavalry.

OBJECTIVE: How did the czars block change in Russia?

1. In the United States, comedians can poke fun at almost anything, including the government. They have no problem if they make jokes about the president or the first family. Senators, cabinet members, and other government officials are also fair game for comedians. Americans take for granted that they live in a free country. One important freedom is the right to criticize the way the government is run. People in other countries, such as the Soviet Union, have not been so lucky. Not until the late l980s have Soviet leaders allowed the people to speak and be heard without fear. In the nineteenth century, Russian leaders often put to death anyone who spoke against them. Writers had to be very careful of what they wrote about the government. The leaders worked to keep people from talking about what was wrong, rather than trying to change Russia for the better. Why might leaders of a country be interested in avoiding change?

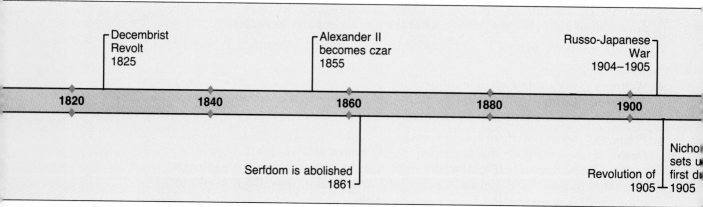

| 1820 | 1840 | 1860 | 1880 | 1900 |

Decembrist Revolt 1825

Alexander II becomes czar 1855

Russo-Japanese War 1904–1905

Serfdom is abolished 1861

Revolution of 1905

Nichol sets u first d 1905

Background: In the late 1980s, Soviet leader Mikhail Gorbachev introduced a plan called glasnost (GLAZ-nohst), which means being open about problems.

THE CZARS: What powers did the Russian czars have?

2. The czars or Russian rulers, had **absolute** (AB-suh-loot) power. "Absolute" means that they did not share power with any other person or group, but rather held it all themselves. They made all laws by personal **decree** (dih-KREE), or order. Government officials made sure these laws were carried out without question. There was no parliament or congress to vote on new laws. Russian nobles and landowners had little voice in the government. People of the middle and lower classes had no voice in government. The czars tried to control every part of Russian society, and they expected to be obeyed.

3. To keep their power, the czars believed they had to silence people who questioned their rule. They feared any uprising that might loosen their hold on Russia. One such uprising happened in St. Petersburg after the death of Alexander I in 1825. Because it took place in December of that year, it has come to be called the Decembrist (dih-SEM-brust) Revolt. There was some confusion as to who would inherit Alexander's throne. A group of army officers took advantage of the confusion to try to take over the government. They hoped to establish a monarchy with a constitution, so that the czar would have to share his power. The new czar, Nicholas I, quickly sent soldiers out to put down the revolt. The group's leaders were hanged, sent to prison, or exiled in far-off Siberia.

4. After the Decembrist Revolt, Nicholas I was afraid to allow any freedom of speech and the press. He started a special secret police to watch for groups that might work against the government. The police would arrest or take the property of any person who had liberal ideas about giving power to the people. The czar had a group of **censors** (SEN-surz) read all books and newspapers. The censors banned any writing that disagreed in any way with the government. They looked for writing that seemed to favor such groups as the Decembrists. Why would the czars want to keep people from reading things that criticized the government? People who wrote books, articles, or poems against the government could be put in prison. Some were sent to Siberia. Even Alexander Pushkin, Russia's greatest poet, was watched very closely.

PEOPLE IN HISTORY

5. Alexander Pushkin (PUSH-kin) was born in Moscow in 1799 to an old Russian noble family. At an early age Pushkin showed an interest in literature and books. His grandmother, who took care of the young boy, would often tell Pushkin stories of his ancestors. One of these ancestors, a great-grandfather, was an African who had come to Russia in the time of Peter the Great. Pushkin always spoke with pride of his African heritage. Pushkin heard Russian folktales from his old nurse, who was a freed serf. He also read many books in his father's library and listened closely to the young writers who often visited his father.

6. Pushkin began his writing career when he published his first piece as a young student of 15. In 1817 he left school to join the foreign office at St. Petersburg. Soon after, Pushkin began to write political verses that contained liberal political ideas. As a result of these works, the government sent Pushkin away to live alone in southern Russia. From 1820 to 1826, Pushkin was forced to live in exile. Many of the letters he wrote to friends were opened and read by the czar's secret police. During this lonely time, Pushkin wrote a large part of his most famous work, the book-length poem *Yevgeny Onegin* (yev-GAY-nee on-YEG-in). In this poem, Pushkin depicts a number of unforgettable characters against a background of Russian life in his time.

7. In the fall of 1826, Nicholas I finally allowed Pushkin to return to St. Petersburg. The czar promised Pushkin that he himself would be the poet's censor. However, Pushkin found the czar's constant watch over him very hard to live with. If Pushkin did

Background: When the death of Alexander I was announced, a rumor arose that he was not dead. Some believed that he was so overcome by illness and worry that he sought peace in a monastery.

389

▲ Russians regard Alexander Pushkin as their greatest literary figure, much as people in English-speaking countries look on Shakespeare.

anything that was out of line, the head of the czar's secret police would scold him.

8. After Pushkin married in 1831, he was forced to take part in the social life of the czar's court. He also had to take a government job. Pushkin refused to give up his poetry and kept on writing. More and more, his works spoke of peasant revolts and Peter ▶ the Great. Why do you think Pushkin admired Peter the Great so much? Pushkin believed that reform was needed in the Russian system. He felt the only way to get change was with the help of both the people and the czar. People in the czar's court began to resent Pushkin. Finally, on February 8, 1837, Pushkin was forced by powerful enemies to fight a duel. Two days later he died of his wounds.

CZARIST REFORMS: What important reforms did Alexander II make?

9. The 1860s brought important reforms to Russia. Czar Alexander II, who came to the throne in 1855, believed that changes were needed to make Russia as modern as the other countries of Europe. However, his advisors warned him that sudden changes could bring down the government. They reminded Alexander II how the rulers of France had been treated in the French revolutions. During his time as czar, Alexander II was caught between a desire to make important changes and fear of giving up too much power.

10. Alexander II's greatest act was freeing the serfs in 1861. However, freeing them solved only part of the serfs' problems. Because few of the freed serfs could raise the money to buy land, most remained as poor as when they were serfs.

11. The reign of Alexander II saw many other reforms. Local assemblies, called **zemstvos** (ZEMZT-vohz), were set up to deal with local needs, such as roads, hospitals, and schools. They also had the power to raise money by taxes. Although the aristocracy led these groups, peasants and townspeople were given a voice as well. Alexander II also reformed the Russian court system and the army. In the courts, all people were treated the same before the law, and trials were to be public. In the army, the term of service was shortened, and people from all classes had to serve. None of these changes, however, touched on the key problem in Russia. People still did not have the right to vote for leaders or have a say in their government. Reforms came from the czar, and he could take them away just as quickly as he made them.

AGAINST THE CZAR: Who were the Russian radicals? Why did Russian radicals fail to change the government?

12. The reforms made by the czars only caused people to want more. Radical uprisings took place again and again and were crushed just as many times. Why didn't the ◀

Background: When Alexander II assumed the throne in 1855, many Russians thought a golden age was in store. In his first days as czar, Alexander reversed the ban on foreign travel and eased censorhip.

czars want to make more reforms? Many radicals who took part in these revolts were members of **minority groups**. Minority groups are groups of people who make up a smaller part of the population. These groups in Russia included Poles, Finns, and Jews. The czars tried to **russify** (RUS-uh-fy) them, or force them to follow Russian customs, language, and beliefs. The Jews were the hardest hit. They suffered through violent attacks, called **pogroms** (poh-GRAHMZ), which were planned by the government itself. Many Jews were killed in the pogroms. Others fled to the United States and Palestine.

▶ **13.** Other radicals who took part in revolts against the czar were young people from noble families. Why would young people from noble families be interested in change? These young people wanted to destroy the present government and set up a new one. They wore cheap clothes like those of workers. Young women wore plain dresses. The men wore blue glasses and
▶ shaved off their beards. Why do you think they dressed like this?

SPOTLIGHT ON SOURCES

14. The desire of Russian young people for change caused family problems. Parents felt that their children were rejecting old values. The break between old and young is the topic of the novel *Fathers and Sons*, by Ivan Turgenev (ee-VAHN toor-GAYN-yef). In this scene, young Arkady is telling his uncle Pavel about his radical friend Bazarov (bat-ZAR-awv).

"He's a nihilist," repeated Arkady.

"A nihilist," said Nikolai Petrovich. That's from the Latin *nihil, nothing,* as far as I can judge; the word must mean a man who . . . who accepts nothing?"

"Say, 'who respects nothing,' " put in Pavel Petrovich, and he set to work on the butter again.

"Who regards everything from the critical point of view," observed Arkady.

"Isn't that just the same thing?" inquired Pavel Petrovich.

▼ In 1881, Czar Alexander II was killed by a bomb thrown under his carriage by a group of radicals. The assassination brought to an end Russia's brief era of reform.

Background: Some radical groups planted bombs in government buildings and set fires in cities. They even tried several times to kill Alexander II until finally, in 1881, he was murdered by a bomb blast.

▲ The colorful costumes of the Ballet Russes (left) contrast with the whiteness of Anna Pavlova's dress. Pavlova was the greatest dancer of the older Russian classical style.

Russian Ballet   Ballet has long been a favorite art form in Russia. In the 1800s, dancers for the Imperial Ballet had armies of admirers, just as rock stars do today. Ballet performances lasted for hours. Theaters sold out for whole seasons. Ballet tickets were handed down from parents to children. Many fans knew their favorite ballets by heart. If a dancer changed a step, they were shocked.

Swan Lake and other famous ballets were created during the 1800's.

In 1909 Sergei Diaghilev (sair-GAY dee-AG-uh-lef) organized a new Russian ballet company in Paris. The Ballets Russes, as the group was called, was a sensation. Crowds gasped at the leaps of the great dancer Vaslav Nijinsky (VAHS-lahv nih-ZHIN-skee). They loved the brightly colored sets and costumes and the beautiful music. Soon the greatest artists of Europe were helping put together shows for the Ballets Russes. The great composers Stravinsky and Debussy and the painter Picasso worked with Diaghilev's group. The Ballets Russes was one of Russia's greatest gifts to twentieth century art.

1. Why was the Ballets Russes so popular in Paris?

2. How might the Russian Ballet have taught people about other parts of Russian culture?

"No, it's not the same thing. A nihilist is a man who does not bow down before any authority [person in power], who does not take any principle [rule] on faith, whatever reverence that principle may be enshrined in [no matter how much people respect it]."

"Well, and is that good?" interrupted Pavel Petrovich.

"That depends, uncle. Some people it will do good to, but some people will suffer for it."

—*Fathers and Sons* by Ivan Turgenev

▶ What authorities would a Russian nihilist in the 1860s not have accepted?

15. In 1905 the radicals had a chance to force the Czar Nicholas II to make major changes. With Russia's defeat in a war with Japan in 1904-1905, the Russian people began to lose trust in their leaders. A large crowd of workers marched to the czar's palace to ask Nicholas II to listen to their pleas for change. Although the workers acted peacefully, the czar's soldiers shot and killed many of them. Bloody Sunday, as the event was called, shocked many Russians. People rioted in the streets. Minority groups banded together against the czar. The peasants, taken by the slogan "All land to the peasants," took over large estates.

16. To quiet the people, Nicholas II set up the first Russian parliament, called the **duma** (DOO-mah). The people were not satisfied, however. Workers staged a general strike that shut down railways, factories, and schools. The strike caused the czar to make more changes. He promised freedom of speech and press and opened election of the members of the duma to nearly all Russian males. These changes made liberals happy, but not the radicals. When radical members tried to pass laws that went against the czar's wishes, Nicholas II stepped in. The czar kept on breaking up the duma until it was run by parties that agreed with him and his government.

▲ Women march in a street of St. Petersburg, the Russian capital, during a demonstration that took place during the Revolution of 1905.

OUTLOOK

17. The Russian czars of the late 1800s wanted to protect their power and not the rights of the Russian people. When Nicholas II interfered with the duma, many radicals lost hope of changing the government from the inside. They searched for new ways to take over the government. The workers' revolts of 1905 set the stage for the Russian Revolution of 1917. This revolution would bring a new government that would lead to the formation of the Soviet Union. How might the history of the region ◀ have been different had the czars agreed to make more radical reforms?

393

CHAPTER REVIEW

VOCABULARY REVIEW

Write the following paragraph on a sheet of paper. Then fill in the blanks with the words that best complete the paragraph.

absolute

censors

duma

minority groups

pogrom

russify

zemstvos

The czars, or Russian emperors, were _____ rulers who held all power themselves. They used _____ to keep people from writing anything against the government. _____ , or non-Russian groups who made up a small part of the population, were treated unkindly by Russian rulers. They were forced to _____ , or follow Russian customs, language, and beliefs. The Jews suffered many violent attacks, or _____ , which were directed by the government. However, the Russian rulers did try to make changes. One was the setting up of local groups called _____ to deal with matters of a local nature. The court system and army were also reformed. Later the government also set up a _____ , or parliament, to which all male Russians could elect representatives.

SKILL BUILDER: OUTLINING

The following is an incomplete outline of the life of Alexander Pushkin. Copy the outline on a separate piece of paper. Then fill in the blanks with the main heads, subheads, or supporting details from the list below. Refer to the **People in History** feature, paragraphs 5–8, if you need help.

Government Work and the Czar's Court

forced into exile

shows an early liking for literature

Childhood

forced to fight a duel

watched closely by secret police

I. Early Life
    A. _____
        1. born to a noble family
        2. _____
    B. Early Writing Career
        1. published his first piece at 15
        2. wrote political verses for a secret society
        3. _____
        4. Wrote Yevgeny Onegin

II. Working Under the Czar
   A. Nicholas I and Censorship
   1. czar agrees to be Pushkin's censor
   2. _____
   B. _____
   1. takes a government post
   2. given special title in czar's court
   3. does not give up writing
   C. Death
   1. becomes unhappy with work
   2. is resented by czar's court
   3. _____
   4. dies of wounds

SKILL BUILDER: CRITICAL THINKING AND COMPREHENSION

▶ **1. Drawing Conclusions:**

a. Why might you conclude that the czars' fear of losing power was greater than their desire to be just rulers?

b. Why did the czars want to russify all minority groups?

c. Democratic change would never take place in Russia as long as the czars were in power. How do the facts in this chapter support this conclusion?

▶ **2. Predicting**

When the czarist government finally came to an end in 1917, from which groups of people do you think the new Russian leaders came?

ENRICHMENT

1. Alexander Pushkin met with Nicholas I after the writer was allowed to return to Moscow. Write the conversation that might have taken place between Pushkin and the czar at their first meeting.

2. Prepare a booklet of pictures that show the great differences in the way of life of the czar and the peasants. You can photocopy pictures from books or magazines or draw the pictures yourself. At the end of the booklet, summarize what you think the pictures tell about Russia under the czars of the 1800's.

3. Reread the **Spotlight on Sources** section of this chapter. Write a short passage about how the "generation gap" in Russia in the 1860s was similar to the "generation gap" in the U.S. in the 1960s. Then discuss how they were different.

4. Research what life in exile in Siberia was like. Russians were sent there for a variety of reasons. Were criminals treated any differently from political prisoners? Were there prison camps there during the 1800s?

CHAPTER 5

The Spirit of Nationalism

▲ This sculpture, representing the Spirit of France, vividly portrays the nationalistic spirit that swept Europe in the 1800s.

OBJECTIVE: How did nationalism become an important force in nineteenth century Europe?

1. In America we sing, "Oh say can you see by the dawn's early light . . . ." But in Sweden they sing, "Thou ancient, unconquered, rock-towered North . . . ." In Portugal people sing, "Heroes of the sea, noble race, valiant and immortal nation . . . ." These are **national anthems**—songs that are the patriotic symbols of countries. The oldest is Great Britain's "God Save the King" (or "God Save the Queen," depending who is on the throne), which dates from 1740. Few other countries have such old anthems. It was only in the nineteenth century that the idea of having a song to honor a country took hold, especially in Europe. At that time people began to identify strongly with the nations they lived in, and they began to show their love of their countries with poems, flags, and songs.

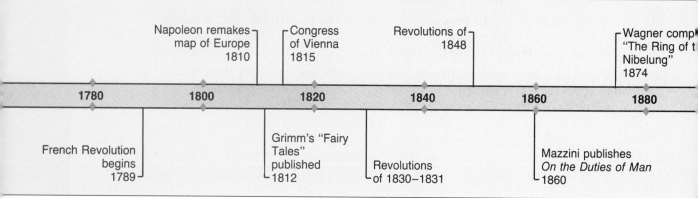

Napoleon remakes map of Europe 1810

Congress of Vienna 1815

Revolutions of 1848

Wagner comp "The Ring of t Nibelung" 1874

1780 — 1800 — 1820 — 1840 — 1860 — 1880

French Revolution begins 1789

Grimm's "Fairy Tales" published 1812

Revolutions of 1830–1831

Mazzini publishes *On the Duties of Man* 1860

Activity: As an introduction to this chapter, ask students to think of some ethnic traditions practiced in their families or in other families whom they know.

DEVELOPMENT OF NATIONALISM: How did nationalism develop in Europe?

2. In Europe during the Middle Ages, no one was loyal to a country. People were loyal to a king, a landowning noble, a bishop, a city government, or some other local authority. Toward the end of the Middle Ages, these local authorities began to lose their power to national monarchs. The national monarchs established powerful kingdoms of France, Spain, England, and Portugal.

3. As the monarchs united their countries, the idea of nationalism began to develop. The first step occurred when all the people in a country became loyal to one person, the monarch. Gradually, people in each country began to be loyal also to their language, history, and culture. They were becoming loyal to their nations.

GROWTH OF NATIONALISM: How did the French Revolution help nationalism to grow?

4. In the late eighteenth century, the French Revolution furthered the growth of nationalism. After the French king and queen were executed, the French people shifted all their loyalty to their nation. They showed how strongly they felt about France by creating a national flag. A national anthem was also written. A national anthem is a song that shows love for one's country. When the French armies went into battle,

they carried the flag and sang the anthem. They fought for their country, as well as for their rulers. How do Americans show love for their country today? ◄

5. France under the leadership of Napoleon I helped to spread nationalism in Europe. Napoleon moved through Europe conquering other countries so that he could place them under French rule. In some countries, Napoleon's rule brought with it a spirit of nationalism. This was particularly true in Germany and Italy, regions that had not been united under one government for centuries. In other countries, such as Spain and Russia, nationalism was used as a tool to help drive out the French armies. By the time Napoleon was defeated, nationalism had grown to be a strong force in Europe. How did the Congress of Vienna prove how ◄ strong nationalism had become?

NATIONALISM AND WRITERS: How did the work of nineteenth century writers help to spread nationalism in Europe?

6. Writers and poets of the nineteenth century had much to do with the spread of nationalism in Europe. The way they wrote, and what they wrote about, aroused the nationalist feelings of the people. These writers and poets were romantics (roh-MAN-tiks), or followers of **romanticism** (roh-MAN-tih-siz-um). Romanticism was a movement in the nineteenth century that

Daily life in . . .

If you wanted to learn the latest news from Paris, London, or Vienna in the 1800s, what would you do? You would pick up a copy of the daily paper. The inexpensive daily newspaper came into being during the nineteenth century. With printing machines making 1,500 copies in an hour, newspapers could be printed and sold cheaply. Daily papers not only told about the latest news events. They also included travel stories and small ads for jobs and medicines.

Some books appeared one chapter at a time in daily newspapers. These included books by Alexandre Dumas and Charles Dickens. Some radical newspapers were sold in France, Italy, and Germany. These papers broke the law because they attacked existing governments, which allowed few liberties to their citizens. Police would often be seen standing around newsstands watching to see if any of these newspapers were being sold.

Background: Refer students to Unit 7, Chapters 4 and 5 for information on the French Revolution and the rise of Napoleon's empire in Europe.

397

placed great value on feelings and on the past. The romantic writers were interested in folk tales and folk songs of different **ethnic** (ETH-nik) groups. An ethnic group is a group of people who share the same language and culture. How would reading stories about your ethnic group affect your feelings about your family's history?

7. Romanticism helped to bring about a **cultural revival** among ethnic groups throughout Europe. A cultural revival is a new interest in the history and customs of a group. In Germany, a movement started to develop German culture. A group of German writers began to write in German about Germany's past. Among these writers were Johann Wolfgang von Goethe (YO-hahn VULF-gahng fawn GUR-tuh), Friedrich Schiller (FREE-drikh SHIL-ur), and the brothers Jakob and Wilhelm Grimm. The Grimm brothers traveled around Germany listening to and collecting folk stories. These stories were published as Grimm's *Fairy Tales* beginning in 1812. How would writing stories in the language spoken by the people help nationalism to grow?

8. The different peoples of eastern Europe were also concerned about the loss of their cultures and languages. The upper classes of national groups like the Czechs, Slovaks, Romanians, and Serbians had always spoken German or French. They imitated the styles of Paris or Vienna. In the 1800s, eastern Europeans started to collect their own people's folktales and ballads as well as popular songs. They studied the ethnic languages and wrote grammars and dictionaries of them. Histories which told of the heroic deeds of the peoples of eastern Europe during the Middle Ages were also written. Some of what was written about these groups had never been told before.

SPOTLIGHT ON SOURCES

9. The writer who helped to develop a spirit of nationalism in Italy was Giuseppe Mazzini (joo-SEP-peh mat-SEE-nee). Maz-

zini wrote that ethnic groups in Europe had the right to rule themselves. In 1860 Mazzini wrote his most widely read book, *On the Duties of Man*. In this book, Mazzini tells why he thinks Italy should become a nation.

> In laboring [working] for our own country on the right principle [for the right reason], we labor for Humanity [all the people in the world]. Our country is the fulcrum [prop] of the lever we have to wield [handle] for the common good. If we abandon [give up] the fulcrum, we run the risk of rendering ourselves useless, not only to humanity but to our country itself. Before men can associate [deal] with the nations of which humanity is composed, they must have a national existence. There is no true association except among equals. It is only through our country that we can have a recognized collective existence [that we can be seen as one group].
>
> —*On the Duties of Man*, Giuseppe Mazzini

Why does Mazzini feel that the Italian states should become one nation?

NATIONALISM AND MUSIC: How did the music of the nineteenth century show the spirit of nationalism?

10. The spirit of nationalism also affected the musical composers of the 1800s. They looked to their countries' histories, myths, and folk songs for ideas for their music. Each ethnic group had a national composer whose music would speak for the many who yearned to be united and free.

11. The composer Giuseppe Verdi (joo-SEP-peh VAIR-dee) did much for the growth of nationalism in Italy. Verdi was one of the greatest **opera** composers in the nineteenth century. Opera is a drama with its words and actions set to music. The music and words of Verdi's opera *Nabucco* increased feelings against foreign rule in Italy. Sometimes the government forced Verdi to change the words of his operas. But the music alone reminded people of the spirit of nationalism.

PEOPLE IN HISTORY

12. Another composer whose operas stirred strong feelings of nationalism was the German composer Richard Wagner (VAHG-nur). Richard Wagner became interested in music as a young man in Leipzig, Germany. Later Wagner created some of the most important operas of the nineteenth century. Wagner had a great love for everything German. He especially admired German history, myths, and literature. This love is shown in the music he wrote.

13. Wagner was not only busy writing music. In the early part of his life, he was also interested in social reform. In 1849 Wagner was forced to flee Germany because he had taken part in the revolution in Dresden in 1848 and 1849. If he had stayed in that city, Wagner would have been put to death.

14. After he left Germany, Wagner began to write his great national opera. He continued to work on it, with interruptions for other projects, after his return to Germany. The name of this masterpiece was *The Ring of the Nibelung*. *The Ring* is not a single opera. Rather, it is a series of four operas intended to be performed over the course of a week. Based on old German and Norse folk legends from the early Middle Ages, it tells a complicated story of gods, goddesses, heroes, villains, giants, dwarfs, a dragon, and a magical ring, helmet, and sword.

15. Wagner finally was allowed to go back to Germany in the 1860s. In 1864 he gained the support of the king of Bavaria. With his help, Wagner was able to build his own theater in Bayreuth (BY-royt). Now Germans could hear German operas in their composer's own theater. *The Ring* was finished in 1874 and performed for the first time at Bayreuth two years later. To this day the Bayreuth Festival is an important celebration each year of Wagner's music and German culture.

▲ In *The Ring of the Nibelung*, Richard Wagner created a world of heroes, heroines, gods, and goddesses that still thrills opera audiences.

OUTLOOK

16. Several centuries passed before the spirit of nationalism finally took hold in Europe. But once it did in the nineteenth century, Europeans would never be the same again. Books, newspapers, and even the songs that they sang reminded people of their desire to belong to one nation. What ◀ would have happened had nationalism died in Europe? The different ethnic cultures that make up Europe today might have died out. The United States also might not have been what it is today, with its mixture of cultural heritages. Think of all the people who have come from the countries of Europe to settle in the United States. Nationalism helped preserve the language and customs of many European groups. What ◀ can you and your family do to keep your ethnic culture alive?

399

CHAPTER REVIEW

VOCABULARY REVIEW

Write each number and word on a sheet of paper. Then write the letter of the definition next to the word it defines.

1. national anthem
2. romanticism
3. ethnic group
4. cultural revival
5. opera

a. a new interest in the history and customs of a group
b. a song that shows love for one's country
c. a group of people who share the same language and culture
d. movement that placed great value on feelings and on the past
e. a drama in which the words are set to music

SKILL BUILDER: UNDERSTANDING A CARTOON

▶ The two cartoons show how nationalism affected Austria and Germany in different ways. Study the cartoons. Look for the symbols used in each one. Think about what the symbols could mean. Then answer the questions.

UNDERSTANDING A DRAWING

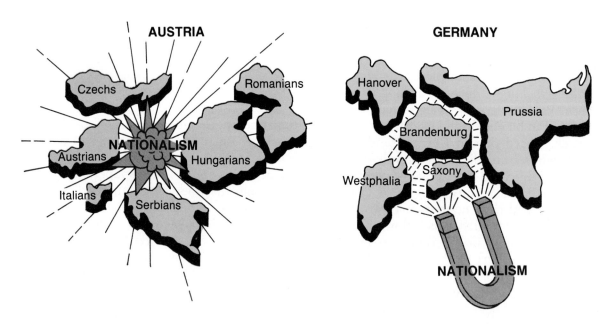

a. Nationalism caused a split in the Austrian empire. How is this shown in the cartoon?

b. What does the magnet stand for in the cartoon on Germany?

c. What generalization can you make about nationalism in the nineteenth century based on these two cartoons?

SKILL BUILDER: CRITICAL THINKING AND COMPREHENSION

1. Drawing Conclusions

a. Without the French Revolution, some of the European countries of today might not have come about. What facts from this chapter lead you to draw this conclusion?

b. What conclusion can you draw about the effect of the romantic movement on nationalism?

c. What conclusions can you draw about the effects, good and bad, of nationalism on human rights?

2. Predicting:

a. Which of the members of the Austrian empire do you think will still have nationalist uprisings after they break away from Austrian rule—the Italian states, the German states, or eastern European groups? Explain your answer.

b. What do you think happened to the music of Verdi and Wagner once Italy and Germany had become nations?

c. What do you think will be the effect of growing national pride on relations between countries? Will growing national feeling lead to tension between countries? Or will it lead to better understanding? Explain the reasons for your prediction.

3. Compare and Contrast

▶ Compare the cultural revival in the 1800s with the earlier cultural revival known as the Italian Renaissance. How are the two movements alike, and how are they different? What interests sparked the beginning of each movement?

ENRICHMENT

1. Imagine that the United States was under the rule of another world power. Write a poem to stir the spirit of nationalism in Americans to fight for their freedom.

2. Operas by Verdi and Wagner are often shown on public television. Watch one of these operas on television. Then be a music critic. Write a report on what you thought of the music, the singers, and the staging of the opera.

3. In the nineteenth century, the prima donna, or the major female singer in an opera, was treated very much like a movie star is today. Research the life of the prima donnas of the nineteenth century operas. Then, as a news reporter of the time, write an article describing your meeting with a prima donna in her home.

4. Romanticism also influenced the art of the 1800s. Look through the paintings by romantic artists of the 1800s in an art book in your school or neighborhood library. How do the romantic paintings show the same traits found in the romantic books of the 1800s?

5. Research the techniques and methods that governments have used to inspire nationalism among their people during times of war or other crisis. List at least three instances from recent news that illustrate these methods.

CHAPTER 6

Germany Emerges

OBJECTIVE: What factors helped to unite Germany?

1. Germany's movement toward nationalism actually began in the minds of its philosophers. In the early 1800s, philosophers such as Georg Hegel pointed out that Germans shared the same language, customs, and history. Hegel thought that making the Germans aware of their heritage would help them unite. Perhaps this idea is what made Napoleon say "The English inhabit the sea, the French the earth, and the Germans the air." Napoleon probably meant that while Britain had a great navy and France a great army, Germany had great thinkers, but no real power. In fact, the German people never seemed to be able to deal with the problems at hand without getting caught up in ideas. As a result, they

▲ Should the German states unite? Liberal leaders hotly debated the issue in the Frankfurt Assembly of 1848.

had never been able to forge themselves into a unified, powerful nation. Then suddenly, after 1850, they changed dramatically. The Germans started looking at the question of becoming a nation with common sense and began finding real answers.

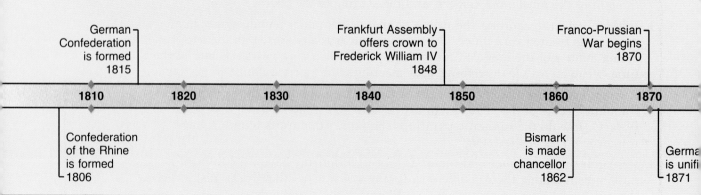

German Confederation is formed 1815

Frankfurt Assembly offers crown to Frederick William IV 1848

Franco-Prussian War begins 1870

| 1810 | 1820 | 1830 | 1840 | 1850 | 1860 | 1870 |

Confederation of the Rhine is formed 1806

Bismark is made chancellor 1862

Germa is unifi 1871

Much of this change had to do with the leadership of a tough and remarkable man. Had Napoleon been alive he would have met his match in Otto von Bismarck.

NAPOLEON AND GERMANY: What part did Napoleon play in bringing the German states together?

2. Without knowing it, Napoleon I took the first real steps toward uniting Germany in the early 1800s. Germany in 1800 was divided among more than 250 independent states, each with its own laws, taxes, armies, money, dress, and ways of speaking German. These states were loosely joined in the Holy Roman Empire, headed by Austria. In 1806 Napoleon, having defeated Austria, dissolved the Holy Roman Empire. His armies took over many of the German states, large and small. By combining many of the smaller states, he reduced the number of German states to about 100. Napoleon then joined these states to form a new

▶ Confederation of the Rhine. How would this confederation better Germany's chances of becoming one nation?

3. New states and a customs union were formed after Napoleon's fall from power in 1815. The Congress of Vienna reduced the number of German states to 38. These 38 states were joined together to form the new German Confederation. Metternich's Austria was the strongest member of the confederation. Prussia was the second strongest member. By the 1830s, many of the German states entered the *Zollverein* (TSUL-fer-yn), or customs union, with Prussia. This allowed the states to trade freely with one another without having to pay taxes on traded goods. Why would this customs union show how unity could help the German states?

FRANKFURT ASSEMBLY: Why did the Frankfurt Assembly fail to unify Germany?

4. German nationalist leaders began to see a need for a united government to fight the country's many problems. They saw that simply bringing together states would not make a nation. A severe **depression** (dih-PRESH-un) hit Germany in 1846. A depression is a time when business activity falls and many people are out of work. **Political repression** (rih-PRESH-un) was also a problem. That is, the people did not have the freedom to say or write what they felt about the government. They also did not have the right to vote, nor did they have a constitutional form of government.

5. In May 1848, about 500 liberal leaders formed an assembly at Frankfurt to write a constitution for all the German states. One of the questions facing the assembly was whether to make Germany a monarchy or a republic. The other was whether to include Austria in the union with all its non-German ethnic groups. In December, after much debate, the assembly drew up a constitution for a new German *Reich* (RYKH), or empire. The constitution called for a

Daily life in . . .

In nineteenth century Germany, a *Gymnasium* (ghim-NAH-zee-oom) was not a place where students played sports. It was a high school that prepared only male students for the university. The cost of going to the Gymnasium was high. One Prussian government official said he spent about a third of his income on schooling for his three sons.

At the Gymnasium, students studied grammar, rhetoric, logic, arithmetic, geometry, astronomy, and music. But by the 1850s, other kinds of schools had opened. The new schools offered training to students in science and more technical subjects. Students who graduated from these new schools could then get jobs in Germany's growing economy.

Background: The members of the Frankfurt Assembly were largely from the middle class, i.e., professors, lawyers, judges, and clergymen.

403

federation of democratic states with an all-German assembly. Only the German parts of Austria were invited to join the new Germany. The king of Prussia, Frederick William IV, was offered the title of "emperor of the Germans." Why do you think Prussia was chosen to lead the states?

6. The Frankfurt plan failed to please everyone, and the assembly fell apart. The members who wanted a German republic walked out. Frederick William IV refused the assembly's offer to be emperor. A believer in the divine right of kings, he thought that to accept a crown from an elected assembly was to "pick up a crown from the gutter." Austria, in turn, would not accept any Germany it did not lead. Most of the members left or were sent home by force. Frederick William IV then tried to organize the German princes, but Austria blocked his efforts. By 1850 the old German Confederation under Austrian leadership was back. How were the results of the Frankfurt Assembly a victory for the conservatives?

REALPOLITIK: How did "blood and iron" unite the German states into one nation?

7. The Frankfurt Assembly made it clear that liberal ideals alone would not work to unite Germany. Nationalists also began to see that a united Germany would only come to be without Austria. What did Austria do that caused the nationalists to make this conclusion? Nationalist leaders were now willing to use even force to get what they wanted. This tough-minded philosophy was known as *Realpolitik* (ray-AL-poh-lih-teek), or the politics of the real world. The hard-nosed Prussian leader who would use *Realpolitik* to finally lead Germany to unity was Otto von Bismarck.

PEOPLE IN HISTORY

8. Bismarck was born in 1815 to a family of *Junkers* (YOONG-kurz), or Prussian landed aristocrats. After studying the law,

Bismarck served in the army. He did not start his political career until 1847, the year he was elected to the Prussian Diet, or parliament. Bismarck had little sympathy for the revolutions of 1848. To him, liberal and democratic ideals threatened the order of things. He believed that kings should rule by divine right and power should rest in the hands of the Junkers. Bismarck worked to preserve that order and to crush anything that got in its way.

9. After Bismarck became a delegate to the Diet of the German Confederation in 1851, his life's goal began to take form. At the meetings with other states of the confederation, Bismarck became aware that Prussia's interests were often at odds with those of Austria, then the most powerful member of the Diet. Bismarck became convinced that Prussia had to bring the German states together without Austria. After three years as minister to Russia and France, Bismarck took the most important step in his career. In 1862 King William I made Bismarck chancellor, or president and chief minister, of Prussia.

10. Bismarck ruled Prussia with an iron fist. He was called the "Iron Chancellor" because he was a strong leader. He decided on a policy of "blood and iron." This meant that he planned to use military force and war, if necessary, to unite Germany. He hated representative government, or "parliamentary chatterboxes," as he called them. Bismarck handed out orders and expected them to be obeyed. He made the army larger and stronger. Through military might, Bismarck made Prussia the leading German state. He also found that force and war worked well in managing to unite Germany.

SPOTLIGHT ON SOURCES

11. When Bismarck became chancellor in 1862, he went before parliament to give his reasons why Prussia should have a stronger army. As you read this piece, look for the

Activity: Discuss with students to what extent world leaders use *Realpolitik* today.

▲ Otto von Bismarck, a strong believer in military power, united Germany in 1871. Why was he called the "Iron Chancellor"?

word or words that show Bismarck's belief in *Realpolitik.*

> Germany is looking to Prussia, not for liberty but for power. Some German states may be looking for freedom. But that is not the goal of Prussia. Prussia must build up her power and keep it ready for the right moment. We have already missed some good chances to act. Since the Congress of Vienna, Prussia has not been satisfied with her borders. The great questions of the day are not decided by speeches and majority votes. That was the mistake we made in the past. The great questions of the day are decided by blood and iron.
>
> —from *Bismarck's Speeches and Letters,*
> Hermann Schoenfeld, ed.

12. An early chance for Bismarck to use *realpolitik* and a stronger Prussian army

came in 1864. With the help of Austria, Prussia went to war against Denmark. The two German powers were fighting for the provinces of Schleswig (SHLES-vik) and Holstein (HOHL-shtyn). Although the people of these provinces were German, they were ruled by the Danish monarchy. The prize Prussia received from this war was the province of Schleswig, while Austria received Holstein. Bismarck, however, wanted both of the northern German states.

13. After winning the short war with Denmark, Bismarck knew Prussia now had to fight Austria. Why did Bismarck think ◄ this fight was so important to his plans for Prussia? As part of his plan, Bismarck won a promise from France that it would stay out of a war between Prussia and Austria. Italy promised to enter the war on Prussia's side. Then Bismarck picked a quarrel with Austria over Schleswig and Holstein. To many people's surprise, in 1866 Prussia's superior army defeated Austria in just a few weeks. Austria's old-fashioned muzzle guns were no match for the deadly needle guns the Prussians used. As a result of this Seven Weeks' War, Prussia put an end to the German Confederation and Austria's role in it. Austria's power over German affairs ended with its defeat. Prussia then set up the North German Confederation of German states in 1867. Look at the map on this page. What did Bismarck still have to do to ◄ unite Germany once he had defeated Austria?

FRANCO-PRUSSIAN WAR: How did war with France lead to a unified Germany?

14. Bismarck's next move was to defeat France and declare war. Why did Bismarck ◄ see France as a threat to Prussia? The Iron Chancellor reasoned that war with France would bring the southern German states into a union with Prussia. Also, he had his eye on gaining the iron-rich French provinces of Alsace and Lorraine. Oddly enough, Napoleon III, who was then emperor of France, was eager for a war with Prussia. He hoped to destroy Prussia's growing

Activity: Discuss with students whether Bismarck's statement that "the great questions of the day are decided by blood and iron" can be applied to the problems of today's world.

405

power and make himself more popular at home in France by means of a victory.

15. Once the Franco-Prussian War began in 1870, it was clear that Prussia would be the winner. Once again, Prussia's powerful army proved its might. France's army was weak and did not have enough supplies for the troops. As in the Seven Weeks' War with Austria, the Franco-Prussian War was over quickly. It lasted only a few months. Napoleon III was captured, and the victorious German army entered Paris. France lost Alsace and most of Lorraine to Prussia. Bismarck made the country pay a huge **reparation** (rep-uh-RAY-shun) of five billion francs. A reparation is a fine paid to make up for the damage done by the loser during a war.

16. Following the German victory, Bismarck held a historic meeting at Versailles, near Paris. Germany, a new and powerful nation, now made its entrance on the stage of world history. This was because Prussia now had the strength Bismarck needed to form a united German Empire. Strong feelings of nationalism had been stirred by the Franco-Prussian War. These feelings had brought the southern German states into the fight—as Bismarck had shrewdly predicted. With the defeat of France, all German states except Austria formed what became known as the Second German Reich. In January 1871, the princes of the German states met in the Hall of Mirrors at the Palace of Versailles, where they proclaimed Germany a unified nation. At this same meeting, the Prussian King William I was offered the title of emperor of the new nation. Why did the new Germany became a monarchy and not a republic?

ALLIANCES AND POLICIES: What steps did Bismarck take to keep Germany united?

17. Now that Germany was a united nation, Bismarck took steps to keep it that

▼ The loosely organized German Confederation of 34 separate monarchies and four free cities was taken over by Prussia after 1866. What was the name of unified Germany after 1871?

Unification of Germany

- Prussia before the Seven Weeks' War, 1866
- Annexed by Prussia in 1866
- Joined with Prussia to form the North German Confederation in 1867
- South German states. Joined with the North German Confederation in 1871
- Boundary of German Reich (Empire) in 1871

0   200 miles
0   300 kilometers

▲ In the Hall of Mirrors of the Palace of Versailles, King William of Prussia becomes Emperor William I of Germany under the watchful eye of Bismarck (in white).

way. In the years following the Franco-Prussian War, Bismarck tried to form alliances with other nations. How would alliances help a new nation like Germany? In 1878, Bismarck called the Congress of Berlin to try to settle a war between Bulgaria (in eastern Europe) and the Ottoman Empire. He failed to satisfy everyone who took part in the congress. But the meeting improved Germany's ties with Austria.

18. In order to protect Germany from Russia and France, Bismarck formed an alliance with Austria and Italy. This alliance was known as the Triple Alliance. Later, Russia agreed to remain neutral (NOO-trul) in case Germany went to war against a third powerful nation. A neutral nation is one that does not take sides in a war. Bismarck's alliance system was not perfect. Yet it kept Germany in a strong position among other nations and helped prevent a major European war.

19. Bismarck also pushed for policies that would strengthen German unity at home. He believed that all people in Germany should think, talk, and act as Ger-

mans. What problems do you think this would cause later on? Under Bismarck's leadership, all of Germany began to use the same kind of money. He also helped to bring all the railroads into one system. This allowed Germany's economy to grow and its people to prosper.

OUTLOOK

20. Many who study Bismarck judge some of his actions as repressive. But it cannot be denied that without Bismarck, Germany probably would not have become a nation at this time in its history. Before Bismarck, German states were divided and not able to share common goals. Under the strong rule of Bismarck, Germany not only became a united nation, but it also grew to become one of the richest and most powerful countries in the world. However, the world would not forget the ways of Bismarck. The time would come when Germany would have to pay for the Iron Chancellor's mistakes.

Ask: Before 1870 emigration from Germany was high, mostly because of the poor economy. After 1872 emigration dropped and immigration to Germany increased. Ask students to explain this change.

407

CHAPTER REVIEW

VOCABULARY REVIEW

Write each of the following words on a sheet of paper. Then write the correct definition for each word. Use the glossary on pages 728-737 to help you.

1. *Zollverein*
2. depression
3. political repression
4. *Realpolitk*
5. reparation
6. *Junkers*
7. *Reich*
8. *Gymnasium*

SKILL BUILDER: COMPLETING A CHART

▶ Fill in the following chart using the information given in Chapter 6.

The Unification of Germany

STEPS	DATE	RESULTS
1. Napoleon dissolves Holy Roman Empire, reduces number of German states to 100		Confederation of the Rhine is formed
2. After Napoleon's fall from power, Congress of Vienna reduces number of German states to 38	1815	
3.	1830s	German states trade freely with one another without having to pay taxes on trade goods
4.	1848	Frankfurt Assembly meets to draw up a constitution for all German states
5. Bismarck allies Prussia with Austria and declares war on Denmark	1864	
6.	1866	Austria's power over German affairs ends
7. Prussia declares war on France	1870	
8. Princes of the German states meet at the Hall of Mirrors in Versailles		Germany is proclaimed a unified nation

Now use the completed chart to answer the questions that follow.

1. Which group did the German states join after Napoleon's fall from power?
2. What trade union did many German states join?
3. After which event did the German states become a unified nation?

STUDY HINT — Create a time line about Otto von Bismarck. Highlight important events in his life. Then write a summary statement that explains the part Bismarck played in the unification of German states.

SKILL BUILDER: CRITICAL THINKING AND COMPREHENSION

1. Fact *versus* Opinion   A fact is something that can be proved true or false. An opinion is what a person or persons believe but cannot prove.

▶ Write the following sentences on a separate piece of paper. Then write *fact* if the sentence presents a fact. Write *opinion* if the sentence offers an opinion. If the sentence is a fact, state whether it is true or false.

a. "The English inhabit the sea, the French the earth, and the Germans the air."

b. The Frankfurt Assembly failed to unite the German states.

c. Germany was united under Otto von Bismarck as its king.

d. Germany could only be united with the help of a strong army.

e. France lost important territory to Prussia because of the Franco-Prussian War.

2. Point of View

▶ How do you think the members of the Frankfurt Assembly felt when the King of Prussia rejected the assembly's offer to be emperor of Germany? Did the members feel they were offering the king a crown "from the gutter"?

3. Making Judgments

▶ Do you think uniting the German states through "blood and iron" was the right way for Bismarck to have achieved his goal? Support your judgment with historical facts.

4. Hypothesizing
What might have happened had Prussia lost the Seven Weeks' War and the Franco-Prussian War?

5. Classifying

▶ Tell whether the following statements are true or false. If a statement is false, change the words in *italics* to make it true.

a. Germany was *completely unified* after the Seven Weeks' War.

b. At the Frankfurt Assembly, the king of *Austria* was asked to head the German states?

c. The Holy Roman Empire was founded by *Napoleon I.*

ENRICHMENT

1. Read about the childhood and early life of Bismarck. Then write a short essay that explains how Bismarck's later views might have been formed by the experiences of his early life.

2. Draw four outline maps of Germany showing how the country's boundaries changed in 1715, 1806, 1815, and 1871.

3. Do library research on Georg Hegel, philosopher. How did his writings contribute to the spirit of nationalism in Germany? Make a brief oral report to the class.

CHAPTER 7

Italy Is United

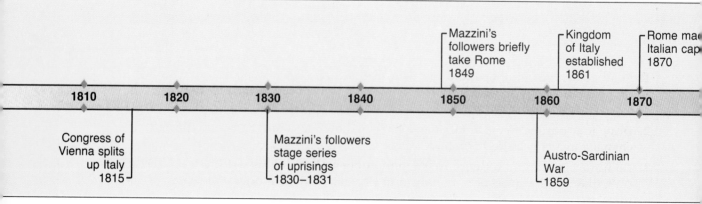

OBJECTIVE: How did strong leaders unite Italy?

1. The Italian patriot Giuseppe Garibaldi fled to New York City after his first attempt to win independence for his country failed. Many distinguished citizens there admired him as a champion of liberty and planned banquets and receptions to honor him. But Garibaldi wanted no official welcome and slipped into the city unannounced on a ferry boat. He refused offers of a free place to stay. Instead he went to Staten Island and took a job in a candle factory. He was clumsy at making candles so he was put to work carrying barrels to the boiling vat. The Italian owner of the factory hated to see such a great man working like that, but Garibaldi insisted. Garibaldi wanted nothing for himself, neither fame nor wealth.

▲ Giuseppe Garibaldi, the leading soldier of the movement for Italian unification, won many admirers by his honesty and unselfishness.

Everything he did was for his country. Four years later, Garibaldi was back in Italy—and this time his revolution succeeded. Thanks to leaders like Garibaldi, the Italian states were able to launch the struggle for independence and unite into a nation.

Mazzini's followers briefly take Rome 1849

Kingdom of Italy established 1861

Rome made Italian cap 1870

1810 1820 1830 1840 1850 1860 1870

Congress of Vienna splits up Italy 1815

Mazzini's followers stage series of uprisings 1830–1831

Austro-Sardinian War 1859

DIVIDED ITALY: Who governed the different parts of Italy after 1815?

2. In 1815, the Congress of Vienna took control of Italy away from France and divided the country into small states and provinces. In the south, Naples and Sicily were joined into the Kingdom of the Two Sicilies. They were returned to the rule of a Bourbon monarch, a relative of the royal families of Spain and France. In central Italy, the Papal States were returned to the pope. The northern states of Lombardy (LAHM-bar-dee) and Venetia (vih-NEE-shuh) became parts of the Austrian Empire. The remaining northern states were independent. Most of them, including Parma (PAR-muh), Modena (MAHD-u-nuh), Lucca (LOO-kuh), and Tuscany (TUS-kuh-nee), had rulers who were friendly to Austria. The most important independent state was the kingdom of Sardinia (sar-DIN-ee-uh). Besides the island of Sardinia, this kingdom included the important areas of Nice (NEES), Savoy, and Piedmont in northwestern Italy near France.

3. Many Italians fought the foreign domination of their country. They wanted a **Risorgimento** (ree-zor-jih-MEN-toh), or revival of the glory Italy had known during ancient Rome and the Renaissance. Patriotic societies were formed to spread nationalistic ideas among the people. To overthrow foreign rulers, a secret society called the **Carbonari** (kar-buh-NAR-ee) was formed. It started rebellions in 1830 and 1831, but these revolts were quickly crushed. Other patriotic groups used letters and pamphlets to carry the message of revolution to the people. One of these patriotic groups was Young Italy, led by Giuseppe Mazzini (joo-SEP-peh maht-SEE-nee).

4. In 1848, Mazzini's followers led uprisings throughout Italy. The next year they seized control of the Papal States and proclaimed a Roman Republic. However, they failed to win the support of most of the peasants and middle class. Austrian troops crushed the rebels in the north, while Louis Napoleon sent French troops to take on the rebels in Rome. There the French army engaged in a two-month battle with an army led by freedom fighter Giuseppe Garibaldi (gar-uh-BAWL-dee). This first attempt to win freedom failed. Both Mazzini and Garibaldi were forced to give up and fled from Italy.

CAVOUR: How did Camillo di Cavour help to unite Italy?

5. After 1849, Count Camillo di Cavour (kah-MEE-loh dee kah-VOOR) became the new leader of the Risorgimento. Cavour

Daily life in . . .

Before the Papal States were united with the rest of Italy, daily life in this region was very restricted. Many of the people's rights were curbed. The Congress of Vienna had abolished religious **toleration** (tahl-uh-RAY-shun), or a government policy that permits people to worship any religion. As a result, after 1815 only the Roman Catholic religion was permitted. As in former times, Jews were forced to live in **ghettos** (GET-ohz), or sections of a city where members of a minority group live because of social, legal, or economic pressure. Jews were also forbidden to own property and were required to attend Catholic church services once a week.

The government was run almost entirely by church officials. Books and newspapers were censored. Anyone expressing opinions not agreed to by the church could be tortured and thrown into prison. The papal government did not want the peasants to learn the ways of the outside world. Education was restricted, and even the construction of railway lines linking the Papal States to the rest of Italy was resisted.

believed deeply in **unification** (yoo-nih-fih-KAY-shun), or the process of uniting the parts of Italy under one government. He decided to make the kingdom of Sardinia the leader of the rest of Italy. In 1852 Cavour became prime minister of Sardinia, which included the important northern region of Piedmont. Cavour built railroads, encouraged the growth of new industries, introduced reforms in the law, and strengthened the military forces. The popularity of the king of Sardinia grew. Cavour's dream of an Italy united under the king of Sardinia was beginning to take shape.

SPOTLIGHT ON SOURCES

6. The leaders of Italian unification did not always agree on the best method of achieving their goal. Mazzini believed that Italy should be a republic like the United States. As a young man, the Italian patriot Giuseppe Garibaldi had also been a strong supporter of the idea of a republic. As he grew older, however, he learned that compromise is sometimes necessary to bring about results. When Mazzini rejected Cavour's idea of uniting Italy under the leadership of the Sardinian king, Garibaldi felt compelled to speak out in favor of Cavour's plan:

> I have been a Republican all my life, but it is not a question of a republic now. I know the Italian masses better than Mazzini, for I have lived with them and lived their life. Mazzini knows the educated classes of Italy and sways their intellects; but there is no making an army from them to drive out the Austrians and the pope; for the mass, for the Italian people, the only banner is 'Unity and the expulsion of the foreigners!'
>
> —*Garibaldi*, by Jasper Ridley. Copyright ©1974 by Jasper Ridley. All rights reserved. Reprinted by permission of Viking Penguin, a division of Penguin Books USA, Inc. and Constable Publishers, London and Curtis Brown, Ltd., London

7. Cavour realized that Italy could not free itself from Austrian control without the help of France. In 1855, Cavour strengthened Sardinia's position when he sided with France in the Crimean War. Three years later, the French emperor, Napoleon III, promised to help drive Austria out of Italy. In return, France would get Savoy and Nice, the French-speaking parts of the kingdom of Sardinia. Cavour hoped to gain control over the northern states of Lombardy and Venetia.

8. In 1859, Cavour cleverly provoked Austria into invading Sardinia. True to his word, Napoleon III sent his army to Sardinia's aid. However, the French emperor then betrayed Cavour's trust by signing a separate peace treaty with Austria. Under the terms of this treaty, France took Nice and Savoy, Sardinia gained Lombardy, and Austria kept control of Venetia.

9. Meanwhile, popular revolts broke out in central Italy. The people of Tuscany, Parma, Modena, and some of the Papal States had driven out their rulers. A plebiscite, or popular vote, was held in 1860, and the people decided to unite with Sardinia. Most of northern Italy was now united in one kingdom.

GARIBALDI IN SOUTHERN ITALY: How did Garibaldi's campaign create the kingdom of Italy?

10. In southern Italy, the struggle for Italian unification was led by Garibaldi. Garibaldi was determined to drive the Bourbons out of southern Italy. With the financial backing of Cavour, he gathered a volunteer army called the Red Shirts. Garibaldi and 1,000 Red Shirts sailed for Sicily, where they defeated an army 20 times larger. Garibaldi then led his army onto the Italian mainland and captured Naples. The victorious army planned to march on to Rome and, possibly, as far north as Venetia.

11. Cavour was alarmed by Garibaldi's plan to attack Rome. The French army had occupied Rome since 1849, and Cavour did not want to go to war with France. To head off Garibaldi, Cavour sent his own army across the Papal States, carefully avoiding Rome. Meanwhile, plebiscites in Sicily and Naples called for union with the north. In the part of the Papal States outside Rome, other plebiscites had the same result. In 1861, the first Italian parliament in history proclaimed the Kingdom of Italy under Victor Emmanuel II of Sardinia. Thousands cheered as Garibaldi and the new king of Italy rode side by side in an open carriage through the streets of Naples.

FINAL STEPS: What steps were necessary to complete the unification of Italy?

11. The unification of Italy was not yet complete. Venetia and a few of the other northern states were still ruled by Austria. Rome was still ruled by the pope and occupied by the French. Italy gained Venetia in 1866 after siding with Prussia against Austria in the Seven Weeks' War. In 1870 the Franco-Prussian War forced France to pull its troops out of Rome, and the Kingdom of Italy promptly took it over. Despite the protests of Pope Pius IX, Rome became the capital of the united Kingdom of Italy in ▶ 1871. Why would the king of Italy prefer to have the capital of his kingdom in Rome?

12. The problems of Italy did not end with unification. Political and financial problems continued to plague the new kingdom well into the twentieth century. Disagreements arose with the popes about how the kingdom of Italy and the papacy should relate to each other. These disagreements were not resolved for many years. There also were continual changes of government. The people of Italy lacked a tradition of democratic rule. The limited monarchy created by the Italian constitution was troubled by corruption. The economic future looked bleak as well. The nation had neither the fertile land to support its growing population nor the coal, iron, and oil needed for industrialization. Many Italians migrated to the United States or to South America. ▶ What role do you think these problems might have played in the rise to power of a strong Italian dictator in the 1920s?

▲ Rising nationalism led to the overthrow of foreign rule and unification of Italy in 1861. What lands were added to Italy after 1866?

OUTLOOK

13. The Unification of Italy was accomplished against great odds. Austria was a powerful force in Italy, and it intended to remain one. It could remain powerful, however, only if Italy stayed divided. Italy was fortunate to have the able and dedicated leadership of Mazzini, Cavour, and Garibaldi in its struggle. Even in the dark years when Mazzini and Garibaldi were forced to leave Italy, the dedication of these men never faltered. Cavour cleverly lured Napoleon III of France into the Italian struggle against Austria. Garibaldi risked his own life in battle and motivated all who served with him. All three men were prime examples of strong leaders. What are the qualities that make a person a strong leader? Which American leaders do you think possess these qualities today?

Background: After Rome became part of Italy, a part of the city was set aside for the pope's use. This part of the city eventually became Vatican City, a small nation-state within the city of Rome.

413

VOCABULARY REVIEW

ghettos   Carbonari

toleration   unification

Risorgimento

1. Many Italians wanted to see a _____ , or resurgence of the glory Italy had known during ancient Rome and the Renaissance.

2. The _____ was a secret society organized to overthrow Italy's foreign rulers.

3. Mazzini, Garibaldi, and Cavour dedicated their lives to achieving the _____ of Italy.

4. A policy of religious _____ permits people of all religions to worship freely.

5. In the Papal States, Jews were forced to live in _____ , or quarters of the cities where members of a minority group live because of social, legal, or economic pressure.

SKILL BUILDER: CREATING A TIME LINE

▶ Below is an incomplete time line. Use the dates and events listed below to complete the time line. The time line at the beginning of this chapter can be used as a reference.

STEPS IN ITALIAN UNIFICATION

1859—Austro-Sardinian War; Sardinia gains Lombardy

1860—Tuscany, Parma, and Modena vote to join the Kingdom of Sardinia

1861—Victor Emmanuel becomes first king of Italy

1866—Italy gains Venetia after Austro-Prussian Seven Weeks' War

1870–1871—Italy gains Rome during Franco-Prussian War

| 1850 | 1860 | 1870 | 1880 |

SKILL BUILDER: CRITICAL THINKING AND COMPREHENSION

1. Fact *versus* Opinion

▶ According to the information presented in this chapter, determine whether each of the following statements is a *fact* or an *opinion*.

a. Mazzini's Young Italy was a better organization than the Carbonari.

b. Count Camillo di Cavour was a clever politician.

c. Life in the Papal States was difficult for Italians who were not Roman Catholic.

d. Italy would have been better off as a democratic republic rather than as a constitutional monarchy.

e. Garibaldi was a military genius on the order of George Washington and Napoleon.

2. Point of View

▶ Read the following quote and identify what Count Cavour's point of view was toward bringing Rome into the new Italian nation.

"The star of Italy is Rome. The Eternal City, around which 25 centuries have accumulated all the glories of the world, must be the capital of Italy."

3. Making Judgments

Do you think the Congress of Vienna was justified in abolishing religious toleration in the Papal States? Why or why not?

4. Hypothesizing

Suppose that Mazzini's and Garibaldi's rebellion of 1848 had been successful. What possible developments might have occurred over the next 5 years as a result of this. Do you think that this might have led to an Italian civil war, with Italians fighting Italians? How do you think Cavour and the king of Sardinia would have reacted? Would other foreign powers, such as Spain, have been tempted to become involved?

ENRICHMENT

1. Garibaldi's defeat of an army 20 times the size of his own would seem to be a good story for a motion picture. Using reference books from the library, find out how he did it. What role did morale and the spirit of nationalism play in this victory?

2. Imagine that you are an editorial cartoonist for a nineteenth-century newspaper. Draw a cartoon expressing your point of view on one of the following:

   a. the revolution of 1848

   b. the role of Mazzini, Cavour, and Garibaldi in the unification of Italy

   c. the entry of Italian troops into Rome in 1870

CHAPTER 8

The Austrian Empire

▲ Francis Joseph was emperor of Austria (later Austria-Hungary) from 1848 to 1916, one of the longest reigns in European history.

OBJECTIVE: How did nationalism cause problems for the Austrian empire?

1. In America, people are citizens of fifty different states. Imagine that, of all of these states, the best jobs could be held only by people from Virginia and Minnesota. From these states would come the people who ran the government, managed the large companies, and became bishops and generals. Virginia and Minnesota would even send out people to govern the other states. If you lived in one of the other 48 states, how would you feel about this arrangement? In the 1800s, there was a similar situation in the Austrian empire. Many different nationalities lived within the empire, each of them with its own territory and its own language. Yet until 1867, all power in the empire was held by only one of these nationalities, the

Germans. After 1867, power was divided between two of the empire's nationalities, Germans and Hungarians. How do you imagine the other nationalities felt about this arrangement? What would you have expected them to do about it?

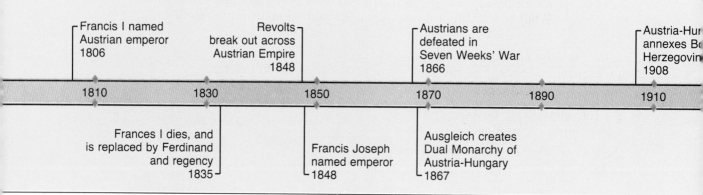

Francis I named Austrian emperor 1806

Revolts break out across Austrian Empire 1848

Austrians are defeated in Seven Weeks' War 1866

Austria-Hur annexes Bo Herzegovin 1908

1810   1830   1850   1870   1890   1910

Frances I dies, and is replaced by Ferdinand and regency 1835

Francis Joseph named emperor 1848

Ausgleich creates Dual Monarchy of Austria-Hungary 1867

Background: Francis Joseph began as a poor ruler who knew little about principles of government. His advisors were older men who always agreed with him to avoid losing their political positions.

UNREST IN THE EMPIRE: Why were feelings of nationalism so strong in the Austrian empire?

2. In 1815, Austria was a land of many peoples. The largest ethnic group was the Germans. Numbering about 12 million, they lived mostly in Austria and Bohemia. Magyars (MAHG-yarz), or Hungarians, numbered about 10 million and lived in Hungary. About 8.5 million Czechs (CHEKS) and Slovaks (SLOH-vahks) and 5 million Poles lived in the northern parts of the empire. In the east and south, Ukrainians (yoo-KRAY-nee-unz), Romanians (roh-MAY-nee-unz), Croats (KROHTS), Serbs, Slovenes (SLOH-veenz), and a small Italian population accounted for an additional 15.5 million people. Each group had its own language and culture. Many wanted self-government within the empire.

3. Amid this nationalist fervor, Austria was ruled by a narrow-minded emperor, Francis I. Francis began his rule in 1806. His bureaucratic government was hostile to reform and suspicious of any new ideas. His philosophy of government was, "Rule, and change nothing." Although he allowed his chancellor Metternich wide powers in dealing with foreign countries, he himself kept a close grip on affairs within the country. His methods for dealing with the empire's ethnic groups was summed up when he said, "Peoples? What does that mean? I know

only subjects!" He tried to control his citizens' discontent by setting up a censorship bureau to make sure that anti-government writings were not printed. When Francis I died in 1835, control was given to a **regency** (REE-jun-see). A regency is a person or group of people who govern when the monarch is unable to do so. In this case the new emperor was mentally disabled. The regency was a group of noblemen who continued the policies of Francis I. Do you think a regency would be likely to undertake any big reform efforts?

UPRISING IN HUNGARY: How did feelings of nationalism lead to revolution?

4. The first revolt in the Austrian empire began in Hungary. Two leaders rose among the Magyars. Count István Széchenyi (IST-vahn SAY-chay-nee) was an aristocrat who favored political, social, and economic reforms. He hoped to lead a national movement to bring about change within the system. At the same time, a more radical leader, Lajos Kossuth, also gained support.

PEOPLE IN HISTORY

5. A lawyer by profession, Lajos Kossuth (LY-ohsh KOH-sooth) was an exciting orator who favored a complete break with Austria. When revolution broke out in

Daily life in . . .

In the 1800s, Vienna was not only the capital of the Austrian empire, but also an important center of European culture. Only Paris and London were larger among European cities. Vienna was known for its beautiful streets and buildings. In the late 1850s the medieval fortifications that surrounded the city were torn down. In their place, a series of eight boulevards was laid out, forming a circle around the center of the city. Called the **Ringstrasse** (RING-shtrah-suh), these boulevards were lined with beautiful public buildings, such as opera houses, libraries, and museums. The buildings were designed to give an impression of **grandeur** (GRAND-yoor), or impressive size. The city attracted scientists and scholars, artists and composers. The tuneful waltzes of Johann Strauss (YOH-hahn SHTROWS) entertained guests at the Hapsburg court, while the symphonies and other works of Johannes Brahms (yoh-HAH-nus BRAHMS) drew the middle class to the concert halls.

Background: The Austrian empire was practically a totalitarian state. Censors banned books that criticized the government. The lower classes paid taxes and served in the army, yet had no voice in government.

417

▲ The Museum of the History of Art is one of the magnificent public buildings on Vienna's Ringstrasse. The statue in the foreground is of Empress Maria Theresa.

France in 1848, Kossuth saw this as a time for Hungary to rise against the Austrians. Speaking before the parliament, he urged the people to remove the "dead hand" of the government in Vienna. Kossuth told them to fight for their liberty. Printed in German and spread throughout the empire, Kossuth's speech inspired revolts not only in Hungary but in other places as well. Why do you think a speech about freedom for Hungary would also be an inspiration for people in other countries?

6. As a result of this revolt, Hungary won almost complete independence from Austria. However, the Magyars refused to share the rights they had won with other nationalities in Hungary. Magyar domination quickly became more repressive than Austrian rule. An army of Croats organized to bring down the Hungarian government. The Austrian government, seeing a way to bring down the new Hungarian government, sent troops to help the Croats. Kossuth responded by declaring complete Hungarian independence from Austria on April 14, 1849.

SPOTLIGHT ON SOURCES

7. Kossuth's speech before the parliament echoed the American Declaration of Independence. Kossuth said, in part:

"The House of Hapsburg has forfeited [given up] its right to the Hungarian throne. We feel a duty to make known the motives and reasons that have impelled us to this decision, so that the civilized world may know that we have not taken this step out of unbounded confidence in our wisdom nor out of revolutionary fervor, but that it is an act of extreme necessity which we have had to adopt in order to save from utter destruction a nation that has been driven to the limits of a most enduring patience."

—from *Selected Speeches of Kossuth,* Francis W. Newman

The Magyars put up a strong fight. However, the revolt was crushed, but not until the Austrians called in a Russian army to

Background: Although he led the Magyars in Hungary, Kossuth was a Slav. He appealed to minor nobles like himself who had inherited honorable family names but little in the way of wealth.

help. By the end of 1849, the Austrians once again ruled Hungary. Kossuth, however, escaped to the United States, where his speeches about freedom and democracy ► won a large audience. Why would a person like Kossuth be popular with the American people?

8. In June of 1848, a congress of Slavic peoples was held in Prague. **Slavs** (SLAHVS) are people whose native language is in the Slavic (SLAH-vik) family of languages. The biggest Slavic country is Russia. Within the Austrian empire, Slavic peoples included the Czechs, Poles, Slovaks, Ukrainians, Serbs, Croats, and Slovenes—just about everyone except the Germans and the Magyars. Slavs from all over the empire met to show their equality with Magyars and Germans. Prague, the city where the meeting took place, was in the northern part of the Austrian empire. It was the capital of the former kingdom of Bohemia, populated mainly by Czechs but with a minority of Germans. During the meetings, anti-German feelings ran high. Marches by Slav radicals led to fighting in the streets of Prague. The local Austrian officials sent in soldiers to put down the fighting and end the Slav Congress.

TWO KINGDOMS: What caused the Austrian empire to be split into two kingdoms?

9. In 1848, Francis Joseph became Austrian emperor. He was only 18 years old when he became emperor. Francis Joseph tried to put the empire back together by stamping out ethnic differences. He made German the language of government and schools. He wanted to get rid of differences in customs and laws. However, his changes only stirred more nationalist feelings among Magyars and Slavs.

10. Austria changed its policy after it was defeated by Prussia in the Seven Weeks' War of 1866. Having lost both land and prestige, Francis Joseph knew he must find a way to hold on to what was left of his empire. To save the empire, he accepted the Compromise of 1867, which made Austria and Hungary equal but united countries. Hungary had its own government, but the two countries had a single foreign policy.

▼ The revolts of 1848 broke out in many different parts of the Austrian empire. Here a group of Polish demonstrators protest the continuing Austrian rule of a part of their country.

Change along the Danube The lands along the Danube River have been swept by political change for hundreds of years. The political turmoil discouraged people from using the river, and it never became the great trade route that its length would suggest.

The map on this page compares the political geography along the Danube today with the political geography of 1867. Read the facts about the changing political geography along the Danube. Think about how political change alters trading patterns when you study the map.

Austria-Hungary covered much more territory in 1867 than today's independent nations of Austria and Hungary.

Other present-day countries that occupy lands that were part of Austria-Hungary in 1867 include the Czech Republic, Slovakia, Poland, Ukraine, Romania, Croatia, and Italy.

In 1867, Austria-Hungary had seaports at Trieste (tree-ES-teh) and Fiume (fee-OO-may).

Trieste is now in Italy. Fiume, now called Rijeka (ree-YEH-kuh), is in present-day Croatia.

Present-day Austria, Hungary, the Czech Republic, and Slovakia are landlocked countries. Landlocked countries have no seaports. Their trade moves on rivers, roads, and railroads, and they generally are poorer than countries on the coastline.

Study the map on this page. Then answer these questions.

1. Name the present-day nations that the Danube River passes through or borders.

2. Which of these nations were parts of Austria-Hungary in 1867?

3. Who controlled the mouth of the Danube River in 1867? Was this nation friendly or hostile to Austria-Hungary? Who controls the mouth of the Danube today?

4. Why do you think the Danube River is not the great trading route its length would suggest?

Change Along the Danube River

— Austria-Hungary in 1867
— Present-day boundaries
AUSTRIA Names of present-day countries

▲ The Royal Palace rises above the Danube River in Budapest, the capital of Hungary. The palace was Francis Joseph's residence when he was in Hungary.

Magyar became the official language of Hungary. This arrangement was called the **Ausgleich** (OWS-glykh), or separation. The empire was now called Austria-Hungary. Francis Joseph was the emperor of Austria and the king of Hungary.

11. While Magyars and Germans were pleased by the new law, other groups like the Slavs felt left out again. Only those who adopted German or Magyar languages and customs were able to get ahead in the new Austro-Hungarian Empire. A bill to give Czechs in Bohemia their own government failed because of Magyar and German opposition. By 1900, Slavic anger was ready to explode. In 1908, Austria-Hungary annexed the provinces of Bosnia (BOZ-nee-uh) and Herzegovina (hurt-seh-goh-VEE-nuh). These provinces were in the Balkan Peninsula on the border between Austria-Hungary and the Ottoman empire. Austria-Hungary had occupied them since 1878 but until now they had remained Ottoman possessions. Both provinces were inhabited by Slavic people related to the Serbs. Serbian nationalists were upset, because they had hoped to add the area to their own kingdom. Austria-Hungary's action not only upset Serbia but also added more dissatisfied Slavs to the empire.

OUTLOOK

12. Nationalism was a strong challenge to the Austrian empire. It is still a powerful force in Eastern Europe today. Nationalism has led to the breakup of Czechoslovakia into the republics of Czech and Slovakia. It has also led to the breakup of Yugoslavia and the Soviet Union. In the former Soviet Union there were more than 200 ethnic groups. The demand of these ethnic groups for self-rule or independence was one cause of the breakup of the Soviet Union into 15 independent republics. Since the breakup, ethnic unrest has continued to plague Russia, Armenia, Azerbaijan, and other newly independent countries. Why do you think national groups and ethnic groups continue to struggle for independence?

421

CHAPTER REVIEW

VOCABULARY REVIEW

Write each number and word on a sheet of paper. Then write the letter of the definition next to the word it defines.

1. regency
2. Slav
3. Ausgleich
4. grandeur
5. Ringstrasse

a. the event that made Austria and Hungary equal but united countries

b. a series of broad boulevards that replaced the old city walls of Vienna

c. a body of people who govern a kingdom in the absence or disability of the monarch

d. impressive size

e. a person whose native language is Slavic, including Czech, Polish, Serbo-Croatian, Slovenian, and Ukrainian

SKILL BUILDING: MAKING A TIME LINE

A time line is a line going from left to right that shows a group of events in chronological order. The purpose of a timeline is to place events in historical perspective.

The following steps will help you make your own timeline entitled "Important Events in the History of the Austrian Empire."

1. Below you will find events to include in your timeline. Eliminate any that do not fit the subject of this timeline.

    1267–Hapsburg rule begins

    1789–French Revolution

    1848–Revolutions break out in Europe

    1848–Zachary Taylor is elected President of the United States

    1848–Francis Joseph becomes Austrian emperor

    1866–Prussia defeats Austria

    Compromise of 1867 is passed

    1908–Austria annexes Bosnia and Herzegovina

2. Take the events you have chosen and draw a timeline. Now place marks on the timeline. The first and last marks will be the first and last events on your timeline. The marks of the remaining events should be spaced so as to give an accurate impression of how many years have passed.

3. Write the date above the mark. Write what happened on that date below the mark. You may want to write what happened on an angle to fit it all in.

SKILL BUILDING: CRITICAL THINKING AND COMPREHENSION

1. Fact *versus* Opinion

▶ Write the letters a through j on a piece of paper. If the statement below is a fact, write (F). If it is an opinion, write (O).

a. The Austrian empire was a land of many cultures and languages.

b. The most nationalistic group was the Poles.

c. The first revolution in the Austrian empire took place in Hungary.

d. Kossuth based his speech before the Hungarian parliament on the American Declaration of Independence.

e. The language and culture of the Magyars was superior to those of the Serbians and the Croats.

f. Most Magyars were pleased by the Compromise of 1867.

g. Francis Joseph treated all ethnic groups in the empire fairly.

h. Austria changed its policy toward its ethnic minorities after it was defeated by Prussia.

i. One way to restore unity in an empire is to stamp out ethnic differences.

j. Kossuth was a more radical Magyar leader than Szechenyi.

2. Point of View

What point of view was Emperor Francis I expressing toward Austria's many ethnic groups when he said, "Peoples? What does that mean? I know only subjects."

3. Making Judgments

In your opinion, what was the most important thing that kept the Austrian empire together in spite of the ethnic differences of the people?

4. Hypothesizing

Reread paragraph 11. What hypothesis can be made about the future of the Austrian empire from the information in this paragraph?

ENRICHMENT

1. Francis Joseph was only eighteen years old when he was crowned emperor of Austria. Imagine that you, too, are to take over high office at a young age. List some of the problems that you might face because of your youth. What might be some advantages of being such a young ruler?

2. Using the information in paragraph 2, make a circle graph that illustrates the percentage each ethnic group made up of the Austrian population.

3. Imagine you are a reporter for a Magyar newspaper assigned to cover a debate between Count Szechenyi and Lajos Kossuth on Hungary's future. Write an article that describes the arguments and points of view expressed by these two leaders in the debate.

CHAPTER 9

Decline of the Ottoman Empire

This scene of a Constantinople market place suggests some of the differences between Ottoman and European ways of life in the 1800s.

OBJECTIVE: What caused the breakup of the Ottoman empire?

1. To most people, fashions or clothing styles are mainly matters of personal taste. In the nineteenth century, however, what people wore might sometimes relate to the survival of an empire! In southeastern Europe, the Ottoman Empire was losing power and influence. Stuck in its traditional ways, it was being left behind. When its leaders finally began a movement for reform and modernization, one of the first steps was to introduce the **fez.** The fez is a brimless hat with a flat top and a tassel. This hat replaced the turban, which could be worn only by Muslims. Anyone could wear the fez. Although this and other reforms were attempted, they only put off the empire's eventual collapse.

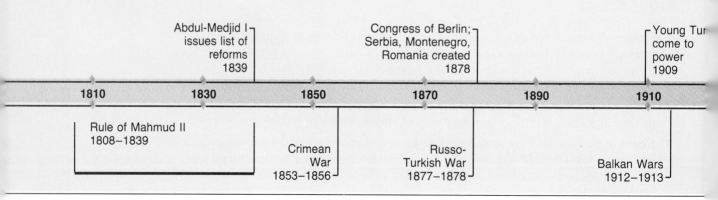

Abdul-Medjid I
issues list of
reforms
1839

Congress of Berlin;
Serbia, Montenegro,
Romania created
1878

Young Tur
come to
power
1909

1810   1830   1850   1870   1890   1910

Rule of Mahmud II
1808–1839

Crimean
War
1853–1856

Russo-
Turkish War
1877–1878

Balkan Wars
1912–1913

PROBLEMS IN THE EMPIRE: What problems weakened the Ottoman empire in the early 1800s?

2. At the beginning of the 1800s, the Ottoman empire covered a huge area. The empire extended as far east as Persia. It stretched over most of northern Africa. It also included all the land in southeastern Europe south of the Danube River. This area of southeastern Europe is known as the Balkans (BAHL-kunz). Locate the Balkans
▶ on the map on the next page. What was the northernmost Balkan nation?

3. As the nineteenth century began, the Ottoman empire was faced with two problems that threatened its unity and strength. The first problem was the lessening influence of the sultan, or emperor, over the empire's many provinces. Many of the **pashas** (POSH-uz), or men of high rank who ruled the provinces, were interested only in increasing their own power. They further weakened the sultan's power by keeping the provinces' tax money for themselves.

4. The second problem facing the empire was the rise of nationalism, especially among the peoples of the Balkans. People of many different nationalities lived in the Balkans. Among them were Greeks, Albanians, Romanians, Serbs, Croats, and Bulgarians. Each nationality had a different language, culture, and history from that of their Ottoman rulers. In addition, most of the people of the Balkans were Christians, while their rulers were Muslims. These differences weakened Balkan loyalty to the Ottoman empire.

5. Under Ottoman rule, the people of the Balkans had few freedoms. They could worship their own religion freely, and they were given control over local affairs. Yet, as Christians, the people of the Balkans were denied rights that were granted to the Muslims. They were not permitted to carry weapons. They could not wear fine clothing, nor could they be seen wearing the color green because it was sacred to Muslims. Their houses could not be grander or bigger than those of the Muslims. The heavy taxes they had to pay supported an army in which they could not serve and a government in which they had no voice.

BALKAN UPRISINGS: How successful were the Balkan revolutions of the early 1800s?

6. In the early 1800s, Balkan leaders began to urge revolt and independence from Ottoman control. Resentment was growing

Daily life in . . .

The Tanzimat period of reform had as large an impact on Ottoman culture as it did on Ottoman law and society. In the fifty years after the first Ottoman printing press was developed in 1835, almost 3,000 books were published. Most books dealt with religion, but poetry was also very popular. In addition to books, the theater provided a place where new ideas could be presented. Many of the earliest plays were produced for foreigners or the non-Islamic population. The first Turkish-language theater was not founded until 1867. However, once the Ottoman theater got underway, it proved to be extremely popular with the people in many parts of the country.

In 1867, a Museum of Antiquities was established and later made a part of the Imperial Museum. Laws were passed that prevented foreigners from removing important archeological finds from the empire. In 1875, a school was opened to train Ottoman archeologists and museum specialists. Pride and interest in Ottoman heritage were outgrowths of the reform period.

School attendance began to soar. Between 1867 and 1895, the number of elementary schools and students attending them more than doubled. By 1895, 90 percent of the boys and over 33 percent of the girls were attending elementary school.

Background: Mahmud's reforms regarding European-style dress did not apply to women. Following Islamic custom, women continued to cover themselves from head to foot except for one or both eyes.

425

among the people of the Balkans. Inspired by the success of the French Revolution, the Serbs and the Greeks were the first to revolt. The Serbs rose up against the Ottomans in 1804. Although their revolt was unsuccessful, the Serbs were given a larger role in local government. The Greek Revolution of 1821 was more successful. With the support of Great Britain, France, and Russia, the Greeks overcame the Ottoman army after several years of bloody fighting. In 1829 Greece became the first Balkan nation to win its independence. Why do you think the nations of Europe were more willing to help the Greeks than the Serbs?

SPOTLIGHT ON SOURCES

7. One of Greece's strongest supporters was the English poet George Gordon Byron. Besides contributing a large amount of money himself, he helped raise money from other English supporters of the Greek cause.

Byron even travelled to Greece in 1823 to fight in the Greek war for independence. He took command of a group of soldiers and helped plan the attack on a Turkish-held fortress. In the following letter to a Greek friend, he explained why he felt he must take up arms for the Greek cause:

> Dear Friend, . . . Greece has ever been for me, as it must be for all men of any feeling or education, the promised land of valor [bravery], of the arts, and of liberty; nor did the time I passed in my youth in traveling among her ruins at all chill my affection for the birthplace of heroes. . . . To see myself serving, by your side and under your eyes, in the cause of Greece, will be to me one of the happiest events of my life.
>
> —from *The Letters of Lord Byron*,
> Mathilde Blind, ed.

Byron died in Greece and became a Greek national hero. Why do you suppose the Greeks honor him?

▼ Strong nationalist feelings in the Balkans pushed back the boundaries of the Ottoman Empire between 1870 and 1914. What new nations arose in the Balkans during this period?

The Balkans, 1870-1914

— Boundary of Ottoman Empire in 1870
— Boundary of Ottoman Empire in 1913 after the Balkan War
▨ Ottoman Empire in 1914
☐ New nations with date of Independence

0   200 miles
0   300 kilometers

OTTOMAN REFORMS: Why did the reforms of the early nineteenth century fail to save the Ottoman empire?

8. As the nineteenth century began, a struggle for the Ottoman throne broke out. The fight pitted the forces of westernization against the forces of religious tradition. Rulers would take the throne, only to be deposed or killed very quickly. By 1808, only one Ottoman male in the ruling line was still alive. He was Mahmud II (mah-MOOD).

PEOPLE IN HISTORY

9. Mahmud II is known as the Peter the Great of the Ottoman Empire. Like Peter, and unlike most earlier Ottoman rulers, Mahmud tried to make the empire more like the nations of western Europe. Mahmud believed that reforms and modernization would help hold the empire together. Mahmud built a new army and strengthened the central government. He set up a postal system and oversaw the publication of the first Turkish newspaper. Mahmud encouraged the learning of European languages. In this way, he hoped to increase contacts with the west and to expose his people to western sciences and technology. Students were sent overseas to study at European universities, while European advisers were brought in to help the empire modernize. New high schools were opened, although Mahmud lacked the money to make free public education available to everyone. Mahmud also introduced European customs and European-style dress. He replaced the traditional turban, the hat worn by Muslims, with the fez. Mahmud's goal was to eliminate differences in appearance between Muslims and non-Islamic people. Why would eliminating differences between Muslims and non-Islamic people be important to the survival of the empire?

10. Although Mahmud could not reverse the decline of the Ottoman empire, he did slow it down. His reforms paved the way for even greater changes that began after his death in 1839. Mahmud's son, Abdul-Medjid I (ab-dool-muh-JEED), succeeded him to the throne of the empire.

11. In 1839, Abdul-Medjid I issued a document called the Hatt-i Sharif (HOT-ee shah-REEF), which outlined his reforms. It abolished capital punishment without a trial and guaranteed all citizens equality before the law regardless of race or creed. This period in Ottoman history is called the **Tanzimat** (TAHN-zee-maht). Tanzimat refers to this reorganization of government and society that took place. All citizens were now eligible for public office. Christians no longer had to pay special taxes and they could serve in the army. The number of schools, newspapers, and books increased. Western manners and ideas became popular.

12. The changes of the Tanzimat period did not succeed in holding the empire together. Most people did not accept the reforms. Most Muslims were happy with the earlier rules and customs. They did not want the Christians to be their equals. Even the Christians were unhappy. Most Christians wanted independence, not a reformed empire. As a result, the empire continued to lose support. The government also sank deeper and deeper into debt, as it borrowed heavily to pay for its reforms.

EUROPEAN INTERFERENCE: How did the nations of Europe take advantage of the Ottoman empire's weakness?

13. The large nations of Europe knew that the Ottoman empire was weak. In fact, the Russian czar described the empire in this way: "We have a sick man on our hands—a man gravely ill. It will be a grave misfortune if one of these days he slips through our hands, especially before the necessary arrangements are made." How would you explain what the czar meant?

14. Russia had its own plans for the "sick man." Russia wanted control of the Dardanelles (dar-duh-NELZ). The Dardanelles connect the Black Sea with the Mediterra-

Ask: Which Russian czar made this quote describing the Ottoman empire as "a sick man"? How do you know?

427

nean Sea. The Dardanelles were Russia's only access to the Mediterranean. As long as the Dardanelles stayed in Ottoman hands, Russian access to the Mediterranean could be cut off at any time. This was unacceptable to the Russians, who also sought a warm-water port for their mighty fleet. To gain control of the Dardanelles, Russia would have to take the Ottoman capital of Constantinople.

15. In its first attempt to gain the Dardanelles, Russia was defeated by the Ottomans during the Crimean War (1853-1856). The war took its name from the Crimean peninsula, on the Black Sea in the southern part of Russia, where most of the fighting took place. The Ottomans were aided in this war by Britain, France, and in the last year of the war, the Italian kingdom of Sardinia. Why would these countries come to the aid of the Ottoman empire? When the Russians tried again, more than twenty years later, they were more successful. In the Russian-Turkish war of 1877–1878, the European nations remained neutral, or not aligned with either side. This time, without European aid, the Ottomans lost. In the Treaty of San Stefano, which ended the war, the Russians let the Ottomans keep Constantinople. However, the treaty forced the Ottomans to give up much of their empire in the Balkan peninsula.

16. The terms of the Treaty of San Stefano pleased only Russia. Great Britain, France, Germany, and Austria-Hungary objected to so much Russian power in the Balkans. They demanded that all European nations agree to any treaty having to do with the Balkan region. Russia gave in and met with the other nations at Berlin in 1878. At the Congress of Berlin, the nations decided to set up three independent Balkan nations: Serbia, Montenegro (mahnt-uh-NEE-groh), and Romania. Bulgaria was granted the right to govern itself but remained within the Ottoman empire. Many of the European powers took control of Ottoman territory. Russia took some land on the south side of the Caucasus Mountains. Austria-Hungary took over the governing of Bosnia and Herzegovina, although for the time being they remained part of the Ottoman empire. The island of Cyprus came under British control.

▼ British cavalry (soldiers on horseback) attack Russian troops in the Crimean War. This was one of the last wars in which cavalry played an important part.

THE BOILING POINT.

▲ As this cartoon from the early 1900s suggests, wars in the Balkan peninsula were a constant threat to the peace of all of Europe.

17. Just before the Russian-Turkish War, a new leader, Abdul-Hamid II (ahb-DOOL hah-MEED), came to power in Turkey. Many hoped that Abdul-Hamid II would reform the government further, and in fact a constitution was put into force at the end of 1876. The constitution provided for a two-house parliament, with one house appointed and the other elected. However, the constitution left so much power in the hands of the sultan that after 1877 parliament did not meet for more than 30 years. During these years, secret societies began to form among Turkish military students who wanted to see a more effective parliament. One secret group, the Young Turks, was finally able to force Abdul-Hamid II off his throne in 1909. The Young Turks set about restoring the Ottoman empire to its former glory.

18. The empire that the Young Turks dreamed of was weakened by several events. Just before the Young Turks came to power, Bulgaria declared its independence. In 1908, Bosnia and Herzegovina were annexed by Austria-Hungary, or made part of Austria-Hungary. The Young Turks were unable to stop these events. Then, in 1912, Greece, Serbia, Montenegro, and Bulgaria attacked Turkey in what was the beginning of the Balkan Wars. Between 1912 and 1913, the Balkan nations succeeded in driving the Ottomans almost out of Europe. By the wars' end, the city of Constantinople and a small area around it were all that was left of the Ottoman empire in Europe. The new Balkan nation of Albania joined the five other independent Balkan states.

19. The Balkan Wars so preoccupied the Young Turk government that no democratic reforms were ever enacted. In their fight to keep what was left of the empire together, the Young Turks set up a **military dictatorship**. In such a government, a leader or groups of leaders of the armed forces had absolute power. Why would this type of government appeal to some people? The dreams of Mahmud II that were first expressed 100 years earlier were forgotten.

OUTLOOK

20. Part of the reason the Ottoman empire declined was the unwillingness of its people to give up their traditional ways. The Ottomans were slow to accept western forms of government, western education, and western agricultural and industrial technology. Many critics today point out that the United States is suffering from many of the same problems. They say the United States is falling behind Japan and some western European nations. These critics say Americans have been slow to adopt Japanese methods of production. They say that American education has been slow to provide students with the skills necessary to survive in a technological world. Do you ◄ think the United States is going to experience a decline like that of the Ottoman empire? Why or why not?

VOCABULARY REVIEW

Write each of the following words on a sheet of paper. Then write the correct definition for each word. Use the glossary on pages 728-738 to help you.

1. pashas

2. fez

3. Tanzimat

4. military dictatorship

SKILL BUILDER: MAKING A CHART

Charts can be useful tools for summarizing and organizing important dates and events in history. Charts present information in brief by making use of rows and columns. To make a chart, first decide what the topic of your chart is and create a title for it. Then decide what information will go in each of the columns of the chart and create headings for each column. Finally, fill in the appropriate information under each heading to complete your chart.

▶ The chart below has been started for you. On a sheet of paper, fill in the missing items.

NATIONALISM IN THE BALKANS

Balkan Nation	Date of Independence	How Independence Was Won
Greece		Revolt from Ottoman Empire
Serbia		Congress of Berlin
Montenegro		
Romania		
Bulgaria		

SKILL BUILDER: CRITICAL THINKING AND COMPREHENSION

 1. Fact *versus* Opinion

▶ Write the letters a through h on a piece of paper. If the statements below are fact, write **F**. If they are opinion, write **O**.

a. Most of the people who lived in the Balkan peninsula were Christians, while their rulers were Ottoman Muslims.

b. The main reason why the Ottoman empire declined was its failure to modernize.

430

c. The success of the French Revolution inspired the people of the Balkans to become independent.

d. Mahmud II introduced more reforms than any other Ottoman ruler.

e. Muslims supported the reforms of the Tanzimat wholeheartedly.

f. Russia failed twice to capture Constantinople.

g. At the Congress of Berlin, many European powers took control of Ottoman territory.

h. In their effort to keep the empire together, the Young Turks made the government more democratic.

2. Drawing Conclusions

▶ Reread the quote from Lord Byron's letter in paragraph 7. How did Lord Byron feel about Greece?

3. Predicting

▶ Reread the quote in paragraph 13. What did the Russian czar think would happen to the Ottoman empire? What did he mean by "necessary arrangements"?

4. Hypothesizing

a. Do you think that if a reform-minded leader like Mahmud II had come along earlier that the Ottoman empire might have been saved? Why or why not?

b. Imagine that the peoples of the Balkans had similar languages, cultures, religions, and histories. What do you think might have happened to the Ottoman empire? Explain why.

ENRICHMENT

1. Draw a map that shows the location of the Aegean Sea, the Dardanelles, the Sea of Marmara, Constantinople, the Bosporus, and the Black Sea. When you have finished your map, explain why the Dardanelles were so important to the Russians.

2. Write a letter to a friend in Europe describing the changes brought about by Mahmud II from the point of view of (a) an Islamic religious leader and (b) a Turkish teenager.

3. Locate George Gordon Byron's poem "On This Day I Complete My Thirty-sixth Year." After reading the poem, summarize what it says about Byron's feelings for Greece and its struggle for independence.

4. Suppose that you are one of the "Young Turks" at about the time that the Young Turks took over the Ottoman government. Write a letter to a friend in western Europe explaining the Young Turk movement. Describe the condition of the Ottoman empire and its government. Then tell what your group hopes to do to make things better.

UNIT REVIEW

SUMMARY

In the nineteenth century, nationalism and liberalism forced changes in the map and the governments of Europe. In Great Britain, the political rights of the people were increased. By the late 1800s, men no longer had to own property to be able to vote or run for office. France experienced a century of turmoil, as republics and empires rose and fell. By the end of the century, however, a republican government was firmly in place. In Russia, change came more slowly. Peasants and serfs were given greater freedom, but it was not until early in the twentieth century that parliamentary government was introduced. Prussia had to wage war with its European neighbors in order to unite the many Germans states into one empire. For Italy, the challenge was to throw out foreign rulers and unite the country under one leader. By 1870, Italy had achieved its goal. The Austrians and Ottomans saw their empires weaken as the many ethnic groups living within their borders demanded independence.

SKILL BUILDER: READING A MAP

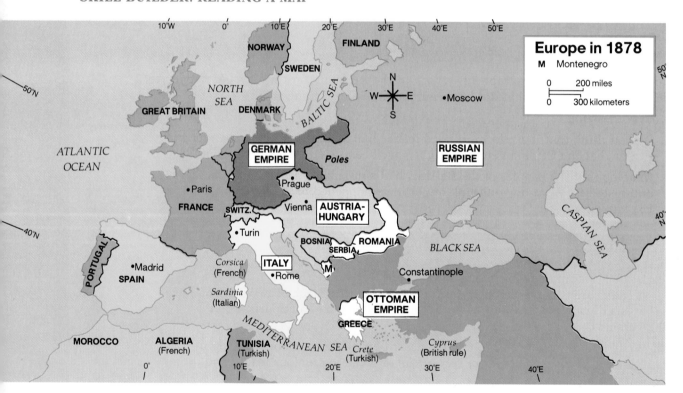

1. Which empire controlled Crete in 1878?

2. Which nations were landlocked in 1878?

3. How many Balkan nations had achieved independence by 1878?

4. Why do you think the British were pleased with gaining control of Cyprus in 1878?

5. Why were the Russians so interested in gaining control of the Dardanelles when they had good ports along the Baltic Sea?

432

SKILL BUILDER: CRITICAL THINKING AND COMPREHENSION

1. Fact *versus* Opinion

1-1. Which one of the following statements is a fact?
   a. The nineteenth century was a time of great progress.
   b. The rulers of Europe during the nineteenth century were wise and able men.
   c. In 1900, France was the only major country of Europe that was a republic.
   d. Otto von Bismarck was the greatest statesman of the nineteenth century.

1-2. Which one of the following statements is an opinion?
   a. The Austrian empire became Austria-Hungary in 1867.
   b. Italian unification was completed in 1870.
   c. Britain had the best government in Europe after 1867.
   d. Czar Alexander II was assassinated in 1881.

1-3. Which of the following statements is a fact?
   a. Napoleon III was a charming person.
   b. The foreign policy of Napoleon III was not well planned.
   c. Napoleon III's reign was a brilliant era in French history.
   d. The Second Empire of Napoleon III lasted 18 years.

2. Cause and Effect

▶ Match the cause in the left column with the effect in the right column.

Cause	Effect
1-1. Prussia quickly defeated France in 1870.	**a.** Greece gained its independence.
1-2. Garibaldi successfully invaded Sicily and Naples.	**b.** The Crimean War was fought.
1-3. The Ottoman empire weakened.	**c.** Almost all British men had the right to vote.
1-4. The Reform Acts were passed by Parliament.	**d.** The Second Empire of Napoleon III collapsed.
1-5. The Congress of Vienna sought to establish a balance of power in Europe.	**e.** The kingdom of Italy came into being.
1-6. Russia wanted an outlet from the Black Sea.	**f.** There were no major European wars for many years after 1815.

ENRICHMENT

1. Write a one-page essay explaining which nation of Europe you would have wanted to live in during the nineteenth century. Be sure to provide reasons for your choice based on historical facts.

2. Use information in the library to help you compare the lives, rights, and roles of women in nineteenth century England with the lives, rights, and roles of women in the Ottoman empire during the same time period. Put the results of your research into a written report.

3. Prepare a book of drawings that illustrates the key events that took place in one European nation during the nineteenth century.

UNIT 9

ESL/LEP Strategy: In small groups, have students create drawings, collages, or other visual displays showing one of the changes brought by the Industrial Revolution. Students can choose an invention, a scientific discovery, a cultural transformation, or a change due to urbanization and socialization.

THE INDUSTRIAL REVOLUTION

OBJECTIVE: Unit 9 will introduce you to a period in history when many important inventions and breakthroughs were made in technology, science, and medicine. You will be able to list and discuss the reasons why an Industrial Revolution changed the course of history throughout the world.

John Kay
invents the
flying shuttle
1733

James Watt
invents the
steam engine
1769

Eli Whitney
invents the
cotton gin
1793

| 1720 | 1740 | 1760 | 1780 | 1800 |

Empress Catherine II
of Russia begins rule
1762

French
Revolution
begins
1789

First steamboat
reach commerc
success is Fulto
Clermont
1807

▲ The women are carding, drawing, and twisting cotton cloth at a textile mill. Why do you think men are not shown?

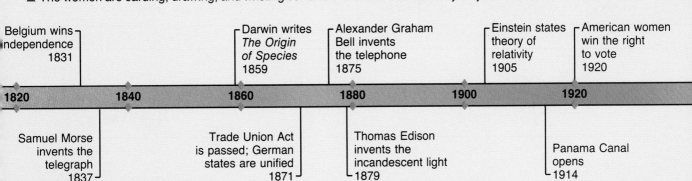

Belgium wins
independence
1831

Darwin writes
*The Origin
of Species*
1859

Alexander Graham
Bell invents
the telephone
1875

Einstein states
theory of
relativity
1905

American women
win the right
to vote
1920

1820   1840   1860   1880   1900   1920

Samuel Morse
invents the
telegraph
1837

Trade Union Act
is passed; German
states are unified
1871

Thomas Edison
invents the
incandescent light
1879

Panama Canal
opens
1914

CHAPTER 1

Industry and Agriculture

▲ This colored engraving shows spinning, reeling, and boiling of yarn to make Irish linen in County Down, Ireland 1783.

OBJECTIVE: How did the changes in industry and agriculture that began in England lead to the Industrial Revolution?

1. At about the same time as the American and French revolutions were taking place, there was another revolution. This revolution was to bring great changes into people's lives in many parts of the world. In fact, this revolution changed the western world from a rural, agricultural society to an urban, industrial society. The change marked the beginning of the modern world. This revolution also helped to bring the slave trade to an end. Before this revolution, the slave trade was an important part of

Great Britain's economy. Afterward, Great Britain no longer needed the income from the slave trade. Instead, world trade of goods produced especially in England made Great Britain one of the wealthiest nations of the world. There were no uprisings or

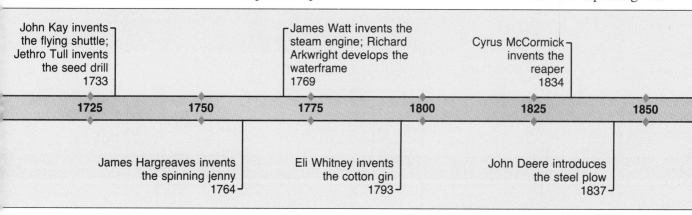

John Kay invents the flying shuttle; Jethro Tull invents the seed drill 1733

James Watt invents the steam engine; Richard Arkwright develops the waterframe 1769

Cyrus McCormick invents the reaper 1834

1725　　1750　　1775　　1800　　1825　　1850

James Hargreaves invents the spinning jenny 1764

Eli Whitney invents the cotton gin 1793

John Deere introduces the steel plow 1837

wars in this revolution, which began in Great Britain during the early 1700s. Instead, this revolution brought a new way of living and making things. For this reason it is known as the **Industrial Revolution.**

COTTAGE INDUSTRY: How were goods made in England before the early 1700s?

2. During the 1600s, England was a nation of farmers. However, many farm families earned extra income by producing goods using hand tools and working in their homes. This simple method of making goods at home is called **cottage industry.** Textiles, or cloth, was one of the leading products of England's cottage industry by the early 1700s. Merchants usually brought raw cotton or wool to a worker's home. There, the whole family often worked together to sort the fibers and spin them into thread, using a hand-operated spinning wheel. Family members then wove this thread into cloth, using a hand-operated loom. The finished cloth was returned to the merchant, who paid the family for its work.
▶ Why do you think textiles were a leading product of the cottage industry?

3. By the early 1700s, the demand for cloth had grown rapidly both in England and in many other lands. England's colonies provided the raw cotton England needed, as well as many other important raw materials, such as lumber, rice, and tobacco. In addition, the colonies became an important market in which to sell textiles and other English goods. The cottage industry was not able to meet this great increase in demand for goods. As a result, England began to search for new ways to produce more goods for its own people and for the colonists.

INVENTIONS: How did new inventions and discoveries help to bring the Industrial Revolution to England?

4. New inventions in England soon changed the way textiles were produced. In 1733, John Kay invented the flying shuttle, a new hand-operated machine that wove cloth at great speed. As cloth was made faster, the demand for thread also grew. In 1764, another machine called the spinning jenny made it possible for one person to spin sixteen threads at a time. The spinning jenny was invented by James Hargreaves. About five years later, Richard Arkwright invented another spinning machine called the water frame. The water frame spun cotton fibers into thread at a speed even faster than the spinning jenny. Then in the 1780s, Samuel Crompton invented the spinning mule. The large spinning mule combined ideas from both the spinning jenny and the water frame to produce a stronger, finer thread.

PEOPLE IN HISTORY

5. Richard Arkwright was a barber and wigmaker from Preston, England. After his water frame became popular, Arkwright built many cotton textile mills and hired hundreds of people to work in them. The water frame needed more than human power to work. By 1771, Arkwright had set up many of his mills along streams to use water power. The mills were also called **factories,** or buildings where machinery was operated by workers to make textiles or other products.

6. One of the most important inventions in England was the **steam engine.** The steam engine was invented in 1769 by a Scotsman named James Watt. The steam engine used coal to produce a new and important source of power for running machines. By the 1790s, the steam engine was used to run Crompton's spinning mule. With the steam engine, textile mills no longer had to be located on rivers or streams to obtain water power. Where do ◀ you think factories were built once the steam engine was invented?

7. As the new textile machines increased the output of cloth, more and more raw cotton was needed. This need for raw cotton led to another important invention. In 1793, an American named Eli Whitney invented

437

the **cotton gin**, a machine that removed the seeds from the cotton fiber. The cotton gin made it faster and cheaper to produce cotton fiber. In the United States, cotton became the chief crop in several southern states. The growing demand for cotton led to the spread of slavery in the southern United States. From 1793 to 1823, the number of slaves brought to the United States from Africa increased by more than one million. Thousands of slaves planted, tended, and harvested cotton in the southern United States. In the United States, slavery continued until the end of the Civil War, when the Thirteenth Amendment to the Constitution finally abolished slavery. In the meantime, the use of slaves allowed U.S. plantation owners to become among the world's largest suppliers of cotton.

▼ The better quality thread made possible by Samuel Crompton's spinning mule increased the profits of textile mills in Great Britain.

8. The textile industry became England's leading industry by the late 1700s. In 1800, textiles made up nearly half of the goods exported from England. English merchants shipped cotton cloth to Africa, India, and Asia, where people now prized this lightweight, washable material. As English merchants and factory owners in the textile industry prospered, other industries also were developing.

9. Two other important industries that developed in England along with the textile industry were coal mining and iron. England had plentiful supplies of iron ore and coal, and new industrial towns sprang up near these resources. In the early 1700s, iron producers discovered how to make a stronger, purer iron. They also began to use coal, which burns hotter than wood, to heat and melt iron ore. With the increased use of coal, England's coal mining industry expanded. In addition, more iron was needed to make the new textile machines.

FACTORY WORKERS: How did the Industrial Revolution change lives?

10. The use of textile machines and the increase of factories changed the lives of many people during the Industrial Revolution. Factories were often crowded, dirty, and unsafe places. Men, women, and children, who may have farmed in the past, left their homes before sunrise each morning to work in a mill or factory. They returned home each evening after working 12 or 14 hours at their jobs. Factory workers were paid low wages for their long hours of hard labor. However, there were some employers who did take care of their employees by building homes for them and educating their children.

11. Working conditions in the coal mines were even worse than those in the factories. Workers spent long, dangerous hours working in mine shafts deep below ground. Mine cave-ins and accidents were common. Yet many of the workers were five- and six-year-old boys. These children often spent 12 hours a day alone in the dark, opening

Activity: Have students research what working conditions are like in today's coal mines. Then have them compare today's working conditions to those in the eighteenth and nineteenth centuries.

438

wooden trap doors for the coal cars. Why do you think children were used for labor in factories and mines?

SPOTLIGHT ON SOURCES

12. Here is one child's account of a British coal mine in the 1800s:

I first saw the coal-pits at night. As I rode over a hill I suddenly perceived before me, in every direction, strange lights, that only seemed to make the darkness deeper. Melancholy sounds, as of groans and sighings, and wild lamentings, came upon my ear . . . I could perceive by the fires, that blazed here and there in a hundred places . . . a wild landscape . . . It was the coal-pits, that these fires were burning by them; and the sounds I heard were the sounds of the machinery by which the coal was drawn up, and of the steam-engines by which the pits were cleared of water.

—from *Growing Up in the Industrial Revolution,* Penny Clarke

AGRICULTURE: How did changes in agriculture help Industrial Revolution spread?

13. Agriculture, too, underwent many changes in England in the 1700s. The potato became such a successful food crop that it helped to increase the food supply. With a

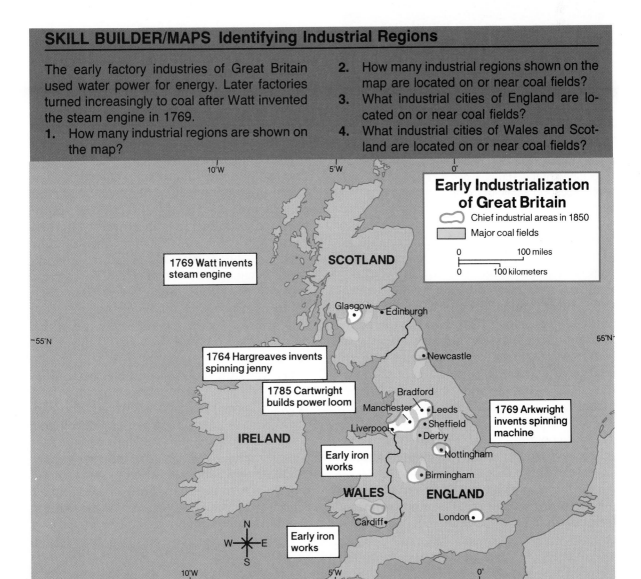

SKILL BUILDER/MAPS Identifying Industrial Regions

The early factory industries of Great Britain used water power for energy. Later factories turned increasingly to coal after Watt invented the steam engine in 1769.
1. How many industrial regions are shown on the map?

2. How many industrial regions shown on the map are located on or near coal fields?
3. What industrial cities of England are located on or near coal fields?
4. What industrial cities of Wales and Scotland are located on or near coal fields?

Early Industrialization of Great Britain

Chief industrial areas in 1850

Major coal fields

0   100 miles
0   100 kilometers

1769 Watt invents steam engine

SCOTLAND

Glasgow   Edinburgh

1764 Hargreaves invents spinning jenny

1785 Cartwright builds power loom

Newcastle

Bradford
Manchester   Leeds
Liverpool   Sheffield
            Derby
                Nottingham

1769 Arkwright invents spinning machine

IRELAND

Early iron works

Birmingham

WALES   ENGLAND

Cardiff   London

Early iron works

▲ Children worked long hours in the mines and factories of the 1800s. Their size let them work in places too small for adults.

better supply of food, England's population increased. In addition, the Enclosure Acts passed by Parliament allowed wealthy landowners to fence off common lands that small farm families had used. As a result, many of these small farmers were forced to ► look for jobs in mills and factories. How were fewer farmers able to produce enough food for the growing population of the new industrial cities? Fortunately, new farming machinery was introduced and new farming methods were developed. These inventions and changes made it possible for farmers to produce larger harvests and healthier livestock than before.

14. One important new method of farming was crop rotation. In **crop rotation** farmers change, or rotate, the crops they plant from field to field each year. During the Middle Ages, European peasants used to plant a field to grain for two years. Then they let the worn-out field lie fallow, or unused, for one year. In the 1700s farmers learned that growing clover for livestock feed renewed worn-out soil better than a year of lying fallow. How do you think a ◄ crop rotation system using clover changed Europe's food supply? How else do you think Europe's food supply changed when corn and potatoes were introduced from America?

15. Along with crop rotation, there were several inventions and improvements in farming tools that greatly increased farm production. One of the most important inventions was the seed drill, invented by Jethro Tull in England in 1733. This machine planted seeds in rows faster than farmers could plant them by hand. In the United States, Henry Blair, a freed African American, invented a seed planter for corn. Two Americans, Charles Newbold and John Deere, improved the plow by creating long-lasting iron and steel blades to replace wooden plows.

16. Other farm machinery was invented that helped the harvesting of crops. The threshing machine, invented by a Scotsman named Andrew Meikle, separated grain from its stalk. In 1834, an American named Cyrus McCormick invented a machine that sped up the harvesting of grain. McCormick's reaper allowed farmers to harvest larger grain crops much faster than they could using scythes, or hand tools for cutting grain. Why do you think the use of the ◄ new farming methods, tools, and machines spread rapidly?

17. The introduction of new crops also improved food production. In the late 1800s, George Washington Carver, who had been born a slave in America, developed new food products. They included soybeans, peanuts, and sweet potatoes. Carver experimented with these new crops and found many ways to use them both as food and as products in industry. What are some peanut ◄ products in common use today?

THE ECONOMY: How did the Industrial Revolution change the economic system in Great Britain?

18. The new machines and factories of the Industrial Revolution could not have been built without **capital.** Capital is wealth used in business to produce more wealth. The people who ran the early factories of the Industrial Revolution worked hard to raise capital. For example, two brothers named Samuel and Aaron Walker started a factory to make tools. Along with working in the factory, Samuel kept his teaching job. Aaron mowed fields and sheared lambs as a part-time job. In this way, the two brothers were able to pay for their families' needs and expand their business. When the business made a profit, they used that money as capital to improve their factory. The capital was used to improve the furnace, build a warehouse, and get a mold so that they could add frying pans to their product line. It was in this slow, well-planned way that some factory owners finally became wealthy.

19. Some business people did not have enough capital of their own to build a factory. In the early days of the Industrial Revolution, people solved this problem by seeking friends or family members as partners. Another way that business people raised money to build factories was to **mortgage** their land. To mortgage means to pledge property to a creditor as a promise for repaying the debt. When a person today ◄ says she is going to get a mortgage to pay for her house, what does that mean?

20. The increase in the exchange of money brought about by the Industrial Revolution led to the growth of banks. Banks held money for customers and exchanged bills for coins. Banks also gave loans to businesses for capital improvements or for meeting payroll. How do banks help people ◄ and businesses today?

▼ The mechanical thresher, invented by Andrew Meikle, made separating grain from stalks easier and faster.

OUTLOOK

21. By the early 1800s, Great Britain was the world's leading industrial nation. Great Britain produced more iron than all other nations together. It had more railroads and sold more textiles than any other nation. Merchants, factory owners, and bankers became an important class in English society. Within a few years, the Industrial Revolution would spread around the world. These changes in industry and agriculture that began in England nearly 300 years ago are still going on today. Businesses continue to seek better ways of producing the high-quality food and manufactured goods that people expect today. Why was the Indus- ◄ trial Revolution so important in shaping the world you live in today? Can you think of some machines and other products you use that have been invented in recent years?

441

CHAPTER REVIEW

VOCABULARY REVIEW

Write each number and word on a sheet of paper. Then write the letter of the definition next to the word it defines.

1. Industrial Revolution
2. steam engine
3. cotton gin
4. factories
5. crop rotation
6. cottage industry
7. capital
8. mortgage

a. a machine that provided a new and important source of power for industry

b. to pledge property to a creditor as a promise for repaying a debt

c. a period of 200 years in which machines and new sources of power were invented to produce large amounts of goods

d. changing the kinds of crops planted in a field from year to year

e. buildings where machinery was operated by workers to make textiles or other products

f. producing goods by using hand tools and working in the home

g. wealth used in business to produce more wealth

h. a machine that removed the seeds from cotton fiber

SKILL BUILDER: READING A TABLE

Read the table and, on a sheet of paper, answer the questions that follow.

Important Inventions of the Industrial Revolution

Inventor	Invention	Country/Year	Significance
John Kay	Flying shuttle	England 1733	Wove cloth at a faster rate
James Hargreaves	Spinning jenny	England 1764	Made more threads faster
James Watt	Steam Engine	England 1769	Power Source
Richard Arkwright	Water frame	England 1769	Spun cotton fibers into thread faster than spinning jenny
Eli Whitney	Cotton gin	America 1793	Separated cotton seeds from cotton fibers
Robert Fulton	Steamboat	America 1807	Transportation
Elias Howe	Sewing machine	America 1846	Sewing and stitching material

1. What was the significance of James Watt's invention?
2. Who invented the cotton gin in what year?

3. How many American inventors are listed?

4. What is the earliest invention on the chart?

5. What is the latest invention on the chart?

6. List in alphabetical order the inventions that were important to the textile industry.

SKILL BUILDER: CRITICAL THINKING AND COMPREHENSION

Write your answers to the questions that follow on a sheet of paper.

1. Sequencing

▶ Arrange the events below in the order in which they happened.

a. Eli Whitney invents the cotton gin.

b. Richard Arkwright sets up the first cotton mill run by water power.

c. John Kay invents the flying shuttle.

d. Elias Howe invents the lock-stitch sewing machine.

e. James Watt invents the steam engine.

2. Compare and Contrast

a. How was farming done in Europe before the 1700s?

b. How did farming change during the 1700s?

3. Predicting

How do you think the world would have been different today if the Industrial Revolution had not taken place?

4. Summarizing

▶ Write a summary statement for each category listed that explains how each helped the growth of the Industrial Revolution.

a. Textile machinery inventions

b. Improved methods of farming

c. Capital and banking

ENRICHMENT

1. Make a list of jobs that you do daily for which no machine has been invented or for which an existing machine could be improved to do the job better. Plan a machine that could do one of these jobs. Draw a diagram of the machine showing how it would work. On a sheet of paper, write a paragraph explaining how the machine would work.

2. The chemical industry grew out of the Industrial Revolution. One of the earliest industrial needs for chemicals was for bleaching textiles. Use the library to research information about the rise of the chemical industry. Prepare a report to present to the class.

The Industrial Revolution Spreads

CHAPTER 2

FACTORY GIRLS PREPARING THE WARP FOR THE WE

▲ This 1841 engraving shows Massachusetts mill workers from the Lowell factories preparing the warp for the weaver.

OBJECTIVE: How did the Industrial Revolution spread throughout the world?

1. Today, the exchange of goods and services between distant lands is not at all unusual. Many Americans own Japanese cars and televisions, and many Japanese enjoy eating at American-owned fast-food restaurants. When people exchange goods, they exchange ideas as well. During the Industrial Revolution, the same thing happened. As the quality and quantity of goods from Great Britain increased, other nations began to learn about England's new indus-

tries. In this way the ideas and inventions of the Industrial Revolution that began in England slowly spread to other countries. Other European nations began to realize that Great Britain was far ahead of them in wealth from exports of goods. Great Britain

William Cockerill builds textile factory in Russia late 1700s

Belgium wins independence 1831

Alfred Krupp builds steel industry in Ruhr Valley c. 1838

Germany takes over Alsace-Lorraine 1870

1760   1780   1800   1820   1840   1860   1880

French Revolution begins; Samuel Slater builds America's first water loom 1789

Belgium builds railroads 1834

German states are unified 1871

444

was also ahead of other European nations in agricultural production. Great Britain continued to be the world's leading industrial and trading nation until about 1870. At that time, the United States and Germany became major competitors to Great Britain's industrial leadership.

INDUSTRIALISM SPREADS: How did new industries develop in other countries?

2. As the textile and coal mining industries grew in Great Britain, the British made gains in wealth and power. British goods such as flannels, linen, cotton, stockings, coal, and iron were sold in many parts of the world. Profits were used to build more factories, dig more mines, and expand industry still further. The British government aided the growth of industry by building up the British navy. The British navy kept overseas shipping routes safe for British traders.

3. Other countries also made money from Britain's growth in manufacturing. British factories needed more raw materials than Great Britain could supply. In the mid-1700s the American colonies increased their trade by supplying lumber, cotton, and other raw materials to Great Britain. Even after the colonies became the independent nation called the United States, they contin-

ued to supply Great Britain with raw materials, as did other nations. The trade contracts often required, these nations often bought the goods manufactured by British factories. Some British **investors** also used their growing wealth to build factories in other countries. (Investors are people who put money into developing businesses to make profits). How might the foreign-owned factories have helped the people in other countries?

4. Some British industry leaders wanted to protect the knowledge, wealth, and power gained from the Industrial Revolution. Therefore, they tried to keep other countries from learning how to build the new machines. Parliament passed laws against the sale of British machinery to other countries. Even the plans for building the machines were kept secret, and skilled workers were not allowed to leave England. Despite these measures, some workers did leave England. One person who left England to go to America was Samuel Slater. Slater had become highly skilled at working on textile machines in England. When he arrived in Providence, Rhode Island, in 1789, Slater built America's first water loom from memory. Little by little **industrialization** was spreading to other lands, despite Great Britain's efforts. (Industri-

Daily life in . . .

Francis Cabot Lowell was an American merchant who learned about manufacturing textiles by visiting cotton mills in England. When Lowell returned to the United States in 1812, he and his partner produced spinning and weaving machines that were better than those Lowell had seen in England. Lowell's mill was the first factory in the United States to take raw cotton grown in America and turn it into finished cloth made by American workers.

Lowell's Waltham factory soon became famous for the good working conditions it provided for its workers. After Lowell's death,

his ideas were continued in a new industrial community set up in the town of Lowell, Massachusetts. Most of the jobs in the Lowell factories were held by women. These factories, unlike many at that time, were clean and safe. The factory workers lived in company-owned boarding houses. They attended company-sponsored classes to obtain an education and met at social gatherings. The Lowell workers also published their own magazine. The success of the Lowell factories helped change many people's minds about the role of women. More women began to enter the workplace.

Background: British laws required the American colonies to buy certain manufactured goods from Britain. Americans could sell only nonmanufactured goods and raw materials to British businesses.

445

Background: In France, dissatisfied textile workers destroyed machinery by throwing wooden shoes into them. *Sabotage* comes from *Sabot*, the French word for a wooden shoe.

alization is the development of industries in which factory workers produce manufactured goods).

BELGIUM: How did industry develop in Belgium?

5. About the same time that industrialization was developing in Great Britain, it was being born across the English Channel in Belgium. The weaving of cloth was hardly a new idea to the people of Belgium. In the region of Flanders, the Flemish people had been handweaving fine woolen goods in their homes for hundreds of years. In fact, much of the raw wool used by this cottage industry was bought from England. When English manufacturers first decided to produce woolen goods, they hired skilled Flemish weavers. The Flemish weavers helped set up the weaving industry in England. At the same time, some British workers and inventors went to Belgium to build machinery needed for large-scale production of textiles. Why do you think Belgium became the second of the European nations to industrialize?

6. The industrialization of Belgium sped up after that nation won its independence from the Netherlands in 1831. As an independent nation, Belgium mined its large supplies of coal for energy and iron ore for building machines. In addition, Belgium became the second European country to build a railroad system. With a good supply of labor, natural resources, and an excellent transportation system, Belgium had become an industrialized nation by the late 1800s.

PEOPLE IN HISTORY

7. William Cockerill was an English textile manufacturer who brought the textile industry to Belgium in the early 1800s. In the late 1700s he helped Russia start a textile industry. Catherine the Great, Empress of Russia, wanted to modernize her country. She hired Cockerill to build a textile factory in Russia using machinery he

had invented in England. Two years after his successful textile business was begun, Catherine died. Her son disapproved of his mother's plans for Russia, and he had Cockerill thrown into prison. Cockerill escaped and settled in Sweden, but he was unable to interest the Swedes in his inventions. He then moved to Belgium in 1799 and introduced Belgian woolen makers to his machinery. Within a few years, Cockerill had built his own textile factories in Belgium. His son, John Cockerill, later built factories in Belgium to produce iron products.

FRANCE: Why did the Industrial Revolution develop so slowly in France?

8. By the 1700s, France had a well-developed textile industry that produced linen and silk cloth, but the growth of industry soon slowed because of wars. French textile mills used the loom and spinning machines to make linen and silk cloth. However, the French Revolution of 1789 and the Napoleonic Wars halted the growth of this industry. Most of France's natural resources, such as coal and iron ore, were used to make weapons for Napoleon's army rather than to build new industries. After the Napoleonic Wars ended, some of France's best coal mines were in areas of France that became part of Belgium. In addition the French government, which had been weakened by the revolutions of 1830 and 1848, could do little to help industries grow and develop.

9. By the mid-1800s, however, the French government encouraged the building of railroads, new road systems, and new industries. During the rule of Emperor Napoleon III, many of the new industries produced guns, cannons, and other weapons. However, when Germany defeated France in the Franco-Prussian War in 1870, Germany took Alsace-Lorraine from France. As a result, France lost this rich coal and iron ore mining region. Once again, industrial growth in France slowed greatly. It was not until the 1900s that France began to rebuild its industrial strength.

Ask: What effect do you think the Franco-Prussian War of 1870 had on the French economy?

446

GERMANY: How did the unification of Germany speed up industrialization in that country?

10. An important early step in the industrialization of Germany was the birth of Friedrich Krupp's steel plant in the Ruhr Valley about 1810. The Krupp family had been making weapons for about 200 years. However with coal- and steam-powered machines, more weapons could be made faster. When Krupp's son Alfred took over the business in the 1840s, he began making ▶ steel weapons in molds called **casts**. How do you think casts help speed up weapons production? Soon the Prussian and Russian armies were placing bulk orders for these fine new weapons.

11. Industrialization spread rapidly after Germany became a united nation in 1871. Germany gained the rich iron and coal resources of Alsace-Lorraine that same year. The new German emperor and his powerful minister, Bismarck, succeeded in making Germany a strong industrial nation. German ships soon equaled those of Great Britain and the United States. The Germans supplied vessels for the world's navies and merchant fleets. The Krupp industries became a world leader in the manufacture of steel. The Ruhr Valley, where Krupp industries and others were located, became a major center of industry in Europe. Germany had a larger railroad system and produced more steel than did either France or Great Britain. Only the United States produced more steel and had a better railroad system than did Germany.

THE UNITED STATES: Why was the United States the first non-European country to industrialize?

12. The natural resources of Great Britain's American colonies were valuable to British industry. One of the most important of these resources was lumber. The huge forests of America supplied the wood used to build Britain's trading ships and navy. Shipbuilding became America's first impor-

▲ The Krupp steelworks, shown in this painting by Heinrich Kley, employed 20,000 workers and controlled Germany's arms industry.

tant industry. At the time of the American Revolution, one out of every three British ships had been built in America. Too, the British textile industry needed America's raw materials of cotton, rice, and **indigo**, which was a dye used to color cloth.

13. After Samuel Slater built the first successful spinning mill in the United States, the textile industry grew rapidly there. The New England states, with their many rivers for water power, became America's major textile manufacturing area. Pennsylvania and the southern states also had important roles. Pennsylvania became a center of iron making and, later, steel production. The city of Pittsburgh became the nation's largest iron manufacturer. The southern states provided food crops and raw materials for northern factories as well as for those in England. What raw materials ◀ did the southern states provide to northern factories?

Activity: Find information about Britain's policies for sending indentured servants and prisoners to the colonies in America. Also find out how the American Revolution caused British prisoners to be sent to Australia.

447

A Geographic View of History

World Industrial Regions Today   Modern industrial development is concentrated in less than 25 percent of the world's countries. People who live in these "developed countries" enjoy a much higher standard of living than people who live in nonindustrial "less-developed countries," or LDCs. Read the following facts about the uneven distribution of industrialization today:

The world's largest industrial regions, all located in the Northern Hemisphere, include seven leading industrial powers: the United States, Russia, Japan, Germany, Great Britain, France, and Italy.

The United States and Canada produce more goods and services than any other part of the world.

The 12-member European Community (EC) has the second-largest concentration of industries. EC membership is open only to industrial countries with democratic forms of government.

Russia and the countries of Eastern Europe have the world's third-largest concentration of industries.

The five New Industrial Countries (NICs), industrialized in the 1970s, include South Korea, Taiwan, Singapore, Brazil, and Mexico. They export goods made with advanced technologies borrowed from older industrial countries.

Reread the facts and study the map and chart. Then, answer the following questions:

1. According to the chart, which country produces the most goods and services? In what region is this country located?

2. What is the name of the 12-member organization that has the second-largest concentration of industries?

3. Why do you think many of today's nonindustrial countries want to become future NICs?

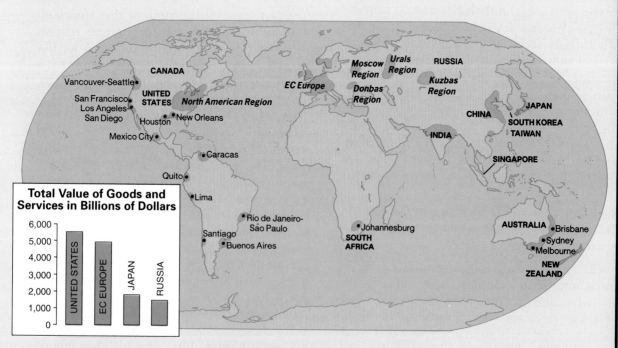

Leading Industrial Regions Today

15. Railroads soon played an important part in the growth of American industry. In the 1860s, the United States government gave railroad companies vast plots of free land on which to build their railroads. Why do you think the United States government did that? The companies then sold the land along the railroad tracks and used this money to help pay their building costs. Farms and towns grew up beside the tracks and became customers for the railroads. By the late 1800s, the United States was linked by railroads from coast to coast. The iron and steel industries expanded with the growth of the railroads. By the end of the nineteenth century, America was the world's leading producer of iron and steel, as well as of many other industrial products. ▶ Why were railroads critical to the development of America as an industrialized nation?

OVERSEAS COLONIES: Why were non-European countries with natural resources taken over by the industrialized nations?

16. By the late 1800s, the growing demand for resources and raw materials led to a fierce competition among the industrialized nations. African and Asian countries with these resources also were markets for manufactured goods made by the industrial powers. Prices went up for rubber, tin, hides, and other overseas resources. The rivalry for these resources often led to conflicts among the industrial nations—and sometimes even led to war. Industrialized nations were eager to win control of the other areas of the world that were rich in natural resources. As a result, the industrialized nations used their wealth and power to gain colonies. These new colonies were meant for the good of the industrialized nations. The industrialized nations cared little about how their actions affected the people and the land they colonized. Large parts of Africa were claimed by England, Germany, France, Belgium, and Italy. The United States, too, joined in this race for overseas colonies by purchasing places such as Alaska. How do you think colonization ◀ might have helped the people who were colonized?

SPOTLIGHT ON SOURCES

17. Many people in the United States and in other industrial nations were worried about their nation's ruling other lands as colonies. However, those who favored overseas colonies won the debate. In the United States, Senator Albert Beveridge of Indiana used the following words to explain why an American empire was needed:

> . . . Shall the American people continue their march toward the commercial supremacy of the world [becoming the leader of world trade]? Have we no mission [duty] to perform, no duty . . . to our fellow [humans]? . . . Shall we occupy [take over] new markets for what our farmers raise, our factories make, our merchants sell . . . [and] new markets for what our ships shall carry?
> —*The Indianapolis Journal,*
> September 17, 1898

Senator Beveridge said that the answer to all these questions had to be "yes."

OUTLOOK

18. As the industrial nations gained new colonies, they used them as new markets and as suppliers of natural resources. By the late 1800s, the balance of wealth and power throughout the world shifted dramatically to favor the industrial nations. The Industrial Revolution had made the nations of Western Europe as well as the United States and Japan the most powerful countries on earth. Today, the nations that became colonies in Africa and Asia in the 1800s have regained their independence. Many of these nations are working hard to become industrialized. Why do you think these countries ◀ want to develop their own industries?

Activity: Write a report about the way Japan became industrialized in the late 1800s.

CHAPTER REVIEW

VOCABULARY REVIEW

Write each of the following words on a sheet of paper. Use the glossary on pages 728-737 to write the definition for each word or term. Then complete the sentences that follow.

industrialization   casts

investors   indigo

1. _____ spread to Belgium after it began in Great Britain.
2. Profits from new businesses began to attract _____ .
3. The cloth was dyed with _____ .
4. The _____ for the weapons allowed each weapon to be the same.

SKILL BUILDER: USING A DICTIONARY

When you are trying to locate words in a dictionary, guide words can help you locate words quickly. Guide words are printed in the upper left-hand and right-hand corners of each page. The upper left-hand guide word tells the first full entry on that page. The upper right-hand guide word tells the last entry that begins on the page.

▶ Imagine that the pair of words below are guide words on a dictionary page. Look at them carefully. Then, skim paragraphs 13 and 14 and choose the words that would be found on that dictionary page. Make sure you list the words in alphabetical order.

map   **mist**

SKILL BUILDER: CRITICAL THINKING AND COMPREHENSION

▲ 1. Summarizing

▶ Read paragraphs 5, 10 and 12. Then summarize each paragraph by writing a one- or two-line headline about each paragraph's content. Write your headlines on a separate sheet of paper.

a. Paragraph 5 _____

b. Paragraph 10 _____

c. Paragraph 12 _____

2. Cause and Effect

▶ Match the cause in column 1 to the effect in column 2.

2-1. The Flemish had been weavers of fine woolens for hundreds of years.

a. The demand for manufactured goods grew rapidly.

2-2. The demand for raw materials grew rapidly.

b. Belgium developed rapidly as an industrial nation.

2-3. Raw materials could be transported quickly from one place to another.

2-4. France lost lands with important natural resources to Germany and Belgium.

2-5. William Cockerill set up textile machinery in Belgium.

c. The Industrial Revolution was slow to take hold in France.

d. Flemish weavers helped set up the weaving industry in England.

e. Factories could keep a steady supply of raw materials.

3. Predicting

▶ Read paragraphs 2 and 3. On a separate sheet of paper, copy the sentence that most likely predicts the future.

a. World trade will continue to grow.

b. People will lose interest in buying foreign-made goods.

c. The nations of the world will benefit equally from the exchange of goods and services.

▶ Read paragraphs 16 and 18. Write the sentence that most likely predicts the future.

a. The nonindustrial nations will probably always accept their colonial status.

b. The balance of wealth and power will eventually favor the non-industrial nations.

c. After regaining their independence, most nonindustrial nations will work hard to become industrialized.

4. Point of View

▶ The names of some industrialists are listed below. Following the names are statements these industrialists could have made. Read the statements carefully. On a sheet of paper, match the industrialist with the statement by writing the industrialist's name next to the letter of the statement.

William Cockerill   Francis Lowell   Samuel Slater

a. "I don't believe that the British should keep the inventions of machinery away from other nations. I will go to America where I will attempt to build the water loom from memory."

b. "It surprises me that I, a textile manufacturer, would have a son interested in producing iron products."

c. "I am convinced that factory workers need decent housing, clean, safe working conditions, and a modest education."

ENRICHMENT

1. Use an outline map of Europe and an Atlas to draw in the coal and iron ore deposits of Europe. Explain why Alsace-Lorraine was frequently taken over by victorious countries in time of war.

2. In 1800 the North Americans and Europeans controlled only 34 percent of the world's land. By 1914 they controlled 84 percent of the world's land. Have a class debate on whether it was positive or negative that industrialized nations colonized many nonindustrialized nations.

3. Research and prepare a report on the development of mass production. How did mass production increase industrial growth of nations?

CHAPTER 3

New Ways To Communicate and Transport Goods

▲ Robert Fulton's *Clermont*, which was 133 feet long and 18 feet wide, averaged five miles per hour on a trip from New York to Albany.

OBJECTIVE: How did the Industrial Revolution bring great changes in transportation and communication?

1. Do you ever look at the labels sewn in your clothing? The sweaters, jeans, and shoes you buy often read "Made in the Philippines," "Made in China," or "Made in Brazil." These countries are thousands of miles away from the United States. How did these items end up in the store where you bought them? Today, clothing, food, machinery, jewelry, and many other products are part of a worldwide trade. In this way, Americans can choose from products made in many countries. People from other countries choose from products made in the United States and other parts of the world. Trade among nations began long before the Industrial Revolution. However, new forms

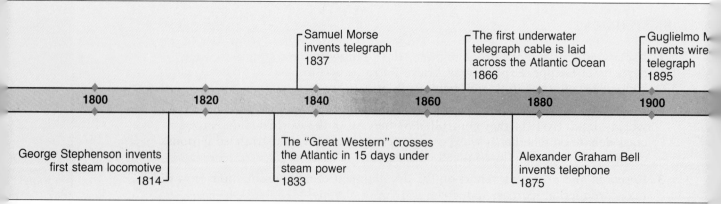

- Samuel Morse invents telegraph 1837
- The first underwater telegraph cable is laid across the Atlantic Ocean 1866
- Guglielmo M invents wire telegraph 1895

| 1800 | 1820 | 1840 | 1860 | 1880 | 1900 |

- George Stephenson invents first steam locomotive 1814
- The "Great Western" crosses the Atlantic in 15 days under steam power 1833
- Alexander Graham Bell invents telephone 1875

Background: Industrialization changed the balance of trade between European countries and their colonies. Machine-made British cotton fabrics far outsold hand-spun muslin and calico fabrics from India.

of transportation and communication allowed trade to expand rapidly after the Industrial Revolution.

TRADE: How did the growing trade among nations help develop a worldwide economy?

2. The rapid expansion in trade helped the spread of the Industrial Revolution. The steamships, canals, and railroads of the industrial age made travel faster and easier. More and more European merchants traded with distant countries and colonies. European merchants imported lumber, tin, rubber, and cotton from these overseas countries for Europe's factories. As this world trade grew and population expanded, the demand for goods increased as well. Factories had to find ways to produce more manufactured goods to keep up with the growing demand at home and in other countries.

3. With the increase in international trade, a worldwide economy began to develop. Countries throughout the world began depending on one another for raw materials and manufactured goods. The economies of many nations began depending on the profits they made from world trade. The money earned from world trade, in turn, helped pay for new inventions and improvements in machinery and transportation. The money earned from world trade also made trading nations wealthier through increased tax income. Industrialists worked hand-in-hand with merchants and traders to keep up with the growing
▶ demand for goods. How do you think these changes in trade and industry helped the world to become more modern?

TRANSPORTATION: What 19th century inventions brought about improvements in transportation?

4. The great changes in trade could not have taken place without improvements in transportation. For many centuries, goods had been transported over land by slow-moving horse-drawn wagons and river vessels. Wind-driven sailing ships were used for transportation across oceans. During the eighteenth century, as trade expanded, particularly between North America and Europe, these sailing ships were slow and undependable. As a result, inventors tried steam power to improve ways of transporting people and goods.

5. In 1807, an American inventor named Robert Fulton launched the *Clermont,* the first successful steam-driven side-paddle vessel. The **steamboat** made travel on water much faster than it had ever been before. In the United States, steamboats were soon sailing up and down the Mississippi River. The steamboats carried cotton from the South and manufactured goods from the North. In 1833, a ship called the *Great Western* crossed the Atlantic Ocean in 15 days using steam power. These new seagoing ships could now transport raw materials, manufactured goods, and people much more quickly across the ocean.

SPOTLIGHT ON SOURCES

6. Steamboats carrying cotton became a common sight on the Mississippi River during the 1800s. Here is how one writer described this trade in cotton:

Although steamboatmen turned their attention to passenger comfort and luxury in the years following the Civil War, it was cargo that would make or break river transportation, and, on the lower Mississippi, "cargo" meant cotton. Planters grew cotton all along the shores of the river in the southern states . . . . Coming in wagon loads to the gin, cotton made its way through neighborhoods and city streets, creating excitement as it passed. Weighing the first bale was a yearly ritual watched with intense interest. At the beginning of each season it was announced who had brought the first bale into town, which agent took it on commission, where it was ginned, and which carrier transported it to its des-

Activity: John Fitch, an American inventor, built several types of steamboats in the 1780s. He tried mechanical oars and then paddle wheels. The public thought of Fitch's steamboats as impractical gimmicks. Select a student to present Fitch's ideas. Have students react to Fitch's ideas.

453

tination [final port]. Stopping at as many as forty or fifty landings between Memphis and New Orleans, carriers loaded hundreds and even thousands of bales on their decks.

—"Steamboats on the Mississippi," Joan W. Gandy and Thomas H. Gandy

7. Railroad trains were another important form of transportation that developed from the invention of the steam engine. In 1814, an English engineer named George Stephenson built the first successful steam **locomotive.** People were amazed in 1830 when Stephenson's engine, the *Rocket,* pulled a train of cars at a speed of 29 miles (47 kilometers) per hour! Traveling by rail was faster and smoother than traveling across land by horse and wagon. Trains were also able to transport much larger quantities of raw materials to factories and manufactured goods to market. How did the development of trains create new jobs for people?

8. Improved ways of making roads also made travel and trade quicker and easier. Before the Industrial Revolution, many trade routes were along hard-packed dirt roads that turned to mud during heavy rain. In England and elsewhere, a few main roads in large cities were made with cobblestones or bricks. In the 1700s, a Scottish engineer named John L. McAdam developed a new method of building roads. McAdam used crushed stones to make a smooth, long-lasting road surface. McAdam's method of building roads is still in use today. What word related to road construction today comes from McAdam's name? With improved building methods, England soon had a network of roads to help towns and factories transport goods to railroad stations and shipping docks.

COMMUNICATION: What inventions helped to improve communication?

9. With the increase in worldwide trade, improved forms of communication were needed almost as much as improved transportation. Inventions in communication in the 1800s led to a **communication revolution.** These inventions in communication allowed faster communication over greater

▼ The *Rocket,* George Stephenson's successful steam locomotive, was the winner of a competition to provide rail service between Liverpool and Manchester, England.

ROCKET

distances, mostly among the industrialized nations. In 1844, Samuel F. B. Morse from the United States invented the **telegraph**. Morse discovered that electrical signals could be sent over wire. By stringing wires from one place to another, coded messages could be tapped out at one end and received at the other. In 1866, the first underwater telegraph cable was laid across the Atlantic Ocean. The Atlantic Cable allowed Americans and Europeans to send messages to each other in a matter of minutes. The telegraph represented a giant step forward in long-distance communication.

10. The telephone was invented by another American, Alexander Graham Bell, in 1875. Bell was searching for better ways to educate deaf people. He came up with the idea of sending speech sounds by electrical currents. His invention, called the telephone, allowed voices, rather than coded messages, to be heard by wire for the first time in history. Bell soon set up telephone companies in the United States and in England. By the early 1900s, the United States and other parts of Europe were linked by long-distance telephone. How do you think the invention of the telephone changed the world forever?

▲ Alexander Graham Bell, inventor of the telephone, places the first long distance call from New York to Chicago in 1893.

PEOPLE IN HISTORY

11. In 1895, an Italian scientist named Guglielmo (goo-lee-EL-moh) Marconi discovered how to send telegraph signals by using airwaves. While experimenting with a telegraph key at his father's home, Marconi discovered that electrical signals could be sent through the air. He then set out to invent an instrument to use these airwaves to send messages. Marconi also figured out how to use an antenna to send messages over greater distances. By 1899, British battleships were using Marconi's **wireless telegraph** to send messages over a distance of 75 miles (121 kilometers). Two years later, Marconi received a message in New Zealand that had been sent from England, thousands of miles away.

OUTLOOK

12. As transportation and communication became quicker and easier, people in distant lands began to be linked closer together. A world market for goods had been developed. Through trade markets and improved communication, ideas also traveled swiftly from one place to another. Americans and Europeans learned more about ways of life in Africa and Asia. Africans and Asians learned more about Europeans and Americans. As a result, the world soon seemed to be a smaller place. How do you learn today about what is happening in other countries? Do you think it is important to know about events everywhere as soon as they happen?

Background: By the early 1900s, home wireless sets had become a major form of entertainment in Europe and the United States.

455

CHAPTER REVIEW

VOCABULARY REVIEW

Write each of the following sentences on a sheet of paper. Then fill in the blank with the word that best completes each sentence.

steamboat

locomotive

communication revolution

telegraph

wireless telegraph

1. Inventions of the _____ allowed people to communicate over great distances much faster.

2. The _____ made shipping faster and more dependable.

3. Messages could be sent long distances on electrical signals through the air with the _____ .

4. With the development of the _____ , faster travel by train over land was made possible.

5. The Atlantic Cable allowed the first long distance communication by _____ from North American to Europe.

SKILL BUILDER: READING A TIME LINE

The Industrial Revolution was a time of invention and the spread of ideas. Often one invention makes another invention possible. Sometimes inventions lead to new needs or new ideas.

▶ Study the time line below to answer these questions.

1. Which was invented first, the wireless, the water loom, or the steam engine?

2. Which two inventions were developed in the same year?

3. How long after the invention of the telephone did Marconi invent the wireless?

4. Between which two events on the time line would you place Eli Whitney's invention of the cotton gin in 1793?

5. Using the time line and information from chapters 1, 2, and 3, explain in a few sentences why you think the development of the textile industry led to the development of the steel industry.

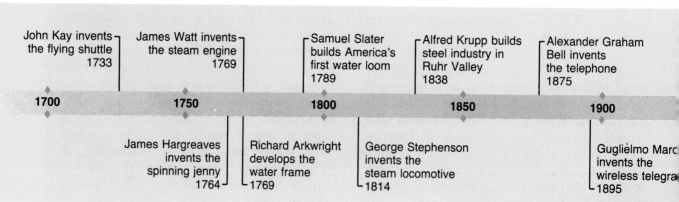

John Kay invents the flying shuttle 1733

James Watt invents the steam engine 1769

Samuel Slater builds America's first water loom 1789

Alfred Krupp builds steel industry in Ruhr Valley 1838

Alexander Graham Bell invents the telephone 1875

1700   1750   1800   1850   1900

James Hargreaves invents the spinning jenny 1764

Richard Arkwright develops the water frame 1769

George Stephenson invents the steam locomotive 1814

Guglielmo Marc invents the wireless telegra 1895

SKILL BUILDER: CRITICAL THINKING AND COMPREHENSION

1. Main Idea

1-1. Copy the sentence that best expresses the main idea of paragraph 4.

a. Sailing ships were used for hundreds of years.

b. Improvements in transportation were needed to meet the growing demand for goods.

c. Industry was not profitable in the nineteenth century.

d. Steam was a better source of power than wind or horses.

1-2. A good title for paragraph 8 would be

a. Building Better Roads

b. The Master Builder

c. English Railroads

d. Cobblestone and Brick

2. Cause and Effect

▶ Match the cause in column 1 to the effect in column 2.

2-1. The Industrial Revolution brought about improvements in travel.

2-2. The steam engine was invented.

2-3. Electrical signals could be sent through the air.

2-4. Improvements were made in communication.

a. The steamboat and locomotive were developed.

b. Business deals could be completed in a single day.

c. Goods could be moved from one place to another more rapidly.

d. Messages could be sent thousands of miles without wires.

3. Fact *versus* Opinion

▶ Read sentences a–e below and decide whether each one is a statement of fact or opinion. Write the letter of each statement on a sheet of paper. Label each statement **F** for fact or **O** for opinion.

a. Transportation improved when steam power was applied to trains and ships.

b. Hard-packed dirt roads were smoother than crushed stone roads.

c. People will someday be able to communicate by reading each other's minds.

d. Improved trains and roads helped to move goods faster from the factories to the docks for shipping.

e. The wireless telegraph is better than the telephone.

ENRICHMENT

1. Find out more about the telegraph, the telephone, or the radio through library research. Write a short history of the invention you have chosen. Tell how the invention was used in the past and explain how its use has changed over the years. Also discuss how this invention affects the world we live in today and how it may affect the world of the future.

2. Research and prepare an oral report with diagrams that explains why and how canals were built in Europe and America during the Industrial Revolution.

CHAPTER 4

Urbanism, Socialism, and Women's Rights

▲ London shows the results of urbanism. The Industrial Revolution caused overcrowding in cities where manufacturing offered people jobs.

OBJECTIVE: How did the growth of cities lead to new social problems and new reforms?

1. In recent years, many cities across the United States have been given new life. Old buildings that once would have been torn down instead have been cleaned up and remodeled. Local officials have worked hard to make downtown areas safer and cleaner. In some places, people have moved back from the suburbs to the city in order to live closer to their jobs. Despite the best efforts of concerned citizens, however, pov-

erty and crime continue to be major problems for most modern cities. However, these problems did not begin recently. They have been with us ever since the Industrial Revolution. Attempts to solve these problems were made over a century ago in the

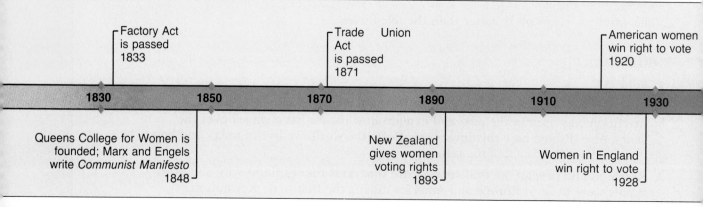

Factory Act
is passed
1833

Trade Union
Act
is passed
1871

American women
win right to vote
1920

1830   1850   1870   1890   1910   1930

Queens College for Women is founded; Marx and Engels write *Communist Manifesto*
1848

New Zealand gives women voting rights
1893

Women in England win right to vote
1928

458

industrial centers of nineteenth-century Europe.

CITIES: How did the Industrial Revolution encourage the growth of cities?

2. In the 1700s and 1800s most of the factory towns were built in areas where coal or iron ore was mined. Factory towns were also built in areas where textile mills used water power from rivers and waterfalls. When railroads and canals were built, and iron and coal could be transported over distances, cities quickly grew around transportation and trade centers. Cities that had been centers of trade in the past now became manufacturing centers whose lifelines were the railroads. This growth and expansion of cities is called **urbanism**.

3. In England and other industrial countries, people from farming areas and small towns poured into the cities to work in factories. This was partly due to the enclosure laws, and partly to the hope for a better life. Shops soon were opened to sell goods to workers and their families. As cities grew larger, more city services were needed. Jobs opened up for police officers, fire fighters, postal workers, and schoolteachers. The first daily newspapers written for the workers soon appeared. Construction boomed as more families arrived in the cities looking for jobs and housing.

4. Europe's population grew from 187 million in 1800 to 274 million in 1850, which added to the growth of the cities. In the century after 1840, nearly 60 million people left Europe to find a better life in North and South America's cities and farmland. More than 34 million Irish, Italians, Russians, Germans, Austrians, and other people from every nation of Europe came to the United States. These **immigrants**, or people who move to a new country to live, brought ideas and skills with them.

URBAN SOCIETY: What problems did workers face in factories and in crowded industrial cities?

5. The industrial cities of Europe grew so rapidly that they could not keep up with the need for housing, water supply, and sewers. Few city governments had enough money to pay for these services. In Europe and the United States, many workers lived in tenements. Tenements were five- or six-story row houses, which were attached to each other, with windows only in the front and back of the building. This low-cost form of housing was used to crowd a great many people into a small area. Often, families of eight or ten people lived in a single room. These crowded housing conditions led to terrible health problems. Crime and disease were part of everyday life for many tenement dwellers.

6. Working conditions in the factories worsened as the factories increased in size and number. Laborers worked long hours, received low pay, were harshly treated, and had uninteresting jobs. Textile mills were

Daily life in . . .

The middle class gained power during the Industrial Revolution. Before the Industrial Revolution, the middle class was a small group of merchants and crafts people. During the Industrial Revolution, more people had a better opportunity to increase their income. As jobs in fields such as accounting, engineering, and law grew, the middle class grew. By the mid-1800s a large number of schools, libraries, and universities were founded to educate the middle class. In addition, as the power and size of the middle class grew, Parliament no longer represented just the landowning upper classes. The middle class had increased its powers, so that it now could influence and take a more active role in government.

Ask: During the first half of the nineteenth century, why did marriage and birth rates tend to go up and down as wages rose and fell?

459

dark and airless. Workers toiled at their jobs 12 to 14 hours each day and sometimes became sick as a result. Most factories used heavy machinery with no safety features to protect the workers. Accidents were common, and workers had no insurance to help their families if they were injured. Insurance is money set aside by contract to cover a person from loss due to things such as illness, injury, or fire. Workers who complained about poor working conditions could expect to lose their jobs. Factory owners could easily find people to take the place of any dissatisfied workers.

SOCIALISM: How did poor living and working conditions lead to the rise of socialism?

7. The troubles of factory workers inspired some people to think about ways to improve life. The gap between the rich and the poor seemed to grow larger with each passing year. The English philosopher John Stuart Mill believed that government should take steps to create a better society. In his book *On Liberty*, published in 1859, Mill called upon the government to educate workers and improve their working conditions. He also believed workers should act together to form **labor unions**. Labor unions are organizations of workers formed to protect workers' rights.

8. As the problems of industrial society grew, a group known as Socialists saw a need for sweeping change. Under **socialism**, the basic means of production and distribution of goods are owned by the people. The government, which represents the people, owns and runs the farms, mines, factories, and stores. Under socialism, private owners no longer control business or make profits by taking advantage of poorly paid workers. Instead, through public instead of private profits the government gives people all needed goods and services.

9. The first socialist thinkers imagined perfect societies called utopias. In a utopia, all people would be free and equal, and all problems would be solved by reason.

Claude Saint-Simon (sahn-see-MOHN) and Charles Fourier (fur-ee-AY) in France and Robert Owen in England were **utopian socialists**. Utopian socialists urged people to set up ideal communities in which everyone would work together for the common good. Several such communities were established in the early part of the nineteenth century, but all of them failed within a few years.

10. Karl Marx was a German economist who wrote about a new kind of socialism. In 1848, Marx and another socialist, Friedrich Engels, wrote a pamphlet called the *Communist Manifesto*. They described "scientific socialism," which they called **communism**. Under communism, free enterprise, or the freedom of private business to form and operate for profit without government control, was to be ended. Instead, the workers would control farming, mining, manufacturing, transportation, communication, and all forms of buying and selling.

SPOTLIGHT ON SOURCES

11. The *Communist Manifesto* outlined the Marxist ideal of a classless society. Marx believed that socialism not only was desirable but was inevitable—that is, it had to happen. In Marx's view, the workers, or **proletariat** (proh-luh-TAIR-ee-uht), would be driven to rise up against the middle-class business owners, or **bourgeoisie** (burzh-wah-ZEE). If necessary, the proletariat would use force to win its political and economic rights. The workers' party, or political groups, then would be free to set up a communist government. Marx called for working people around the world to take swift action:

> . . . The history of all . . . society is the history of class struggle . . . . Of all the classes that stand face to face with the bourgeoisie today, the proletariat alone is a really revolutionary class . . . . Let the ruling classes tremble at a Communist revolution. The proletarians have nothing to lose but their

Background: Charles Fourier wanted to set up utopian communities called **phalansteries**. The utopian community of Brook Farm, set up in the 1840s near Boston, was based on Fourier's ideas.

460

chains. They have a world to win. Working men of all countries, unite!
—*Communist Manifesto,* Karl Marx

12. A communist revolution never took place in Western Europe. Although Marx believed that workers of many nations would join together, nationalism was more powerful than class unity. Writing in 1848, Marx did not foresee that advances in science and medicine would improve the lives of workers in the cities. He also could not know that the governments of Europe would work for reform during the second half of the nineteenth century. Therefore, communism gradually lost its appeal to most workers in Western European nations.

REFORMS: How did the lives of workers change in the last half of the nineteenth century?

13. Advances in education, science, and technology improved the lives of many people in the later 1800s. Safety features were slowly added to machines to reduce injury. Improvements in education occurred because of the need for workers skilled in building and repairing machines. Other workers needed education in bookkeeping, the tracking of goods in stock, and the shipping of goods based on orders. Better systems of sewage disposal were developed. Food and water supplies became cleaner and safer. Medical science learned to treat or prevent such diseases as smallpox and diphtheria, which once claimed many lives. While many people still died at an early age by today's measures, people did begin to live longer, healthier lives.

14. As workers gained a higher standard of living, they began to demand political and social reforms. For example, they wanted the right to form unions to bargain with factory owners for better wages and working conditions. Workers in England won this right under the Trade Union Act of 1871. Sometimes workers would strike, or walk off the job, to force managers to bargain with union leaders. Change was slow, but the lives of workers began to improve.

15. Child labor laws were another important reform of the nineteenth century. Parliament passed a law in 1802 against hiring children younger than the age of nine. However, this law was not enforced until the Factory Act was passed in 1833. According to the Factory Act, children between the ages of nine and 13 could not work longer than nine hours a day in the textile factories. Young workers between the ages of 13 and 18 could not work more than 12 hours a day. England's child labor laws set the example for similar laws later passed in Western Europe and the United States.

WOMEN'S RIGHTS: What new opportunities did women gain during the Industrial Revolution?

16. The movement for women's rights also began during the Industrial Revolution. Until the nineteenth century, women

▼ When the Industrial Revolution came to England, there were no traditions that prevented the use of children as laborers.

Background: Britain's Queen Victoria was a firm opponent of the women's movement. Her attitude helped prevent Englishwomen from getting the vote until the twentieth century.

461

▲ Claude Monet's famous painting "Field of Poppies" is a good example of how the Impressionist painters tried to show the effect of the subtle play of light on a landscape.

Impressionism   During the late 1800s, industrialization brought changes not only to Europe's economy, but in painting as well. Impressionism was a new style of painting that suggested a different way of looking at the world. The name of the new style came from a painting entitled "Impression, Rising Sun" by the French artist Claude Monet. Most of the first Impressionists were French. They included Edouard Manet, Edgar Degas, and Pierre Auguste Renoir. In 1874, these artists and others exhibited their work in Paris. Although the new art style was at first laughed at by the public, it had a lasting influence on the next generation of artists.

The Impressionists tried to create their impressions of nature as quickly and directly as possible. Impressionist painters were more interested in light and color than in subject matter. They often used rough brush strokes, ignoring outlines and details, to highlight the changing effects of light. Some of these artists painted the same scene at different times of the day in order to show the effects of sunlight on a place. For example, Monet's series called "Rouen Cathedrals" (1894) shows a lovely stone church in different tones and colors from early morning to late evening.

1. How did the Impressionist painters get their name?

2. What effect might the invention of photography have had on painters during the late 1800s?

worked at home or in small shops. Women could not vote and had few property rights. When factories opened, women were hired to work longer hours than men for lower pay. However, as more and more women entered the workplace, they began to demand more equal treatment.

PEOPLE IN HISTORY

17. Mary Wollstonecraft (WUL-stun-kraft) (1759–1797) was an early leader of the women's rights movement. In the 1780s, Wollstonecraft and her sisters started a school for young women. In her book *Thoughts on the Education of Daughters* (1787), she described how young girls were harshly treated and poorly educated. In her most famous book, *Vindication of the Rights of Women*, she wrote that women should receive the same schooling as men. With proper education, she insisted, women could enter into government and business on equal terms. Many people at that time thought Wollstonecraft's ideas went too far against the traditions of society. Yet her writings helped build the foundation of the fight for women's right to vote and equal job opportunities.

18. The struggle for women's rights was a long and difficult one. Queen's College for Women was founded in London in 1848. In 1870, the British government began hiring women for certain jobs. Women's **suffrage**, or the right to vote, remained a key issue for many years. In 1893, New Zealand became the first country to give women full voting rights. After many years of struggle, American women won the vote in 1920. British women, too, finally gained the right to vote in 1928. With a voice in government, women had a better chance to gain such goals as equal pay and job training.

OUTLOOK

19. The Industrial Revolution brought about many changes in the way people

▲ Mary Wollstonecraft, an English writer and passionate voice for women's rights, published *Vindication of the Rights of Women* in 1972.

lived. As cities grew, the problems of poverty and crime grew as well. People often lived in crowded, unsanitary conditions, and they were so poorly paid that they had little hope of finding something better. Illness or injury could be disastrous, for there was no such thing as health or unemployment insurance. Not surprisingly, new ideas about government and society arose as the gap between rich and poor continued to grow wider. Some thinkers, such as Marx and Engels, predicted that the entire system would fall apart. For most people today, however, the quality of life has been greatly improved as a result of the Industrial Revolution. The average working day today is about half as long as it was in the late 1800s. Many workers today enjoy paid vacations and receive pensions when they retire. In ◄ what other ways are most workers today better off than they were in the 1800s?

CHAPTER REVIEW

VOCABULARY REVIEW

Write each of the following sentences on a sheet of paper. Then fill in the blank with the word that best completes each sentence.

urbanism	utopian socialists	proletariat
socialism	suffrage	bourgeoisie
immigrants	communism	labor unions

1. People who leave their homeland to move to another country are called _____ .

2. Under _____ , the basic means of production are owned by the public.

3. _____ is the term Marx used to mean workers.

4. People who wanted to set up perfect societies in which the public owns all means of production were called _____ .

5. The middle-class business owners in the 1800s were known as the _____ .

6. _____ is the right to vote.

7. The movement of large numbers of people into cities is called _____ .

8. Under _____ ,workers control all farming, mining, manufacturing, communication, and all buying and selling.

9. _____ are organizations of workers that help improve working conditions and benefits in factories.

SKILL BUILDER: USING A PRIMARY SOURCE

British factory workers labored for long hours each day, and factory life was often difficult. Yet the Industrial Revolution, in time, improved the lives of the British people. One historian who lived during the Industrial Revolution explained how it changed the people's lives.

> . . . the manufacturer [factory worker] is both in a more comfortable and in a less dependent situation than the agricultural labourer [farm worker] . . . . There has been a great diminution of mortality [large reduction in the death rate], and . . . this . . . has been greater in the manufacturing towns than in the country [farming areas] . . . . The peo- ple live longer because they are better fed, better lodged [housed], better clothed, and better attended [cared for] in sickness, and . . . the improvements are owing to [caused by] that increase of national wealth which the manufacturing system [Industrial Revolution] has produced.
>
> —"Southey's Colloquies," Thomas Babington Macaulay

▶ This primary source tells about life during the Industrial Revolution. It was written by a historian who lived in that era. Read the source carefully. Then on a sheet of paper, write the answers to the questions that follow.

1. Does the writer think factory workers are better off or worse off than farm workers?

2. Write the sentence which explains that British people were living longer as a result of the Industrial Revolution.

464

3. In what other ways did British people's lives improve according to this writer?

SKILL BUILDER: CRITICAL THINKING AND COMPREHENSION

1. Generalizing

▶ Write a generalization for each group of facts.

Group A

Workers moved from farms into cities when factories were built.

Factory cities were built where raw materials were mined.

Railroads caused the growth of some cities.

The increase in manufacturing brought about increased trade, which aided the growth of cities.

Group B

Living conditions in cities were crowded.

Living areas were not clean.

Disease spread rapidly among workers.

The crime rate was high in areas where workers lived.

2. Summarizing

▶ Summarize paragraphs 13–15 by answering the following question.

How did the lives of workers change because of the social, political, and economic reforms of the Industrial Revolution?

3. Fact *versus* Opinion

▶ Copy the following statements. Write *Fact* following each statement of fact and *Opinion* following each statement of opinion.

a. Under socialism, property is owned by the government.

b. Utopian socialism was a good idea that should have worked.

c. Karl Marx thought that the working classes would take over the factories.

d. Socialism was a very important force in Western Europe.

e. Advances in science and medicine were the most important changes of the Industrial Revolution.

4. Making Judgments

Do you think all the changes brought about during the Industrial Revolution made society better? Why or why not?

ENRICHMENT

1. Write a letter inviting a speaker from your local labor board to talk to your class about laws that govern working conditions today. After the person has spoken to the class, draw a chart or a table that compares and contrasts today's working conditions with those during the Industrial Revolution.

2. Make a drawing of an ideal factory town showing how areas for living would be kept separate from industrial areas. Show where there will be parks, and include a business district with stores and restaurants. You will also have to decide whether the people will live in apartment buildings or in single-family homes.

CHAPTER 5

Science and Medicine in the 1800s

▲ Louis Pasteur was a pioneer in medicine. He first proved that many diseases were caused by germs or bacteria.

OBJECTIVE: In what ways did science and medicine help the growth of the Industrial Revolution?

1. Today, most Americans go to a local clinic or their doctor for a health checkup every year. Children are vaccinated against measles, polio, mumps, and other diseases. Adults often get flu shots when doctors predict that disease will spread. When people are in an accident or have a serious health problem, they are taken to nearby hospitals. If they need an operation, skilled doctors and nurses will treat them. Even if they only have a headache or a cold, people take medicine to help make them feel better. It is difficult to imagine what people's lives were like without such health care. Yet most of these advances in medicine first began only a century ago. Medical science probably advanced in response to certain unhealthful conditions that developed during the Industrial Revolution.

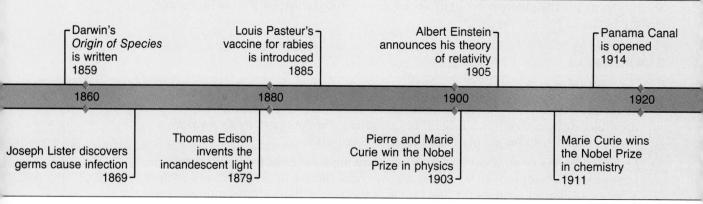

Darwin's *Origin of Species* is written 1859

Louis Pasteur's vaccine for rabies is introduced 1885

Albert Einstein announces his theory of relativity 1905

Panama Canal is opened 1914

1860 — 1880 — 1900 — 1920

Joseph Lister discovers germs cause infection 1869

Thomas Edison invents the incandescent light 1879

Pierre and Marie Curie win the Nobel Prize in physics 1903

Marie Curie wins the Nobel Prize in chemistry 1911

Activity: Have students prepare a chart that compares cities today with cities in the early 1800s. Have them focus on such items as streets, lighting, housing, sanitation, and transportation.

MEDICINE: How did advances in medical science improve people's lives during the years of the Industrial Revolution?

2. In the nineteenth century, large cities grew up around centers of industry. As the population of these cities grew, large numbers of people needed to be fed, clothed, and housed. Disease spread rapidly in these overcrowded cities. The Industrial Revolution might have slowed its pace if many workers had been lost to disease. However, medical science was making discoveries about how diseases spread.

3. Louis Pasteur was a French chemist who helped bring about great changes in medicine. Pasteur made many important discoveries while trying to solve some of the problems faced by French industry. In 1865, Pasteur saved the silk industry in France by finding ways of killing the **bacteria** responsible for spreading silkworm disease. (Bacteria are germs invisible to the naked eye.) Pasteur also helped the wine industry by discovering that heat destroys the bacteria that turn wine sour.

4. Pasteur's experiments also proved that bacteria were responsible for many diseases in people and animals. He then was able to cure or prevent many diseases. Pasteur's experiments also proved that tuberculosis could be spread by drinking milk that had been infected with bacteria. As a result, all the milk people drink today is **pasteurized**, or heated to destroy the bacteria that cause tuberculosis.

5. Scientists in other countries also contributed to the great advances in medicine during the Industrial Revolution. Robert Koch, a German scientist, identified the exact germs that cause cholera and tuberculosis. In 1867, Joseph Lister, an English doctor, discovered how to kill germs that caused infections. Before this discovery, operations were dangerous because patients often died as a result of infection. Lister's discovery made operations safer and more successful. Another English scientist named Alexander Fleming discovered that certain kinds of bread mold were able to kill bacte-ria. Fleming's experiments led to the discovery of penicillin, a drug still used today to cure many diseases.

6. Another major advance in medical science took place in the early 1900s during the building of the Panama Canal in Central America. The Panama Canal was a very important improvement in the world's ocean transportation system. This canal provided a new, direct passage for ships from the Atlantic to the Pacific ocean. However, building of the canal was halted when hundreds of workers began dying of a mysterious disease called **yellow fever**. The symptoms of yellow fever are a fever, vomiting, and the yellowing of the eyeballs and skin. A team of scientists led by Walter Reed, an American doctor, went to Panama to try to learn how the disease was spread. A Cuban doctor named Carlos Juan Finlay finally discovered that yellow fever was spread by mosquitoes in Panama's hot and humid climate. By destroying the mosquitoes' breeding grounds, scientists were able to control the spread of yellow fever. How ◄ did the work of Reed and Finlay aid the completion of the Panama Canal in 1914?

ENERGY AND POWER: How did the need for new sources of power help bring about advances in science?

7. Electricity and other sources of power were vital to the growth of industry and trade. Before the Industrial Revolution, people used their own muscles or the power of animals to run simple machines. However, muscle power was not enough to drive heavy machinery and run large factories. How do you think the development of elec- ◄ tricity helped to advance the Industrial Revolution?

8. Scientists from many countries made important discoveries that increased the use of electrical power. In 1800, an Italian scientist named Allesandro Volta invented one of the first electric batteries. In 1831, Michael Faraday, a British scientist, built the first electric generator. In the United States, Thomas Edison, Alexander Graham

Background: The people of France built the Pasteur Institute in Paris as a monument to Louis Pasteur. It is one of the world's most important medical research centers.

467

Bell, and Lewis Howard Latimer found new ways to use electricity.

PEOPLE IN HISTORY

9. Lewis Howard Latimer, an African American, became one of the pioneers in the field of industrial inventions. Latimer worked with two other great scientists, Thomas Edison and Alexander Graham Bell. As a young man, Latimer served in the Union navy during the Civil War. He then became a draftsman and drew up the plans for new factory machinery. By 1876, Latimer was an expert electrical engineer, and he worked with Bell on several projects. A few years later, Latimer joined the United States Lighting Company in Connecticut. There he invented one of the first **incandescent** bulbs, a light powered by electricity. (Incandescent means white hot.) Later, he worked with Thomas Edison on many of the great inventions made in Edison's laboratory.

10. The use of atomic energy was pioneered by a Polish scientist named Marie Curie. Together with her husband, a French physicist, Marie Curie discovered the **radioactive** elements radium and polonium. (Something that is radioactive gives off radiant energy in the form of alpha, beta, or gamma rays.) In 1903, the Curies won the Nobel Prize in physics. Marie Curie contin-

ued her scientific research after her husband's death. In 1911, she won the Nobel Prize in chemistry. As director of the Radium Institute of Paris, she conducted important research on radioactivity and radium therapy. Marie Curie died in 1934 from the effects of radiation, after a lifetime of studying radioactive materials.

NEW SCIENTIFIC THEORIES: What new scientific ideas were developed during the late 1800s?

11. Albert Einstein was a German-born scientist whose discoveries changed people's understanding of the universe. Einstein's scientific work on the relationship between matter, space, motion, and time resulted in his **theory of relativity.** Einstein's discoveries paved the way for the use of atomic energy as a power source.

12. Charles Darwin was an English scientist whose theories changed the way many people think about the world. On a five-year trip around the world, Darwin studied plants and animals in South America, Australia, and many islands in the Pacific Ocean. In his book *The Origin of Species* published in 1859, Darwin stated his **theory of evolution.** According to Darwin's theory, animals and plants slowly evolve, or develop and change, over long periods of time. Weak forms of life slowly die out, and stronger forms survive by adapting to changing

Daily life in . . .

Thomas Edison, an American, was one of the greatest inventors in history. He patented more than a thousand inventions and helped improve the inventions of many other people. Edison's inventions included the record player, the motion picture camera, and street lighting. Edison did not believe scientists and inventors had to work alone. He hired well-known scientists like Lewis Howard Latimer to work with him in his laboratories in New Jersey. In Edison's well-equipped labs, teams of scientists worked around the clock on various projects. Lab members were encouraged to share their ideas and to help each other as much as possible. Edison's workshops marked the start of the modern industrial research laboratory. In industrial research labs, teams of workers systematically work together to solve a problem. Why do you think working in teams might be more productive?

conditions. This process is called **natural selection**, or survival of the fittest.

SPOTLIGHT ON SOURCES

13. Darwin described his theory of evolution as follows:

> As many more individuals of each species are born than can possibly survive, and as consequently [as a result], there is a frequently recurring [happening again] struggle for existence, it follows that any being, if it vary however [only] slightly in any manner profitable to itself [that helps it], under the complex and sometimes varying conditions of life, will have a better chance of surviving, and thus is naturally selected. From the strong principle of inheritance, any selected variety will tend to propagate [pass along] its new and modified form.
>
> —*On the Origin of Species*, Charles Darwin

14. Darwin's ideas have been used in many different ways. Scientists used the theory of evolution to explain the changes that seem to have taken place in living things throughout the earth's long history. Some economists used Darwin's ideas to explain the way in which businesses compete. They said that the "fittest" businesses would naturally succeed, and businesses that were unfit to survive would just as naturally fail.

15. People also used Darwin's scientific ideas to explain certain theories about society and government. Social Darwinists argued that the universe is made to reward hard work and punish laziness. They wrongly said that poor people were responsible for their own poverty. Social Darwinists believed governments and wealthy individuals should not change the natural way of things by aiding needy people. Some people used the phrase "survival of the fittest" to explain why weaker people are sometimes left to suffer. They falsely claimed that "superior" people had a

▲ Marie Curie shared the Nobel Prize with her husband in 1903. She won the Nobel Prize again in 1911, the first woman so honored.

"natural right" to rule the world. How ◀ might this misunderstanding of Darwin's theory contribute to social injustice?

OUTLOOK

16. Many great discoveries in science and medicine improved people's lives in industrial nations during the later years of the Industrial Revolution. New methods of curing and preventing diseases helped save people's lives. Discoveries in electricity and atomic energy set the stage for events that occurred in the twentieth century. As a result of improved communication, people in other parts of the world soon learned about these great medical and scientific discoveries. How did these discoveries help people of nonindustrialized lands? Why are medical discoveries today still shared among nations?

Background: Some believe that Hitler's theory of "Aryan Superiority" was based on Social Darwinism. Point out to the class how this illustrates the potential for misuse of scientific theories.

469

CHAPTER REVIEW

VOCABULARY REVIEW

Write each of the following sentences on a sheet of paper. Then fill in the blank with the word that best completes each sentence.

bacteria

pasteurized

theory of evolution

natural selection

yellow fever

incandescent

radioactive

theory of relativity

1. _____ were the invisible germs that were responsible for spreading the silkworm disease.

2. Darwin's _____ states that animals and plants slowly change over long periods of time.

3. When milk is heated to destroy the bacteria that can cause tuberculosis, it is _____ .

4. The process in which weak forms of life slowly die out and stronger forms survive is called _____ .

5. Something that is white hot is called _____ .

6. Einstein's discussion of the relationship between matter, space, motion, and time is called the _____ .

7. A disease caused by the mosquito that produces fever and yellowing of the skin is _____ .

8. Radium is very _____ .

SKILL BUILDER: MAKING A TIME LINE

Thomas Alva Edison was a genius in technology. The phonograph and motion pictures were two of Edison's inventions that changed people's ways of living.

Look at the list of years below. Next to each year is a statement about an accomplishment of Thomas Edison. On a sheet of paper, construct a time line using the information given below.

1847–Thomas Alva Edison is born.

1877–Phonograph is invented.

1882–A central light and power station in New York City is designed by Edison.

1889–Edison invents the first successful motion picture device.

1931–Thomas Alva Edison dies.

SKILL BUILDER: CRITICAL THINKING AND COMPREHENSION

1. Sequencing

▶ Rewrite the following events in the order in which they happened.

a. The Panama Canal opens.

b. Marie Curie receives the Nobel Prize in chemistry.

c. Darwin's theory of evolution is published in his book *The Origin of Species*.

d. The Curies win the Nobel Prize.

e. Latimer becomes an expert electrical engineer.

f. Lister discovers how to kill germs that cause infections.

g. Faraday builds the first electric generator.

2. Drawing Conclusions

▶ Reread paragraphs 3, 4, 5 and 6. Copy the sentence that draws the best conclusion from the information in those paragraphs.

a. Bacteria are dangerous.

b. Through careful scientific research, dangerous bacteria can be controlled.

c. All diseases are spread by bugs.

3. Point of View

▶ Copy the following statements that express points of view. After each statement, write the name of the person who probably would have expressed that point of view.

Louis Pasteur   Alexander Fleming

Thomas Edison   Lewis Latimer

Charles Darwin   Marie Curie

a. Only the strongest will survive.

b. My discovery will help prevent death from infection.

c. If you heat the wine, it will no longer turn sour.

d. I do not believe in slavery.

e. Scientists should work in teams and share their ideas.

f. Radioactive elements can be dangerous to your health.

4. Hypothesizing

a. Write a sentence explaining what you think was Louis Pasteur's working hypothesis that led to his pasteurizing milk.

b. Write a sentence explaining what you think was Carlos Juan Finlay's working hypothesis that led to the discovery of how yellow fever was spread.

ENRICHMENT

1. Find out the meaning of the word *volt*, and why it came from Allesandro Volta's name.

2. Write a brief essay expressing your opinion regarding Social Darwinism. Do you think hard work should be rewarded and laziness punished? Why? Share your opinion with your classmates.

471

UNIT REVIEW

SUMMARY

The period from the early 1700s to the early 1900s saw a major change in the course of history. This change was called the Industrial Revolution. During this time, many nations in the western world changed from rural, agricultural economies to urban, industrial economies. Industrialization meant using machines, powered by water or by steam engines, to produce more goods at lower cost. New inventions caused textile weaving to become a major industry. As textile factories grew, cities grew around them. Although new machinery improved agriculture, people poured into cities in search of factory jobs. Living and working conditions were often poor in crowded industrial cities. With the invention of the steam engine and improvements in methods for making steel, heavy industry developed. As industry spread, the need for raw materials and new markets caused European nations to set up colonies in America, Asia, and Africa. Scientific and medical discoveries were stimulated by industrial needs and by health problems in overcrowded cities. Urbanism led to movements for social reform. Trade unions developed and women struggled for the right to vote. Transportation, communications, and improvements in living standards advanced dramatically in industrialized nations. Your way of life today is almost entirely dependent on changes that occurred during the Industrial Revolution.

SKILL BUILDER: READING A GRAPH

▶ Study the graph below. Then select the word or phrase that best completes each sentence that follows. Write your answers on a sheet of paper.

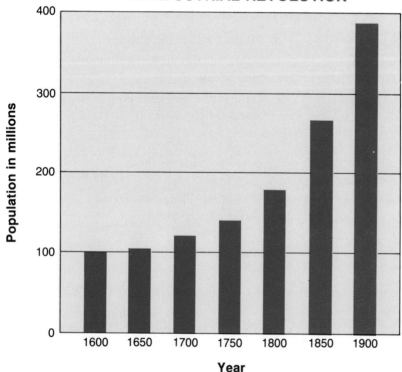

EUROPEAN POPULATION DURING
THE INDUSTRIAL REVOLUTION

Source: *Atlas of World Population History*,
Colin McEvedy and Richard Jones, Penguin Books,
Middlesex, England, 1978

472

1. Between 1650 and 1750 the population of Europe _____
   a. almost doubled   b. increased by 41 million   c. increased by 144 million

2. Between 1750 and 1850 the population of Europe _____
   a. increased by 30 million   b. almost doubled   c. increased by 200 million

3. Between 1650 and 1850 the population of Europe _____
   a. increased by 171 million   b. almost tripled   c. increased by 130 million

4. Between 1850 and 1950 the population of Europe _____
   a. more than tripled   b. increased by 302 million   c. almost doubled

5. Between 1950 and 2050 the population of Europe will have increased at a rate that is _____ than the rate of increase between 1850 and 1950.
   a. slower   b. faster   c. much faster

SKILL BUILDER: CRITICAL THINKING AND COMPREHENSION

1. Making Judgments

▶ Read the paragraph below. Then select the statement that makes the best judgment about the paragraph.

1-1.   The Industrial Revolution began when water power was first used to run machines in textile factories. This meant that a textile factory had to be built beside a river or waterfall. Soon the machines in many factories were run by steam engines.
   a. During this time many rivers and waterfalls dried up.
   b. Steam engines could be built almost anywhere.
   c. Steam engines would only work beside a river or stream.
   d. Rivers and streams were needed for drinking water.

2. Sequencing

▶ List the events in each group below in the order in which they happened.

a. Samuel Morse invents the telegraph.
   Thomas Edison invents the light bulb.
   Alexander Graham Bell invents the telephone.

b. The Krupp family builds steel mills in the Ruhr Valley.
   William Slater builds a textile mill in America.
   Eli Whitney invents the cotton gin.
   The Trade Union Act is passed in England.

c. Charles Darwin writes *On the Origin of Species*.
   Karl Marx writes *The Communist Manifesto*.
   Albert Einstein publishes his theory of relativity.

ENRICHMENT

Make a chart of scientific discoveries and inventions that occurred during the Industrial Revolution. Use the library to find information about twelve important breakthroughs. Make a small drawing to illustrate each discovery or invention, and draw connecting arrows to show how one breakthrough led to another.

ESL/LEP Strategy: Prior to beginning this unit, list on the chalkboard facts students already know about colonialism and imperialism. At the end of this unit, ask students to add new information about how imperialism was one of the causes of World War I. Ask students to add what they know about the effects of imperialism on their countries of origin.

IMPERIALISM LEADS TO WORLD WAR I

OBJECTIVE: Unit 10 will show how rival European and Asian powers rushed to colonize different parts of the world, and how this rivalry led to World War I.

British start
Opium War
in China
1839

Suez Canal
is built
1869

Triple
Alliance
is formed
1882

1800 **1820** **1840** **1860** **1880**

Monroe Doctrine
is issued
1823

Treaty of
Nanjing is
signed
1842

Indian National
Congress party
is formed
1885

▲ Queen Victoria is proclaimed "Empress of India" on January 1, 1877, in Delhi, India.

ited States
s Spanish-
erican War
1898

Japan wins
Russo-Japanese
War
1905

Triple
Entente
is formed
1907

Germans sign
Treaty
of Versailles
1919

1900

1920

oxer Rebellion
takes place
in China
1900

Muslim League
is formed
1906

World War I
begins
1914

CHAPTER 1

Imperialism and Africa

▲ The Zambezi River in Africa plunges 355 feet over Victoria Falls. Why do you think the falls were named in 1855 for a British queen?

> **OBJECTIVE:** Which European nations took over Africa in the late 1800s and how were the lives of Africa's peoples changed as a result?

1. Deep in the heart of Africa is a magnificent waterfall. Its blue and white waters form beautiful misty rainbows as they plunge with a mighty roar into the deep valley floor below. Africans long ago named this waterfall Mosi Oa Tunya, meaning "smoke that thunders." Today, however, it is known throughout the world as Victoria Falls. Why is one of Africa's greatest natural wonders named after a British queen? Like many other places in Africa, it was given a new name by one of the European nations that took over Africa in the late 1800s. In the 1800s industrial nations of Europe swept through the continent taking control and making changes. The invaders told native Africans what laws to obey, where to live, which language to speak, and what taxes to pay. Imagine how life must have changed for Africans as outsiders took charge of their lands.

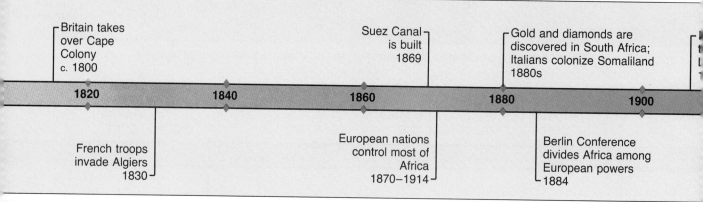

Britain takes over Cape Colony c. 1800

French troops invade Algiers 1830

1820

1840

Suez Canal is built 1869

1860

European nations control most of Africa 1870–1914

Gold and diamonds are discovered in South Africa; Italians colonize Somaliland 1880s

Berlin Conference divides Africa among European powers 1884

1880

1900

IMPERIALISM: Why did industrialized nations want new territories?

2. Imperialism (im-PEER-ee-al-izm) is a national policy of taking control of another nation or territory. During the years from 1870 until 1914, nations in Europe took control of nearly all of Africa and parts of Asia. At the same time, the United States and Japan also entered the competition for overseas possessions.

3. The major cause of imperialism was the Industrial Revolution. By 1870 Europe, the United States, and Japan had industries that demanded more raw materials than these nations could supply. So they looked to other parts of the world to find them. ▶ What are some raw materials the United States must import today? The industrialized nations also needed new markets for their growing output of manufactured goods. They created new markets by taking control of countries in Asia and Africa. Factory owners and merchants were earning large profits in industrialized nations and looked to Africa and Asia as places to invest their profits and make even more money.

4. In addition to economics, nationalism, or the feeling of pride in one's nation, was a strong motivator of imperialism. People in industrialized nations were proud of their strong nations and believed that by taking control of other lands they could make their nations even stronger. Many people in imperialist nations also believed that their way of life was superior to that of others. They were eager to take their medicines, scientific discoveries, and new inventions to the rest of the world. Religion was another motivating factor. Some people believed that they had a duty to spread Christianity to other lands.

IMPERIALISM IN ACTION: What methods did European nations use to build their empires?

5. The imperialist nations had three methods of building an empire. In most cases, an imperialist nation sent its army into a territory to set up a **colony** (KAHL-

uh-nee). Local leaders were replaced with foreigners from the more powerful nation, which completely controlled and directly governed the colony. Or an imperialist nation might set up a **protectorate** (proh-TEK-tuh-ret) that forced a ruler to submit to foreign rule. The native ruler of a protectorate usually kept his title but lost power. Occasionally an imperialist nation only demanded special rights to carry on business and trade in certain locations. Where an imperialist nation had these rights, the area was called a **sphere of influence.**

6. Whichever way a European country chose to govern its African possessions, the goal was the same: to make the colony pay for itself, while earning money for the home country. European countries took a number of measures to ensure that this goal was met. Where minerals were plentiful, they set up mines. For example, mining operations were started in the Belgian Congo (Zaire, today), where copper was found, and in South Africa, where diamonds could be mined for profit. In other areas Europeans encouraged the production of profitable farm products such as rubber or peanuts.

7. The imperialist powers also raised money through taxes, which the Africans had to pay in cash. In order to get cash, many Africans were forced to take jobs in the mines or on the large farms, called plantations, owned by Europeans.

EUROPE AND AFRICA: How were European nations able to take over most of Africa?

8. Inventions made during the Industrial Revolution helped Europeans overpower African peoples between 1870 and 1914. For example, new railroads and steamships made it possible for an imperialist nation to send armies and supplies to Africa quickly. In addition, new and deadly weapons such as repeating rifles and machine guns were used to defeat the Africans, who lacked modern weapons.

9. New medicines also helped Europe take over African lands. Early European explorers could not travel into the interior

Activity: Ask volunteers to recall their reading about the Industrial Revolution in Unit 9. **Ask:** What changes did this revolution bring to Europe and the United States?

477

▲ American journalist Henry M. Stanley finds the missing Scottish explorer David Livingstone at Lake Tanganyika in 1871.

ain began financing explorers to find out more about Africa. Britain soon claimed much of the land in Central and East Africa. Henry Stanley, an American, made an important journey into Central Africa in the 1870s to explore the Congo River for King Leopold II of Belgium. Leopold set up a company to rule the Congo, a land rich in copper and rubber.

12. Germany and other European nations began to move into East Africa in the 1880s. A scramble for Africa began as the rival European nations rushed to claim control over more and more areas in Africa. To settle the conflicting claims that arose, Germany called a meeting at Berlin in 1884. Fourteen European nations sent representatives to the Berlin Conference, but no African peoples were invited. Why do you think ◄ Africans were excluded? The Europeans agreed on how they would divide up Africa. Look at the map on the bottom of page 479 to see how Africa was divided among the European nations. Without ever considering tribal loyalties or the rights of African peoples, the Europeans had carved up Africa for themselves.

NORTH AFRICA: Which imperialist powers from Europe gained colonies in North Africa?

13. In North Africa, the two chief imperialist powers were France and Britain. In 1827 the French consul to Algeria was slapped in the face by the governor of Algiers. In 1830 the French took Algiers, removing the governor from office. By 1848 France had colonized Algeria and in 1881 Tunisia became a French protectorate. By 1900, several European nations tried to gain control of Morocco. With a combination of clever diplomacy and a show of military strength, France won the struggle. Except for a small part that went to Spain, Morocco became a French protectorate.

of Africa because of the threat of tropical diseases. By the late 1800s, however, Europeans had developed medicines and vaccines to protect them from some diseases.

CENTRAL AND EAST AFRICA: How did explorers open up these parts of Africa to imperialism?

10. Until the mid-1800s, Europeans knew little about the interior of Africa. Then in the 1850s David Livingstone, a Scottish doctor and missionary, became the first European to travel across the interior of Africa. His reports about the land and the people he saw in Africa were of great interest to Europeans. They were excited by Livingstone's account of his trip up the Zambesi (zam-BEE-zee) River and his discovery of a magnificent waterfall. Livingstone named the waterfall Victoria Falls, for Queen Victoria of England.

11. Political and business leaders in Brit-

14. Britain became alarmed when a French company built the Suez Canal in 1869. The canal is a vital waterway that allows ships to travel from the Mediterranean Sea to the Red Sea. Whoever con-

Activity: Have students speculate about why North Africa is considered part of the Middle East region and the rest of Africa—Sub-Saharan Africa—is a region unto itself.

478

trolled the canal could control trade over the route. To end French competition in the area, Britain quietly bought up stock in the company that ran the canal. Britain gained controlling shares of the Suez Canal in 1875. Then, in 1882, Britain turned Egypt into a British protectorate. How did controlling Egypt protect the Suez Canal for Britain? From Egypt, the British army moved south into the Sudan. After a long struggle, the British defeated the Sudanese army in the 1890s.

15. If you look at the map at the bottom of this page, you will see that Italy and Spain held small portions of North Africa. In the 1880s Italy colonized much of Somaliland and Eritrea (er-uh-TREE-uh). In 1895 Italy sent troops to take over Ethiopia near the Red Sea. The Ethiopians pushed back the Italians. The ancient kingdom of Ethiopia remained independent. In 1911 Italy also took over Libya on the Mediterranean Sea. Spain controlled small parts of North Africa.

WEST AND SOUTH AFRICA: How were the lands of West and South Africa affected by European imperialism?

16. Britain and France took over most of West Africa. When the European nations and the United States ended the slave trade in the early 1800s, many freed slaves settled in the British colony of Sierra Leone. Other freed slaves moved to the new, independent nation of Liberia. After 1870 the British conquered Nigeria and the Gold Coast, and the French took the Ivory Coast, Dahomey, and French Guinea. Portugal claimed a small colony on the Atlantic coast.

17. At the southern tip of Africa was a land that became a battleground between Africans and Europeans. The weather in South Africa was pleasant and the soil good for farming. As a result, settlers were attracted to the region. South Africa was the home of several African peoples in 1652 when Dutch settlers started the Dutch Cape Colony. In 1814-1815 the British took over

▼ By 1900 nearly all of Africa had been claimed and divided into colonies by European powers. Which colonies were claimed by Germany in 1914? Which were claimed by Great Britain?

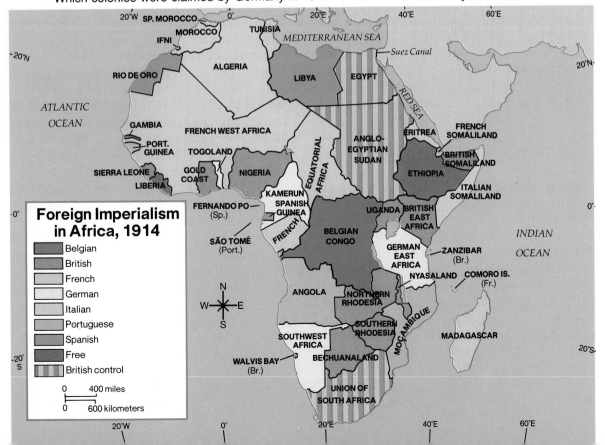

Foreign Imperialism in Africa, 1914

- Belgian
- British
- French
- German
- Italian
- Portuguese
- Spanish
- Free
- British control

0   400 miles

0   600 kilometers

the Cape Colony from the Dutch by a treaty of the Congress of Vienna..

18. Descendants of the Dutch settlers, called **Boers** (BOHRZ), did not want to live under British rule. (*Boer* is a Dutch word meaning "farmer.") The British had made English the official language of South Africa. They also favored fair treatment of the native African peoples, which the Boers thought was against God's will. As a result, in the 1830s about 10,000 Boers moved north in protest, carrying all their belongings in covered wagons. Following this Great Trek north, the Boers set up two republics called Transvaal (trans-VAL) and the Orange Free State. The Boers soon came in conflict with the **Zulus** (ZOO-looz), a farming people who were expanding their empire into the same region.

PEOPLE IN HISTORY

19. In the early 1800s, Shaka ruled the Zulu nation northeast of the area where the Boers set up republics. Shaka was a clever military leader who built a large army that he used to control the 50,000 people in his nation. Shaka taught his soldiers new ways of fighting with short, sharp spears and trained them to move quickly. Shaka's army conquered other tribes in the region and fought the Boers who moved into Zulu land. Shaka trained his army so well that even after his death in 1828, the Zulus fought the Boers and British for many years. The British finally defeated the Zulus in 1879.

20. In the 1880s, the discovery of gold and diamonds in the Boer republic of the Transvaal brought new conflict to South Africa. Treasure seekers flocked to the Transvaal from all parts of the world. One of them, Cecil Rhodes, made a fortune in the diamond mines there. In 1890, Rhodes became prime minister of the British Cape Colony. He expanded British control northward, acquiring a land later named Rhodesia in his honor. In 1899 the Boers declared war on the British. Although the Boers were

outnumbered, they fought for three years before they laid down their arms. In 1910, Britain combined the Boer republics with the British territories to form the Union of South Africa.

SPOTLIGHT ON SOURCES

21. Many African peoples fought to defend their freedom. Chief Macemba of Tanganyika spoke these words to the Germans who took over his land:

> I have listened to your words but can find no reason why I should obey you—I would rather die first . . . . If it be friendship you desire, then I am ready for it, but to be your subject, that I cannot be . . . . If it should be war you desire, then I am ready, but never to be your subject.
> —from *The African Past*, Basil Davidson

OUTLOOK

22. Have you ever been curious about your ancestors? If so, you will understand why Alex Haley, an African American writer, wanted to trace his roots in The Gambia, which is in West Africa. Haley went to The Gambia to learn more about his past. There he found people who could tell stories of village life in the old days. These stories included information about one of Haley's ancestors who was taken as a slave long ago. In 1976 Haley published a book called *Roots* that tells what he learned about his history. Haley's experience shows that people in The Gambia have held on to their tradition of passing down their history through storytelling. In spite of many years of control by imperialist nations, not all African traditions had died. However, some of the changes brought by Europeans eventually led to the growth of African nationalism. In colonial schools, Africans learned Western ideas about liberty, equality, and the rights of people. Soon many Africans would begin to fight for their independence.

A Geographic View of History

Climate Regions and Colonial Exports of Africa   European nations wanted colonies in Africa to make money by exporting, or selling to other countries, Africa's many minerals and agricultural products. Africa is a continent with a variety of climates. Climate plays a large part in determining where agricultural products can be grown. The map on this page shows Africa's climate regions and some of the products produced in Africa during colonial times. Read the following facts about Africa's climate regions and exports during colonial times. Then, on a sheet of paper, answer the questions that follow.

Facts

In the tropical Belgian Congo, Africans worked almost like slaves to mine copper and diamonds.

In West Africa, large plantations of palm trees and cocoa trees were planted near the coast. Palm and cocoa trees thrive on high temperatures and rain.

Coffee and tea were in great demand in Europe. Both crops grow well in hilly and mountainous areas.

Africa's desert climates are too dry for crops, but irrigation can make these lands productive. During colonial times, cotton was grown on irrigated land.

1. What type or types of climates are found in the area that was the Belgian Congo? What minerals did the Belgians export?

2. What agricultural products came from British and French West Africa? Which one of these products grows in a climate region called "tropical with a dry season"?

3. What type of climate does most of North Africa have? What agricultural products came from North Africa? What technique was used to grow crops in dry North Africa?

4. Where were coffee and tea produced? What climate region do these crops need?

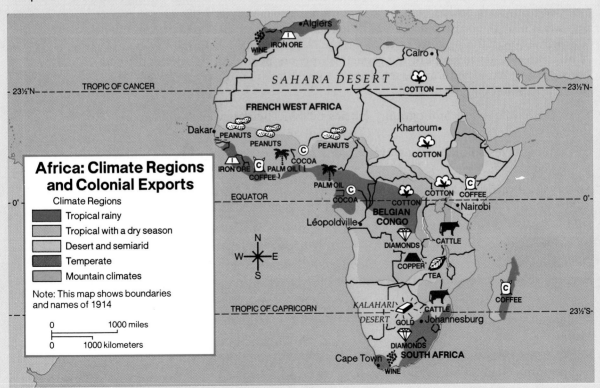

Africa: Climate Regions and Colonial Exports

Climate Regions
- Tropical rainy
- Tropical with a dry season
- Desert and semiarid
- Temperate
- Mountain climates

Note: This map shows boundaries and names of 1914

0   1000 miles
0   1000 kilometers

481

CHAPTER REVIEW

VOCABULARY REVIEW

Write each number and word on a sheet of paper. Then write the letter of the definition next to the word it defines.

1. imperialism
2. colony
3. protectorate
4. sphere of influence
5. Boers
6. Zulus

a. a nation that has a local ruler but is really ruled by another nation

b. Africans who had a nation northeast of the Boer republics

c. territory governed directly by an outside power

d. a nation's policy of taking control over another nation or territory

e. land within a nation where another nation has special rights to do business

f. descendants of Dutch settlers in South Africa

SKILL BUILDER: WRITING FOOTNOTES AND BIBLIOGRAPHIES

When you write a report, you may need to use footnotes and make a bibliography. A *footnote* is an explanation below the text on a page. It may tell the source of a quotation or give additional information about something in the text. A number in the text matches the number of the footnote. A *bibliography* is an alphabetical listing of all sources used to prepare the report. It appears at the end of the report and names the title and author of each source, as well as its publisher, city of publication, and copyright date.

▶ Read the footnote and bibliography entries below. Then answer the questions that follow.

Shaka taught his soldiers new ways of fighting with short, sharp spears and new improved shields.[1]

Footnote: Donald R. Morris, *The Washing of the Spears: A History of the Rise of the Zulu Nation under Shaka* (New York: Simon and Schuster, 1965), p. 47.

Bibliography: Morris, Donald R. *The Washing of the Spears: A History of the Rise of the Zulu Nation under Shaka.* New York: Simon and Schuster, 1965.

Bibliography: Zaner, John. "More Blood than Brains: 'Shaka Zulu' Comes to the TV Screen." *Weekday Magazine*, 19 December 1984, p. 46.

a. On what page of Morris's book is there information about Zulu methods of fighting?

b. Where can you find a review of a TV program called "Shaka Zulu"?

c. When was *The Washing of the Spears* published?

d. List two differences between the forms of a footnote and a bibliography entry.

STUDY HINT Make an outline of the colonization of Africa in the 1800s and early 1900s by European nations. Check your outline against the map on page 479.

SKILL BUILDER: CRITICAL THINKING AND COMPREHENSION

1. Classifying

▶ Number a sheet of paper from one to seven. Write the letter or letters of the person or country that each of the following statements describes.

a. David Livingstone   **d.** France

b. Germany   **e.** Britain

c. Henry Stanley   **f.** Italy

1. Made Algeria into a colony and Tunisia a protectorate

2. First European to travel across the interior of Africa

3. Began to move into East Africa in the 1880s

4. Took over Somaliland and Eritrea

5. Explored the Congo for King Leopold II of Belgium

6. Turned Egypt into a protectorate in 1882

7. Named Victoria Falls for Queen Victoria of England

2. Cause and Effect

▶ Read each of the statements of causes below. Then write a result of each cause.

a. Factories in industrialized nations produced a growing output of goods.

b. The British took over the Cape Colony.

c. David Livingstone traveled through Africa's interior.

3. Fact *versus* Opinion

▶ The paragraph below contains facts and opinions. Read the paragraph and then answer the questions that follow it.

(A) E.A. Ritter's biography *Shaka Zulu* was first published in 1955 and **(B)** is still in print; **(C)** it is a highly popular tale **(D)** that shows the author's great familiarity with the details of Shaka's life; **(E)** the book has no table of contents or index; and **(F)** that lack makes the book difficult to use for research.

a. On a sheet of paper, write the letters of three facts from the paragraph.

b. Write the letters of three opinions from the paragraph.

c. Write the letters of two opinions that are supported by facts in the paragraph. Also write the supporting facts.

d. Write the letter of one opinion not supported by fact in the paragraph.

ENRICHMENT

1. Find out more about the Zambesi River and Victoria Falls. Make a map of the river and draw in and label important geographical features along the river.

2. Choose one former African colony. Research the history of that colony. Find out, for example, which country controlled it, what products it produced, what improvements came to the colony, and what problems arose. Make a chart telling what you found out.

CHAPTER 2

China and the West

▲ Chinese peasants captured many cities during the Taiping Rebellion. The rebellion opened China to foreign imperialism.

OBJECTIVE: How did the imperialist nations weaken China?

1. Today, the widespread use of drugs is a serious problem that worries many Americans. Drugs that are brought into the United States against the law are a threat to Americans' health and safety. Imagine, then, what might happen if several other nations became more powerful than the United States. Suppose these nations forced the United States to trade its cars, computers, and wheat for drugs. Fortunately, this is only an imaginary scene for the United States. About 150 years ago, however, the Chinese people faced just such a problem. One of the chief products that Europe sold to China was drugs. European nations forced China to trade its silks and tea for opium, a habit-forming drug. At the time,

European nations were practicing imperialism, as you have read. In China, as in Africa, great changes resulted from European imperialism. The very basis of Chinese civilization was worn away. China's independence as a nation was severely threatened.

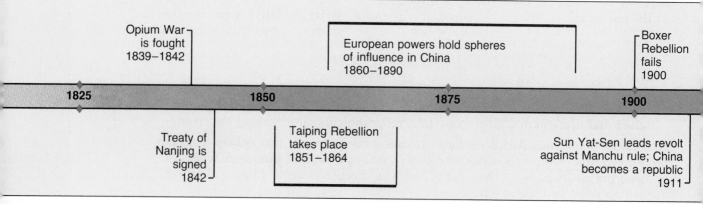

Opium War
is fought
1839–1842

European powers hold spheres
of influence in China
1860–1890

Boxer
Rebellion
fails
1900

1825   1850   1875   1900

Treaty of
Nanjing is
signed
1842

Taiping Rebellion
takes place
1851–1864

Sun Yat-Sen leads revolt
against Manchu rule; China
becomes a republic
1911

Background: Opium was first introduced into China in the late 1600s and its use spread quickly. The Chinese government tried to stop the growing, selling, and importing of opium in the 1700s.

THE WEAK MANCHU RULERS: What chain of events in China opened the door to imperialism?

2. In 1644, people from Manchuria conquered China and set up the Manchu, or Ching, dynasty. By the 1800s the Manchu power was weakened by corruption. Also, the population of China was growing rapidly, reaching 300 million by the 1800s. There was not always enough food to feed so many people. These problems led to a number of rebellions against the Manchu government. Europeans saw these troubles as a way to gain advantages in China.

3. British traders had begun to trade for China's silks, tea, and porcelain in the 1600s. However, the Manchu rulers had carefully limited British access to China. These rulers also had refused to treat the British traders as equals, since the Chinese people believed that they were superior to other people.

4. By the 1830s, the British found a product to trade with China that led to a war. The British bought opium in other places and took it to China to trade for Chinese products. The Manchu rulers soon saw that the growing use of opium was very harmful to their people. They tried to stop the opium trade. In 1839 a Chinese official wrote to England's Queen Victoria about the problem. "Let us ask," he wrote, "where is your conscience? . . . Since it [opium] is not permitted to do harm to your own country, then even less should you let it be passed on to the harm of other countries—how much less to China!"

5. Soon afterward, the Chinese government seized $6 million worth of opium that was to have been sold through Canton. The British used this action as an excuse to start the Opium War, which lasted from 1839 until 1842. The Chinese military could not match the superior weapons of the British and by 1842 the Chinese had lost the war.

6. The Treaty of Nanjing ended the war in 1842. It forced China to lower its tax on all traded goods and to open four other ports to British traders. Within a short time, China was forced to give several other nations most of the trading rights it had granted to Britain.

7. China was further weakened by a peasant uprising known as the Taiping (TY-ping) Rebellion, which lasted from 1851 to 1864. Its leaders promised reforms, such as more equal ownership of land. The rebels were able to gain control of more than half of China. Finally, though, they were crushed by the Ching rulers.

8. As the Taiping Rebellion raged, Britain and China again went to war. With France's help, Britain defeated the Ching army. Following this defeat, China had to open additional ports to foreign trade. The Chinese government was forced to accept Western nations as equals and to agree to protect Christian missionaries in China. The Chinese were also forced to allow foreigners to use the laws of their own nations in governing their Chinese territories.

9. As a result of the war, the imperialist powers realized just how weak China had become. They saw their chance to take over large territories in China. Russia forced China to give up land along the Sea of Japan. There, in 1860, Russia built the port of Vladivostok (vlad-uh-vuh-STAK) as an important trading center. Why do you think ◄ this was a good port for trade? In the 1880s–1890s the French took over Indochina, land that is now the nations of Vietnam, Laos, and Cambodia. Japan, too, soon became interested in Indochina, especially Korea. For a long time China had controlled Korea's foreign affairs and trade. In 1894 Japan and China went to war over Korea. Japan easily won the war. China had to give Korea its independence and also had to give up the island of Formosa and other territory to Japan.

SPHERES OF INFLUENCE: How did imperialist powers rule parts of China?

10. Some nations became worried that China might soon collapse as a nation, so they proposed a plan. Each foreign nation would set up its own sphere of influence in

Ask: Have students recall their earlier reading about European trade with China. What products did Europeans especially want from China and the East Indies? (silk, spices, porcelain)

485

China. Within its sphere of influence, the foreign nation had the right to build railroads, open mines, and lease large amounts of land from the Chinese government.

11. Great Britain, France, Germany, and Russia held spheres of influence in all parts of China. The United States, which was emerging as a world power at the end of the nineteenth century, also wanted to trade with China. For this reason, the United States did not want to see China carved up by imperialist powers. In 1899 the United States proposed freedom of trade among the spheres of influence in China. The United States' **Open Door policy,** as it was called, went into effect soon afterward.

THE BOXER REBELLION: What were the causes and results of this uprising?

12. The Chinese people were deeply angry at the foreign nations for dividing their country into spheres of influence. They disagreed, however, over what to do. Some argued that the only way to make China strong again was to accept Western ideas.

Others felt strongly that they had to drive the foreigners out of their land. Some Chinese people who wanted to drive out the foreigners formed a secret group known as the Righteous Harmonious Fists. Europeans called members of this group **Boxers**.

SPOTLIGHT ON SOURCES

13. The leaders of the Boxers asked the Chinese people to join them:

Attention: all people in markets and villages of all provinces of China— now, [because] Catholics and Protestants have vilified [spoken harshly against] our gods and sages [wise persons], have deceived [lied to] our emperors and ministers [officials] above, and oppressed [treated cruelly] the Chinese people below . . . . This forces us to practice the . . . magic boxing [revolt] so as to protect our country, [drive out] the foreign bandits . . .

—from *China's Response to the West*, by Ssu-Yu Teng and John K. Fairbank

▼ By the early 1900s, the world's major powers had divided China into spheres of influence and won control of China's trade. What foreign power controlled trade at Shanghai?

Foreign Spheres of Influence in China About 1900

- British sphere of influence
- French sphere of influence
- German sphere of influence
- Japanese sphere of influence
- Russian sphere of influence

Note: This map shows present-day country names and boundaries

0   400 miles
0   600 kilometers

14. In 1900 the Boxers began an uprising in northern China. Boxers killed many foreign missionaries whom the Boxers hated for opposing ancestor worship and other age-old Chinese beliefs. The Boxers also surrounded the European section of Beijing and kept the Europeans contained for several months. To protect their citizens, several foreign powers, including the United States, sent troops to free the foreign section and defeat the Boxers. Then the foreign nations forced the Empress Tz'u-hsi (TSOO-SHEE) to sign a treaty giving the European nations even greater power than before. European nations now could station their soldiers in China and send ships to protect their ports.

15. After the failure of the Boxer Rebellion, many Chinese realized there was a desperate need for change in the government of China. While many nations had industrialized, life in China had remained the same. The inventions and improved farming and manufacturing methods brought about by the Industrial Revolution were foreign to China. The Chinese, understandably, had a strong reluctance to adopt Western ways. Empress Tz'u-hsi had refused to allow any reforms, so when she died in 1908, China was ripe for change. In 1911 Chinese revolutionaries overthrew the Manchu dynasty and set up a republic. The man who led the revolt was Sun Yat-sen (SOON-YAT-SEN).

▲ Tz'u-hsi was China's last great empress. After her death, the Manchu Dynasty was overthrown and China became a republic.

PEOPLE IN HISTORY

16. Sun Yat-sen, a man who was called the "father of new China," was the son of peasant parents. Sun studied medicine in Hong Kong but decided that he was more interested in helping his country than in becoming a doctor. He tried many times to start a revolution, but failed. Sun left China and began using his energy to raise money for a revolution. Finally, in 1911, the revolution began and Sun returned to China. Sun became the first president of the Republic of China. Sun was determined to bring peace to China and to base his government on democratic ideas. What rebellion in China in June of 1989 had a similar goal? Until his death in 1925, Sun worked to make China into a strong, modern nation.

OUTLOOK

17. Today, China is one of the largest nations in the world. It has more than one billion people, about one quarter of the world's population. The Chinese call their country Chung-kuo, which means Middle Kingdom or Central Country. In the past they thought of their land as the center of the world. By the early 1900s Sun Yat-sen would say of China, "Today we are the poorest and weakest nation in the world and occupy the lowest position in [world] affairs. Other men are the carving knife and serving dish; we are the fish and the meat."

Activity: Have students read an encyclopedia entry on Empress Tz'u-hsi and write a short essay describing how the empress gained power and kept it in China for almost 50 years.

487

CHAPTER REVIEW

VOCABULARY REVIEW

Write each of the following words on a sheet of paper. Then write the correct definition for each word. Use the glossary on pages 728–737 to help you.

Boxers

Open Door policy

SKILL BUILDER: INTERPRETING LINE GRAPHS

Study the line graph below. Then answer the questions that follow on a sheet of paper.

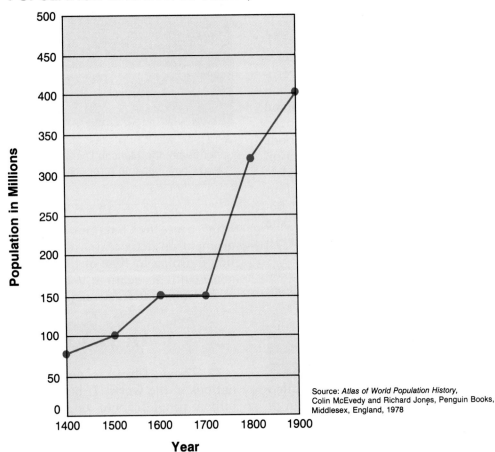

POPULATION GROWTH IN CHINA, 1400-1900

Source: *Atlas of World Population History,* Colin McEvedy and Richard Jones, Penguin Books, Middlesex, England, 1978

1. What years does the graph cover?
2. What was China's population in 1600? in 1850?
3. Make a generalization about China's population between 1400 and 1850?
4. China's population doubled between 1740 and 1850. What might have been one reason for this great increase?

488

SKILL BUILDER: CRITICAL THINKING AND COMPREHENSION

1. Summarizing

▶ Reread paragraphs 7–8 about the Taiping Rebellion. Choose the statement below that you think is an accurate summary of the paragraph. Write the letter of your choice on a sheet of paper.

a. During the Taiping Rebellion (1851–1864), peasants got control of over half of China before they were crushed.

b. The Taiping Rebellion was a religious uprising.

c. Although the Manchus put down the rebellion, they lost ground to the Europeans, who attacked during the uprising.

2. Generalizing

▶ Read the sentences below, which are based on information in this chapter. Then, on a sheet of paper, write a generalization about China based on these sentences.

Great Britain's sphere of influence included areas north of Hong Kong and west of Shanghai.

Russia's sphere of influence was in China's large northern provinces of Outer Mongolia and Manchuria.

Germany's sphere of influence went from Kiachow Bay inland along the Yellow River.

France's sphere of influence went along the southern coast.

3. Compare and Contrast

▶ Answer the questions that follow on a sheet of paper.

a. State one similarity between the attitude of the United States and the attitude of European powers toward trade with China.

b. State one way in which the Taiping Rebellion and the Boxer Rebellion differed.

4. Point of View

▶ Reread paragraph 1 in this chapter. On a sheet of paper, write the letter of the statement below that best represents the point of view of the author.

a. The imperialists were unfair to force China to trade drugs for goods.

b. The drug problem in the United States today is very much like the situation in China 150 years ago.

c. The Chinese themselves caused the problems they had with European countries.

ENRICHMENT

1. Do research on the Taiping Rebellion. The Taipings were against foot-binding, slavery, opium-smoking, gambling, and the use of tobacco and wine. They were for the equality of men and women and the distribution of property equally among the Chinese people. Imagine you are a Chinese peasant. Write a journal entry explaining why you support the rebellion against Manchu rule.

2. Read more about Sun Yat-sen in an encyclopedia or a biography. Take notes for a class discussion on Sun. Chapter Review Answers

CHAPTER 3

Japan's Power Grows

▲ Commodore Matthew Perry took four warships into Tokyo Bay in 1853 to force Japan to open its ports to American traders.

OBJECTIVE: How was Japan able to resist imperialist nations and become a world power?

1. You have probably walked into a post office or other United States government building and seen a photo of the President. In the 1890s, when Japanese students arrived in school each day, they saw a picture of the emperor. Next to the picture was a message from the emperor that described the importance of education. A message from the emperor carried great weight in Japan because the emperor was considered to be divine. He was the symbol of Japan's long tradition as a nation. By the 1890s, education in Japan had become very important as part of a crash program to modernize the nation. The Japanese believed that education would create a trained nation that could compete with other industrial powers. To the Japanese, education also meant learning Japan's ancient traditions and values. The Japanese were determined to keep their traditions and become a modern industrial nation at the same time.

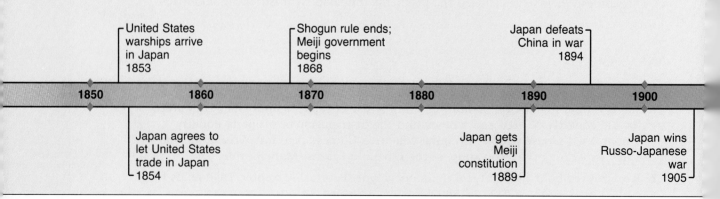

United States warships arrive in Japan 1853		Shogun rule ends; Meiji government begins 1868		Japan defeats China in war 1894	
1850	**1860**	**1870**	**1880**	**1890**	**1900**
	Japan agrees to let United States trade in Japan 1854			Japan gets Meiji constitution 1889	Japan wins Russo-Japanese war 1905

490

OPENING JAPAN: What changes did the arrival of American warships bring to Japan?

2. You have read in Unit 5 that in the 1600s the Tokugawa family became the shoguns, or rulers of Japan. In the 1600s and 1700s, the shoguns closed off Japan from the rest of the world. No foreign traders could come to Japan, and no Japanese could travel to other lands.

3. The Tokugawa shoguns ruled Japan through a system of feudalism. The people of Japan were divided into social and economic classes. The nobles held the highest position and controlled the samurai. Next came the peasants. Merchants occupied the lowest class.

4. Over the years this class system began to break down. Business and trade within Japan increased, and the importance of merchants grew. Some merchants soon rivaled nobles in wealth. The merchants came to resent their low standing in society. At the same time, some nobles began to favor the overthrow of the Tokugawa shogun. They believed the emperor should again be the true ruler of Japan.

5. The situation came to a head in 1853, when four American warships steamed into Tokyo harbor. Their commander, Commodore Matthew Perry, carried a written message from the United States government. The message demanded that Japan open its ports to American trading ships. The shogun's government did not want to agree to Perry's demands. Yet it knew that China had been attacked and defeated when it refused to open its ports to British traders. Therefore, in 1854, Japan signed a treaty giving American merchants and ships the right to trade in two Japanese ports. Several European nations then forced Japan to ► sign similar trade treaties. When, if ever, does a nation have the right to force another nation to do business with it?

6. After these trade treaties were signed, a group of powerful nobles decided that they had to act to keep foreign nations from taking control of Japan. In 1868 they forced the shogun to resign. They then re-

stored the imperial government. The new emperor, who took control of the government, was only fifteen years old. He took the name **Meiji** (MAY-jee), meaning "enlightened government." During his forty-five-year rule, Japan became a modern country and the first industrialized nation in Asia.

7. From the beginning, the leaders of the Meiji government decided to modernize Japan while at the same time keeping Japanese culture. Japanese officials were certain that modernization was the only way to make Japan strong enough to remain free from foreign control. The leaders believed further that Japan must become a strong nation in order to safeguard its own culture. What was happening in Africa in the 1800s ◄ to break down the traditional cultures, and how could Japan safeguard its own culture? The Meiji government brought foreign experts to Japan to teach Western skills. It sent Japanese officials abroad to study Western society and Western governments as well as businesses, school systems, and military forces. How would these actions make Japan stronger?

SPOTLIGHT ON SOURCES

8. One of Japan's leaders in the 1800s explained how Japan became modernized and stayed free of foreign control:

From the beginning, we realized fully how necessary it was that the Japanese people should not only adopt Western methods, but [that they] should also speedily become competent [be able] to do without the aid of foreign instruction . . . . In the early days we brought many foreigners to Japan to introduce modern methods, but we always did it in such a way as to enable the Japanese students to take their rightful place in the nation after they had been educated.

—from *Japan: Selected Readings*, Hyman Kublin, ed.

491

MEIJI REFORMS: In what ways did Japanese society change under Meiji rule?

9. The Meiji officials believed that their first task was to reshape Japanese society. One of the first acts of the government was to abolish feudalism in Japan. The nobles had to give up their control over the samurai and the peasants. The nobles also had to turn over their large landholdings to the emperor. The emperor paid the nobles for these lands and gave many of them important posts in his government. The laws, too, were changed so that they applied equally to all groups in Japan.

PEOPLE IN HISTORY

10. Japan set up a strong centralized government under the new emperor. Prince Ito (EE-toh), one of the most powerful Meiji leaders, planned the new government. Born into a wealthy noble family, Ito joined the group of nobles who forced the shogun from power and restored the emperor. In 1885 Ito became the **prime minister**, the head of the officials who advised the emperor. What nations today have a system of government with a group of ministers, headed by a prime minister, who gave advice to a ruler or head of government. Before Ito reached this high rank, he had worked to set up the new government he was to lead. In 1882 Ito visited Western nations to study their **constitutions**, or plans of government. He especially admired Germany's new constitution and used it as the basis for the constitution he wrote for Japan. (Ito became Japan's first prime minister under this new constitution.)

THE NEW CONSTITUTION: What kind of government was set up by the Meiji constitution?

11. The Meiji constitution gave the emperor nearly all the power in the government. For example, he had the power to select the prime minister and all the officials who ran the government and advised him. A lawmaking body called the diet had, in fact, few powers. The emperor and his officials could both make laws and reject laws passed by the diet.

12. In 1889 the constitution was presented to the people as a gift from the emperor. Most Japanese accepted the gift. As a result, Japan did not have to face the unrest or uprisings that weakened nations such as China. Instead, Japan was able to grow steadily stronger at home and develop into a powerful nation in world affairs.

Daily life in . . .

If you had been a woman in Japan at the end of the 1800s, you would have had some bold new choices before you. As Western ideas took hold in Japan, so too did Western styles. Some Japanese women and men began wearing Western-style clothing. For a woman, this meant putting away the kimono, or robe, and putting on a long dress such as the ones worn by women in Western nations. Gone were the wooden sandals; in their place were leather shoes.

As Japan became modernized during the Meiji rule, the place of women in Japanese society improved. Women could now enter shrines and temples to worship. Also, women were now allowed to work outside the home, which increased the labor force for Japan's new industries. In addition, when the Meiji government announced that education was a must for children, they meant for girls, too. Not many nations at the time provided public education for girls. Japanese girls could go to free elementary schools and many went on to high schools, where they had to pay only small tuition fees. In some cases, they were able to attend colleges.

Background: The Japanese government set up compulsory education in 1872 and ordered textbooks to be written on Western models. Japan's leaders wanted an educated populace with a desire for progress.

NEW INDUSTRIES IN JAPAN: How did Japan become industrialized?

13. The most important part of Japan's plan for becoming a modern nation was to develop its own industries and to keep control of them. Here, too, the Meiji government borrowed many of its ideas from Western industrialized nations. It imported factory machinery and brought in experts from other nations. The government also built many of Japan's new factories, steel mills, railroads, and shipyards. The government helped pay for the new roads and telegraph lines that soon linked Japan's growing cities. Why do you think Japan refused to finance its new industries with money invested by people from other nations? In addition to controlling its own industries, Japan now had many products to trade with other nations for the iron ore and oil that it needed to run its new factories and machines.

14. By the 1880s, there was a new group of wealthy business families in Japan, called the **zaibatsu** (ZY-baht-soo). The Meiji government sold most of Japan's major industries to these powerful families. Families such as Mitsubishi and Mitsui were among the zaibatsu. Each zaibatsu controlled companies in all areas of business. For example, one zaibatsu owned banks, mines, insurance companies, textile factories, and shipping lines.

15. The Meiji government's plan to modernize Japan brought many changes. It ended feudalism, as you have read. It led to the building of factories, railroads, and ships. One of the other vital changes was the setting up of a new education system. Elementary schools, high schools, and colleges were set up throughout Japan. Japanese students studied Japanese history and language, arithmetic, science, and geography, as well as morals and gymnastics. In morals classes students were taught loyalty to their family, nation, and emperor and to be proud of Japan. In gymnastics, students practiced military drills to increase their physical fitness.

JAPANESE IMPERIALISM: How did Japan become a world power with overseas holdings?

16. As Japan grew stronger, the Meiji government began to take a greater interest in Japan's relations with other nations. It began to build its military strength with the help of the zaibatsu. These business families controlled factories that produced weapons for Japan's growing army. They also built ships and guns for its navy. The zaibatsu worked with Japan's political and military leaders to build up the nation's military forces. Japan's major industries now included the manufacturing of weapons and ships.

17. Japan soon became an imperialist nation. Why did a nation that so fiercely resisted foreign control want to impose control on other nations? Part of the reason was that Japan wanted to win the respect of the European imperialist nations that were colonizing China. Morever, Japan now

▼ By 1875 Japan was the most powerful nation in Asia. What Asian lands did Japan conquer and annex between 1875 and 1910?

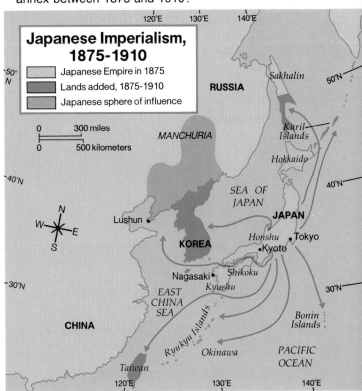

Japanese Imperialism, 1875-1910

- Japanese Empire in 1875
- Lands added, 1875-1910
- Japanese sphere of influence

0 300 miles
0 500 kilometers

RUSSIA
Sakhalin
MANCHURIA
Kuril Islands
Hokkaido
SEA OF JAPAN
JAPAN
Lushun
KOREA
Honshu
Tokyo
Kyoto
Nagasaki
Shikoku
EAST CHINA SEA
Kyushu
CHINA
Ryukyu Islands
Bonin Islands
Okinawa
PACIFIC OCEAN
Taiwan

ESL/LEP Strategy: Write the words *samurai, feudalism, shogun,* and *imperialist* on index cards. Have students define the words on the other side. Students can form teams to drill with the cards.

493

The Arts and Artifacts

▲ Hiroshige was the most famous ukiyo-e artist. What do the drawings "Tokaido Bridge" and "A Sudden Shower at Ohashi" tell you about life in Tokyo in the early 1800s?

Hiroshige's Drawings of Tokyo The Japanese people have a special love for the beauty of nature. This love of nature appears in Japanese art throughout the centuries. Until the 1700s, most Japanese artists painted scenes of waterfalls, seashores, and mountains on silk for the wealthy nobles. Then, during the 1700s and 1800s, Japanese artists developed a way of using carved and colored blocks of wood to print their paintings on rice paper. The method was cheaper and allowed more Japanese people to buy the lovely woodblock drawings, called **ukiyo-e** (oo-kee-oh-YAY).

The most famous ukiyo-e artist was Hiroshige (hir-uh-SHEE-gay). Born in 1797 in Tokyo, he loved the people and sights of his city. By Hiroshige's time, Tokyo was a busy city, filled with shops, markets, and public parks. Hiroshige's drawings of Tokyo soon became well known in all of Japan. Japanese visitors to the city often took his drawings back to their villages to remind them of Tokyo's wonders.

Hiroshige's art showed Tokyo's streets, its bridges, and its rivers. Often rain, mist, and snow added to the beauty of the scene. Many of Hiroshige's drawings also showed people enjoying special evenings of fun, with parades in the streets and the sky filled with brightly colored fireworks. They showed children and their parents at family picnics in the park. Other drawings depicted young women and men boating on a lake or young lovers walking together on a moonlit night.

Many Japanese families collected Hiroshige's drawings. People today know more about Tokyo than any other Japanese city of the 1800s because of Hiroshige's art.

1. Why did ukiyo-e art become popular in Japan?

2. What subjects did Hiroshige choose for his drawings?

3. How have Hiroshige's drawings helped people learn about Tokyo of the 1800s?

Activity: Lead a discussion about ukiyo-e art. Ask students to suggest art they have seen that creates the same effect—beauty that also gives the viewer information about a subject.

494

needed raw materials and markets for its industrial products. Japan also needed to import food for its growing population. Japan's leaders thought that the gaining of colonies in Asia would help solve these problems.

18. Korea was one area in which Japan tried to expand its trade. However, China, which controlled Korea, was not about to allow the Japanese to move into Korea without a fight. Japan and China then went to war. Japan won an easy victory over China and as a spoil (or profit) of the war, Japan gained the island of Formosa from China. China's long rule in Korea ended. In 1910 Korea became a Japanese protectorate. How was Japan, a small nation, able to defeat the large nation of China?

19. Ten years after defeating China, Japan won an even greater victory over Russia. Russia and Japan had become rivals in Asia. Both countries wanted to take over Chinese-controlled Manchuria, which was rich in such natural resources as iron and other minerals. When Russia occupied Manchuria, Japan decided to attack the Russian navy at Port Arthur and in 1904 the Russo-Japanese War officially began. Both Japan and Russia sent large armies into Manchuria. The Japanese won several important land battles and naval victories against the Russians.

20. In 1905 the two nations ended the war by signing the Treaty of Portsmouth. The treaty gave to Japan both Port Arthur and Russia's sphere of influence in Manchuria. Japan also won control of the southern half of the Russian island of Sakhalin (SAK-uh-leen). Japan's victory over Russia marked the first time an Asian nation had defeated a European nation on European turf. With this victory, Japan became a world power. It also joined the other world powers as an imperialist nation.

OUTLOOK

21. Have you ever shared a job with someone and found that the two of you had

▲ The Emperor Meiji moved his court into Tokyo Castle in 1868. Under his rule, Japan emerged as a modern, industrial nation.

different methods of working? Nations, like people, have different methods of doing things. China and Japan both were pushed into the modern world by threats from Western powers, but they responded to the threats in different ways. Japan's leaders dealt with the pressure from the West by moving quickly to become an industrialized nation. They set up a strong central government that helped build the new industries Japan needed to become a world power. Japan built up a modern army and navy and by 1900 was an imperialist nation. Its victories in wars with China and Russia also proved that Japan was one of the world's strongest nations.

Background: Point out that Japan turned itself from a feudal nation into a modern power in a very short time. By 1904 it was able to challenge and defeat Russia using its modern army and navy.

CHAPTER REVIEW

VOCABULARY REVIEW

Write each of the following words on a sheet of paper. Then write the definition for each word. Use the Glossary on pages 728–737 to help you.

1. Meiji   **3.** constitution   **5.** ukiyo-e

2. prime minister   **4.** zaibatsu

SKILL BUILDER: INTERPRETING A BAR GRAPH

► The following bar graph shows the spread of Japanese rule during the years 1895 to 1910. Study the graph and then answer the questions.

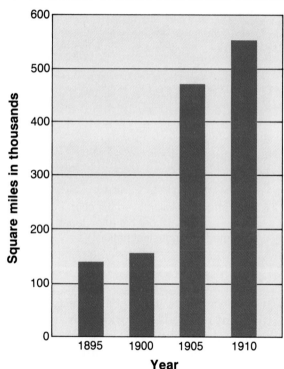

JAPANESE TERRITORIAL EXPANSION, 1895-1910

Source: *Atlas of World Population History*, Colin McEvedy and Richard Jones, Penguin Books, Middlesex, England, 1978

1. Look at the vertical axis. What does the figure 200 mean?

2. In 1894 the size of Japan was approximately 143,000 square miles (372,000 square kilometers). In 1895 Japan gained Formosa.
  a. About how many square miles (square kilometers) did Japan rule in 1895?
  b. About how many square miles (square kilometers) was Formosa? (HINT: Subtract 143,000 square miles (372,000 square kilometers) from your answer to **a.**)

3. In 1905 Japan took control of Russia's sphere of influence in Manchuria. Japan also took over the southern half of Sakhalin Island. About how many square miles (square kilometers) did Japan rule in 1905?

4. In 1910 Korea became a protectorate of Japan. About how many square miles (square kilometers) did Japan rule by 1910?

SKILL BUILDER: CRITICAL THINKING AND COMPREHENSION

1. Main Idea

a. Reread paragraph 9 from this chapter. Then write the topic sentence from the paragraph on a sheet of paper.

b. Reread paragraph 15 from the chapter. Write the main idea of the paragraph. Then write at least three details that support the main idea.

2. Sequencing

▶ Put the following events in the correct sequence.

a. Japan defeats Russia and gains Port Arthur, Manchuria, and part of Sakhalin.

b. Commodore Matthew Perry arrives in Japan to open it to trade with other nations.

c. Japan gets a new Meiji constitution.

d. Japan ends shogun rule and begins the Meiji government.

e. Prince Ito travels to Western nations to study their governments.

f. Japan gains the island of Formosa from China.

3. Drawing Conclusions

▶ Read the following paragraphs in this unit: Chapter 2, "China and the West," paragraph 15; Chapter 3, "Japan's Power Grows," paragraph 7. Then select the conclusion from the choices below that follows logically from the two paragraphs you read. Write the letter of your choice on a sheet of paper.

a. The heads of government in China and Japan in the late nineteenth century agreed to adopt Western ideas and skills.

b. The heads of government in China and Japan in the late nineteenth century rejected Western ideas.

c. The heads of government in China and Japan in the late nineteenth century disagreed about the need to adopt Western ideas.

4. Making Judgments

Do you think Japan's adoption of Western ways was an important cause of its becoming an imperialist power? Why or why not?

ENRICHMENT

1. Hiroshige's drawings of Tokyo tell us much about the way Japanese city-dwellers lived in the 1800s. Make a series of drawings about life in your city or community. In choosing what to draw, hypothesize about what people in the future might want to know about your community.

2. You have read how Prince Ito, the Meiji leader, traveled to Europe. While he was in Germany, he became a good friend of Otto von Bismarck. Review Unit 8, Chapter 6, which discusses the rule of Bismarck. Then create on paper a conversation the two leaders might have had. In the conversation, the two leaders should share their views of each other's countries and governments. (You may wish to read more about Japan and Germany in the late 1800s before beginning this assignment.)

Great Britain in India

▲ An 1857 rebellion by Indian soldiers ("sepoys") of the East India Company led the British government to take over rule of India.

OBJECTIVE: What were the effects of British colonization in India?

1. What would happen if one day a large foreign company based in the United States announced its sole distribution of a rare new resource? The resource had the properties of gold and the usefulness of oil. The foreign company, the XYZ Corporation, worked on the discovery and development of this new resource for years. In the process, it established a power base throughout the United States. The XYZ Corporation found it could make greater demands on the people and companies who began to depend on its product. Eventually, XYZ began to have power over local governments as well.

Profits, however, did not stay in the United States. Instead, the enormous profits made on this highly desirable new resource were sent to the foreign country. In the mid-1800s an actual British company, called the East India Company, had this kind of con-

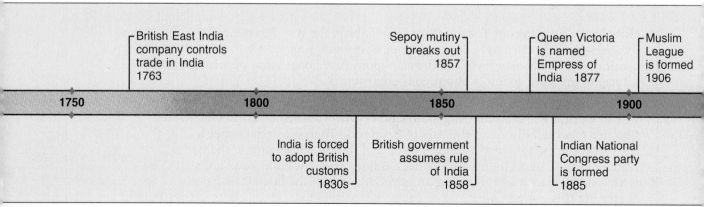

British East India company controls trade in India 1763

Sepoy mutiny breaks out 1857

Queen Victoria is named Empress of India 1877

Muslim League is formed 1906

1750   1800   1850   1900

India is forced to adopt British customs 1830s

British government assumes rule of India 1858

Indian National Congress party is formed 1885

trol over trade and government in India. Gradually, its influence led to Britain's domination of India until 1945, when India finally achieved independence from the British Empire.

THE BRITISH EAST INDIA COMPANY:
How did this business company come to rule India?

2. In 1498 the Portuguese explorer, Vasco da Gama became the first European to reach India by sailing around Africa. His journey was quickly followed by others. For many years the Portuguese, the Dutch, the British, and the French clashed over who would control the spice trade in India. By the 1700s only two rivals remained, Britain and France. This rivalry in India, and around the world, led to the Seven Years' War, which Britain won in 1763. Following the war, the British East India Company took full control of trade in India. (The British East India Company was owned by a group of British business people who traded in Indian spices, silks, and dyes.)

3. Gradually the East India Company expanded the territory under its control and became involved in the actual governing of India. This was possible, first, because the Mogul rulers at the time were weak leaders. Furthermore, India was a land of many states ruled by local princes, called **rajahs** (RAHJ-uhs). The caste system further divided the people. Religious conflicts also arose between Hindus and Muslims.

4. By the mid-1800s, the British East India Company controlled most of north India. The Company built trading posts to protect its traders and created an army made up of Indian soldiers called **sepoys** (SEE-pois). Sometimes, the Company used this army to take over new areas of India. Other times, it made agreements with local rajahs, who allowed the Company to trade in their lands. In return, the rajahs were allowed to keep their thrones.

5. In the 1830s the British East India Company decided to make certain changes that would help it rule India more easily. In

1836 the Company made English the official language and required Indian schools to teach Western history, literature, and science. British missionaries were allowed to set up Christian schools and to try to convert Indians to Christianity. According to corporate policy, Indians were not allowed to hold high-level jobs in the company.

6. The Indian people saw their language, culture, and religious beliefs threatened by this growing foreign domination. The more the British tried to impose their culture, the more resentful Indians became. A spirit of nationalism began to take hold. Inspiring this nationalism were the ideas of Ram Mohan Roy (rah MOH-hon ROH-ee).

PEOPLE IN HISTORY

7. Ram Mohan Roy was a Hindu scholar who lived from 1772 until 1833. Roy taught that Indian society needed some important **reforms**, or improvements, in order to become an independent nation. For example, Roy opposed the Hindu custom of **suttee** (suh-TEE), which called for a wife to kill herself when her husband died. He also worked to end such ancient Hindu customs, as the killing of infant girls, child marriages, and the caste system. As a result of Roy's teachings, the British outlawed some of these Hindu practices in the 1830s. Roy's teachings spread slowly through the country. Nearly fifty years passed before the spirit of nationalism would become a strong force in India.

THE SEPOY MUTINY: How did this revolt bring changes in India's colonial government?

8. In 1857 a revolt broke out among the sepoys. The British called the revolt the Sepoy Mutiny. A **mutiny** (MYOOT-uh-nee) is a revolt by soldiers against their officers. Indians called it the First War of Indian Independence. Why do you think the British ◀ and Indians had different names for the uprising? The immediate cause of the revolt was a new rifle issued to the sepoys. The cartridges had been greased so the bullets

ESL/LEP Strategy: Have students make a sketch that illustrates each of the following words: *rajah, sepoy, suttee, mutiny.*

499

would slide out more easily. To use this rifle, the sepoys had to bite off part of the cartridge. Rumors spread that beef fat and pork fat had been used to grease the bullets, which outraged Hindu and Muslim soldiers. (Hindus believe that cows are sacred and Muslims are not allowed to eat pork.) Both groups felt the British had insulted them and their religious beliefs.

9. This incident with the new rifles fueled India's resentment of the British. The sepoy revolt spread and nearly brought an end to British rule in India. Finally, though, the British were able to crush the revolt.

10. After the Sepoy Mutiny ended in 1858, the British government decided to end the rule of the East India Company and to govern India directly. By this time India was Britain's most important colony. Under the new arrangement, Britain ran about three fifths of India, while the rest still was governed by local rulers. The local rulers of the Indian states were allowed to keep full power over their own people. However, a British official called a **resident commissioner** now was responsible for the rulers' relations with each other and with other nations. To make British control complete, Britain's ruler, Queen Victoria, was crowned Empress of India in 1877.

SPOTLIGHT ON SOURCES

11. Rudyard Kipling, a British writer born in India, wrote a poem that expressed the British view of imperialism.

> Take up the White Man's [European's] burden [duty]
> Send forth the best ye [you] breed [have]
> Go bind [pledge] your sons to exile [to live in other lands]
> To serve your captives' [people being ruled] need. . . ."
> —"The White Man's Burden,"
> Rudyard Kipling

How do you think Indians felt about Kipling's views?

▲ A British officer rides in style in this eighteenth century painting. British officials ruled India from 1774 to 1947.

IMPERIAL INDIA: What were Britain's economic policies in India?

12. The chief goal of the British government in India was to help British business. The government encouraged India's farmers to grow more cotton for Britain's new cloth-making factories. Indians were not allowed to weave their own cotton into cloth or import machinery to make cloth. For hundreds of years, weaving cotton had been the way many Indian families earned their living. Now many families had no work. At the same time, another problem arose. Many farmers who planted cotton stopped growing food crops resulting in a reduced amount of food available for India's fast-growing population. Low food supplies caused hunger and starvation in much of India in the late 1800s.

13. The British did make some changes in India that could be seen as improvements for the Indian people. For example, the

Activity: Have students research such traditional Indian crafts as cloth weaving.

British dammed rivers and built canals to bring water to farmlands to grow more crops. The British built many railroads to help move food and supplies to all parts of the country. These railroads and new telegraph lines also helped to tie the country together. In addition the British ended wars between the rulers of the Indian states and prevented many conflicts between Hindus and Muslims. They brought the many different peoples of India under the authority ▶ of one government. Were these improvements a fair exchange for the problems caused by British rule?

14. The British also introduced changes in education that benefited the Indians. The British started elementary schools, high schools, and colleges. Indian students studied to become teachers, lawyers, doctors, and business people. These educated Indian men and women soon formed a growing middle class. The members of India's middle class studied Western history and culture, as well as science and math. They also learned Western ideas about freedom and democracy. It was this group of educated people that would lead the nationalist movement in India.

RELIGIOUS DIVISIONS: Why was Britain able to maintain power in India into the 1940s?

15. Because of the deep religious division between Hindus and Muslims, nationalism spread slowly in India. In 1885 a group of reformers, whose ideas dated back to the teachings of Ram Mohan Roy, formed a new political party called the Indian National Congress. At first, this party worked for more self-government for Indians. Later, the party would work for complete independence from Britain. How do you think an ▶ organized political party helped spread ideas of nationalism?

16. Most members of the Indian National Congress were Hindus. Although India's Muslims were worried by Hindu control of the Congress party, they favored many of the Congress party's ideas. Yet in 1906 the Muslims started the Muslim League to im-

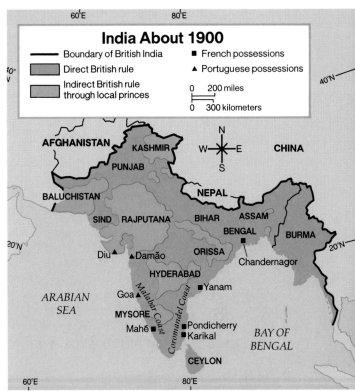

The British Empire in India lasted from 1763 to 1947. What parts of India did the British rule indirectly through local princes?

prove the lives of the Muslims in India. About 1920, Mohandas K. Gandhi (mohuhn-DAS K. GAHN-dee) became the Hindu leader of the nationalist movement. Gandhi and others worked for many years to bring about independence for India. But in the early 1900s, the Hindu and Muslim nationalist leaders were still too divided by religion to work together effectively for reform.

OUTLOOK

17. Why is it sometimes difficult for people of different beliefs to work together, even if they have a common goal? Many years of British rule in India affected both Hindus and Muslims. By 1900, both groups were eager to be independent of Britain, yet they had trouble working together to achieve that goal. In which nations today do ◀ religious differences cause civil strife?

Ask: How did a program of hand spinning and weaving begun by Gandhi help the Indian nationalist movement? (It made India self-sufficient economically in the textile industry; it advanced political freedom by challenging the British textile industry.)

501

CHAPTER REVIEW

VOCABULARY REVIEW

Write each number and word on a sheet of paper. Then write the letter of the
definition next to the word it defines.

1. rajah
2. suttee
3. sepoy
4. mutiny
5. resident commissioner
6. reforms

a. Hindu custom in which a wife would kill herself when her husband died

b. improvements in society

c. revolt by soldiers against their military officers

d. title of a local Indian ruler

e. British official who acted as a bridge between local Indian rulers and other nations

f. Indian soldier in the British East India Company army

SKILL BUILDER: INTERPRETING A TIME LINE

Note the dates on the time line below of key events and political leaders from
Chapter 4. These persons and events played an important role in the growth of a
nationalist movement in India. Read the time line carefully and then answer the
questions that follow.

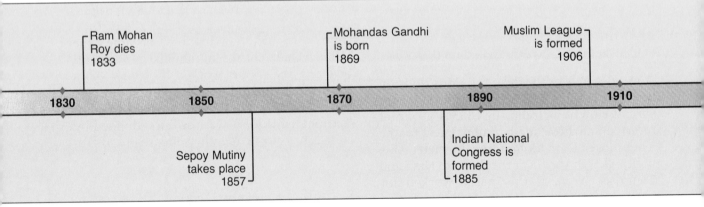

1. Did Indian nationalists Mohandas Gandhi and Ram Mohan Roy work together? Explain your answer.

2. Which political party was formed first—the Indian National Congress or the Muslim League?

3. Gandhi died in 1948. Did most of Gandhi's career take place during or after the reign of Queen Victoria?

4. When did the Sepoy Mutiny take place? Could the Muslim League have been involved in the mutiny? Why or why not?

SKILL BUILDER: CRITICAL THINKING AND COMPREHENSION

1. Main Idea

▶ Write the letters of the statements that best support the main idea, below.

Main idea: The Sepoy Mutiny was a turning point in Britain's relationship with India.

a. India had many Hindus and Muslims.

b. Hindu and Muslim soldiers revolted when they thought they would have to touch animal fat.

c. The real cause of the mutiny was Indian anger over British attempts to change Indian culture.

d. The British government decided in 1858 to rule India directly.

e. Queen Victoria ruled Britain for a long time.

2. Spatial Relationships

▶ Use the map on page 501 to answer the questions that follow.

a. Which two of the following countries were not part of India in 1900: Afghanistan, Nepal, Burma, Ceylon?

b. Was more of India ruled directly by the British or indirectly through local princes?

c. Were there more French or Portuguese possessions within India?

d. The distance from the easternmost end to the westernmost end of British India in 1900 was about how many miles or kilometers?

3. Cause and Effect

▶ On a sheet of paper, write the letter of each cause listed below. Then next to the letter write an effect that resulted from the cause. Use information from this chapter to help you state the effect.

a. Ram Mohan Roy opposed the Hindu customs of suttee and child marriage.

b. The British government encouraged India's farmers to plant cotton.

c. The British introduced their system of education to India.

d. Indian nationalists made increasing demands for self-government.

4. Hypothesizing

▶ Hypothesize about what India would have been like in the early 1900s if: the British never imposed their language, culture, and religious beliefs on the Indian people, the Sepoy Mutiny never took place, Ram Mohan Roy was never born.

ENRICHMENT

1. Find out more about the Sepoy Mutiny. Imagine that you were present during the mutiny. Write an eyewitness account of the event.

2. India was called the "jewel in the crown," meaning that it was Britain's most prized colony. Find out more about the ways India was important to Britain. Then write a short essay explaining why India was the "jewel in the crown."

CHAPTER 5

Imperialism Spreads

OBJECTIVE: How did strong nations apply imperialism to Southeast Asia and the Pacific?

1. Is your locker overflowing with books, your sweats, and maybe a stale lunch? What would you think if a school board member adopted a rule limiting what you could keep in your locker and how you could arrange those things? Since these new rules created more space, the official then enforced a rule where students had to double up using lockers. Then, the school took over the vacant lockers, using them to store supplies from a business that belonged to the board members. The imperialist nations acted much this way toward the lands and peoples they took over in the late 1800s. Every major industrial nation was involved in the claiming of faraway places. The in-

▲ Queen Liliuokalani (1838–1917) resisted American imperialism in her Hawaiian kingdom. Her name means "Lily of Heaven."

dustrial nations took control of those lands, told the people how they had to live, and used those places to benefit themselves. The United States joined in this race for possessions by claiming Puerto Rico and some islands in the Pacific. The European powers

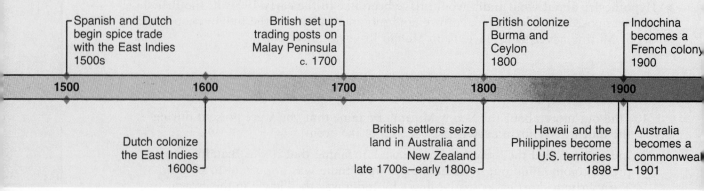

Spanish and Dutch begin spice trade with the East Indies 1500s

British set up trading posts on Malay Peninsula c. 1700

British colonize Burma and Ceylon 1800

Indochina becomes a French colony 1900

| 1500 | 1600 | 1700 | 1800 | 1900 |

Dutch colonize the East Indies 1600s

British settlers seize land in Australia and New Zealand late 1700s–early 1800s

Hawaii and the Philippines become U.S. territories 1898

Australia becomes a commonweal 1901

took control of smaller parts of Southeast Asia and of most of the Pacific Islands.

THE DUTCH, BRITISH, AND FRENCH:
Why did these powers start colonies in Southeast Asia?

2. In the age of exploration during the 1500s, the Portuguese, Spanish, and Dutch started a rich trade in spices with the East Indies, which is today called Indonesia. By the 1700s, Europeans had colonized these distant places. When the Dutch took control of the East Indies, they built plantations on which to grow sugarcane, rice, tea, and coffee. These crops were exported along with such raw materials as rubber and tin. The people of the East Indies provided the labor force for the Dutch settlers, who in turn owned and operated these businesses for the benefit of the Netherlands.

3. The British, too, were interested in starting colonies in Southeast Asia. In the 1700s, British merchants set up trading posts in the southern part of the **Malay Peninsula** (may-LAY puh-NIN-suh-luh), which stretches south from mainland Southeast Asia. In the early 1800s, the British built a trading settlement at Singapore. The location of this island off the southern tip of the Malay Peninsula made it the most important trading center in Southeast Asia. Find Singapore on the map on page 727. ▶ Why was Singapore an important stop on the shipping routes between Asia and Europe? In the mid 1800s, the British moved north into Burma to protect the eastern border of their empire in India. As they had done in other colonies, the British built railroads and started schools in Burma. They also built dams and canals that enabled Burma's farmers to grow more rice.

4. The British colonized the islands of Ceylon and Borneo in Southeast Asia. Using troops to fight against the Dutch and then against local chiefs, the British captured Ceylon about 1800. Find Ceylon, now called Sri Lanka (sree LAN-kuh), on the Atlas map on page 727. ▶ Why would the colonists of India want to control the island of Ceylon?

The British planted Ceylon's first rubber trees and developed rubber plantations. They turned Ceylon, which was also rich in rubies and sapphires, into a major producer of rubber and tea. The British also built trading posts on the northwestern coast of the island of Borneo. That island has some of the world's richest deposits of petroleum and diamonds. Look at the map on page 508. What other European power held land ◀ on Borneo during the 1800s?

5. As industrialism developed, France, too, became involved in the race for colonial possessions in Southeast Asia. The French had been interested in the Eastern part of Indochina (the large peninsula south of China) since the 1700s, when French missionaries had first made contact with the Indochinese. By the 1800s, the French were sending troops to Indochina to defeat the Vietnamese who objected to foreign rule. By 1900, Indochina was a French colony.

6. The French made many changes in Indochina. They built roads and railroads and dug canals to bring water to farmlands to increase rice production for export. They opened mines that produced tin and coal needed by France's industries. Plantations were started on which to grow rubber, tea, and coffee for export. These changes improved French lives but not the lives of the peasant farmers native to Indochina, who were expected to work long hours for low pay. But the French—unlike the British in India—tampered little with the local government. They allowed educated Indochinese to continue to hold high government posts in the colony.

THE PHILIPPINES AND HAWAII: How did the United States come to control these islands?

7. Spain was an early rival of the Dutch in the exploration and colonization of Southeast Asia. Spanish ships arrived in the Philippine islands in the 1500s. Very quickly a flourishing trade developed that made the Philippines an important source of Spanish wealth. The native people, called

Background: Today, the area of the world known as Southeast Asia includes the lands of Burma, Thailand, Laos, Kampuchea, Vietnam, Malaysia, Singapore, Indonesia, and the Philippine islands.

Filipinos (fil-uh-PEE-noz), adopted many aspects of Spanish culture, including the Catholic religion. The Philippines remained under Spanish control until the United States defeated Spain in 1898 in the Spanish-American War. As a result of the war, the Philippines became a territory of the United States. Filipinos hoped that the United States would offer them independence. But the United States decided to use the islands as a base for expanding American trade in the Pacific. The Philippines did not become independent until 1946.

SPOTLIGHT ON SOURCES

8. Many Americans did not want the United States to adopt a policy of imperialism. This is how President William McKinley justified his decision to control the Philippines:

> I have been criticized a great deal about the Philippines, but I don't deserve it. I didn't want the Philippines . . . . I prayed. . . . And one night it came to me . . . that we could not give them back to Spain . . . that we could not turn them over to France or Germany—our commercial rivals in the Orient [Asia] . . . that we could not leave them to themselves because they were unfit for self-government . . . that there was nothing left for us but to take them all and to educate the Filipinos and uplift and civilize and Christianize them . . .
>
> —from *Modern Times,* C. J. H. Hayes

▶ How are McKinley's remarks representative of imperialist ideas of the 1800s?

9. The United States soon grew interested in making Hawaii an American territory. Throughout the many years of trade with the Far East, trading ships of all nations had routinely stopped at the Hawaiian Islands for fresh provisions and water. Then, with the first successful use of ocean-going ships in 1817 and the use of steam-powered vessels, Hawaii became a major

refueling stop. The United States saw the islands as a crossroads of trade and a source of potential wealth. In the early 1800s, the first of several American business concerns established large sugarcane and pineapple plantations in Hawaii. Before long these companies became wealthier and more powerful than the local government. Upon ascending the Hawaiian throne in 1891, Queen Liliuokalani (lih-LEE-uh-woh-kuh-LAN-ee) tried to end this growing American control, but the powerful American business groups were able to force her from power. In 1898 the United States Congress made Hawaii an American territory, and in 1959 Hawaii was admitted to the union as the fiftieth state.

SMALLER PACIFIC ISLANDS: Why did imperialist nations need islands in the Pacific?

10. Imperialist nations needed islands in the Pacific that would serve as **coaling stations,** or places where steamships could stop to take on coal for fuel. The use of steamships had increased trade among all parts of the world. As imperialist nations of the 1800s developed trade routes across the Pacific, they took control of many islands as refueling stops. Moreover, to protect the trade routes, colonizing nations built military bases on many of these islands. By 1900 most islands in the Pacific were controlled by foreign nations. Germany, a latecomer to imperialism, controlled the northern Solomon islands and parts of New Guinea, western Samoa, and the Caroline, Marshall, and Mariana islands, while Great Britian held Australia, New Zealand, Fiji, and the southern Solomon islands.

AUSTRALIA AND NEW ZEALAND: Which European nation colonized these lands?

11. After the British captain James Cook explored the coast of Australia in 1770, Great Britain claimed the continent as its own. The first wave of British settlers arrived in New South Wales in Australia in 1788. Soon, the British had established six

▲ Miners and other settlers flocked to Australia after gold was discovered in Port Phillip colony in 1851. The gold rush was a turning point in Australian history.

colonies on the continent. In the process, however, the British settlers came into conflict with Australia's original inhabitants, the aborigines. The settlers seized land belonging to the aborigines for use as sheep and cattle ranches. The more land the British took, the deeper they moved into the continent. The aborigines were defenseless against both the weapons and the European diseases introduced into their country by these settlers. As a result, they were soon subdued by the settlers, who then began demanding from Britain the freedom to govern themselves. In 1901 the British holdings in Australia were joined together into the Commonwealth of Australia, which functioned as an independent nation within the British Empire. The first Australian constitution provided for a parliamentary form of government.

12. Captain Cook had also explored the coast of New Zealand on his famous expedition. In the early 1800s British traders, whalers, and seal hunters, as well as missionaries from Australia, ventured to New Zealand. Soon the native Maori tribes, like the aborigines of Australia, were overrun.

The fact that in the 1840s the British government had signed a treaty with the Maori agreeing to protect native rights was overlooked. By the early 1900s, New Zealand had become a self-governing nation within the British Empire.

OUTLOOK

13. At first, imperialist nations wanted colonies for raw materials and markets. But later, they began to want lands for other reasons. As world trade grew, the imperialist powers took over the islands of the Pacific to use as refueling stations and bases of defense for their navies. Nations gloried at seeing their flags fly over foreign lands, regardless of the cost to the natives of those lands. Imperialism became a means of expressing national pride and power. Britain's empire became the largest in the world with the colonizing of Australia and New Zealand. But by the early 1900s, imperialism had reached its strongest point. What nations in the world today still rule ◀ other countries?

507

CHAPTER REVIEW

VOCABULARY REVIEW

Write the following paragraph on a sheet of paper. Then fill in the blanks with the words that best complete the paragraph.

Filipinos   coaling stations   Malay Peninsula

 Southeast Asia and the Pacific Ocean interested imperialist powers. The British, for example, took over land on mainland Southeast Asia and the __1__ . One group of islands in the Pacific Ocean, the Philippines, was a colony of Spain. __2__ were disappointed that the United States did not make their land independent when it took over the Philippines from Spain in 1898. Many islands in the Pacific Ocean were important to European naval powers, who wanted the islands for __3__ .

SKILLBUILDER: READING A MAP

Study the map below and then answer the questions that follow.

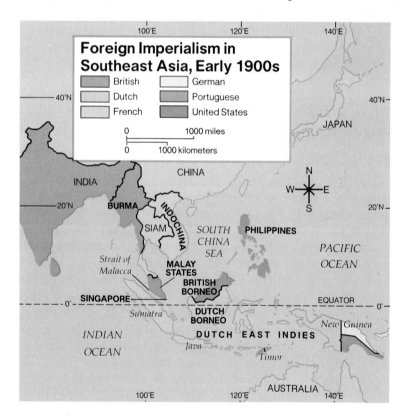

1. Which people controlled southern Borneo, western New Guinea, western Timor, and the islands of Java and Sumatra?

2. Which people controlled India, Burma, southeastern New Guinea, northern Borneo, and the Malay States?

3. Which country in mainland Southeast Asia was totally independent?

4. Which imperialist power had the least territory in Indochina?

STUDY HINT Read about Captain James Cook in paragraph 11 of this chapter on page 506. Use reference materials such as encyclopedias and the *Reader's Guide to Periodical Literature* to discover more about how Cook changed the face of the Pacific.

SKILLBUILDER: CRITICAL THINKING AND COMPREHENSION

▲ 1. Summarizing

▶ Read paragraph 2 of this chapter. Decide which of the points listed below accurately summarizes the main idea of paragraph 2. Write the letters of your choice on a sheet of paper.

a. By the 1700s the Dutch had won control of the spice trade in the East Indies.

b. The Dutch colonized the East Indies in order to increase trade for the benefit of the mother country.

⬤ 2. Generalizing

▶ Read paragraphs 3 and 4 of this chapter. On a sheet of paper explain which of the following generalizations based on those paragraphs is most valid and why.

a. Britain was mainly interested in colonies in Southeast Asia as a source of converts to Christianity.

b. Britain was mainly interested in colonies in Southeast Asia as sources of raw materials and places for trading posts.

c. Britain was mainly interested in colonies in Southeast Asia because it wanted to develop land for the benefit of the people who lived in the colonies.

◣ 3. Compare and Contrast

Read paragraphs 3, 6, and 12 of this chapter. Then, write a paragraph comparing and contrasting French and British methods of colonization. Use information in Chapter 4 of this unit to help you recall British methods in India.

4. Fact *versus* Opinion

▶ Write the letters of the statements below. Then identify each of the statements, which are based on information in the chapter, as a *fact* or an *opinion*. For each statement of fact, tell how you would check that the statement was true. For each statement of opinion, state whether it is supported by facts in the text.

a. The Dutch wanted the East Indies as a source of food and raw materials.

b. The United States, as President McKinley said, was justified in making the Philippines a United States territory.

c. Nations grabbed some Pacific islands not only as sources of raw materials, but also for other reasons.

ENRICHMENT

1. In 1838 James Brooke, a British adventure-seeker who had served in the army of the British East India Company, arrived in North Borneo. Find out about what happened to Brooke and how he influenced the history of Borneo. Give a brief report to the class.

2. Through library research, find out more about the culture of Australia's aborigines and New Zealand's Maori. Take notes on your research and prepare a brief talk for the class.

CHAPTER 6

Economic Imperialism in Latin America

▲ The Monroe Doctrine of 1823 warned that the United States would no longer allow European interference in the Americas.

OBJECTIVE: How did European and American involvement in Latin America reflect a new kind of imperialism?

1. Often when people go shopping they are tempted to buy something that they cannot afford. Sometimes people borrow money from friends or even take out a bank loan that they know they will have trouble repaying. This problem of spending money you don't have is the basic economic problem of **scarcity** (SKER-suh-tee). It applies to individual people and to nations. Nations, especially young struggling nations, often have a scarcity or lack of funds. They have to borrow money from other nations in order to get their economies started. If they cannot repay these loans, their young governments are in danger of collapse. Sometimes their very independence is at stake.

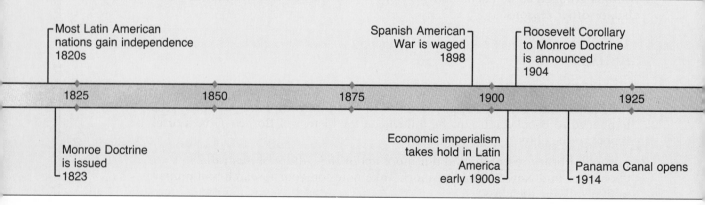

Most Latin American nations gain independence 1820s

Spanish American War is waged 1898

Roosevelt Corollary to Monroe Doctrine is announced 1904

| 1825 | 1850 | 1875 | 1900 | 1925 |

Monroe Doctrine is issued 1823

Economic imperialism takes hold in Latin America early 1900s

Panama Canal opens 1914

Activity: After students have read the first paragraph of the chapter, have them brainstorm reasons why a young nation would have to borrow money.

This type of situation arose in the 1800s, when the newly independent nations of Latin America were developing their governments and industries. Latin American nations borrowed billions of dollars that they later had trouble repaying.

AFTER INDEPENDENCE: What problems did the new nations of Latin America face?

2. Most Latin American nations won their independence in the 1820s. But the years of fighting had destroyed many farms and businesses and had left Latin Americans unprepared for self-government. In many new nations of Latin America, **caudillos** (kow-THEE-ohs), or military dictators, took control with the support of the army. The rule by caudillos led to uprisings and to many changes of government.

3. Knowing that the governments of Latin America were unstable, Spain urged its European allies to help it regain control of its former colonies. Only Austria was willing, but was not prepared to embark on such a mission alone.

4. England had strong economic reasons for not wanting Latin America to revert to Spanish control. Many British businesses and bankers had invested large sums in Latin America. If Spain regained control of Latin America, these British investments would be threatened.

5. England approached the United States about making a joint declaration to protect the independence of the new Latin American nations. The United States considered and then rejected this request, preferring to issue its own strong policy statement known as the **Monroe Doctrine**. In 1823 President James Monroe warned that the United States would not allow any nation to regain its colonies in the Americas.

SPOTLIGHT ON SOURCES

6. Here is part of what President Monroe wrote in that doctrine of 1823:

We should consider any attempt on their part to extend their system to any portion of this hemisphere as dangerous to our peace and safety. The American continents are henceforth not to be considered as subjects [places] for future colonization.

How is interference in another nation's ◄ affairs, however good the intention, also a kind of imperialism?

ECONOMIC IMPERIALISM: How did industrialized nations gain control of the economies of Latin America?

7. By the late 1800s many businesses and small industries were being started in Latin America and roads, railroads, shipyards, mines, plantations, hospitals, and schools were being built. The young Latin American governments lacked the funds to finance this growth. But investors from industrialized nations were eager to lend the billions of dollars required to develop the Latin American economies. They knew their investments would yield huge returns, or profits. Latin America was rich in copper, tin, rubber, iron ore, gold, and oil— precisely the raw materials the European countries needed most at that time.

8. Most nations of Latin America came to depend on foreign investments to keep their economies going. These investments represented a new kind of imperialism called **economic imperialism**. Now foreign nations were in control of the economies, instead of the politics, of Latin America. What problem would this situation breed?

9. The failure of some Latin American nations to repay their debts had repercussions. Revolts were common in Latin America. Rulers who had borrowed heavily from foreign banks often were overthrown. Many times the new government would not or could not repay the money owed foreign banks. Foreign banks then refused to lend more money to the new government until it paid the earlier debt—or until it was overthrown by a ruler who would pay the debt.

Background: Foreign investors bought many plantations, mines, and railroads in Latin America just when these growing industries were beginning to show a profit. The Latin American laborers, who were paid very low wages, did not benefit from these profits and neither did the Latin American economy.

511

But sometimes foreign nations sent troops
▶ to collect the money by force. Why do you think such European military intervention in Latin America began to worry the United States?

THE SPANISH-AMERICAN WAR: How did the United States gain its territories?

10. In the mid-1890s revolts against Spain broke out in the Spanish colonies of Cuba and Puerto Rico. Many Americans admired these people in their fight for freedom, but American investors who owned businesses in Cuba grew concerned about their investments. In 1898 the United States sent the battleship *Maine* to Cuba to protect American citizens living there. When the *Maine* mysteriously exploded in Havana harbor, the United States declared war against Spain.

11. The United States quickly won the Spanish-American War. Cuba was given its independence but the United States was given the power to intervene in Cuba to protect American lives and property. This so-called **Platt Amendment** was written into the Cuban constitution of 1900. The United States also was given Puerto Rico in the Caribbean Sea and the Philippines and Guam in the Pacific Ocean. The nation that had issued the Monroe Doctrine was now itself guilty of imperialism.

SKILL BUILDER/MAPS Identifying Climate Regions

Climate regions are areas of the earth's surface sharing similar climates. Temperatures and rainfall patterns are used to define climate regions. Tropical climates are hot all year. Temperate climates have warm summers and cool or cold winters.

1. Where in Latin America is the climate hot and rainy throughout the year?

2. Where in Latin America is the climate temperate, with cool winters and warm summers?

3. Where in Latin America is the climate tropical, with alternating wet and dry seasons?

4. Where in Latin America is the climate too dry for growing crops without irrigation?

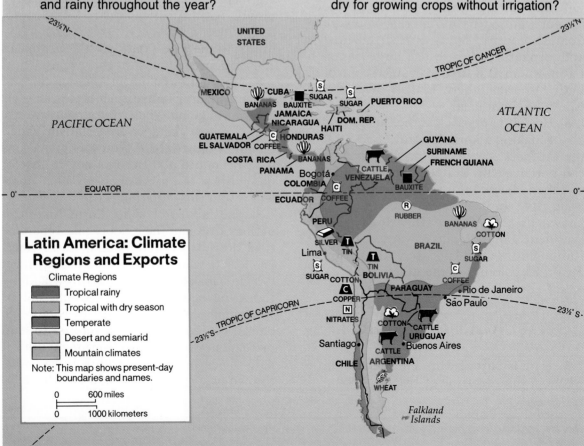

Latin America: Climate Regions and Exports

Climate Regions
- Tropical rainy
- Tropical with dry season
- Temperate
- Desert and semiarid
- Mountain climates

Note: This map shows present-day boundaries and names.

0   600 miles
0   1000 kilometers

THE BULLY FROM THE NORTH: How did the United States earn Latin American distrust

12. The United States proceeded to build a naval base on Cuba and a second naval base on Puerto Rico. Why would these actions make Latin Americans begin to distrust the United States? The main purpose of both bases was to protect the canal that the American government intended to build across the isthmus of Panama. Such a canal would provide a much-needed shortcut for U.S. ships from the east coast to the U.S. holdings in the Pacific. President Theodore Roosevelt offered Colombia, which owned Panama, a $10 million cash payment and $250,000 a year for a strip of land on which to build the Panama canal. But Colombia turned down the offer.

13. In 1903 a revolt broke out in Panama with the active assistance and cooperation of the United States. The United States recognized Panama as an independent nation in exchange for the right to build a canal across the isthmus of Panama. But Latin Americans were outraged by Roosevelt's tactics for acquiring this land.

14. In 1904 in his message to Congress, President Roosevelt announced a bold new policy, known as the **Roosevelt Corollary** to the Monroe Doctrine, that made the United States a kind of police force of the Caribbean. This policy barred any European nation from sending troops into Latin American countries. But it also promised that U.S. troops would act on behalf of European investors if Latin American nations failed to honor their debts.

SPOTLIGHT ON SOURCES

15. President Roosevelt spoke the following words to Congress in 1904:

> Chronic wrongdoing . . . may in America . . . ultimately require intervention by some civilized nation, and in the Western Hemisphere the adherence of the United States to the Monroe Doctrine may force the United States, how-

▲ This 1905 cartoon is titled *The World's Constable*. What United States foreign policy is the cartoon poking fun at?

ever reluctantly, . . . to the exercise of an international police power.

How do you think Latin Americans felt about the United States' self-appointed role as the police force of the Caribbean?

OUTLOOK

16. Presidents Roosevelt, Taft, and Wilson wanted to promote the best interests of both the United States and Latin America. But the Roosevelt Corollary, which was meant to prevent European military takeovers in Latin America, fanned the fires of Latin American distrust. Latin Americans worried that the real aim of the Roosevelt Corollary was to give the United States control over Latin America. When, if ever, is ◄ the intervention of one nation in another nation's affairs justified?

Background: In 1914 the Panama Canal was opened to the ships of all nations. In 1921, two years after Roosevelt's death, the U.S. government paid $25 million to Colombia, ostensibly as a gift. Latin Americans regarded this "gift" as an apology for the way in which the United States had acquired the Canal Zone.

CHAPTER REVIEW

VOCABULARY REVIEW

Write each of the following words on a sheet of paper. Then write the correct definition for each word. Use the glossary on pages 728-737 to help you.

caudillo

Monroe Doctrine

Platt Amendment

economic imperialism

Roosevelt Corollary

scarcity

SKILL BUILDER: MAKING AN OUTLINE

Use paragraphs 2, 7, 8, and 9 of this chapter to construct an outline on economic imperialism in Latin America. Copy the outline below on a sheet of paper. Then fill in the blanks.

   I. Problems facing Latin American nations after independence
      A. _____
      B. _____
      C. _____

  II. How foreign investors gained control of Latin American economies
      A. Latin American nations needed money to develop economies.
      B. _____
      C. _____

 III. Failure to repay loans
      A. Causes
         1. _____
         2. _____
      B. Repercussions
         1. Foreign investors refuse more loans.
         2. _____

SKILL BUILDER: CRITICAL THINKING AND COMPREHENSION

 **1. Classifying**

▶ On a sheet of paper, write a title for each set of information below.

  a. European nations realize new Latin American nations are weak. Spain asks for help taking back former colonies in Latin America. United States reacts by saying it won't allow imperialist nations to retake colonies in Latin America.

  b. After Spanish-American War, United States gets Spanish territories in the Caribbean and Pacific. United States takes over Hawaii in 1898.

2. Sequencing

▶ Reread paragraphs 10 and 11 of this chapter. Then, on a sheet of paper, write the letters of the following steps in correct sequence.

   a. The *Maine* exploded in Havana harbor.

   b. The United States declared war against Spain.

   c. Cuba rebelled against Spanish rule.

   d. The Platt Amendment was written.

   e. American investors who owned businesses in Cuba grew concerned about their investments.

3. Drawing Conclusions

▶ Read each group of statements below. Draw a conclusion from each group of statements. Write your conclusions on a sheet of paper.

   a. Cuba started a revolution against Spanish rule in the mid-1890s. American investors had many investments in Cuba.

   b. By the early 1900s the United States was building up a Pacific empire. The United States needed an easier way for its navy to get from the East Coast to the West Coast to defend its Pacific empire.

4. Point of View

▶ Reread the excerpts from the Monroe Doctrine in paragraph 6 and the Roosevelt Corollary in paragraph 15. On the basis of these excerpts, answer the questions below. Write your answers on a sheet of paper.

   a. Which President believed that a nation sometimes has a moral duty to intervene in another nation's affairs?

   b. Which President believed that a nation has a right to intervene only when its own peace and security are at stake?

   c. How did President Roosevelt feel about taking aggressive action against other nations? Use words from his speech to support your answer.

ENRICHMENT

   1. Do library research to read more about the explosion of the United States battleship *Maine* and how some American newspapers responded to this event. (Use the *Reader's Guide to Periodical Literature* to help get you started. Then imagine you are a newspaper editor in 1898. On a sheet of paper, write a brief article for your newspaper, giving your opinion of how the United States should respond to the event.

   2. Research the building of the Panama Canal. Write a description of how some part of the canal was constructed.

   3. Make an outline map of Central America. Label nations and events in Central America in the early 1900s involving United States intervention. You may wish to use encyclopedias or other sources to find out more about United States actions during this period.

CHAPTER 7

The World at War

▲ The unsuspecting Archduke Franz Ferdinand greets a Serbian citizen moments before the fatal shot that started World War I.

OBJECTIVE: What were the causes of World War I, and which nations fought in this war?

1. The bombing of London by German airships was a common occurrence during World War I. Picture this scene on a street in Britain's capital of London in 1915. German airships have bombed the city. Two women bend over a person lying injured on the pavement. The women lift the person into a waiting horse-drawn ambulance, which they quickly drive to the nearest hospital. The women are not nurses or ambulance drivers. They had been students at a business school when the war began in 1914. They had responded to a poster urging women to join the London volunteer ambulance service. They learned to drive a horse-drawn ambulance and to give first aid. While British soldiers and nurses were on the battlefields in France, Britain needed its citizens to help out at home. Never before had entire populations been so involved in war. An entire generation of young men went off to fight. Women in

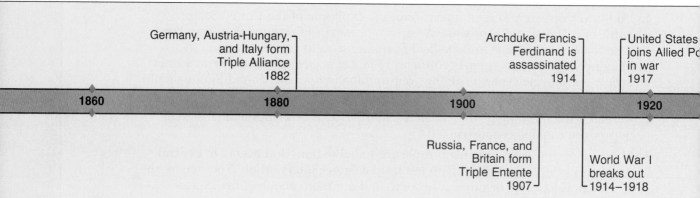

Germany, Austria-Hungary, and Italy form Triple Alliance
1882

Archduke Francis Ferdinand is assassinated
1914

United States joins Allied Po in war
1917

1860   1880   1900   1920

Russia, France, and Britain form Triple Entente
1907

World War I breaks out
1914–1918

large numbers began to do work most had never done before. World War I caused lasting changes in the way people lived.

CAUSES OF THE WAR: How did nationalism, a system of alliances, and an arms race among European nations lead to World War I?

2. The growth of nationalism in Europe was one cause of World War I. As you learned in Unit 8, nationalism had become a powerful force in the Balkan peninsula. Locate Romania, Bulgaria, Greece, Serbia, Montenegro, and Albania on the map on page 518. These areas, together with the nearby parts of Austria-Hungary and the Ottoman Empire, make up the Balkans. You also read in Unit 8 about the breakup of the Ottoman Empire, which had formerly controlled most of the Balkans. Peoples of the Balkans had become nations in their own right, and from time to time fighting erupted as groups fought for territory. The whole area was ready to explode.

3. Another cause of World War I was the arms race that had developed in Europe. An arms race is a rivalry among nations to gain the greatest military power. Most countries developed industries to produce guns, cannons, and other modern weapons. Many European nations also began to form re-serve armies. In case of trouble, these re-serves would be **mobilized** (MOH-buh-lyzd), or called to active duty to serve in the army. Weapons and trained soldiers were supposed to give a country a sense of security. Instead it appeared, that Europeans were heading for war.

4. New alliances among European countries created a warlike atmosphere. In 1882 Germany, Austria-Hungary, and Italy formed the **Triple Alliance**. According to this agreement, each nation promised to come to the aid of the others if they were attacked. France, in 1894, signed a similar agreement with Russia. In this treaty, both nations promised that if either one of them was attacked, the other would go to its aid. Then, in 1907, Britain joined France and Russia to form the **Triple Entente** (ahn-TAHNT), which was an agreement among the three nations to cooperate with one another.

THE BALKANS: Why did this area interest many European nations?

5. Trouble in the Balkans played a large role in tensions in Europe in the early 1900s. This trouble included nationalism and the interest of other Europeans in the area. Serbia became the leader of Slavic nationalism. Slavs, as you know, are peoples spread over Eastern Europe whose

Daily life in . . .

As the war dragged on, people struggled to stay alive in the crumbling towns of Europe. Here is an account of how one young Belgian managed to survive:

"We stayed in the cellar among the coal for five days and nights as the Germans bombarded our city. When the shelling stopped at last, my mother fled with us children to a run-down neighborhood that was a distance from the fighting. In a few weeks, we ran out of food. We chewed on candle ends. There was no gas for heat or lights, so we went to bed early and huddled together under all the covers we had. During the days we stood in lines at the bakeries and groceries, hoping that there would be a bit of bread or meat left to buy. One day an old man in the neighborhood dug up the garden behind our house. We watched him intently. He scattered small mysterious things on the ground. The next week—a miracle!—green things peeped out of the ground, and in a few weeks he brought us the first tiny carrots from this garden. For four long years this garden lived, and so did we."

Ask: How does this arms race compare to the United States-Soviet nuclear arms race since World War II?

517

languages stem from the same root. Serbia's goal was to become the leader of a large South Slavic kingdom. Many of the people who would be part of such a kingdom lived in Bosnia, Herzegovina, and other parts of Austria-Hungary. As a result, Austria-Hungary was alarmed by Serbian nationalism. Russia, a Slavic nation, backed Serbia's goal. Russia was also interested in the Balkans because it wanted to gain control of the outlet from the Black Sea into the Mediterranean Sea, which was part of the Ottoman Empire.

6. Britain was concerned about Germany's interest in building a railroad through the Balkans. The German emperor, Wilhelm II, wanted to build a "Berlin-to-Baghdad" railroad connecting Germany
▶ and the Ottoman Empire. Why would Germany want such a railroad? Britain was worried about trouble in the Balkans because this area was so near the Suez Canal. The Suez Canal was Britain's main route to its colonies in Asia.

THE WAR BEGINS: How did the alliances of Europe's nations lead them into war?

7. The murder in the Balkans of the heir to Austria's throne started a chain of events that plunged Europe into war. On June 28, 1914, Archduke Francis Ferdinand of Austria visited Sarajevo (SAR-uh-yeh-voh), the capital of Bosnia. As the archduke and his wife rode in an open car, a Serbian nationalist fired two shots, killing the Austrians. The Austrian government believed that Serbia was behind the murders. On July 23, 1914, Austria sent Serbia a list of demands that Serbia refused to meet.

8. The alliances between the European nations now caused the conflict to spread quickly. Austria-Hungary mobilized its army to threaten Serbia. This move alarmed Russia, which in turn began to mobilize its armies so that it could come to the aid of Serbia. France promised its ally Russia that it would support Serbia. On July 28, 1914, Austria-Hungary declared

▼ World War I was fought between the Allies and the Central Powers. What European nations sided with the Allies in the war? What European nations sided with the Central Powers?

war on Serbia. Germany, too, declared war on Serbia because of an agreement with Austria-Hungary.

9. Other nations were quickly drawn into the war. The Russian mobilization presented Germany with a problem. The German army had a battle plan for any war with Russia and its ally France. The plan called for Germany to invade Belgium, a **neutral** (NOO-trul) country, in order to get quickly to France. "Neutral" means not taking sides. After quickly defeating the French army, the Germans would then move east to deal with the slower-moving Russians. But should Germany wait to put its plan into action until the Russians had mobilized and declared war? If Germany waited, it would have to fight France to the west and Russia to the east at the same time. The Germans decided to attack rather than to wait. On August 1, Germany declared war on Russia and and then on France. Following its war plan, Germany quickly invaded Belgium. This invasion caused Britain, which had a longstanding agreement to protect Belgium, to join the conflict. Britain declared war on Germany on August 4.

THE WESTERN FRONT: Why did the Allies and the German armies fight a war in the trenches?

10. When the war began, both sides expected to win a quick victory, but this was not to happen. On one side were the **Allied Powers**, or Allies. The Allies included France, Britain, Russia, and Serbia. On the other side were the **Central Powers**. The Central Powers were Germany and Austria-Hungary. The Ottoman Empire and Bulgaria joined the Central Powers soon after the war began, and Italy and Japan joined the Allies. The United States was the last major nation to enter the war, joining the Allies in 1917. Before the war ended, thirty-one countries had entered the fighting, making it truly a worldwide war.

11. Germany had the best-trained army in Europe, and it moved fast. The German

▲ The entry of American soldiers into the war helped the Allies defeat Germany along the Western Front.

army conquered Belgium in just three weeks and moved on into France. By the first week of September 1914, the German forces were within 40 miles (64 kilometers) of Paris, the French capital. Then the German army was stopped at the Marne River by French and British troops. This important victory for the Allies doomed Germany's plan for a quick victory in France.

12. After the German army was halted, the fighting reached a **stalemate** (STAYL-mayt), meaning that neither side was able to advance. Instead, the opposing armies dug a line of trenches that stretched nearly 300 miles (480 kilometers) from the Belgian coast to the border of Switzerland. This line of forts and trenches, which bordered Germany on the west, was called the **Western Front**. For the next four years, bloody fighting continued all along the Western Front. Neither side gained much territory in this trench warfare. For example, in 1916 the Germans tried to end the stalemate by

Background: In April 1917, German submarines destroyed 875,000 tons of shipping headed for Great Britain. The British changed their naval tactics and gradually overcame the German threat to their food supply. However, by the end of 1917, Germany had destroyed more than 8,000,000 tons of Allied shipping.

519

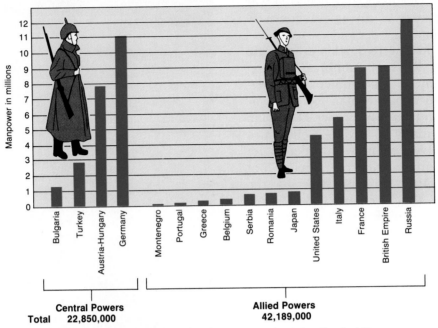

TROOP STRENGTH OF CENTRAL AND ALLIED POWERS IN WORLD WAR I

Central Powers
Total   22,850,000

Allied Powers
42,189,000

▲ The Allied Powers had almost twice the troop strength of the Central Powers, as the above chart states. Why did it take the Allies four years to win the war?

launching a huge attack against the French forts at Verdun (vur-DUN). After ten months of fierce fighting, Verdun remained in French hands at a cost of more than 750,000 German and Allied soldiers' lives. The stalemate on the Western Front lasted until large numbers of American forces arrived in 1918.

NEW WEAPONS: What powerful new weapons were first used in World War I?

13. Many new and deadly weapons were used for the first time in World War I. Machine guns and giant cannons forced both sides to seek protection in the trenches. The British used the first armored tanks in 1916 to protect their soldiers from machine-gun fire. Germany, too, soon began using tanks. Both sides developed fighter planes. All of these weapons greatly increased the number of soldiers who were killed in the land battles of World War I. On the seas, German submarines used torpedoes to sink British warships. They also threatened merchant ships of neutral nations such as the United States.

THE EASTERN FRONT: Why did the Russians drop out of the war?

14. The fighting between the German and Russian armies on the Eastern Front took a heavy toll on both Russia and Germany. Find the **Eastern Front** on the map on page 518. Approximately how long was this line? ◄ Fighting the Russian army weakened Germany, because the long front required so many German troops. Even so, German and Austrian troops managed to win the important battles along the Eastern Front. Russia's army was the largest in Europe, but it was poorly trained and lacked skilled generals. More than one million Russian soldiers were killed. The Russian people lacked food and became weary of fighting.

15. In 1917 a series of events began that took Russia out of the war. In March a revolution forced the czar and his government from power. Later that same year, a second revolution put Vladimir Lenin (VLAD-uh-meer LEN-un) and his Communist party in control. Lenin decided that Russia must stop fighting. Lenin and other revolutionaries wanted to bring a Communist government to Russia, and they needed peace to do so. Early in 1918, Russia signed a treaty with Germany that gave Germany a large part of Russia's territory in return for peace. Now Germany could use all of its army to fight on the Western Front.

THE UNITED STATES: Why did the United States enter World War I?

16. From the very start of World War I, most Americans wanted to stay out of the conflict. This became more and more difficult. The United States wanted to be able to trade with all nations. In January 1917, Germany announced that it would sink the ships of any nation that tried to enter British ports with supplies. After several American ships were sunk, President Woodrow Wilson of the United States warned Germany to end this warfare. Germany refused. Then the United States learned of a secret message that moved President Wilson to end his neutral position in the war. In March 1917, the United States discovered a secret telegram that revealed Germany had been working to make Mexico a German ally. Why would this action alarm the United States? Wilson asked Congress to declare war on Germany, and Congress did so on April 6, 1917.

THE WAR ENDS: How were Germany and its allies finally defeated?

17. The United States' entry into the war gave extra strength to the Allied Powers. Within a short time, American troops and war supplies began to reach the European battle fronts. By the fall of 1917, more than one million American soldiers were fighting on the Western Front.

SPOTLIGHT ON SOURCES

18. The arrival of American soldiers gave new hope to the war-weary Allies. This is how a British nurse described her feelings when she saw these Americans:

. . . They looked larger than ordinary men. Their tall, straight figures were in vivid [strong] contrast to the under-sized armies of pale recruits [new soldiers] to which we had become accustomed. Then I heard an excited exclamation from a group of Sisters [nurses] behind me. "Look! Look! Here are the Americans!" The coming of relief made me realize how long and how intolerable [terrible] had been the tension, and with the knowledge that we were not, after all, defeated, I found myself beginning to cry.
—*Testament of Youth*, Vera Brittain

19. In the spring of 1918, the Germans began a powerful attack along the Western Front but eventually lost heart as events overwhelmed them. Strengthened by American troops, the Allies counterattacked. By August 1918, it was clear that Germany's armies could not win. Bulgaria and then the Ottoman Empire surrendered. On November 3, a revolution broke out in Germany and Wilhelm II was forced to flee. The leaders of the new German government asked for an **armistice** (AR-muh-stihs), or a halt in the fighting. On November 11, 1918, Germany and the Allies signed an armistice agreement, ending the biggest war in Europe's history.

OUTLOOK

20. You have read of the causes that led to World War I. At the same time these factors pushed nations into conflict, there were efforts to help nations cooperate. In 1899 and again in 1907, representatives from many nations met in the Netherlands to work on ways for nations to settle disputes without war. A third meeting was being planned when World War I broke out. Europe had endured so many wars that you might think people there would not want another. Why do you think the forces for war in 1914 were so strong that they overpowered efforts for peace?

CHAPTER REVIEW

VOCABULARY REVIEW

Write the following paragraph on a sheet of paper. Then fill in the blanks with the words that best complete the paragraph.

armistice   stalemate   mobilized   Western Front

Triple Alliance   Eastern Front   Allied Powers

neutral   Triple Entente   Central Powers

    By the early 1900s there were signs in Europe that war could break out at any time. Nations joined in alliances. Germany, Austria-Hungary, and Italy formed the ___1___ and Britain, France, and Russia formed the ___2___ . When World War I did break out in 1914, some nations, such as Belgium, tried to remain ___3___ . Germany, Russia, Austria-Hungary, and France ___4___ their troops. The ___5___ included France, Britain, Russia, and Serbia, while the ___6___ included Germany and Austria-Hungary. The war was fought along two major lines, the ___7___ that stretched from the Belgian coast to Switzerland, and the ___8___ , that reached from the Baltic Sea to the Black Sea in Eastern Europe. In a long ___9___ German and Allied forces faced each other over trenches with neither side gaining ground. The war ended in 1918 when the combatants agreed to stop fighting by signing an ___10___ .

SKILL BUILDER: CREATING A TIME LINE

Create a time line for four months in 1914 entitled "The Beginning of World War I." Use events in paragraphs 7 through 11 of this chapter for your time line. Read the paragraphs and make a list of events that occurred from June through September of 1914. Then arrange the events and their dates on your time line. Use a sheet of paper for your time line and for your answers to the questions that follow.

  1. Which event set off the chain of events that led to a full-scale war?

  2. Which was the first nation to declare war during the period of the time line?

  3. When and where did the French and British stop the German advance?

SKILL BUILDER: CRITICAL THINKING AND COMPREHENSION

 1. Classifying

► Write the following headings on a sheet of paper. Then classify the statements that follow the headings by writing them under the correct heading.

Headings

Alliances as a Cause of World War I

Nationalism as a Cause of World War I

Statements

Balkan peoples wanted their own nations.

Germany, Austria-Hungary, and Italy formed the Triple Alliance.

Russia and France signed a mutual aid agreement in 1894.

Germany and Italy became unified nations in the 1800s.

Serbian Slavs wanted a Slavic nation in the Balkans.

Britain had an agreement to protect Belgium.

2. Spatial Relationships

▶ Refer to the time line on page 516 to answer the questions that follow.

a. How long did the Triple Alliance exist before the Triple Entente was formed?

b. How long did these two alliances in Europe last compared with the length of World War I?

c. Do you think World War I was a long or short war? Explain your answer.

3. Predicting

▶ Think about what you have read of the causes and outcome of World War I. Consider the questions below and then make a prediction about what was to happen in Europe in the first years after the war. Write your prediction on a sheet of paper.

a. Will there be an effort to make an international peace organization?

b. Will nationalism continue to be a strong force in Europe?

c. Will a Slavic kingdom be created in the Balkans?

4. Making Judgments

▶ Refer to information in this chapter to make judgments that answer the following questions. Write your answers on a sheet of paper.

a. Do you think World War I could have been prevented if an international organization like the United Nations had existed then, where countries could have talked over their disagreements?

b. Do you think World War I could have been prevented if each national group had its own nation in 1914?

ENRICHMENT

1. Imagine you were a member of a Slavic group in the Balkans before World War I. How would you feel about being ruled by Austria-Hungary, a nation with different languages and cultures? Write a short essay explaining "Why I Am Proud to Be a Serb (or other national group)." Prepare for your essay by reading an encyclopedia entry on one of the Balkan areas discussed in this chapter.

2. Read *All Quiet on the Western Front* by the German writer Erich Maria Remarque. This novel is a short, simply told, dramatic story of a young German recruit in World War I.

3. Read more about battles fought during World War I. Make an outline map of Europe similar to the map on page 518 in this chapter. Mark the sites of battles and their dates on the map as you read about them in your research.

CHAPTER 8

After World War I

▲ In 1918, world leaders gathered at Versailles Palace in France to sign the Treaty of Versailles, officially ending World War I.

OBJECTIVE: What were the results of World War I and the peace treaties that ended the war?

1. The nightmare was over. It had been called "the war to end all wars." It had been the bloodiest, most destructive war in human history. Everything about human life seemed sadly changed. Everywhere people felt that such a disaster must not happen again. Even though the war had many causes, people felt that someone should be blamed. When a war ends, the heads of all the nations involved usually meet to work out a peace. World War I had involved many nations with different interests. The leaders of all the governments would have to meet at a peace conference, a meeting where they must settle their differences in order to make a lasting peace. Could they avoid blaming someone and move forward together? In the first months after the armistice of 1918, such a meeting began in France. However, this peace conference was unusual in one important way. Unwisely, the losers in the war were not even invited.

Paris Peace Conference opens January 18		Germans sign Treaty of Versailles June 28	
January 1919	**April 1919**	**August 1919**	**November 1919**
	German officials refuse to sign "war guilt" clause; Allies threaten to invade Germany late May		Austria-Hungary signs peace treaty with Allies; Austria, Hungary, Czechoslovakia, Yugoslavia are born; Poland regains independence, September

Background: The November 1918 armistice ended the fighting but an official treaty was needed to end the war. The treaty also would set out terms to avoid more conflict.

THE PARIS PEACE CONFERENCE: Who were the leaders and what were their plans?

2. On January 18, 1919, representatives of 27 countries met in Paris to write the terms of the peace settlement after World War I. Only the winners were at the peace conference. The nations that had lost the war—Germany and its allies—were not invited. Russia, which had made a separate peace with Germany, also was absent. The leaders of the Allies controlled the peace conference. President Woodrow Wilson of the United States played a leading role. The British prime minister David Lloyd George and the French premier Georges Clemenceau (ZHORZH klay-mahn-SOH) also played important roles.

PEOPLE IN HISTORY

3. President Woodrow Wilson had been a college teacher who had taught history. He strongly believed that only just and fair peace terms would bring lasting peace. For this reason, Wilson was certain that the peace treaty should not punish the losing nations. He summed up his ideas in these words: "Peace without victory." What does this phrase mean to you?

4. In a speech to the United States Congress a year earlier, Wilson had already stated the kind of peace terms he favored. Wilson listed **Fourteen Points,** or basic ideas, for a lasting peace for all people. The first point stated that the peace treaties must be open agreements debated and signed in public. Wilson thought that secret agreements between nations were dangerous. In other points, Wilson called for freedom of the seas for all nations, and for free trade among nations. He also asked for a cutback in all nations' armed forces, and for the peaceful settlement of disputes over colonies. Another important point stated that each of Europe's nationality groups had the right to have its own nation, a principle called **self-determination.** Wilson felt that the most important idea was the fourteenth point. In it, he proposed that a world organization be set up to keep peace.

5. The leaders of France and Britain soon made it clear that they had different ideas from Wilson's. Clemenceau argued that Wilson's program was unfair to France. Clemenceau insisted that Germany must be punished. He reminded Wilson that the French had lost more soldiers and property than had any other nation during the bloody fighting on the Western Front. Clemenceau stressed the great hardships the French people now faced with so much of their country destroyed. Therefore, he felt that Germany had to be weakened in order to keep it from ever again attacking France. Lloyd George of Britain was less interested in taking revenge on Germany. Instead, he felt that a "balance of power" must be kept in Europe. By this phrase Lloyd George meant that France should not become too strong or Germany become too weak.

PEACE TREATIES: What terms were the Central Powers forced to accept?

6. The Germans had hoped for a peace treaty based on Wilson's Fourteen Points. Instead, they received very harsh peace terms in the **Treaty of Versailles.** This happened because Wilson was forced to give in on many of the Fourteen Points. He did so in order to reach agreement on what he believed was his most important proposal, a world organization for peace called the **League of Nations.** Alsace and Lorraine, which Germany had taken in 1871, were returned to France. Germany also lost territory to Belgium, Denmark, Poland, and Lithuania. This included giving Poland a strip of land, known as the Polish Corridor, between two parts of Germany. Germany also lost all its colonies in Africa, Asia, and the Pacific. These colonies were made **mandates** (MAN-dayts) of the League of Nations. A mandate was a territory that was governed but not owned by a League country. The League later assigned these mandated lands to the Allies to govern. Wilson's idea that all nations should cut back the size of

Background: The League of Nations was a weak association of independent nations. The league lacked the power to enforce its decisions. It did settle some boundary disputes.

525

their army and navy was applied to Germany alone.

SPOTLIGHT ON SOURCES

7. A **"war guilt" clause** in the Versailles treaty forcing Germany to accept the blame for causing the war read as follows:

> The Allied and Associated Governments [nations who fought for the Allies] affirm and Germany accepts the responsibility of Germany and her allies for causing all the loss and damage to which the Allied and Associated Governments and their nations have been subjected as a consequence of the war imposed upon them by the aggression of Germany and her allies.

This part of the treaty caused the most trouble. The German people deeply resented the idea that they alone had been responsible for the war. They were convinced that they were being blamed only because they had lost the war. In the future, Germany would seek revenge for this blow to its national pride.

8. Germany also had to pay an enormous sum of money according to the "war guilt" clause as reparations. Reparations, you remember, are money paid for causing damages. Britain and France wanted Germany to pay not just for war damages but also for all the costs of fighting the war. Wilson argued against this idea. Eventually a commission ruled that Germany should pay $33 billion to the Allies in yearly payments. In May, 1919, the first German representatives sent to sign the Treaty of Versailles resigned rather than sign it. They believed that the large reparations, in addition to the other treaty terms, were too harsh. Finally, however, the Germans were forced to sign the treaty when the Allies threatened to invade Germany.

▼ The map of central and eastern Europe was redrawn after World War I. What nations were reduced in size as a result of the war? What new countries came into being after the war?

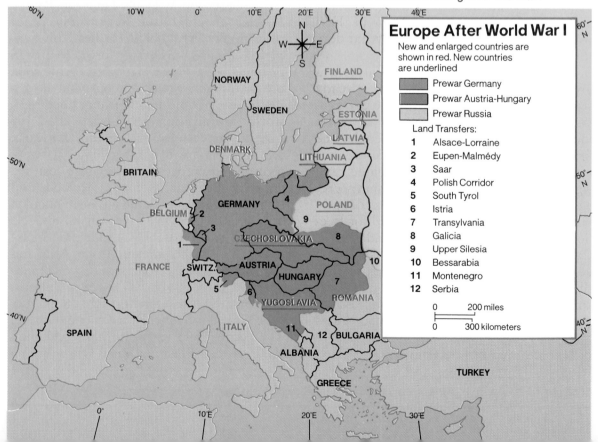

9. Separate peace treaties were signed between the Allies and the other Central Powers. The terms of these treaties were just as harsh as those placed on Germany. Before the war, Austria-Hungary had been a large empire, with a population of 50 million. Under the terms of the peace treaty, it was split into three nations, Austria, Hungary, and the new nation of Czechoslovakia (chek-oh-sloh-VAH-kee-uh). Large amounts of its territory also went to Romania; to the new Serbian-led kingdom of Yugoslavia (yoo-goh-SLAH-vee-uh) in the Balkans; and to Poland, which again became an independent nation. Locate Yugoslavia and Poland ► on the map on page 526. Where was the Polish Corridor?

10. Other treaties broke up the Ottoman Empire and recognized territories lost by Russia. In Europe, the Ottoman Empire kept only Asia Minor and a small area at the end of the Balkan Peninsula. The Ottoman Empire's lands in the Middle East became mandates of the League of Nations. The Allies treated Russia, their former ally, like the defeated nations. You will recall reading that Russia had dropped out of the war early in 1918 and signed a separate peace treaty with Germany. Later that year Finland, Estonia, Latvia, and Lithuania declared their independence from Russia. In a peace treaty, these nations were recognized as independent countries.

THE PROBLEMS OF PEACE: How did creating new boundaries divide people?

11. Nationalism in Europe remained a serious problem after the war. Wilson's ideal of people's rights to self-determination had helped create several new nations. Yet in many parts of Eastern Europe and the Balkans, two or three nationality groups lived together in one area, so that self-determination for everyone was impossible. For example, the new nations of Poland and Yugoslavia contained nearly one million Germans. Czechoslovakia, another new country, had three million German-speaking citizens. Romania had a large Hungarian minority. Peace treaties tried to protect the rights of these groups living in other countries. However, promises by these new nations to treat all their people equally were not enforced.

12. The peace settlement stirred up deep anger and resentment in Germany, much of which was directed toward the Allies. However, the German people also were angry at the leaders of the new German republic, for accepting the peace terms. The government of the German republic lost the support of many of its people from the very beginning. Soon new leaders appeared in Germany who gained support by attacking the Versailles treaty and promising to end its terms. In less than 20 years, Germany would overturn many of the terms of the Treaty of Versailles.

13. Even though Woodrow Wilson had helped write the Treaty of Versailles, the United States Senate never voted to accept it. Many Americans were against the treaty because they were afraid the League of Nations would drag the United States into future wars in Europe. Some senators were willing to accept the treaty if President Wilson would give up the League of Nations clause. However, the President refused to compromise. As a result the United States, which now was the most powerful nation in the world, rejected the Treaty of Versailles and did not join the League of Nations.

OUTLOOK

14. You have read that Germany resented the terms of the Treaty of Versailles and that creating new boundaries in Europe divided people. The United States refused to join the League of Nations, which weakened the League. People have looked back at these results of the 1919 peace conference and said that these problems were to blame for other problems that came later. Try predicting some news for the future. Think of a trouble spot in the world today. What ◄ effect or effects do you think this trouble spot's problems will have on the world?

Ask: Was the United States Senate correct in voting against joining the League of Nations and refusing to approve the Treaty of Versailles?

527

CHAPTER REVIEW

VOCABULARY REVIEW

Write each of the following sentences on a sheet of paper. Then fill in the blank with the word that best completes each sentence.

Fourteen Points   self-determination

League of Nations   Treaty of Versailles

mandates   reparations

"war guilt" clause

1. The _____ was an organization formed to work for world peace.

2. Territories governed but not owned by the League of Nations were called _____ .

3. Wilson's ideas on how to bring about a lasting peace were called _____ .

4. The agreement that officially ended World War I was called the _____ .

5. A part of the treaty that placed the blame for World War I on Germany was called the _____ .

6. _____ is the right of a group to form its own nation.

7. Money paid for causing damages is called _____ .

SKILL BUILDER: INTERPRETING CARTOONS

Study the following cartoon, which deals with the subject of reparations. Then write your answers to the questions that follow the cartoon on a sheet of paper.

1. Which figure in the cartoon represents the United States?

2. Which figure represents Germany and Austria-Hungary?

3. Look at the figure on the right. What attitude does he have about giving up the contents of his bag? Now look at the figure on the left. What attitude is shown by the expression on this figure?

4. Is the cartoonist for or against the payment of reparations? Explain.

SKILL BUILDER: CRITICAL THINKING AND COMPREHENSION

▲ 1. Summarizing

▶ On a sheet of paper, summarize in one paragraph the terms of the Treaty of Versailles. Organize your summary around these general areas:

a. loss of German home territory

b. loss of German colonies

c. reduction of German armed forces

d. acceptance of guilt placed on Germany

e. payment of reparations

➡ 2. Cause and Effect

▶ Write the letter of each effect listed below. Then write a cause that led to the effect.

a. The new nations of Czechoslovakia and Yugoslavia were created.

b. The leaders of the German republic lost the support of many Germans.

c. The United States Senate never approved the Treaty of Versailles.

d. Lithuania, Finland, Estonia, and Latvia were recognized as independent countries.

◢ 3. Fact *versus* Opinion

▶ Identify each of the following statements as a fact or an opinion. If the statement is an opinion, write a related fact. If the statement is a fact, write a related opinion.

a. The victorious Allies were wrong not to invite all the parties who had fought in World War I to the peace conference.

b. President Wilson was foolish to think he could achieve "peace without victory."

c. President Wilson was willing to compromise on any of his Fourteen Points except his plan for a League of Nations.

d. Germany was right to seek revenge for the blow to its national pride.

4. Hypothesizing

▶ Listed below are three of President Wilson's goals in the Fourteen Points that were rejected. For each goal, write a hypothesis of how Germany might have been affected differently if the goal had been met instead of rejected.

a. The armed forces of all nations are to be cut back.

b. All colonial disputes shall be resolved without bias toward any one country.

c. Germany shall be responsible only for reparations to cover direct damages to property and civilians. (not for all costs of the war). (including pensions to former soldiers and families of soldiers).

ENRICHMENT

1. Imagine you are a German-speaking person living in western Poland after the Treaty of Versailles. How would you feel about your home being separated from Germany? Write a letter expressing your feelings to a newspaper editor.

2. The League of Nations was to many Americans the most controversial of Wilson's Fourteen Points. Do library research on this idea. Then write a statement expressing your opinion about the United States' rejection of the League of Nations. Do you agree or disagree with the action the Senate took?

SUMMARY

During the period from the mid-1800s to 1914, the economic and political impact of the Industrial Revolution was felt around the world. Great Britain, France, and Germany had grown in economic strength and national pride. Nationalism was an expression of national rivalry and ambition. Industry's growing hunger for raw materials and markets turned nationalism into imperialism. Between 1870 and 1914, almost all of Africa and parts of Asia had been colonized by European powers. Earlier, Great Britain had begun to colonize Australia and New Zealand. European powers had won spheres of influence in politically weak China. The United States opened trade with Japan in 1854 and China in 1900. Japan had used western knowledge to industrialize, while avoiding control by Europeans. By 1875, Japan was the strongest nation in Asia, and had begun its own empire. The United States won control of the Philippines after a war with Spain in 1898. Nationalism and colonial rivalry created dangerous trends in Europe after 1880. Industry could now produce new and powerful weapons on a large scale. European nations were soon caught in an arms race. Rivalry and fear persuaded the major powers to split into two alliance systems. Tensions rose until finally, in 1914, Europe was engulfed in World War I. In 1917, the United States entered the war, turning the tide against Germany. In 1918 Germany signed an armistice. The peace conference that followed failed to create a permanent peace. Instead, it sowed the seeds of World War II.

SKILL BUILDER: READING A MAP

▶ Study the map below. Then answer the questions that follow the map.

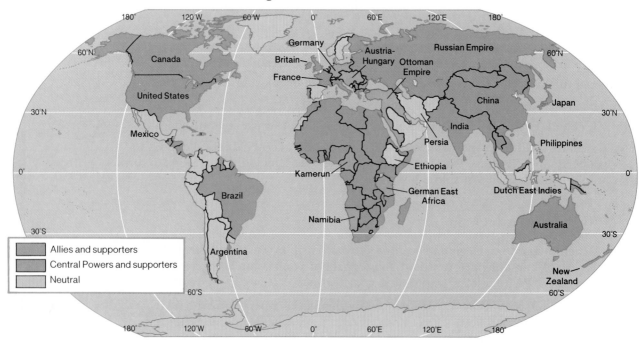

Taking Sides in World War I

1. Which countries were known as the Central Powers?

2. Which African countries supported the Central Powers?

3. Which country in the Middle East supported the Central Powers?

4. Which nation bordering the United States remained neutral?

5. Which side—Central, Allied, or Neutral—had the largest total land area?

SKILL BUILDER: CRITICAL THINKING AND COMPREHENSION

1. Sequencing

▶ Arrange the following events in the order in which they happened.

a. Sun Yat-sen leads a revolt against Manchu rule in China

b. British settlers seize land in Australia and New Zealand

c. Archduke Ferdinand is assassinated

d. American warships arrive in Japan

e. Germany, Austria-Hungary and Italy form the Triple Alliance

f. Berlin Conference divides Africa among European powers

g. German officials refuse to sign the "war guilt" clause

h. British government assumes rule of India

i. French troops invade Algiers

j. Russian Revolution takes place; United States enters World War I

2. Predicting

▶ Read each paragraph below. Select the statement that best predicts the outcome.

2–1. Germany, Austria-Hungary, and Italy had formed an alliance in which they agreed to help one another in any war. Russia, England, and France had a similar agreement. In July of 1914, Austria-Hungary declared war on Serbia, a Slavic area with cultural ties to Russia.
a. England and France will go to war with Russia to prevent war with Serbia.
b. Russia will invade Serbia to come to its defense.
c. Russia will mobilize; Germany will declare war on Serbia.
d. France will invade Serbia in support of its ally, Russia.

2–2. By 1875, Japan had become a powerful industrial nation. Japan had avoided being controlled by western powers. Because Japan was situated on a number of islands that were poor in natural resources for industry, it needed an empire in the Pacific. In 1898 the United States took possession of the Philippines.
a. Japan and the United States will share rule of the Philippines after 1900.
b. Japan and the United States will eventually fight over control of the Pacific
c. Japan will fight China in 1894 for control of the Philippines
d. Russia will control the Philippines after the Russo-Japanese War in 1905.

ENRICHMENT

Make a map showing three stages in the fighting of World War I. Show: (1) the route of Germany's attack on France; (2) the stalemated trench warfare on the Western front, with an indication of the Eastern Front, in 1916; (3) the Western Front in August of 1918, after the United States had joined the fighting.

UNIT 11

ESL/LEP Strategy: Divide students into the two groups who fought World War II, the *Allies* and the *Axis*. As they read the unit, have students take notes pertaining to their group. After students read the unit, ask each group to prepare a dialogue that one of the leaders from their side may have had with a leader from the other side. Then, have students perform their dialogues for the class.

THE WORLD TORN APART

OBJECTIVE: The Allies were unable to bring a lasting peace to Europe and other lands after World War I. During the 1920s and 1930s, rulers came to power in Italy, Germany, and Japan who started nations on the road to another world war.

Mussolini becomes
Fascist leader
of Italy
1922

Lenin
dies
1924

Great
Depression
begins
1929

1922　　　**1924**　　　**1926**　　　**1928**　　　**1930**

Kemal Atatürk
elected president
of Turkey
1923

Stalin starts
First Five-Year
Plan
1928

Japan
invades
Manchuria
1931

▲ Like these workers in an aircraft factory, millions of women worked in factories during World War II.

Hitler becomes
ruler of
Nazi Germany
1933

Franco leads revolution
against Spanish Republic;
Rome-Berlin Axis is formed
1936

France
falls to
Germany
1940

Atomic bomb is
dropped on Japan;
Japan and Germany
surrender 1945

| 1932 | 1934 | 1936 | 1938 | 1940 | 1942 | 1944 |

Italy invades Ethiopia;
India gains partial
self-government
1935

Germany invades
Poland; France
and England
declare war
1939

Japan attacks Pearl
Harbor; U.S. declares
war
1941

CHAPTER 1

The World, 1920 to 1939

▲ Joyous celebrations took place in many countries at the end of World War I. Many people believed that this had been the "war to end all wars."

OBJECTIVE: In what ways were the years between World War I and World War II a time of both new hopes and great troubles?

1. Imagine that you have survived a terrible disaster, such as an earthquake, a huge fire, or a hurricane. The world around you has fallen apart. Friends and relatives have been killed. Buildings are destroyed and food is scarce. You make it through this time by hoping that things will improve. For weeks you dream of better times, sure that things could not get worse. Then, just when you think things are starting to look good, they become worse than you ever imagined. It seems that this terrible time will never end. In fact, you probably would be glad if all this was just a bad dream. Yet this nightmare really happened to millions of Europeans and Americans after World War I. They had survived the horror of the war and now had high hopes for an era of peace, progress and prosperity. Some of these hopes came true for a time. Then, ten years later, the Great Depression shattered

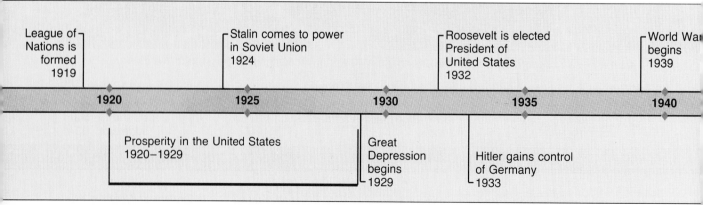

League of Nations is formed 1919

Stalin comes to power in Soviet Union 1924

Roosevelt is elected President of United States 1932

World War begins 1939

1920   1925   1930   1935   1940

Prosperity in the United States 1920–1929

Great Depression begins 1929

Hitler gains control of Germany 1933

all their dreams. People became desperate for jobs, housing, and even food. No matter how hard they tried, they could not make ▶ enough money to live on. How would you take care of yourself and your family if this happened to you? What might you do to try to change things?

ESTABLISHING PEACE: What hopes did the European nations have to prevent another World War?

2. One of the hopes of people after World War I ended was that they would be free to decide how their countries should be governed. This freedom is called **self-determination**. New independent countries such as Yugoslavia, Poland, and Czechoslovakia were created, uniting people of the same national and cultural background. At the same time, many existing countries gained democratic governments. However, the ideals of democracy and self-determination were applied only in Europe. The European nations did not give independence to their colonies in Africa, the Middle East, or Asia. In fact, instead of granting freedom to the colonies captured from Germany and Turkey, the Allies took control of them.

3. Another great hope people had after the war was for world peace. The League of Nations was formed. Member nations agreed to settle their disputes peacefully to prevent small conflicts from turning into another world war. These nations also tried to prevent war by cutting down on their supplies of weapons. This reduction in military power is called **disarmament** (dis-AR-muh-munt).

4. Europeans wanted to avoid another World War at any cost. Millions of people had died in World War I. In this first "total war," new bombs, tanks, and other weapons had been used to kill and injure millions of people. In 1934 in England, a group of people went from house to house asking questions for the "Peace Ballot." Millions of English people replied that they did not want to take part in a European war ever again. In France, a similar peace movement was on the rise.

5. World War I also changed the place of women in European and American society. During the war, women had become an important part of the military effort, working in war-related jobs. Women, by necessity, had to do many jobs from which they once had been excluded. After the war, many women hoped to continue in a more active role outside the home. They also began to enter universities in greater numbers. Most important, women won the right to vote in national elections in many countries. They therefore gained a more active voice in politics.

THE POSTWAR WORLD: What actually happened to the hopes of people and nations after World War I?

6. What developed after the war was often quite different from what people hoped and dreamed. The Treaty of Versailles, which ended the war, forced Germany to pay huge amounts of money and goods to the nations it had invaded. The United States asked its allies to repay loans that it had made to them during the war. How ◀ could countries rebuild after the war if they had to pay large amounts of money to other countries?

THE GREAT DEPRESSION: How was the whole world affected by the Great Depression?

7. During the 1920s, the United States enjoyed great prosperity. In Europe, however, the nations were suffering from inflation, unemployment, and the damages of war. Inflation takes place when the supply of money grows much faster than its actual worth. As a result, prices go up, and people suffer. Inflation can cause great hardship to everyone, but especially to the poor. Another problem was war damage. Many factories in Germany, France, and Belgium had been destroyed by the fighting. European nations depended on Germany paying them money to rebuild, yet Germany was

▲ Many people had high hopes for the League of Nations. How does this cartoon express these hopes? What might allow the cat to get the bird?

even worse off than these other nations. By 1923, a disastrous inflation had made German money so worthless that a single loaf of bread cost a wheelbarrowful of money. As a result, American loans were needed to help keep Germany and other European countries solvent during the 1920s.

8. Hopes for better times were shattered suddenly in October, 1929—the start of the **Great Depression.** The Great Depression was a worldwide collapse in business and industry that lasted from 1929 to 1939. It began when the stock market in New York City crashed, causing a chain of events that plunged the world into economic ruin. First, many American banks failed, and millions of people lost all of their money. Then, failing American banks recalled money that they had loaned to European banks. This caused European banks to fail as well. These bank failures hurt many people and businesses that had invested money in them. Worse still, those who had money now stopped investing it in business and industry. As a result, world industrial production and international trade fell sharply.

SPOTLIGHT ON SOURCES

9. In 1933, in the depth of the Great Depression, one worker out of every four in the United States and Britain did not have a job. Without jobs, families lost their homes, and many did not have enough to eat. Here

Daily life in . . .

For many people in the United States, the 1920s was a time of **prosperity** (prah-SPAIR-uh-tee). The feeling of prosperity was helped by the new practice of buying things using credit. Prosperity is a state of economic well-being. By 1929, five times as many items were bought using credit as in 1920. Americans paid five to ten dollars down and paid the rest in monthly payments. People were able to have things they wanted. By 1929, Americans had used credit to buy most household goods. Using credit payments made life easier, but it also turned out to be dangerous.

The stock market crashed in 1929 because Americans had bought stocks on credit, the same way they had bought homes, cars, and refrigerators. But when the Stock Exchange told investors they must pay up their credit purchases, these investors did not have the money. Because the stock market did not have this money coming in, the prices of stocks crashed. Many banks and companies went out of business, and people lost their jobs. Without jobs people were not able to pay off their credit. As a result, many Americans lost their homes, their cars, and their life savings.

Activity: Bring to class books with pictures of life in Europe during the Great Depression. Have students discuss each photo and describe what it shows about life during the depression.

is how a woman in Britain described her life during the Depression.

If only he had work. Just imagine what it would be like. On the whole, my husband has worked about one year out of twelve and a half. His face was lovely when I married him, but now he's skin and bones. When I married he was robust [healthy] and he had a good job. . . .

He fell out of work about four months after I was married, so I've hardly known what a week's wage was. Through all the struggling I've still not lost my respectability. About three or four years ago I could even manage to win a competition for the best-kept home for cleanliness and thrift. The bedclothes were all mended, but they were clean. . . . My eldest boy has trousers on at the moment with six patches on them; I just tell him he'll be all the warmer, especially in winter. . . .

I do the washing every other week, because I find I can do a large amount of clothes with the same amount of coal and soap, but it is more tiring. . . .

. . . I wouldn't like to live a minute of my life over again. With all the struggling, you can't manage. . . . The only hope we have got is the hope to come. I've lived for hope . . . for thirteen years.

—From *Time to Spare*, Felix Greene, ed.

RECOVERY: What actions did countries take to recover from the Great Depression?

10. Countries tried to help themselves recover from the Great Depression in a number of ways. One approach was to put **protective tariffs** on all foreign goods. Protective tariffs are taxes on foreign goods that make them more expensive. The tariffs were supposed to encourage people to buy less costly **domestic goods**. Domestic goods are products made within a country. Even though these countries improved sales of goods at home, they lost a lot of foreign markets. With fewer foreign markets for

▼ In a street in New York, bread and coffee are distributed to jobless people in 1930. During the Depression, many people did not have enough to eat.

their goods, people making the goods lost their jobs.

PEOPLE IN HISTORY

11. Like the rest of the world, the American people faced great hardships in the years after the Great Depression. When Franklin D. Roosevelt became President of the United States in 1933, he faced the worst economic crisis in his country's history. In order to turn around this economic crisis, he began a program called the New Deal. Under the New Deal, the government spent public money on such programs as the Civilian Conservation Corps (CCC). These programs put to work hundreds of thousands of people who had been unemployed. The New Deal also was responsible for Social Security, which provided for the most basic needs of older Americans.

12. Roosevelt often spoke to the Ameri-

▼ Franklin D. Roosevelt delivers one of his "Fireside Chats." These friendly, informal radio programs helped people cope with difficult times.

can people on the radio, telling them that the government understood the difficult problems people were facing. These speeches were called "fireside chats." Roosevelt also believed that America would have to support the British and French if war broke out in Europe. When World War II began in 1939, he sent ships and ammunition to Great Britain. He also began to build up the American military forces. Finally, in December of 1941, Roosevelt asked Congress to declare war on Japan after the Japanese had attacked Pearl Harbor in Hawaii.

EFFECTS OF THE DEPRESSION: How did governments around the world change because of the Great Depression?

13. As economic conditions worsened, the hope for democracy in many other countries was threatened. Governments were weak and unstable, particularly in nations like Germany, Austria, and Spain, where there had been no democracy before the war. People were becoming desperate for change and were willing to try political extremes and harsh new kinds of government. **Fascism** (FASH-izm) became popular in Germany, Italy, and Spain. Under fascism, a single party controls the government. This fascist party has total power over the people and uses war and racism to gain greater support from the people. In 1922, Italy became a fascist nation led by Benito Mussolini (beh-NEE-toh moos-oh-LEE-nee). In Germany, the Nazi party gained control in 1933 led by its fascist dictator Adolf Hitler. After a three-year civil war, a fascist general, Francisco Franco (fron-SEES-koh FRON-koh), seized power in Spain in 1939.

14. As the Great Depression continued, many governments grew fearful as unrest spread among jobless workers. As labor strikes, riots, and protests for change became common, governments also grew more fearful of revolutions. In many cases, governments responded to this growing unrest with harsh measures. In fascist coun-

▲ September 1, 1939, German tanks surged into Poland. Britain and France declared war on Germany, but they could not get help to Poland in time, and it was quickly conquered.

tries labor unions were outlawed and their leaders were arrested.

15. By the late 1930s, the Great Depression also had helped set the stage for another great war. Fascist countries soon learned that by rebuilding their military power they also created jobs. Germany, Italy, and Japan set out on a path of world conquest. Japan began in 1931 by taking Manchuria from China. In 1935 Mussolini's Italy invaded the African nation of Ethiopia, which it quickly conquered. Ethiopia appealed to the League of Nations for aid, but with no result. Knowing now that the League of Nations would not stop them, the aggressor nations attacked one country after another. In 1937 Japan began a war against China in which it occupied large parts of the country. Hitler's Germany took over Austria in 1938 and Czechoslovakia and a piece of Lithuania in 1939, while Italy took Albania. When Germany invaded Poland in 1939, however, France and Britain realized they had to halt the spread of fascism. On September 3, 1939, they declared war on Germany, and World War II began.

OUTLOOK

16. World War I was said to be "the war to end all wars." People hoped that a series of treaties plus the League of Nations would be able to prevent any new wars from breaking out. Yet in 1939 the world found itself in an even greater war. The League of Nations had not been able to keep the peace because at that time countries were not able to work together. The Great Depression of the 1930s led several countries to turn to fascism. These fascist countries soon began to build strong military forces and this increased the risk of war. Yet many people believed nations would never fight another world war. They felt the new weapons of World War I were too terrible ever to use again. As you know, they were replaced by even more powerful weapons. Today, people say that a nuclear war would be a war to end all wars. Is this similar or different from what people thought after World War I? Do you think the situation today is different from then and if so, how? ◄

539

CHAPTER REVIEW

VOCABULARY REVIEW

Write each number and word on a separate sheet of paper. Then write the letter of the definition next to the word it defines.

1. disarmament
2. domestic goods
3. League of Nations
4. fascism
5. prosperity
6. protective tariffs
7. Great Depression
8. self-determination

a. the worldwide collapse in businesses and industries from 1929 to 1939.

b. products made within a country

c. taxes on imported foreign goods

d. economic well-being

e. reducing armed forces and weapons

f. a form of government in which a single party rules with total power over the people and uses war and racism to gain support from its people.

g. the right of people to decide on their own form of government.

SKILL BUILDER: USING A GRAPH

Look at the following graph that shows figures of unemployment in the United States from 1920 through 1940. Using the graph and the chapter for information, answer the questions that follow the graph.

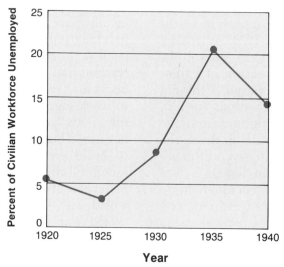

UNEMPLOYMENT IN THE
UNITED STATES, 1920-1940

1. How many years are shown on the graph?
   a. 3
   b. 20
   c. 5

2. In 1925 the unemployment figures were
   a. low
   b. high
   c. not given on graph

3. In 1933 the unemployment figures were
   a. low
   b. high
   c. not given on graph

4. The period between 1930 and 1935
   a. shows a sharp decrease in unemployment
   b. shows a sharp increase in unemployment

c. shows that unemployment remained steady

5. You may conclude that in 1935 the economic situation in the United States was
   a. good
   b. bad
   c. better than in 1925

SKILL BUILDER: CRITICAL THINKING AND COMPREHENSION

1. Main Idea

▶ Reread paragraph 7. Write a sentence stating the main idea of the paragraph.

2. Generalizing

▶ Read the following statements of fact.

Many factories in Germany, France, and Belgium had been destroyed during the war. One person out of every four in Great Britain could not find a job.

▶ Choose which generalization connects these facts.

   a. Europe was an inexpensive place to live.

   b. The European economy suffered from unemployment and the damage of war.

   c. High unemployment is the result of war.

3. Compare and Contrast

This chapter presents many facts and ideas about life in the United States and Europe in the years 1920 to 1939. One way of understanding what happened during this time is to compare and contrast the information. Write two facts or ideas that show how life in the United States and Europe was similar during this period. Then write two facts or ideas that show how life was different.

ENRICHMENT

1. Research life in Italy and Germany during the 1930s. In what ways were they similar and different? In your research, look for information on the government and economies of the two countries. Also look at their military power, the rights of citizens, and the popularity of their rulers. Write a report that compares and contrasts the rise of fascism in Germany and in Italy.

2. Imagine that you were made dictator of one of the countries mentioned in this chapter. Write a speech outlining how you would rule that country during the 1930s. Tell how you would solve your country's economic and political problems.

3. Prepare a report on the League of Nations. Tell what the organization accomplished and what problems it was unable to solve.

CHAPTER 2

Russia Turns to Communism

▲ Lenin seized control of Russia in 1917. His dictatorship made Russia a one-party Communist nation called the Soviet Union.

OBJECTIVE: How did the Communist party gain power in Russia, and what great changes did the Communists make in the lives of the people?

1. Not until 1988 did the Communist government allow maps of the Soviet Union to be published with correct, detailed information on them. Why would the rulers of this powerful country try to keep such information a secret? As the world's leading Communist nation, the Soviet Union believed that the capitalist nations of Europe were determined to stop the spread of communism. The Communist rulers of the Soviet Union also were influenced by their own early history. When the Russian Revolution began in 1917, Britain, France, and the United States had sent soldiers to Russia to aid the armies fighting against the Communists. In this chapter you will read about the Russian Revolution and how the Communist dictatorship was established.

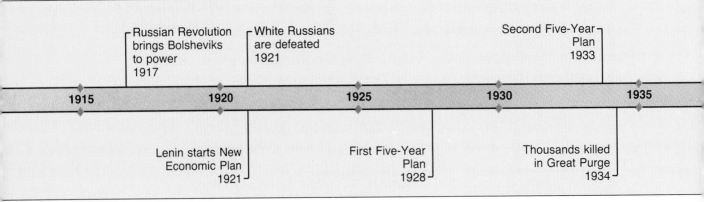

Russian Revolution brings Bolsheviks to power 1917

White Russians are defeated 1921

Second Five-Year Plan 1933

1915 — 1920 — 1925 — 1930 — 1935

Lenin starts New Economic Plan 1921

First Five-Year Plan 1928

Thousands killed in Great Purge 1934

THE RUSSIAN REVOLUTION: How did the Bolsheviks overthrow the Provisional Government and set up a Communist dictatorship led by Lenin?

2. The hardships and suffering of the Russian people in World War I led to the overthrow of Czar Nicholas II and brought the Communists to power. By 1917, Russia's armies had lost many battles, and Germany had conquered large parts of Russia. Millions of Russian soldiers had been killed, and their families back home lacked food and fuel. As a result, the war became very unpopular. The peasants on the farms and city workers now demanded "bread and peace." When Czar Nicholas refused to listen to them, strikes and riots broke out in several Russian cities.

3. In March 1917, workers in Petrograd staged a strike, demanding food and an end to the war. The czar's troops sent to crush the strike joined the workers. As a result, Nicholas II was forced to give up his throne. ▶ Why could the czar no longer stay in power when the army turned against him? A new government was formed called the Provisional Government. The Provisional Government promised the people greater freedom, and it set a date for free elections. Meanwhile, workers and soldiers in the cities set up local **soviets** (SOH-vee-ets), or councils, to govern their areas.

4. The Provisional Government soon became unpopular with the people because it refused to end the war with Germany. At the same time, a revolutionary group called the Bolsheviks (BOL-shuh-viks) were planning to overthrow the government. The Bolsheviks had gained control of many of the city soviets. In November 1917, the Bolsheviks were ready to start uprisings and use force to seize power. On November 6, the Bolsheviks marched on the headquarters of the Provisional Government in Petrograd and arrested its leaders. The Russian Revolution had begun.

5. The Bolsheviks now controlled the Russian government under their leader Vladimir Ilyich Lenin (VLAD-uh-meer ILL-ee-itch LEN-in). At this time, the Bolsheviks became known as Communists. They began to change Russia into a Communist nation based on the ideas of Karl Marx. As head of the Communist party, Lenin had nearly total power, and he used it ruthlessly to change Russia's political and economic system. Led by Lenin, the Communist government took over all land, factories, mines, railroads, banks, and other property. Private ownership of property was now outlawed. Peasant farmers were forced to give much of their crops to the government. The Communists set up a secret police force to hunt down Russians who opposed the revolutionary government. Lenin's government also agreed to give up large amounts of Russian territory in order to end the war with Germany.

PEOPLE IN HISTORY

6. Lenin had long been a supporter of Communist ideas. He was born into a Russian noble family and received a good education. However, when Lenin was 17 years old, his brother was executed for plotting to kill the czar. Lenin now became a bitter foe of the czar and the ruling nobility of Russia. Lenin studied law, but he soon became more interested in Marxist ideas and communism. Lenin then worked to spread Communist ideas among Russian workers. As a result, in 1896 he was exiled to Siberia. In 1900, Lenin and his wife fled from Russia to escape arrest by the czar's secret police.

7. Lenin believed that revolution could be successful in Russia only if it was led by a small, well-organized group. Therefore, in the early 1900s, Lenin had organized his followers into the Bolshevik party. When the government of Czar Nicholas II was overthrown in 1917, Lenin was living in Switzerland. The German government provided a special train for Lenin's secret trip home. Why did Germany want to help Lenin? After all, Germany was still fighting against Russia in World War I. However, Germany's leaders believed that Lenin

ESL/LEP Strategy: Write each sentence from paragraph 3 on a separate index card. Have students work in groups to arrange the sentences in the order that makes the most sense. Ask a volunteer from each group to explain the order they chose.

543

▶ would stir up trouble and possibly cause the czar's government to collapse. Did their plan work?

8. The Communists faced difficult times after they took control of the Russian government. Many of the nobles and large landowners hated the Communists. The peasants, too, were angry because they were forced to give their crops to the Communist government. Many people also feared the Communist government's total control over
▶ their lives. What might people do when they fear and hate a government? In a civil war from 1917 to 1921, the **White Russians**, as the enemies of the Communists were called, fought to overthrow the Communist dictatorship. Britain, France, and the United States supported these groups and sent soldiers to help in the fight. However, the Communist armies defeated the White Russians by 1921.

POST CIVIL WAR: What steps did Lenin take to rebuild the Russian economy?

9. The end of the civil war in 1921 left Russia in terrible shape. Hundreds of thousands of people had been killed in the years from 1917 to 1921. Many of Russia's farms and factories had closed, and many workers now lacked jobs. Crop harvests were poor, and several million Russians had died from hunger and disease. Lenin knew that he must take strong steps to save the Russian Revolution and rebuild Russia.

10. One of Lenin's first steps was to plan the development of Russia as a stronger, more industrial nation. To achieve this goal, Lenin set up the **New Economic Policy** (NEP). Under NEP, the government continued to follow Communist ideas. The government still owned all basic industries, but it also allowed some private ownership of property. NEP lasted until 1928, and the Communist government used it successfully to rebuild Russia's economy.

11. At the same time, Lenin moved to strengthen the country in other ways. Because the nation included several major national groups, Lenin set up four republics in Russia and changed the nation's name to the Union of Soviet Socialist Republics, or the Soviet Union. Lenin also organized the Communist party into a strong, tightly run group. When Lenin died in 1924, the Soviet Union was once more becoming an important power in the world.

JOSEPH STALIN: What policies did Stalin use to strengthen communism, and how did he turn the Soviet Union into a total dictatorship?

12. Joseph Stalin, the Secretary-General of the Communist party, became ruler of the Soviet Union after Lenin died. Stalin believed that harsh measures were needed to turn the Soviet Union into a strong industrial and military power. In 1928, Stalin began the first **Five-Year Plan**. The plan focused on expanding heavy industries like steel mills, oil refineries, and machinery plants. Stalin also reorganized farming in the Soviet Union. All small farmers were required to join **collectives** (koh-LEK-tivz), or large farms owned and run by the government. The government set a quota, or fixed amount of crops, each collective farm must produce and turn over to the government.

13. Stalin's first Five-Year Plan succeeded in expanding Soviet industries, but at the expense of the Soviet people. Factory workers in the cities lacked decent housing, clothing, and other consumer products. Soviet farmers were even worse off. Many prosperous peasant farmers, known as **kulaks** (KOO-lahks), refused to join collective farms. Many of them burned their crops and destroyed their farm animals rather than turn them over to the Communist government. Stalin declared the kulaks enemies of communism and ordered millions of them killed or imprisoned. Stalin also forced the collective farmers in the Ukraine, the country's richest farming area, to give nearly all of their grain to the government for export. The result of this policy was a famine in which millions of people in the Ukraine died of starvation.

544

▲ Joseph Stalin became ruler of the Soviet Union in 1924. His harsh rule forced factory workers to produce heavy industrial goods.

SPOTLIGHT ON SOURCES

14. Stalin's goal was to build a strong industrial economy. He remembered the words of a pre-revolutionary poet, who said, "Thou art poor, Mother Russia, but thou art plentiful. Thou art mighty, but thou art helpless, Mother Russia!" Stalin added:

In the past we had no fatherland and could have none. Now, however, that we have overthrown capitalism and the workers wield power in our country, we have a fatherland and shall defend its independence. Do you want our Socialist [Communist] fatherland to be beaten and to lose its independence? If you do not want that, then you must abolish its backwardness and develop a really Bolshevik pace in the establishment of its Socialist [Commu-

nist] economy. There are no other ways. That is why Lenin said in the time of October—'Either die or overtake and surpass the advanced capitalist countries' . . . . We are fifty or a hundred years behind the advanced countries. We must make good this lag in ten years. Either we accomplish this or we will be crushed.

—*A History of Soviet Russia*, Georg von Rauch

15. Stalin's rule of the Soviet Union continued throughout the 1930s. A second Five-Year Plan began in 1933, with the same aims as the first Plan. During the 1930s, Stalin also gained absolute power within the Communist party. Stalin used force and terror to silence party members who criticized his actions or his policies. Stalin used the secret police to arrest millions of party members. Stalin's campaign to crush all opposition was called the **Great Purge**. Leading Communist party members were tried for treason and executed. Millions of others were sent as slave labor to desolate camps in the Arctic regions.

OUTLOOK

16. The Russian people lived through some of the darkest and most difficult years in their nation's history from 1917 to 1939. During World War I, more Russian soldiers were killed and more people's homes and farms were destroyed than in any other country. Then the Russian Revolution began in 1917 and brought the Communist party to power. When the Communists tried to take control of all private property, a bloody civil war began that raged for several years. In 1921, Lenin laid the foundation of single-party Communist rule in the Soviet Union. After Lenin, Stalin became the Soviet ruler. Under Stalin, during the 1930s, millions of peasants were killed, and the Soviet people faced starvation and terrible hardships. How do you think these years affected the Soviet people? How might the memory of these years still influence people's lives today?

CHAPTER REVIEW

VOCABULARY REVIEW

Write each of the following sentences on a sheet of paper. Then fill in the blank with the word that best completes each sentence.

soviets   Five Year Plan
Bolsheviks   Great Purge
White Russians   collectives
New Economic Policy   kulaks

1. Many _____ were imprisoned or killed for refusing to join collectives.

2. _____ , or local councils, governed during the years of the Provisional Government.

3. All farmers were required to give up their own land and join government owned _____ .

4. A revolutionary group called the _____ was planning to overthrow the Provisional Government.

5. Stalin's campaign to crush all opposition was called the _____ .

6. _____ were enemies of the Communists in Russia's civil war.

7. The _____ was an attempt to industrialize industry in Russia rapidly.

8. Under the _____ some private ownership of property was allowed.

SKILL BUILDER: DIAGRAMS

Use the diagram to complete the statements on the next page.

GOVERNMENT OF THE SOVIET UNION
Soviet Constitutional Government

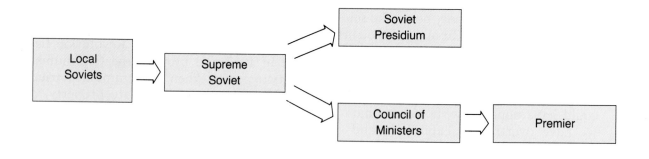

Organization of Communist Party

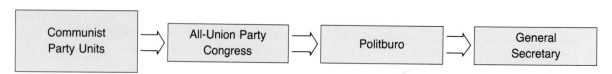

1. The Council of Ministers is chosen by the _____ .

2. Local election districts that choose delegates to the Supreme Soviet are called _____ .

3. The Communist party leader in the Soviet Union is called the _____ .

4. When Communist party delegates from all parts of the Soviet Union meet, the group they form is called the _____ .

5. The group of people chosen by the All-Union Party Congress to decide policies and plans is known as the _____ .

SKILL BUILDER: CRITICAL THINKING AND COMPREHENSION

1. Classifying

▶ Read each statement. Which statement was made by Karl Marx, and which statement was made by Lenin? Explain your answer on a separate sheet of paper.

   a. "It is not a conflict of ideas but of material or economic factors that bring about changes."

   b. "Peace, land, and bread" and "all power to the soviets."

2. Sequencing

▶ On a separate sheet of paper write the following events in the order in which they happened.

   a. Russia ends the war with Germany.

   b. The first Five-Year Plan begins.

   c. Stalin carries out the Great Purge.

   d. Lenin becomes leader of the Communist government.

3. Drawing Conclusions

▶ Read paragraphs 12 and 13. What are your conclusions about how the people felt toward the government? Explain your answer in detail on a separate sheet of paper.

4. Hypothesizing

▶ The New Economic Policy established by Lenin helped to revive the failing economy in Russia by allowing a limited amount of private enterprise. When Lenin died and Stalin became leader, the NEP was ended. If the NEP program had not been ended, how do you think the Soviet Union's economy might have developed?

ENRICHMENT

1. Write a report on the art that was created in the Soviet Union during the first years of the Russian Revolution. Include information about how this art was different from past styles and for what purposes it was used by artists such as Kazimir Malevich, El Lissitzky, Naum Gabo, and Antoine Pevsner.

2. Write a report on the life of Karl Marx. Include in your report information about his background, education, ideas, and writings. Be sure to describe the importance of Marx's ideas about government and society.

CHAPTER 3

Fascism in Italy and Spain

▲ Benito Mussolini ruled Italy as a fascist dictator from 1922 to 1943. Mussolini was formally known as *Il Duce* ("the Leader").

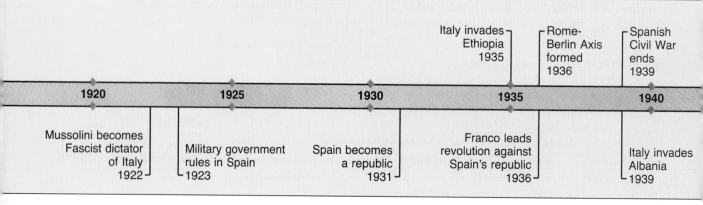

OBJECTIVE How did fascist dictators gain control of Italy and Spain in the years after World War I?

▶ **1.** What if Congress were disbanded one day and the President announced that he would govern alone? What if the President went on national television and said that the Constitution was no longer in force? And what if just about everybody thought that it was a great idea? Picture it: thousands of Americans rush into the streets of Washington, D.C., and shout, "Long live the President!" and "Hang the Congress!" The same day, the editors of the nation's major newspapers disappear and are found dead a week later. Meanwhile, nobody tries to stop

the President. The army and the police have the United States under total control. Clearly, this is a wild notion. But these things actually happened in Italy and Spain in the 1920s and 1930s. The problems in those two countries were so great that many

				Italy invades Ethiopia 1935	Rome-Berlin Axis formed 1936	Spanish Civil War ends 1939
1920		**1925**		**1930**	**1935**	**1940**
Mussolini becomes Fascist dictator of Italy 1922		Military government rules in Spain 1923	Spain becomes a republic 1931		Franco leads revolution against Spain's republic 1936	Italy invades Albania 1939

people were willing to give up their freedom for jobs and security.

FASCISM IN ITALY: How did fascism develop in Italy?

2. During the years following World War I, Italy's economy was very weak. Thousands of Italians were unemployed, many factories were closed, and food prices were high. The Italian government became less and less able to deal with the severe problems facing the country. At the urging of the Italian Communist party, the labor unions went on strike and tried to force the government to raise workers' wages. Soon the strike became violent. The property-owning classes began to fear a Communist revolution in Italy.

3. In 1919, the **Fascist party** (FASH-ist) was organized in Italy. Its members were determined to keep Italy from becoming a communist country. The Fascists believed that the state—the nation—must be all-powerful. Rights of individuals or groups were less important than those of the state. The party took its name from a symbol of authority called a "fasces." The fasces was a group of rods tied around an axe.

PEOPLE IN HISTORY

4. Known as Il Duce (EEL DOO-chay) (the leader), Benito Mussolini began the National Fascist Party in Italy in 1919. He also organized his Fascist followers into a fiercely nationalistic and often violent group known as "Black Shirts." Mussolini was elected to the Italian Parliament in 1921. In 1922, thousands of Black Shirts marched on Rome and demanded political power. When the army told the king it could not stop the Black Shirts, the king agreed to name Mussolini prime minister. In this way, the Fascists took over the entire country without firing a shot.

5. Under Mussolini, all political parties except the Fascist party were outlawed. Civil liberties came to an end. The secret police arrested and often killed anyone who dared to criticize Mussolini or his policies. Labor unions and strikes were forbidden. All newspapers, books, and radio broadcasts were controlled by the Fascists. Many people welcomed fascism, even if it meant a loss of freedom, because Mussolini also brought new prosperity and order to Italy. Mussolini provided much-needed jobs

Daily life in . . .

During the Spanish Civil war, many brutal acts were committed on both sides. The complete destruction of the small Basque town of Guernica (GWAIR-ni-kuh), however, was one of the worst. It was a forecast of events to come in World War II. The German air force, in support of Franco, bombed Guernica for three hours. This bombing marked the first time in modern history that an undefended city had been totally destroyed. For the Germans it was a practice run in military tactics and training. For the people of Guernica, it was an unspeakable horror. An eyewitness wrote:

"I arrived at Guernica on April 26, at 4:40 p.m. I had hardly left the car when the

bombardments began. The people were terrified. They fled, abandoning their livestock [farm animals] in the marketplace. The bombardment lasted until 7:45. During that time, five minutes did not elapse [go by] without the sky's being black with German planes. The planes descended [came down] very low, the machine-gun fire tearing up the woods and roads, in whose gutters, huddled together, lay old men, women, and children . . . Fire enveloped [spread through] the whole city. Screams of lamentation [great sadness] were heard everywhere, and the people, filled with terror, knelt, lifting their hands to heaven as if to implore [pray for] divine protection . . ."

through road-building and public works programs, as well as by expanding war industries. He ended riots and street fighting and improved Italy's economy.

SPOTLIGHT ON SOURCES

6. In an early speech Mussolini described fascism in these words:

> Fascism . . . has already passed over . . . the decayed [rotted] body of the Goddess of Liberty . . . For the Fascist, everything is in the State and nothing human . . . exists . . . outside the State . . . Fascism is totalitarian [controls everything] and the Fascist state . . . gives strength to the whole life of the people . . . Our formula is this: "Everything within the State, nothing outside the State, nothing against the State."
> —from *Encyclopedia of Great Quotations*, George Seldes, comp.

ITALIAN EXPANSION: Where did Mussolini's armies take over new lands for Italy?

7. At first, the Fascist rule seemed successful. However, poverty, joblessness, and hunger returned to Italy in the 1930s. Mussolini felt that Italy needed colonies to solve the nation's economic problems. In 1935, the Italians invaded the African nation of Ethiopia, claiming that the Ethiopians had provoked the attack. The Ethiopians were no match for the Italian army and soon surrendered. The League of Nations demanded that Mussolini withdraw his soldiers, but he refused.

8. In 1936, Mussolini made a pact, or agreement with Hitler, Germany's new dictator. This agreement was called the **Rome-Berlin Axis**. In April 1939, Mussolini invaded and conquered Albania. The Adriatic Sea was called "an Italian lake" after that, because Italy controlled that entire area of the Mediterranean. This time, the League of Nations did not try to stop Mussolini. Mussolini sided with Germany in

World War II. As the war drew to a close in 1945, Mussolini was executed.

SPAIN: What were the causes of unrest in Spain that led to several changes in government?

9. Compared with other European industrial countries, Spain was an undeveloped agricultural society. The people who farmed the land and worked in small factories were generally quite poor. In the early 1920s, Spain faced harsh economic conditions that the king and his weak government could not solve. As a result, a bitter struggle began with unionized workers and peasants against the property-owning class. The sympathies of the army were with the property-owning class. This struggle between opposing forces was similar to the situation in Italy. However, in Spain, the struggle ended in violence and bloodshed. In 1923, an army general led a military takeover of the government. However, the military government failed to solve Spain's problems, and a republic was proclaimed in 1939. Why might a military government ◄ have trouble solving complicated economic problems?

10. Spain's new republican government drafted a constitution that provided equal rights for all citizens and the separation of church and state. However, few improvements in Spanish life resulted. The republic was no more successful in solving inflation and unemployment than the military government had been. Many people wanted to restore the monarchy. In addition, the republican government angered many people in Spain when it threatened the the Catholic Church. Catholicism had been Spain's official religion for centuries. The republican government tried to reduce the power of the church.

CIVIL WAR: How did the Spanish Civil War lead to the fascist dictatorship of Franco?

11. By 1936, Spain was sharply divided into two groups: the **Left**, formed of Socialists, Communists, workers, and liberals;

Activity: Have students discuss the differences between the Fascist government in Italy and the Communist government in the Soviet Union. How were they similar and different?

550

▲ General Francisco Franco established a repressive fascist dictatorship in Spain. Franco won a long and bitter civil war with German help.

and the **Right**, formed of army leaders, landowners, monarchists, Catholic groups, and conservatives. In July 1936, a revolution against the republican government was begun by army troops. Their leader was General Francisco Franco (fron-SEES-koh FRON-koh). Franco's followers, the Right, were known as the Rebels, or Nationalists. The Left, those who fought against Franco to save the Republic, were called Loyalists, or Republicans.

12. The Rebels and Loyalists waged a bitter and bloody civil war that lasted for almost three years. Both sides committed acts of horrible brutality. In addition to heavy loss of life on the battlefield, many innocent civilians were killed.

13. The Spanish Civil war became a kind of preview of World War II as several countries outside of Spain became involved. Franco was aided by the governments of Germany and Italy. Hitler tested new weapons and tactics in Spain, and German and Italian troops fought there side by side. The Loyalists were helped by the Soviet Union. Britain, France, and the United States decided to ignore the war, allowing the winning fascists to take over. In 1939, Franco forced the last of the Loyalist forces to surrender in Madrid.

14. Franco became chief of state, commander in chief, and head of the only legal political party, the Fascist Falange (fuh-LANJ). No other political parties were allowed. Labor unions also were outlawed. The Catholic Church was restored to a position of influence. However, Franco found that, with all his power, he was in charge of a ruined and divided country. Although his sympathies were with the Rome-Berlin Axis, Franco decided not to join the Germans and the Italians in World War II. He had too many problems at home. How ◄ might Franco's decision to stay out of World War II have affected the results of his dictatorship? Instead, Franco began programs to help modernize Spain's agricultural economy and increase production. Franco did do much to improve conditions in his country. Stability gradually returned to Spain, but the repressive dictatorship under Franco severely limited the people's freedoms.

OUTLOOK

15. During the 1920s and 1930s in many democratic countries, their governments seemed unable to solve their growing problems of unemployment and poverty. In Italy and Spain, weak democratic governments were replaced by fascist dictatorships. These fascist leaders took total control of their nations and ended many freedoms for their people. Mussolini took control in Italy. Franco took control in Spain. Although Mussolini's rise to power was easier, the dictatorship in Italy was cut short by involvement in World War II. Franco's rise was more difficult, but his rule lasted longer. Do you think America could ever ◄ become a dictatorship? Why or why not?

Activity: Have students look at the map of Spain on page 728. Ask students how Spain's location, with the Pyrenees mountains in the north made it easier to remain neutral in the world wars.

551

CHAPTER REVIEW

VOCABULARY REVIEW

Write the following words on a separate sheet of paper. Then find these words in the glossary on pages 728–738. Write the definition for each word.

1. Fascist party
2. Rome-Berlin Axis
3. Left
4. Right

SKILL BUILDER: OUTLINING

Copy the outline below about Spain in the 1920s and 1930s and complete the missing items.

I. Spain was an undeveloped agricultural country
    A. Most of the people were farmers.
    B. _____

II. The Spanish government was too weak to solve the country's problems.
    A. The workers and the peasants began a struggle against the property-owning class.
        1. _____
        2. _____
    B. An army general led a military takeover of the government in 1923.
        1. _____
        2. _____

SKILL BUILDER: CRITICAL THINKING AND COMPREHENSION

1. Summarizing

▶ Read carefully and explain the importance of each event. Use a separate sheet of paper.

a. In 1936, Mussolini made a pact with Hitler, Germany's dictator, called the Rome-Berlin Axis.

b. In Italy, the secret police arrested and often killed anyone who dared to criticize the state.

c. In Spain, the republican government angered many people when it threatened the power of the Catholic church.

d. Italy and Spain became Fascist countries in the 1920s and 1930s.

2. Predicting When you predict, you look ahead and make a guess about what may happen next. Good predictions are based on facts. You can often use what you have read to make a good prediction.

552

► Read the paragraphs below. Then answer the questions on a separate sheet of paper.

2-1. During times of war, atrocities are committed by both sides. However, these atrocities often have different consequences, depending upon which side wins the war.

    a. What do you think would be the consequences for soldiers and their commanders who lose a war?

    b. What do you think would be the consequences for the winner?

2-2. Religion is an important aspect in the lives of many people. Perhaps religion is even more important when one religion has long been accepted as the official religion. What might happen if a government decided to abolish the nation's official religion?

3. Spatial Relationships

► Read the list of events that happened in Italy during the 1920s. Then write a list of the events that were taking place in Russia during these same years.

a. In 1921, Mussolini was elected to the Italian parliament.

b. Mussolini was named prime minister of Italy in 1922.

c. Mussolini arrested all those who were against his government and set up a dictatorsip in Italy.

4. Making Judgments

► Tell whether you *agree* or *disagree* with each of the following statements. If you disagree, change the underlined words to make the sentence a statement with which you agree.

a. The Black Shirts were members of the German Nazi party.

b. A Fascist party was first organized in Spain.

c. The Italians invaded the African country of Morocco.

d. Unlike many other Western European countries, Spain was an advanced industrial society.

e. The state religion of Spain was Islam.

f. Franco decided not to join the Germans and Italians in World War II.

ENRICHMENT

1. In both Italy and Spain, the people were divided between groups that included workers on one side and the landowners, business leaders, and industrialists on the other. For example, the Fiat and Pirelli companies encouraged Mussolini to take power and helped him financially. In Spain, most wealthy landowners supported Franco. Did these situations reflect the ideas of Karl Marx that you studied in Unit 9, Chapter 4? Write a paragraph explaining how Marx might have explained or described the events that took place in Italy and Spain.

2. Write a report about the role of Germany and Italy in the Spanish Civil War. In your report, include information about the political and military value of this German and Italian involvement. Explain which side they supported and why, and discuss how the Spanish Civil War was a "little world war."

CHAPTER 4

The Nazis in Germany

▲ Adolf Hitler was known for his dynamic style of speaking. His uncanny ability to sway crowds gave him great power over many Germans.

OBJECTIVE: How did Hitler become dictator of Germany and gain total control over the lives of the German people?

1. People often complain about high prices. They talk about the high price they had to pay for a used car or for furniture. ▶ Yet, how would you and your family be able to live if all prices increased every week? This is what happened in Germany in 1922 and 1923. The German government printed so much paper money that money lost its value. For example, the price of a stamp to mail a letter went from one pfennig to ten million marks during these two years. People carried their money in shopping bags in order to have enough to buy food for supper. Soon it was almost impossible for ordinary Germans to buy anything. Many families faced great hardship, and almost every family found its life savings completely wiped out. As a result, many Germans were willing to listen to a leader with extreme ideas who promised a better life. This leader, Adolf Hitler, eventually became dictator of Germany.

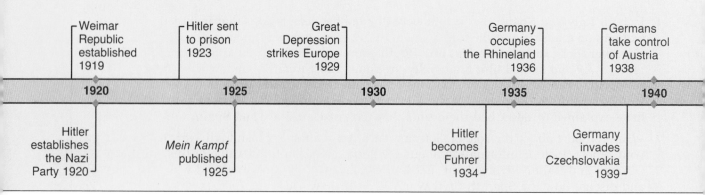

Weimar Republic established 1919

Hitler sent to prison 1923

Great Depression strikes Europe 1929

Germany occupies the Rhineland 1936

Germans take control of Austria 1938

1920 | **1925** | **1930** | **1935** | **1940**

Hitler establishes the Nazi Party 1920

Mein Kampf published 1925

Hitler becomes Fuhrer 1934

Germany invades Czechoslovakia 1939

554

THE WEIMAR REPUBLIC: What problems faced the new democratic government in Germany?

2. In 1919, the German nation had just been defeated in World War I. Some parts of Germany were still occupied by Allied armies. German soldiers were returning home, bitter and unhappy. Many of them were not able to find jobs. During this difficult time, the main hopes of the German people were focused on the city of Weimar. In January 1919, the German national assembly met at Weimar to set up a new democratic government known as the **Weimar** (VY-mar) **Republic**.

3. From the start, however, the Weimar government was weakened by serious economic problems. Germany's economy was in ruins, but Germany was expected to pay reparations to the victorious Allies. The Weimar government had to borrow huge amounts of money from other nations. Even more serious, however, was the government's decision to print more paper money than the treasury could cover. This action quickly led to runaway inflation in Germany in 1922 and 1923 that shattered the public's confidence in its government.

4. The Weimar government seemed helpless to solve the country's problems. Extreme groups formed that weakened the government more and soon challenged its power to rule. The Communist party gained many members by promising to give all power to the people. The National Socialist party gained many followers among war veterans and workers by blaming the government for accepting the harsh terms of the Treaty of Versailles.

PEOPLE IN HISTORY

5. Adolf Hitler was born in a small Austrian town near the German border. He dropped out of high school and went to Vienna to study art. When World War I started, Hitler joined the German army and was wounded in battle. After the war, like many former soldiers, Hitler became interested in politics. In 1920, he joined the National Socialist German Workers party, called the Nazi (NOT-see) party. "Nazi" comes from the German pronunciation of the first two syllables of "National."

HITLER'S RISE TO POWER: How did Hitler become dictator of Germany?

6. Hitler's Nazi party strongly opposed the German Communists. Hitler and his followers believed Germany must again become a strong military power and revenge its defeat in the war. Hitler soon began traveling around Germany giving speeches. He blamed Germany's problems on the Communists, the Jews, and the Weimar government. Many Germans wanted to believe him, since they needed someone to blame for their troubles.

7. Hitler was an exciting speaker. He promised the German people that the Nazi party would find them jobs and restore the nation's economy. He vowed to tear up the Versailles treaty and end Germany's reparations payments.

SPOTLIGHT ON SOURCES

8. In 1924, Hitler wrote a book called *Mein Kampf* (*My Struggle*). In it he claimed that Germans were members of an Aryan master race destined to conquer the whole world. However, Germany could achieve its greatness only by acquiring more "living space." He explained the need for more territory in this way:

> Germany has an annual increase in population of nearly nine hundred thousand souls [people]. The difficulty of feeding . . . [these] new citizens must [will] grow greater from year to year and ultimately [finally] end in catastrophe, unless ways and means are found to forestall [keep away] the danger of starvation and misery in time . . . .

The National Socialist movement must strive to eliminate [end] the disproportion [difference] between our population and our area . . . between our historical past and the hopelessness of our present impotence [powerlessness] . . . .

We National Socialists must hold unflinchingly [firmly] to our aim in foreign policy, namely, to secure for the German people the land and soil to which they are entitled on this earth.

—*Mein Kampf*, Adolf Hitler

9. In the national election of 1930, the Nazi party received more votes than any other party. In 1933, President von Hindenburg appointed Hitler **chancellor,** or prime minister. Thus, Hitler came to power legally. What other dictator also was appointed to head his country's government? Within two months, Hitler forced the German legislature to give up its authority and made himself absolute dictator of Germany. In 1934, Hitler took the title of **Führer** (FEW-rer), or Leader.

THE THIRD REICH: How did Hitler's dictatorship affect the lives of the German people?

10. In 1934, Hitler announced the formation of what he called the Third Reich. The German word **Reich** (RYK) means "empire." Hitler boasted that his Third Reich would last for a thousand years. It lasted only 12 years. Yet in those few years Hitler changed the history of Germany and the world.

11. After he gained power, Hitler acted quickly to end all opposition to his rule. He organized thousands of Nazi party members as Storm Troopers. The Storm Troopers broke up meetings of rival political parties and silenced anyone who spoke out against the Nazis. Hitler also organized a

▼ Nazi aggression against neighboring nations in the 1930s built a stronger Germany at first but later led to defeat in World War II. What lands did Germany annex between 1934 and 1939?

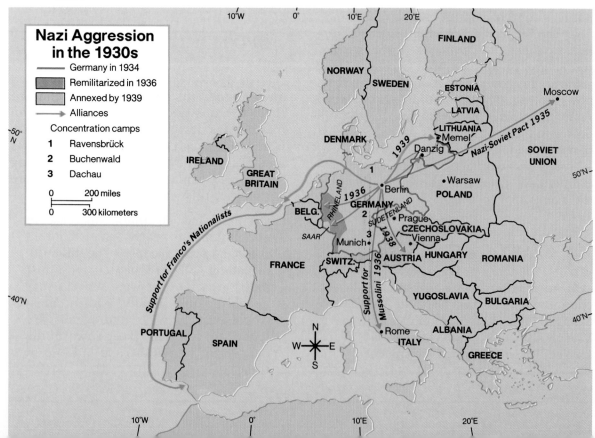

secret police force known as the Gestapo (guh-SHTAH-poh) to brutally hunt down the Führer's enemies. To win the support of the German people, he used **propaganda** (prop-uh-GAN-duh), a one-sided presentation of information. His propaganda minister declared that if a lie is told often enough, people will believe it is true. In speech after speech, Hitler used lies—lies about the Communists and lies about the Jews—to win over the German people. The Nazis even burned all books that discussed ideas Hitler considered to be dangerous.

12. Hitler next turned to the task of ridding Germany of Jews. Although only one percent of the population was Jewish, Hitler believed that the Jews were responsible for most of Germany's problems. In 1933, Jews were forbidden to hold political office. In 1935, the Nuremberg Laws took away the citizenship rights of Jews. Jews were forbidden to teach in any school, work in hospitals, or marry non-Jews. Jews were not allowed to own property, and they were forced to live in **ghettos,** or separate sections of German cities. In 1938, Hitler arrested thousands of Jews and sent them to prison camps.

13. Hitler's economic programs helped Germany. Farm production increased and many industries returned to full production. When Hitler came to power in 1933, six million German workers were without jobs. By 1938, German industries had expanded so rapidly that nearly all workers were employed. Many of the new jobs were created as a result of Hitler's efforts to rearm Germany with planes, tanks, and weapons needed for war.

GERMAN AGGRESSION: What European nations did Hitler take over in the 1930s?

14. Finally, to fulfill his goal of more living space for the German people, Hitler set out on a policy of **aggression** (uh-GRESH-un). Aggression means to use force to take over other countries. First, in 1936, Hitler sent troops to occupy the Rhineland. The Rhineland is a part of western Germany where, to protect France from attack,

German troops had not been allowed since World War I. This move was a violation of the Treaty of Versailles. Then, in 1938, Hitler ordered his army to march into Austria. Without a shot being fired, the Nazis took control of Austria. This, too, was a violation of the Versailles treaty. Hitler's next target was the Sudetenland (soo-DAY-ten-land), the parts of Czechoslovakia along the German border where many German speaking people lived.

15. In September 1938, Hitler held a meeting at Munich with the leaders of Great Britain, France, and Italy. The leaders agreed to have Hitler take the Sudetenland in return for his promise not to demand more territory. Hitler soon broke this promise, however. In March 1939, the German army occupied the rest of Czechoslovakia.

16. Hitler was able to conquer these lands because other European nations did not try to stop him. Many leaders of Europe believed Hitler would limit his aggression. They also believed that Germany had a right to take these lands. In addition, leaders like British prime minister Neville Chamberlain felt that the Versailles treaty was unfair to Germany. When Chamberlain gave in to Hitler's demands, he was following a policy that became known as **appeasement** (uh-PEEZ-munt). Appeasement means giving in to demands by an aggressor nation, hoping to prevent war.

OUTLOOK

17. Germany's takeover of Czechoslovakia in 1939 alarmed the world. Hitler's word and his intentions could no longer be trusted. Unfortunately, the rest of the world had let their armies and navies decline during the Great Depression, and were not ready for war. Food, clothing, shelter, and jobs had become more important to governments than tanks and guns. What if Britain and France had kept their armed forces strong? Do you think Hitler would have tried to conquer Europe? Could the League of Nations have stopped him?

ESL/LEP Strategy: Ask students to define *propaganda* and to give examples of Nazi propaganda and of present-day propaganda.

557

CHAPTER REVIEW

VOCABULARY REVIEW

Write the words in the left hand column on a piece of paper. Then write the letter of the definition next to the word it matches.

1. Chancellor
2. Fuhrer
3. Reich
4. propaganda
5. ghetto
6. aggression
7. appeasement

a. one-sided information
b. Empire or State
c. prime minister
d. giving into demands by an aggressor nation
e. the use of force to take over other countries
f. leader of Nazi Germany
g. it's part of a city a minority group is forced to live in

SKILL BUILDER: USING PRIMARY SOURCES

Before Adolf Hitler became dictator of Germany, he was arrested for trying to overthrow the government. While in jail, he wrote a book called *Mein Kampf* (*My Struggle*) in which he presented his ideas. These paragraphs are taken from his book. Read them and answer the questions that follow.

The question of the inner causes of the Aryan's [German's] importance can be answered to the effect that they are to be sought less in a natural instinct of self-preservation than in the special type of its expression. . . . [The] self-sacrificing will to give one's personal labor and if necessary one's own life for others is most strongly developed in the Aryan. The Aryan is not greatest in his mental qualities as such, but in the extent of his willingness to put all his abilities in the service of the community. In him the instinct of self-preservation has reached its noblest form, since he willingly subordinates his own ego to the life of the community and, if the hour demands, even sacrifices it.

One blood demands one Reich. Never will the German nation possess the moral right to engage in colonial politics until, at least, it embraces its own sons within a single state. . . . Their sword will become our plow, and from the tears of war the daily bread of future generations will grow. . . . *For oppressed territories are led back to the bosom of a common Reich, not by flaming protests, but by a mighty sword.*

▶ Choose the correct answer.

1. To Hitler, what made Aryans superior to others was their willingness to
   a. make sacrifices for the common good.
   b. serve in the army.
   c. keep in good physical shape.

2. Hitler believed that Aryans were
   a. more intelligent.
   b. more noble and virtuous.
   c. better managers.

3. Hitler planned to win territory by
   a. armed force.
   b. complaining to the League of Nations.
   c. making speeches.

4. The responsibility of Germany's leader, according to Hitler, was to
   a. make swords.
   b. build up Germany militarily.
   c. run the schools.

SKILL BUILDER: CRITICAL THINKING AND COMPREHENSION

1. Main Idea

▶ On a separate piece of paper match the paragraph number in column 2 to its main idea in column 1.

Main Idea	Paragraph Number
a. Hitler came to power legally, when the Nazis received more votes than any other party.	7
	16
b. Most of Western Europe tried to appease Hitler.	9
	3
c. The Weimar Republic had to borrow huge sums of money from other nations.	10
d. Hitler pledged to restore Germany's economy and destroy the Versailles treaty.	
e. Hitler said the Third Reich would last for a thousand years.	

2. Generalizing

▶ Write a paragraph explaining how you think propaganda works. Why do people come to believe propaganda?

3. Cause and Effect

▶ On a separate piece of paper write *cause* or *effect* for each set of statements:

3-1. a. The German people often carried their money in shopping bags.
b. The German government printed so much money that it lost its value.

3-2. a. The German government had to borrow a lot of money.
b. The government had to pay for war reparations.

3-3. a. Hitler believed the Jews were responsible for many of Germany's problems.
b. The Jews lost their citizenship.

4. Fact *versus* Opinion

▶ On a separate piece of paper, write a *fact* sentence and an *opinion* sentence about the following subjects from this chapter.

a. *Mein Kampf*
b. Nazi party
c. Storm Troopers
d. Nuremberg Laws

ENRICHMENT

1. Prepare a report on the life of Hitler before he became dictator.

2. Imagine that you are a United States newspaper reporter stationed in Germany after Hitler came to power. Write an article for your readers back home describing how life has changed for the German people.

CHAPTER 5

Militarism in Japan

OBJECTIVE: Why did military leaders gain control of Japan and set out to conquer an empire in East Asia during the 1930s?

1. If you made a list of the cars Americans buy today, you would find that many are Japanese. The same would be true of other products such as television sets, motorcycles, stereos, and many electronic products. Over the last 20 years, Japan has become one of the United States' largest trading partners, as well as one of our closest political allies. However, American relations with Japan were not always as friendly. In 1941, the United States declared war when Japan bombed the navy's base at Pearl Harbor. This surprise attack almost destroyed the American Pacific fleet. At the same time, Japan attacked British colonies

▲ Hirohito, riding a white horse, is accompanied at a military ceremony by his honor guard. Hirohito was emperor of Japan during World War II.

at Singapore and Hong Kong. Why did Japan attack Britain and the United States? What did Japan hope to gain by going ◀ to war? The answers lie in the events that were going on in Japan during the 1920s and 1930s.

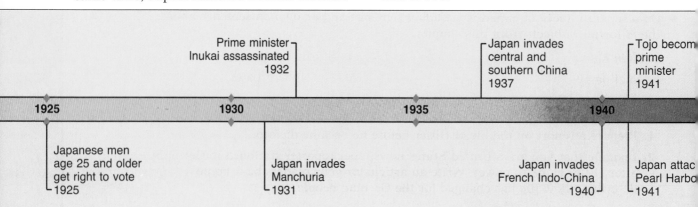

	Prime minister Inukai assassinated 1932	Japan invades central and southern China 1937	Tojo becom prime minister 1941
1925	**1930**	**1935**	**1940**
Japanese men age 25 and older get right to vote 1925	Japan invades Manchuria 1931	Japan invades French Indo-China 1940	Japan attac Pearl Harbo 1941

JAPAN AND THE MILITARY: What events led to the rise of the military in Japan during the 1930s?

2. During the 1920s, Japan's emperor lost much of his traditional power in running the government, as did the nobles and the military. Democratic reforms, or changes in government, gave the Japanese people more political power. All men over the age of 25 were given the right to vote. Political parties were allowed to nominate candidates to run for election to the Diet, or Japanese parliament. The prime minister, once chosen by the emperor, was now chosen by the political party having a majority in the Diet.

3. The growth of democracy in Japan came to a halt, however, during the Great Depression. Because Japan had few natural resources, it depended heavily on its trade with other nations. Japan needed to import food to feed its large population, and coal, oil, and iron ore to keep its industries running. To pay for these imports from other countries, Japan exported cotton, silk, and manufactured goods. Then, during the 1930s, the Great Depression caused a slump in worldwide trade. Japan's revenue from trade fell by nearly 50 percent, and the Japanese economy was devastated. Japan became desperate for food and resources. Many Japanese factories and businesses closed, and many workers lost their jobs.
▶ Under these conditions, what kind of government often appeals to people?

4. Japan's military leaders and the nobles who had controlled the nation in the past now began to regain their old power. The new democratic government seemed unable to solve the problems caused by the economic crisis in Japan. As a result, the nobles and leaders of the army criticized the Diet and the prime minister and blamed them for Japan's problems.

SPOTLIGHT ON SOURCES

5. In 1927, leaders of the Japanese army drew up a plan for conquering Asia. The Chinese got hold of the plan and published it in a document called the Tanaka Memorial. A section of the Tanaka Memorial follows.

Manchuria is politically the imperfect [difficult] spot in the Far East. For the sake of self-protection as well as the protection of others, Japan cannot remove the difficulties in Eastern Asia unless she [Japan] adopts a policy of "Blood and Iron." But in carrying out this policy we have to face the United States which has been turned against us by the policy of China . . . . In the future if we want to control China, we must first crush the United States just as in the past we had to fight in the Russo-Japanese War. But in order to conquer China we must first conquer Manchuria and Mongolia. In order to conquer the world, we must first con-

Daily life in . . .

When public education was first introduced in Japan during the 1870s, many people worried that it might weaken respect for Japanese values and traditions. When the military took control in Japan, they made sure that patriotism and nationalistic pride were emphasized in schools. Japanese children were taught about the glorious victories and heroic acts of the Japanese army. The government showed special movies to make sure the children's loyalty was with the army. In Japan's stores, most of the toys were soldiers, tanks, rifles, airplanes, battleships, and other war toys. In this way, the Japanese military government used the schools to spread propaganda to support the war effort.

Background: The Japanese have a long tradition of obedience to authority, dating back to the earliest years of Japan's history and continuing through feudal times.

561

A Geographic View of History

The Geographic Setting of Japan

Japan is a small country with few natural resources. Yet, it has a large population of about 123 million, or roughly half as many people as live in the entire United States. Read these facts about the advantages and disadvantages of Japan's geographic setting. Think about how Japan is able to support so many people as you study the map below.

Japan is about the size of California. Only 20 percent of the land is flat enough for farming and settlement. The remaining land is 80 percent mountainous.

Japan is densely populated. Especially crowded are the lowland areas in southern Honshu and along the shores of the Inland Sea.

The climate is subtropical in the south and temperate in the north. Farmers can grow two and sometimes three crops a year in the warmest areas.

Modern Japan produces only a small fraction of the resources needed by a modern industrial nation. Nearly all oil, coal, iron ore, copper, cotton, wool, food, and other resources are imported.

A skilled and well-educated labor force uses the imported raw material to produce automobiles, computers, and other high-value manufactured goods.

A warm ocean currents keeps Japan's ports ice-free and open for trade all year.

Study the map again and answer these questions on a separate sheet of paper.

1. Name the islands of Japan.

2. Which of Japan's four main islands is the largest?

3. Name three urban-industrial cities located on or near the shores of Japan's Inland Sea.

4. Name some cities located in the lowland areas of southern Honshu.

5. What advantages favor the development of Japan as an industrial nation?

6. What geographical disadvantages has Japan had to overcome in order to industrialize?

7. Why do you think more people live in southern Japan than in northern Japan?

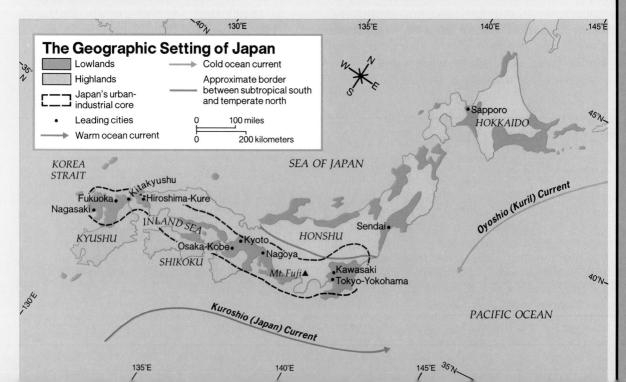

The Geographic Setting of Japan

Lowlands
Highlands
Japan's urban-industrial core
Leading cities
Warm ocean current
Cold ocean current
Approximate border between subtropical south and temperate north
0   100 miles
0   200 kilometers

KOREA STRAIT
SEA OF JAPAN
Sapporo
HOKKAIDO
Kitakyushu
Fukuoka
Hiroshima-Kure
Nagasaki
INLAND SEA
KYUSHU
Osaka-Kobe
Kyoto
HONSHU
Sendai
Oyoshio (Kuril) Current
SHIKOKU
Nagoya
Mt. Fuji
Kawasaki
Tokyo-Yokohama
Kuroshio (Japan) Current
PACIFIC OCEAN

quer China. . . . We shall seize the resources all over China. Having China's entire resources at our disposal we shall proceed to conquer India, Asia Minor, Central Asia, and even Europe. But to get control of Manchuria and Mongolia is the first step.

The Tanaka Memorial, 1927

6. Japan's military leaders became more and more powerful as they gained widespread support among the people. They promised that they would solve Japan's problems by taking over lands in East Asia and establishing an empire there. This Japanese empire would give Japan the resources it needed and provide a market for Japan's manufactured goods. These military leaders also began to use force to gain control of the government. Terrorists assassinated several important businessmen and political leaders who believed the army would destroy democracy in Japan. After

the murder of Prime Minister Inukai in 1932, the military leaders took control of Japan.

JAPAN ON THE MARCH: What lands were taken over as part of Japan's empire in East Asia?

7. Japan's military leaders now began to carry out their plan for restoring the nation's economy and greatness. The plan involved taking control of all the land in East Asia and making it a colony of Japan. The first move was against China. The Japanese military planned to seize Manchuria (man-CHOOR-ee-uh), a region of northern China rich in coal, iron ore, and other natural resources. See the map below. At this time, China was governed by weak political leaders. It was torn by a civil war between the Nationalists and Communists as well as by fighting among rival warlords. Therefore, China was the perfect target for Japan's imperialist plans. In spite of treaty prom-

▼ Between 1910 and 1940 Japan annexed Germany's islands in the Pacific and began to think of China and Southeast Asia as future colonies. What lands did Japan conquer in the 1930s?

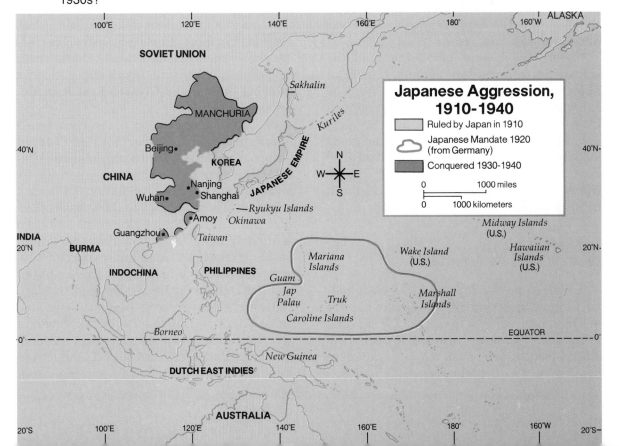

▲ Japanese soldiers move into Manchuria in 1931. After conquering Manchuria, Japan set up a puppet government there headed by the former emperor of China, Pu Yi.

ises that Japan would not attack China, Japan invaded northern China in 1931. Within a short time, the Japanese seized the Chinese province of Manchuria. However, this was only the beginning of Japan's war of conquest in East Asia.

8. Both the League of Nations and the United States protested Japan's seizure of Manchuria. Their protests did not stop the Japanese, however. Instead, Japan resigned from the League of Nations and began a second invasion of China. Using Manchuria as a base, the Japanese army moved into central and southern China in 1937. After heavy fighting, Japanese forces captured most of China's major coastal cities.

JOINING THE AXIS: Why did Japan become an ally of Germany and Italy?

9. To escape the Japanese, the Nationalist Chinese government moved the capital of China far inland to the city of Chongqing. From there, China continued to resist the steady southward push of the Japanese armies, but with little success. The Japa-

nese eventually gained control of most of the eastern coast of China. In September 1940, the Japanese invaded French Indochina (Vietnam, Laos, and Cambodia). At first, many Vietnamese welcomed the Japanese as liberators. However, instead of freeing the French colonies, Japan made them part of its own empire. Japan now called its growing empire the **Greater East Asia Co-Prosperity Sphere**.

10. Japan's aggression in Asia worsened relations between Japan and the United States. The United States **condemned** (kun-DEMD), or spoke out against, Japan for its invasion of China in violation of treaty promises. Then, in 1940, to show its displeasure, the United States began an embargo against Japan. This meant that the United States stopped the sale and export of war materials to Japan. However, this embargo had little effect on Japan. By then the Japanese were busy making plans to seize still more territories in the Pacific that would give them the raw materials they needed. However, the American action did anger the Japanese, who responded by signing an al-

Ask: Should the nations of the world have acted to halt Japan's aggression in China during the 1930s? Why, or why not? If so, what kind of action should they have taken?

▲ Japanese warplanes bombed Pearl Harbor in Hawaii on December 7, 1941. The surprise attack brought the United States into World War II on the side of the Allies.

liance with Hitler and Mussolini called the **Rome-Berlin-Tokyo Axis.**

PEOPLE IN HISTORY

11. Japanese militarists completed their control of the government in 1941 when General Hideki Tojo (TOH-joh) became prime minister. Tojo had made his career in the military. After World War I, he served as military attache (at-uh-SHAY), or technical expert, on the Japanese diplomatic staff in Germany. Later, he headed the Japanese secret police. Tojo also helped plan Japan's invasion of China when he became minister of war. As Japan planned its policy of aggression in the Pacific, Tojo favored war with the United States and Great Britain if necessary. It was Tojo who ordered the Japanese attack on the American naval base at Pearl Harbor, Hawaii, on December 7, 1941. Most of the United States' Pacific fleet was in the harbor when Japanese war planes attacked without warning. This attack on American naval vessels brought the United States into World War II. In the same week, attacks were launched against the Philippine Islands, the British colonies of Hong Kong and Singapore, and the independent kingdom of Thailand. In the weeks that followed, Japan took control over these areas and other parts of Asia as well.

OUTLOOK

12. Japan's rapid growth as a major military and industrial nation was an astonishing accomplishment. Japan had only begun to modernize its industry in the late 1800s. Yet by the 1930s, Japan was a major world power and possessed a large empire in East Asia. Japan was the first nation in Asia to become industrialized. Japan was the first Asian nation to conquer an empire and establish colonies to provide the resources and markets it needed. Why do you think ◄ the people of this small island nation were able to do these things? What island nation of Europe was the first country to industrialize and establish colonies?

565

CHAPTER REVIEW

VOCABULARY REVIEW

Write each of the following words on a piece of paper, and then write the definition for each word. Use the Glossary on pages 728–738 to help you.

1. Greater East Asia Co-Prosperity Sphere
2. condemned
3. Rome-Berlin-Tokyo Axis

SKILL BUILDER: READING A TIME LINE

Look at the time line below which features events connected with the rise of fascism and militarism in Japan and Germany in the 1920s and 1930s. Study the time line to answer the following questions:

1. What role does the Great Depression seem to play in the rise of fascism, by its position on the time line?
2. Which event occurred first, the Japanese invasion of Manchuria or the assassination of Prime Minister Inukai?
3. Starting from his first effort to gain power, how many years did it take for Hitler to finally become dictator of Germany?
4. How soon after coming to power did Hitler order his troops to occupy the Rhineland?
5. According to the time line, which country was first to move against another nation during this period, Japan or Germany?
6. The period of appeasement of Hitler began with Germany's occupation of the Rhineland and lasted for three years. What event brought this period to a close?
7. Which event on the time line marks the beginning of World War II?
8. How many years elapsed between the time Hitler came to power and the outbreak of World War II?
9. How many years elapsed between Japan's first invasion of China and its later invasion of a different part of the country?

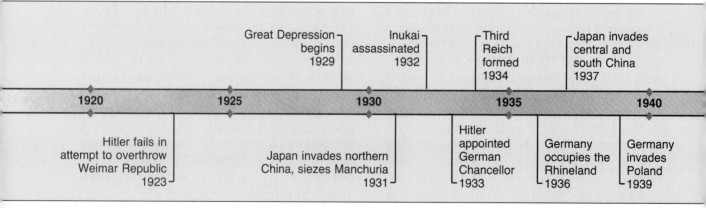

Great Depression begins 1929 · Inukai assassinated 1932 · Third Reich formed 1934 · Japan invades central and south China 1937

1920 · 1925 · 1930 · 1935 · 1940

Hitler fails in attempt to overthrow Weimar Republic 1923 · Japan invades northern China, siezes Manchuria 1931 · Hitler appointed German Chancellor 1933 · Germany occupies the Rhineland 1936 · Germany invades Poland 1939

SKILL BUILDER: CRITICAL THINKING AND COMPREHENSION

1. Classifying

▶ Divide a sheet of paper into three columns. Head the columns *Japan, China,* and *United States.* Write each of the following descriptions beneath the correct heading.

a. Began modernizing in the late 1800s.

b. Invaded and conquered Manchuria.

c. Resigned from the League of Nations after the Manchurian invasion.

d. Needed to import food to feed its people.

e. Placed an embargo on Japan.

f. Was torn by fighting between Nationalists and Communists during the 1930s.

2. Sequencing

▶ On a sheet of paper, rearrange the following events in the order in which they took place.

a. Manchuria is attacked by the Japanese.

b. Japanese invade Indochina.

c. Japanese men age 25 and older gain the right to vote.

d. Prime Minister Inukai is assassinated by terrorists.

e. Japan attacks Pearl Harbor.

3. Contrast and Compare

▶ Complete the following statements on a separate sheet by selecting the correct response.

a. In the 1930s, Japan's government became increasingly _____ , while China's government became more _____ .

b. In 1940, the nations of _____ were fighting World War II, while _____ was still at peace.

4. Point of View

▶ Identify the points of view below with the people or nations. Who held these opinions in the 1930s?

4-1. Territorial expansion would solve Japan's problems.

4-2. Japan should follow moderate policies.

4-3. The Japanese invaders were welcomed as liberators at first.

4-4. The best way to deal with an aggressor nation is to set up an embargo.

a. Prime Minister Inukai

b. Vietnam

c. United States

d. militarists

ENRICHMENT

1. Prepare a research report on Japanese resources and industries today. Identify the resources that Japan must import. Discuss the major industries in Japan. Present your report to the class.

2. Today, Japan is one of the richest nations in the world, yet it still has problems. Some of these include a shortage of affordable housing, and overcrowded cities. Look through some newspapers and find an article about Japan's problems today. Write a two-paragraph summary of the contents of the article.

CHAPTER 6

Other Nationalist Struggles

▲ Mohandas Gandhi, left, gained the support of millions of Indians in his campaign of nonviolent resistance to British rule.

OBJECTIVE: In what ways did the spirit of nationalism lead to the struggle for independence from the 1920s to 1940s?

1. In 1930, 78 people began a march down a dirt road in India, heading for the ocean 24 miles (38.6 kilometers) away. In front was a small man holding a long bamboo pole. Mohandas K. Gandhi, the group's leader, knew exactly what he was doing. The British government had placed a heavy tax on salt. To show his opposition, Gandhi went to the sea to collect the tax-free salt the ocean washed up. As the marchers passed through villages, hundreds joined them. When Gandhi reached the sea, his followers numbered in the thousands. Within days, protests against British rule broke out all over India. Gandhi's march was a sign that not only India, but many other nations in Africa, the Middle East, and Asia would seek independence.

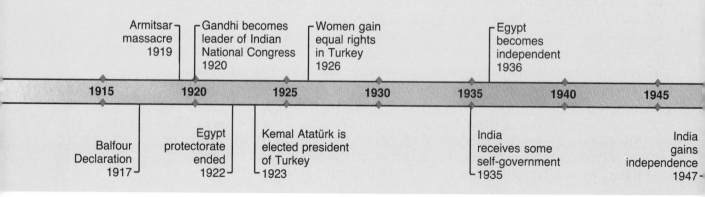

Armitsar massacre 1919 — Gandhi becomes leader of Indian National Congress 1920 — Women gain equal rights in Turkey 1926 — Egypt becomes independent 1936

1915 — 1920 — 1925 — 1930 — 1935 — 1940 — 1945

Balfour Declaration 1917 — Egypt protectorate ended 1922 — Kemal Atatürk is elected president of Turkey 1923 — India receives some self-government 1935 — India gains independence 1947

568

SELF-DETERMINATION: How did the movement toward independence begin to grow?

2. Nationalist movements gained strength in many lands during World War I. Many colonial people had actively supported the war efforts of their European "masters." In return, they demanded the right to rule their own lands. For many colonial people, the war raised doubts about the so-called superiority of European culture. People in India and Egypt now took greater pride in the great civilizations of their past.

3. At first it seemed that the European powers would grant independence to their colonies after World War I. In 1918, President Woodrow Wilson of the United States published his Fourteen Points. This list of the goals for peace included granting independence and equal rights to many groups in Europe. The ideals set forth in the Fourteen Points were eagerly welcomed by people of all nations. Unfortunately, however, these principles were not applied to countries outside Europe. The treaties that ended World War I generally failed to bring democracy and self-determination to these ▶ other peoples. Why do you think the writers of the peace treaties overlooked these non-European countries?

INDIA: What role did Gandhi play in India's struggle for independence?

4. India had been a British colony for over half a century when World War I began. As part of the war effort, India contributed large sums of money and provided 1.5 million troops to military service. Indian soldiers fought bravely, and they returned home filled with ideas of liberty and self-determination. After the war, many Indians continued to demand independence from Great Britain. In 1919 violent protests broke out in the city of Amritsar. Nearly 400 Indians were killed and another 1,200 wounded when British soldiers opened fire on a crowd of unarmed demonstrators. The British government did not bring the soldiers to justice. However, the Congress Party held an independent investigation, led by Mohandas K. Gandhi.

5. In 1920, Gandhi became the leader of the Indian National Congress, India's most important political party. Gandhi was a lawyer who had studied in England. In 1893, he went to South Africa, where for over 20 years he worked to end discrimination against Indians who lived there. After the massacre at Amritsar, he devoted his life to the struggle for independence. His integrity and personal courage earned him the title of **Mahatma** (muh-HAHT-muh), or "great soul."

6. Gandhi believed that independence could be achieved through **satyagraha,** or "truth force." In practice, this came to mean peaceful resistance to the British authorities. Gandhi's philosophy was based on **civil disobedience** (SIV-ul dis-uh-BEED-ee-unz). He urged the Indian people not to attack the British. Instead, they should refuse to pay taxes, to serve in the government, or to obey British laws. Laborers were urged not to work for foreign employers, and students were encouraged not to attend British schools.

7. The principle of civil disobedience was soon adopted by the Indian National Congress. Even so, violent uprisings continued to break out. In 1922, Gandhi was sentenced to prison. He was released after two years. Gandhi went on several extended fasts. How might this have brought attention to ◀ India's struggle? In the 1930s, Britain began to grant more self-government to India. India's provinces gained greater freedom, and a national legislature was elected. However, Gandhi and the Congress Party insisted India must be independent. When World War II broke out, Gandhi urged the Indian people not to take part unless India was granted its independence. In 1942, the British government jailed the Congress Party's leaders for the rest of the war.

8. When the Second World War ended, the British decided to give India its independence. However, millions of Muslims

Activity: Have students research the nonviolent tactics used by Martin Luther King, Jr. in the struggle for civil rights in America and compare them with those used by Gandhi.

569

The Arts and Artifacts

▲ The village artists often painted directly on the walls of their homes. When they could afford paper, they first outlined their drawings, then filled them in with color.

The Painting of Bihar Gandhi began his campaign for India's independence in northeast India in the state of Bihar. He did so because the culture of ancient India was still strong there. The villagers there still practiced traditional ways of spinning cotton and creating works of art. For nearly 3,000 years, lovely paintings had been produced by the women of these Hindu villages along the sacred Ganges River. Every young girl was taught how to make these brightly colored paintings by her mother, her grandmothers, and other women of the village.

The subjects of these paintings were Hindu gods and their lives. Creating this art was considered a religious act. In fact, they usually prayed to the gods as they worked at their art. Women of all castes celebrated the Hindu religion in their paintings.

Because most villagers were poor farmers, they used simple materials to create their art. Their paint brushes were made of bamboo tipped with cotton. Their colors came from dried vegetables, ground stone, and clay.

The beautiful drawings were an important part of the villagers' lives. They were used by young women as wrappings on gifts used in religious ceremonies. They decorated the letters in which unmarried girls proposed marriage to their future husband. Large paintings were made to cover the walls of the room where a wedding was to take place. In this way, the women's paintings and art provided great beauty and expressed the deep religious beliefs that gave strength to India as it struggled for independence.

1. How did women in these villages of India learn to create their beautiful art?

2. Why were these paintings such an important part of the villagers' lives?

3. What kind of brushes and paints did the women use in their drawings and paintings?

did not wish to belong to a country that was made up mostly of Hindus. Rioting broke out all over India. The Congress Party agreed reluctantly to allow a separate Islamic nation, called Pakistan, to be separated from India. On August 15, 1947, India and Pakistan became free nations after two hundred years of British rule. Gandhi continued his efforts to end the fighting between Hindus and Muslims. However, in January 1948, Gandhi was shot to death by an assassin who opposed his dream of Hindus and Muslims living together in peace.

▲ The standard of living improved for many Indians during Jawaharlal Nehru's 17 years as Prime Minister.

PEOPLE IN HISTORY

9. Jawaharlal Nehru (juh-WAH-hur-lal NEH-roo) was, along with Mahatma Gandhi, the leading figure in the creation of modern India. Like Gandhi, Nehru studied law in England before devoting his life to the struggle for Indian freedom. Like Gandhi, he was jailed eight different times between 1921 and 1945. Nehru and Gandhi differed in their hopes for India. Gandhi favored a return to a simple agricultural way of life. Nehru wanted to create an industrial state with a modern economy. Nehru also was more interested than was Gandhi in India's relations with other countries. He disagreed with Gandhi about India's part in World War II, but out of loyalty he supported Gandhi. As a result, he spent much of the war in a British jail. In 1947, Nehru became the first prime minister of independent India.

THE OTTOMAN EMPIRE: How was the Turkish empire broken up after World War I, and how was modern Turkey created?

10. The weak Ottoman Empire sealed its doom in 1914 when it sided with the Central Powers in World War I. A few days after the signing of the armistice, British and French troops marched into Constantinople, the Turkish capital. In 1920 the Treaty of Sèvres split up the huge Ottoman Empire.

The empire now included only Asia Minor and a small area of land around Constantinople. The remainder of the vast lands of the Ottoman Empire were placed in the temporary control of foreign powers under the mandate system set up by the League of Nations. The Ottoman lands in the Middle East were divided among Iraq, Transjordan, and Palestine, which became British mandates, and Syria and Lebanon, which became French mandates.

11. A strong nationalist movement soon grew in Turkey. In 1919, a Greek army had seized land in Turkish Anatolia, and the sultan of Turkey had not opposed this action. Led by Mustafa Kemal (MOOS-tah-fah kuh-MAL), a group of patriotic nationalists known as the Young Turks forced the Greek army to leave in 1921. Kemal then overthrew the sultan's government, ended the Ottoman Empire, and set up the republic of Turkey, with its capital at Ankara. Under a

Activity: Show students pictures of Nehru and of the popular "Nehru jacket" worn in the 1960s.

571

new peace treaty Kemal negotiated in 1923, Turkey regained lands it earlier had lost to Greece. It also got back part of Armenia. To prevent future conflict, nearly 1.5 million Greeks living in Turkey moved to Greece. The large population of Turks living in Greece moved to Turkey.

12. Kemal was elected the first president of Turkey in 1923 and served in this office until his death in 1938. Under Kemal's leadership, Turkey was modernized. New industries were started, and railroads were built. Schools were opened to educate the people. Kemal became known as Kemal Atatürk, or father of the Turks.

PALESTINE: Why did tensions grow between the Arabs and Jews in Palestine?

13. Palestine had long been the Holy Land of Christianity, Judaism, and Islam. **Zionism** (ZY-uh-niz-um) was the Jewish nationalist movement organized in 1897 to establish a Jewish homeland in Palestine. When World War I broke out, Britain won the support of Arabs by making vague promises of future independence for all Arab provinces of the Turkish empire. Yet in 1917, Lord Balfour, the British foreign secretary, also issued an official statement approving a national homeland for the Jews

▲ Jewish immigration into Palestine increased as a result of Zionism. Ships such as this one carried settlers eager to establish new homes.

in Palestine, where many Arabs lived. The Balfour Declaration defended the rights of Arab communities to exist in Palestine, too. Arab leaders felt betrayed by Britain.

Daily life in . . .

Kemal Atatürk modernized almost every aspect of Turkish life. He improved public health and education. He introduced the western calendar and encouraged both industry and the arts. He also ended the control of Islam over the state. Among his most striking accomplishments was the emancipation of women. Before World War I, Turkish women were veiled at age 14, married a year or two later, and then seldom left their homes the rest of their lives. All Turkish women wore black garments and completely covered their faces. Kemal Atatürk changed many of these customs.

He encouraged women to give up the veil and wear European-style clothes. Women were given the right to divorce their husbands while men lost the right to divorce their wives without the woman's consent. The practice of having many wives was ended. In 1926, the new law code gave women equal rights to property and in all legal matters. A few years later, women received the right to vote and hold office. By the 1930s, women were elected to the Grand National Assembly. Women also became teachers, physicians, lawyers, and judges.

Background: Kemal compelled the people of Turkey to adopt family names in 1934. Some first names had become so common that pupils in schools had to be designated by number.

14. During the 1920s and 1930s, tensions increased between Arabs and Jews in the British mandate of Palestine. The Jewish population increased as many Jews fled to Palestine to escape Hitler's persecution. The Arabs refused to accept the Jewish settlers.

▶ Why did Palestine remain a troubled land?

SPOTLIGHT ON SOURCES

15. The Balfour Declaration of 1917 intensified the rivalry between Arabs and Jews in Palestine. Zionists thought the Balfour Declaration promised a Jewish state and argued that Palestine was the land of the Jewish tribes of Israel. The Arabs argued that Palestine had already been pledged to them as an independent state and that Arabs had lived there for 1200 years. Was the Declaration clearly worded?

> His Majesty's Government view with favor the establishment in Palestine of a national home for the Jewish people, and will use their best endeavors [efforts] to facilitate [help] the achievement of this object [goal], it being clearly understood that nothing shall be done which may prejudice [interfere with] the civil and religious rights of existing non-Jewish [Arab] communities in Palestine or the rights and political status enjoyed by Jews in any other country.
>
> —*The Balfour Declaration*, 1917

EGYPT: How did Egypt achieve its independence from the British?

16. Egypt had been controlled by Great Britain since Britain bought control of the Suez Canal in 1875. In 1914, the British army made Egypt a British protectorate. When World War I broke out, the Egyptian economy was hurt by British restrictions on exporting cotton and grain. Many Egyptians were angered by Great Britain's wartime use of Egyptian resources.

17. Although the protectorate was officially ended in 1922, the British remained

▲ The last of the British troops left the Suez Canal zone in 1956. Why might Britain have been interested in keeping soldiers there?

in control of Egypt. They were determined to defend their interest in the Suez Canal. As a result, Egyptians continued to protest British control of their government. In 1936, the Egyptian and British governments reached an agreement. British troops were to be removed from Egypt, except for 10,000 soldiers in the Suez Canal Zone.

OUTLOOK

18. During the 1920s and 1930s, nationalist movements brought independence to many peoples. India and Egypt gained their independence from the British. Turkey became a modernized nation after the Ottoman Empire was broken up. In Palestine, the Jews began their struggle to set up a Jewish nation, but the Arabs also claimed this land. Is nationalism as important in the world today? Why or why not? ◀

Background: In 1918 there were 55,000 Jews and over 500,000 Arabs living in Palestine, an approximate ratio of one to ten. By 1932 the ratio had risen to one Jew for every four Arabs.

CHAPTER REVIEW

VOCABULARY REVIEW

Write each of the following words on a sheet of paper. Then write the correct definition for each word. Use the glossary in the back of the book to help you. Then copy the sentences below and fill in the blanks with the correct word.

1. civil disobedience

2. Zionism

3. Mahatma

4. satyagraha

The Indian leader _____ Gandhi believed that independence could be achieved through _____ . This led him to recommend a policy of _____ to his followers. In the Holy Land, _____ led to a movement among Jews to return to Palestine.

SKILL BUILDER: READING A MAP

Use the information on the map below to answer the following questions.

a. What three continents included lands controlled by the Ottoman Empire?

b. Name several independent nations which were once a part of the Ottoman Empire.

c. Name four bodies of water which bordered the Ottoman Empire.

d. In what direction would you travel to get from the capital of the Ottoman Empire at Constantinople to the Atlantic Ocean?

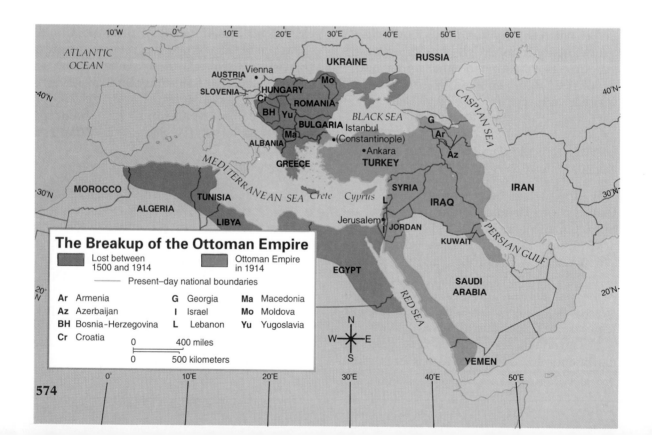

The Breakup of the Ottoman Empire

Lost between 1500 and 1914   Ottoman Empire in 1914

Present–day national boundaries

Ar Armenia   G Georgia   Ma Macedonia
Az Azerbaijan   I Israel   Mo Moldova
BH Bosnia-Herzegovina   L Lebanon   Yu Yugoslavia
Cr Croatia

0   400 miles
0   500 kilometers

SKILL BUILDER: CRITICAL THINKING AND COMPREHENSION

▲ **1. Summarizing**

▶ Match the newspaper headlines below with the event you think they summarize.

Headlines

1-1. "British Shoot Down Unarmed Indians"

1-2. "British to Let Jews into Palestine"

1-3. " 'Young Turks' Take Charge"

1-4. "Wilson 'Wows' World with 14 Points"

Events

a. Kemal Ataturk gains power in Turkey.

b. The Balfour Declaration encourages Jewish settlement in Palestine.

c. Egypt declares war on Israel.

d. Wilson publishes his plan for peace treaties.

e. British crush riot at Amritsar.

2. Drawing Conclusions

a. What conclusion did Gandhi reach after the Amritsar Massacre?

b. What conclusion do you think many Jewish people drew from the Balfour Declaration?

c. What conclusion did the people in many British colonies draw about their ability to govern their own countries?

3. Making Judgments

a. Do you think the Arabs were correct in feeling angry when news of the Balfour Declaration was announced? Why or why not?

b. Do you think it was fair for the Allies to strip the Ottoman Empire of all its possessions except Constantinople and Anatolia? Why or why not?

4. Spatial Relationships

▶ Anatolia, modern-day Turkey, has often been called the land bridge to Asia. Study the map on page 574 and answer the questions below.

a. In which direction would you travel to get from Turkey to central Asia?

b. Which sea lies between Russia and Turkey? Why have Russians and Turks often fought to control this sea?

c. Constantinople controls the straits that connect which two bodies of water?

d. The modern capital of Turkey is Ankara. Is Ankara a seaport or an inland city?

ENRICHMENT

1. Research the Arab and Zionist positions on the Palestine controversy. Consult maps of the period and point out how the land was supposed to be divided. Then stage a debate to decide which argument was more convincing.

2. Imagine that you are a merchant living in India in the early 1920s. You are more prosperous than most Indians. Gandhi has called upon you to refuse to pay taxes and to take part in a peaceful demonstration against the British government. You do not like the British, but your business and your safety could be at risk. Write a diary entry describing your thoughts and feelings about Gandhi's advice.

CHAPTER 7

World War II

▲ German soldiers parade through Paris in June, 1940. In only two months; Hitler's armies defeated the French and drove the British out of France.

> **OBJECTIVE:** How did German and Japanese aggression lead to war in Europe and in the Pacific?

1. "France has fallen," screamed newspaper headlines in June 1940. The largest army in Europe had been crushed by Hitler's army and air force. Supposedly invasion-proof, the French Maginot line of underground forts gave way as the German army rolled on into France. Now Great Britain alone stood in the way of Germany's conquest of Europe. In the Far East, Japanese soldiers, sailors, and marines spread the flag of the rising sun across the Pacific, China, and southeast Asia. No nation seemed strong enough to oppose the Axis powers. Day after day, newspapers around the world and radio broadcasts carried stories of new Axis victories. The defeated nations of Europe now realized how their policy of appeasement had failed. They had been beaten by the strongest armies the world had ever known. Many believed the end of the world's democracies was in sight. But through sacrifice, industrial might and skill, the Allies eventually would rebuild their military strength and smash the Axis powers.

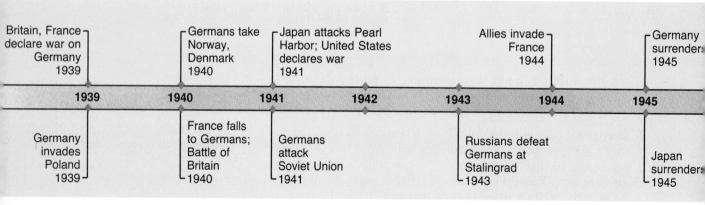

Britain, France declare war on Germany 1939	Germans take Norway, Denmark 1940	Japan attacks Pearl Harbor; United States declares war 1941		Allies invade France 1944		Germany surrenders 1945
1939	**1940**	**1941**	**1942**	**1943**	**1944**	**1945**
Germany invades Poland 1939	France falls to Germans; Battle of Britain 1940	Germans attack Soviet Union 1941		Russians defeat Germans at Stalingrad 1943		Japan surrenders 1945

Activity: Review and discuss the failure of the League of Nations and its meaning for Germany, Great Britain, and France.

THE WAR IN EUROPE: What countries were invaded by Hitler's armies in Western and Eastern Europe?

2. In the spring of 1939, Great Britain promised Poland, Greece, Turkey, and Romania that if Hitler attacked them, the British would come to their aid. Britain and France also tried to gain the support of the Soviet Union, but Stalin turned to the Germans instead. In August 1939, Stalin and Hitler signed the Nazi-Soviet Non-Aggression **Pact**. In this pact, or treaty, the two leaders agreed not to attack each other. They also agreed to divide Poland and the Baltic nations between the Soviet Union and Germany. Less than two weeks later, Nazi troops entered Poland. As they had pledged, France and Britain declared war against Germany. However, they were too late to save Poland, which also was invaded by the Soviet Union in September 1939.

3. With Stalin as his ally, Hitler now had a secure eastern flank. Thus, after the invasion of Poland, Hitler moved to conquer Western Europe. The Germans had used a new kind of war to quickly defeat Poland. This was the **blitzkrieg** (BLITS-kreeg), or lightning war. In this type of warfare, dive bombers attacked from the air to support tank assaults on the ground. Then infantry, or foot soldiers, usually followed to occupy the invaded territory. The Germans used the same method to strike deep into other countries. In early 1940, they took Norway and Denmark. On May 10, 1940, the German blitzkrieg spread across the borders of Belgium, the Netherlands, and Luxembourg. On June 16, the Germans occupied Paris, the French capital. A week earlier, Italy, under its Fascist leader, Mussolini, entered the war on the Axis side. On June 22, 1940, France surrendered.

4. After France fell to the Nazis, Great Britain was left alone in the fight against Germany. The British had a new leader, Winston Churchill. Churchill did not trust Hitler, and had vowed to oppose Hitler's aggression. In 1940, the British believed that the Germans were preparing to invade their country, too. In fact, Hitler was planning such an invasion. In the summer of 1940, the Germans began to attack Britain from the air. The air raids continued for months and came to be known as the Battle of Britain. Britain's air force was outnumbered by the Germans by nearly three to one. Yet with the help of radar, a newly invented tracking device, British pilots knew ahead of time when the Germans were coming. As a result, the British were able to shoot down two German planes for every British plane lost. In late summer of 1940, Hitler changed tactics and ordered his air force to bomb London. The bombing of London was called the Blitz. Although many people were killed and many homes and businesses were destroyed, the morale, or spirit, of the British people was not broken. The Blitz lasted until June 1941 and extended to other British cities. When he failed to destroy the British air force, Hitler realized that he would not be able to invade Britain and broke off the attack. Instead, Hitler turned his attention to the Soviet Union.

5. Hitler had been secretly planning a **campaign** (kam-PAYN), or series of military operations, against the Soviet Union since the summer of 1940. Hitler did not trust the Soviets even though they were Germany's ally. Therefore, on June 22, 1941, Hitler launched his campaign against the Soviet Union. It was the blitzkrieg all over again. The Germans tried to take Leningrad and Moscow, but the Red Army slowed them down. Although the Germans overran the Ukraine and held much Soviet territory, the winter weather of 1941 forced them to stop.

6. In July 1942, the Germans renewed their effort to conquer the Soviet Union. Now German armies advanced toward Stalingrad with over a million men. They captured the port of Sebastopol and laid siege to Stalingrad. However, after months of fighting, the Germans were unable to take Stalingrad, and they then were forced to retreat. Thousands of Germans were trapped around Stalingrad and surrendered. During the German invasion, mil-

Background: The German soldiers faced the Russian winter in their summer uniforms. The Russians, on the other hand, were, in the words of an American journalist, "fully prepared for winter."

lions of Soviet soldiers and civilians were killed, but the Red Army stopped Hitler. Then in the summer of 1943, the Red Army began to push the Nazi armies back to Germany.

THE UNITED STATES: Why did the United States enter the war on the side of the Allies?

7. The United States was not willing to enter the war at first. In 1935, Congress passed the Neutrality Act, which prohibited the shipment of weapons to either side. However, President Roosevelt realized that America would have to help the Allies if ▶ Hitler was to be stopped. Why would American aid be needed? As early as 1939, the United States was selling arms to France and Britain on the cash-and-carry plan. This meant the French and British paid cash in American ports for the supplies they needed. Then they carried them back on their own ships. Finally, when France surrendered to Germany, the American people

were shocked out of their isolationism. When the Nazi bombings of Britain reached their height in 1940, nobody knew if Britain would be able to survive. Therefore, Roosevelt came up with a plan to help Britain. The plan was known as the **Lend-Lease program**. Under this plan, Roosevelt gave Churchill 50 warships for the British navy to use in its fight against the Germans. In return, Britain gave the United States a 99-year lease on several islands in the Atlantic, allowing American naval bases to be established there.

8. The United States finally entered the war on December 8, 1941. In a surprise air attack the day before, Japanese planes had bombed the United States fleet at Pearl Harbor in Hawaii. Half of the ships in the United States Navy were destroyed. Three days after the United States declared war on Japan, Japan's allies, Italy and Germany, declared war on the United States. By now, 38 countries were involved in World War II.

▼ The Axis powers overran much of Europe and North Africa before their defeat by the Allies in 1945. What countries of Europe escaped conquest by the Axis powers in World War II?

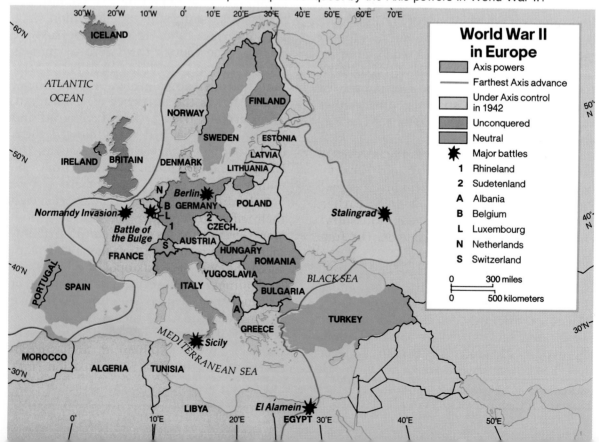

THE PACIFIC: What were the major campaigns fought in the Pacific?

9. The war in the Pacific began with many Japanese victories. The United States was not yet ready to fight Japan, since the Japanese had destroyed most of American Pacific fleet. For this reason, the Japanese were able to wage their war with little opposition, and they quickly seized Hong Kong and Singapore, and invaded the Philippines. In Southeast Asia, Japanese armies marched into Thailand and then Burma until they nearly reached India. To the south, they overran the Dutch East Indies north of Australia.

10. At this point, the Japanese advance in the Pacific finally was ended. In June 1942, Japan attacked Midway Island, a strategic naval base in the Pacific Ocean. However, the American Navy was prepared for the invasion and crippled the Japanese fleet, instead. Why was the battle of Midway the ◄ turning point of the war in the Pacific? After Midway, the Allies began to force the Japanese to retreat. The **strategy** (STRAT-uh-gee), or military plan of attack, the Allies used was called island-hopping. Capturing one island at a time, the Allies took over the Japanese empire in the Pacific and slowly closed in on Japan itself. During these years of fighting, the cost in lives on both sides

SKILL BUILDER/MAPS Absolute and Relative Location

All places on the earth have both an absolute location and a relative location. Absolute location is the precise latitude and longitude of a place. Latitude and longitude are shown by marks on the sides of the map. Relative location is where a place is in reference to other places. Nearness, direction, and land and sea connections are aspects of relative location.

1. What is the absolute location of Japan?
2. What is the relative location of Japan in reference to the mainland?
3. What islands were "stepping stones" for the Allies as they closed in on Japan?
4. Iwo Jima and Okinawa are tiny islands. Why did Japan and the Allies fight for them?

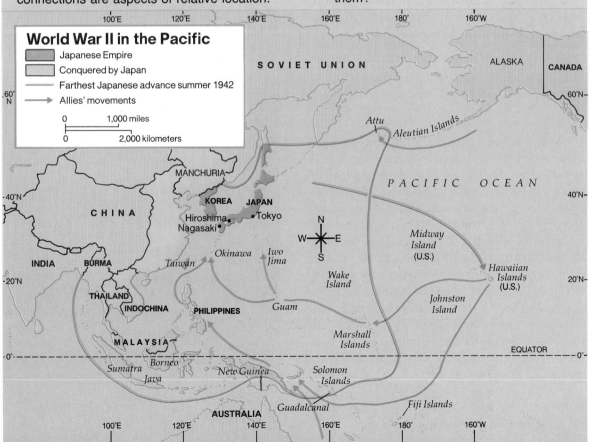

World War II in the Pacific

- Japanese Empire
- Conquered by Japan
- Farthest Japanese advance summer 1942
- Allies' movements

0   1,000 miles
0   2,000 kilometers

was staggering. Finally, in October 1944, Americans started to bomb Japan.

NORTH AFRICA: What desert battles were fought in North Africa?

11. Another region of the world that saw bloody fighting in World War II was North Africa. After the Italians attacked the British forces in Egypt in September 1940, a major campaign began there. The German and British armies did most of the fighting in North Africa, and they fought desert tank battles in Libya and Egypt. At El Alamein (al-uh-MAYN), in 1942, the Germans were finally forced to retreat. American troops also took part in this struggle. The campaign, called Operation Torch, was the first fighting between American and German troops in World War II. After El Alamein, the victorious Allied forces then moved from North Africa to Sicily and Italy. The Italians were defeated when the Allies captured Rome in June 1944. By now the Germans were retreating from the Soviet Union, and the Japanese were on the defensive. The Allies now were preparing their final and greatest campaign of the war, the invasion of Western Europe.

ALLIED WAR PLANNING: How did the leaders of the Allies work together to win the war?

12. When the Allies declared war on Germany, they needed to plan a common strategy against Hitler and to decide how to bring about peace after Hitler was defeated. First, Churchill and Roosevelt met aboard a warship in the Atlantic Ocean. There they signed the Atlantic Charter. The Charter supported the right of all people to choose their own government. It also proposed a world organization be established to keep the peace. Soon after, the Allies agreed that Germany, Italy, and Japan must be forced to accept unconditional surrender. In November 1943, Roosevelt, Churchill and Stalin met at Teheran. At Teheran, they agreed

to launch the Allied invasion of Western Europe.

SURRENDER: What events led to the Allied victory in World War II?

13. The Allied invasion took place on June 6, 1944, known as D-Day. The invasion was the largest in history. Within a month, more than one million Allied soldiers landed on the beaches of Normandy in France. The Germans resisted the invading armies, but by December the Germans had been pushed back to their own border.

SPOTLIGHT ON SOURCES

14. Can you imagine the feelings of the Allied soldiers who crossed the English Channel to invade France? Robert Capa was a Hungarian-born photographer who recorded many of the events of the war with

▼ D-Day, June 6, 1944, saw the Allies invade Nazi-held Europe. More than 100,000 soldiers and 5,000 ships took part in the invasion.

his camera. Here is how he described the scene.

> At 4:00 A.M., we were assembled on the open deck. The invasion barges were swinging on the cranes ready to be lowered. Waiting for the first ray of light, the two thousand men stood in perfect silence; whatever, they were thinking, it was some kind of prayer . . . . None of us was at all impatient [tired of waiting], and we wouldn't have minded standing in the darkness for a very long time. But the sun had no way of knowing that this day was different from all others, and rose on its usual schedule. The first-wavers [the first to go ashore] stumbled into their barges, and—as if on slow-moving elevators—we descended [went down] onto the sea. The sea was rough and we were wet before our barge pushed away from the mother ship.
>
> —*Images of War*, Robert Capa

15. As the Allied armies pressed from the west, the Russian armies moved against Germany from the east. The Russians were on German soil in January 1945 and reached Berlin in April. In March, the American army crossed the Rhine River into Germany. The German capital of Berlin fell to the Allies on May 2, and the German forces surrendered on May 7. A week before Germany surrendered, Hitler committed suicide. The war in Europe was over.

16. On April 12, 1945, President Roosevelt died, and Vice-President Harry Truman became president. One of Truman's most difficult decisions concerned the war against Japan. His military advisers told Truman that an invasion of Japan would cost over one million American lives. However, by July 1945, the first atomic bomb was successfully test-exploded. Truman then ordered that atomic bombs be dropped on the Japanese cities of Hiroshima and Nagasaki. Nearly 80,000 people died at Hiroshima and 60,000 at Nagasaki. On August 15, 1945, Japan surrendered.

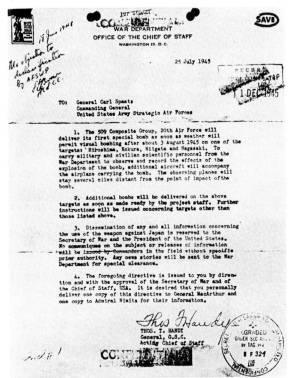

▲ This letter authorized the United States Army Air Force to drop the first Atomic bombs on Japan in August 1945. Within two weeks, the war ended.

OUTLOOK

17. World War II was one of the most terrible conflicts in modern history. Both sides used new methods of mass destruction. Bombing raids on cities killed hundreds of thousands of men, women, and children. The atomic bomb was more terrible still, destroying whole cities in a blinding flash of death. After the war ended, Allied armies discovered that six million Jews and millions of other people had been murdered in Nazi concentration camps. Hitler's racist policies had resulted in genocide, or the murder of people. These tragic events, however, made people everywhere vow that such things would never happen again. Why do you think World War II was such a terrible tragedy? Do you think it changed the way people think about war? Could another world war ever take place?

Background: Roosevelt, Stalin, and Churchill met in early February 1945 at Yalta, in Russia, and agreed to divide Germany into occupation zones. They pledged their countries would join the United Nations.

581

CHAPTER REVIEW

VOCABULARY REVIEW

Write each of the following words on a piece of paper, and then write the definition for each word. Use the Glossary on pages 728–740 to help you.

1. pact
2. blitzkrieg
3. campaign
4. Lend-Lease program
5. strategy

SKILL BUILDER: MAKING A TIME LINE

Copy the blank time line on a separate sheet of paper. Unlike the time line at the beginning of the chapter, this time line is divided into months. Place the dates and events below in the proper order on the blank time line. The events you will place on the time line are all from 1939, the first year of World War II in Europe.

a. Germany takes over Czechoslovakia–March 15
b. Germany invades Poland–September 1
c. Poland surrenders–September 27
d. Soviet Union invades Poland–September 17
e. Britain and France declare war on Germany–September 3

| Jan. 1939 | Mar. 1939 | May 1939 | July 1939 | Sept. 1939 | Nov. 1939 | Jan. 1940 |

SKILL BUILDER: CRITICAL THINKING AND COMPREHENSION

1. Cause and Effect

Match each of the causes below with the effect you think it fits.

Causes

1-1. Poland is invaded by Germany.
1-2. France is defeated by Germany.
1-3. Japan attacks the United States at Pearl Harbor.
1-4. Atomic bombs are dropped on Japan.
1-5. The Allies defeat Germans and Italians in North Africa.

Effects

a. World War II begins.
b. Japan surrenders.
c. Britain is left alone to fight the Germans.
d. The Allies invade Italy from North Africa.
e. France and England declare war on Germany.
f. The United States declares war on Japan.

2. Generalizing

▶ Match the generalizations below with the person or event from your chapter that you think is best described.

2-1. He wanted to conquer the world, but took his own life in April 1945, as the Allies defeated his armies.

2-2. He became president of the United States when former President Franklin Roosevelt died and was responsible for ordering the first atomic bombing in history.

2-3. This 1944 invasion marked the biggest military operation in history and led to the Allied reconquest of France.

2-4. He became prime minister of England and led that nation during World War II.

a. Franklin Roosevelt

b. Winston Churchill

c. The Allied landings in Normandy in France

d. Harry S Truman

e. Adolf Hitler

3. Predicting

a. Do you think Britain would have lost World War II if the United States had not helped?

b. Do you think Germany would have attacked the United States if Britain had been defeated?

c. Would the Japanese have surrendered if the atomic bombs had not been dropped on their cities?

d. What do you think would have happened if the Germans had defeated the Russians?

4. Hypothesizing

a. Do you think the United Sates would have gone to war against Japan and Germany if Pearl Harbor had not been attacked?

b. What do you think would have happened if Hitler had been killed earlier in the war?

ENRICHMENT

1. Read about the London Blitz in books about World War II. Then pretend that you are living in London during the Blitz and write a letter to a friend in the United States describing what conditions are like and how you are managing to survive.

2. Give a brief oral report about one of the following battles of World War II: Dunkirk, Battle of Britain, the Coral Sea, Midway, Guadalcanal, El Alamein, Stalingrad, Battle of the Bulge, Rangoon. You will find encyclopedias and books on World War II useful in gathering information for your report.

UNIT REVIEW

The years after World War I were troubled times in Europe and throughout the world. Existing problems became much worse with the onset of the Great Depression in 1929. Nationalist movements had important effects in India, Turkey, Palestine, and Egypt. In Europe, Fascist dictators took over all the power of the Italian, German, and Spanish governments. Hitler became dictator of Germany in 1933. His Nazi party used propaganda and force to rule. Mussolini became dictator of Italy in 1922. In Spain, after a civil war, Franco set up a fascist dictatorship in 1939. In Russia and Japan, too, strong groups seized control. In 1917, the Communist party, led by Lenin, overthrew the czar's government. In Japan, army generals gained control. In the 1930s, several of these countries increased their military power and began taking over nearby lands. Finally, in 1939, Germany's invasion of Poland led to World War II.

SKILL BUILDER: READING A MAP

▶ This map shows the two sides that fought in World War II. Look at the map key, study the map, and then answer the questions below on a sheet of paper.

Taking Sides in World War II

1. What were the two sides that fought in World War II?
2. Name the Axis powers and list the countries they conquered.
3. Name two countries in Asia that supported the Allies during the war. Why do you think those nations favored the Allies?
4. Name two countries in Europe that were neutral in the war.
5. Which side included the most nations? In what part of the world were most of those nations located?

584

SKILL BUILDER: CRITICAL THINKING AND COMPREHENSION

 1. Cause and Effect

▶ For each pair of statements below, select the effect that matches the cause.

1-1. a. Ghandi and Nehru led the strong nationalist movement in India.
b. Britain granted India some self-government in the 1930s.

2-1. a Japan conquered Manchuria and then invaded southern and central China.
b. Military generals took control of the Japanese government.

 2. Fact versus Opinion

▶ For each statement below, write F if it is a fact and O if it is an opinion.

a. After Turkey became a republic, Kemal Ataturk wanted to modernize that country.

b. Franco's attack against the republican government of Spain caused the Spanish civil war.

c. India should have been given its independence by the British when World War II began.

d. The people of the Soviet Union were better off under the communist government than under the czar.

3. Hypothesizing

▶ Read each of these statements and then make a hypothesis that you think explains the statement.

a. World War II was one of the bloodiest wars in history.

b. The Jewish people wanted to establish a homeland in Palestine.

c. The Great Depression made it possible for dictators to gain power in several countries.

d. Japan conquered many lands in Asia and in the Pacific, but was defeated in World War II.

ENRICHMENT

1. World War I was the first war that involved most of the major nations of the world. World War I was called "the war to end wars." Yet, 20 years after it ended, World War II broke out. Here are some of the events that happened after World War I: (1) Hitler became dictator of Nazi Germany; (2) Mussolini became dictator of Italy; (3) The Great Depression lasted from 1929 to 1939; (4) Army generals ruled Japan. Using the information in this chapter and other sources, choose one of the events and explain how it helped to cause World War II.

2. Hitler was a cruel dictator, but he also was a master of propaganda. By totally controlling all the news and information in Germany, Hitler gained the support of most of the German people. Suppose you were a reporter interviewing Hitler. Make a list of the questions you would ask him. Then write the answers you think Hitler would have made. Read your questions and answers again. Put a check mark in front of any item that you think is propaganda.

UNIT 12

ESL/LEP Strategy: Have students work together to prepare an illustrated glossary of the vocabulary words in this unit. Ask them to gather pictures, information, or firsthand accounts of life during the post-World War II era.

THE POST-WAR WORLD

OBJECTIVE: Unit 12 will give you an opportunity to compare and contrast the effects of World War II in Europe, Asia, and the United States. You will be able to outline and describe the steps taken by countries in Europe and Asia in order to build their economies and save their people from poverty and despair.

The United Nations is established 1945

NATO is founded; West and East Germany become nations; Communists win power in China; Mao Zedong rules Communist China 1949

Soviet leader Stalin dies; Workers in East Germany revolt; Elizabeth II becomes British queen 1953

| 1949 | 1951 | 1953 | 1955 | 1957 |

America's Marshall Plan begins 1947

Korean War begins 1950

Krushchev becomes Soviet leader 1955

The Soviet Union launches Sputnik; European Common Market is set up 1957

▲ The photo shows a rally in Peking, China. This rally is in support of the leader Mao-Tse Tung.

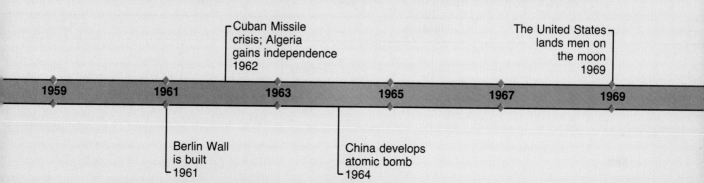

Cuban Missile
crisis; Algeria
gains independence
1962

The United States
lands men on
the moon
1969

1959   1961   1963   1965   1967   1969

Berlin Wall
is built
1961

China develops
atomic bomb
1964

CHAPTER 1

Effects of World War II

▲ General Douglas MacArthur was the postwar leader of U.S. forces in Japan. He and his aides wrote Japan's new constitution.

OBJECTIVE: What happened to defeated Japan and Germany, and how did the nations of Europe work together to recover from World War II?

1. "Close relatives, brothers and sisters and cousins, got together, and using sheet iron and scorched poles . . . built small huts . . . . At this time the joy and relief that they were still alive began to wear thin . . . as time went on the huts could scarcely keep out the rain, nor could they protect so many people crushed into such a narrow space. . . . [By December, cold] winds were blowing; sleet was falling; and it became impossible to live in the huts. Carpenters and day laborers came from other parts of the city and people gave them the material with which to build [temporary houses]. . . ." This quote describes Nagasaki, Japan, at the end of World War II. The writer was Takashi Nagai. He was a scientist who lived in Nagasaki, one of two cities destroyed by atomic bombs in August 1945. Throughout the world, many peoples also faced ordeals of recovering from the war.

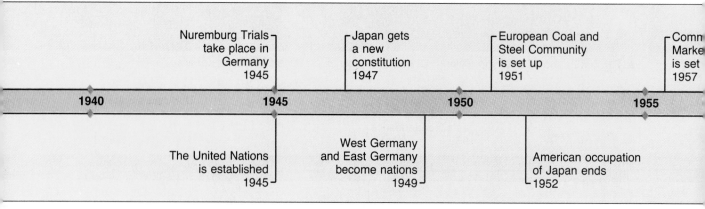

	Nuremburg Trials take place in Germany 1945		Japan gets a new constitution 1947		European Coal and Steel Community is set up 1951		Comm Marke is set 1957
1940		**1945**			**1950**		**1955**
	The United Nations is established 1945		West Germany and East Germany become nations 1949			American occupation of Japan ends 1952	

JAPAN: What changes did the occupation of Japan by American troops bring to that country?

2. In 1945, many of Japan's cities lay in ruins. Many of its people were homeless and hungry. More than 2 million Japanese had died during the war. The large empire that Japan had conquered was gone. Yet the Japanese had depended on that empire for their food and raw materials. After Japan surrendered, it was occupied by American troops. The commander of the American forces, General Douglas MacArthur, carried out President Truman's plan for a peaceful Japan. Japan's war leaders were tried and punished as war criminals. Japan was not permitted to have an army or navy.

3. General MacArthur also ruled Japan while a new democratic government was being set up. In 1947 a new constitution restored the Japanese Diet, whose members now were elected by all the people. Japanese women received the right to vote for the first time. In 1951, the United States and many other nations signed a final peace treaty with Japan. Japan now regained its independence and promised never again to fight a war. The United States agreed to defend Japan, and the American occupation ended in 1952.

4. During the years after the war, Japan received large amounts of aid from the United States. This aid helped Japan re-build its industries. The Japanese no longer had to spend huge amounts on their armed forces. Instead, this money was invested in new factories and machinery. During the 1950s, Japan expanded its trade with other countries. The United States became one of Japan's most important markets. Japan's skilled work force and modernized industries soon made Japanese products popular throughout the world. Japanese democracy also grew strong during these years. In this way, Japan was transformed from a wartime enemy controlled by the military into a democracy and a close ally of the United States.

GERMANY: Why was Germany divided into the two nations of West Germany and East Germany?

5. After Germany surrendered in 1945, the Allied armies ruled that country. Germany was divided into several parts. The Soviet Union ruled eastern Germany, and Britain, France, and the United States controlled western Germany. Like Japan, Germany's economy and its people had suffered heavy loses in the war. It was a land of bombed-out homes and factories and cities. Yet the Allies were unable to agree on how to treat Germany. The Soviet Union believed Germany should be forced to pay for the damage it had caused other countries. Therefore, the Soviet armies seized factory

Daily life in . . .

A worker in Milan, Italy, kissed his family good-bye, picked up his suitcase, and hopped on a train for West Germany. When he arrived in the city of Dusseldorf in West Germany he got a job in a steel mill there. The young Italian worked hard and earned more than he ever had before. No longer was he jobless, as he had been in Milan. He spent three years as a steel worker in West Germany. During those three years, he sent most of the money he earned back home to his family. He made some good friends among the Germans he worked with. However, most of his time away from the job he spent with other Italians who were working in the steel mill. The idea of workers from one country getting jobs easily in another country was new in Europe in the 1950s. Yet this was only one example of how the Common Market and events in postwar Europe were bringing peoples closer together.

Background: The post-World War I bitterness caused by the Treaty of Versailles and the depression caused by German attempts to pay war debts to the allies were partly responsible for Hitler's rise.

589

equipment and machines to send back to the Soviet Union. The Soviets also insisted that Germany should be punished for starting the war. They felt that Germany should be kept weak, and not allowed to rebuild its farms and factories. The United States, Britain, and France disagreed, believing that such policies would only lead to yet another war. Instead, they felt Germany needed a democratic government and a strong economy. Therefore, these nations helped rebuild businesses and industries in

▶ western Germany. Why do you think the United States and the Soviet Union held such different views about how to deal with Germany?

6. In 1949, the United States, Britain, and France agreed to combine their parts of western Germany into an independent nation called West Germany. The Soviet Union then established a government under its control in East Germany, as this land now was known. In this way, Germany became a divided nation. West Germany was ruled by a democratic government elected by the people. East Germany was ruled by a Communist government controlled by the Soviet Union.

7. The Allies were, however, in agreement that the Nazis should never again be allowed to rule Germany. They called for a formal trial to make Nazi leaders accountable for their inhuman actions during the war. These trials were held at the International War Crimes Court in Nuremberg, beginning in 1945. Twenty-two top Nazi leaders were tried for crimes against humanity, and 19 were found guilty.

PEOPLE IN HISTORY

8. At the center of the judge's bench at the Nuremberg war-crimes trials sat a short, balding man. At home in England, he had a long career as a judge. At Nuremberg he was the president, or head, of the three judges who tried the cases against the Nazi leaders. His name was Sir Geoffrey Lawrence. The Nazi leaders on trial were accused of terrible crimes. The court defined these crimes as "crimes against peace" and "crimes against humanity."

9. The most horrible of these crimes was the torture and murder of 6 million Jews in German concentration camps. This inhuman action against the Jewish people became known as the **Holocaust** (HOL-uh-kawst). The interest of the whole world was focused on the trial. Lawrence listened carefully and conducted the trial fairly. The Nazis' main defense was that they were only doing their duty and following orders. Lawrence and the other judges, however, ruled there were moral laws that came before duty to any nation; obeying orders was no excuse. Lawrence was praised for the way he conducted the trial, but he never became famous. The Nuremberg Trial, however, will always be a reminder that laws and orders that violate higher moral laws must never be obeyed.

▼ Not until after the war was the full extent of Nazi cruelty unveiled. Six million Jews had been murdered in the death camps.

The Breakup of Germany

Germany in 1937
Germany in 1945
American zone
British zone
French zone
Soviet zone
S Saar

0   100 miles
0   200 kilometers

▲ Germany was divided into four postwar zones. Each zone was ruled by one of the Allies. Which zones later became West Germany?

EUROPE RECOVERS: In what ways did postwar nations of Western Europe work together to restore their economies?

10. Even before the war ended, the Allies saw that they would have to help war-torn Europe in its recovery efforts. To help accomplish this task, the Allied nations formed the United Nations Relief and Rehabilitation Administration, or UNRRA. This organization supplied food, medicine, fuel, and clothing to aid war survivors. UNRRA also provided seeds, fertilizer, farm machinery, and tools for Europe's farmers. In addition, in the first few months after the war, UNRRA aided many **refugees** (REF-yoo-jeez), or people who had been forced to leave their homeland.

11. When the war ended, the nations of Western Europe realized that they must work together in order to rebuild. This meant that they had to set aside their feel-

ings of nationalism and begin to work for a more united Europe. The rebuilding of the steel industry in Western Europe is one example of the benefits of international co-operation. Iron ore and coal are needed to make steel. France was rich in iron ore. Belgium and West Germany were rich in coal. Yet each country had high tariffs, or taxes, that limited trade of these materials. For example, a French steel mill had to pay tariffs in France on coal from Belgium. Therefore, in 1950, French foreign minister Robert Schuman proposed a plan to help Western Europe produce steel cooperatively. His plan called for an end to tariffs on coal, iron ore, and steel in Western Europe. France, Italy, Belgium, West Germany, the Netherlands, and Luxembourg agreed to Schuman's plan. In 1951, they joined together to create the European Coal and Steel Community, or ECSC.

12. The success of six ECSC nations in working together led in 1957 to the formation of the European Economic Community, also called the **Common Market**. The goal of the Common Market was to reduce and then end all tariffs on all products traded among nations of Western Europe. In this way, the Common Market nations hoped to make Western Europe a large and important economic bloc whose economies worked together. Investors, or people who put money into businesses, would be encouraged to help factories and industries expand in Western Europe.

13. The European Common Market was proof that Western Europe had recovered from World War II. Factories and mines greatly increased their output. Employment was high, as the growth in industry and farming created new jobs. Trade among members of the Common Market was thriving. In 1959, Great Britain, Austria, Denmark, Switzerland, Sweden, Portugal, and Norway organized the European Free Trade Association, or EFTA. EFTA, too, reduced tariffs and expanded trade among its members. Later, Great Britain, Ireland, Spain, Portugal, Denmark, and Greece joined the Common Market.

Background: Charles de Gaulle resisted Great Britain's membership in the Common Market for years. He once remarked: "But—it's an island."

591

The Arts and Artifacts

▲ In 1945, Iwo Jima was the site of a fierce battle between Japanese and U.S. troops. A war memorial in Washington, D.C. is modeled on the photograph snapped in battle.

The Iwo Jima Memorial Is there a statue of a famous person or a monument to a great event in your city or town? Monuments and statues honor people or events that are very important to a community. In Washington, D.C., there is a statue of five American Marines raising the American flag. This monument salutes the courage of the Marines and honors those who were killed in World War II. It also tells a small part of the story of a famous battle—the Battle of Iwo Jima in 1945. Iwo Jima was the bloodiest battle the Marine Corps ever fought. More than 6,000 Americans and 20,000 Japanese were killed in the fighting on this Pacific island. The Marine Corps monument in Washington is a statue made from a photograph taken during the battle. It shows a proud moment of victory—the raising of the United States flag atop the highest hill on Iwo Jima.

Forty years after the battle, 200 Americans and 130 Japanese met again on Iwo Jima. They had come to put up a different kind of monument. This was a monument to peace built to remind the world that nations, like people, can forgive. At the base of this monument is a simple statement of peace: ". . . We pray together that our sacrifices on Iwo Jima will always be remembered and never repeated."

1. Who is honored by the Iwo Jima monument in Washington, D.C.?

2. Why do you think the new monument built in Iwo Jima celebrates peace, not just victory?

592

SPOTLIGHT ON SOURCES

14. In the agreement that set up the Common Market, the goals of its members were explained in these words:

> . . . (1) to end forever the conflicts that so long divided the nations of Europe; (2) to raise living standards and speed technical progress; (3) to restore the weight [power] and importance of Europe in world trade; (4) to abolish outdated [no longer useful] trade barriers which split Western Europe into small protected markets; to make possible large-scale operations in the increasing number of industries in which it is essential. . . . (7) to set up the institutions which will form the basis for a future United States of Europe.
>
> Treaty Establishing the European Economic Community, Article 3, 1957

▶ Why do you think these nations wanted to someday set up a "United States of Europe"?

THE UNITED NATIONS: Why was this organization formed?

15. In 1945, the United Nations was created to help nations prevent future wars. The 51 member nations agreed to ask the United Nations, or UN, to settle disputes among them. The UN also was to help end disease, furnish food and aid to nations in times of disaster, and safeguard basic human rights. To carry on its work effectively, the UN is made up of two major bodies. The General Assembly has representatives from every nation. It debates problems that are brought before it and then suggests how they might be solved. The Security Council has 15 members, including five permanent members—the United States, the Soviet Union, Great Britain, France, and China. The main responsibility of the Security Council is to maintain peace throughout the world.

16. As more nations gained their independence in the 1950s and 1960s, member-ship in the United Nations increased. However, the Security Council often was unable to act because each of its permanent members had the power of **veto** (VEE-toh), or the right to reject decisions by the Council. (If any of the five permanent members vetoes any decision, it cannot be passed.) As a result, the General Assembly became more important and gained the right to take action when the Security Council was made ineffective by a veto.

17. The United Nations took an active part in maintaining peace around the world. For example, the UN sent peacekeeping forces to the Middle East in 1947 to help in dividing Palestine. When the creation of Israel in Palestine led to war between Israel and the Arab nations, UN forces helped restore peace. UN forces also helped to end the fighting between India and Pakistan in 1949. UN troops went to Korea in 1950 and helped fight a war there. During the 1960s, the UN helped to restore peace to the Congo and Cyprus.

OUTLOOK

18. At the close of World War II the once-powerful nations of Japan and Germany were weak and defeated nations. United States troops occupied Japan and helped that nation to recover from the war. The Allies disagreed, however, on how to treat Germany. As a result, Germany was divided into two separate countries. After the war, the nations of Western Europe learned how to work together to help rebuild their economies. In fact, the European Coal and Steel Community was so successful that the Common Market was set up. Another important step in the strengthening of nations after the war was the creation of the United Nations. The role of the UN was to help keep peace throughout the world and to prevent future wars. How do you think ◀ Western European nations benefited by working together? Can you think of an example of nations that are helping each other today?

Ask: Today Germany and Japan challenge the economic power of the United States and its Western European allies of World War II. Was it a good idea to rebuild the defeated nations of World War II?

593

CHAPTER REVIEW

VOCABULARY REVIEW

Write each number and word on a sheet of paper. Then write the letter of the definition next to the word it defines.

1. refugees
2. Holocaust
3. veto
4. Common Market

a. In Europe after World War II, these people had been forced to leave their homelands.

b. Organization of Western European nations formed to reduce and end tariffs on products traded with each other.

c. The torture and murder of 6 million Jews in German concentration camps.

d. The right of the permanent members of the Security Council to reject the Council's decisions.

SKILL BUILDER: USING PRIMARY SOURCES

The United Nations Educational, Scientific and Cultural Organization (UNESCO) was established in 1946. UNESCO encourages artists, scholars, scientists, and students to travel to other countries and share ideas. The purpose of the agency is to promote international cooperation. It also encourages worldwide respect for justice, law, human rights, and freedoms for all people. The passage that follows is from the Charter of UNESCO, which was drawn up on November 4, 1946:

. . . Since wars begin in the minds of [people] it is in the minds of [people] that the defenses of peace must be constructed; that ignorance of each other's ways and lives has been a common cause throughout the history of [humankind] of that suspicion and mistrust between the peoples of the world . . . that the great and terrible war which has now ended was a war made possible by the denial of the democratic principles of the dignity, equality, and mutual respect of [individuals] and by the propagation [spread] in their place through ignorance and prejudice of the doctrine of the inequality of [people] and races; that the wide diffusion [spread] of culture and the education of humanity for justice and liberty and peace are indispensable [necessary] to the dignity of [humankind] . . .

▶ According to the Charter of UNESCO, tell whether the following statements are *true* or *false*. If a statement is false, change the words in italics to make it true.

1. *Wars* begin in the minds of people and here must the defenses of peace be built.

2. *Low living standards* have been a common cause throughout history of mistrust among peoples of the world.

3. One of the causes of *World War I* was the idea that men and races are unequal.

4. All people in all countries should have justice, *liberty* and peace.

5. The defenses of peace must be constructed *on all national borders*.

SKILL BUILDER: CRITICAL THINKING AND COMPREHENSION

1. Classifying

▶ Practice your classifying skills by completing the table below, which describes post-war Germany and Japan. Copy the table onto a sheet of paper and use the information in this chapter to fill in the blanks.

	Germany	Japan
Occupying nation(s)		
Postwar government(s)		
When occupiers left		

2. Sequencing

▶ Write the following events in the order in which they happened.

a. In order to disarm Germany, Soviet troops seized German factory equipment and machines and shipped them to the Soviet Union.

b. Bombings and battles destroyed many European and Japanese cities.

c. The European Coal and Steel Community was formed to help Western European countries increase their production of steel.

d. The United Nations was formed.

e. The European Economic Community was formed.

3. Compare and Contrast

a. Compare the views of Great Britain, the Soviet Union, France, and the United States about how to treat the defeated leaders of Nazi Germany.

b. Contrast the ideas of the Soviet Union and the United States about how Germany should be treated after the war.

ENRICHMENT

1. Imagine that you are a newspaper reporter in Europe after World War II. Your assignment is to write a feature story describing to readers in your home town what it is like to be a student in a city that has been bombed. Before you write, do library research or use information from the chapter to learn about the city you will be reporting from. If possible, use photographs from magazines, newspapers, or encyclopedias to illustrate your story.

2. When might it be necessary or right to break a law or disobey a government in the name of a higher moral law? List examples.

3. Form a study group with several students. Bring to class news items about the United Nations you may have read in newspapers or magazines. Arrange a bulletin board display of these news items.

CHAPTER 2

The New Superpowers

▲ In 1961, United States President Kennedy and Soviet Premier Nikita Khrushchev met in Vienna for two days. Why are such meetings important?

OBJECTIVE: How did the United States and the Soviet Union become superpowers and why did rivalry develop between these nations?

1. The opposite ends of the earth are called the North Pole and the South Pole. For this reason, people sometimes refer to nations that are very different from each other as being poles apart. After World War II, two of the Allies who had fought together during the war followed very different policies and soon were poles apart. The Soviet Union and the nations that it controlled were often referred to as the East. The United States and the nations that supported its policies were referred to as the West, or western nations. The Soviet Union and the United States were much stronger than all other countries. These nations were strong in terms of size, wealth, natural resources, and powerful military forces. Because of their great power, the United States and the Soviet Union became known as **superpowers**. Before long, these countries were locked in an intense rivalry.

Post-war U.S. economy prospers
late 1940s–1950s

Soviet Union
launches Sputnik
1957

| 1950 | 1955 | 1960 | 1965 |

Soviet Union
tests atomic
bomb
1949

U.S. astronau
land on mo
19

THE UNITED STATES: How did the United States become such a powerful post-war nation?

2. During the war, U.S. farms and factories had expanded rapidly to provide the weapons and food needed for the American armed forces and U.S. Allies. American industries provided the planes, tanks, weapons, and ships that brought final victory to the Allies. As a result, few cars, household goods, furniture, and other consumer goods were produced during the war. After the war, as American soldiers returned home, the American economy shifted to peacetime production. Now American industry turned out a steady stream of new houses, cars, refrigerators, and washing machines. People had not been able to buy any of these things during the war. Now the demand was so great that people often waited over a year for a new car to arrive.

3. American industries also produced machinery and industrial products to send to the nations of Western Europe. Many of Europe's factories and industries had been destroyed in the war. The United States now exported vast amounts of steel, machine tools, and other materials that Europe needed to rebuild its economies. As a result, the late 1940s and 1950s were boom years in the United States.

4. American farm production continued to grow rapidly after the war. American farmers grew record crops of corn and wheat in these postwar years. Many European farms had been destroyed, and Western Europe now depended on the United States for much of its food as it recovered from the war.

5. The economy of the United States became the strongest in the world. There were several reasons why the American economy grew so strong. The United States had abundant supplies of important natural resources such as iron ore, coal, oil, and copper. It also had a large and well-educated workforce. Further, the United States had not been bombed or damaged during the fighting in World War II. It was free to concentrate on developing its industries rather than rebuilding them. The American economic system known as **capitalism** was based on freedom of opportunity, which was a great motivator in developing new industries. Under a system of capitalism, there is private ownership of property and means of production. Individuals are free to own and operate businesses and to work in any jobs for which they are qualified. Why would this system motivate individuals to work hard to produce more? Large American businesses called corporations were owned by thousands of investors who bought stock in those businesses. Under this system American businesses were able to produce the goods and products needed by Americans and by other post-war nations.

Daily life in . . .

After the war, many new communities were built near large cities. The Sanchez family was a typical family in one of these communities, or suburbs. Each weekday morning the Sanchez children walked to the new school, which had been especially built for the community. But they weren't the only students in the family. Their father was a student at the local college. Having joined the army upon graduating from high school, he had fought bravely in the war in Europe. Now a post-war program called the G.I. Bill of Rights made it possible for Mr. Sanchez and other U.S. veterans of the war to continue their studies. During the war Mrs. Sanchez had worked in a factory that produced fighter planes. In peacetime, Mrs. Sanchez decided to continue working at the factory, which now manufactured passenger planes. While the G.I. Bill paid her husband's tuition, it was Mrs. Sanchez's paycheck that supported the family.

SOVIET UNION: How did the Soviet Union rebuild its power and become a post-war leader of the Communist countries?

6. The Soviet Union suffered great losses in World War II. Soviet armies had fought bitter battles against the German invaders, battles that destroyed many Soviet cities and towns. Soviet farms and factories were heavily damaged. Major railroads, highways, and communication systems were nearly destroyed. More than 20 million Russians were killed during the war. When the fighting ended, the Soviet economy was near collapse.

7. The communist government of the Soviet Union made the rebuilding of the nation's economy its most important post-war task. Soviet soldiers in eastern Germany shipped German machinery to Russia to help rebuild Soviet industries. What other measures did the communist government take to rebuild the Soviet economy? It seized complete control of the nation's economy. A few government agencies decided what to produce, how much to produce, what price to charge, and so forth. Factories and major means of production were taken over by the state. The post-war communist government led by Joseph Stalin also concentrated its efforts on rebuilding heavy industries, which include steel, iron, machinery, and industrial equipment. Heavy industries were needed to build new factories and businesses in the Soviet Union. These industries were also needed to produce planes, ships, and weapons to rebuild the Soviet army and navy.

▼ On August 21, 1968, the Soviets invaded Czechoslovakia. Soviet tanks are shown below stationed at a busy intersection in Prague.

PEOPLE IN HISTORY

8. Joseph Stalin, the secretary-general of the Communist party, ruled the Soviet Union from 1928 until his death in 1953. Stalin was born in a worker's family in the Russian province of Georgia. He studied to be a priest, but became more interested in revolutionary politics. Because he led protests against the czar's government, Stalin was sent to prison in Siberia in 1903. After he escaped from Siberia a year later, he joined the Bolsheviks. For the next twelve years he worked with the Bolsheviks, plotting the overthrow of the czar. After the Russian Revolution, Lenin appointed Stalin secretary-general of the Communist party in 1922. Following Lenin's death in 1924, a struggle for power began that lasted several years. Stalin emerged as Lenin's successor when he assumed sole leadership of the Soviet Union in 1928.

9. Soviet rulers, determined to prevent any future invasion of their nation, kept their armies in the nations of Eastern Europe after the war. Communist governments controlled by the Soviet Union soon seized control of Poland, Hungary, Czechoslovakia, Romania, and Bulgaria. These Soviet-controlled nations became known as **satellite nations.** Satellite nations are countries whose political and economic systems are controlled by a more powerful country.

By succeeding in its plan to control these nations along the European border of Russia, the Soviet Union drew an invisible border between Eastern and Western Europe. This dividing line was called "the Iron Curtain." Only Yugoslavia and Albania, which also were ruled by communist-led governments, refused to follow the orders of the Soviet Union. Yugoslavia instead chose to depend on democratic nations in the West for aid. Albania remained a small, isolated nation without allies.

10. The satellite nations of Eastern Europe served the Soviet Union in useful ways. They were an important market for Soviet products as well as a source of supply of munitions, oil, and other natural resources and products needed by the Soviet Union. In years when Soviet harvests were poor,

---

▼ The Soviet Union expanded its borders after World War II. What Eastern European countries were affected by the Soviet expansion?

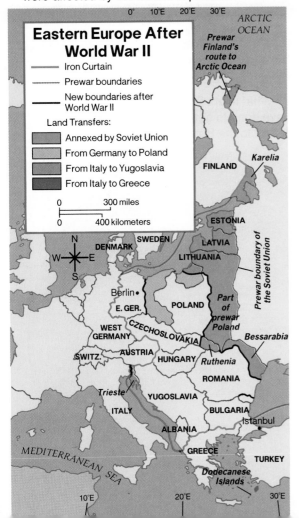

Eastern Europe After World War II

— Iron Curtain

------ Prewar boundaries

—— New boundaries after World War II

Land Transfers:

Annexed by Soviet Union

From Germany to Poland

From Italy to Yugoslavia

From Italy to Greece

0   300 miles

0   400 kilometers

the rich grain fields of Romania and Hungary supplied the Soviet people with much-needed wheat. In addition, the communist-controlled Eastern European nations functioned as important military allies of the Soviet Union.

SUPERPOWER RIVALRY: What other post-war factors and events contributed to the growing rivalry between the Soviet Union and the United States?

11. Ideology (eye-dee-AHL-uh-jee) was a major difference between the two superpowers. Ideology is the body of ideas on which a particular political, social, or economic system is based. In the Soviet Union, the Communist party believed that the purpose of government was to set up a political and economic system that would guarantee equal distribution of wealth and property among all peoples. To this end, the Soviet leaders totally controlled the nation's economy by deciding what goods would be produced based on what goods were most needed by the nation. The wishes of the individual were not important. Communists objected to free enterprise, wherein a few people pocketed the profits while the workers worked many hours a week for low wages. They believed that the good of the many was more important than the good of the few or the one.

12. The United States, on the other hand, strongly believed in private ownership of property, as you have read in paragraph 5. The American government did not control the nation's economy. It had only limited power to regulate business and industry. In contrast to the Communists, most Americans believed that the focus on the individual safeguarded the rights of the many. Why do you think it might be difficult for each of these countries to understand the other's point of view?

13. Another post-war rivalry between the superpowers developed over the issue of atomic weaponry. During World War II the United States had tested and used the atomic bomb against Japan. The fact that the United States was the only post-war

599

A Geographic View of History

Global Rivals   NATO and the Warsaw Pact were military defense alliances formed by the two superpowers after World War II. NATO (North Atlantic Treaty Organization) was formed in 1949 and now includes the United States, Canada, and 14 European nations. CEMA (Council for Economic and Mutual Assistance) was formed by the Warsaw Pact nations in 1955. It had 11 Communist member nations before it dissolved in 1991.

The map on this page is a polar map centering on the North Pole. It shows how NATO and CEMA tried to protect the United States and the Soviet Union during the Cold War era. Read the facts about these two countries and their military alliances. Think about how politics and geography influence each other as you study the map and read these facts.

The United States and the Soviet Union emerged from World War II as rivals.

Each superpower formed a mutual defense alliance with neighboring nations. Members of each alliance agreed to consider an attack on any member as an attack on all.

The shortest air route between Moscow and Washington, D.C., the capitals of the two superpowers, is over the Arctic Ocean. Missiles and modern aircraft can fly across the partly frozen ocean in minutes.

The threat of Soviet air attacks gave new military importance to Greenland, Canada, and Alaska on the Arctic shores of North America. All were equipped with radar, anti-aircraft, and anti-missile equipment to destroy approaching enemy aircraft.

Nine out of ten Soviet citizens lived in the European part of the Soviet Union.

Now use the above facts and the map to answer the following questions. Write your answers on a separate sheet of paper.

1. The Arctic Ocean lies to the north of both the Soviet Union and North America. What NATO members watched Soviet activities along the Arctic Ocean?

2. Why would Western Europe have feared a Soviet land attack more than the United States?

3. What might Europe's Warsaw Pact nations have done to get to the Mediterranean Sea? To get to the Persian Gulf?

The Superpowers and Their Allies

NATO members (United States, Belgium, Canada, Denmark, France, West Germany, Greece, Iceland, Italy, Luxembourg, Netherlands, Norway, Portugal, Spain, Turkey, United Kingdom)

CEMA members (Soviet Union, Bulgaria, Cuba, Czechoslovakia, East Germany, Hungary, Mongolia, Poland, Romania, Vietnam)

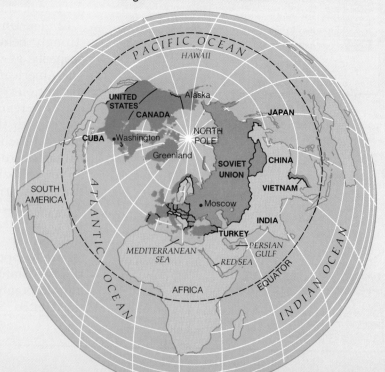

▶ nation with nuclear weapons worried the Soviet Union and many other nations. The Soviet Union determined to develop nuclear weapons of its own in order to restore the balance of power. Soviet spies soon passed along American secrets about nuclear weapons to Communist leaders in Russia. Once the Soviets had developed nuclear weapons, the Soviet Union and the United States started a fresh race to make still more destructive weapons. Each wanted to have the superior defense. In this way the rivalry between the two superpowers continued to grow. Why might such a rivalry be dangerous?

SPOTLIGHT ON SOURCES

14. In 1949, the Soviet Union tested its first atomic bomb. The Communist government's great effort to develop its own nuclear weapons is described here by Nikita Khrushchev (nih-KEE-tuh KHROOSH-chef), who became the Soviet premier, or ruler, in 1953.

> The most urgent military problem facing us after the war was the need to build nuclear weapons. We had to catch up with the Americans . . . [We] saw that the [Americans] were mobilizing against us, that they had already accumulated [built up] hundreds of atomic bombs, and that the prospect of military conflict with the United States was all too possible and not at all encouraging for our side. Stalin ordered that all our technological efforts be directed toward developing atomic weapons of our own . . . We had exploded a bomb on the ground but not yet in the air. It was only a prototype [a model]; the U.S. had already used its bombs against Japanese cities.
> —from *Khrushchev Remembers: The Last Testament,* Strobe Talbott, ed. and trans.

15. The exploration of outer space was another area in which the United States and the Soviet Union soon became rivals. During World War II, scientists had developed rockets for firing weapons. The two superpowers saw that space exploration would greatly increase their prestige in the world and would serve a military purpose as well. In the late 1950s, the Soviets began an impressive series of achievements in space. In 1957 the Soviet Union successfully launched Sputnik, the first small artificial satellite, into space. Two years later, the Soviets landed the first rocket on the moon. In 1961, the first Soviet space capsule with a Soviet cosmonaut, or space traveller, on board orbited the earth. The Soviet space program was admired throughout the world.

16. The United States reacted to these events with alarm. In 1961, President John F. Kennedy ordered a large increase in government spending on research and exploration in space. Funds for improving education in math and science were also made available. The United States' efforts were rewarded soon when American astronauts orbited the earth. In 1969, a United States team of astronauts were the first humans to land on the moon and explore its surface. Why was this event so important to ◀ Americans?

OUTLOOK

17. After World War II, the United States and the Soviet Union developed in very different ways. In the United States, the nation's economy boomed as houses, cars, furniture, and other peacetime goods were made for American consumers. In the Soviet Union, the emphasis was on rebuilding factories and building up the armed forces. Communist ideas about government and economic systems were vastly different from democratic ideas of government and from the capitalism practiced in the United States. The arms race and the space race led to important discoveries. Would these dis- ◀ coveries have been made sooner if the two superpowers had cooperated and shared ideas?

ESL/LEP Strategy: Ask students to role play the likely reaction of U.S. leaders to the news that the Soviets had developed an atom bomb (paragraph 14) and to Soviet achievements in space (paragraph 15).

601

CHAPTER REVIEW

VOCABULARY REVIEW

Write each of the following words on a sheet of paper. Then write the correct definition for each word. Use the glossary in the back of the book to help you.

1. superpowers
2. capitalism
3. satellite nations
4. ideology

SKILL BUILDER: READING A CIRCLE GRAPH

The circle graph below contains information about the four regions of the Soviet Union that produce steel. Read the graph and answer the questions that follow it.

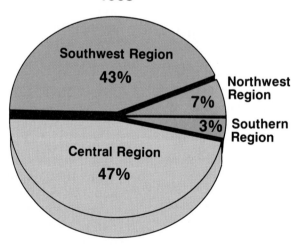

STEEL PRODUCTION IN THE
SOVIET UNION BY REGION
1963

Source: *A Geography of the U.S.S.R.*, John Cole,
Penguin Books, 1967 (England)

1. What is the title of the graph?
2. Into how many sections is the graph divided?
3. Which region of the Soviet Union produced the most steel in 1963?
4. According to the graph which region of the Soviet Union produced the least steel in 1963?

SKILL BUILDER: CRITICAL THINKING AND COMPREHENSION

1. Main Idea

▶ Re-read the quote by Nikita Khrushchev in paragraph 14 of this chapter. Which of the following statements best states the main idea of the quotation?

  a. The United States had many atomic bombs and the Soviet Union had only a prototype of an atomic bomb.

  b. Stalin wanted the Soviet Union to have more atomic bombs than the United States had.

  c. Stalin wanted the Soviet Union to have as many bombs as the United States in case of a conflict between the two nations.

2. Spatial Relationships

▶ The United States and the Soviet Union are both large nations. Use the map on page 600 to understand the geographic relationships between the two nations. Then answer the questions that follow.

  a. Which nation is larger in terms of land mass, the United States or the Soviet Union?

  b. Would the United States or the Soviet Union have more chance for border disputes with neighbors? Why?

  c. Which part of the United States is the Soviet Union nearest to?

  d. Which of the two nations has the colder climate? On what evidence from the map did you base your answer?

3. Drawing Conclusions

The Soviet Union suffered heavy losses in the war. How do you think the loss of over 20 million men in the war affected Soviet industry? Cite reasons for your answer from the chapter text.

4. Point of View

Some people would argue that the United States needs to develop more powerful and destructive weapons for reasons of defense. Others would argue that the spending of money on defensive weaponry is immoral when there are so many starving and homeless people in the world. How do you feel about this issue? Write your opinion in a brief paragraph.

ENRICHMENT

  1. Imagine you are a political cartoonist. Draw a cartoon to show the rivalry between the United States and the Soviet Union. Think of a symbol you could use to represent each nation.

  2. Read more about the United States during the early 1950s. Write a short description about some important developments during the period. Some examples of important subjects are women in the workforce, farming, weapons development, television, and sports.

CHAPTER 3

A Cold War Between the Superpowers

▲ Potsdam Conference, 1945: Harry S Truman and Joseph Stalin were the leaders of the two superpowers when the Cold War began.

OBJECTIVE: What was the Cold War and what were some major events in the Cold War?

1. "A shadow has fallen upon . . . the Allied victory. . . . This is certainly not the liberated Europe we fought to build up. Nor is it one which contains the essentials of permanent peace." These words were spoken in 1946 by Winston Churchill, then Prime Minister of Great Britain. He was expressing his disappointment that the ending of World War II had not brought real peace but only new conflicts and dangers. In the years that followed World War II the two superpowers, the United States and the Soviet Union, appeared to be challenging each other in many parts of the world. The rivalry between the Soviet Union and the United States became known as the **Cold War.** There were no military battles or bombings in the Cold War. No actual fighting took place. Instead, it was a war of

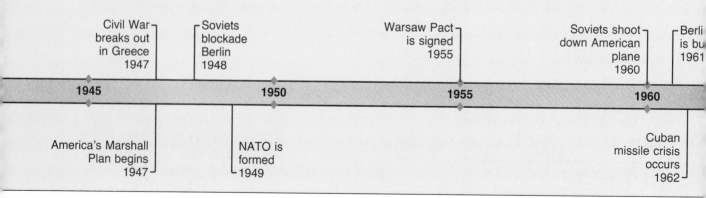

Civil War breaks out in Greece 1947	Soviets blockade Berlin 1948	Warsaw Pact is signed 1955	Soviets shoot down American plane 1960	Berli is bu 1961
1945	**1950**	**1955**	**1960**	
America's Marshall Plan begins 1947	NATO is formed 1949		Cuban missile crisis occurs 1962	

Ask: What is your understanding of relations between the United States and the Soviet Union today? Ask students if they think the two nations are friends or rivals.

604

words and threats, a struggle between the two superpowers for power and influence. With each year of the Cold War, the world became more divided between the Communist and non-Communist nations.

THE TRUMAN DOCTRINE AND CONTAINMENT: What policies did the United States follow to prevent the spread of communism?

2. When World War II ended, the United States worried about the Soviet Union's takeover of the lands in Eastern Europe. As you know, these lands included East Germany, Poland, Czechoslovakia, Hungary, Romania, and Bulgaria. By 1947, all these countries were firmly ruled by Communist governments that were dominated by the Soviet Union.

3. In 1947, a civil war broke out in Greece when Greek communists tried to seize control of that country and stopped free elections. The same year Great Britain found that it could no longer afford to help the Greek government. The Greek government turned to the United States for aid. At the same time, the Soviet Union demanded land from Turkey. Turkey borders both Greece and the Soviet Union. The Soviets demanded that Turkey share the control of two important straits, or waterways. These straits, the Bosporus and the Dardanelles, connect the Black Sea to the Mediterranean. Why do you think the Soviet Union would want to control these waterways? The United States became alarmed by these events and feared that the Soviet Union was trying to take over Turkey and Greece.

4. President Truman of the United States decided to take strong action to stop Soviet influence in Greece and Turkey. In March 1947 Truman announced that the United States would spend $400 million in military aid to Turkey and Greece. The United States considered efforts to spread communism a threat to democracy. Truman further announced that the United States would continue to "support free people who are resisting subjugation [takeover] by armed minorities [small groups] or by outside pressures." Truman's statement became known as the **Truman Doctrine.** Under this plan, the United States promised to give food, machinery, and supplies to all free nations that were threatened by communism. The Truman Doctrine had important immediate results. It helped Turkey to remain independent and enabled the Greek government to defeat the Communist rebels.

5. The Truman Doctrine led to a new **foreign policy** for the United States. Foreign policy is the way a nation deals with other nations. This new American foreign policy was known as the policy of **containment.** The government of the United States wanted to contain, or hold back, the Soviet Union from gaining control of any more lands. The policy of containment was aimed at stopping the Soviet Union from spreading communism to other nations.

PEOPLE IN HISTORY

6. Harry S Truman had been raised on a Missouri farm. As a young man he fought in World War I. After the war he became a country judge and later was elected a United States Senator from Missouri. Truman was selected in 1944 to run as Vice-President when President Franklin Delano Roosevelt was up for re-election. When Roosevelt died suddenly in April 1945, Truman became President. Truman later told reporters that when this happened, "I felt like the moon, the stars, and all the planets had fallen on me." Yet Truman took over as President and carried on the war until victory was won. Truman won the admiration of many Americans for his strong stand against Soviet communism and was re-elected President in 1948.

7. To help European nations recover after the war, the United States agreed to give these nations large amounts of aid. In 1947 the **Marshall Plan** provided $17 billion in aid to help these nations strengthen their economies. Sixteen nations in Western Eu-

Activity: Have students discuss their opinions of the use of aid to win allies. **Ask:** Why might a nation be reluctant to accept foreign aid from either the United States or the Soviet Union?

605

rope took part in the plan. Such American foreign aid also was intended to help increase trade and cooperation among European nations. Any nation receiving aid under the Marshall Plan had to agree to drop all trade barriers. The United States offered Marshall-Plan aid to the nations of Eastern Europe as well. However, those nations refused the offer. The Cold War intensified.

SPOTLIGHT ON SOURCES

8. Unlike the Truman Doctrine, the Marshall Plan—which was written by George C. Marshall, President Truman's Secretary of State—was nonpolitical. Any needy nation could apply to the United States for aid under this plan. The offer of aid was made to the Soviet Union, but the Soviet Union declined the offer. U.S. motives for giving aid so freely are described in this portion of the Marshall Plan:

> . . . The United States should do whatever it is able to do to assist in the return of normal economic health in the world, without which there can be no political stability and no assured [certain] peace. Our policy is directed not against any country or doctrine but against hunger, poverty, desperation, and chaos [complete disorder]. Its purpose should be the revival [restoring]

of a working economy in the world. . . . Any government that is willing to assist in the task of recovery will find full cooperation, I am sure, on the part of the United States government.
> —from *Congressional Record,* June 30, 1947

THE BERLIN BLOCKADE: What happened when the Soviet Union challenged the West in Berlin?

9. In 1948, Germany became the scene of one of the most serious conflicts of the Cold War. As you have learned, in the period right after World War II, Britain, France, and the United States controlled the western part of Germany and the Soviet Union controlled the eastern part. Deep inside the eastern part of Germany was the former German capital of Berlin. Berlin—like the rest of Germany—was divided among the four World War II allies. Locate Berlin on the map on page 610. The section of the city known as West Berlin was run by Britain, France, and the United States. East Berlin was run by the Soviet Union.

10. In the years following the war, several attempts were made to reunite the four occupied zones of Germany. Little progress was made. Therefore, in 1948, Britain, France, and the United States decided to unite their zones into one country, called West Germany. They also merged their sec-

Daily life in . . .

The winter of 1948 and 1949 was the most active time of the Berlin Airlift. The skies were often crowded with transport and cargo planes that brought much-needed supplies. Berliners called the big transport planes "raisin bombers" because of the food they carried. Sacks of flour and coal were unloaded constantly at the landing sites. Still, Berliners had to do without essentials. Electricity was rationed, or limited in use. Berliners were told, for example, that they would have power for only a few hours each day.

The Berlin Airlift lasted as long as the blockade of Berlin—321 days. The Soviet hope to "starve" the Western powers out of Berlin remained unfulfilled. Finally the Soviets allowed the Western powers to govern their sector of Berlin as they wished—without Soviet participation. On May 26, 1949, the Soviets removed the blockade. Transports from West Germany were again allowed to travel across East Germany to reach West Berlin.

▲ Children in West Berlin wait for a plane to land during the Berlin airlift. How was the airlift an example of cooperation among the Allies?

tors of Berlin, which lay in Soviet-controlled East Germany. The Soviet Union opposed a strong, united Germany because it feared that a strong Germany might someday again attack the Soviet Union. As a result, the Soviet Union shut down all roads and rail lines to Berlin. No trucks or trains with food supplies could get through to the city. In this way, the Soviets hoped to force the Western powers out of Berlin.

11. The United States saw the blockade as a threat to the freedom of Western Europe. In response, American and British planes began to fly food, fuel, clothing, and supplies into West Berlin. These flights were known as the **Berlin Airlift.** The airlift brought 2.5 million tons of supplies to Berlin in 277,000 flights that continued for almost a year. Finally, in May 1949, the Soviet Union ended the Berlin blockade. Later in 1949, Germany was formally divided into two separate nations and Berlin was informally divided into two separate cities. The Soviet Union set up the Communist nation of East Germany and the Western nations set up the democratic nation of West Germany.

NATO AND THE WARSAW PACT: What military defense agreements did the Soviet Union and the United States form in Europe?

12. The Berlin blockade strengthened relations between the United States and Western Europe. To prepare militarily in case the Soviet Union tried to take over more of Europe, in 1949 the United States, Canada, and 10 Western European nations set up the North Atlantic Treaty Organization (NATO). NATO was a military defense agreement founded on the principle that "an armed attack against one or more of [these allies] in Europe or North America should be considered an attack against them all."

13. In response to the birth of NATO, the European communist nations formed a military defense agreement against a possible attack from the United States or other NATO members. This agreement was called the Warsaw Pact. Warsaw Pact members included the Soviet Union, East Germany, Poland, Czechoslovakia, Hungary, Roma-

Activity: Have students read more about the Berlin Airlift in encyclopedias or school library books. Then ask volunteers to describe some of the effects of the blockade and airlift on Berliners.

▲ The Berlin Wall, built of concrete and barbed wire in 1961, divided East and West Berlin until the autumn of 1989. Why was it a dramatic symbol of the Cold War?

nia, and Bulgaria. With the formation of NATO and the Warsaw Pact, the division of power in Europe was made clear. Eastern Europe formed the Communist bloc (group) of nations. Western Europe formed the democratic bloc.

14. The Cold War thawed briefly in 1960 when President Eisenhower of the United States and Premier Khrushchev of the Soviet Union agreed to meet. A summit meeting was scheduled for late in the year. But in May 1960, the Soviet Union announced it had shot down an American spy plane over Soviet territory. Eisenhower admitted that a spy plane had been sent to take pictures of Soviet military bases, and agreed to stop all such flights over the Soviet Union. Yet Khrushchev refused to attend the summit meeting. Relations between the two superpowers again grew cold.

THE BERLIN WALL: Why did the Soviet Union and East Germany build this barricade?

15. Since the end of World War II, Berlin had become a symbol of the split between Western Europe and Eastern Europe. Hundreds of East Germans left East Germany annually by walking across the boundary line into West Berlin. They fled for several reasons. For example, West Berlin had a higher standard of living than did East Germany. Many East Germans wanted to be reunited with their families in the West. Others were seeking economic and political freedom.

16. In 1961, East Germany took steps to prevent its citizens from leaving the country. One morning Berliners awoke to the sight of a barbed-wire fence that separated East from West Berlin. Soviet tanks and East German police patrolled the 15-mile (24-kilometer) border that divided the city. Only a few well-guarded checkpoints where authorized people could cross existed along this border. Soon, the barbed-wire fence was replaced with a wall. Why would a wall ◀ more completely cut off contact between people in East Berlin and people in West Berlin? The Berlin Wall stood for nearly 30 years as a harsh reminder of the effects of the Cold War.

▲ This U.S. Air Force photograph taken in 1962 proved the existence of a secret Soviet missile base in Cuba. Why was this discovery so alarming to Americans?

THE CUBAN MISSILE CRISIS: Why did the United States and the Soviet Union nearly go to war in the early 1960s?

17. In 1962, just two years after the Soviets had shot down the U.S. spy plane, the Soviet Union and the United States had another serious **confrontation,** or clash. This confrontation was over Cuba, an island 90 miles (145 kilometers) off the southern coast of Florida. In 1959, Cuba had become a communist nation with close ties to the Soviet Union. In 1962, the Soviets secretly built a missile base in Cuba for launching nuclear missiles. When the United States learned about this secret base, it took swift action. President Kennedy demanded that the Soviet Union remove the missile base. Kennedy also ordered a U.S. air and naval blockade of Cuba to prevent Soviet arms shipments from reaching Cuba. Several Soviet ships carrying missiles sailed toward Cuba nonetheless.

18. People throughout the world were concerned and alarmed that the Cuban Missile Crisis, as it was called, would lead to nuclear war. Finally, on October 28, six days after the U.S. blockade began, Kennedy and Khrushchev reached agreement. The Soviet Union ordered its ships to turn around. Khrushchev agreed to **dismantle,** or take apart, the Soviet missile base in Cuba; halt construction of other bases in Cuba; and remove Soviet weapons from Cuba. In return, the United States agreed to end the blockade and not to invade Cuba once the Soviets withdrew. Why do you ◄ think Kennedy and Khrushchev each backed down to negotiate a peaceful end to the Cuban Missile Crisis?

OUTLOOK

19. Fear and distrust after World War II created tensions between the Soviet Union and the United States. After 1962 the tensions began to ease as the United States and the Soviet Union looked for ways to solve their differences. What advice would ◄ you have given President Kennedy during the Cuban Missile Crisis?

Activity: Have students locate Cuba on the atlas map on page 724. Ask students to imagine living in Florida during the Cuban Missile Crisis. Have them write a short paragraph explaining how they might have felt living so close to a tense spot in the Cold War.

CHAPTER REVIEW

VOCABULARY REVIEW

Write each of the following words on a sheet of paper. Then write the correct definition for each word. Use the glossary on pages 728–740 to help you.

1. Truman Doctrine
2. Cold War
3. foreign policy
4. containment
5. Berlin Airlift
6. confrontation
7. dismantle
8. Marshall Plan

SKILL BUILDER: READING A MAP

► The questions that follow are based on the map of Berlin at the bottom of this page. Answer questions 1–5 to test your skill at reading a map.

1. What is the title of the map? What does the title tell you about the history of the city?

2. Where was the Berlin Wall located? Why was the wall built?

3. Which countries occupied the zones of West Berlin? Which country occupied East Berlin?

4. What do the circles along the boundary between East and West Berlin represent?

5. Which country surrounded Berlin?

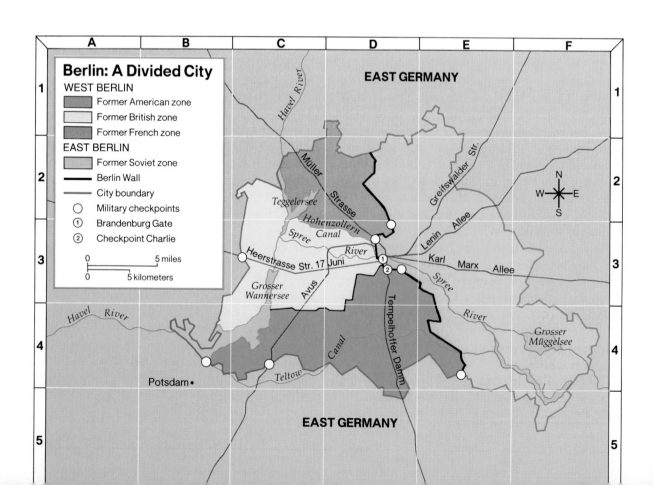

Berlin: A Divided City

WEST BERLIN
- Former American zone
- Former British zone
- Former French zone

EAST BERLIN
- Former Soviet zone
- Berlin Wall
- City boundary
- ○ Military checkpoints
- ① Brandenburg Gate
- ② Checkpoint Charlie

0   5 miles
0   5 kilometers

EAST GERMANY

▶ Now test your skill at locating places on a map. This map has a grid, or vertical and horizontal lines, that cross at regular intervals creating squares. In this way, each square can be identified by a letter and a number. For example, the Brandenburg Gate in the center of the map is located in a square where the space for the letter **D** and the space for the number **3** meet. Use the letters and numbers of the grid to answer questions 6-7.

    6. Is there a military checkpoint in the square created by letter **D** and number **5**?

    7. Is the square created by letter **F**, number **1** inside or outside the city boundary?

SKILL BUILDER: CRITICAL THINKING AND COMPREHENSION

1. Summarizing

▶ Read paragraphs 2, 3, 4, and 5 from this chapter. Write a summary statement that describes U. S. foreign policy in 1947.

2. Cause and Effect

▶ Match the cause from column 1 with its effect in column 2.

Causes

2-1. The Soviet Union demanded land from Turkey.

2-2. The Soviet Union shot down an American spy plane over Soviet territory.

2-3. People from East Berlin were crossing over to West Berlin in large numbers.

Effects

a. Khrushchev refused to attend a summit meeting with President Eisenhower.

b. Under Soviet pressure, the East Germans constructed the Berlin Wall.

c. President Truman offered to help small countries threatened by communism.

3. Making Judgments

▶ Write a judgment of the action described in the following paragraph.

    In the late 1950s, the United States secretly began sending spy planes on flights over Soviet territory. The spy planes were designed to fly at very high altitude, so that the Soviet Union could not shoot them down. However, by May 1960, the Soviets had developed a missile that succeeded in shooting down one of the spy planes. Why or why not was the Soviet Union justified in shooting down the U.S. spy plane?

4. Point of View

In 1962 the United States confronted the Soviet Union over Soviet missiles in Cuba. The Soviet Union backed down and removed the missiles. However, it was a very tense time. Do you think the United States made a wise move in challenging the Soviet Union over the Cuban missiles? Why or why not?

ENRICHMENT

    1. Find two or more adults to interview about the Cuban Missile Crisis. Ask them to recall their feelings about the events. Write their responses on a piece of paper. Compare your interviews with those of another student in the class.

    2. Imagine you were in West Berlin during the airlift. Write a diary entry for a day of your life in the blockaded city.

CHAPTER 4

Crisis and Change in Europe

▲ Large crops of wheat are produced in Ukraine. Ukraine is sometimes called the breadbasket of Eastern Europe.

OBJECTIVE: In what ways did the nations of Western Europe grow stronger in the 1950s and 1960s and why did unrest spread in Eastern Europe?

1. During the 1950s and 1960s, the nations of a divided Europe began to recover from the shock of World War II. Western Europe, remembering the lessons of two world wars, moved toward economic unity. Eastern Europe, recovering slowly, found itself part of a new empire controlled by the Soviet Union. The nations of Eastern Europe had been struggling toward democracy before the war. As they recovered, they found that they were no longer free to explore that path. The contacts they once had with the rest of Europe were broken. The Cold War had drawn a line through Europe. The line separated the Western democracies from nations that the Soviet Union had forced into Communism. However, the memory of freedom was still alive in East

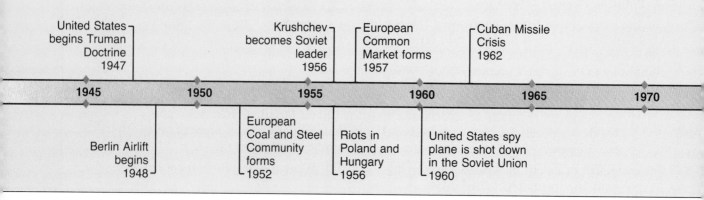

United States begins Truman Doctrine 1947

Krushchev becomes Soviet leader 1956

European Common Market forms 1957

Cuban Missile Crisis 1962

1945   1950   1955   1960   1965   1970

Berlin Airlift begins 1948

European Coal and Steel Community forms 1952

Riots in Poland and Hungary 1956

United States spy plane is shot down in the Soviet Union 1960

612

Germany, Poland, Hungary, and Czechoslovakia. These nations tried to move toward more democracy and independence. The Soviet Union responded with tanks and troops. Western Europe would shine as a beacon of hope.

THE SOVIET UNION: What policies did the Soviet Union follow under Khrushchev?

2. In 1953, the long rule of Joseph Stalin in the Soviet Union ended. After Stalin's death, a struggle among Soviet leaders ended with Nikita Khrushchev as the new ruler. Khrushchev began to relax some of the harsh policies Stalin had used. The Soviet economy under Stalin had built heavy industry and neglected the needs of the Soviet people. Now Khrushchev included the production of more consumer goods in the Soviet Five-Year Plan. Khrushchev also made agriculture more important in his plan for the economy. He allowed farmers on Soviet collective farms to grow crops of their own. He also gave managers of factories as well as collective farms more power to run their operations. These changes resulted in increased production in Soviet farms and factories during the late 1950s and early
▶ 1960s. Why would the Soviet workers have been motivated to produce more?

3. Khrushchev also ended some of the worst conditions that Stalin had caused in his years of dictatorial rule. Some of the prisoners in Soviet forced-labor camps were freed by Khrushchev. Their crime had been to criticize Stalin and his harsh policies. In 1956 Khrushchev declared that Stalin had betrayed the Communist party and that he had oppressed the Soviet people. Khrushchev now also allowed some Soviet writers and artists to visit other countries. However, Khrushchev remained a tough leader who fully controlled both the Communist party and the Soviet Union. Even so, he let the world learn how Stalin had ruled the Soviet Union in the early 1950s as the Cold War had begun.

UPRISINGS IN EASTERN EUROPE: Why did revolts take place in the Soviet satellite nations?

4. During the 1950s, relations between the Soviet Union and its satellite nations of Eastern Europe grew steadily worse. The people in many of these countries disliked their governments. They were tired of the hardships and difficult lives they led under Communist rule. Even more important, the people of these Eastern European nations missed the freedom they had enjoyed as independent nations. And many of them believed that the Soviet Union would never allow them to become free nations again.

Daily life in . . .

In the United States anyone who wants to travel from Washington to Boston can do so just by buying a train ticket. Compare the situation of someone in France who wanted to go from Paris to Rome shortly after the end of World War II. He had to get a passport from the French government, a visa from the Italian government, and he had to buy Italian money. To move goods from one country to another was equally complicated. It could take as much as eight days for a truck loaded with grinding wheels to travel from Manchester, England, to Milan, Italy. Tariffs and other border fees, plus the driver's expenses, could amount to the equivalent of $5,000, in six different currencies. These were the conditions in Europe shortly after the end of World War II. As the debate on unity progressed, the vision of a Europe where people and goods could move freely began to appeal to popular imagination. Then a step was taken that helped many manufacturers. The barrier that separated Europe's coal and iron mines and from the factories that needed both to produce steel was the first to go.

▲ Gomulka, the man standing at the left, witnessed the signing of a 1956 pact that clarified the status of Soviet forces in Poland.

5. During the 1950s, several revolts broke out in the nations of Eastern Europe. In 1953, an uprising by workers in East Germany was crushed by Soviet tanks. Khrushchev's new policies led other Eastern European countries to hope for reform. In 1956, Polish workers demanded better wages and working conditions. Riots broke out in Poznan (POHZ-nawn) and other cities. A new Communist leader, Wladyslaw Gomulka (VLAD-ih-slav goh-MOOL-kuh) agreed to improve workers' lives and give them a greater voice in managing factories. The Soviet Union accepted these changes but Khrushchev refused to allow further political changes. Poland remained a Soviet satellite nation.

PEOPLE IN HISTORY

6. Gomulka had joined the Communist party in Poland in the 1920s, when the party was illegal. During the German occupation of Poland in World War II, Gomulka secretly reorganized the Communist party. When the Soviet army occupied Poland after the war, Gomulka was given a high post in the Polish government. Then Stalin purged the Communist party in Poland and jailed Gomulka. When the Polish riots broke out in 1956, Khrushchev decided the people would listen to Gomulka and chose him to head the new government. Gomulka abolished collective farms in Poland and improved relations with Poland's church leaders. However, the reforms did little to improve living standards for the Polish people. Later, when riots again took place in Poland, Gomulka was forced to resign.

7. The people of Hungary also demanded more freedom, and in 1956 they replaced their Soviet-controlled government. The new leader of Hungary, Imre Nagy (IM-ree NAHJ), was an independent Communist who now asked the west for help and called for free elections. Khrushchev acted promptly and sent Soviet troops who overthrew Nagy's government. Bloody battles were fought, but the Hungarian revolt was crushed by Soviet soldiers. Hungary remained a Soviet satellite nation.

8. The peoples of Eastern Europe remained ruled by Communist parties and controlled by the Soviet Union during the rest of the 1950s and 1960s. Yet unrest and discontent continued among the people there. In 1968, the Communist government in Czechoslovakia tried to grant more freedom to its citizens. Again, Soviet troops were sent to overthrow the Czech government and put a pro-Soviet ruler in power. The Soviet Union continued in firm control of Eastern Europe.

WESTERN EUROPE: How did Germany, Britain, and France recover from the war and rebuild their economies in the 1950s and 1960s?

9. West Germany became the leading economic power in Western Europe in the years after it became an independent nation. The German people were determined to forget the war years and to work hard to rebuild their part of the now-divided German nation. The West German government was headed by Chancellor Konrad Adenauer (KON-rad AH-duhn-ow-er) from 1949 to 1961. Under Adenauer, West German industries grew rapidly, producing steel, cars, and machinery that were sold to many other countries. West Germany's trade grew as rapidly as its industries, and by the end of the 1960s it was one of the world's leading industrial nations. West Germany's rapid and amazing change from a ruined, defeated nation to a great industrial country became known as the German "economic miracle."

10. West Germany became a close ally of the United States and the West during the Cold War. In 1955, Germany joined NATO. Adenauer was opposed to communism, and he disliked the policies of the Soviet Union. He particularly hated the Soviet control over East Germany. Adenauer dreamed of someday reuniting the two parts of Germany. However, the leaders of West Germany who came to power after Adenauer's death tried to improve West Germany's relations with the Soviet Union. In 1969, Chancellor Willy Brandt (VIH-lee BRAHNT) agreed to accept the borders of all nations of Eastern Europe. He also recognized East Germany as an independent nation. In this way, the division of Germany into two separate nations now seemed permanent. Why might the leader of Germany need to be especially concerned about East-West relations?

11. Great Britain emerged from the war a much weaker nation. It had lost its overseas empire of colonies that had provided much of its wealth. Its economy had been seriously hurt during the war. The British people voted into power a new government in 1945 ruled by the Labor party. The Labor government was in office for the next six years and used its power to set up a **welfare state** in Britain. In a welfare state, the government provides for the basic needs of the people. The Labor government provided free medical and health services, low-cost public housing, and increased pensions and jobless benefits. The Labor government also nationalized, or took over the ownership of, the nation's coal mines, iron and steel industries, railroads, and telephone and electric services. Yet most British industries still were owned by private companies. When the Conservative party regained power in 1951, it accepted the welfare state reforms. In foreign policy, too, both parties strongly supported the West in the Cold War. British armed forces also played a key role in NATO.

12. During the 1950s and 1960s, Britain often faced difficult times. Nevertheless, some of its past glory was recalled when Queen Elizabeth II came to the throne in 1953. The British Commonwealth of Na-

▼ Queen Elizabeth II was only 25 years old when she became Queen of England. Why has the royal family remained so popular in England?

Ask: Why do you think the English people were so eager to replace their government with one which promised a welfare state?

615

▲ Algerian independence was granted after eight years of violent rebellion. This parade took place as part of the celebration of the 20th anniversary of the start of the Revolution.

tions was another link to Great Britain's past. Most of the nations of the British empire that gained their independence in these years joined the Commonwealth.

13. The people of France, too, found life difficult in the years after the war. France's economy was badly damaged as a result of the German occupation and the fighting. However, Marshall Plan aid helped French farmers and factory owners to recover. The French government also nationalized certain industries such as coal and gas. By the mid-1950s, France was beginning to build a stronger economy. Yet, the most difficult problem France faced after the war was its government. The French National Assembly elected by the people had many political parties, including a strong Communist party. However, no single party had enough votes to rule, and French governments were made up of coalitions, or members of several parties. These governments often were voted out of office. France's weak governments led to a demand for change. In 1958, General Charles de Gaulle, a wartime hero, was given power by the National Assembly

to draft a new constitution for France. De Gaulle created a strong Presidency with power to pass laws and a new National Assembly with fewer powers. The French people voted in favor of de Gaulle's plan.

14. De Gaulle was elected the first president of the new French Republic. One of his first acts was to end France's fight to keep its colony of Algeria. French settlers in Algeria opposed that nation's struggle for independence. France, however, withdrew its troops and granted Algeria independence in 1962. However, de Gaulle strongly believed that France was still a great nation. In fact, he wanted to make France the leader of Western Europe. De Gaulle feared that the United States might not be able to defend Europe. He also decided to improve France's relations with the Soviet Union, since he believed that Germany might someday again be France's chief enemy. For this reason, de Gaulle withdrew France from an active role in the NATO alliance. Why might France's foreign policy have ◄ caused problems for its western allies? In 1968, a wave of unrest among the French

Activity: Students might research additional facts about the Algerian revolution and find out why France finally granted Algeria independence.

people against de Gaulle's use of power in France finally led him to resign from office in 1969.

A THAW IN THE COLD WAR: In what ways did relations between the superpowers and their allies slowly improve by the late 1960s?

15. After more than 25 years of hostility and tension, relations between the East and West gradually began to change. In the early 1960s, Soviet leader Khrushchev had talked about **peaceful co-existence** (PEES-fuhl ko-ig-ZIST-unts). By this he meant that the superpowers would have to learn to live together even though they distrusted each ▶ other. What steps might be taken to strengthen the trust between East and West?

16. The confrontation between the United States and the Soviet Union during the Cuban Missile Crisis caused leaders on both sides to see the great need to try to end the Cold War. As a result, the Soviet and American leaders began to hold **summit meetings** more often. Summit meetings are private conferences between the heads of the two superpowers. These meetings were a sign that the superpowers now preferred talks to confrontation. To prevent a nuclear war being caused by an accident on either side, a "hot line" telephone was installed that connected Moscow and Washington, D.C.

17. Another sign of a thaw in the Cold War was a series of talks held about reducing the nuclear weapons of both sides. These SALT talks (Strategic Arms Limitation Talks) were aimed at limiting the number of nuclear warheads and missiles among the NATO and Warsaw Pact nations. By the end of the 1960s, the SALT talks were making progress. A thaw in the Cold War marked the beginning of a new stage in the relationship between the Soviet Union and the United States. This stage was known as **detente** (day-TAHNT), or the easing of strained relations. Detente offered hope for a more peaceful future. Yet the rivalry between East and West continued.

▲ The peaceful demonstration shown above took place in Bremerhaven, Germany, to protest the presence of nuclear missiles there.

OUTLOOK

18. The 1950s and 1960s were years of great change in Europe. In the Soviet Union, the brutal dictatorship of Stalin was replaced by Khrushchev's more moderate policies. In the Soviet satellite nations of Eastern Europe, growing unrest led to several unsuccessful revolts. Soviet control tightened after each revolt. In Western Europe, West Germany was successful in building up its trade and industries and became a major industrial nation. Britain and France remained weaker countries during these years. The Soviet Union and the United States slowly began to end the confrontations of the Cold War. Yet the two superpowers and their allies in Europe remained apart as hostile rivals. Why did ◀ the nations on both sides still distrust one another? What issues did each side still have to resolve with the other?

617

CHAPTER REVIEW

VOCABULARY REVIEW

Write the following sentences on a sheet of paper. Then use your vocabulary words to fill the blanks.

welfare state   summit meetings

peaceful co-existence   detente

1. Great Britain tried to care for its population by becoming a _____ that provided for the basic needs of the people.

2. As a means of making sure peace was kept, leaders of nations would often hold _____ to discuss economic, social or military issues.

3. The goal of many nations was to live together in _____ without war.

4. The easing of tensions between countries is called _____ .

SKILL BUILDER: CREATING A TIME LINE

Follow these steps to create a time line. Be sure the lines are evenly spaced. Use the time line at the beginning of this chapter as an example.

1. Title your time line: *Events in Eastern Europe.*

2. Draw a line five inches long and mark each inch-mark with a year like this:

1945   1950   1955   1960   1965   1970

3. Mark each year between the five-year marks with a small line.

4. Review Chapters 3 and 4. Position each of the following events correctly on the time line you have created.

1948–Berlin Airlift begins

1962–Cuban Missle Crisis

1956–Riots occur in Poland and Hungary

1956–Khrushchev becomes Soviet leader

1960–United States spy plane is shot down in the Soviet Union

1947–Communist rebels try to take over Greek government; United States begins Truman Doctrine

1952–European Coal and Steel community forms

1957–European Common Market forms

SKILL BUILDER: CRITICAL THINKING AND COMPREHENSION

1. Generalizing

▶ Read paragraphs 7 and 8 of this chapter. Choose the statement on the next page that best forms a generalization of paragraphs 7 and 8. Write the generalization on a sheet of paper.

a. After World War II, the Soviet Union took control of almost every aspect of life in Eastern Europe.

b. After World War II, the Soviet Union directed the industries of Eastern Europe in order to build up heavy industry for the Soviets.

c. After World War II, Eastern Europe wanted to accept the Marshall Plan but the Soviets would not let them.

2. Contrast and Compare

▶ Compare and contrast the development of business and industry in Western Europe with its development in Eastern Europe. In what ways were the problems of business and industrial development and growth similar? How were the means of solving these problems different? Write your comments on a sheet of paper.

3. Fact *versus* Opinion

▶ On a sheet of paper, write the letters **a.** through **d.**. Then write *fact* or *opinion* to label each of the statements below.

a. Polish people were right to revolt against their government.

b. In 1956 the Poles revolted, partly because of their low wages and poor working conditions.

c. The Poles were not afraid of the Soviet threat to use tanks against rioters.

d. The people of Poland would be better off today if the 1956 riots had never taken place.

4. Hypothesizing

▶ Practice your skill at making a hypothesis. Read the question below and follow the directions. Write your answer on a sheet of paper.

What do you think might have happened in Europe if Eastern European nations had been allowed to trade freely with Western European nations after World War II? Find facts in the chapter to support your hypothesis.

ENRICHMENT

1. Write a short story describing what it might have been like to be a teenager in one of the countries of Eastern Europe after World War II. Include information about the availability and variety of clothing, television shows, and the type of work your father or mother may have done. If you need further details for your story, use a recent encyclopedia.

2. After the Hungarian revolt of 1956 was crushed, many Hungarians came to the United States as refugees. Locate and interview persons who left Hungary at this time. Ask them to tell about their experiences and how they escaped. Report your findings to the class.

3. Make a newspaper clipping file of articles about Western and Eastern Europe. Use the map on page 726 to list the nations of Europe. Look for articles about trade, art, culture, sports, fashion or human-interest stories from nations on your list. Pick two or three articles you think are the most interesting and share them with the class.

CHAPTER 5

Communism in China and Korea

▲ Mao Zedong, the first ruler of Communist China, talks with peasant leaders. What mood do you think the artist was trying to express?

OBJECTIVE: How did the rivalry between the United States and the Soviet Union influence events in China and Korea after the war?

1. The growing rivalry between the United States and the Soviet Union after World War II had a major impact in Asia as well as in Europe. In 1945, China was still fighting a civil war. Korea was trying to recover from years of harsh Japanese rule. The United States and the Soviet Union, with their sharply different outlooks, both tried to influence what would happen in these Asian countries. During the years of the Cold War, both nations tried to win allies in Asia. The division of China after 1949 led to the Soviet Union becoming an ally of Communist China. The United States supported its ally, Nationalist China in Taiwan. Korea was divided between the two superpowers. Finally, the rivalry of the superpowers in Asia caused them to become

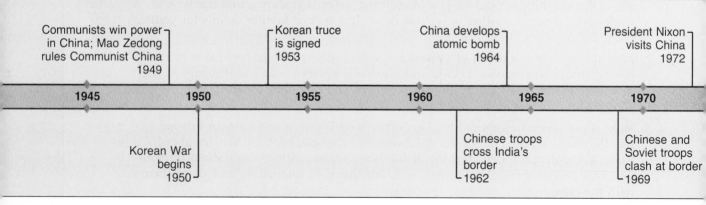

Communists win power in China; Mao Zedong rules Communist China 1949

Korean truce is signed 1953

China develops atomic bomb 1964

President Nixon visits China 1972

| 1945 | 1950 | 1955 | 1960 | 1965 | 1970 |

Korean War begins 1950

Chinese troops cross India's border 1962

Chinese and Soviet troops clash at border 1969

620

involved in a war. Korea became the battle ground.

CHINA'S CIVIL WAR: Who won the civil war in China and how did it lead to the creation of Communist China and Nationalist China?

2. Before World War II, the Chinese had been fighting a civil war for over 15 years. Japan's invasion of China in 1937 succeeded partly because China had been so weakened by this war. Then, when World War II ended in 1945, the civil war began again. The Communist Chinese armies and the Nationalist Chinese armies fought for four more years. Finally, in 1949, the Communists won the war. The Chinese Communists then took control of all of mainland China. The Nationalist Chinese fled to the large island of Taiwan off the coast of China.

3. The Nationalists and the Communists set up separate nations. Now there were two Chinas, the People's Republic of China on the mainland, ruled by the Communists, and the Republic of China on Taiwan, ruled by the Nationalist government. Mao Zedong (MOU dzuh-DOONG) became the ruler of the People's Republic, now known as Communist China. Chiang Kai-shek (CHYANG ky-SHEK) became head of Nationalist China on the island of Taiwan. Each government claimed it ruled the true China. The Soviet Union supported Communist China and gave it military and economic aid. The United States recognized Nationalist China and set up **diplomatic relations** with it. Diplomatic relations are the ways two nations manage affairs between them. The United States had no diplomatic relations with Communist China.
▶ Why are diplomatic relations important?

PEOPLE IN HISTORY

4. Mao Zedong, known as "Chairman Mao" in China, was a hero to his people. For many years, he was the leader, or chairman, of the Chinese Communist party. Mao Zedong was born in 1893 to a well-to-do peasant family. As a young man, he helped start

the Chinese Communist party. When the Nationalists nearly defeated the Communists in China's civil war in 1934, Mao led his followers into northern China. This retreat became known as the Long March. Mao then organized and built up his Communist forces there. When the People's Republic, or Communist China, came into being in 1949, Mao became the ruler of that Communist nation.

5. Mao's goals were to make China a modern industrial nation and to set up a **classless society**. China had long had several classes or social levels. At the lowest level was nearly all of China's population—the peasant farmers. All other classes had more wealth. Industries that had been owned by wealthy families were taken over by the government. Land that had been owned by landlords was divided among the peasant farmers. Many Chinese moved from rural areas into growing cities. At first the military controlled local governments. Soon these local governments came under control of civilians who were members of the Communist Party. Although China's large population included people with many different views, Mao's leadership was not seriously questioned.

SPOTLIGHT ON SOURCES

6. A Western writer described what a Chinese peasant's life was like during the 1950s.

"Thin and reed-like from the famines and droughts of his youth, he lives on a daily ration of just over a pound of rice and one teaspoon of meat, and grows his own cabbage and beans in his backyard. . . . He usually walks to work, which is organized by a committee of the natural leaders of his village and occasionally inspected by [Communist] officials from the county town. . . . Once a week he must go to a political "pep talk" meeting, and once a month he can see . . . a government film, exalting [praising] the collective life, or recalling the worse aspects of the old life before 1949. . . . Gradually his life is becoming better . . . . Who can know what he really feels, how in his heart he weights the good against the bad consequences [results] of Communist rule?

—Anatomy of China: An Introduction to One Quarter of Mankind, Dick Wilson

THE CHINESE-SOVIET SPLIT: What caused the break between Communist China and the Soviet Union?

7. "There cannot be two suns in the sky" is an old Chinese saying. Yet, after World War II, China and the Soviet Union were both giants in the Communist world. Could there be two suns in the Communist sky? Could both these countries share in the leadership of the world's Communist nations? By the late 1950s, the answer was clear. The two Communist giants, the Soviet Union and the People's Republic of China, were quarreling. An important conflict broke out between them over Commu-

nist ideology. The leaders of the Soviet Union and the leaders of China all were Communists, but they had different ideologies. The Soviet Communists decided to make less effort to spread communism by causing revolutions in other countries. The Soviets believed that other countries would come to accept communism without revolutions or war. This idea was called peaceful co-existence. The Soviets believed that communism and other systems of government could co-exist, or live side by side. The Chinese Communists did not accept these ideas. Instead, they continued to believe they must spread Communism by world revolution.

8. The Chinese Communists were especially interested in causing revolutions in the nations of the **Third World**. Third World nations are the developing nations in Africa, Asia, and Latin America. Many of them are nations that once were colonies of European nations. Most of them were not allies of the United States or allies of the Soviet Union. Even so, the Soviet Union knew that trying to cause revolutions in Third World nations might bring it into conflict with the United

▼ At this site near Canton, students and intellectuals work for three days each month planting trees. Communist China requires everyone to work part-time at such tasks.

Activity: Have students read about China's commune system started in the 1950s. Then organize a class discussion in which students explain how workers in communes are organized.

States. It also knew that any conflict that threatened the United States' interests might start a nuclear war.

9. The Soviet Union's idea of peaceful co-existence troubled Communist China for another reason. The Soviet Union seemed to be becoming friendlier with the Western nations. After the Cuban missile crisis in 1962, the Soviet Union and the United States began to try to reduce the tensions of the Cold War. Communist China disliked this Soviet effort, since it might leave China alone in its struggle with the West.

10. As the Soviet Union's split with Communist China grew, the Soviets stopped helping China develop nuclear weapons. The Soviet Union had helped Chinese scientists to develop atomic reactors that could make nuclear materials for peaceful uses and for weapons. To the Chinese, it appeared that the Soviets did not want China to become a nuclear power. The Chinese developed nuclear weapons and exploded a test bomb in 1964.

11. Communist China and the Soviet Union also quarreled over the long border they share. Study the map on this page which shows this border. In the late 1800s, Russia had taken huge areas of land from China along this border. China wanted some of this land back. However, the Soviet Union refused, declaring that the border must stay as it was. In 1969, the armies of the two nations clashed at several points along the border, and tensions increased between the two countries.

EFFECTS OF THE SPLIT: What did the break between Communist China and the Soviet Union mean for the world?

12. Communist China also played a role in events in many other parts of the world. Sometimes Chinese policies supported the Soviet Union, but sometimes they did not. In several nations of Asia, Africa, and Latin America, Communist China encouraged Communist-led revolts. China also provided

▼ China and the Soviet Union shared a long land boundary in Asia. Which Chinese cities were located near the border between the two countries? Which Soviet cities?

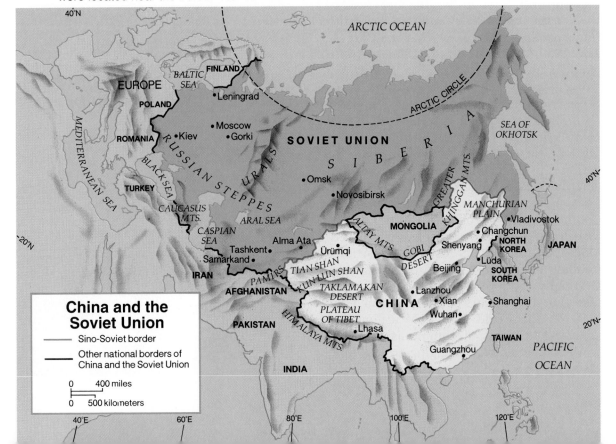

China and the Soviet Union

— Sino-Soviet border

━ Other national borders of China and the Soviet Union

0   400 miles

0   500 kilometers

weapons and military advisers to help these nations win their independence.

13. In 1962, Communist China quarreled with India over the border between the two countries. Chinese troops crossed into India to seize territory. This action put the Soviet Union in a difficult position. The Soviet Union was a friend of India as well as an ally of China. Therefore, the Soviets did not support either nation. However, India received aid from Britain and the United States, and China was forced to withdraw its soldiers.

14. By the 1960s, although China was developing as an industrial nation, Mao felt that the revolution was slowing down. He believed that a classless society could only be created by constant struggle. Because the Chinese government tried to control so many aspects of life, a huge **bureaucracy** (byoo-RAH-kruh-see) had grown up. A bureaucracy is all of the officials and assistants who manage a government. Mao felt that the bureaucracy was too powerful and too comfortable. It had almost become a special, privileged class.

15. In 1966, Mao started what he called the Cultural Revolution. Its aim was to weaken the bureaucracy and restore revolutionary values. Mao knew that the Chinese army and large numbers of Chinese youth would support him. Students and young workers gathered from all over China. Huge rallies were held in Beijing. Mao organized them into groups that were called Red Guards. A small red-covered book, *The Sayings of Chairman Mao*, became a guide for action. In the next three years the Red Guards caused serious disorder in China. Local governments were overthrown and Communist party officials unfriendly to Mao were dismissed. Schools were closed. Many cultural leaders lost their positions. Conflict often broke into street fighting. Gradually, by 1969, the disorders had quieted. For three years Mao had turned his back on the world in a final attempt to achieve the ideals of communism. Meanwhile, the world was changing around him. Mao Zedong's China would change too.

16. In the late 1960s, China seemed isolated and alone in the world. It had split with the Soviet Union. It had no diplomatic relations with the other superpower, the United States. Then in 1971 the United Nations General Assembly voted to recognize the People's Republic as China's representative instead of the Nationalist government on Taiwan. The following year an unusual event took place. President Nixon of the United States traveled to China. Because Mao was now very old, Nixon met with the new leader of the Chinese government, Zhou Enlai (JOH-en-LY). The two leaders agreed to talk about improving relations between their countries. These talks led to more trade and cultural contacts between China and the United States. Communist China had ended its isolation and become independent of the Soviet Union. What would be the advantage to the United States of this development? What would be the advantage to China? ◀

▼ Richard Nixon's 1972 visit to the People's Republic of China opened the door to increased trade between China and the United States.

DIVIDED KOREA: How was Korea split into the two nations of North Korea and South Korea?

17. Korea is an ancient nation with its own language and customs. However, for centuries it had often been ruled by other countries. Japan, China, and Russia had fought to control Korea. In 1910, Japan invaded and occupied Korea. When Japan was defeated in World War II, Korea regained its independence. The Soviet Union and the United States sent forces to Korea when the war ended. There were Soviet soldiers in the north and American soldiers in the south. The two superpowers were unable to agree about what kind of government to set up for a united Korea. As a result, Korea was divided along the 38th parallel. A Communist government was set up in North Korea. A democratic government was set up in South Korea.

18. In 1950, a war broke out suddenly in the Korean peninsula. Fighting began at the 38th parallel when North Korean soldiers invaded South Korea. The United States and 15 other United Nations members sent troops to Korea. The United Nations force was led by General Douglas MacArthur of the United States. When it appeared the United Nations forces were winning, Communist China sent troops to help North Korea. After the war had gone on for three years, a **truce** finally ended the fighting in 1953. A truce is an agreement to stop the fighting. No peace treaty was signed to end the Korean War because both sides could not agree on peace terms. The 38th parallel still separates North and South Korea. Troops patrol the border on both sides.

19. The bloody fighting in Korea destroyed large parts of North and South Korea. Thousands of Korean families were separated and became refugees. Bomb craters and burnt-out villages dotted the countryside. Cities and towns were in ruins. Korea was the first country in which the Cold War had turned into actual fighting.

▲ The Korean War was a conflict between Communist and non-Communist forces for control of the Korean Peninsula. What was the result?

OUTLOOK

20. In 1949 a Communist government took over all of China except the island of Taiwan. During the 1950s and 1960s, Communist China became an important nation in Asia. At first, it was aided by the Soviet Union, but later the two countries became rivals for the leadership of the Communist world. Mao Zedong tried to make China a classless society. His belief in the value of revolutionary struggle led to the Cultural Revolution. Mao continued to be an inspiring figure to the Chinese. Zhou Enlai saw that it was necessary for China to take part in the modern world. Why did China and ◄ the Soviet Union quarrel over ideology? Which nation is the leader of the Communist world today?

CHAPTER REVIEW

VOCABULARY REVIEW

Write each of the following words on a sheet of paper. Then write the correct definition for each word. Use the glossary on pages 728–738 to help you.

truce   diplomatic relations

bureaucracy   Third World

classless society

SKILL BUILDER: USING PRIMARY SOURCES

Ding Ling was a Chinese writer who discussed the suffering caused by the Chinese Cultural Revolution of the late 1960s in her writing. During the Cultural Revolution, like millions of others, she was imprisoned and accused of being an enemy of the revolution. She was imprisoned in a small cell and isolated from other people, but she still believed in the revolution and hoped that help would come. Read the following selection. Then answer the questions below.

"I had no pen, I had no paper. If I had something that I wanted to say to someone, there was no one else in the room but myself. It was isolation, complete and absolute isolation. From the day of my birth I had never experienced isolation like that. Before, during the Cultural Revolution, if during the daytime I had been abused or beaten or was forced to suffer in some other way, still at nightime I could return to my own shed, but shut up alone in that room, one had the choice of sitting facing the wall or of pacing about between the walls. That loneliness was like a poisonous snake, gnawing away at my heart."

from *The Gate of Heavenly Peace*, by Jonathan D. Spence. Copyright © 1981 by The Jonathan D. Spence Children's Trust. All rights reserved. Reprinted by permission of Viking Penguin, a division of Penguin Books USA, Inc.

1. To what animal does Ding Ling compare the effects of loneliness?

2. How many people were imprisoned with Ding Ling?

3. Does the writer think her current imprisonment is worse than her previous jailing?

4. What important tools was the writer not allowed to have?

5. What two choices of action did the writer have?

SKILL BUILDER: CRITICAL THINKING AND COMPREHENSION

 1. Classifying

▶ Classify the two groups of sentences below by giving each group a title. Write your titles and the sentences that belong to the titles on a sheet of paper.

1-1. a. The Chinese Nationalists and Communists fought in the 1920s and 1930s.

b. After World War II, the Communists defeated the Nationalists.

STUDY HINT: Make a Venn diagram comparing the Soviet Union and Communist China. Draw two large, overlapping circles. In the area where the circles overlap, write how the countries are alike. In the other parts of the circle, write the ways the countries are not alike.

1-2. a. After World War II, the Soviet Union sent troops to North Korea, and the United States sent troops to South Korea.

b. Two Koreas emerged.

2. Sequencing

▶ Two of the items in the list below are not in the proper sequence. Copy the sentences on a sheet of paper and put them in sequence.

a. China became a republic in 1912.

b. Chiang Kai-shek became the Nationalist leader.

c. Dr. Sun Yat-sen and his followers started the Nationalist party.

d. The Chinese civil war was halted when the Japanese invaded China.

e. In 1949 the Nationalists fled to the island of Taiwan.

3. Drawing Conclusions

▶ After World War II ended, the Nationalists and the Communists took up their fight. Read paragraph 18 of this chapter. Which of the statements below do you think is a logical conclusion you could draw about paragraph 18? Write the letter of your choice on a sheet of paper.

a. The United States was very eager to get North Korean troops out of South Korea.

b. The United Nations took the lead in sending troops to Korea in 1950.

c. Communist China sent North Korean troops into South Korea in 1950.

4. Point of View

▶ Read the source quoted in paragraph 6 of this chapter that describes a Chinese peasant's life after 1949. Choose the statement below that you think best states the point of view of the author of the source.

a. The author thinks the life of the Chinese peasant was greatly improved after the Communists took over in China.

b. The author thinks the Chinese peasant believes his life is better under the Communist government in China.

c. The author does not know how the Chinese peasant feels about his life now, but the author thinks the peasant's life has improved a little.

ENRICHMENT

1. Read about the "Long March" Mao Zedong led his followers on in the 1930s when they hid in the hills of central China. Use encyclopedias or library biographies of Mao Zedong. Help organize a class discussion on how Mao held his followers together under difficult conditions.

2. Interview family or friends who remember the Korean War. Take notes on their memories of the war. Then write an essay on the war from the point of view of people in the United States.

UNIT REVIEW

The years following World War II were full of international hope and tension. Memories of the devastation rained on Japan by two atomic bombs made thoughts of beginning any future nuclear wars "unthinkable." Hopes were high that the United Nations, set up in 1945, would protect the peace and prevent future wars. Japan was placed under American military rule. Germany was divided and placed under the rule of the four Allied armies. Great Britain, France, and Italy were severely weakened as a result of the war. As Japan and the great European prewar powers declined, the United States and the Soviet Union emerged as the world's two new "superpowers." Efforts to spread their conflicting ideologies led to a "Cold War." Aid from the United States assured the rebuilding and survival of West Germany and Japan as industrial democracies. NATO committed the United States to military action in Europe should a member nation be attacked. Communist governments, backed by Soviet troops or aid, gained control of Eastern Europe, mainland China, and Cuba. During the Korean War, the Cold War heated up into a "hot war" and threatened world peace. Tensions also rose high over communist actions involving Greece, Berlin, Taiwan, and Cuba. A nuclear arms race and a race to control space between the two superpowers added to world tensions. How would a superpower benefit by winning a nuclear arms race or a space race?

SKILL BUILDER: READING A MAP

▶ Study the map below. Then answer the questions that follow the map.

1. What were the largest communist neighbors of the People's Republic of China?
   a. India, Mongolia, and Burma
   b. Mongolia and India
   c. Mongolia and the Soviet Union

2. Which non-communist neighbors of the People's Republic of China face the Pacific Ocean?
   a. Thailand, the Philippines, and India
   b. The Philippines, Taiwan, and Japan
   c. Vietnam, the Philippines, and Japan

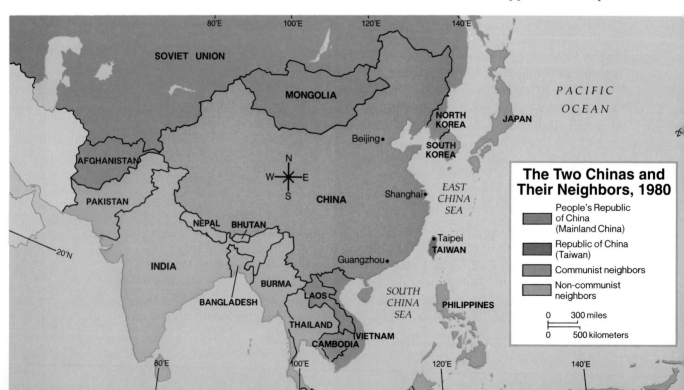

The Two Chinas and Their Neighbors, 1980

People's Republic of China (Mainland China)

Republic of China (Taiwan)

Communist neighbors

Non-communist neighbors

0   300 miles
0   500 kilometers

3. What are the three largest nations on the map?
   a. Mongolia, Burma, and Japan
   b. India, China, and Mongolia
   c. India, China, and the Soviet Union

4. What are the two smallest nations on the map?
   a. South Korea and Taiwan
   b. Taiwan and Bhutan
   c. Taiwan and Cambodia

5. What nations border North Korea?
   a. South Korea and China
   b. South Korea and Japan
   c. Japan and China

6. Which nations are islands?
   a. Taiwan, South Korea, and Japan
   b. Taiwan, Japan, and the Philippines
   c. Taiwan, Vietnam, and the Philippines

SKILL BUILDER: CRITICAL THINKING AND COMPREHENSION

1. Point of View

▶ Write the letters **a** to **d** on a sheet of paper. Read each statement and choose the person who would be most likely to hold that opinion. Write the name of that person next to the letter.

Harry S. Truman	Joseph Stalin	Charles de Gaulle
Mao Zedong	John F. Kennedy	Wladislaw Gomulka

a. The United States is a paper tiger.

b. Algeria should be given its independence.

c. Any small nation threatened by communism will receive aid from the United States.

d. An attack by Cuba on any nation in the Western Hemisphere will be viewed as an attack by the Soviet Union on the United States.

2. Fact *versus* Opinion

▶ Write the letters **a** to **d**. Then write **fact** or **opinion** for each of these statements.

a. The Soviet Union was bound to take over Eastern Europe after World War II.

b. Japan had depended on its Asian empire for almost all of the raw materials for its industries.

c. If Khrushchev had not foolishly put missiles in Cuba, communism might have spread to Western Europe.

d. The establishment of the Common Market meant that Europe had recovered from World War II.

ENRICHMENT

1. Research and write a report on the area of Eastern Europe called the Sudetenland (now part of Czechoslovakia). Be sure to include in your report your thoughts about how important international upheavals may affect populations of small areas caught in between.

2. With a classmate, prepare and present an imaginary debate between Harry S. Truman and Joseph Stalin about what might happen if Germany and Japan once again became major world powers.

UNIT 13

ESL/LEP Strategy: Explain the meanings of *independence* and *interdependence*. List on the chalkboard the regions that are discussed in this unit. After they read the unit, have students work in groups to make a list of the countries that have achieved independence in each region and the reasons why the regions are interdependent.

MODERN NATIONALISM

OBJECTIVE: In Unit 13, you will learn how the nations of Africa, South America, Asia and the Middle East are facing the responsibilities of independence in a modern world.

The Philippines becomes a republic 1946

Vietnamese defeat the French; U.S. aid to South Vietnam begins 1954

Castro comes to power in Cuba 1959

Indira Gandhi becomes prime minister of India 1966

| 1945 | 1950 | 1955 | 1960 | 1965 | 1970 |

Pakistan and India gain independence 1947

Jomo Kenyatta jailed by British 1953

Black protestors killed in Sharpeville, South Africa 1960

First U.S. combat troops to Vietnam 1965

East Pakistan becomes the independent nation of Bangladesh 1971

An oil derrick, symbol of the rising importance of the oil-rich nations, looms above a group of camels in a desert of the Middle East.

October War fought;
OPEC imposes oil
embargo
1973

Egypt and Israel
sign peace agreement
1979

Ferdinand Marcos flees
Philippines; Corazon
Aquino becomes president
1986

1975 **1980** **1985** **1990** **1995** **2000**

U.S. agrees to
pull troops out of
South Vietnam
1973

Black majority
rule comes to
Zimbabwe
1980

Nelson Mandela is
released from prison;
Namibia wins independence
1990

Persian Gulf War
1991

CHAPTER 1

South Asia

▲ The peace of a Buddhist temple in Sri Lanka stands in sharp contrast to the bitter conflicts in that country.

OBJECTIVE: What has slowed the growth and development of the nations of South Asia?

1. On a clear day in August 1988, a C-130 transport lifted off from an airfield at Bahawalpur (buh-HAH-wuhl-poor), Pakistan, with no trouble. It climbed easily to 5,000 feet. Suddenly, there was a burst of smoke. The plane exploded and crashed to the ground. Dead were Muhammad Zia ul-Haq (ZEE-uh ool-HAK), Pakistan's president, and 29 others. At first, this tragedy was believed to have been an accident. Then it was found to be an intentional act by people opposed to the president. Violence had once again brought change to South Asia. Pakistan has not been alone among South Asian nations in its experience of violent political upheaval and change. Since World War II, some South Asian nations have seen their governments change from democracies to military dictatorships. Free market economies have become planned ones. The instability of these nations can often be traced to ethnic and religious conflicts. The sources of these conflicts go back many years.

India and Pakistan win independence 1947

East Pakistan becomes the independent nation of Bangladesh 1971

Indira Gandhi killed; Rajiv Gandhi named prime minister 1984

Rajiv Gandhi assassinated 1991

1945   1955   1965   1975   1985   1995

Ceylon gains independence from Great Britain 1948

Indira Gandhi becomes prime minister of India 1966

General Zia seizes power in Pakistan 1977

Benazir Bhutto becomes the first woman to lead an Islamic nation 1988

SRI LANKA: How has nationalism torn the nation of Sri Lanka (formerly Ceylon) apart?

2. In 1948, after almost 400 years of colonial rule, Ceylon gained its independence from Great Britain. Although Ceylon joined the British Commonwealth, the people ruled themselves. In its first years as an independent nation, Ceylon was troubled by conflicts between two ethnic groups, the Sinhalese (sin-gul-LEEZ) and the Tamils (TAM-ulz). The Sinhalese are Buddhists, while the Tamils are Hindu. The Sinhalese felt that the new nation should adopt their language, Sinhala, as the official language. The Tamils felt that if their language was lost, their religion might be, too. The government in control of Ceylon after the war tried to unite the two groups and recommended that both languages be used.

3. In 1956, however, the Sri Lanka (sree-LAN-kuh) Freedom Party won the election and enacted a law making Sinhala the country's official language. Fighting broke out between the Sinhalese and the Tamils in 1958. During the fighting, the prime minister was **assassinated**, or murdered, by a secret attack. His widow, Sirimavo Bandaranaike (sih-rih-MAH-voh ban-dah-rah-NY-kuh), took his place. Bandaranaike promoted the idea that one language and one culture were necessary to unite the nation. In this way, she believed, people would work for the good of the nation, not just their own group. She even **nationalized** Christian schools to eliminate any additional religious conflict. To nationalize is to give ownership of or control to the national government. Despite Bandaranaike's efforts, tension and conflict persisted.

4. In 1972, a new constitution was written, and the people voted to change the name of their country to the Democratic Socialist Republic of Sri Lanka. In 1977, Junius R. Jayewardene (jay-wahr-DEE-nee) became the nation's leader. A new party, the Tamil United Liberation Front, was formed to represent the interests of the Tamil population. The TULF demanded that provinces in the north and east be made into the independent state of Tamil Eelam. They asked that Tamil Eelam be given self-determination. Jayewardene refused to give in to TULF demands. Why might he have been reluctant to give in? ◄

5. Pressures for Tamil independence increased. By 1983, groups of Tamils, such as the Liberation Tigers of Tamil Eelam, turned to acts of **terrorism** (TEHR-or-izm) to achieve independence. Terrorism is the use of violence to bring about a change by force or threat. Many innocent Sinhalese civilians were killed. The army retaliated by killing Tamil civilians who were thought to be helping the extremists. This only made the situation worse.

6. In 1987, President Jayewardene and Prime Minister Rajiv Gandhi (GAHN-dee)

Daily life in . . .

Bombay is a rich port city on India's west coast. It is also the film capital and financial center of the country. With a population of 10 million people, Bombay faces difficult problems with overcrowding and traffic. Most people live in one-room tenements called hutments. Often the space is shared by many members of one family. Traffic is so bad that some people must leave home hours before they need to be at work if they are to arrive on time.

One important job in Bombay is that performed by the *dabbawallahs* (dab-uh-WAHL-luz). Each day they pick up lunches at the homes of the workers. They carry these lunches to the railroad stations. Trains then carry the lunches into the city. Once the lunches reach the city, other dabbawallahs pick them up and deliver them to the workers. By foot, bicycle, and handcart, dabbawallahs carry thousands of lunches every day.

▲ Tea is grown on huge plantations in Sri Lanka. Harvesting the tea is done by hand, as it has been for centuries.

of India signed an agreement giving the Tamil areas of Sri Lanka greater **autonomy**. Autonomy is the right of self-government. Tamil was also recognized as one of the country's official languages. The agreement called for an end to the fighting and a surrender of arms by the Tamil extremists. The Indian army was to provide assistance, if necessary, to enforce the agreement. Although the agreement seemed fair, both Tamil extremists and Sinhalese nationalists rejected it. To the extremists, the agreement did not go far enough. To the Sinhanese nationalists, it gave away too much. As a result, Sri Lanka today finds itself buried in ▶ a violent conflict with no end in sight. What other options might have ended the conflicts?

PAKISTAN: How were the countries of Pakistan and Bangladesh created?

7. The story of Pakistan's independence is closely connected to the story of India's independence. Before 1947, Pakistan was part of India. The Indian population was eager to see India rid itself of British control. However, Muslims feared the Hindu majority would not let them have a say in the government when India became independent. A movement that called for a separate and independent Muslim state began. The British agreed that it would be best to partition, or divide, the country into two or more separate political units. When India became independent in 1947, Pakistan was created as a separate country of the British Commonwealth.

8. Since the Muslim population was concentrated on two different sides of India, Pakistan itself consisted of two states. These states were almost a thousand miles apart. Look at the map on page 636. Which state ◀ was bigger? East Pakistan had more than half the nation's population but received less economic support from the government than West Pakistan. The reason for this was that the government of the new country was based in West Pakistan and was dominated by West Pakistanis. How might the distance ◀ between the two areas have added to the problem of governing them fairly?

9. By the late 1960s, Pakistan was being torn apart by unrest and rioting. In 1971, a civil war broke out. The East Pakistanis were helpless against a much stronger West Pakistani military. Thousands were killed, and millions fled to India. This brought India into the war and ultimately led to the defeat of West Pakistan. By the end of 1971, East Pakistan had become the independent country of Bangladesh (bang-luh-DESH). With a large population and few resources, Bangladesh today is one of the world's poorest nations.

10. Political unrest has continued to plague Pakistan. When General Zia ul-Haq seized power in 1977, most traces of democracy disappeared in Pakistan. Elections

▲ Crowds greet Benazir Bhutto as she travels through Sri Lanka. Bhutto has won a place in history as the first female prime minister of an Islamic nation.

were postponed indefinitely, and Islamic law began to replace civil law. President Zia was killed in August 1988. After his death, the first regular elections were held in Pakistan in 11 years. The party of Benazir Bhutto (BEN-uh-zeer BOO-toh) gained the most seats in government. Bhutto became the first female prime minister of an Islamic country. Bhutto strengthened Pakistan's economy and improved foreign relations. In 1990, she was accused of favoritism and was removed from office. A new election brought a rival party to power.

INDIA: How has India progressed since becoming an independent nation?

11. When India celebrated its first independence day on August 15, 1947, the newly independent nation faced many problems. Although Pakistan had been created to reduce the conflict between Hindus and Muslims, many Muslims still lived in India. They felt that they had little power in government. The Indian government, led by Prime Minister Jawaharlal Nehru (juh-WAH-har-lal NAY-roo), tried to resolve this problem by dividing India into various states. Each state was made up of people who spoke the same language and followed the same religion. These states had their own governments, much like states in the United States. However, in some states the population continues to change. The states created by Nehru no longer represent one religion or one culture. New state borders are still being drawn today. Why might it be ◀ difficult to stabilize these boundaries in a country such as India?

12. Nehru's government began an ambitious program to raise the standard of living throughout India. In 1951, the first of several Five Year plans was approved. These plans were carefully designed to improve India's agricultural production, industries, education, and public health. India's food production increased remarkably as a result. India has also been successful in building up its industries. India now exports large quantities of such items as iron ore, steel, and chemicals in addition to cloth, clothing, and jewelry.

SPOTLIGHT ON SOURCES

13. A new Indian constitution that went into effect in 1950 introduced many changes to India. The rigid caste system that had gripped India for centuries was loosened. The new constitution forbade racial discrimination, even against the lowest class, ▶ the untouchables. Do you think all Indians were glad for the new equality of classes? The following account, written by an Indian journalist, gives the reaction of one woman.

> In the same village I walked into the house of a grey-bearded Sikh (SEEK) peasant. Though not too impressive or clean, his house is big. In the courtyard two beautiful big bullocks are standing with a bright yellow cloth covering their backs . . . . The man has sufficient land, and according to him everything is fine . . . . Just then a woman comes in . . . . Mistaking me perhaps for an emissary [representative] of the government, she lets forth a torrent of complaints . . . .
>
> "But why are you so angry?" I ask mildly as soon as I can get in a word.
>
> "Why?" she repeats. "The government has given land to *Harijans* (Untouchables) in this village. The result is that they will not do our work. And now I, a *Jat* woman. . . . "I have to dirty my hands making cowdung cakes. Is this a Jat's work?"
>
> "But don't you want the condition of *Harijans* also to improve?" I ask.
>
> "Why should it?" is the forceful reply with the full weight of conviction behind it. "*Harijans* were born to do menial jobs. . . . Am I meant for this—do I deserve it?" and she holds out her dirty hands to invite sympathy.
>
> —from *Blossoms in the Dust,* Kusum Nair

▼ In 1947, India and Pakistan gained independence from British rule. When did Bangladesh break away from the rest of Pakistan and become a separate nation?

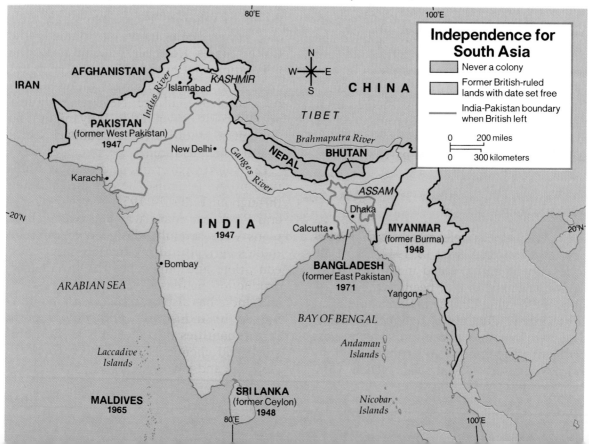

Independence for South Asia

- Never a colony
- Former British-ruled lands with date set free
- India-Pakistan boundary when British left

0   200 miles
0   300 kilometers

IRAN

AFGHANISTAN

KASHMIR

Islamabad

CHINA

TIBET

PAKISTAN (former West Pakistan) 1947

Indus River

Brahmaputra River

New Delhi

NEPAL

BHUTAN

Karachi

Ganges River

ASSAM

Dhaka

20°N

INDIA 1947

Calcutta

MYANMAR (former Burma) 1948

Bombay

BANGLADESH (former East Pakistan) 1971

Yangon

ARABIAN SEA

BAY OF BENGAL

Andaman Islands

Laccadive Islands

MALDIVES 1965

SRI LANKA (former Ceylon) 1948

Nicobar Islands

PEOPLE IN HISTORY

14. Nehru died in 1964, and two years later his daughter Indira Gandhi (IN-dee-rah GAN-dee) became prime minister. Gandhi helped to strengthen and modernize India. During the 1950's, India had not become involved in the cold war between democratic and Communist countries. In 1962, a border dispute with Communist China had resulted in an invasion of India by the Chinese. As a result of this brief but alarming encounter, India began to build up armaments. During Indira Gandhi's time in office, India developed the technology to produce nuclear weapons and launch space satellites. How might the ability to produce these weapons change the way India is regarded by other countries in the world?

15. Gandhi's greatest problem was the continuous fighting between India's religious and ethnic groups. At one point she declared **martial law**. When martial law is declared, the military is called upon to enforce all laws and maintain order. In addition, Gandhi had some of her opponents put in jail, and she restricted other freedoms. It seemed as if India's democracy were being replaced by a dictatorship. The situation became more complicated in 1984, when Sikhs who wanted to establish an independent state took over the Golden Temple at Amritsar (am-RIT-sur). They used the temple as a base for raids on villages in the area. Gandhi sent soldiers in to drive the Sikhs out of the temple. More than 600 Sikhs were killed in the fighting. India's population of 14 million Sikhs was outraged. Sikhs serving in the Indian army rebelled. On October 31, 1984, several Sikh bodyguards shot and killed the prime minister.

16. Indira Gandhi's place was taken by her son Rajiv. For a time, Gandhi managed to reduce the violence between Sikhs and Hindus. But by 1988, terrorism was on the rise. In 1989, amid charges of corruption, Gandhi was forced from office. Two years

▲ Indira Gandhi, shown here with her father, Jawaharlal Nehru, lost her life as a result of the Sikh issue. Why might this problem continue?

later, while campaigning to return to government, Gandhi was assassinated by Sri Lankan guerrillas. Today, India is struggling to improve its economy. But outbreaks of violence hamper progress. In 1992, violence erupted as Hindus and Muslims destroyed one another's religious sites.

OUTLOOK

17. Gaining independence from foreign powers is often a difficult process. South Asia was no exception. Ruling themselves turned out to be an even greater challenge for these countries. A major problem has been meeting the demands of the many different religious and ethnic groups who live in each country. Mohandas Gandhi had led the movement for Indian independence without violence. What advice do you think ◄ Gandhi would give to the governments of South Asia if he were alive today?

637

CHAPTER REVIEW

VOCABULARY REVIEW

Write each of the following sentences on a sheet of paper. Then fill in the blank with the word that best completes each sentence.

martial law   terrorism

assassinated   nationalized

autonomy

1. Indira Gandhi was _____ , or murdered, in an attack by some of her Sikh bodyguards in 1984.

2. Some Tamils in Sri Lanka have engaged in _____ , or the use of violence to bring about a change by force or threat, to gain independence for their people.

3. In 1987, the Tamil areas of Sri Lanka were given greater _____ , or the right of self-government.

4. When _____ is declared, the military is called upon to enforce all laws and maintain order.

5. Bandaranaike _____ Christian schools to reduce religious conflict.

SKILL BUILDER: OUTLINING

Reread paragraphs 2 through 6. Then complete the following outline about Sri Lanka. Part of the outline has been completed for you.

I. **Early Years of Independence**
   A. Conflicts arose between the Sinhalese and the Tamils.
   B. _____

II. **Ceylon in the 1950s**
   A. Sri Lanka Freedom Party makes Sinhala the country's official language.
   B. _____
   C. Tension and conflict persist between Tamils and Sinhalese.

III. _____
   A. _____
   B. Tamil United Liberation Front forms to represent the interests of the Tamil population and demands that provinces in the north and east be given independence.
   C. _____

IV. **Sri Lanka in the 1980s**
   A. Groups of Tamils turn to acts of terrorism to achieve independence.
   B. _____
   C. Both Tamil extremists and Sinhalese nationalists reject the agreement and violence continues.

SKILL BUILDER: CRITICAL THINKING AND COMPREHENSION

1. Summarizing

▶ Reread paragraphs 8 through 10. Write a summary telling what these paragraphs are about.

2. Cause and Effect

▶ For each cause given below, write an effect that resulted from it.

    a. India enters the civil war in Pakistan.

    b. Communist China invades India in 1962.

    c. In 1983 groups of Tamils turn to terrorism to achieve independence in Sri Lanka.

3. Hypothesizing

▶ Think about what you have learned about problems the independent nations in South Asia have faced recently. Form a hypothesis about the underlying cause for most of the problems. How would you test this hypothesis?

4. Fact *versus* Opinion

▶ On a sheet of paper, write the numbers 1 to 6. Then write *fact* or *opinion* for each of the following statements. Review the chapter if you need to refresh your memory on any of these topics.

    a. Nehru's grandson was prime minister of India.

    b. The Tamils in Sri Lanka have used terrorism to achieve their aims.

    c. Rajiv Gandhi should have been firmer with the Sikh terrorists.

    d. India should stop spending so much money fighting the Sikhs.

    e. Benazir Bhutto became prime minister of Pakistan through an election.

    f. If East and West Pakistan were closer together, the civil war would not have taken place.

ENRICHMENT

1. Imagine that you are a Muslim living in India in 1945. Write a letter to the editor of your local newspaper explaining why you support the partition of India.

2. Stage a trial of the killers of Indira Gandhi. Characters in the play should be (1) the defendants, (2) their two attorneys, (3) two prosecuting attorneys, and (4) the judge, with the rest of the class serving as jury. The prosecutors should argue that the killers should be convicted of murder and should argue for the punishment they think is appropriate. The defense attorneys should explain why the killers thought of themselves as patriotic Sikhs who do not deserve severe punishment. You will need to look in magazines and newspapers to find out how many people were involved, what their backgrounds were, and other information necessary for the trial.

CHAPTER 2

The Middle East

▲ The airport in Riyadh, the capital of Saudi Arabia, is typical of structures built recently in the oil-rich nations of the Middle East.

OBJECTIVE: How have nationalism and religion shaped the Middle East of today?

1. Winning the lottery! It's practically ▶ everyone's fantasy. What would you do if you and a group of your friends suddenly won a $40 million prize? You might buy some expensive clothes, the most sophisticated audio equipment, or a new home for your family. You and your friends might think about building a gym or meeting house where you could get together in your spare time. You might save some of it for college or vocational school for yourself or members of your family. Middle Eastern nations hit a similar jackpot when they organized to control the supply and price of oil in the 1970s. As billions of dollars flowed in, decisions had to be made about how to best use their new-found wealth. Many of these oil-rich nations made decisions that enabled them to rise from poverty to positions of wealth and world influence. What ◀ problems might a country face if its people suddenly became wealthy?

1940	1950	1960	1970	1980	1990	2000

Jordan and Syria gain independence 1946

Nasser elected president of Egypt; Conflict over Suez Canal 1956

October War is fought; OPEC imposes an oil embargo 1973

Palestinian uprising begins 1987

Middle East peace talks continue 1992

State of Israel is founded 1948

Six-Day War is fought 1967

Israel and Egypt sign a peace treaty 1979

Iran-Iraq War 1980–1988

Persian Gulf War 1991

NEW ARAB NATIONS: What Middle East nations gained their independence after World War I?

2. Promises of self-determination made by the Allies at the end of World War I raised Middle Eastern hopes for independence. Iraq became the first Arab nation to win its independence in 1932. The British left Egypt in 1936, and France gave Lebanon its independence in 1941. Five years later, the British granted independence to Jordan, and the French withdrew from Syria. Saudi Arabia was the only Middle Eastern territory that had escaped European control altogether. Before 1932, the land of Saudi Arabia had been a collection of independent kingdoms. In 1932, these kingdoms were united and Saudi Arabia was created.

3. Although independence was welcomed by these countries, it often created conflicts of ideals. In 1952, a group of young Egyptian soldiers, called the Free Officers, seized power in Egypt from King Farouk. The man who became the country's new leader was Colonel Gamal Abdel Nasser (guh-MAHL AB-dul NAH-sur). Nasser was elected president in 1956. Nasser's chief objective was to end foreign control of business in Egypt. He nationalized major industries and divided large landholdings among the poor. Although he crushed any opposition to his policies, Nasser was popular with the Egyptian people. He became a symbol of independence to the Arab world. What qualities ◄ does a leader need to be both powerful and popular?

4. Nasser followed an independent course in foreign affairs. Although Egypt accepted economic assistance from the Western powers, it bought arms from Czechoslovakia, a Soviet-bloc state. To show its disapproval, the United States in 1956 went back on its promise to help Egypt build the Aswan Dam. In retaliation, Nasser seized control of the Suez Canal from private British and French companies. Western countries, fearing the canal would be closed off to them, launched an attack against Egypt. After a short conflict, a United Nations army was sent in to keep the canal open. Nasser lost the battle but won greater Arab support. Why might support ◄ for Nasser have increased after the Suez conflict?

5. In his effort to achieve Arab unity, Nasser arranged for Egypt and Syria to become one nation in 1958. The United Arab Republic (U.A.R.) was proclaimed, with Nasser as its ruler. However, the distance between Egypt and Syria, as well as differences in economic ideas, prevented the union from being successful. The Syrians were not satisfied with Nasser's control of their country and left the U.A.R. in 1961.

Daily life in . . .

In the deserts of the Middle East, water is the key to life. Without it, there is no farming and not enough grass for livestock. Middle Eastern countries use different means to deal with their lack of water. In Israel, parts of the Negev Desert are used for farming. Water is brought to the Negev through the National Water Carrier, a system of pipes, tunnels, and canals. This system runs 88½ miles (142 kilometers) from the Sea of Galilee southward. Israeli scientists have also found a way to drip water and minerals straight to plant roots. In this way, almost no water is wasted.

In Saudi Arabia and other countries on the Persian Gulf, drilling for oil led to the discovery of underground water. Arabs around the gulf also use oases, where underground springs feed the soil. In 1977, a Saudi prince announced a new way to solve the water problem. He planned to have an iceberg towed from the Antarctic to the Red Sea. The prince's idea has yet to be tried.

Although the U.A.R. did not last long, Nasser had shown that Arab countries could work together for common goals.

ISRAEL: How has Jewish nationalism brought Arab countries together in a common cause?

6. The first stirrings of Jewish nationalism began to surface in the late 1800s. At that time, **anti-Semitism**, or hostility toward Jews, seemed to be increasing all over Europe. In Germany, Jews were no longer permitted to hold public office. In France, the Dreyfus affair appeared to be a clear-cut case of strong anti-Jewish feeling. Pogroms, organized massacres of helpless people, were carried out against Jews in Russia. Many Jews became convinced that they would never be accepted by other Europeans. These Jews began a movement called Zionism, which aimed at reestablishing a Jewish homeland in Palestine. Zionism spread rapidly throughout Europe.

▼ Many Israeli farmers work in a kibbutz—a community where property, labor, and living quarters are shared.

7. The first groups of Jewish immigrants arrived in Palestine in 1882. On November 2, 1917, the Zionist movement received the backing of the British government when Foreign Secretary Arthur Balfour issued the Balfour Declaration. As you read in Unit 11, this declaration stated Britain's official approval of the establishment of a national home for the Jewish people in British-controlled Palestine.

8. The Balfour Declaration encouraged many Jews to move to Palestine after World War I. By 1935, they numbered about 300,000. The growing Jewish population was not welcomed by the native Arab population. However, the Nazi slaughter of millions of Jews in World War II brought increased world support for a Jewish state. In 1947, the United Nations voted to partition Palestine into two states, one Jewish and one Arab. This plan was accepted by the Jews but rejected by Arabs in the Middle East. Why do you think this plan was unpopular with the Arabs? ◀

9. On May 14, 1948, the new state of Israel was born. The next day, Lebanon, Syria, Iraq, Jordan, and Egypt attacked Israel, hoping to drive the Israelis out of Palestine. However, they learned that the Israelis were well trained and determined to remain. By 1949, Israel had won the war and increased the size of its territory. The fighting forced thousands of Palestinian Arabs to flee their homeland into Syria, Jordan, and Lebanon. The problem of what to do with the Palestinian refugees became a source of conflict between Israel and neighboring Arab nations.

ARABS AND ISRAELIS: How has a lack of Arab unity affected Israel?

10. Since the 1960s, the Arabs and Israelis have engaged in two wars. The June 1967 war, called the "Six-Day War," was the most important for Israel. Israel won control of the West Bank of the Jordan River, the Golan (GOH-lahn) Heights, the Sinai Peninsula, and the Gaza Strip. The new lands gave Israel more secure borders. The

Ask: Why would violence against Jews lead to increased support for a Jewish state?

victory also showed that without unity, Arabs had little chance of driving the Israelis out of the Middle East.

PEOPLE IN HISTORY

11. Golda Meir moved to Palestine in 1921. She became involved in government and played an important role in helping to form the state of Israel in 1948. In 1969, Meir became Israel's first female prime minister. Under Meir, Israel beat back a surprise attack by Egypt and Syria in a conflict known as the October War of 1973.

12. In 1970, Anwar el-Sadat (AHN-wahr el-suh-DAHT) became president of Egypt. After the October War, Sadat decided to present a more **moderate,** or less extreme, view toward Israel. Sadat believed that Egyptians and Israelis could work out their differences. In 1979, Sadat met with Israeli Prime Minister Menachem Begin (meh-NAHK-uhm BAY-gin) and U.S. President Jimmy Carter. They signed a treaty under which Israel agreed to return the Sinai Peninsula to Egypt in exchange for peace. Many Arabs were upset about the treaty because they believed that Sadat had abandoned the Palestinian cause. In 1981, Sadat was killed by Muslims who claimed that he was a traitor to Arabs and Islam.

13. Peace with Egypt brought some relief, but tensions inside Israel increased during the 1980s. In 1987, Palestinians living in the occupied lands of Israel began an uprising called the *intifada.* Israel tried to put down the uprising without much success. Then, in 1989, the Soviet Union's decision to allow Jews to emigrate raised new possibilities. Suddenly, hundreds of thousands of Russian Jews poured into Israel. In addition, Israel staged a rescue operation that brought 14,000 Ethiopian Jews to Israel in 1991. Israelis welcomed the newcomers, but worried about how their economy would withstand the expense of resettling the immigrants. How do you think mass immigration affected the conflict between Israelis and Palestinians?

OIL: How did OPEC affect the price of oil from the 1970s to the 1990s?

14. Huge reserves of oil are the major source of wealth in the Arab countries of the Middle East. In the 1970s, Arab countries used the Organization of Petroleum Exporting Countries (OPEC) to keep world oil prices high. OPEC is a **cartel,** or a group that joins together to limit competition. By limiting the amount of oil they sold, OPEC countries sent oil prices soaring in the 1970s. Then in 1973, OPEC led an **embargo,** or a ban, on shipments of oil to nations that supported Israel during the October War.

15. By the 1980s, OPEC's influence had weakened. Many countries located new oil suppliers and became less dependent on OPEC. In the face of decreased earnings, the countries of OPEC became less unified and began increasing oil production. However, oil prices remained fairly high.

▼ Today, sources for oil are found in the countries shown in the graph below. Which group supplies the most oil?

WORLD PETROLEUM PRODUCTION

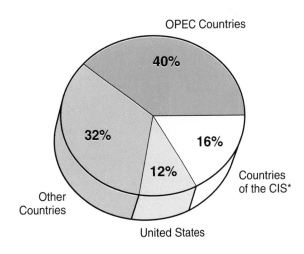

OPEC Countries 40%

Other Countries 32%

United States 12%

16% Countries of the CIS*

Total World Production: 22.2 billion barrels per day

* CIS = Commonwealth of Independent states
Source: *The 1993 Information Please Almanac*, Houghton Mifflin Co., Boston.

Background: Although the Arab oil fields are important to many countries, the leaders of the countries in the Persian Gulf refuse to have other countries station troops in the area to protect the fields.

643

A Geographic View of History

Oil in the Middle East In 1947, coal was the world's chief energy source. Today, coal has been replaced by oil. The oil-rich Middle East has gained new importance as a result of this change.

Read these facts about oil in the Middle East. Think about them as you study the map of oil fields and pipelines below. Then answer the questions that follow.

The Middle East produces more oil than any other region in the world. An estimated 14 million barrels of oil are produced there each day.

Five Persian Gulf nations dominate Middle East oil production. They are Saudi Arabia, Iran, Iraq, Kuwait, and the United Arab Emirates.

Three nations on the Mediterranean side of the Middle East produce little or no oil. They are Israel, Jordan, and Lebanon.

The Persian Gulf is the chief outlet for tankers carrying oil from terminals in the Middle East.

Pipelines offer other outlets for Middle East oil. Pipelines carry oil through Saudi Arabia, Turkey, Syria, and Jordan.

Most of the oil-producing countries in the Middle East belong to OPEC. Names of OPEC members are underlined on the map.

In 1973, Middle East OPEC members cut off oil supplies to supporters of Israel. Their cutoff led to gasoline and oil shortages throughout the world.

Now use the map below to answer the following questions. Write your answers on a separate sheet of paper.

1. Who are the leading oil producers in the Middle East?

2. Which of the oil-producing countries are members of Opec?

3. Where are most of the Middle East oil fields located?

4. Why is the Persian Gulf so important?

5. Why is the Middle East always in the news?

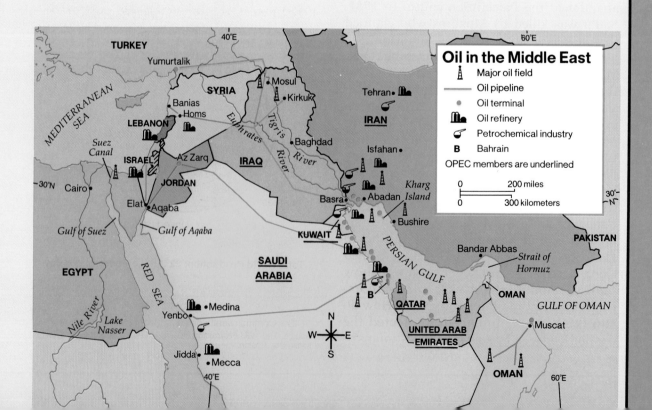

IRAN: How has religion made nationalism stronger in the Middle East?

16. Religious beliefs and principles have also played a large part in Middle East conflict. Islam has always been an important part of daily life in Arab countries. As countries modernized, however, they adopted many western ways. Some Islamic fundamentalists grew concerned. The fundamentalists believed that strictly adhering to the ways of Islam was best.

17. The most powerful fundamentalist in the Middle East was the Ayatollah Ruhollah Khomeini (koh-MAY-nee). Khomeini came to power in Iran in 1979 when opposition to the rule of Reza Shah Pahlavi (PAL-uh-vee) spread. Under Khomeini, an Islamic revolution began. The shah fled Iran and went to the United States. The Iranians rejected everything western and considered the United States an enemy.

SPOTLIGHT ON SOURCES

18. Public protests in Iran were frequent in the last years of the shah's reign. Fereydour Hoveyda, the former Iranian ambassador to the United Nations, describes a 1978 demonstration:

> On Sunday, December 11, hundreds of thousands of people held a procession in the center of Tehran. . . . Huge portraits were carried high. Slogans against the Shah rippled in the wind. . . ."Death to the Shah!" "Victory is near," "Khomeini is our leader," and so on. People from all walks of life could be found in the throng. . . .
>
> Next day the people of Iran flooded on the main streets of their principal towns in millions. Except in Esfahan, where violent clashes occurred, they all showed the same calm, the same discipline, and above all the same determination. But the Shah and his advisers seem not to have realized the deep significance of these events.
>
> —*The Fall of the Shah,* Fereydour Hoveyda

19. In 1979, Iran took a number of Americans **hostage** and demanded the return of the shah. The United States refused. After 444 days of captivity, the hostages were set free. During the hostage crisis, a border dispute prompted Iraq to attack Iran. The Iran-Iraq War lasted from 1980 to 1988 and caused much damage and loss of life, but no border changes.

THE PERSIAN GULF WAR: How did the Persian Gulf War lead to Middle East peace talks?

20. In August 1990, the world watched as Iraqi dictator Saddam Hussein invaded oil-rich Kuwait. With UN approval, the United States organized an international coalition to fight Hussein. Coalition forces began their attack on January 17, 1991. After just a few days, much of Iraq's defenses were destroyed. In desperation, Iraq launched Scud missiles at Saudi Arabia and at neutral Israel. Incredibly, Iraqi Scuds failed to cause major damage and failed to draw Israel into the war. Within six weeks, the coalition liberated Kuwait. Hussein remained in power, however, threatening the stability of the region.

21. After the war, the United States used its influence to promote Middle East peace talks. The peace talks began in October 1991. Delegates from Israel, Egypt, Lebanon, Jordan, and Syria attended. There was also a delegation of Palestinians. It was hoped that the talks would bring stability and order to the region.

OUTLOOK

22. Years of fighting have settled few problems in the Middle East. The issues that divide the nations of the Middle East are so complex that it will take a long time to work them out. Although not all countries of the region participated, the Middle East peace talks offered the hope of a future without war. Why do you think the ◄ United States is eager to end the conflicts in this region?

ESL/LEP Strategy: Ask students to imagine they are newspaper reporters covering the protest described in paragraph 19. Have them write a 100-word newspaper article describing events in Iran.

645

CHAPTER REVIEW

VOCABULARY REVIEW

Write each number and word on a sheet of paper. Then write the letter of the definition next to the word it defines.

1. cartel
2. embargo
3. hostage
4. anti-Semitism
5. moderate

a. hostility toward Jews
b. less extreme
c. a group that forms to limit competition
d. a person held by one party in a conflict as a pledge that promises will be kept or terms met by another party
e. a ban

Copy the sentences below and fill in the blanks with a vocabulary word.

A movement known as Zionism arose in Europe as a result of increasing _____ . Organized persecution that took the form of _____ in Russia encouraged Jews to seek a new homeland in Palestine. Life in the Middle East has been marked by conflict, with Arab and Israeli leaders moving back and forth between extreme and _____ positions. In the 1970s, the _____ known as OPEC led an _____ on shipments of oil to nations that supported Israel. Anti-western feelings erupted in Iran in the 1970s, when 53 Americans were taken _____ .

SKILL BUILDER: INTERPRETING A TIME LINE

Use the following time line to answer the questions below.

1. How long did the United Arab Republic last?
2. How many years after the Balfour Declaration was issued did Israel become a state?
3. When did France give up its last colony in the Middle East?
4. Which Middle East nation established a monarchy?

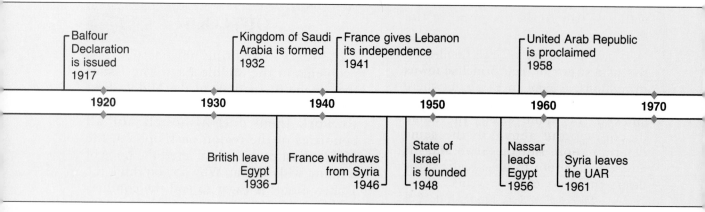

Balfour Declaration is issued 1917		Kingdom of Saudi Arabia is formed 1932	France gives Lebanon its independence 1941		United Arab Republic is proclaimed 1958	
1920	**1930**	**1940**	**1950**	**1960**	**1970**
	British leave Egypt 1936	France withdraws from Syria 1946	State of Israel is founded 1948	Nassar leads Egypt 1956	Syria leaves the UAR 1961

646

STUDY HINT   Make a list of all the events mentioned on the time line on page 640. Then list one outcome or result for each of the events.

SKILL BUILDER: CRITICAL THINKING AND COMPREHENSION

1. Main Idea

▶ Determine which item in each category below does NOT fit the category. Write that item on a sheet of paper.

1-1. Members of OPEC
  a. Saudi Arabia
  b. Kuwait
  c. Iran
  d. Israel

1-2. Arab leaders
  a. Anwar Sadat
  b. Gamal Abdel Nasser
  c. Golda Meir

2. Cause and Effect

▶ Determine which sentence in each pair of sentences is a cause. Write the sentence on a sheet of paper.

a. Arab nationalism grew stronger after World War I. Egypt, Syria, Lebanon, and Libya broke free from European rule.

b. Israel won control of the West Bank, Golan Heights, the Sinai Peninsula, and the Gaza Strip. Israel engaged in the Six-Day War with Arab nations.

c. OPEC nations agreed to limit the amount of oil they would sell. The price of oil jumped to record highs.

3. Generalizing

▶ On a sheet of paper, write the word that belongs in each blank.

3-1. _____ was important for the beginnings of both modern Egypt and Israel.
  a. nationalism
  b. Islam
  c. Judaism

3-2. The Ayatollah would NOT have disagreed with the shah of Iran on the issue of _____ .
  a. adopting western customs
  b. the price of oil
  c. adopting western law
  d. the importance of Islam in daily life

4. Point of View

Write a paragraph from the point of view of a Zionist. Explain why you want to live in Israel. Next, write a paragraph from the point of view of a Palestinian. Explain why you want part of Israel to be an independent Palestinian state.

ENRICHMENT

1. Use four outline maps of the Middle East and colored pencils to show the changing borders of Israel. On the first map, show Palestine before Israel became a nation. On the second map, show Israel in 1948. On the third map, show Israel after the Six-Day War. On the fourth map, show Israel as it is today. Label the countries that surround Israel.

2. For one week, cut out all the newspaper articles about the Middle East that you can find.

647

CHAPTER 3

Conflict in Southeast Asia

OBJECTIVE: Why has Southeast Asia seen so much conflict since the end of World War II?

1. After World War II, the nations of Southeast Asia had historic decisions to make. All had suffered greatly under the Japanese occupation and were eager for peace and independence. But in almost every case, they found themselves in more conflict after the war. Their leaders couldn't decide on what kind of government to have. Some wanted Western-style democracies with close ties to Europe and America. Others wanted Communist governments with close ties to China and the Soviet Union. The world powers, meanwhile, took great

▲ Ferdinand Marcos greets enthusiastic crowds at his inauguration as president of the Philippines on December 30, 1965.

interest in these conflicts: to control resource-rich Southeast Asia would greatly increase their power. Before long, much of the region would become a battlefield between the opposing forces of eastern and western powers.

The Philippines gains independence 1946	U.S. Congress passes Gulf of Tonkin Resolution 1964	Vietnam invades Cambodia 1979	Fidel Ramos elected president of the Philippines; Thailand's Democratic party wins a majority in election 1992	
1945	**1955**	**1965**	**1975**	**1985**	**1995**
	Indonesia declares independence 1949	Ferdinand Marcos becomes president of the Philippines 1965	Vietnam becomes Communist; Khmer Rouge begins reign of terror in Cambodia 1975	Ferdinand Marcos flees Philippines; Corazon Aquino becomes president 1986	Cease-fire agreement signed in Cambodia 1991

THE PHILIPPINES: How did Ferdinand Marcos interfere with a new democracy in the Philippines?

2. The first nation in Southeast Asia to gain its independence after World War II was the Philippines. On July 4, 1946, the Philippines became a republic. What do you think was the first challenge facing the Philippines? Fighting had destroyed half of the nation's cropland and much of its livestock. Almost a million people had been killed. Manila lay in ruins. **Speculators** (SPEK-yuh-layt-urz), or people who buy or sell in hope of making a profit, took advantage of the young government. The slow pace of reform upset many people, particularly farmers. It was not until 1953 that the Philippines elected its first effective leader, Ramon Magsaysay (mag-SY-sy).

3. Magsaysay went to work creating an honest and open government. He also defeated the Hukbalahap, or Communist land-reform movement. Before Magsaysay was able to complete his reforms, he was killed in an air crash in 1957. In 1965 Ferdinand Marcos was elected president. During his first term in office, Marcos built roads, schools, and bridges. He started a land reform program that gave ownership of land to poor tenant farmers. Marcos also provided poor farmers with technical assistance and money.

4. A major problem with the Marcos government was that it was corrupt. Marcos took a huge portion of tax money for his friends and himself. His family and friends held important government positions whether they were qualified or not. By 1972, Filipinos were tired of corruption in government. Demonstrations by angry citizens led Marcos to declare martial law. Martial law allows leaders to control the people by using military force. All newspapers and television were put under Marcos's control, and opposition leaders were arrested. Among them was Senator Benigno Aquino (ah-KEE-noh). Martial law lasted until 1981. By then, Marcos had changed the constitution so he could remain in power. Leaders who

opposed Marcos, such as Aquino, were sent into exile, or removed from the country. What do you think would happen if a United States leader declared martial law?

5. In 1983, Benigno Aquino tried to return from exile to the Philippines to prepare for elections scheduled for 1984. However, Aquino was assassinated as he stepped off the plane at the airport. Many people blamed President Marcos and the army. In 1985, the head of the Philippines army and 25 other people went on trial for the murder of Aquino. When the nation's supreme court dropped the charges, demonstrations against the government broke out. Distrust of Marcos grew with rumors that he and his family had hidden billions of dollars overseas. This money had clearly come from the nation's treasury and missing foreign aid. Marcos's popularity was at an all-time low.

6. In 1986, President Marcos held elections to prove that his power was still strong. His opponent was Aquino's widow, Corazon. According to international observers, Marcos and his followers lost, but this did not stop the pro-Marcos Philippine National Assembly from proclaiming him the winner. Most people, however, did not believe that he had won honestly. Demonstrations against Marcos became so powerful that he was forced to leave the country. How does the United States Constitution safeguard our election process?

PEOPLE IN HISTORY

7. Corazon Aquino became the new president of the Philippines in February of 1986. Aquino was born on January 25, 1933, north of Manila. She came from a family of wealthy land owners. When she was a teenager, she was sent to the United States to attend Roman Catholic convent schools in Philadelphia and New York City. In 1954, Aquino graduated from Mount St. Vincent College in New York and continued her law studies in Manila. While Aquino was supportive of her husband's career, she had

Background: Corruption in Philippine government reached new heights under Marcos. It is estimated that they took $500 million in government money every year. The government is now suing for this money.

649

▲ Corazon Aquino was president of the Philippines from 1985 to 1992. Despite widespread popularity, her government faced a number of coup attempts.

never thought of becoming a political leader herself. However, she quickly proved herself to be a strong and hard-working president. Aquino released many political prisoners. She appointed a group of leaders to develop a more democratic constitution. She also had the army swiftly end an attempt by Marcos supporters to take over the government.

8. Although life in the Philippines improved under Aquino's leadership, the country still faced many problems, including a weak economy and widespread poverty. Aquino's government was subject to a number of coup attempts by military dissidents and by a Communist guerrilla movement. After surviving a seventh coup attempt, Aquino decided not to run for president in upcoming elections. In 1992, Aquino's defense secretary Fidel Ramos was elected president.

INDONESIA: How is Indonesia trying to improve its economic condition?

9. Indonesia, a largely Islamic nation of islands, had to fight for its independence from the Netherlands. During World War II, the Japanese took control of Indonesia and imprisoned the colony's Dutch leaders. After Japan surrendered in 1945, Indonesia declared its independence from the Netherlands and chose Sukarno (soo-KAR-noh) as its president. However, the Netherlands did not want to give up the colony. After a long war, Indonesia won independence in 1949.

10. The Indonesians had trouble agreeing on a form of government to adopt. Sukarno responded by starting a system called "guided democracy." In this system, Sukarno was head of state, head of government, and head of the armed forces. Sukarno had started as a national hero in the fight for independence. However, he was not a wise economic leader. Indonesia has great natural resources such as rubber, petroleum, and coffee, but Sukarno did not train his people in industrial development. He also spent too much money on the armed forces and sports stadiums. Under his leadership, Indonesia came close to bankruptcy.

11. In 1965, there was an attempted Communist takeover. General Suharto (soo-HAR-toh) quickly defeated the rebels, killed thousands of Communists, and by 1967 forced Sukarno out of power.

12. Suharto was elected president in 1968 and has maintained power through an army-controlled government. Under Suharto, Indonesia's economy has improved even though it is still in debt. The discovery of oil and the government control over the oil industry have improved income from oil exports. Suharto have also encouraged good relations with Western nations that have supplied economic aid to Indonesia. In 1990, Indonesia established trade relations with China. Why do you ◄ think good trade relations are important to Indonesia?

13. Before World War II, Vietnam, Laos, and Cambodia were all part of the French colony of Indochina. During the war they fell into Japanese hands. The Vietnamese organized a resistance movement against Japan. Their organization was called the Viet Minh and its leader was Ho Chi Minh (HOH CHEE MIN). Although Ho Chi Minh was a Communist, he believed that independence for Vietnam could only be gained if all political groups united in a **coalition.** A coalition is a temporary alliance of separate parties for joint action. When the Japanese surrendered in 1945, Ho Chi Minh gained control of northern Vietnam and then declared independence for the entire nation.

14. The French fought to regain control of Vietnam. However, through intense guerrilla warfare lasting from 1946 to 1954, the Viet Minh defeated the French forces. At an international conference held in Geneva in 1954, Vietnam was temporarily divided into two nations. North Vietnam was headed by Ho Chi Minh. South Vietnam had a French-backed government. In addition, elections to reunite Vietnam were called for 1956. South Vietnamese president Ngo Dinh Diem (nyoh din DIHM) opposed the idea of national elections, claiming that the Communists would undermine fair elections in the north. No agreement was reached between North and South Vietnam, and no elections were held. Vietnam remained a divided nation.

15. Once divided, Vietnam did not remain peaceful. In the late 1950s, North Vietnam began to support the **Vietcong,** or Communist rebels, in South Vietnam. The United States responded by sending supplies and military advisers to South Vietnam. Under President Lyndon Johnson, however, U.S. involvement increased dramatically. In 1964, the United States claimed that a North Vietnamese ship fired on a U.S. ship in the Gulf of Tonkin off the coast of North Vietnam. The U.S. Congress passed the Gulf of Tonkin Resolution, which gave the President broad powers of war. By the end of 1965, almost 200,000 U.S. troops were fighting in South Vietnam. Casualties on both sides were heavy. The war soon became very unpopular with many people in the United States because it seemed impossible to win.

16. The **guerrilla warfare** tactics of the Vietcong proved to be highly effective against U.S. technology and firepower. Guerrilla warfare involves small bands of fighters who engage in surprise attacks and then retreat. In addition, South Vietnam's government enjoyed less and less support from the people. Critics felt the government of South Vietnam was corrupt.

17. In 1968, the scope of the war grew larger. In one large assault, called the Tet Offensive, large numbers of U.S. installations throughout South Vietnam

▼ Because of his role in freeing Viet Nam from France, Ho Chi Minh was respected by many Vietnamese, even those who were not Communists.

▲ American soldiers were at a disadvantage fighting against the Vietnamese guerrillas because of their lack of familiarity with the jungle terrain.

were attacked. After the attack, President Johnson announced that he believed the war was "unwinnable." By 1969, opposition to the war was so strong in the United States that the new President, Richard Nixon, announced a new policy called **Vietnamization.** The job of fighting would be handed over to the South Vietnamese army as U.S. troops were gradually withdrawn. As the United States withdrew troops from Vietnam, it began destroying Vietcong bases and supply routes inside neighboring Cambodia and Laos.

18. Exhausted by years of fighting, North and South Vietnam agreed to negotiate an end to the war. In 1973, they signed the Paris Accords, which called for a cease-fire and the return of U.S. prisoners of war. The United States agreed to withdraw all its troops. However, after the United States pulled out, fighting continued among the Vietnamese. By April 1975, the Communists controlled the entire country.

19. The rest of Indochina became Communist soon after North Vietnam gained control of the South. By 1975,

Communist guerrillas in Cambodia, called the Khmer Rouge, had won control of the country. The Khmer Rouge began a reign of terror, killing anyone they believed to be an enemy of the revolution. The people who lived in the cities were moved to rural areas. There, they were forced to work on communal farms under army supervision. The harsh conditions and resulting famine killed more than 2 million people.

20. In 1979, Vietnam invaded Cambodia and drove the Khmer Rouge west. The Khmer Rouge then launched a guerrilla war, conducted from bases in Thailand. During the late 1980s, Vietnam began pulling out its forces from Cambodia. By 1991, a UN-sponsored cease-fire agreement set up a national council to govern the country. Elections were scheduled for 1993, while a UN peace-keeping force helped Cambodia prepare for the transition.

21. After the Vietnam War, Vietnam was faced with overwhelming economic problems. Efforts to relieve these problems during the 1970s and 1980s proved ineffective. In addition, the Soviet Union began to decrease the amount of aid it offered to Vietnam. In the early 1990s, Vietnam began to experiment with free-market reforms to improve its economy. In addition, Vietnam announced efforts to help the United States find out about the fate of U.S. prisoners of war who had been

▶ missing since the Vietnam War. What effects do you think the fall of the Soviet Union had on Vietnam?

22. Laos, bordering Vietnam and Cambodia, was established as a neutral state when the French left Indochina in 1954. In 1975, however, it became Communist after years of conflict between pro-Western and Communist forces. Since the withdrawal of Western aid in 1975, Laos remains one of the poorest countries in Southeast Asia. In the early 1990s, Laos adopted a new constitution that dropped references to socialism. Laos has also been trying to implement free-market reforms to improve its economy.

▼ Thousands of refugees live in camps like these. What solutions can you think of for the refugee problems that Southeast Asia faces?

THAILAND: What challenges has Thailand faced since the end of World War II?

23. During World War II, Thailand was forced to become Japan's ally. After the war, Thailand's independence was restored, and since that time, the nation has had both elected and military governments. Thailand has had some Communist uprisings, but as a member of the Southeast Asia Treaty Organization (SEATO), it has remained pro-Western. During the Vietnam War, Thailand allowed the United States to use Thai air bases to launch attacks on Communist forces.

24. The aftereffects of the Vietnam War have left Thailand with many problems. Since 1975, thousands of refugees from Vietnam, Laos, and Cambodia have fled to Thailand. The Thai government has kept refugees in camps and provides them with food, clothing, and shelter.

25. In 1991, the military staged a bloodless coup and appointed a temporary government. But when a military leader was appointed prime minister, pro-democracy demonstrations broke out demanding an end to military rule. During a large demonstration in Bangkok, the military fired into the crowd, killing about 100 people. The prime minister resigned and new elections in 1992 gave the democratic party a slim majority.

OUTLOOK

26. After World War II, many colonies in Southeast Asia were granted their independence. However, wars broke out over the kinds of governments these countries should have. Both the United States and the Soviet Union wanted to influence the politics of these emerging nations. After the fall of communism in the Soviet Union, a number of Southeast Asian countries appeared to adopt more democratic governments. What effects do ◀ you think free-market reforms and more democratic governments will have on Southeast Asian nations?

ESL/LEP Strategy: Have students form groups. Give each group a slip of paper with the name of a key figure from Chapter 3. The groups should compile a list of word clues to the person's identity. Have groups list their clues on the chalkboard while the class tries to guess the person's identity.

653

CHAPTER REVIEW

VOCABULARY REVIEW

Write each of the following words on a sheet of paper. Then write the correct definition for each word. Use the glossary on pages 728–740 to help you.

1. speculators
2. coalition
3. Vietcong
4. guerilla warfare
5. Vietnamization

SKILL BUILDER: READING A MAP

Maps are pictures of the world's land areas. They show more than the shape of the land. They can also be used to find out what an area is like. Look at the map below. On a sheet of paper, write answers to the questions that follow.

1. What does the small map in the corner show?
2. What does the map key show about borders?
3. Which countries formed French Indochina in 1954?
4. Which countries were Communist before 1965?
5. What is the DMZ?

SKILL BUILDER: CRITICAL THINKING AND COMPREHENSION

 1. Classifying

► Listed below are statements about two Southeast Asian countries, the Philippines and Vietnam. Beside each statement write (P) if it applies to the Philippines and (V) if it applies to Vietnam.

a. Martial law was declared here in 1972.

b. Before World War II, this was a colony of France.

c. This country invaded Cambodia in 1979.

d. Popular demonstrations forced the leader of this country to flee after an election.

2. Sequencing

▶ Reread paragraphs 2 through 8 and put the following sentences in their correct order.

a. Benigno Aquino was assassinated at the airport in Manila.

b. Manila lay in ruins.

c. Marcos declared martial law.

d. Marcos and his followers lost the election, but the Philippines legislature proclaimed him the winner.

e. Corazon Aquino became president.

3. Drawing Conclusions

▶ Reread paragraphs 13 and 14 and list only the sentences which draw the correct conclusions from the facts.

a. The Vietnamese were as opposed to Japanese domination as they were opposed to French domination.

b. The French would have been willing to give up Indochina if Ho Chi Minh was replaced as leader of the opposition.

c. Ho Chi Minh wanted Vietnam to have a coalition government after it gained its independence.

▶ Reread paragraphs 9 and 10 and list only the sentences which draw the correct conclusions from the facts.

d. Sukarno had the support of nations such as the Soviet Union and China.

e. The government of Suharto has helped improve Indonesia's economy and its relations with the West.

f. Sukarno pushed too hard for rapid industrialization.

4. Making Judgments

▶ Indicate which of the following sentences are correct by writing *true* or *false* next to each statement.

a. At the end of World War II, most nations in Southeast Asia made a smooth adjustment to democracy.

b. Filipinos rejected Ferdinand Marcos because they felt his government was corrupt.

c. Dutch supported the Indonesian movement for independence.

d. The turning point of the Vietnam war was the Tet Offensive.

e. Since World War II, Thailand has become an important ally of the United States.

ENRICHMENT

1. Use library resources to find out more about one of the Southeast Asian leaders mentioned in this chapter. Before you begin, make a list of questions you would like to ask. Then write an imaginary interview with this leader that provides the answers to your questions.

2. Use library resources to prepare an economic activity map of Southeast Asia. Find out what resources each country has and what products it produces. Create symbols for the products and resources and put them in their correct location on your map. Label all countries and include a map key.

CHAPTER 4

Freedom Movements in Africa

▲ Jomo Kenyatta, the first president of Kenya, worked hard to improve the country's economy and standard of living.

OBJECTIVE: How has independence affected life in African countries?

1. Jailed for his role in the fight for black rights in South Africa, Nelson Mandela became a symbol of the injustice of apartheid, or separation of people by race. At his trial, he explained why he chose to fight. "All lawful modes of expressing opposition to [white rule] had been closed by legislation [law]," Mandela said. "We were placed in a position in which we had either to accept a permanent state of inferiority, or to defy the government. We chose to defy the law." In 1990, after serving a term of almost 28 years, Mandela was released. The government of South

Africa was showing signs of change. After World War II, most African nations won their independence. Since then, they have been struggling to develop stable economies and governments. How might stable government contribute to a stable economy? ◄

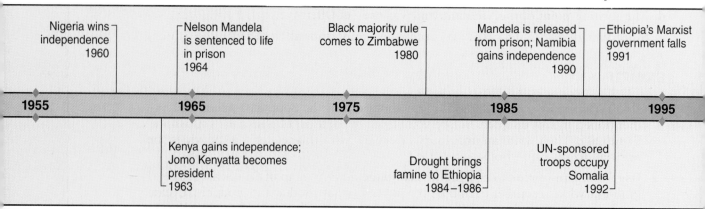

Nigeria wins independence 1960	Nelson Mandela is sentenced to life in prison 1964	Black majority rule comes to Zimbabwe 1980	Mandela is released from prison; Namibia gains independence 1990	Ethiopia's Marxist government falls 1991
1955	**1965**	**1975**	**1985**	**1995**
	Kenya gains independence; Jomo Kenyatta becomes president 1963	Drought brings famine to Ethiopia 1984–1986	UN-sponsored troops occupy Somalia 1992	

ESL/LEP Strategy: Ask students to role play Nelson Mandela at his trial. Have them review the statement he made at the trial (see paragraph 1) and express Mandela's ideas in their own words.

656

NATIONALISM: Why did African nations demand independence after World War II?

2. "Uhuru!" (freedom) was the cry of thousands of Africans as World War II came to an end. Many Africans felt that independence should be their reward for helping the Allies defeat the Axis powers in North Africa. Declarations like the Atlantic Charter further encouraged African hopes for freedom. The Atlantic Charter had been drawn up in 1941 by United States President Franklin Roosevelt and British Prime Minister Winston Churchill. It declared that the world's future depended on people being free to choose their own form of government.

3. The Soviet Union also encouraged independence by reminding Africans that Europeans had used African land to promote European wealth for years. The Soviets spread Marxist ideas and promised Africans a government in which all citizens would share in the nations' wealth.

4. Finally, Western countries began to call for an end to colonialism. They saw that Africans were willing to fight for their freedom. The westerners realized that the colonial system could not last much longer. The question was: How would power be transferred effectively to the Africans?

5. Independence came for the African colonies in the decades after World War II. Several African countries won freedom from Great Britain. These countries were Ghana, Gambia, Nigeria, Kenya, Southern Rhodesia (now Zimbabwe), Northern Rhodesia (now Zambia), Tanzania, Malawi, and the Sudan. Among the countries that gained independence from France were Morocco, Tunisia, Chad, Guinea, Dahomey (now Benin), Mali, Mauritania, Senegal, and Madagascar (now Malagasy). Portugal gave up Angola and Mozambique in southern Africa.

6. In some countries, the transfer of power came peacefully. In Nigeria, the British gradually increased the role of Nigerians in the government through a series of written constitutions. Independence came in 1960 without war. Gambia, which had served as an Allied navy base in the war, was given powers of self-government by the British governor. In 1965, Gambia became an independent country. It has a multiparty, democratic government.

7. Elsewhere independence came as a result of long and painful struggle. In the east African country of Kenya, tension began to grow in the early 1950s. British farmers occupied rich lands that the Kikuyu (ki-KOO-yoo) people regarded as their own. As their population grew, the Kikuyu demanded the right to move into this area, which had been set aside for white people. Instead of working with the Kikuyu to solve this problem, the British passed strict laws to keep them in line. Jomo Kenyatta, (JO-mo ken-YA-ta) a Kikuyu nationalist leader who had gone to school in Great Britain, spoke out against the British. He called for an end to **segregation,** the enforced separation of the races. Kenyatta also demanded

Daily life in . . .

Radio is an important source of information and entertainment in Africa today. "Africa Number 1," a radio station in Libreville, Gabon, plays a mixture of African, American, and European music. Unlike most African stations, which are government owned, "Africa Number 1" is a private business. On Saturday nights, millions of Africans tune in to "Africa Dance," a show of nonstop dance music. Some villages have parties at which people gather together to dance to radio music. While black American music is popular, African music groups get the loudest and most enthusiastic response. Most African music is written for dancing. Words are sung in English, French, or in one of the many tribal languages.

▶ voting rights for his people. Why do you think the British refused to leave Kenya?

8. By 1952, Kenyan anger turned into violence. Kikuyu terrorists, called Mau Mau (MAOW MAOW), began killing both British landowners and Kenyans who worked for the landowners. In 1953, Kenyatta was jailed on suspicion of being the Mau Maus' leader. As the violence continued, the British saw that major changes had to be made in their attitude towards Kenya. Blacks slowly won control of the government. In 1963, Kenya became independent and Jomo Kenyatta was elected president. Kenya's government has generally encouraged a free-market economy. In 1992, giving in to international pressure, Kenya held its first multiparty elections in 26 years.

9. Southern Rhodesia declared its independence from Great Britain in 1965, but prejudice and racial struggles continued to cause problems. Southern Rhodesia's government was in the hands of a white minority that began to pass laws restricting black peoples' rights. The white government came under attack from two rebel groups, the Matabele (muh-TAH-buh-lee), led by Robert Mugabe (moo-GAHB-ee), and the Shona (SHOH-na), led by Joshua Nkomo (en-KOH-moh), who outnumbered the Matabele. After years of war, blacks won majority rule in 1980 and changed the country's name to Zimbabwe. Mugabe was elected prime minister, promising to work with opponents. However, fighting between the Shona and the Matabele went on for several years. In 1986, Nkomo merged his forces with Mugabe's. In elections in 1990, Mugabe won another term as prime minister. However, Zimbabwe faces serious economic problems. In 1992, severe drought created even more difficulties.

SOUTH AFRICA: Why have black South Africans been unable to win full rights?

10. South Africa is a nation where the black majority has been oppressed by a small white minority. South Africa, a self-governing dominion of Great Britain until 1961, has practiced racial segregation for hundreds of years. Beginning in 1912, the government started passing laws limiting the rights of blacks and other non-whites. This policy of separating the races by law is called **apartheid** (uh-PAR-tayt), a word that means "separate." Apartheid defined four distinct racial groups: whites, blacks, Asians, and people of mixed racial heritage. Until the early 1990s, blacks had almost no voice in the government and were forced to live in segregated homelands away from white communities. These homelands contained the poorest land in the country. If a black South African needed to leave a homeland area to go to work, he or she had to have a pass. Without a pass, blacks risked being jailed. Criticism of the government and its policies was severely restricted within the country. In addition, the South African government extended apartheid to Namibia, a country on its western border that it controlled.

SPOTLIGHT ON SOURCES

11. Alan Paton, a South African novelist, wrote several books about his country's troubled racial situation. In *Cry, the Beloved Country*, published in 1948, he describes a white youth's thoughts about South Africa.

> It is hard to be born a South African. One can be born an Afrikaner [Boer, or of Dutch descent], or an English-speaking South African, or a coloured man, or a Zulu. One can ride, as I rode when I was a boy, over green hills and into great valleys. One can see, as I saw when I was a boy, the reserves of the Bantu people and see nothing of what was happening there at all. . . . One can read, as I read when I was a boy, the brochures about lovely South Africa, that land of sun and beauty sheltered from the storms of the world, and feel pride in it and love for it, and yet know

nothing about it at all. It is only as one grows up that one learns that there are other things here than sun and gold and oranges. It is only then that one learns of the hates and fears of our country. . . .

—Reprinted by permission of Charles Scribner's Sons, an imprint of Macmillan Publishing Company, from *Cry, the Beloved Country*, by Alan Paton. Copyright 1948 by Alan Paton; copyright renewed © 1976 Alan Paton

PEOPLE IN HISTORY

12. By the 1950s, black people began to call for better wages and many social changes. Black groups formed to protest the government's policies. One group was the African National Congress (ANC), led by Nelson Mandela (man-DEL-uh). Mandela used his skills as a lawyer to defend blacks against unfair treatment by the government. As leader of the ANC, Mandela orga-

nized a series of nonviolent protests in the early 1950s. The police responded to the protests with violence, and soon the marches turned into open street battles. In 1960, in the township of Sharpeville, the police fired on blacks marching to protest laws requiring passes. Sixty-nine blacks were killed and another 180 hurt.

13. After Sharpeville, Mandela and other black leaders decided to increase the pressure on the South African government. The ANC turned to **sabotage** (SAB-uh-tajh), or destructive action designed to hurt an enemy. The ANC blew up railroads and public buildings. From 1962 to 1990, Mandela was imprisoned for sabotage and for planning to overthrow the government.

14. Many countries used **boycotts** to try to force the South African government to end apartheid. A boycott involves refusing to have business dealings with a certain country or group. In 1986, the United States imposed **sanctions** discouraging U.S. companies from doing business in

▼ In the 1950s and 1960s, many African colonies won their freedom. What present-day countries of Africa never experienced colonial rule by European powers?

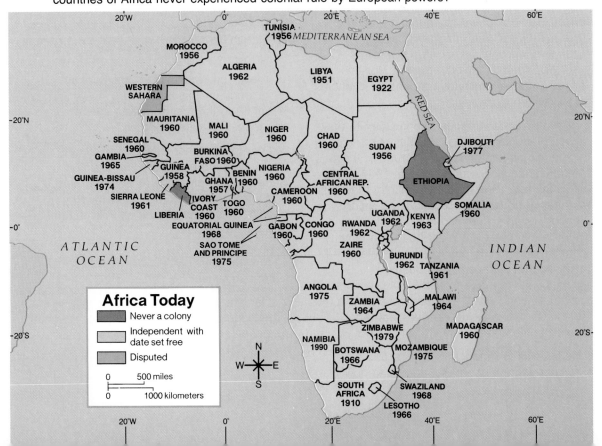

The Arts and Artifacts

▲ As president of Senegal, Senghor worked to improve the agriculture of his country and protested against international trade policies that were unfair to developing nations.

When you think of weapons that are used to fight revolutions and bring about social change, you might think first of powerful weapons such as tanks and guns. However, one of the most powerful weapons for change is the written word.

Leopold Sedar Senghor (seng-GOHR), now a world-famous poet, used his talent to help his people understand and be proud of their African heritage. Senghor, born in 1906, grew up in Senegal, West Africa, a country that was at the time under French control. As a child Leopold loved school and decided to become a teacher. As he grew older he began to write poetry. Leopold and other African poets believed that all races had valuable contributions to make to world civilization. He saw in African culture a certain passion and spirituality that is lacking in European and American life and culture.

On a visit to America in the late fifties, Senghor wrote a poem that described how African Americans could contribute to culture and life in New York City. A brief excerpt from this poem is given below.

"New York! I say New York, let black
    blood flow in your blood,
Let it rub the rust from your steely
    joint, like a life-giving oil"

Leopold Senghor was praised across the world. Through his poems the people of Senegal were given an African insight of life and the world. Loved and respected by his people, Senghor was elected President of Senegal in 1960.

1. In what ways can African culture enrich European culture?

2. Can you think of any poems or songs that Americans could use as symbols of national purpose or identity?

South Africa. Sanctions are measures designed to force a nation to change its policies.

15. Finally, in the 1980s and 1990s, the South African government showed signs of change. During the 1980s, several apartheid laws were repealed, including the pass laws and the law banning the ANC. In 1990, black leader Nelson Mandela was released from prison by Prime Minister Frederick de Klerk. That same year, Namibia gained independence. Soon, laws concerning ownership of property were scrapped, as were laws classifying South Africans into racial categories. Although progress has been made, South Africa has a long way to go before it achieves complete equality. Members of the ANC have clashed with another black activist group, the United Democratic Front (UDF), as well as with supporters of the Inkatha party. In addition, the white Conservative party, which is opposed to reform, is a growing force in South Africa. The government of South Africa must come to terms with the differences among these groups in order to bring peace and stability to South Africa.

PRESENT-DAY AFRICA: What challenges have African nations faced since World War II?

16. Since 1960, many African countries have met with new opportunities and difficult new problems. Some countries have had trouble setting up stable governments. Power struggles have led to revolts and civil wars. The problems of blending different cultures, each rich in honored traditions, are challenging. Many nations lack the money and technical knowledge to develop their own resources. Many are deeply in debt from having borrowed heavily from world banks. Some experts fear that this debt crisis could hold back their economies for many years.

17. Ethiopia is a country where political and economic troubles are connected. In the late 19970s, a Marxist government took power in Ethiopia. Large farms and planta-

tions were taken over by the government. However, crop production fell off sharply. When a huge drought hit Ethiopia from 1984 to 1986, **famine** struck. Famine is an extreme scarcity of food. Nations throughout the world sent aid, but distribution was hampered by rebels who were fighting against the government. In 1991, rebel forces finally defeated the Marxist government. They now face the task of rebuilding Ethiopia's economy and government. Another country plagued by famine and civil war is Somalia. Fighting among various Somali factions reached a climax in the early 1990s. In 1992 and 1993, international forces led by the United States occupied parts of Somalia with the mission of distributing food and medical aid.

18. Some countries, like Cote d'Ivoire (koht deev-WAHR) in central Africa, have prospered since independence. Cote d'Ivoire, meaning "ivory coast" in French, got its name from early trading in ivory there. Today Cote d'Ivoire has one of the strongest economies in Africa. Some business are owned by the government, while others are in private hands. Money from crops such as coffee and cocoa has enabled the country to modernize. The people of Cote d'Ivoire have one of the highest per capita incomes of any black African nation. Since 1960, President Felix Houphouet-Boigny (HOO-fway-BWAH-nyee) has led the country toward stability and prosperity.

OUTLOOK

19. After World War II, some African countries won independence through peaceful means, while others had to fight for freedom. The experiences of these new nations over the last 25 years have shown that independence does not necessarily bring prosperity. It may bring responsibilities that countries are not prepared for. War and hunger still threaten millions of lives in Africa every year. Why do you think the United States faced few of these problems in the 1780s?

CHAPTER REVIEW

Write each of the following sentences on a sheet of paper. Then fill in the blank with the word that best completes each sentence.

boycotts	famine	segregation
sanctions	sabotage	apartheid

1. In Kenya, Jomo Kenyatta called for an end to _____ , or the enforced separation of the races.

2. The South African policy of separating the races by law is called _____ .

3. After the Sharpeville massacre, the African National Congress turned from nonviolence to acts of _____ , blowing up bridges, railroads, and public buildings.

4. _____ involve refusing to have business dealings with a certain country.

5. _____ are measures designed to force a nation to change.

6. Between 1984 and 1986, Ethiopia was struck by _____ as a result of a huge drought.

SKILL BUILDER: USING A CHART

The following chart gives information about 10 countries in Africa. Information about the United States is given for comparison. Use the chart to answer the questions at the top of the next page.

FACTS ABOUT COUNTRIES

Country	Population (in millions)	Life Expectancy male	Life Expectancy female	Literacy (percentage)	Average Income (per person in dollars)
Egypt	53.3	60	60	45	655
Ethiopia	48.2	38	39	35	110
Kenya	23.3	53	58	47	230
Zaire	33.2	50	53	55/53	140
Chad	4.7	42	45	17	160
Ghana	14.3	50	54	30	410
Liberia	2.4	53	54	20	310
Nigeria	111.0	48	52	30	520
Zambia	9.7	66	59	66	540
United States	256.0	72	78	99	18,400

Source: *The World Factbook*, U.S. Government Printing Office, Washington.

Look at the map on page 659. Locate each country that you read about in Chapter 4 and name one leader that worked for independence in that country. Review the text if you need help.

1. Which African country has the highest average income per person?

2. Which African country has the highest literacy rate?

3. Compare the "life expectancy" and the "literacy" columns. Do the two sets of figures seem to be related? Explain your answer.

4. Which country has the lowest life expectancy? What situation in that country might explain this?

SKILL BUILDER: CRITICAL THINKING AND COMPREHENSION

▲ 1. Summarizing

1-1. Reread paragraph 1 and determine which of the following sentences gives the better summary of the paragraph.
   a. Mandela was jailed by the South African government for destroying the economy.
   b. By releasing Nelson Mandela from jail, the South African government showed it was willing to change some of its policies.

1-2. Reread paragraph 2 and determine which of the following sentences gives a better summary of the paragraph.
   a. Hopes for African nationalism were high following World War II.
   b. Roosevelt and Churchill started the African movement for freedom.

■ 2. Spatial Relationships

▶ Look at the map of Africa on page 659. Does the location of South Africa enable it to affect shipping in the area? Why or why not? Why do you think the South African government tries to influence what happens in such countries as Namibia and Botswana?

❯ 3. Predicting

▶ Reread paragraphs 10 through 15. On a sheet of paper, list the ways in which the South African government discriminated against black people. Then tell what you think conditions for blacks in South Africa will be like ten years from now.

▤ 4. Hypothesizing

a. Reread paragraph 18. On a sheet of paper, list what you found out about the economy of Cote d'Ivoire. Then tell how you think its economy might affect other countries in the area.

b. What do you think was the single most important factor in bringing about African independence? Give reasons for your answer.

ENRICHMENT

1. Choose five African countries and find out how each nation got its name and what its flag looks like. Make a chart of the names and their origins. Then make color drawings of the flags.

2. African nations have a rich cultural heritage of art, literature, music, and social life. Choose one African nation and do research on its art or social customs and how this culture is preserved today. Write a report on your research.

CHAPTER 5

Latin America's Role

▲ The city of Brasilia—shaped like a bow and arrow when viewed from the air—is famous for its modern architecture.

OBJECTIVE: How are Latin American nations working to solve the problems that they face today?

1. Which ethnic backgrounds are represented in your school—Asian, African, European, Hispanic? People with Hispanic backgrounds make up about 9 percent of our country's population. Hispanics are the fastest-growing ethnic group in the United States today. Immigrants from nations in the Western Hemisphere made up over 70 percent of the total number of immigrants to the United States in 1991. More than half of that percentage came from Mexico. For these immigrants, as it was for those who came before them, the United States is a land that presents new opportunities. For some, it also offers a refuge from political oppression. These new North Americans in turn bring their music, food, and social customs to enrich the cultural life of the United States.

⌐Kubitschek is elected president of Brazil 1955	Oil deposits are discovered in Mexico; Argentina falls under military rule 1976⌐	⌐Argentina invades the Falklands 1982	⌐Brazilian President Carlos Menem puts down military uprising 1990

1955	**1965**	**1975**	**1985**	**1995**

Castro comes to power in Cuba 1959	Alfonsin is elected president of Argentina 1983	Brazil elects a civilian government for the first time in 21 years 1985	

Ask: Why would the United States seem to be an attractive place to Latin American immigrants?

CHANGING GOVERNMENTS: Why have the governments of Latin America changed so often?

2. The history of Latin America has been one of almost constant turmoil and change. This turmoil can be traced to Latin America's colonial heritage. The Spanish and the Portuguese did not encourage their Latin American colonies to practice self-government. Instead, they kept firm control over the colonists' lives. With no democratic traditions to guide the people, military dictators often took power after the colonies gained their independence. If the people became dissatisfied with their government, their only option was to overthrow it. However, one dictator was usually succeeded by another. Until the 1980s, half of the Latin American countries were ruled by military dictatorships. In addition, the sharp contrasts in standards of living that existed in colonial times still exist in many ▶ parts of Latin America today. How might these differences in standards of living also lead to political unrest?

3. The political history of Brazil is in many ways typical of politics in other Latin American countries. Since World War II, Brazil has been ruled by dictators, military leaders, and leaders chosen through democratic elections. Some of these leaders de-

voted their energies to improving Brazil's economy while others were concerned mainly with keeping themselves in power.

4. Brazil is the largest country in South America, and it is very rich in natural resources. Its potential for development is enormous. One leader who made genuine progress in improving Brazil's economy and government was President Juscelino Kubitschek (KOO-buh-chek). Kubitschek was elected in 1955 and served until 1961. During that time, he helped many new industries get started in Brazil, including the steel, automobile production, and shipbuilding industries. By the beginning of the 1960s, Brazil had become one of the major industrial nations among the world's developing countries.

5. The project that was most important to Kubitschek was the building of a new national capital in Brasilia, deep in the interior of the country. It was Kubitschek's hope that the relocation of the capital would bring economic growth to a huge area of undeveloped wilderness. The national capital moved from Rio de Janeiro to Brasilia in 1960. Today Brasilia is a thriving city with striking modern architecture.

6. During Kubitschek's administration, democracy flourished. People's rights were protected, and freedom of speech allowed criticism of the government. However, this

Daily life in . . .

Brazil's efforts to modernize are coming in conflict with a small but vocal group of Amazon Basin Indians known as the Kaiapo. Numbering about 3,600, the Kaiapo have lived in this tropical rain forest region for thousands of years, raising crops. The discovery of gold and forests of mahogany on their land has brought offers of big money from prospectors and lumber companies. Until recently, the Amazon region was relatively untouched by modern civilization. As this region becomes more developed, the rain forest is beginning to

disappear. It is being replaced with highways, cattle ranches, mines, and hydroelectric dams.

The concern of the Kaiapo is twofold. They want to protect their habitat, and they want to make sure that they are paid fairly for the resources taken from their lands. The Kaiapo have done what few of Brazil's Indians have done. They have traveled to the seat of white power, Brasilia, to protest government policies they oppose. Dressed in their body paint and headdresses, the Kaiapo have learned to use white political ways to protect their way of life.

Background: Brazil and Paraguay together are building the world's largest hydroelectric dam, The Itaipu Dam, on the Parana River at a cost of $15 billion. Borrowed money is paying for this project, to be completed in the 1990s.

atmosphere of openness did not last. Military leaders became worried that the government favored Marxism. By 1964, the military had seized power, dominating Brazil's government until 1985. Political parties were outlawed and the powers of Congress and the courts were reduced. Newspapers and television were **censored**, or examined, edited, and controlled, by the government. Critics of the government often disappeared without a trace. When a depression struck Brazil's economy in the mid-1970s, public dissatisfaction with the government forced the military to relax its control. A policy of *abertura* (ah-bair-TYOO-rah) was begun. *Abertura* meant "opening" the door to democratic reforms.

7. In 1985, Brazil elected its first civilian government in 21 years. The new president-elect was Tancredo Neves. But Neves died shortly after the election and Jose Sarney (sahr-NAY) became president. Sarney began to restore democracy to Brazil, enacting a new constitution in 1988. In 1989, Fernando Collor de Mello was elected president. Collor's main goals were to reduce inflation and debt. However, in 1992, he resigned amid charges of bribery. The future of Brazil rests on how it resolves a number of issues, including population growth, an unstable government, and a poor economy. Which of these issues might be most difficult to solve?

GROWING DEBTS: Why are large debts a problem for so many Latin American nations?

8. During the 20th century, Latin American governments realized that the way to raise the standard of living for their people was to promote industrial growth. Many people of Latin America were living in severe poverty. Public services such as sewer systems, schools, and highways needed to be built quickly. However, to accomplish this the Latin American nations had to borrow huge amounts of money, particularly from the United States. In 1984, Brazil owed foreign banks $93 billion. In 1985, Argentina's debt amounted to $48 billion

and was growing at a rate of $150 million a month. Latin American countries expected to have no problem repaying the loans because their economies would be growing. Many did experience periods of growth, but government upheavals and a worldwide **recession** in the early 1980s brought improvement to a halt. (A recession is a period of reduced economic activity.) Latin American countries were unable to pay all of their debts, and their economies began to suffer. Inflation forced the people to pay high prices for basic needs such as food, housing, and clothes. How can problems caused by a growing debt be avoided?

9. Argentina, the second-largest country in South America, has to deal with a growing debt, political instability, and military coups. For many years following World War II, Juan Peron, a popular dictator, was in charge of the country. In 1973, elections were held, and Peron became president. When Peron died in 1974, his widow Isabel, his third wife, succeeded him. In 1976, the military seized power and ruled Argentina for almost eight years. The military government took away many of the measures that had protected Argentina's industries from foreign competition. As a result, many of the country's largest companies went bankrupt.

10. In 1982, Argentina's military government challenged British rule of the Falkland Islands, which are located off the coast of Argentina. This action was taken partly to turn the country's attention away from the failing economy. After ten weeks of war, Britain defeated Argentina.

11. The poor economy and Argentina's defeat in the Falklands forced the military government to hold elections in 1983. Civilian government was restored with the election of Raul Alfonsin. Alfonsin resigned the presidency in 1983 because he failed in his main goal of reducing debt and inflation. Newly elected President Carlos Menem took office and put through a tough new program. Menem was able to put down a military uprising in 1990, but has failed to halt rising inflation.

Background: Juan Peron ruled Argentina from 1946-1955 and 1973-1974. His first wife, Eva, played an important role in his government and was wildly popular. Peron, however, stole much of Argentina's wealth.

SOCIAL CONDITIONS: How have economic
and social conditions changed in Latin
America in recent years?

12. Adequate living conditions are not available for many people in Latin America. Latin American cities are crowded, and housing shortages are common. There are not enough doctors to provide medical care to the poor, and there is little chance for the poor to go to school.

13. Severe poverty is a problem both in the cities and in the country. The greater part of the wealth in most Latin American countries is held by a very small group of people. Living in the cities are large groups of people who cannot find work and who lack skills for modern-day jobs. In the country, living conditions are often worse than in the cities. Many people do not own land but rent it. When crops are bad, times are very hard for small farmers. Modern farm machinery is too expensive for most Latin American farmers to buy.

14. Latin America is a region rich in natural resources, but poor in skilled labor. Although many Latin Americans have been trained as engineers, scientists, and technicians, there are still not enough of these skilled workers. Yet Latin Americans often will not allow foreign investors to help them develop their natural resources. They reason that foreign companies would develop their own products in Latin America. They fear that these companies would use Latin American labor but the profits would not stay in the country to help Latin Americans.

15. In Mexico, a relatively stable government has brought about many positive changes for the Mexican people. Mexico is a democracy, but it has only one political party with any influence. This is the Institutional Revolutionary Party (PRI), which has been in power for over fifty years. Recent presidents of Mexico have been successful in their efforts to bring their country into a leadership position among developing nations. The Mexican government has given much attention to education. As a

▲ Mexico City is the oldest city in North America, and one of the most highly populated cities in the world.

result, Mexico has sharply increased its literacy rate in recent years. Public health programs are in place to educate people about proper nutrition and how to fight disease. The average life expectancy for Mexicans has increased.

16. In 1974, large oil deposits were discovered in southern Mexico. This resulted in a period of sudden prosperity. The Mexican government borrowed huge sums from foreign banks to finance development projects. In the early 1980s, the price of oil fell, and Mexico found itself deep in debt. The government has taken steps to stabilize Mexico's economy, but large-scale unemployment and a major earthquake in Mexico City in 1985 have slowed progress.

COMMUNISM: Why is communism a threat
to the stability of Latin America?

17. Democratic governments exist in some Latin American countries. However,

Ask: What steps will Latin American nations have to take in order to improve the standard of living?

communism and repressive military dictatorships have gained a strong foothold in a number of Latin American countries. Many of the democratic governments, in Central America especially, are weak. The military is really the power behind the president in these countries.

18. Cuba was the first country in Latin America to experience a Marxist revolution. Corruption plagued the Cuban government throughout the 1940s and 1950s. The dictatorship of Fulgencio Batista (buh-TEES-tuh) outlawed criticism and made protest an extremely dangerous and often fatal activity. In spite of the danger, opponents of Batista organized a revolutionary movement under the Marxist leadership of Fidel Castro.

PEOPLE IN HISTORY

19. Fidel Castro was a Cuban revolutionary who became a symbol for the Socialist Revolution. Castro led his first attack against the Batista regime in 1953. The attack failed, and Castro and his followers organized a guerilla campaign and overthrew Batista. On January 1, 1959, Batista was forced to leave Cuba. Castro, now Cuba's leader, promised to end corruption, bring back democracy, and hold new elections.

20. Castro was a very popular leader. He raised salaries, gave land to the poor, and cut the cost of services such as electricity. He also seized all farms, industries, and sugar plantations, many of which were owned by business people from the United States. These actions forced the United States to break diplomatic relations with Cuba in 1961. Why do you think that the ◄ United States was so angry with Castro? However, when Castro turned to the Soviet Union for assistance, he lost the support of many Cubans. A million people fled Cuba when, in 1961, it became the first nation in the Americas to have a communist form of government. The United States

▼ Political problems plague the many small nations of Central America and the Caribbean. What nations in Central America face both the Pacific Ocean and the Caribbean Sea?

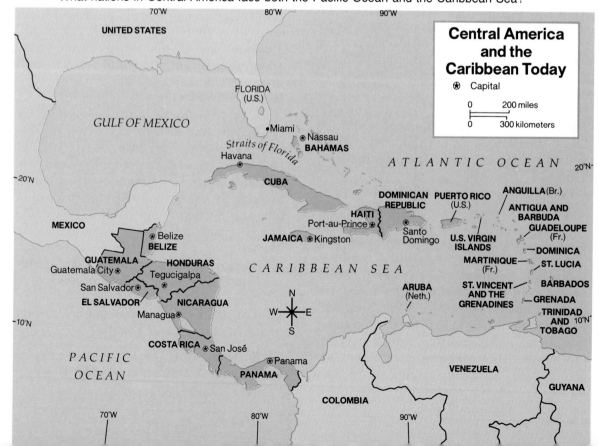

cut off all trade with Cuba, hoping to force Castro out of office.

SPOTLIGHT ON SOURCES

21. In 1961, the United States tried to overthrow Castro by training Cuban exiles to invade Cuba and supplying them with weapons. Two weeks before the invasion took place, President John F. Kennedy issued a statement. It explained why the United States regarded the situation in ▶ Cuba as threatening. Do you think Kennedy's concerns were reasonable?

> The present situation in Cuba confronts the Western Hemisphere with a grave and urgent challenge. This challenge does not result from the fact that the Castro government in Cuba was established by revolution. The hemisphere rejoiced at the overthrow of the Batista tyranny, looked with sympathy on the new regime, and welcomed its promises of political freedom and social justice for the Cuban people. The challenge results from the fact that the leaders of the revolutionary regime betrayed their own revolution, [and] delivered that revolution into the hands of powers alien to the hemisphere. . . . It is the considered judgment of the Government of the United States of America that the Castro regime in Cuba offers a clear and present danger to the . . . Americas.
>
> —from *America in the Cold War*, edited by Walter LaFeber. Copyright © 1969 by John Wiley.

22. The invasion, which has been called the Bay of Pigs, was a complete failure. Castro's army quickly defeated the invaders. The Soviet Union declared that it was committed to defend Cuba's independence from American intervention. In 1962, the Soviets began to secretly ship nuclear missiles to Cuba. These missiles had a range long enough to hit American cities. As you have read in Unit 12, Kennedy discovered the Soviet action and forced the Soviets to remove the missiles. However, the Cuban Missile Crisis nearly resulted in war. The threat of invasion has caused Castro to distrust the United States ever since.

23. Until the fall of communism in the Soviet Union and Eastern Europe, Cuba relied on the billions of dollars of aid the Soviet Union sent each year. Since the breakup of the Soviet Union, Cuba has maintained a Communist government, with Castro at its head. But the country's economy has suffered without aid from the Soviet Union. How has the breakup of the ◀ Soviet Union affected Cuba?

24. The United States has been actively involved in Caribbean Basin affairs in the 1980s and 1990s. During the Cold War, the United States tried to encourage democracy and fight the spread of communism. In 1983, U.S. forces invaded Grenada, an island nation in the Caribbean, and brought down Grenada's Marxist government. The United States also sent money and military aid to the **contras,** a group of Nicaraguans who tried to overthrow Nicaragua's Marxist government. In addition, the United States sent aid to El Salvador and Guatemala in an attempt to keep their weak democratic governments in power.

OUTLOOK

25. Many people criticize the United States for interfering in Latin American affairs. They claim that it causes anti-American feelings among Latin Americans. As a result of this policy they argue that the United States often supports Latin American governments that are as oppressive as any communist government. Supporters of American intervention in Latin American affairs argue that such involvement helps stop the spread of communism. They claim that the United States is helping people who want democracy but feel powerless to get it. Why are the politics of Latin America ◀ of special interest to the United States?

Background: Fidel Castro was an excellent baseball player. He went to Pittsburgh, Pennsylvania, and tried out for one of the Pirates' farm teams. When he did not make the team, he returned to Cuba.

669

CHAPTER REVIEW

VOCABULARY REVIEW

Write each number and word on a sheet of paper. Then write the letter of the definition next to the word it defines.

1. recession
2. censor
3. contras
4. *abertura*

a. to repress; to examine, edit, and control
b. a rebel group of Nicaraguans trying to oust Nicaragua's communist government
c. a period of reduced economic activity
d. a policy of opening the door to democratic reform

SKILL BUILDER: INTERPRETING A TIME LINE

Use the time line below to answer the following questions.

1. How long did the military rule Argentina?
2. Which Latin American nations has the United States invaded since the 1950s?
3. Which Latin American leader was responsible for the construction of Brasilia?
4. How long after Castro came to power did the United States break off relations with Cuba?
5. Which Latin American leader has been in power longest? How long has he been in power?

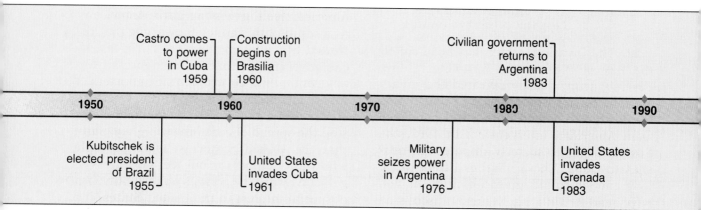

Castro comes to power in Cuba 1959 — Construction begins on Brasilia 1960 — Civilian government returns to Argentina 1983

1950 — 1960 — 1970 — 1980 — 1990

Kubitschek is elected president of Brazil 1955 — United States invades Cuba 1961 — Military seizes power in Argentina 1976 — United States invades Grenada 1983

SKILL BUILDER: CRITICAL THINKING AND COMPREHENSION

1. Classifying

▶ Reread the chapter. List the countries of Latin America under the correct headings.

a. Countries with Communist Governments   **b.** Countries with Debt Problems

▶ Write a heading for each of the following sets of information.

c. Kubitschek, Sarney, Alfonsin   **d.** Batista, Castro, revolution

2. Generalizing

▶ The generalization below is followed by three statements. Write *valid* if the statement supports the generalization, write *invalid* if it does not support the generalization.

Generalization: Latin America's efforts to modernize have failed.

a. Even though it is rich in natural resources, Latin America does not have enough people with the skills to develop these resources.

b. Fear of foreign control has kept some Latin American countries from allowing foreign businesses to develop the natural resources.

c. Improvements made through huge loans have not enabled Latin American countries to repay these loans, let alone made the countries rich.

3. Making Judgments

▶ Reread paragraphs 18-23. Then write answers to the following questions. Give reasons for your answers.

a. Did Batista deserve to stay in power?

b. Were Castro and his followers justified in conducting a guerrilla campaign to take over the Cuban government?

c. Did President Kennedy have sound reasons for considering Cuba a threat?

4. Fact *versus* Opinion

▶ Reread paragraphs 18-23. Write *fact* or *opinion* for each of the following statements.

a. Castro took complete power in Cuba.

b. The United States should never have backed the Bay of Pigs invasion.

c. Cuba and the United States have had little contact since the early 1960s.

d. The Soviet Union gave aid to Cuba.

ENRICHMENT

1. Follow events in one Latin American nation for a week by cutting out newspaper or magazine articles that relate to this nation. At the end of the week, write a summary of the latest developments.

2. Select a Latin American country that was not discussed in this chapter, and locate resources in the library that will tell you about this country's government and economy. Then write a report based on your research.

UNIT REVIEW

SUMMARY

By the time World War II ended, most world governments had come to believe in self-determination for all people. This factor, combined with the growth of nationalism, led to independence for countries all over the world. However, independence did not always bring peace and prosperity. War, revolutions, and terrorism continue in many parts of the world. In South Asia, conflicts between different ethnic and religious groups have caused unrest and violence. In South Africa, inequality for non-whites is still a serious problem. After independence, conflicts between Communist and non-Communist forces created war and instability in Southeast Asia. Israel became a new nation in the Middle East after World War II, but border disputes with the Palestinians have kept the area in a state of conflict. Mexico, Brazil, and some countries of Central America have established democratic governments. These regions contain some of the world's most valuable resources. What happens in these regions is important to the countries that exist there and also to a world dependent on their resources.

SKILL BUILDER: READING A MAP

Use the map to answer the questions. Write your answers on a sheet of paper.

1. What is the capital of Iraq?
2. Which countries labeled on the map have coastlines on the Red Sea?
3. Why might Lebanon easily become involved in the struggles between Israel and the Palestinians?
4. What countries have coastlines on the Persian Gulf?
5. If Iran wanted to attack Iraq's oil tankers as they sail east through the Persian Gulf, where would Iran have the best chance of finding one? Why?

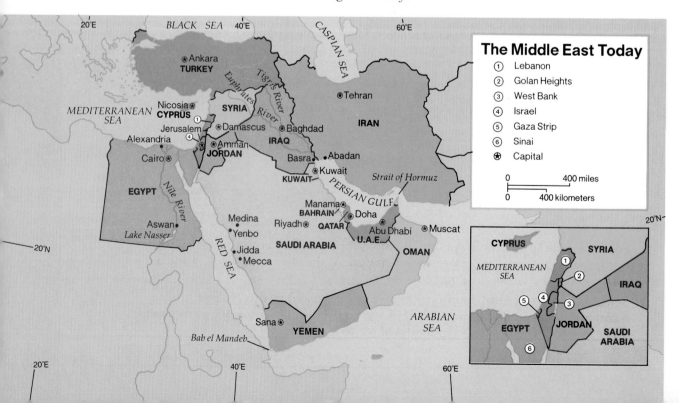

SKILL BUILDER: CRITICAL THINKING AND COMPREHENSION

 1. Classifying

▶ Classify the following countries according to what region they are located in.

Brazil   Ethiopia   Cuba   Argentina
Cambodia   Mexico   The Philippines   Zimbabwe

2. Making Judgements

▶ Number your paper **a** through **e**. Indicate which of the following sentences are correct by writing *true* or *false* next to each letter. Base your judgments on information you find in Unit 13.

a. At the end of World War II, few thought the nation of Israel should be founded.

b. In Central America, democracy has always been successful.

c. In Sri Lanka, conflicts between the Tamils and the Sinhalese have been a continuing problem.

d. Racial conflicts are not a problem in Africa, since so many different races live together there.

e. The discovery of oil deposits in Mexico solved all its financial problems.

3. Fact *versus* Opinion

▶ Write the letters **a** through **d**. Then write an **F** for fact or an **O** for opinion for each of these statements.

a. Communist countries such as the Soviet Union supported Marxist governments throughout the world.

b. President Marcos took government funds for his personal use.

c. The United States should stop interfering in the affairs of Latin American nations.

d. The government of South Africa has begun to change its policies about apartheid.

e. Islam is an influential religion in Iran.

4. Generalizing

▶ Re-read the "Spotlight on Sources" feature in Chapter 1, paragraph 13. Write a generalization based on this source reading.

ENRICHMENT

1. Divide into two groups. One group should research the views and programs of Corazon Aquino. The other should research the views and programs of Ferdinand Marcos. Then hold a mock news conference. One person from the Aquino group should interview Marcos. A person from the Marcos group should interview Aquino.

2. Make a Modern Nationalism Challenge game. Form two teams. Each team should write five questions having to do with the material presented in Unit 13 on one side of 3 x 5 index cards. Write the answers on the back of each card. Put all the cards in a box. Mix them up and take turns asking each team to answer one of the questions.

UNIT 14

ESL/LEP Strategy: Ask students to make flashcards for the vocabulary words in this unit. Have them write the word on one side and the definition on the other. When students finish, discuss how some words have different meanings for each student.

GLOBAL CHALLENGES IN THE AGE OF TECHNOLOGY

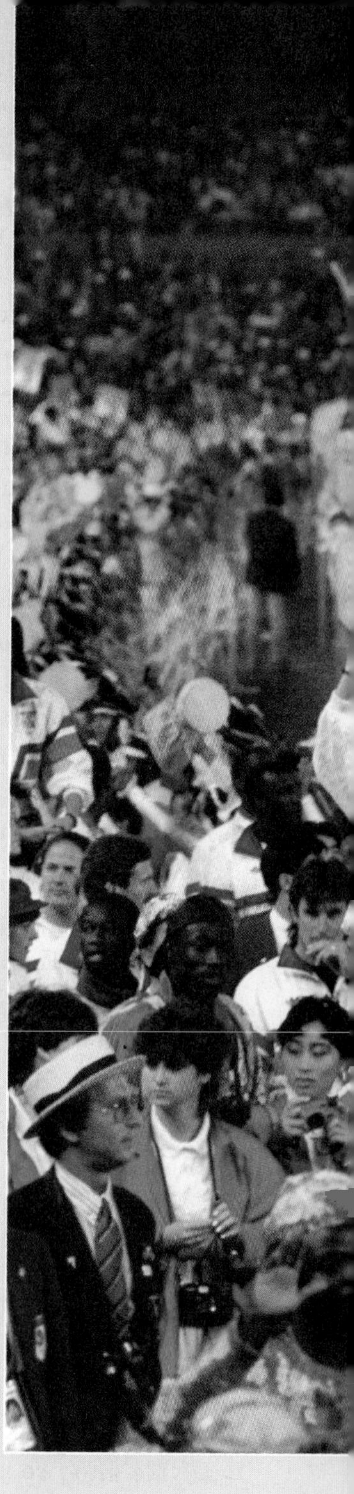

OBJECTIVE: Important changes have taken place among the major nations of the world in recent years. Why are the developments in these countries important in shaping the world's future?

European Community is formed 1957

Nixon becomes the first U.S. President to travel to Communist China 1972

1955 | 1960 | 1965 | 1970 | 1975

U.S. astronaut John Glenn orbits the earth 1962

Deng Xiaoping becomes leader of Communist China 1978

▲ Every four years athletes from around the world gather in a spirit of friendly competition at the Olympic Games.

┌Margaret Thatcher is
elected prime minister
of Great Britain
1979

┌Gorbachev becomes
general secretary of
the Soviet Union
1985

┌Soviet Union breaks
up into 15 independent
republics
1991

World population┐
expected to reach
6.1 billion
2000

1980   **1985**   **1990**   **1995**   **2000**

┌Ronald Reagan
becomes
U.S. President
└1980

George Bush is
elected President
of the United States
1988┘

Persian
Gulf War
1991┘

┌Bill Clinton becomes
President of the United States
└1992

CHAPTER 1

Western Europe Prospers

OBJECTIVE: How have Western European countries become world leaders in industry and trade under democratic governments?

1. Great Britain and France are separated by a narrow body of water called the English Channel. For centuries, the Channel protected the British island nation from invasion by sea. The Chunnel has changed that. The Chunnel is a 31-mile (50-kilometer) long underwater tunnel that connects Great Britain and France. Trains and cars carry passengers through the tunnel. Then, special high-speed trains at either end of the tunnel take people to London or Paris. For the first time in

▲ People from all over the world visit Paris to see its beautiful art, buildings, and monuments, such as the Arc de Triomphe.

history, Great Britain is linked directly to Europe. In the past, the British regarded the English Channel as an important defense. For more than 900 years, the Channel prevented European armies from invading Great Britain. Today, however,

European Community or "Common Market" is organized 1957

Margaret Thatcher is named British Prime Minister 1979

Mitterrand is elected president of France 1981

John Major takes over as British prime minister 1990

1955   1965   1975   1985   1995

European Community holds first direct elections to European Parliament 1979

Germany reunified 1990

Great Britain has close ties with the nations on the continent of Europe. In fact, the new tunnel is a symbol of the growing unity and close ties among the nations of Western Europe.

EUROPEAN UNITY: In what ways are the nations of Western Europe working together today?

2. The experience of two devastating wars had persuaded the people of Western Europe to move toward unity. The countries of Western Europe include several of the world's leading industrial nations. The peoples of Western Europe enjoy freedom and live under democratic governments they elect. They are among the best-educated and most productive people in the world. Yet less than 50 years ago, at the end of World War II, much of Western Europe lay in ruins. During the 1950s and 1960s, the countries of Western Europe worked hard to rebuild their governments, their cities, and their economies. The experience of two devastating wars persuaded the people of Western Europe to move toward greater unity. In order to solve the many problems they faced, the people of these countries tried to forget their past wars and rivalries. They put aside their feelings of nationalism and began to work together. During these years, they also joined together to form the NATO alliance to defend themselves against the threat of Soviet expansion.

INTERDEPENDENCE: How can growing economic cooperation reduce the risks of war among nations?

3. Since World War II a major revolution in economic cooperation has taken place among European nations. In 1957, six countries of Western Europe formed the European Community in order to increase production and trade. Today, Germany, France, Great Britain, Italy, Spain, Greece, and six other countries belong to this European Community. Five other nations— Sweden, Norway, Austria, Switzerland, and Iceland—belong to a separate trading group that also works with the European Community. How had these countries acted toward each other in the past?

4. The purpose of the European Community is to encourage **free trade** in Western Europe. Free trade means there are no tariffs on products traded among member countries. In addition, the member countries agreed to put a tariff on all goods imported from nations outside the European Community. By combining the efforts of many countries, the European Community has become one of the world's largest markets. The Community turns out more goods and services each year than either the United States or Japan. It produces nearly one fourth of the world's manufactured goods. In fact, the European Community accounts for nearly 20 percent of international trade, making it the largest trading power in the world. Its success has encouraged other countries, including Sweden, Austria, and Turkey, to apply for membership.

5. The actions of the European Community go beyond free trade. During the early 1990s, the Community adopted regulations have made it easier for businesses and industries to set up offices and factories in member nations. Other areas the European Community hopes to regulate include transportation, energy, environmental protection, education, and technology. In addition, by the end of this century, many of the member countries may be using the same **currency** (KUR-ren-see), or money. Putting these policies into action is often difficult. Policies that benefit one nation may not benefit another. Compromise and communication are essential if the Community is to succeed.

6. The countries of the European Community have also set up the beginnings of a common government for the people of Western Europe. In 1979, voters in member nations elected delegates to a European Parliament. However, the European Parliament does not have the power to enforce the laws it makes. Many Europeans hope that

Activity: Have students consult an encyclopedia or reference book on Italy, Spain, or Greece to prepare a brief report on these members of the European Community.

677

some day the Community will form a
▶ United States of Europe. What might be
the advantages of this type of union?

GREAT BRITAIN: What important changes have been made in the lives of the British people in recent years?

7. During the 1980s, the Conservative party gained the majority in the House of Commons. Its leader, Margaret Thatcher, became prime minister. This Conservative government has made some changes in the socialist economy of Great Britain. Thatcher strongly believed that people should work hard, save money, and be responsible for improving their own lives. She also believed that the British government had gained too much power over its citizens' lives. For example, the government owned many of Britain's most important industries, including shipbuilding, steel manufacturing, mining, and air transport.

▼ Margaret Thatcher headed the British government from 1979 to 1990. Her forceful manner won her the name *Iron Lady*.

Thatcher believed that these industries would be run better and make larger profits if private companies took them over. Therefore, she asked the government to sell many of these industries to private groups. Nearly 20 percent of the British people bought shares of stock in these new companies. Thatcher also believed that the power of British labor unions had become too great. In the mid-1980s, several long strikes by coal miners and truck drivers caused hardships in Great Britain. When Thatcher refused to accept the unions' demands, most people supported her action. As a result, British unions were weakened.

8. Thatcher's policies to cut expenses and reshape Britain's economy enjoyed considerable success. However, Thatcher's opposition to many elements of European unity and her support of an unpopular tax led to her resignation in 1990. John Major, the new Conservative party leader, became prime minister. In 1992, despite high unemployment and other troubles, Major led the Conservatives to a fourth straight election victory.

PEOPLE IN HISTORY

9. Margaret Thatcher was the daughter of a grocery store owner. She attended Oxford University, where she studied chemistry. At Oxford she became interested in politics and joined the Conservative party. After her marriage in 1950, she ran for Parliament but was defeated. For the next few years she raised her children and earned a law degree. However, she also remained active in politics. In 1959, she was elected to Parliament as a Conservative party member from London. After serving as Minister of Education for several years, Thatcher became the leader of the Conservative party in 1975.

10. When Thatcher became prime minister of Great Britain in 1979, she was the first woman ever to hold this high office. She won reelection in 1983 and 1987, when the Conservative party won majorities in Par-

678

liament. When she left office, she had served as prime minister longer than any other British leader in the last 160 years.

FRANCE: In what ways have the lives of the French people improved in recent years?

11. During the early 1980s, the government of France was controlled by the Socialist party. The French people elected François Mitterrand (fran-SWAH mee-teh-RAHN), a Socialist, as president in 1981. The Socialist party in France favored government ownership of the country's most important businesses and industries. Like most European countries, France's government had long owned the nation's railroads and airlines, coal mines, electricity, and gas. The government also partly owned several of France's largest businesses, including oil, auto manufacturing, chemicals, and iron and steel mills. In the early 1980s, Mitterrand's government took over other industries as well. However, the government allowed the managers of these companies to run them without strict government controls. The French government also spent large sums of money helping French businesses plan new products and modernize their factories.

12. As a result of these government policies, the French people enjoyed a new prosperity during the 1980s. French farmers grew record amounts of wheat and corn. In fact, France produced more farm products than any other Western European nation. As a result, the incomes of French farmers grew rapidly. French workers, too, were among the most skilled in Europe. Their increased output of products and services resulted in a steady increase in their incomes. Mitterrand's government also cut inflation sharply by the late 1980s. This meant that many French workers now could afford to buy houses, cars, and other high-priced products.

13. Mitterrand's socialist government became more conservative during the late 1980s. In the election for the French parliament in 1986, the Socialists were narrowly defeated by the Conservatives, and a Conservative became prime minister. However, Mitterrand remained president of France. In 1988 Mitterrand was re-elected, and the Socialists again attained a majority in parliament. The Socialist party's main goal now was to modernize France's industries. Even though the French government sometimes was divided among opposing parties, France remained a strong and united nation.

GERMANY: How did East and West Germany become reunited?

14. When Germany was defeated in World War II, it was divided into two countries, West Germany and East Germany. East Germany was ruled by a Communist government as a satellite of the Soviet Union. West Germany became a democracy and an ally of the nations of Western Europe and the United States. In 1955 West

▼ People in Germany enjoy shopping in a variety of stores. Before reunification, East Germans had limited access to consumer goods.

The European Community Today   Six of Europe's squabbling nations decided to set aside ancient rivalries after World War II and begin cooperating. They set up what is now called the European Community and may one day become the "United States of Europe."

The map on this page shows the development of the European Community. Read these facts about the European Community today. Think about them as you study the map. Then answer the questions that follow.

Founding members of the European Community were Belgium, France, West Germany, Italy, the Netherlands, and Luxembourg.

Six other nations joined after 1970. In 1990, East Germany was accepted into the Community as part of reunited Germany. Many other nations have applied for membership.

The European Community has no capital city. Most meetings take place in Brussels or Luxembourg, and the European Parliament often meets in Strasbourg, France.

The members of the European Community have loose political links. The Community has a civil service to help draw up regulations. But major decisions are made by national governments. The European Parliament has few powers.

Member nations use many different languages and currencies. One day, they may share a common currency.

One goal of the Community is to eliminate the need for passports or other documents for travel between member countries.

Now use the map to answer the questions below. Write your answers on a separate sheet of paper.

1. Who were the six original members of the European Community?

2. Which six countries joined the European Community after 1970?

3. What obstacles must be overcome in order to create a United States of Europe?

The European Community Today

- Original members
- Members joining after 1970

0   500 miles
0   800 kilometers

Germany became a member of NATO. During the 1950s and 1960s, West Germany rebuilt its businesses and industries so that they were among the strongest of any nation. West Germany's ability to develop a strong new economy in such a short time was called Europe's "economic miracle."

15. West Germany soon became the wealthiest country in Western Europe. It produced more steel, chemicals, electronic products, cars, and engineering machinery than any other European nation. West Germany also exported more products than any other country of Western Europe. Nearly 40 percent of Germany's industrial production was sold to foreign nations.

16. During the 1970s and 1980s, West Germany's government was headed by two able leaders. Helmut Schmidt (HEL-moot SHMIT) of the Social Democratic party served as chancellor from 1974 to 1983. Helmut Kohl of the Christian Democratic Union became chancellor in 1983. Under both leaders, the government played an active role in managing the nation's economic growth.

17. During this time, West German workers gained new rights. In large West German companies, the workers began to help determine production goals, wages, working conditions, and management staff. German workers continued to be one of the most productive work forces in Europe. They enjoyed one of the highest **standards of living** in the world. A people's standard of living is the amount of goods, comforts, and luxuries they can afford to buy.

18. Many Germans had hoped that one day East and West Germany would be reunited. But few expected reunification to come as suddenly as it did. In the late 1980s, a sense of crisis began to grow within East Germany. By 1989, crowds were openly protesting against the East German government and Communist party leader Erich Honecker. In October 1989, the Communist party removed Honecker and chose a new leader. But protests ▶ continued. Why do you think people continued to protest?

SPOTLIGHT ON SOURCES

19. On November 9, 1989, East Berlin radio suddenly announced that East Germans could travel freely to the West. Slowly at first, then in a flood, East Germans advanced toward the Berlin Wall. West Berliners lined the wall to welcome East Germans as they crossed. West Berlin's mayor declared:

> "The whole city and all its citizens will never forget November 9, 1989. For 28 years since the wall was built we have yearned for this day. We Germans are now the happiest people on earth. [November 9] was not yet the day of re-unification, but it was a day of reunion."

20. Events moved rapidly after that. East Germany held elections and chose the country's first democratic government. Then, East and West German leaders decided that East Germany would join West Germany under West Germany's democratic system of government. On October 3, 1990, Germany was reunited.

21. Reunification brought many challenges. East Germany's Communist economy was in tatters and many industries in the East needed to be modernized. Some West Germans resented the higher taxes they had to pay in order to rebuild the East. German leaders promised that the hardships would be temporary. They were confident that Germany's strong economy would pull the country through.

OUTLOOK

22. The countries of Western Europe are among the richest and most productive in the world. Britain, France, and Germany, Europe's leading industrial powers, are leading the effort to create a strong European Community. Their main goal is to improve the economy and raise the standard of living. How do you think Europe's ◀ economy affects the United States?

681

CHAPTER REVIEW

VOCABULARY REVIEW

Write each of the following sentences on a sheet of paper. Then fill in the blank with the word that best completes each sentence.

currency   free trade   standard of living

1. In countries with _____ , there are no tariffs, or taxes, on imported products.

2. Money that is used to buy goods and services is called _____ .

3. When people have a high _____ , they can afford to buy the products they need as well as many comforts and luxuries.

SKILL BUILDER: READING A PRIMARY SOURCE

The European leaders who created the European Community often said that their goal was to unite Europe's nations. They hoped that in the future the Western European nations would join together to form a United States of Europe. This is how a leading French planner of the European Community explained this goal.

"Americans should understand better than anyone the benefits for Europe and the world of the peaceful revolution that is taking place in Europe, for America too is a common market [one large market] whose states apply common laws through their common federal institutions [the nation's government]

Europe is on the way to achieving economic unity, but we must have no doubt that in due course [in the future] it will move toward unity in foreign policy and defense. What is gradually emerging is a great new entity [group of nations], the United States of Europe."

1. Where is the "peaceful revolution" mentioned by the writer taking place?

2. In what country do the states and the nation's government already form a common market?

3. Does the author favor or oppose the creation of a United States of Europe?

SKILL BUILDER: CRITICAL THINKING AND COMPREHENSION

 1. Classifying

▶ Divide a sheet of paper into three columns. Head the columns *Great Britain, France,* and *Germany*. Write each of the following descriptions beneath the correct heading.

a. François Mitterrand was elected president in 1981.

b. It was divided into two parts and occupied by foreign troops from 1945 to 1990.

c. Margaret Thatcher served as prime minister from 1979 to 1990.

d. It developed a strong new economy in such a short time that it was called Europe's "economic miracle."

e. It produced more farm products than any other Western European country.

f. The Conservative party sold many government-owned industries to private groups.

2. Generalizing

▶ Read each pair of statements and then make a generalization using the information they provide.

2-1. a. The nations of Western Europe tried to forget their past rivalries and wars.
    b. The people of Western Europe tried to put aside their feelings of nationalism.

2-2. a. The European Community turns out more goods and services than either the United States or Japan.
    b. The European Community produces nearly one fourth of the world total of manufactured goods.

2-3. a. East Berliners flooded into West Berlin when they heard that the border had been opened in 1989.
    b. West Germans welcomed East Germans who crossed the border in November 1989.

3. Drawing Conclusions

▶ Read each pair of statements below and use this information to form a conclusion about the meaning of these statements.

3-1. a. West Germany had the strongest economy in Europe in the 1980s.
    b. German reunification combined the resources and people of the two Germanies.

3.2. a. At the end of World War II the countries of Western Europe were in ruins.
    b. Today, Western Europe is one of the richest regions in the world.

3.3. a. Margaret Thatcher was the first woman ever to serve as prime minister of Great Britain.
    b. Margaret Thatcher served as prime minister longer than any British leader in the last 160 years.

4. Point of View

▶ Read each statement and write (T) if it correctly gives the point of view of the people of Western Europe and (F) if it does not.

a. The European Community will weaken the economies of its member countries.

b. The European Parliament will help countries move toward political unity.

c. It is important for people in Western Europe to have a high standard of living.

ENRICHMENT

1. Have the class hold a mock election for members of the European Parliament. Have two students campaign for each seat from the 12 member nations. Students should prepare a list of issues they want the parliament to consider concerning both their nation and Western Europe as a whole. The whole class then should hear the opposing candidates and vote for the 12 delegates.

2. Ask students to imagine that they live in united Germany. Assign half the students to represent former West Germans and half to represent former East Germans. Then, have them write letters describing what they like and dislike about reunification. Ask volunteers to read their letters aloud.

CHAPTER 2

The Soviet Union Dissolves

▲ President Boris Yeltsin of Russia led the resistance to the coup. Why was the resistance against the coup successful?

OBJECTIVE: What events led to the breakup of the Soviet Union and what problems do the people of the region face as they struggle to create a new order?

1. Beginning in the mid-1980s, the people of the Soviet Union were enjoying more freedom than ever before. President Mikhail Gorbachev had introduced a number of reforms that gave people more decision-making power and more freedom of expression. Then, on August 19, 1991, tanks rumbled through the streets of Moscow. Communist hard-liners announced that they were taking control of the Soviet government. Gorbachev's reforms had angered these uncompromising leaders.

Hard-liners swept Gorbachev aside in a sudden **coup d'état** (KOO day-TAH)—a government takeover by force. But the Soviet people had tasted freedom and they refused to accept the coup. Boris Yeltsin (YEHL-tsin), president of the Russian

1975	1980	1985	1990	1995

Soviet forces move into Afghanistan 1979

Gorbachev named general secretary of Soviet Union 1985

Soviet forces leave Afghanistan 1989

Most Eastern European satellite nations remove Communist governments 1989–1991

Solidarity pushes for change in Poland 1980

Gorbachev steps down; Soviet Union dissolves as republics declare independence 1991

Russian economy continues to decline 1992

republic, the Soviet Union's largest unit, led the resistance to the coup. Climbing onto a tank in front of the Russian government's headquarters, Yeltsin asked soldiers to ignore the commands of the coup leaders. He urged workers to stop working and go on strike. Yeltsin declared that the democratic reforms that Gorbachev had initiated were "irreversible"—they could not be taken back. Public support of Yeltsin was overwhelming. Rather than risk civil war, the hard-liners backed down. Gorbachev returned to office—but Yeltsin had established himself as the leader of the reform movement. By the end of the year, Gorbachev had resigned and the Soviet Union had disappeared. It had broken up into 15 separate republics.

THE SOVIET ECONOMY: Why did the Communist system fail to bring prosperity to the Soviet people?

2. After World War II, the Soviet Union became one of the world's two "superpowers" along with the United States. The Soviet Union had a centrally controlled government that operated under one political party—the Communist party. The party, headed by the General Secretary, controlled the government. Under its Communist system, the Soviet Union had a planned economy. The government owned all the industries. It also controlled all the farms, grouping them into large units where farm people worked together in teams. A state planning commission decided what items factories would produce, what crops farmers would grow, and what jobs people would perform. The government also set the prices at which goods would be sold. This system had been started in the 1920s and 1930s in order to force the rapid growth of industry to serve the needs of the nation—not the needs of the one consumer. Why might Communist leaders think such a system would lead to rapid economic growth?

3. A huge **bureaucracy** was created to carry out the Soviet system of central, or nationwide, planning. A bureaucracy is an organization that creates rules, gives directions, and keeps records necessary to carry out a government's plans. The Soviet bureaucracy was made up of officials of both the government and the Communist party. Many Communist party officials received high salaries and special privileges. These officials had access to the best food, clothing, and apartments available. They received superior health care and their children went to top schools. This situation angered ordinary people and caused resentment against bureaucratic and party officials. In addition, as the Soviet bureaucracy grew in size, it became slow and inefficient. Bureaucrats often showed little interest in helping the Soviet people. Yet the government and party depended on the bureaucracy to plan and direct the jobs of factory workers, office workers, and farmers. Do you think bureaucracies in the United States are more responsive to people's needs?

4. The Communist leaders of the Soviet Union used much of the nation's resources and wealth to build up heavy industry. The government built factories that produced machinery, trucks, and buses. They also produced a great deal of military goods, including tanks, missiles, and nuclear weapons. As a result, factories turned out few consumer goods for the Soviet people.

5. By the 1960s and 1970s, it was clear that the Soviet Union faced serious economic problems. Many city families had to live in tiny apartments. There were constant shortages of meat, fruit, milk, and other foods. Often people would stand in line for hours to find that a government-run store was out of toothpaste or shoes. Cars, television sets, and other luxuries were not available in great quantities. Which of these shortages was most serious?

6. Another issue facing the Soviet people was the poor quality of the products that were available. Factories and farms all had to meet **quotas**. A quota is a set number of goods a factory must make. If a factory's quota was 50,000 raincoats, the raincoats

▲ Mikhail Gorbachev is pictured attending a parade in Cuba with Fidel Castro. How do you think the breakup of the Soviet Union has affected Cuba?

had to be produced, whether the factory
► had proper materials or not. Why would such a system make it hard for workers to produce high-quality goods?

PEOPLE IN HISTORY

7. During the 1970s and 1980s a series of leaders tried and failed to improve life in the Soviet Union. Finally, in 1985, Mikhail Gorbachev (GOHR-buh-chawf) became General Secretary of the Communist party and the leader of the Soviet Union. Gorbachev, at age 51, was one of the youngest leaders ever to head the Soviet government. He soon made it clear that he wanted a new generation of leaders with new ideas to control the Communist party and to rule the nation.

8. Gorbachev was born in a small village in southern Russia. The son of peasant farmers, Gorbachev studied law at Moscow State University. He then served in several posts in Stavrapol, a city near his village. He soon became leader of the Communist

party in Stavrapol. In 1970, Gorbachev was elected a member of the Supreme Soviet. Nine years later, he became a member of the **Politburo** (POH-liht-byoo-roh), the top group of Communist officials who ran the country. In 1985, Gorbachev became Secretary General, the most powerful position in the government. Then, in 1990, he was also elected president.

PERESTROIKA: What was Gorbachev's plan to improve Soviet industry and farming?

9. To the older leaders of the Soviet Union, Gorbachev's plans were revolutionary. They were based on the belief that important changes had to be made if the Soviet people were to have better lives. Gorbachev called his plan for change *perestroika* (peh-res-TROY-kuh). *Perestroika* is a Russian word meaning "to rebuild." One of the most important changes was to limit central planning of Soviet farming and industry. Workers, farmers, and members of the bureaucracy were to be allowed to make many of the decisions affecting the work they did. For example, factory managers and workers were to cooperate to improve the products they made. Workers who produced more goods were to receive higher wages. Individual farm workers and leaders of the collective farms were to work together to increase the size of crops. Families who produced more than their quota of crops could sell these crops on the open market to earn extra money. Soviet citizens also were permitted to start small businesses of their own, such as hair salons and restaurants. In allowing the Soviet people more economic freedom, Gorbachev did not, however, intend to end communism and endorse capitalism.

10. Despite the efforts of perestroika, the Soviet economy was clearly in decline. By the early 1990s, production continued to drop in many industries. Reform-minded Soviet economists told Gorbachev his programs had to go further, urging him to allow factories and businesses to set prices for goods themselves. Their proposals, however, threatened to move the Soviet Union's planned economy closer to a market economy. A market economy is one in which producers and buyers decide about production, distribution, and price. These types of changes were opposed by many government and party leaders. In addition, any attempt to make the economy more efficient was likely to lead to some unemployment. Gorbachev did not believe that the Soviet people were ready for such changes. Yet economic conditions continued to worsen.

FOREIGN POLICY: How did the rising hopes of the people of Eastern Europe force Gorbachev to ease Soviet control?

11. Dramatic changes occurred in the relations between the Soviet Union and the satellite nations of Eastern Europe. Eventually, Gorbachev was forced to change Soviet policy toward the satellite nations. During the 1950s and 1960s, the Soviet army had moved in to crush movements for freedom in East Germany,

▲ One of the issues the newly independent countries face is how to divide the Soviet Union's military resources.

Hungary, and Czechoslovakia. In the early 1980s, Soviet leaders had pushed the Polish government to take stern action against **Solidarity** (sahl-ih-DAR-ih-tee), a trade union that had challenged the government's iron rule. During the late 1980s and early 1990s, Gorbachev was forced to take a different approach. From 1989 to 1991, most of the nations of Eastern Europe replaced their Communist rulers with freely elected governments. Gorbachev stood by as one nation after another threw out its Communist-style economy. Eastern Europe's nations began market-oriented reforms that often went far beyond those tried in the Soviet Union. Finally, in 1991, Gorbachev formally ended the Warsaw Pact military alliance.

12. Gorbachev's policy of openness extended to the countries of the West. The weakness of the Soviet Union helped to bring the Cold War to an end. In the past, there had been temporary thaws in the

687

▲ Lech Walesa, the popular leader of the Polish Solidarity movement, speaks at a rally for workers' rights.

Cold War. For example, the early 1970s had been a time of *détente*, an easing of tensions. But in 1979, Soviet troops had moved into Afghanistan, a nation on the Soviet Union's southern border, and Cold War tensions soared again. For the next 10 years, Soviet troops struggled to crush a rebellion against the pro-Soviet Communists who ran Afghanistan's government. Supported by the United States and other nations, Afghani rebels continued to fight. In 1989, Gorbachev pulled Soviet forces out of Afghanistan.

13. The Soviet pullout from Afghanistan was one of a number of steps that brought the Soviet Union and the rest of the world closer to the end of the Cold War. Gorbachev also had to reduce Soviet troop levels in Eastern Europe and reduce aid to pro-Soviet governments in Cuba and other nations. He also agreed to talks with the United States that led to sweeping arms reductions. In 1987, Gorbachev and U.S. President Ronald Reagan signed a treaty to destroy medium-range nuclear missiles. Four years later, Gorbachev and U.S. President George Bush signed a more ambitious treaty called the Strategic Arms Reduction Treaty, or START. Under START, both sides agreed to large reductions in strategic (long-range) nuclear missiles. For the role he played in helping to reduce Soviet aggressiveness, Gorbachev was awarded the Nobel Peace Prize in 1990.

THE END OF THE SOVIET UNION: Why did the Soviet Union break up into 15 independent nations?

14. Gorbachev's domestic and foreign policy reforms won him respect and recognition abroad. He was not as popular with the people of the Soviet Union, however. Gorbachev's limited economic reforms were not effectively raising the standard of living. In fact, the Soviet Union produced fewer goods in 1990 than it had the year before. The following year, production dropped still further. Some Soviet citizens called for a complete transition to a free-market economy. Others said Gorbachev had gone too far already and that his reforms had destroyed a Communist system that had at least kept people fed.

15. Gorbachev was also confronted with a growing spirit of nationalism in the 15 republics of the union. One republic, Russia, was far larger than any other. In the days before communism, Russia had created the Russian Empire and ruled over neighboring lands. Those same lands were supposed to be self-governing republics within the Soviet Union. But the reality was that the Soviet government based in Russia controlled almost every aspect of the economy and government. More and more people in the other republics began to protest for freedom and self-rule. To stop the growing unrest, Gorbachev agreed to a Union Treaty in 1991. The Union Treaty promised to increase the power of the republics and reduce the power of the Soviet government. But only nine Soviet republics agreed to the treaty. The six others demanded full independence. In the end, the Union Treaty never went into effect. The day before it was to be signed, hard-line Communist leaders staged their coup d'état.

16. Once the coup had been put down, Gorbachev accepted the outright independence of three of the republics— Estonia, Latvia, and Lithuania. These republics had been independent before World War II. During the war, the Soviet Union occupied and annexed them. Now, they were free once again.

17. As a result of the coup, Gorbachev lost most of his influence and political power. Power continued to shift from the central Soviet government to the 12 remaining republics. The Communist party, which had been disgraced by the involvement of its top leaders in the attempted coup, was banned by Russian President Boris Yeltsin. By the end of 1991, the republics agreed to dissolve the Soviet Union.

SPOTLIGHT ON SOURCES

18. In 1991, Gorbachev had to resign his post as the last president and general secretary of the Soviet Union. His fellow citizens had mixed emotions about his departure. An independent journalist, Yuri Shchekochikin, discussed his own feelings:

> "Gorbachev is a mystery. It is not clear whether he is a reformer or destroyer, a worthy holder of the Nobel Peace Prize or the man who disrupted a country that covers one-sixth of the Earth's surface. He tried to reconcile [harmonize] the irreconcilable: communism and democracy. He gave the slaves freedom, and they ended up cursing him."

19. Eleven of the 12 newly independent nations decided to form a loose confederation called the Commonwealth of Inde-

pendent States, or CIS. The country of Georgia declined to join. The Commonwealth is an attempt by the former republics to coordinate policy on some issues, such as nuclear weapons. The members of the CIS maintain their own military forces and their own foreign policies. Each nation has a seat in the United Nations. Russia occupies the former Soviet Union's seat on the Security Council.

20. More than 200 different ethnic groups, or nationalities, lived in the former Soviet Union. With the authority of the Soviet Union gone, violent religious and ethnic conflicts broke out in a number of regions. The territorial dispute between Azerbaijan and Armenia pitted Muslims and Christians against one another. In Moldova, people of Romanian origin quarreled with people of Russian origin. A number of ethnic minorities living in Russia, Georgia, and Tajikistan demanded self-rule. Would civil wars break out in the ◄ republics? Would these new nations splinter into even tinier nations?

OUTLOOK

21. The people living in the newly independent republics have faced great challenges since the breakup of the Soviet Union. In several of the republics, there have been violent clashes among various ethnic groups. The economic reforms begun by Russia, Ukraine, and other republics have caused economic hardship for many. Germany, the United States, and other democratic nations have offered money, food, and additional help. At the dawn of a new era, many people in the former Soviet Union look to the future with hope. For the first time since 1917, they are experiencing the freedom that democracy can bring. At the same time, they are experiencing the challenges that come with a truly free society. Why are most countries ◄ eager to see the newly independent republics succeed?

Ask: What changes would you have recommended if you had been a Communist party official in the Soviet Union?

689

CHAPTER REVIEW

VOCABULARY REVIEW

Write each of the following sentences on a sheet of paper. Then fill in the blanks
with the word that best completes the sentence.

Solidarity   bureaucracy   Union Treaty

quotas   Politburo   *perestroika*

1. The Soviet government set _____ on factory goods produced.
2. The top group of Communist officials who ran the Soviet Union was called the
3. _____ was Mikhail Gorbachev's policy of rebuilding the structure of Soviet society.
4. In the early 1980s, Soviet leaders urged Poland to suppress _____ , a trade union.
5. The Soviet Union depended on the _____ to plan and direct the jobs of workers and farmers.
6. The _____ , a plan for reshaping the Soviet Union into a looser grouping of republics, was not put into effect.

SKILL BUILDER: READING A MAP

Study the map below and then answer the following questions.

1. Name three nations that were once satellites of the Soviet Union.
2. Which is the largest newly independent nation to emerge from the Soviet Union?
3. Which newly independent countries border the Caspian Sea?
4. Which countries are north of Iran?
5. Which region is located in eastern Russia?

The Breakup of the Soviet Union

	Former Soviet Union		Satellites of the former Soviet Union		—— Present–day boundaries	
Ar Armenia	**Be** Belarus	**G** Georgia	**La** Latvia	**Mo** Moldova	**Tu** Turkmenistan
Az Azerbaijan	**Es** Estonia	**K** Kyrgyzstan	**Li** Lithuania	**Ta** Tajikistan	**Uz** Uzbekistan

Compare and contrast conditions and policies in the Soviet Union before and after Mikhail Gorbachev came to power. Then, compare conditions before and after the breakup of the Soviet Union. How has the economy changed? How has the government changed?

SKILL BUILDER: CRITICAL THINKING AND COMPREHENSION

▲ 1. Main Idea

▶ Select the letter of the statement that best expresses the main idea of the paragraph.

1-1. The main idea of paragraph 5 is:
  a. The Soviet Union faced serious economic problems in the 1960s and 1970s.
  b. Consumer goods were in short supply in the 1960s and 1970s.
  c. New housing was scarce in the last two decades.

1-2. The main idea of paragraph 7 is:
  a. A series of leaders managed to improve life in the Soviet Union in the 1970s and 1980s.
  b. Mikhail Gorbachev provided new leadership in the Soviet Union.
  c. In 1985 Mikhail Gorbachev became leader of the Soviet Union.

1-3. The main idea of paragraph 10 is:
  a. Economists did not approve of Gorbachev's reforms.
  b. Gorbachev and reform-minded economists disagreed about how to solve the Soviet Union's economic problems.
  c. Gorbachev did not think the Soviet people were ready for change.

1-4. The main idea of paragraph 20 is:
  a. Muslims and Christians in the former Soviet Union did not get along.
  b. Ethnic and religious disputes have exploded into violence in the newly independent republics.
  c. The Soviet Union contained more than 200 different nationalities.

2. Sequencing

▶ Review paragraphs 11, 12, and 13, which discuss foreign policy. Then place the events below in the correct chronological order.

  a. Soviet troops pull out of Afghanistan.
  b. Gorbachev and Bush sign START pact.
  c. Soviet troops move into Afghanistan.
  d. Soviets pressure Poland to act against Solidarity trade union.
  e. Satellite nations abandon communism.

3. Compare and Contrast

▶ Review paragraphs 2 and 9. Write a short essay comparing how Soviet farming and industry were run before and after Gorbachev's reforms.

4. Making Judgments

  a. The former Soviet republics have faced demands from ethnic groups for greater rights and self-rule. Imagine that you are a government leader in one of those republics. What problems would you face if you gave in to the demands? What problems would you face if you resisted the demands?

ENRICHMENT

1. Use the *Readers' Guide to Periodical Literature* to research articles about the economic reforms being carried out in Russia or Ukraine. Write a report on how those reforms are affecting the people who live there.

2. With a group of classmates, put together a news sheet on the current status of the newly independent republics. Each group member should choose one republic. Next, find a newspaper article on the republic. Then, summarize the articles and lay them out on a poster-size sheet of paper. Use more than one piece of paper if your group has many articles.

CHAPTER 3

China Modernizes

▲ In Peking, parking lots are provided for bicycles. Why might bicycles be an advantage over cars in a large, crowded city?

OBJECTIVE: What changes have China's Communist leaders made in agriculture and industry to try to improve the people's lives?

1. Today, more people live in China than in any other country in the world. By the early 1990s, China's population had reached 1.2 billion people. Nearly 22 percent of the world's total population was Chinese. The Communist rulers of China decided that the government must control this population growth. If it did not, they thought China could not produce enough food or goods for its people. During the 1970s, the Chinese government ordered the people to limit the size of their families. Families who agreed to have only one child were rewarded. They received monthly cash payments, free child care, housing, and better jobs. In this way the government tried to overcome the ancient Chinese custom of having large families and make one-child families popular. Family planning is one of the changes in Chinese society that you will read about in this chapter.

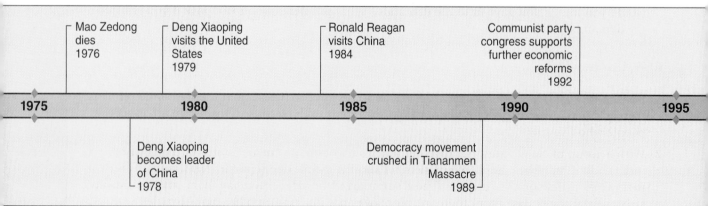

Mao Zedong dies 1976

Deng Xiaoping visits the United States 1979

Ronald Reagan visits China 1984

Communist party congress supports further economic reforms 1992

1975   1980   1985   1990   1995

Deng Xiaoping becomes leader of China 1978

Democracy movement crushed in Tiananmen Massacre 1989

CHINA'S COMMUNIST RULERS: In what ways did China's Communist leaders weaken the country?

2. China is one of the oldest civilizations in the world, dating back nearly 4000 years. However, in the past 50 years it has gone through many revolutionary changes. These changes began when the Chinese Communist party gained control of China in 1949. Since then, Communist leaders have tried several different plans to reform Chinese society. When one plan failed, China's rulers then began another. Often these plans were extreme and were carried out harshly. As a result, the Chinese people faced years of unrest and sometimes cruel treatment by their government.

3. Most of the Chinese people are farmers. Under Communist control, the farmers worked on large **communes**, or government-run farms. Strict government controls over these communes was often unsuccessful, and poor harvests and food shortages became common. In the towns and cities, China's government-owned businesses and industries were not able to make enough products to meet China's needs. Production quotas, or goals, were set so high by the government that workers knew they could not meet them. Also, under the Communist government, all workers in the same jobs received equal wages. As a result, workers were discouraged from caring about their jobs or the quality of their work.

PEOPLE IN HISTORY

4. Deng Xiaoping (DENG shah-oh-PING) became the leader of Communist China in 1978. As a young man, Deng went to France to study. There he became very interested in the ideas of communism. When he returned to China he joined the Communist party and helped the Communists defeat the Nationalists in China's civil war. After the Communist Party came to power in China in 1949, Deng held many important posts. However, he was forced to leave the government when extremists took control of China in the 1960s. Deng never forgot these years, called the Cultural Revolution, and how they weakened China.

THE FOUR MODERNIZATIONS: What was Deng Xiaoping's plan to make China a modern industrial country?

5. Under Deng, a new plan for a better life for China and its people began. This plan was called the **Four Modernizations**. Deng was convinced that China must rebuild its economy by introducing some of the ideas of capitalism. What were the four major parts of Chinese life that Deng believed needed to be modernized? Deng's plan called for modernizing and improving (1) farming, (2) industry, (3) science and technology, and (4) the military forces. The goal of Deng's plan was to make China one of the world's most powerful nations by the year 2000.

FARMING: How did changes in farming improve the lives of farm families?

6. During the 1980s, many important changes were made in farming communities in China. The quota system was continued. However, each family was allowed to grow crops beyond the quota, which could be sold on the open market. The **profit motive** was introduced. This meant that the money received from selling these extra crops belonged to the family. The family could spend this money as it wished. Many families used this money to buy houses or start small businesses.

7. The reform in Chinese farming was a great success. Farmers' income doubled during the 1980s. This achievement was very important, for it greatly improved the lives of the 800 million people living on China's farms. This meant that the farmers now favored Deng's reforms and created a base for other economic changes. With their support, China could follow its new plan to modernize industry, science, and the army.

Background: During the Cultural Revolution of the late 1960s, millions of Chinese were jailed and executed. Many of these were teachers, doctors, and other professional people.

693

▲ This woman is working as a welder in a factory in Nanning, China. How might her job have changed since the Deng government came into power?

9. The government also encouraged the people to set up small businesses. Soon small, privately owned restaurants, factories, building firms, beauty shops, and bus companies appeared throughout China. These small businesses could not hire more than seven to ten workers, but they were free to keep the profits they earned. In China's rural areas, small, private businesses grew to supply the needs of the farm communities.

10. China turned to other nations to help the country to become industrialized. The Deng government invited foreign companies to set up plants and factories in China. These businesses were to be **joint ventures**. This meant that they were to be owned partly by the foreign companies and partly by the Chinese government. By the 1990s, hundreds of firms from Hong Kong, Germany, Japan, the United States, and other nations were doing business in China. U.S. companies were writing computer software, selling hamburgers, and marketing shampoo, among other activities. In turn, the Chinese were learning how capitalists run businesses.

INDUSTRY: What new freedoms were allowed workers in factories and businesses?

8. The Deng government introduced many important changes in industry. Most factories and businesses still were owned by the government. However, many factories now signed contracts with the government similar to those signed by the farm communes. In these agreements, factories were allowed to produce more than their government quotas. They were then able to sell these extra products to pay bonuses, or additional wages, to the workers. Another important reform was the power given to factory managers to hire and fire workers. This power led to better, more efficient production, because poor workers would not be kept on the job. As a result of these reforms, China's total output of goods and services increased by almost 9 percent each year in the 1980s and early 1990s.

SCIENCE AND TECHNOLOGY: How did the Chinese people benefit from advances in science?

11. China made major advances in modernizing science and technology in the 1980s. During the 1960s and 1970s, many scientists, doctors, and engineers had been forced to leave their jobs and work as field laborers in the country. As a result of this anti-education attitude, the advance of technology in China came to a halt. Under Deng Xiaoping's Four Modernizations plan, schools and colleges were reopened. Teachers returned to their classrooms, and young people could once again study science, medicine, and engineering.

12. China made important advances in space technology and in developing nuclear weapons during the 1980s. China signed agreements with several foreign companies to use Chinese spacecraft to launch commu-

Activity: Have students make a chart showing the organization of the Chinese Communist party and government. Be sure they understand that party members hold the key posts in the government structure.

nications satellites. The Communist government also began to build more nuclear power plants to generate energy for new industries. However, China made its most important technology gains in the buildup of its military forces.

SPOTLIGHT ON SOURCES

13. The Chinese people were expected to work hard to help the government carry out its plan to make China into a modern nation. The Communist party's official newspaper, the *People's Daily*, explained why great effort and loyal support by the people were needed.

> "China is a large country with a poor foundation. In order to catch up with the living standard and labor productivity [output] of the economically developed [industrialized] countries, we must make arduous efforts [work very hard] for several decades or longer. We solved the long-standing problems of feeding and clothing the 800 million peasants, and the peasants have gradually become well off. The living standard of the people in urban areas [cities] has also improved markedly in recent years. Hard work and vigorous efforts to make the country prosperous are the fine tradition of our nation. We must lay a solid foundation for making the country powerful and the people rich, which has been the long-cherished aspiration [lovingly held goal] of generations of Chinese people."
>
> —from *People's Daily*

RESISTING POLITICAL CHANGE: Why have political reforms lagged behind economic reforms?

14. Deng's Four Modernizations plan has brought many changes to China. But for all of China's economic reforms, political life has remained mostly unchanged. Movements for democratic reform occurred in the 1970s and 1980s. But the Communist government quickly repressed them.

15. A new period of rebellion began in the spring of 1989. It began as millions of people marched to Beijing and other cities to protest for political reform. The marchers included ordinary workers, students, and even members of the Communist party bureaucracy. At first, the government allowed these peaceful demonstrations. Thousands of students and other citizens camped out in Tiananmen (tyen-AHN-min) Square in Beijing, and held discussions about democracy and freedom.

16. But soon Chinese leaders decided that the democratic movement had gone too far. In the darkness before dawn of June 4, 1989, political leaders sent the military to sweep the students and workers from Tiananmen Square. Troops allowed protesters to file out of the square. But violence broke out in the streets nearby. Suddenly, tanks and troops opened fire on civilians. Hundreds of protesters died during the bloody crackdown. Leaders of the protest were jailed.

17. The fighting at Tiananmen Square brought harsh criticism from many countries. But China's leaders remained firmly against increasing democratic freedoms. Many world leaders supported China's shift to a market economy. However, many of them were deeply troubled by China's hard-line crackdown on democracy.

OUTLOOK

18. The 1990s have brought economic change to China. A few people in China hope that as China's economic power continues to grow, the power of the Communist party will wither away. But hard-liners in the government insist that they will fight against this so-called "peaceful evolution." For the most part, China's future depends on the people who succeed Deng Xiaoping and his followers. Do you think China will become more ◀ democratic in the future?

CHAPTER REVIEW

VOCABULARY REVIEW

Write each of the following sentences on a sheet of paper. Then fill in the blank with the word that best completes each sentence.

joint ventures   Four Modernizations   communes   profit motive

1. By using the _____ the government allowed farm families to grow extra crops and sell them to earn money.
2. Deng Xiaoping's plan for rebuilding China's economy is called the _____.
3. Most of China's population works on large government-run farms, or _____.
4. _____ are businesses that are partly owned by foreign companies and partly owned by the Chinese government.

SKILL BUILDER: READING A PRIMARY SOURCE

Women in China gained more freedom and greater opportunities in recent years. Read this report from a Beijing newspaper and then answer the questions below.

"In 1949 women made up only 7.5 percent of all workers in state-owned enterprises [businesses]. The percentage rose to 21 percent in 1965 and 36 percent in 1983. In addition, one third of China's scientists are women, and women have begun to take leadership roles in a number of fields. . .Women's liberation [freedom] depends, in the final analysis, on economic status. It seems a vast majority are in favor of women playing a major role in modernization."

1. How much of China's work force did women make up in 1983?
2. In what profession were women especially important?
3. What does the writer mean by stating that women's freedom depends on their economic status?

SKILL BUILDER: CRITICAL THINKING AND COMPREHENSION

▲ 1. Main Idea

▶ Select the letter of the statement that best describes the main idea of each paragraph mentioned.

1-1. Paragraph 5
    a. Deng promised the people to make China a strong nation.
    b. Deng decided that China's economy must be modeled on capitalism.
    c. Deng developed a plan for rebuilding China's economy.

1-2. Paragraph 8
    a. Industrial production increased during the 1980s and 1990s.
    b. The Chinese government introduced many important changes in industry that greatly increased production.
    c. Factory workers now were not kept on their jobs if they did poor work.

2. Cause and Effect

For each cause given below write an effect that resulted from it.

a. China could not produce enough food for its people.

b. Deng's reforms introduced the profit motive for farm families.

c. Foreign companies that invested in joint ventures brought their own ways of doing things to China.

3. Compare and Contrast

Copy this chart on a sheet of paper. Fill in the information under the heading **China Under Deng Xiaoping** for each of the four subjects.

	China Under Mao Zedong	China Under Deng Xiaoping
Farming	Farmers worked on communes and produced crop quotas set by the government.	
Industry	Workers held jobs for life, received equal wages for the same jobs; factory had to meet government production quota	
Science and Technology	Scientists and engineers were forced to work as farm laborers on communes.	
Political Life	People had little freedom to express opinions or choose leaders.	

4. Fact *versus* Opinion

Write each statement on a sheet of paper. Then write *fact* if the statement is fact and write *opinion* if the statement is an opinion.

a. China's population is the largest in the world.

b. Deng Xiaoping began the Four Modernizations program in order to build up China's economy.

c. By inviting foreign companies to invest in China, Communist leaders were admitting that communism had failed.

d. The Tiananmen Massacre shows that Communist leaders will do anything to stay in power.

ENRICHMENT

1. Do research in periodicals on China's current leaders and policies. What changes have taken place since the 1989 uprising? What has remained the same?

2. In China's government center at Beijing, "wall posters" were used by the government and by critics to state their views on life in China. Make posters that express your views about changes you think should be made in China.

697

CHAPTER 4

Japan Becomes an Economic Superpower

▲ Emperor Akihito and wife are greeted by children in traditional dress. Respect for authority plays an important part in Japanese life.

OBJECTIVE: How did Japan become a strong industrial country and the world's leading trading nation?

1. In February 1989, the leaders of 154 nations went to Tokyo to attend the funeral of Emperor Hirohito of Japan. Emperor Hirohito had ruled in Japan for 62 years. During his reign, Japan recovered from overwhelming defeat in war to become one of the most advanced industrial countries in the world. People in the United States and many other countries now drove Japanese-made cars and used Japanese-made cam-

eras and VCRs. They listened to music on Japanese-made stereos and watched their favorite programs on Japanese-made TVs. Japanese businesses were building factories in many of these countries to make computers, microwave ovens, and video cameras.

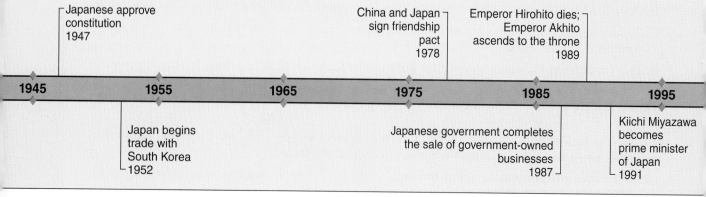

Japanese approve constitution 1947

China and Japan sign friendship pact 1978

Emperor Hirohito dies; Emperor Akhito ascends to the throne 1989

1945 1955 1965 1975 1985 1995

Japan begins trade with South Korea 1952

Japanese government completes the sale of government-owned businesses 1987

Kiichi Miyazawa becomes prime minister of Japan 1991

People all over the world became very interested in Japan. Many of them wondered how Japan had become such an important country. In this chapter you will read about the remarkable growth of Japan in the years following World War II.

JAPAN'S ECONOMY: How have businesses and industries in Japan made the country powerful?

2. In the years after World War II, Japan rebuilt its factories and businesses. Soon Japan's economy began to grow at the fastest rate of any nation in the world. In 1950, for example, Japan was not able to produce enough goods to provide for its people's needs. By the late 1980s, Japan was making so many products that it was the leading trading nation in the world. It produced and sold 25 percent of all the cars in the world, 90 percent of the world's TVs, and 50 percent of the world's ships.

3. During the 1970s and 1980s, Japan's economy became the second most productive in the world. Only the United States had industries and businesses that produced more than Japan. Yet Japan is a small island nation in East Asia with a population of 124 million people. Most of its land is mountainous, and it has few natural resources. Thus, Japan has to import resources from other countries. It imports nearly all the coal, iron ore, copper, oil, and other raw materials used by its industries. Japan also has to import much

▶ of the food its people need. How has Japan been able to pay for all things it imports? Japan manufactures many high-quality goods to export, or sell, to other countries.

4. The workers and managers in Japan's businesses and factories work closely together. They regard their companies almost like a family. They believe that their own success depends on how well their company does in business. In all large Japanese companies, workers and managers hold jobs for life. They receive bonuses, or extra pay, for doing excellent work. When the company needs to cut its costs, it retrains its workers

for other jobs, rather than firing them. As a result, Japanese workers are very productive. The goods they produce are so well made that they are in great demand in many other countries.

5. Several large groups of companies, called *keiretsu* (KAY-ret-soo), control a large part of Japan's economy. The companies in such a group typically include a large bank, a car-making company, a chemical firm, a steel plant, a shipbuilding company, a trading company, and so on. Mitsubishi and Mitsui are examples of *keiretsu*. However, many individual companies also play an important part in Japan's industrial production. You probably have heard of some of these companies, such as Sony, Honda, and Sharp.

6. The Japanese government provided help and guidance to businesses. The Ministry of International Trade and Industry (MITI) played an important part in shaping Japan's economy. MITI helped the nation's industries plan for the future. It also helped Japanese businesses work together to develop new products. All of Japan's businesses are privately owned. The last government-owned businesses, the railroads and the nation's airline, were sold to the public in 1987.

7. Today, Japan's businesses and government are planning ways to keep their country's economy strong in future years. During the 1970s and 1980s, the Japanese built up their heavy industries, such as steel, car-making, and shipbuilding. However, these industries required Japan to import huge amounts of iron ore, oil, coal, and other materials. In the 1980s, Japan saw that Taiwan, South Korea, and Singapore could produce these same products at a lower cost. As a result, Japanese businesses began phasing out heavy industries and switching to more profitable high-technology products.

8. High-technology products require fewer imported materials and made good use of Japan's well-educated work force. The new high-technology products included supercomputers, advanced computer soft-

Ask: Why do workers try so hard to do a good job? How do workers feel about their companies? How does Japan's system compare with that in the United States?

699

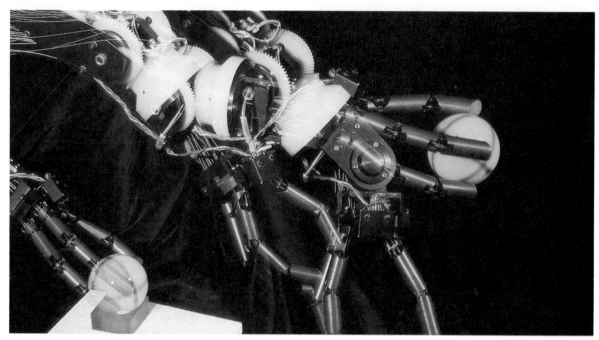

▲ This robotic hand can perform many delicate tasks. Why might the study of robots lead to better understanding of the human brain.

ware, and high-definition TV. Japanese factories also began using robots, lasers, and computer-controlled machinery to produce these items.

SPOTLIGHT ON SOURCES

9. The leaders of Japan's government and industries have developed a plan to keep Japan's economy strong and powerful in the future. Their plan is to produce artificial intelligence computers. Artificial intelligence computers are computers that will be able to understand speech and to solve complex problems—in short, to think. Here is how one writer described the plan:

> The Japanese have named their miracle product "the Fifth Generation Computer System." Their miracle product will be an information processing system [computer] that has the capacity [is able] "to reason." Users of these computers will be able to speak to them, show them pictures and graphs, and give them handwritten messages. Since the Japanese intend to produce and market these new systems at a low cost, they will be available [used] everywhere—in homes, offices, restaurants, farms, and small shops.
> —from *The Power Economy,* John O. Wilson

Do you think these artificial intelligence ◄ computers will replace workers?

JAPAN'S GOVERNMENT: How has Japan's democratic government benefited the people?

10. Japan's democratic government has been as important as Japan's businesses and industries in making the nation prosperous. The Japanese constitution of 1947 provides for a Diet, or lawmaking body, elected by the people. The Diet elects the prime minister from the political party with the most members in the Diet. The emperor is a symbol, or sign, of the country's unity, but he has no real power. In 1989, Emperor Akihito (ak-kee-HEE-toh) came to the throne when his father, Emperor Hirohito, died.

Activity: Have students do research on the fascinating subject of artificial intelligence computers and report on some possible uses for this technology of the future.

700

▲ A Japanese family enjoys a card game. How do their clothes and the decoration of the room reflect the combination of traditional and Western ways in Japan today?

PEOPLE IN HISTORY

11. Emperor Akihito was born in 1933 and raised at the imperial court in Tokyo. He was educated by an American, who taught Akihito Western ideas. As a student, Akihito became very interested in science and sea life. He also traveled to many other countries. As crown prince, he spent his life preparing to become the future emperor. Akihito's rule as emperor will be known in Japan as the Era of Achieving Peace.

12. The Liberal-Democratic party has run Japan's government since 1946. It gets strong support from the voters. Several other parties have won seats in the Diet, but they have not had enough votes to form a government. The Liberal-Democratic party contains rival groups that compete for power. In recent years, it has been troubled by bribe-taking and other scandals. Prime Minister Kiichi Miyazawa (kee-EE-chee mee-yah-ZAH-wah), who took office in 1991, struggled to restore the party's good

name. He also met with the leaders of many other major industrial countries to discuss trade between Japan and those nations.

JAPANESE SOCIETY: What is life like for the people in Japan today?

13. The family has remained the most important group in Japanese society. Members of the family depend on each other and consider the family's needs more important than those of its individual members. Japanese parents are proud of their children and make sure they study hard in school. They expect their children to obey and to respect them. In most families, the mother spends the most time with the children and is closest to them. Many Japanese women now have jobs, but they still are the center of family life. The father often works long hours, and he spends less time with the children.

14. By the 1980s, most Japanese families lived in large cities or towns. Land and houses were so expensive in Japan that most families lived in small apartments of

▲ A family-like spirit is present in Japanese industries. Managers work closely with the people they supervise. Employees exercise together daily.

one or two rooms. Yet the Japanese enjoyed a high living standard in spite of their small, crowded apartments. They earned good wages and were able to buy cars, video cameras, and other luxuries. Many families were able to send their children to college. Japanese families also saved a larger part of their income than the people of most other nations. These savings provided money for Japanese industries and for investment in other countries.

15. School and education are very important to the Japanese people. Children in Japan are expected to learn and succeed in school. Japanese students attend school 240 ▶ days a year. How does this compare with the number of school days in the United States? From the first grade on, Japanese children also have two hours of homework each day. Students in Japan study hard and are among the best educated in the world. Few students drop out of school. In fact, 94 percent of all students graduate from high school, and 37 percent of these high school graduates go on to college or technical school. Education in Japan helps to decide a person's position in society. Students with the highest grades from the best colleges are hired by the most important businesses and government agencies. These students are expected to become the future leaders of Japan.

JAPAN AND THE WORLD: How have Japan's relations with other countries changed in recent years?

16. During the 1980s, Japan faced serious problems in its relations with other countries. The United States imported nearly 40 percent of the goods exported by Japan. Yet Japan limited the amounts of certain products such as cars, meat, and chemicals it imported from the United States. The result was that the United States had a large **trade deficit** with Japan. A trade deficit means that a country buys more goods from other nations than it sells to those nations. By 1987 Japan also had invested over $500 billion in the United States and other countries. Japan used this money to buy important companies, major banks, and large

Ask: Why is schooling so important in Japan? Do Americans consider school to be this important? How does a person's schooling affect his or her life in each of these countries?

▲ Shipping has always been important to Japan, an island country. Why might an increase in exports make shipping even more important?

office buildings in countries such as the United States. Japan also set up factories in these countries. As a result, some nations began to worry that Japan might gain too much control over their economies.

17. Japan has been taking a more active role in world affairs. During the 1980s, Japan started a major foreign-aid program. It used some of the large sums earned from exports to help the developing countries of Africa and Asia. Moreover, Japanese businesses have set up factories in countries such as Malaysia and Singapore.

18. The end of the Cold War had an impact on Japanese foreign policy. After World War II, Japan and the United States became military allies. U.S. troops were stationed in Japan for defense purposes. Both countries agreed that the Soviet Union and its large army were a threat to Japan. With the Soviet Union gone, Japan has been working with Russia to solve territorial disputes over several Pacific ▶ islands. How might the breakup of the Soviet Union affect relations between the United States and Japan?

OUTLOOK

19. Japan, a small country with 124 million people, has become an economic superpower. All around the world, people ride to work in Japanese cars and watch sporting events and movies on Japanese television sets. They take pictures with Japanese cameras and listen to music on Japanese compact disc players. Trade is a very important aspect of Japan's economy. As an island nation with few natural resources, it must import raw materials to keep the factories working. Japan is dependent on countries that export these raw materials and on countries that buy its exports. A worldwide economic slump in the early 1990s caused a decline in Japan's growth. Some large businesses had to reduce the number of people they employed. In the midst of the slump, Japan carefully planned new products and ideas for the future. Why is careful planning ◀ important in times of economic decline? Do you think Japan will maintain its position as an economic superpower in the future?

Background: The United States trade deficit grew, from a deficit of $28 billion in 1981 to over $170 billion in 1989. In this same period, Japan's trade surplus grew from $8.7 billion to over $120 billion.

CHAPTER REVIEW

VOCABULARY REVIEW

Write each of the following words on a sheet of paper. Then write the correct definition for each word. Write each word in a sentence.

keiretsu

trade deficit

SKILL BUILDER: MAKING A TABLE

The table below compares Japanese society with American society. Use the information in this chapter to complete the table.

	United States	Japan
Education	Students attend school 180 days each year	
Trade	Low tariffs, few trade barriers	
Natural Resources	coal, iron ore, copper, oil, and many other resources	

SKILL BUILDER: CRITICAL THINKING AND COMPREHENSION

1. Generalizing

▶ Write the number of the paragraph in the chapter that is described by each of these generalizations.

a. The *keiretsu* are powerful industry groups in Japan.

b. School and getting an education are very important in Japan.

c. The government has been as important as business and industry in making Japan a prosperous country.

d. Japan is now playing a larger role in world affairs, especially in giving help to the poorer nations of the world.

2. Cause and Effect

▶ Select the effect that matches the cause.

1-1. Japan is switching to the production of high-technology products.
   a. More imported materials will be needed.
   b. Foreign workers will be needed.
   c. More Japanese workers with scientific and technical training will be needed.

1-2. The Japanese constitution provides that the members of the Japanese Diet are elected by the people.
   a. The prime minister, who is elected by the Diet, represents the people.
   b. The prime minister is chosen by the emperor.
   c. The majority of the Diet is elected by the people.

1-3. Japan limited the amount of certain products that it imported from the United States.

    a. The United States imported few products from Japan.

    b. The United States had a large trade deficit with Japan.

    c. Japan had a large trade deficit with the United States.

1-4. Other Asian countries built up their heavy industries and competed with Japanese industries.

    a. Japan began to grow more farm products.

    b. Japan decided to switch to more profitable high-technology products.

    c. Japan increased its exports of heavy machinery to other Asian countries.

3. Predicting

▶ Read the predictions below and explain why you agree or disagree with them.

    a. The United States will continue to import more products from Japan than it exports to Japan.

    b. The Japanese will succeed in developing artificial intelligence computers.

4. Hypothesizing

    a. Why might Japan become the leader of the Third World countries?

    b. What would happen if the United States decided to sharply cut imports from Japan?

ENRICHMENT

1. Use the Reader's Guide to Periodical Literature, the World Almanac, and other reference sources to find additional information on Japanese investments in the United States. Find examples of banks, office buildings and other real estate, and manufacturing companies. Prepare a report on your findings. As part of the report, make a table to show to the class.

2. Take a survey of members of your homeroom. The object of the survey is to find out how many Japanese products are owned by them and their families, and what kind they are. Classify each product by brand name, or the company that produced it, as well as by the kind of product that it is. Present your findings in a report to the class.

3. In the 1930s, Babe Ruth and other members of the New York Yankees visited Japan. Since that time, baseball has been the most popular sport there. Baseball as it is played in Japan is different in important ways from the way it is played in the United States. Research and prepare a report on baseball in Japan. Tell the differences between Japanese and American baseball. Tell what you think these differences show about the cultures and attitudes of the two countries.

4. Work with several other students to research and prepare a report on Japanese home and family life. Include descriptions of Japanese houses and furniture. Tell about the relationship of husband, wife, and children. Describe Japanese food, and tell how the family entertains its guests. Finally, tell what each member of the family does for recreation.

CHAPTER 5

The United States Moves Ahead

▲ Fireworks on the Mall in Washington, D.C.: What historic event did the United States celebrate on July 4, 1976?

OBJECTIVE: In what ways have the American people improved their lives and helped maintain peace in the world?

1. In 1991, the American people celebrated the 200th birthday of the Bill of Rights. During those 200 years, the United States had grown from a loose alliance of 13 small states into a large and powerful nation. By 1900, the United States had begun to influence world events. By the 1950s, it had become the leader of the democratic nations of the world. The United States had always been a nation of immigrants—the home of a people who had come from other lands, a mixing bowl of different races and different traditions.

The American people had built their nation on the ideals of freedom and opportunity for all citizens. On that 200th birthday, Americans voiced their determination to continue working toward equality of opportunity for all Americans.

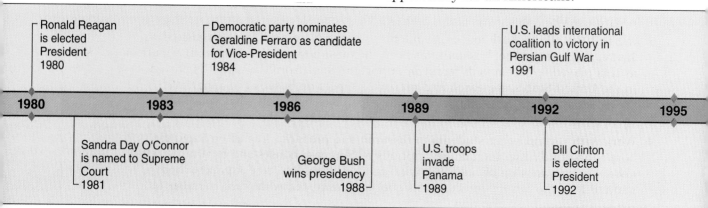

Ronald Reagan is elected President 1980

Democratic party nominates Geraldine Ferraro as candidate for Vice-President 1984

U.S. leads international coalition to victory in Persian Gulf War 1991

| 1980 | 1983 | 1986 | 1989 | 1992 | 1995 |

Sandra Day O'Connor is named to Supreme Court 1981

George Bush wins presidency 1988

U.S. troops invade Panama 1989

Bill Clinton is elected President 1992

Ask: Why is the United States called "the land of opportunity"? What are this nation's great ideals? Why has it sometimes been difficult to achieve these ideals?

THE AMERICAN ECONOMY: How did American business, industry, and farming change in the 1980s and 1990s?

2. Since the end of World War II, the American economy has been one of the strongest and most productive in the world. During these years, the United States produced more goods and services than any other country. As the American economy grew, there were changes in the kinds of work people did. Heavy industries, such as iron and steel mills, machinery, and manufacturing became less important. As a result, fewer Americans now worked in factories and more than half of the American labor force worked in business offices, banks, and stores.

3. During the 1990s, more Americans held jobs than ever before. The number of workers grew from 85 million in 1970 to more than 120 million in 1992. However, for many Americans, their jobs were less secure than they had been in the 1970s. U.S. industry often found itself competing against foreign industries. Many foreign factories were more modern than U.S. factories. In many cases, foreign workers earned considerably less than U.S. workers. Because U.S. goods often were more expensive, American companies found their market shares declining.

4. The growing number of women workers was another major change in the labor force. Two-worker families became common. By the 1990s, more than 50 percent of all workers were women—many of whom had children and were working to help support their families. One in every seven families was headed by a single woman. Because women often were paid lower wages than men, many one-parent families lived in or close to poverty. In the 1990s, although most women still worked in factories, stores, and offices, a growing number had become lawyers, accountants, and doctors.

5. In the boom years that followed World War II, most Americans enjoyed prosperous times. More families than ever before were able to buy their own homes. By the 1990s, 65 percent of the American people owned their own houses or apartments. Americans owned more cars than the people of any other country. Most people had to borrow money to make big purchases such as homes and cars. However, many people seemed to have money for leisure activities such as sports, entertainment, and travel.

6. Not all U.S. workers shared equally in the general prosperity of the 1980s. Many Hispanics and African Americans had difficulty finding jobs, and many others were poorly paid. The incomes of African-American and Hispanic families often were lower than those of other families. However, many African Americans and Hispanics made important gains in these years. Some took special job training to acquire new skills. Others attended colleges and became doctors, lawyers, teachers, and business leaders.

7. U.S. farmers faced serious difficulties in the 1980s and 1990s. Most farms in America were now run by large companies. Most families on small farms could not compete with the large corporate farms. As a result, many farmers had to sell farms that had been in their families for generations. The corporate farms produced more wheat, corn, soybeans, and other crops than ever before. In fact, the large company farms grew more grain and other crops than America needed. This meant that farmers grew surplus crops that were sold to the people of other countries. Should family farms have been forced out ◀ of business, or should they have been protected by the government?

AMERICAN GOVERNMENT: What role did the President and Congress play in changing Americans' lives?

8. Ronald Reagan was elected President in 1980 and again in 1984, winning the majority vote. Reagan believed the federal government should cut taxes on American industries and spend less on **social pro-**

ESL/LEP Strategy: Copy paragraph 3 onto reproducible paper omitting every fifth word (or paragraph 5, omitting every seventh). Provide a word bank with the missing words. Have students work in groups to find the word that best fits in each blank.

707

grams. Social programs are government programs that help needy groups of people to improve their lives. Reagan believed that if businesses paid lower taxes, they would be able to expand and provide more jobs for American workers. Congress passed much of Reagan's program and made sweeping changes in the tax system. During the Reagan years, after a rough start, the economy grew.

9. Reagan's Vice-President, George Bush, was elected President in 1988. In office, Bush continued Reagan's program of holding down the cost of social programs. Then, in the early 1990s, the country slipped into a **recession,** or sharp economic downturn. After a time, many people lost faith in Bush's ability to turn the economy around.

10. In the presidential election of 1992, voters were presented with three choices. President George Bush led the Republican ticket, Arkansas Governor Bill Clinton was the Democratic candidate, and Texas businessman Ross Perot ran as an independent candidate. Clinton won the election by an electoral landslide. He and his running mate, Al Gore, promised to bring changes that would improve the U.S. economy and change the health care system.

GAINS BY WOMEN AND MINORITIES: How did women and minorities gain a more active role in public life?

11. Women made major gains in U.S. politics during the 1980s and 1990s. In 1984, Democratic Congresswoman Geraldine Ferraro became the first woman to run for Vice-President on a major party's ticket. After the election of 1992, there was a total of six women serving in the Senate and 47 serving in the House of Representatives—the highest numbers ever. These numbers represented an increase in public support for women in the federal government. In addition, women were elected in record numbers to positions in state and local governments.

▲ In the 1992 presidential race, Bill Clinton ran a tough campaign that focused on the economy. Here, he is shown with his wife Hillary.

PEOPLE IN HISTORY

12. In 1981, Sandra Day O'Connor was appointed a Supreme Court justice, making her the first woman to serve in this position. O'Connor had previously served as state senator and as a judge in Arizona's highest courts. Her talent and skill were rewarded when she was chosen to serve on the United States Supreme Court.

13. African Americans and Hispanics played a growing role in U.S. government during the 1980s and 1990s. In the 1984 and 1988 presidential elections, Jesse Jackson was a leading candidate for the Democratic party's nomination. Since the 1960s, African Americans and Hispanics have served in presidential cabinet posts and other important government positions. In addition, many Hispanics and African Americans have made gains in state and local government.

AMERICAN SOCIETY: How did life improve and what challenges did Americans face?

14. The population of the United States grew to 256 million in 1992. Included were more than 29 million African Americans, 22 million Hispanics, 7 million Asians, and 2 million Native Americans. Hispanics and people aged 65 and over have become the two fastest-growing groups.

15. About 8.6 million people immigrated to the United States in the 1980s. Many arrived from Asia. Even more came from Mexico, Central America, South America, and the Caribbean. Newcomers face many difficulties. They often lack good housing and work at the lowest-paying jobs. Like immigrants of the past, they hope to build a better life.

WORLD AFFAIRS: How has U.S. foreign policy changed from the 1980s to the 1990s?

16. Today, the United States faces a vastly different world from the one it confronted in the past. The end of the Cold War and the breakup of the Soviet Union during the early 1990s have made the United States the unchallenged world leader.

17. Arms control was a major issue in the final years of the Cold War. During the 1980s, President Reagan increased military spending. After Mikhail Gorbachev came to power in the Soviet Union, the two leaders negotiated reductions of nuclear weapons. After the breakup of the Soviet Union, the United States began talks on this issue with the newly independent countries.

18. The United States took an active role in the Western Hemisphere throughout the 1980s. President Reagan sent troops to the island of Grenada in 1983 to help remove its leftist government. In 1989, President Bush sent troops into Panama to oust right-wing military leader Manuel Noriega. In Nicaragua, the Reagan administration backed armed rebels, called contras, against the leftist government.

19. Events in the Middle East posed new opportunities for the United States. In 1990, Iraq invaded the country of Kuwait.

With UN support, the United States built an international coalition, or association, to remove Iraqi forces from Kuwait. On January 17, 1991, the Persian Gulf War began. In six weeks, the coalition's military forces drove Iraq out of Kuwait. The United States then used its influence to promote peace talks between Israel and its Arab neighbors.

20. In its unchallenged role, the United States found itself being called upon to solve problems throughout the world. For example, in 1992 and 1993, American forces occupied portions of the African nation of Somalia to try to stop massive starvation caused by fighting among rival groups.

21. The United States faced two major economic problems in the 1980s and 1990s. It suffered a trade deficit, selling too few goods abroad to pay for imports. It also ran up a massive **budget deficit**—the government took in too little money to pay for its spending. Tax cuts and military spending during the 1980s caused the deficit to grow even larger. The United States had to borrow billions of dollars from other nations to pay its bills.

OUTLOOK

22. At the dawn of a new era, the United States finds itself in a position of world leadership. Despite some economic setbacks, the United States continues to be one of the world's leading nations. Its traditions of freedom and opportunity continue to inspire people. African Americans, Hispanics, and women have made gains that have led to more job opportunities and fuller equality. However, the problems of poverty and homelessness remain to be solved. Americans also are becoming more aware of the critical need to balance the budget and clean up the environment. What do you think the ◄ United States must do to keep its position of world leadership?

Background: Entertainment comprises one of America's leading exports. Rock and country and western music records, motion pictures, television programs, and live concerts by pop music superstars not only earn many billions in foreign exchange, they also spread American culture throughout the world.

709

CHAPTER REVIEW

VOCABULARY REVIEW

Write each of the following words on a sheet of paper. Then write the correct definition for each word.

recession

Persian Gulf War

social programs

SKILL BUILDER: READING A LINE GRAPH

Study the graph and then answer the questions.

1. What period of time is covered on this graph?

2. How many autos are represented by each mark on the left-hand side of the graph?

3. In which year were auto exports from Japan to the United States the largest?

4. In which year did auto exports from Japan reach more than 3 million for the first time?

5. In how many years were more than 3 million autos exported from Japan to the United States?

6. In which year was the smallest number of autos exported?

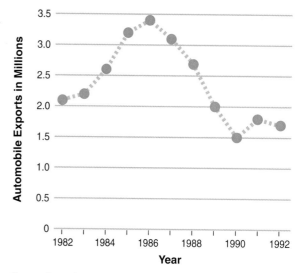

JAPANESE AUTOMOBILE EXPORTS TO THE UNITED STATES, 1982–1992

Source: Japan Automobile Manufacture's Association, Inc..

SKILL BUILDER: CRITICAL THINKING AND COMPREHENSION

 1. Classifying

▶ Copy the descriptions below grouping them under the correct category of: American government, American foreign policy, or American economy.

a. With UN approval, the United States took a leading role in the Persian Gulf War of 1991.

b. By the 1990s, more than 50 percent of all American workers were women.

c. Jesse Jackson was a candidate for the Democratic party's nomination in 1984 and 1988.

d. In 1983, American troops were sent to the Caribbean island of Grenada.

e. Most farming in America was done by large companies and small farm families were not able to compete.

f. Sandra Day O'Connor was chosen by President Reagan as the first woman ever to serve on the Supreme Court.

STUDY HINT Read the People In History on page 708. This biography of Sandra Day O'Connor tells about her important role in recent American history. Think about what she has accomplished. How is O'Connor an example of an important subject discussed in the chapter?

2. Spatial Relationships

▶ Read each statement below. After each write **C** if the place is close to the United States or **F** if it is far away.

a. During the 1990s, many immigrants came from Asia.

b. Many immigrants came to the United States from Mexico.

c. Large numbers of people came from South America to the United States.

3. Drawing Conclusions

▶ Read each pair of statements below and then write the conclusion you form from this information.

3-1 a. Foreign workers earned considerably less than American workers.

b. American goods were often more expensive than foreign goods.

3-2 a. In 1984, Congresswoman Geraldine Ferraro ran for Vice-President on the Democratic ticket.

b. Many women served in Congress and in high state and city offices.

4. Hypothesizing

▶ Read each statement below and then write a sentence in which you form a hypothesis about why the statement is true.

a. In recent years, millions of immigrants have come to the United States from many other parts of the world.

b. During the 1980s, the United States took an activist role in the Western Hemisphere.

c. The United States has a huge budget deficit.

d. In the early 1990s, many American workers felt less secure about their jobs.

ENRICHMENT

1. Prepare a classroom display of highlights of the nation's bicentennial celebration of the Bill of Rights. Include a list of the Bill of Rights (the first ten amendments to the Constitution). The display can include drawings or pictures of the people who supported the Bill of Rights. Make a cartoon drawing showing the freedoms protected by these amendments. You may wish to write brief summaries of recent court cases in which one of the amendments has been upheld.

2. Reread paragraphs 1 to 10 in this chapter. Then make a chart entitled "The United States Today." Head one part "Important Achievements" and head the other part "Problems to Be Solved." Then under each of these headings include the achievements and problems you think are the most important.

CHAPTER 6

The Challenge of the Future

▲ Lasers are intense beams of light produced by stimulating atoms. The new technology has many industrial and medical applications.

OBJECTIVE: What challenges must people around the world tackle now and in the future?

1. At midnight on December 31, 2000, the world will enter a new century, the year A.D. 2001. It will be the start of a new millennium, or the first day of the next 1,000 years. Think back to what was happening in the world about 1,000 years ago. How much has the world changed over that 1,000 years? Have those changes affected the way you live today? How much do you think the world will change over the next 1,000 years? These are important questions for you to think about. Finding answers to these questions will help you to understand the importance of the past. You will also understand how the past is connected to the present and to the future. Most importantly, finding the answers to these questions will help you to think about what you would like your role to be in the future.

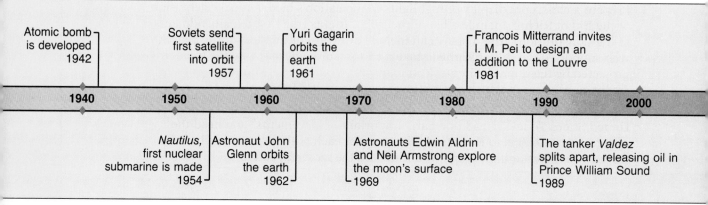

Atomic bomb
is developed
1942

Soviets send
first satellite
into orbit
1957

Yuri Gagarin
orbits the
earth
1961

Francois Mitterrand invites
I. M. Pei to design an
addition to the Louvre
1981

1940	1950	1960	1970	1980	1990	2000

Nautilus,
first nuclear
submarine is made
1954

Astronaut John
Glenn orbits
the earth
1962

Astronauts Edwin Aldrin
and Neil Armstrong explore
the moon's surface
1969

The tanker *Valdez*
splits apart, releasing oil in
Prince William Sound
1989

TECHNOLOGY AND INDUSTRY: How has modern technology improved the lifestyle of people in industrialized nations?

2. The technology that started with the Industrial Revolution in the 1700s eventually revolutionized the methods of manufacturing goods for a world-wide market. Standardization of parts, the assembly line, and mass production made it possible for early industrial societies to produce more goods than non-industrial societies. Lasers (LAY-zurs), computers, and other technologies have further increased productivity. Lasers are intense beams of light that can do precise cutting and sealing. Lasers are used in industry, in surgery, and in other fields.

3. Just as there was a Stone Age and a Bronze Age thousands of years ago, people today say that this is the Computer Age. The Computer Age probably will continue into the twenty-first century. Some people fear that many jobs will be lost because of computers. In fact, jobs *have* been lost because of the greater efficiency of the computer. However, new kinds of jobs, such as programmers, computer repair, software development, and computer sales have formed because of the computer. In the twenty-first century, the nations that continue to develop computer technology and encourage computer education will probably do best economically.

4. Think about the nations of the world today. Have you noticed that people in the more industrialized nations are often better clothed, fed and sheltered than people in non-industrialized nations? People must be able to satisfy their basic needs of food, clothing and shelter before they can take time to develop other goods. The technology that led to the Agricultural Revolution helped to free people from struggling to meet only their basic food needs. With less time needed for farming, people had more time to create new inventions, from spinning machines and telephones to automobiles and space crafts. Ever since the Industrial and Agricultural revolutions, advances

in the industrialized world have taken place rapidly. By contrast, many people in nations that have remained largely agricultural continue to struggle for their basic needs. Why do you think this is so? How might industrialized nations help agricultural nations?

TECHNOLOGY AND ENERGY: How has modern technology provided new energy sources?

5. During the Industrial Revolution, water power and steam power from coal were the major forms of energy. This energy was used to power factory machines, trains, and ships. Oil was known but had little value as a resource until major oil production began in the mid-1800s. The main product of the oil industry at that time was kerosene, used for lamps. With the development of gasoline-powered automobiles in the early 1900s, oil production increased rapidly. World War I also increased the demand for fuel oil to power the wartime tanks, ships and airplanes. Oil quickly became a major source of energy for the industrial nations. After World War I, fuel oil was used to power tractors and other farming equipment. This led to more improvements in crop production in industrial nations. In addition, roads were built, using by-products of oil. New roads improved transportation systems and trade in industrialized nations of the world. Today oil is a major source of energy for transportation, heat and factory power. However, oil is a non-renewable resource. The supply of oil is declining and scientists expect oil supplies to run out in the early part of the twenty-first century.

6. In recent years some people have placed hope in nuclear power as the power of the future. The development of the atomic bomb in 1942 led scientists to discover the power of nuclear energy. By 1954 the United States made the first use of controlled nuclear energy through the *Nautilus*, which was the first nuclear-powered submarine. By the late 1950s nuclear power

Activity: Students who are interested in technical careers might do research to find out more about how technology is changing the world of work.

713

plants were being built to supply electrical energy to people in the United States. Nuclear energy, formed by splitting atoms, creates huge amounts of heat. The heat is used to make steam which moves the generators that create electricity.

7. There have been disagreements among people in many parts of the world about the safety of nuclear power. People who favor nuclear energy like it better because it takes less nuclear fuel to create greater energy than oil, coal, or natural gas. People also favor nuclear energy because it does not pollute the air as it releases heat. People who oppose nuclear energy say that nuclear power plants are far too costly to build. They also say that nuclear power plants are far too dangerous to humans as well as wildlife if a meltdown should occur and ▶ radiation is released. What do you think about the use of nuclear energy?

8. Probably one of the most critical issues facing the world in the twenty-first century

is the energy issue. The industrial world cannot survive without energy sources. Nations that are slowly becoming industrialized are also beginning to use more and more energy. Yet the supply of energy is limited. Many scientists and inventors today are tackling the energy issue. They are trying to find new, safer, cleaner, and less expensive ways to provide energy to the world. Some scientists continue to experiment with using **solar energy**, or energy from the sun. Other scientists hope to tap energy from the powerful flow of water in the ocean. Still other scientists are discovering how to develop energy from **nuclear fusion**. In nuclear fusion, atoms are combined rather than split. Nuclear fusion can create greater heat energy than nuclear fission. Nuclear fusion also is safer because it does not produce radioactivity. In recent years scientists have been more successful with nuclear fusion experiments. Combined research and development of nuclear fusion may prevent an energy crisis that otherwise would surely develop in the twenty-first century. How can you help conserve energy ◀ daily? How would the world change if all sources of energy were suddenly used up?

TECHNOLOGY AND THE ENVIRONMENT: How have advances in technology both helped and threatened the environment?

9. Advances in technology have helped improve the way we use earth's resources in some ways. The Agricultural Revolution was just the beginning of finding better ways to grow crops. Today, it takes less land to yield much greater harvests of food than it did just 100 years ago. In the past farmers often wore out the soil. Today farmers replace the lost nutrients in the soil with fertilizers. Scientists have learned how to grow hardier plants that better resist disease and drought. In the past flood waters could ruin crops and communities. Today, large dams help control rivers so that damage from floods is often kept in check. In the past, lumber jacks stripped forests bare of trees. Today, industrialized nations know

▼ One or more nuclear reactors lie at the heart of a modern nuclear power plant. The reactors are encased in concrete.

how to selectively cut grown trees and re-plant tree seedlings so that forest land is not

▶ destroyed. What other examples can you think of where scientific discoveries and technology have improved and protected our environment?

10. On the other hand, this knowledge has not always been put to use. The effects of technology have damaged the planet earth. Garbage and waste products have been dumped into the ocean. This practice has harmed marine life and spoiled the beaches in many parts of the world. **Pesticides** that have been used to protect crops have caused illness in birds, animals and humans. Pesticides are chemicals that are used to kill insects. Exhaust fumes from automobiles and burn-off from factories that use coal and oil have polluted the fragile air you breathe. In fact, pollution from coal has been directly linked to causing **acid rain**. Acid rain forms when the sulfur burn-off from coal combines with rain water to create sulfuric acid. The acid kills trees in forests thousands of miles from the polluting factories. Even something as simple as salt, used to melt ice and snow on roadways in winter, can pollute our water supply.

11. A dramatic example of modern technology threatening the earth occurred in the coastal waters of Alaska on March 24, 1989. The supertanker *Valdez* ran aground on a reef in Alaska's Prince William Sound. Prince William Sound is a major fishing ground for salmon, herring, shrimp, and crab. It is also home to wildlife such as seals, sea otters, birds, and whales. The broken hull of the ship released over 10 million gallons of oil into the sound. The oil slick quickly spread over 1,600 square miles, killed wildlife, and damaged 800 miles (1,280 kilometers) of shoreline. Similar oil spills have caused damage in other parts of the world. Modern technology

▶ and industry cannot be reversed. What should industrialized nations of the world do to protect the earth from air pollution, water pollution, and other types of pollution?

▲ Forests around the world are being destroyed by unregulated cutting and increasing air pollution.

SPACE TECHNOLOGY: How has space technology changed people's perceptions of the world today?

12. Like earlier explorations of the earth, the exploration of the solar system has occurred because humans are naturally curious. Curiosity has also led to scientific and technological discoveries which have allowed people to travel into space. Space exploration began in 1957, when Soviet scientists sent the first small satellite into orbit around the earth. Since that time, the Soviet Union and the United States have become leaders and rivals in space exploration. In 1961, Soviet cosmonaut Yuri Gagarin was the first person to orbit the earth in a spacecraft. Then John Glenn, an American astronaut, orbited the earth in 1962. In the late 1960s, the United States began the Apollo program. The aim of Apollo was to land American astronauts on

The Arts and Artifacts

▲ I.M. Pei's invisible roof is a successful blend of technology and art. Glass for the 71-foot pyramid was specially made by a French company.

The Louvre's "Invisible Roof"

The Louvre is one of the greatest art museums in in the world. The Louvre is a huge palace in Paris. It was built mostly in the time of Louis XIV. In 1981 the President of France, Francois Mitterand, invited the American architect, I.M. Pei, to design an addition to the Louvre to improve its use as a museum. The Louvre had no central entrance, and visitors often felt lost in its endless rooms and corridors. I.M. Pei, a Chinese American, was at first shocked by the idea of making any changes in the historic building. Then he decided to take on the challenge. Pei chose to excavate, or dig out, the large courtyard so that the needed improvements could be built underground. In that way, the addition would not change the outside of the palace itself.

Pei put only one new structure above the surface of the courtyard, a "roof" for a new central entrance. The entrance takes visitors to different parts of the museum through underground passages. Pei told his assistants that the "roof" must be simple, beautiful, and must not block any view. He told them that he wanted the roof to be "invisible."

For the invisible roof, Pei and his staff created a pyramid of clear glass panels mounted on a delicate steel frame. The task of making the frame as light as possible, was given to a company in Canada that made rigging for racing yachts. The frame was held in place by a network of cables inside the pyramid. At first the French people were not sure what to think of this ultramodern addition to their historical museum. However, they have come to accept it as representing mutual respect between modern architecture and the magnificent architecture of the past.

1. How did I.M. Pei preserve the beauty of the past while making an improvement in the Louvre for the present?

2. What might you have done if you had been asked to improve the Louvre as a museum?

the moon, and bring them safely back to earth. In 1969 two American astronauts, Edwin Aldrin and Neil Armstrong, landed on the moon and explored its surface. This historic success was shared by millions of people all over the world as they watched the landing on television.

SPOTLIGHT ON SOURCES

13. Astronaut William Anders, who flew the Apollo mission in 1968, described his feelings at the sight of earth from space.

"We were fighter pilots and test pilots out to do a job. But all of us either transcended [rose above] that or were jerked out of it by the view of the Earth as a sphere [globe] about the size of your fist at the end of your arm. When these views [of earth] came back on television or in photographs, mankind [people] could see for the first time that it existed on a very small, fragile, and finite [limited] Earth."

—from *The View from Space*, Ron Schick and Julia Van Haaften

14. Astronaut Anders was not the only person struck by the smallness of earth in the vast expanse of space. Millions of television viewers also saw how tiny the earth is. The pictures made people around the world realize that earth is the only known place where humans can comfortably survive. Therefore, in the late 1900s many people have joined groups such as the Sierra Club and the National Wildlife Association to help protect the earth's environment and wildlife.

15. In the last ten years, space probes have been sent to the far reaches of the solar system. These probes have sent back photographs to earth of planets such as Jupiter, Saturn, and Uranus. The photographs and other data have brought scientists much new information about the atmospheres and surfaces of these planets. Improved knowledge about the climate of Venus

has given scientists a new approach to understanding changes in Earth's atmosphere.

16. The space program has also led to improved scientific information about the earth and improved awareness of cultures around the globe. Some satellites circling the earth provide daily information about cloud patterns. Therefore weather forecasting is more accurate. Satellites also scan the earth for new sources of coal, oil, and natural gas. Other satellites relay signals to television sets so that people around the world can see world events as they happen. People today, especially in industrialized nations, can know more than ever before about people and cultures from other parts of the world. How might this knowledge ◄ improve relations among people around the world? How might the improved relations help prevent nuclear warfare?

OUTLOOK

17. The history of the world is a history of challenges faced by various groups of people. Often the challenges were military. Sometimes they were religious or political. People and nations today have their own set of challenges as they look forward to the twenty-first century. Certainly the advances humans have made in areas such as industrialization, communication, agriculture, education, and medicine have improved the quality of life. However, millions of people, mainly in non-industrialized nations of the world, are unable to meet basic human needs. Many are hungry, and many starve to death each year. What can be done to ◄ help those people? In industrialized nations there is the real danger of pollution that goes with technological advancement. Since the earth is the only place for humans ◄ to live, what needs to be done about pollution? These are just a few of the challenges that you will face as the future leaders of the world. What role do you think you would ◄ like to play in making the planet earth a cleaner, healthier and safer place to live?

CHAPTER REVIEW

VOCABULARY REVIEW

Write each of the following sentences on a sheet of paper. Then fill in the blank with the word that best completes each sentence.

lasers   pesticides

solar energy   acid rain

nuclear fusion

1. _____ are chemicals used to kill harmful insects.

2. Some people heat their homes by placing _____ panels on their roofs to collect energy from the sun.

3. Sulfur from burning coal combines with water droplets in clouds to produce _____ .

4. _____ are so exact that they are used in delicate eye surgery. Patients recover quickly because no incision is needed.

5. Heat produced from joining atoms is called _____ .

SKILL BUILDER: READING A MAP

Study the map below. Then answer the questions that follow.

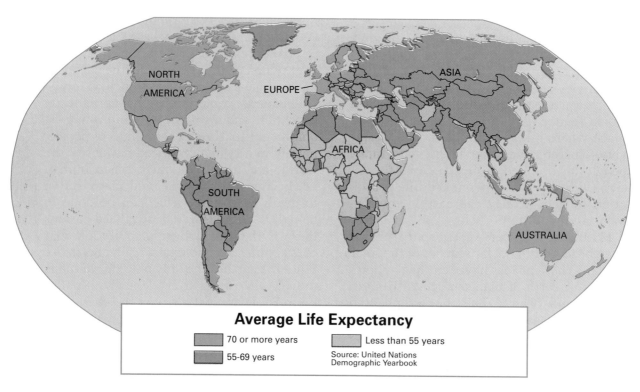

Average Life Expectancy

- 70 or more years
- 55-69 years
- Less than 55 years

Source: United Nations Demographic Yearbook

STUDY
HINT

Look at the three photographs in Chapter 6. What does each photo tell you about the effects of technology on the world?

1. What is the title of the map?

2. Is life expectancy longer or shorter in industrialized nations than in non-industrialized nations?

3. Which continents or parts of continents have an average life expectancy of 70 or more years?

4. Which continent has the largest area of life expectancy less than 55 years?

5. What other continent has the same overall life expectancy as South America?

SKILL BUILDER: CRITICAL THINKING AND COMPREHENSION

▲ 1. Summarizing

▶ Write a summary statement that describes the main sources of energy available to the world today.

2. Cause and Effect

▶ Rewrite each cause. Next to each cause write the effect that matches it.

Cause

2-1. The Valdez ran aground on a reef.

2-2. Burning coal emits sulfur.

2-3. Oil supplies are being used up quickly.

Effect

a. New forms of energy must be found.

b. Oil has polluted Prince William Sound.

c. Acid rain is destroying forests.

3. Predicting

▶ Answer the following questions.

a. What do you think will happen if pollution of the earth is not held in check?

b. Do you think nuclear power plants will continue to be built? Why?

4. Making Judgments

▶ Use your judgment to answer the following questions.

a. What are the advantages and disadvantages of living in an industrialized nation?

b. What do you think is the most pressing issue for the twenty-first century? Why?

ENRICHMENT

1. Gather newspaper and magazine articles about current pollution problems. Make a short oral report that summarizes your findings.

2. Write a comparison of life 1,000 years ago to life today in a region of your choice. Include agriculture, clothing, shelter, jobs, family life-style, government, and trade. Then write a description of how life will be in that region 1,000 years from now.

UNIT REVIEW

SUMMARY

The major nations of the world changed rapidly in the 1980s and 1990s. Most Western European countries have benefited from the European Community, which promotes freer trade. In 1991, the world witnessed the breakup of the Soviet Union. Communism suffered big setbacks both in the Soviet Union and in Eastern Europe, where the former satellite nations turned to democracy. In China, Communist rule continued, although economic reforms brought greater prosperity to many. Japan has built a strong economy, becoming a powerful trading nation. High-quality Japanese goods are sold throughout the world. The United States, now the world's only superpower, enjoys a relatively high standard of living. However, the country must work to reduce its trade and budget deficits. In addition, women and minorities benefit from increased opportunities in education and employment.

SKILL BUILDER: READING A GRAPH

▶ The graph below shows the growth in the world's population since 1950. Study the information on the graph and then answer the questions below.

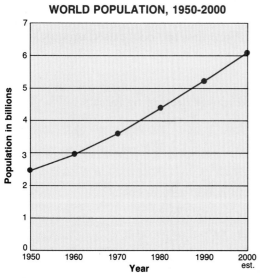

WORLD POPULATION, 1950-2000

Sources: *Demographic Yearbook-1983*, The United Nations, New York, N.Y., 1986
The World Almanac and Book of Facts, World Almanac, New York, N.Y.

1. For what period of time is world population growth shown?

2. What was the population in the earliest year shown on the graph? What is the population in the last year shown?

3. In what year did world population go over 3 billion for the first time?

4. How much did population increase between 1950 and 1990? How much more will it increase by the year 2000?

5. It took nearly 200 years, from the year 1650 to the year 1850, for world population to grow from 500 million to 1 billion. How many years did it take for the population to grow from 2.5 billion to more than 6 billion?

SKILL BUILDER: CRITICAL THINKING AND COMPREHENSION

○ **1. Generalizing**

▶ Read each pair of statements. Then make a generalization using the information they provide.

1-1 a. After the collapse of the Soviet Union, the Russian republic banned the Communist party.
b. In the former satellite nations of Eastern Europe, democratic governments replaced Communist ones.

1-2 a. The breakup of the Soviet Union left the United States the only remaining superpower.
b. The United States occupied parts of Somalia in the early 1990s.

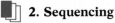

2. Sequencing

▶ Read each pair of statements and decide which event described happened first.

2-1. a. George Bush was elected president of the United States.
  b. Margaret Thatcher became the first woman to serve as prime minister of Great Britain.

2-2. a. Communist China began its plan of the Four Modernizations.
  b. Japan's economy became the second largest in the world.

2-3. a. Deng Xiaoping became leader of Communist China.
  b. Helmut Schmidt became chancellor of West Germany.

3. Predicting

▶ Read each statement below and then make a prediction about what it means for the future of each country.

a. In the 1990s, many different ethnic groups in the former Soviet Union demanded more power to control their own affairs.

b. In Japan, education determines the kind of job a person has as well as his or her position in society.

c. In the United States, many African Americans and Hispanic Americans attended college and became doctors, lawyers, teachers, and business leaders.

4. Making Judgments

▶ Read each group of statements and then make a judgement about the problem they describe.

a. Exploring space increases knowledge and brings improvements in medicine and other benefits to humanity. However, space exploration costs billions of dollars that could be used to help needy people. Should the United States continue its space program?

b. China has begun economic reforms that have raised the nation's standard of living and given people new opportunities. China is also a Communist country that allows its people few political freedoms. What should the United States policy be toward China?

ENRICHMENT

1. Every night on television, reporters describe current events that are taking place in the United States and in nations all around the world. Watch one of these news programs. As you do so, on a sheet of paper write down events occurring in one of the countries you read about in this chapter. When the program is ended, study the events you listed. Then use your notes to write a short paragraph telling how these events compare with the ways things were in that country in the early 1980s.

2. Think about some of the problems people living in these nations faced in the early 1990s. Also think about some of the things they achieved during this time. Suppose you were an adviser to the President in the year 2020. Write a short report to help the President understand what people's lives were like in the 1990s. Explain why it is important for the nation's leader to know this history.

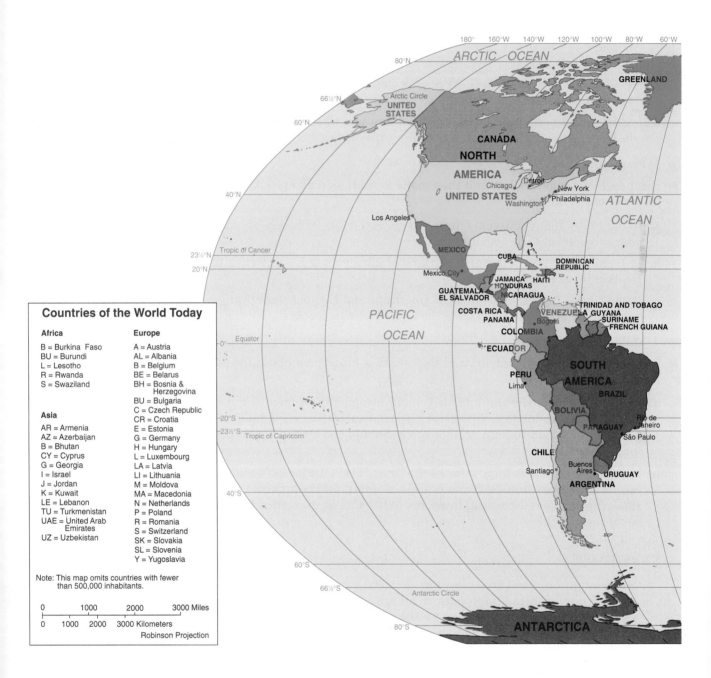

Countries of the World Today

Africa

B = Burkina Faso
BU = Burundi
L = Lesotho
R = Rwanda
S = Swaziland

Asia

AR = Armenia
AZ = Azerbaijan
B = Bhutan
CY = Cyprus
G = Georgia
I = Israel
J = Jordan
K = Kuwait
LE = Lebanon
TU = Turkmenistan
UAE = United Arab
     Emirates
UZ = Uzbekistan

Europe

A = Austria
AL = Albania
B = Belgium
BE = Belarus
BH = Bosnia &
     Herzegovina
BU = Bulgaria
C = Czech Republic
CR = Croatia
E = Estonia
G = Germany
H = Hungary
L = Luxembourg
LA = Latvia
LI = Lithuania
M = Moldova
MA = Macedonia
N = Netherlands
P = Poland
R = Romania
S = Switzerland
SK = Slovakia
SL = Slovenia
Y = Yugoslavia

Note: This map omits countries with fewer
than 500,000 inhabitants.

0	1000	2000	3000 Miles

0	1000	2000	3000 Kilometers

Robinson Projection

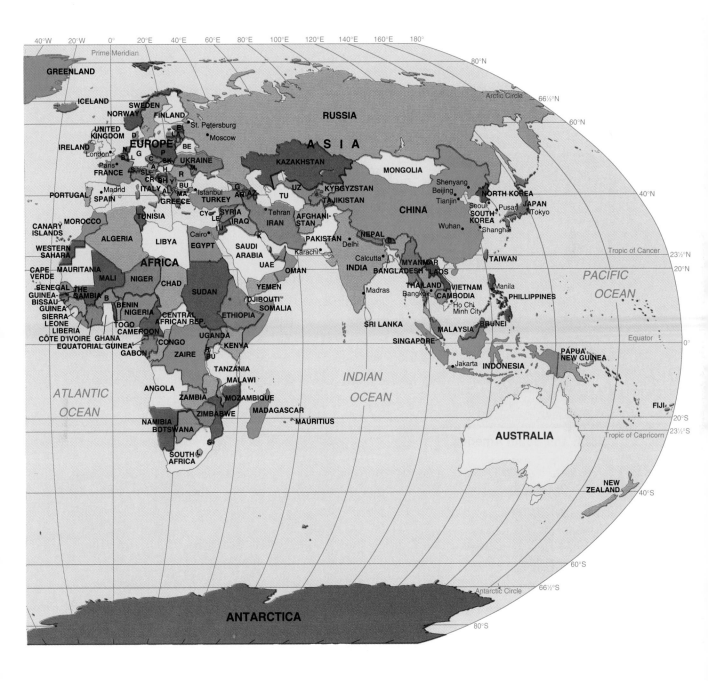

40°W 20°W 0° 20°E 40°E 60°E 80°E 100°E 120°E 140°E 160°E 180°

Prime Meridian

80°N

GREENLAND

Arctic Circle 66½°N

ICELAND

SWEDEN 60°N

NORWAY **FINLAND**

St. Petersburg

RUSSIA

UNITED Moscow
KINGDOM

IRELAND **EUROPE** **A S I A**

London• **KAZAKHSTAN**

Paris• **UKRAINE** **MONGOLIA**
FRANCE

Shenyang 40°N
PORTUGAL Madrid• **ITALY** **UZ** **KYRGYZSTAN** Beijing• **NORTH KOREA**
SPAIN **GREECE** **TURKEY** **TU** **TAJIKISTAN** **CHINA** Tianjin• **SOUTH** **JAPAN**
Istanbul **KOREA** •Tokyo
Seoul• •Pusan
TUNISIA **SYRIA** Tehran• **AFGHANI-** Wuhan• •Shanghai
CANARY **CY** **IRAQ** **IRAN** **STAN**
ISLANDS **MOROCCO** **LE** **NEPAL** Tropic of Cancer 23½°N
ALGERIA **LIBYA** Cairo• **PAKISTAN** Delhi• **TAIWAN** 20°N
WESTERN **EGYPT** **SAUDI** Karachi• **MYANMAR**
SAHARA **AFRICA** **ARABIA** **INDIA** **BANGLADESH** **LAOS** **PACIFIC**
CAPE **MAURITANIA** Calcutta• **THAILAND** **VIETNAM** Manila• **OCEAN**
VERDE **UAE** **OMAN** **CAMBODIA**
MALI **NIGER** **YEMEN** Madras• Bangkok• **PHILLIPPINES**
SENEGAL **CHAD** **DJIBOUTI** Ho Chi
GUINEA- **THE** **SUDAN** **SOMALIA** Minh City
BISSAU **GAMBIA** **NIGERIA** **CENTRAL** **ETHIOPIA** **BRUNEI**
GUINEA **BENIN** **AFRICAN REP.** **SRI LANKA** **MALAYSIA**
SIERRA **TOGO** **CAMEROON** **UGANDA** **SINGAPORE** Equator 0°
LEONE **GHANA** **CONGO** **KENYA** **PAPUA**
LIBERIA **EQUATORIAL GUINEA** **ZAIRE** **NEW GUINEA**
CÔTE D'IVOIRE **GABON** Jakarta• **INDONESIA**
TANZANIA
MALAWI
ATLANTIC **ANGOLA** **INDIAN** 20°S
ZAMBIA **MOZAMBIQUE** **OCEAN** **FIJI**
OCEAN **ZIMBABWE** **MADAGASCAR**
NAMIBIA **MAURITIUS** Tropic of Capricorn 23½°S
BOTSWANA **AUSTRALIA**
SOUTH
AFRICA **NEW** 40°S
ZEALAND

60°S

Antarctic Circle 66½°S

ANTARCTICA

80°S

723

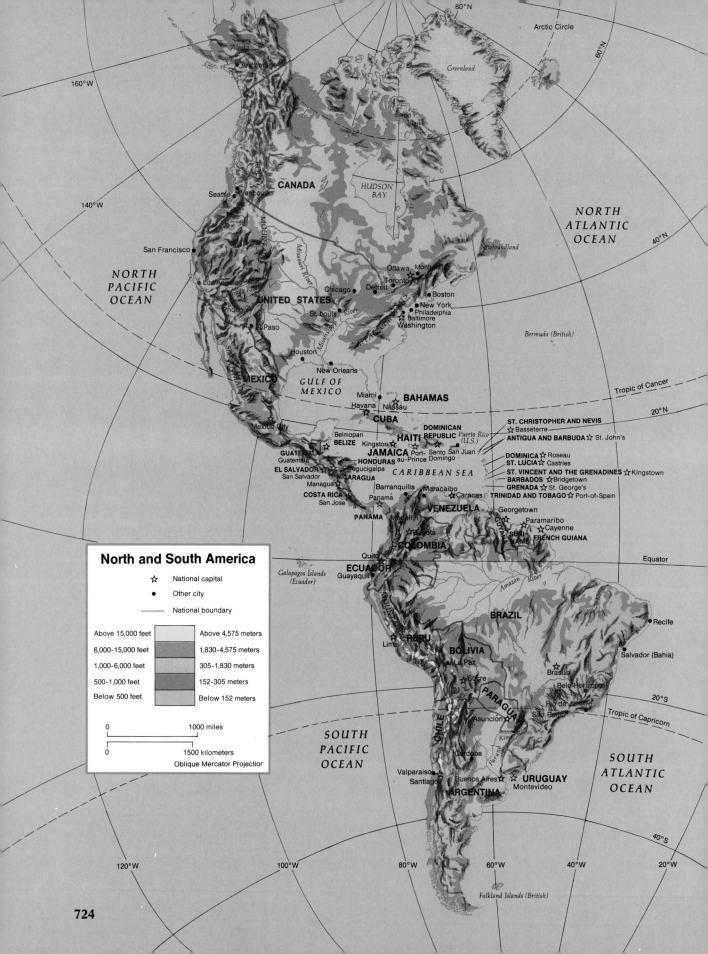

North and South America

☆ National capital

● Other city

— National boundary

Above 15,000 feet		Above 4,575 meters
6,000-15,000 feet		1,830-4,575 meters
1,000-6,000 feet		305-1,830 meters
500-1,000 feet		152-305 meters
Below 500 feet		Below 152 meters

0   1000 miles

0   1500 kilometers

Oblique Mercator Projection

NORTH ATLANTIC OCEAN

NORTH PACIFIC OCEAN

SOUTH PACIFIC OCEAN

SOUTH ATLANTIC OCEAN

CARIBBEAN SEA

GULF OF MEXICO

HUDSON BAY

Arctic Circle

Tropic of Cancer

Equator

Tropic of Capricorn

CANADA

Alaska

Greenland

Baffin Island

Newfoundland

Bermuda (British)

Anchorage

Seattle · Vancouver

San Francisco

Los Angeles

Phoenix

El Paso

UNITED STATES

Missouri River

St. Louis · Ohio River

Chicago ·

Detroit

Ottawa · Montreal · Toronto

· Boston

· New York

· Philadelphia

☆ Baltimore

Washington

Mississippi

Houston ·

New Orleans ·

MEXICO

Mexico City ☆

Belmopan ☆

GUATEMALA

Guatemala

EL SALVADOR

San Salvador ☆

HONDURAS

Tegucigalpa

NICARAGUA

Managua ☆

COSTA RICA

San Jose ☆

PANAMA

BELIZE

Miami ·

Havana ☆ · Nassau

BAHAMAS

CUBA

HAITI

JAMAICA

Kingston

Port-au-Prince

DOMINICAN REPUBLIC

Santo San Juan

Domingo

Puerto Rico (U.S.)

ST. CHRISTOPHER AND NEVIS

☆ Basseterre

ANTIGUA AND BARBUDA ☆ St. John's

DOMINICA ☆ Roseau

ST. LUCIA ☆ Castries

ST. VINCENT AND THE GRENADINES ☆ Kingstown

BARBADOS ☆ Bridgetown

GRENADA ☆ St. George's

TRINIDAD AND TOBAGO ☆ Port-of-Spain

Barranquilla ·

Panamá ☆

Maracaibo ·

Caracas ☆

VENEZUELA

Georgetown ☆

Paramaribo ☆

Cayenne ☆

FRENCH GUIANA

SURINAME

GUYANA

Medellín ·

Bogotá ☆

COLOMBIA

Quito ☆

ECUADOR

Guayaquil ·

Galapagos Islands (Ecuador)

Amazon River

BRAZIL

Recife ·

Salvador (Bahia) ·

Lima ☆

PERU

BOLIVIA

La Paz ·

Sucre ☆

Brasília ☆

Belo Horizonte ·

Rio de Janeiro ·

São Paulo ·

PARAGUAY

Asunción ☆

Paraná River

CHILE

Valparaíso ·

Santiago ☆

Córdoba ·

Buenos Aires ☆

Montevideo ☆

URUGUAY

ARGENTINA

Falkland Islands (British)

160°W   140°W   120°W   100°W   80°W   60°W   40°W   20°W

80°N   60°N   40°N   20°N   20°S   40°S

Africa

☆ National capital

• Other city

〜〜〜 National boundary

Above 15,000 feet	Above 4,575 meters
6,000-15,000 feet	1,830-4,575 meters
1,000-6,000 feet	305-1,830 meters
500-1,000 feet	152-305 meters
Below 500 feet	Below 152 meters

0 200 400 600 800 miles

0 200 400 600 800 kilometers

Lambert Azimuthal Equal-Area Projection

ASIA

EUROPE

Prime Meridian
0°

20°E

40°W

20°W

40°N

Azores
(Portuguese)

Madeira Islands
(Portuguese)

Tangiers
Rabat
Casablanca •
MOROCCO

Algiers

Tunis
TUNISIA
☆ Tripoli

MEDITERRANEAN SEA

Alexandria •
Cairo ★

Suez Canal

Canary Islands
(Spanish)

WESTERN
SAHARA

ALGERIA

LIBYA

EGYPT

Tropic of Cancer
23½°N

20°N

RED SEA

Nile River

CAPE VERDE

Nouakchott ☆

MAURITANIA

Timbuktu •

NIGER

CHAD

SUDAN

Khartoum •

DJIBOUTI

GULF OF ADEN

• Praia

SENEGAL
☆ Dakar

MALI

Niamey
BURKINA
FASO

Kano •

Blue Nile

White Nile

Djibouti •

GAMBIA
Banjul ☆
Bissau ☆
GUINEA-
BISSAU

Bamako ☆

Ouagadougou ☆

N'Djamena •

Addis Ababa •

ETHIOPIA

GUINEA

Niger River

BENIN

Conakry ☆
Freetown ☆
SIERRA
LEONE

IVORY
COAST

GHANA

TOGO

Niger River

NIGERIA

CENTRAL
AFRICAN REP.

SOMALIA

Monrovia ☆

Abidjan •

Porto
Novo
Lome ☆
Accra ☆

Ibadan •
Lagos •

CAMEROON

Bangui ☆

Mogadishu •

LIBERIA

Malabo ☆
EQUATORIAL
GUINEA

Yaoundé ☆

Zaire (Congo) River

UGANDA

KENYA

GULF OF
GUINEA

SÃO TOMÉ
AND PRINCIPE

Libreville ☆
GABON

CONGO

ZAIRE

Kampala ☆

Kigali ☆
RWANDA
BURUNDI
Bujumbura ☆

Nairobi ☆

INDIAN

☆ Victoria

Equator
0°

0°

ATLANTIC

OCEAN

Brazzaville ☆
Kinshasa ☆

Mombasa •

OCEAN

SEYCHELLES

Luanda ☆

TANZANIA

Dar es Salaam •

COMOROS
☆ Moroni

ANGOLA

ZAMBIA

MALAWI

Lusaka ☆

Lilongwe ☆

MOZAMBIQUE

MOZAMBIQUE CHANNEL

☆ Antananarivo

Windhoek ☆

BOTSWANA

ZIMBABWE

Harare ☆

MADAGASCAR

Tropic of Capricorn
23½°S

NAMIBIA

Gabarone ☆

Pretoria ☆
Johannesburg •

Mbabane ☆
Maputo ☆
SWAZILAND

23½°S

Maseru ☆
LESOTHO

Orange River

• Durban

SOUTH
AFRICA

Cape Town ☆

40°S

W

20°W

0°

Prime Meridian

20°E

40°E

725

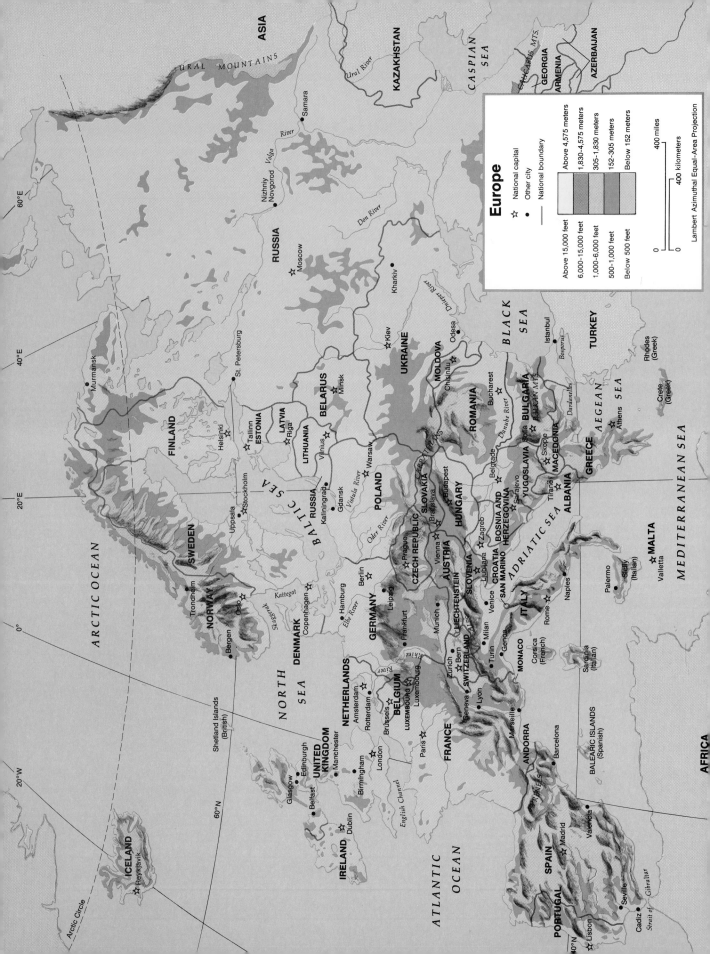

ASIA

URAL MOUNTAINS

Ural River

KAZAKHSTAN

Volga River

Samara

Nizhniy Novgorod

Don River

RUSSIA

☆ Moscow

CASPIAN SEA

CAUCASUS MTS.

GEORGIA
ARMENIA
AZERBAIJAN

Kharkiv ●

Dnieper River

Kiev ●

UKRAINE

MOLDOVA
☆ Chişinău

Odesa ●

Istanbul ●

Bosporus

BLACK SEA

TURKEY

Rhodes (Greek)

Crete (Greek)

Murmansk ●

St. Petersburg ●

Helsinki ☆

FINLAND

Tallinn ☆
ESTONIA

LATVIA
Riga ☆

LITHUANIA
Vilnius ☆

Minsk ●

BELARUS

Warsaw ☆

Bucharest ☆

ROMANIA

Danube River

Belgrade ●

Sofia ☆

BULGARIA

BALKAN MTS.

Skopje ●
MACEDONIA

Tiranë ☆
ALBANIA

GREECE
Athens ☆

AEGEAN SEA

ARCTIC OCEAN

NORWAY

SWEDEN

Uppsala ●

Stockholm ☆

BALTIC SEA

Kaliningrad ●
(RUSSIA)

Gdansk ●

Vistula River

POLAND

Oder River

Prague ☆
CZECH REPUBLIC

Bratislava ☆
SLOVAKIA

Budapest ☆
HUNGARY

Vienna ☆
AUSTRIA

LIECHTENSTEIN

SLOVENIA
Ljubljana ☆

Zagreb ☆
CROATIA

BOSNIA AND HERZEGOVINA
Sarajevo ☆

SAN MARINO

YUGOSLAVIA

ADRIATIC SEA

Trondheim ●

Bergen ●

Oslo ☆

Kattegat

Skagerrak

DENMARK
Copenhagen ☆

Hamburg ●

Elbe River

Berlin ☆

Leipzig ●

GERMANY

Frankfurt ●

Munich ●

Rhine River

Zurich ●
Bern ☆
SWITZERLAND
ALPS

Venice ●
Milan ●
Turin ●
Genoa ●

ITALY

Rome ☆

Naples ●

Corsica (French)

Sardinia (Italian)

Palermo ●

Sicily (Italian)

MALTA
☆ Valletta

MEDITERRANEAN SEA

NORTH SEA

Shetland Islands (British)

NETHERLANDS
Amsterdam ☆
Rotterdam ●

BELGIUM
Brussels ☆

LUXEMBOURG
☆ Luxembourg

Paris ☆
FRANCE

Lyon ●

Geneva ●

Marseille ●

MONACO

ANDORRA

Barcelona ●

BALEARIC ISLANDS (Spanish)

Glasgow ●
Edinburgh ●
UNITED KINGDOM
Belfast ●
Manchester ●
Birmingham ●
London ☆

IRELAND
Dublin ☆

English Channel

PYRENEES

Madrid ☆
SPAIN
Valencia ●

ICELAND
Reykjavík ☆

Arctic Circle

ATLANTIC OCEAN

Lisbon ☆
PORTUGAL

Seville ●
Cadiz ●
Strait of Gibraltar

AFRICA

60°E

60°N

40°E

20°E

0°

20°W

60°N

40°N

GLOSSARY

A

abertura (ah-bair-TOO-rah) (Spanish word) An open door policy to democratic reform.

aborigines (ab-uh-RIJ-uh-neez) The original inhabitants of a country.

absolute (AB-suh-loot) Complete; perfect; no limitations or restraints.

absolute monarch (MON-ark) A King or Ruler with no restrictions.

absolute power Complete control.

acid rain (AS-ehd RAYN) Rain contaminated by chemical by products of industry.

acropolis (uh-KRAHP-uh-lis) A fortified hilltop area in an ancient Greek city-state.

Age of Reason The period in the 1700s when experience and reason replaced religious beliefs and traditions as the basis of many people's ways of thinking; the Enlightenment.

aggression (uh-GRESH-un) An unprovoked, often hostile attack by one country against another.

agora (AG-uh-ruh) The marketplace or place of assembly in an ancient Greek city.

allegiance (uh-LEE-juns) Devotion or loyalty to one's group or country.

alliance (uh-LY-uns) A friendship or agreement formed for mutual benefit.

alloy (AL-oi) A substance that is a mixture of two or more metals.

alms (AHMZ) Charity sometimes given to the poor in the form of money or food.

alphabet (AL-fuh-bet) The letters of a written language, arranged in their customary order.

amphitheater (AM-fuh-thee-uh-ter) A huge arena where the Romans held public events.

Anatolia (an-uh-TOH-lee-uh) A peninsula in Asia, now part of Turkey; also called Asia Minor.

ancestor worship (AN-ses-tur WUR-ship) The practice of honoring as divine an individual or group from which one is descended.

anesthetics (an-uhs-TEHT-iks) Substances that produce a loss of bodily sensations.

animism (AN-uh-miz-um) A belief that all things (including items such as trees, rocks, and man-made objects) have souls and conscious life.

anthropologists (an-thruh-PAL-uh-jists) Scientists who study the physical and cultural characteristics, origins, race distribution, environment and social relations of human beings.

anti-Semitic (an-tee-suh-MIT-ihk) Showing hostility toward or discrimination against Jews.

apartheid (uh-PART-hayt) A policy in the Republic of South Africa that legally separates and classifies people by skin color.

appeasement (uh-PEEZ-ment) The policy of giving into the demands of an aggressive power to keep the peace.

arch (ARCH) A curved structure spanning the top of an opening or doorway serving as a support for the wall above the opening.

archaeologist (ar-kee-AHL-uh-jist) A scientist who studies ruins and other remains of ancient peoples.

archipelago (ar-kuh-PEL-uh-goh) A large group of islands.

architect (AR-kuh-tekt) A person who designs buildings and oversees their construction.

aristocracy (ar-uh-STAH-kruh-see) Government by a privileged few, usually of inherited wealth and social status.

armada (ar-MAH-duh) A large fleet of warships.

Aryan (AIR-ee-un) A modern name for a group of early invaders of India and their language; in the 1930s and 1940s the term was used by Nazis to refer to non-Jewish Caucasians.

assassinated (uh-sas-i-NAY-ted) An important leader murdered for political reasons.

astronomers (uh-STRON-uh-murs) Scientists that study the origin, motion, and other characteristics of heavenly bodies.

astronomy (uh-STRON-uh-mee) The science that examines planets and other heavenly bodies.

atone (uh-TOHN) To do something that will make up for a wrong done.

atrium (AY-tree-uhm) The central hall of a Roman house.

Ausgleich (OWS-glykh) The separation in 1867 of Hungary from Austria, forming Austria-Hungary, two nations with one ruler.

autonomy (aw-TAHN-uh-mee) The power or right of self government.

B

back to basics Stressing the importance of basic subjects such as reading, spelling, and arithmetic.

Balance of Power A means of keeping peace by making sure that no nation or group of nations becomes so powerful that it can dominate others.

banished (BAN-ishd) Forced to leave a country; expelled.

baptism (BAP-tiz-um) A Christian ceremony or ritual that uses water to signify spiritual rebirth.

728

barbarians (bar-BAIR-ee-enz) A name given to foreigners by the ancient Greeks and Romans. They felt that other people were inferior, lacking in refinement and learning.

barons (BAR-uns) Members of the nobility.

barter economy (BAR-tur i-KAN-uh-mee) A system of trade by exchanging goods or services, rather than money.

Bastille (bas-TEEL) A fortress jail in France, whose fall in 1789 marked the beginning of the French Revolution.

batik (buh-TEHK) An Indonesian method of decorating cloth.

Berbers (BUR-berz) A nomadic group of North African Muslims.

Berlin Airlift (bur-LIN) A response to the Soviet blockade of roads and rail lines to Berlin, by American and British planes, which flew food, fuel, clothing, and supplies into West Berlin.

bishop (BISH-up) A high-ranking church official.

Black Death The bubonic plague, which killed millions of people in medieval Europe.

blitzkrieg (BLITS-kreeg) German "lightning war"; sudden, swift attacks for quick victory.

Boer (boor) A descendant of Dutch colonists in South Africa; also called Afrikaner.

Bolsheviks (BOL-shuh-viks) The original members of the Communist Party in Russia.

borough (BUR-oh) A town or urban district in Great Britain that elects a member to parliament.

bourgeoisie (BOOR-jwa-zee) The social class between the very wealthy and the poor; middle class.

Boxers (BOK-serz) A group of Chinese belonging to a secret society who tried to drive foreigners out of China and abolish Christianity in the late nineteenth century.

boyars (baw-YAHRS) Members of the Russian aristocracy until the rank was abolished by Peter the Great.

boycott (BOI-kot) Refusal to buy goods.

bubonic plague (byoo-BAH-nik PLAYG) A contagious disease that was carried by fleas from infected rats and transmitted to humans.

Buddhism (BOOD-izm) A religion in Eastern and Central Asia started by Gautama Buddha.

budget deficit (BUHJ-it DEF-uh-sit) The imbalance created when the government takes in less money than it spends.

bureaucracy (byoo-RAH-kruh-see) A body of appointed or hired government officials who follow a set routine.

C

calculus (KAL-kyuh-lus) A method of computation.

caliph (KAY-lif) A title for the religious and civil head of a Muslim state and successor of Muhammad as civil and spiritual head of Islam.

calligraphy (kuh-LIG-ruh-fee) Fancy or elegant style of handwriting.

campaign (kam-PAYN) A series of military operations designating phases of a war.

capital (KAP-uh-tul) Seat of government in a country; also, money and goods used to make more goods.

capitalism (KAP-uh-tul-izm) An economic system under which people are free to own and develop their own property in order to make a profit.

caravel (KAR-uh-vel) A small fifteenth and sixteenth century ship with broad bows, high narrow poop, and lateen sails.

Carbonari (kar-bo-NAH-ree) A secret society of the nineteenth century whose purpose was to unify Italy.

cartel (car-TEL) An international organized group controlling prices or production in some field of business.

caste system (KAST SIS-tum) An ancient practice in India by which people are born into a social class and cannot move out of it.

castes (KASTS) Hindu groups in Indian society that are divided by work. Each caste has its own customs and jobs that are passed on from parents to children.

catacombs (KAT-uh-komz) Underground cemeteries where Christians hid from persecution by Roman emperors.

caudillo (kow-THEE-lyoh) In Latin America, a leader, especially a military dictator; Spanish for "strong man."

cedar (SEE-duhr) A tall tree of the pine family whose wood is known for its fragrance and durability.

censor (SEN-suhr) To examine, edit, and control information in order to keep objectionable ideas from reaching the public; also, a person who censors.

Central Powers In World War I, the alliance of Germany, Austria-Hungary, the Ottoman Empire, and Bulgaria.

centralized government (SEN-truh-lyzd GUV-ur-munt) Government in which the power comes from one central place or person.

chancellor (CHAN-suh-lur) A government official; may be either the highest person in the government, as in the German empire, or a lower official, as in the British cabinet.

chinampas (chin-NAM-pas) Rafts covered with roots, weeds, and mud on which the Aztecs planted some of their crops; floating gardens.

chivalry (SHIV-al-ree) The rules or code of behavior for knights.

circumnavigate (sur-kum-NAV-uh-gayt) To go completely around (the earth)

city-state Self-ruling state consisting of a city and its surrounding territory.

civilization (siv-uh-luh-ZAY-shun) An advanced state of society.

civil disobedience (dis-uh-BEE-dee-uns) Gandhi's philosophy that urged people to disobey unjust laws and refuse legal responsibilities.

civil servant Government employee.

civil service A group of workers hired to carry out the government's work.

civil war A war fought between groups of the same country.

clan A group of families that are related to each other, but other members can be adopted. In ancient Japan, each clan had its own god, who was believed to be the founder of the clan.

classical (KLAS-i-kul) Characteristic of ancient Greece and Rome; an artistic or literary style characterized by simplicity, balance, dignity, and emotional restraint.

classless society (KLAS-les suh-SY-uh-tee) The ultimate goal of Communist principles, in which all class differences will disappear and complete equality will exist.

clergy (KLUR-jee) Those trained to carry out the functions of a church, such as priests and monks.

coalition (koh-uh-LISH-un) A temporary alliance of persons, parties, or countries for joint action.

coaling stations (KOL-ing STAY-shuns) Places where steamships could stop to take on coal for fuel.

codes of Hammurabi (KODZ uv hah-moo-RAH-bee) 282 laws written on clay tablets and on display throughout Babylon.

Cold War War of words between the Soviet Union and the United States after World War II.

collectives (kuh-LEK-tivs) Large farms worked by the people in common; often under government direction.

colony (KAHL-uh-nee) A settlement of people governed by a foreign nation.

Common Market Agreement made after World War II among six nations of Western Europe eliminating tariffs on the goods they import from one another.

commonwealth (KAHM-un-welth) A government founded on law and the people's agreement.

commune (KAHM-yoon) In ancient Greece, a group of leading citizens; in China, a government-run farm.

communication (kuh-myoo-nih-KAY-shun) The sending and receiving of messages and other information.

communism (KOM-yuh-nizm) An economic system based on government ownership of all industry.

concordat (kun-KAWR-dat) A compact, covenant or agreement between a pope and a government about church affairs.

Concordat of Worms (kun-KAWR-dat uv WURMZ) The compromise of 1122 that ended the fight between popes and emperors over investiture.

condemned (kun-DEMD) To be pronounced guilty; convicted.

confrontation (kon-frun-TAY-shun) Face to face opposition; a challenge.

conservatives (kon-SUR-vuh-tivs) Those who preserve existing conditions and ways and resist change.

constitution (kon-stuh-TOO-shun) A system of principles, usually a document, by which a nation or an organized group of people is governed.

constitutional monarchy (kon-stuh-TOO-shun-ul MAN-ark-ee) A government where the king supports the constitution, thus confining the king's power to its system of principles.

consul (KAHN-suhl) In ancient Rome, one of two elected officials who enforced the laws.

Consulate (KAHN-suhl-it) The government of France from 1799 to 1804.

containment (kuhn-TAYN-muhnt) The American Cold War policy of preventing the spread of Soviet power.

Contras (KAHN-truhz) A group of Nicaraguan guerrillas supported by the United States government.

convert (kun-VURT) To change from one belief, faith or religion to another.

corporation (kaw-puh-RAY-shun) A business company whose identity remains the same regardless of changes in its ownership or work force.

cottage industry (KOT-ij IN-dus-tree) The system of making goods at home.

cotton gin A machine that separates the seeds, hulls, and foreign material from cotton.

Counter Reformation (KOUN-tur ref-ur-MAY-shun) Reforms in the Catholic church.

count (KOUNT) A European nobleman.

coup (KOO) A sudden and highly successful act.

coup d'état (KOO-DAY-ta) The sudden, violent overthrow of a government.

credit (KRED-it) The trust that a person will pay back the money he or she borrows.

Creoles (KREE-olz) People of European descent born in Latin America.

crop rotation (KROP roh-TAY-shun) Method of farming by which a different crop is planted on the same piece of land each year. Some types of plants deplete the nutrients in the soil; other plant types replenish the soil, thus rotation.

crucifixion (kroo-suh-FIK-shun) To put to death by nailing or binding the hands and feet to a cross.

crusades (kroo-SAYDZ) During the Middle Ages, expeditions by Christians to the East to fight the Turks over possession of the Holy Land.

cultural revival (KUL-chuh-rul ri-VY-vul) Bringing back, refreshing, or renewing the institutions and expressions of a culture.

culture (KUL-chur) The features or way of life of a civilization, also the expression of that way of life through music, literature, painting, sculpture, and architecture.

cuneiform (kyoo-NEE-uh-form) Wedge-shaped markings in clay; a system of writing in ancient Mesopotamia.

czars (ZARS) Rulers of Russia before the Russian Revolution overthrew the monarchy in 1917.

D

Daimyos (DY-myohs) The great lords or powerful landowners of feudal Japan.

date The oblong edible fruit of an Old World plant; the time at which an event happens.

decentralized government (dee-SEN-truh-lyzd GUV-ur-munt) A system of government in which power is spread out among many local places and people.

deductive method (di-DUKT-iv METH-ud) The reasoning process by which a conclusion follows logically from the facts given.

delegate (DEL-uh-gayt) Person or representative with the power and responsibility to act for another.

delta (DEL-tuh) A fan-shaped or triangular area of land made by deposits of mud and sand at the mouth of a river.

democracy (di-MAK-ruh-see) A government ruled by the people through elected representatives.

depression (di-PRESH-un) A period of low economic activity.

desert (DEZ-urt) An arid, barren area of land where rainfall is less than ten inches a year.

desertification (dez-urt-uh-fi-KAY-shun) The change of semi-desert land into a true desert.

dialogue (DY-uh-log) An exchange of ideas and opinions between two or more persons.

dictator (dik-TAYT-ur) A person who rules a nation with absolute power.

diet (DY-ut) An assembly that meets to make decisions on religious or political matters.

diocese (DY-uh-sis) An administrative district of the Roman empire; later, the district over which a bishop has authority.

diplomatic relations (dip-luh-MAT-ik rih-LAY-shunz) The ways that two nations peacefully handle affairs between them.

Directory (duh-REK-tuh-ree) The form of government set up in France in 1795.

disarmament (DIS-ARE-muh-munt) The elimination or scaling down of a nation's military strength and equipment.

dissidents (DIS-ih-dints) People who openly differ or disagree with an opinion, group or government.

doctrines (DOK-trinz) Rules or policies maintained by a government or political leader.

domestic goods (duh-MES-tik) Products that are made or grown at home.

domestication (duh-mes-tuh-KAY-shun) The taming of animals.

duchy (DUCH-ee) The territory belonging to a duke or duchess.

Duma (DOO-ma) The first Russian parliament called together by Czar Nicholas II after the revolution of 1905.

Dvoryane (dvor-YAH-nuh) Russian landowners at the top of the class system created by Ivan the Terrible.

dynastic cycle (dy-NAS-tik Sy-kul) The rise and fall of dynasties.

dynasty (DY-nas-tee) A long line of rulers from the same family.

E

Eastern Front The line of forts and trenches that stretched from the Baltic Sea to the Black Sea in Eastern Europe.

ecclesiastical (i-klee-zee-AS-ti-kul) Relating to or concerned with the church.

economic imperialism (ek-uh-NAM-ik im-PIR-ee-ul-izm) The state of one country controlling the economic systems of other countries.

edicts (EE-dikts) Decrees or orders given by an authority backed or supported by law.

elector (i-LEK-tur) A person entitled by their office to participate in an election; one qualified to vote in an election.

embargo (im-BAR-goh) A government order preventing merchants' ships from entering or leaving ports.

emigrate (EM-uh-grayt) To leave one's country and live in another.

emperor (EM-pur-ur) Supreme ruler of an empire.

encyclopedia (in-sy-kluh-PEE-dee-uh) A work that contains information on all branches of knowledge.

enlightened despot (in-LYT-end DES-pot) An autocrat who shows interest in the common people.

enlightenment (in-LYT-n-munt) A period in Europe, beginning in the late 1600s, when ideas from the Scientific Revolution spread to other areas of thought.

ephors (EF-awrs) Five elected Spartan magistrates who had power over the king.

equanimity (ek-wuh-NIM-uh-tee) Serenity of mind; contentment.

ethnic group (ETH-nik) A group of people who share a common tradition, language, religion, and way of life.

excommunicated (eks-kuh-MYOO-nuh-kaytid) Expelled from the church membership.

explorations (eks-pluh-RAY-shun) A search conducted for purposes of discovery.

extended family (ik-STEN-did) A family that includes several generations of relatives living together or near one another.

F

factory (FAK-tuh-ree) A building used or suitable for manufacturing.

famine (FAM-un) A great lack or absence of food in an area.

fascism (FASH-izm) A system of government which is highly militaristic, nationalistic, racist, and intolerant of opposition.

Fascist party (FASH-ist) A political group advocating the ideas of fascism.

federation (fed-uh-RAY-shun) A group of city-states that gives up individual sovereignty to a central authority but retains certain limited power.

Fertile Crescent (FERT-uhl KRES-uhnt) A rich farming area stretching in a curve from the Tigris-Euphrates valley through Syria to Palestine.

feudalism (FYOOD-ul-iz-uhm) The system of government in the Middle Ages, based on personal loyalties between lords and vassals.

fez A brimless flat-crowned hat that usually has a tassel and is made of red felt.

fief (FEEF) A piece of land under the feudal system.

filial piety (FIL-ee-ul PY-uh-tee) A central idea of Confucius's teachings: children and young people must honor and love their parents and all older family members.

Filipinos (fil-uh-PEE-nohs) Natives or inhabitants of the Philippine Islands.

Five Year Plan Centralized economic planning introduced by Stalin in 1928 to industrialize the Soviet Union and increase agricultural production as rapidly as possible.

foreign policy (FOR-in POL-ih-see) A country's plan or pattern of relations with other countries.

Forum (FAWR-um) Former marketplace that, under Augustus, was built up into the main business section of the city.

Four Modernizations (mad-ur-ni-ZAY-shunz) Four proposed areas of improvement in the People's Republic of China: agriculture, industry, national defense, and science and technology.

Fourteen Points List of U.S. war aims drawn up by President Wilson during World War I.

freemen Persons enjoying civil or political liberties.

free trade Trade based on the unrestricted international exchange of goods without high tariffs.

friar (FRY-ur) A member of one of several Roman Catholic religious orders for men in which monastic life is combined with preaching and other priestly duties.

Führer (FYOOR-ur) (German word) Title given to Adolph Hitler, fascist dictator of Germany.

G

ghetto (GET-oh) Originally a section of European cities where Jews were forced to live. The word now refers to a section of a city where people of particular races or religions live apart from others.

glacier (GLAY-shur) Large mass of ice and snow that slowly moves over the land.

gladiator (GLAD-ee-ayt-ur) A person who engaged in a fight to the death for public entertainment in ancient Rome.

Golden Age of Greece A period of great prosperity and culture in Greek history.

grandeur (GRAN-jur) The quality or state of being grand, magnificent, awe inspiring.

gravity (GRAV-uh-tee) The force that pulls objects toward each other. The amount of force depends upon the mass and distance of the objects. Isaac Newton discovered the law of gravity around 1687.

Great Depression (di-PRESH-un) World wide economic slowdown of the 1930's, causing massive unemployment.

Great Purge (PURJ) In Russia, the killing or deporting to labor camps in the 1930's of millions of people, both in and out of the Communist party.

guerrilla warfare (guh-RIL-uh) Warfare conducted by small bands of fighters, not part of a regular army, who launch surprise attacks and then quickly disappear.

guilds (GILDS) Organizations of businessmen or skilled workers.

guillotine (GIL-uh-teen) A machine, popular in France, used to behead a person by means of a heavy blade.

gymnasium (jim-NAY-zee-um) In some countries, a high school that prepared only male students for the university.

H

haiku (HY-koo) A poetic form popular in Japan for over 300 years.

Hellenistic Age (hel-uhn-IS-tik) In ancient Greece and the Middle East, the historical period from the death of Alexander the Great in 323 B.C. to the conquest of Greece by the Romans in 31 B.C.

hereditary (huh-RED-uh-ter-ee) Traits passed from ancestor to descendant through genes.

heresy (HER-uh-see) An opinion or belief which differs from the official teachings of a church.

heretic (HER-uh-tik) A person who believes or teaches heresy or heretical doctrine.

hierarchy (HY-uh-rar-kee) The arrangement of persons or things by rank or class.

hieroglyphics (hy-ur-uh-GLIF-iks) An ancient Egyptian system of writing in which a picture or symbol stands for a word.

Hinduism (HIN-doo-izm) The major religion of India.

Holocaust (HAL-uh-kawst) The organized killing of six million Jews by the Nazis during World War II.

hostage (HAS-tij) A person taken prisoner for ransom or terms.

Huguenots (HYOO-guh-nats) French Protestants.

humanists (HYOO-muh-nists) People who study human interests and values instead of theology.

I

icons (EYE-kanz) Pictures of religious figures such as Christ and the saints.

ideology (eye-dee-AWL-uh-jee) A systematic body of concepts or ideas.

immigrants (IM-uh-grunts) People who come to a country from other lands.

imperialism (im-PIR-ee-ul-izm) The policy of extending a nation's power and influence beyond its borders.

Inca (ING-kuh) The ruler of the Native American empire in Peru.

incandescent (in-kuhn-DES-uhnt) White hot.

Indies (IN-deez) The islands of Indonesia in Southeast Asia (East Indies) and of the Caribbean Sea (West Indies).

indigo (IN-dih-goh) A blue dye, or the plant of the pea family that the dye comes from.

inductive method (in-DUK-tiv) Reasoning that starts from facts and goes to a general idea.

indulgence (in-DUL-juns) Pardon for sins granted to a person who had made sacrifices or payment.

Industrial Revolution (in-DUS-tree-ul rev-uh-LOO-shun) The change from the making of goods at home with hand tools to the manufacture of goods in factories with machines.

industrialization (in-DUS-tree-ul-iz-ay-shun) The process of making or becoming industrial.

infidel (IN-fuh-del) A person who does not believe in a particular religion.

inflation (in-FLAY-shun) A rise in prices and salaries that lessens the purchasing power of money.

Inquisition (in-kwuh-ZISH-un) An inquiry or investigation conducted by the church in the Middle Ages, to discover and punish heresy.

investiture (in-VES-tuh-chur) The power to place Church officials in office.

investors (in-VEST-ors) People who give or commit money to a project or idea in the hope of gaining profits.

irrigation (ir-uh-GAY-shun) Bringing water to dry land through canals, ditches or pipes.

isthmus (IS-mus) Narrow strip of land joining two larger bodies of land.

J

jaguar (JAG-war) A large cat found in tropical America.

javelin (JAV-uh-lin) A light spear.

joint venture (VEN-chur) A risk, as in business, that is shared.

Judaism (JOO-duh-izm) The Hebrew religion.

Junkers (YOONK-urz) Members of the Prussian landowning aristocracy.

jury (JOOR-ee) A group of people sworn to make a decision in a legal matter.

K

Kabuki (kah-BOO-kee) A Japanese play set to music, and dance with fanciful costumes.

kami (KAH-mee) (Japanese word) Special object or occurrence in nature, considered to be sacred.

kulaks (koo-laks) Prosperous peasant farmers of Russia who refused to join the collective farms.

L

labor union Organization formed by workers to advance its members' interests in respect to wages and working conditions.

laser (LAY-zur) A device which produces an intense beam of light.

Law Code A systematic statement of a body of law or rules of conduct.

League of Nations An alliance of nations for a common purpose of promoting peace. Forerunner of the United Nations.

Left Liberal position as distinguished from conservative (Right).

legions (LEE-junz) Groups of 3000 to 6000 soldiers in the ancient Roman army.

Lend-Lease program World War II U.S. program that sent allies food, medicines, and other material.

liberalism (LIB-uhr-uhl-iz-uhm) The political attitude favoring changes and reforms that guarantee people's rights and freedoms.

limited monarch (LIM-it-id MON-ark) A ruler or king with restricted power.

locomotive (lo-kuh-MOT-tiv) An engine that moves under its own power.

logic (LUH-jik) The science of correct reasoning describing valid relationships among propositions.

longships Strong, fast ships used by the Vikings. The ships were decorated with the shapes of snakes and dragons.

lord One having feudal power and authority over others.

M

Magna Carta (MAG-nuh KAR-tuh) The first written document that limited the power of British monarchs, signed in 1215.

Malay Peninsula (MAY-lay puh-NIN-soo-luh) A peninsula in southeast Asia extending from Singapore to the Isthmus of Kra.

mandates (MAN-dayts) Commissions granted by the League of Nations to member nations to administer conquered territories as guardians on behalf of the League.

Mansa (MAN-suh) A West African name for king.

manufactured (man-yoo-FAK-churd) Raw materials made into useful goods by hand or machine.

martial law (MAR-shul) The law enforced by the military in an occupied territory or during an emergency.

medieval (mee-dee-EE-vul) Relating to or characteristic of the Middle Ages.

megaliths (MEG-uh-liths) Huge stones used in prehistoric monuments.

Meiji (MEYE-jee) "Enlightened government," the name chosen in 1868 by the 15-year-old-emperor of Japan. He ruled for 45 years. Japan became a modern industrial state under his leadership.

memoirs (MEM-warz) Stories of personal experience.

mercenaries (MUR-suh-ner-ees) Soldiers for hire; professional soldiers.

merchants (MUR-chunts) People who buy and sell goods for profit; traders.

Messiah (muh-SY-uh) In Judaism, the promised and expected deliverer of the Jews. In Christianity, Jesus is regarded as the deliverer promised by prophesy.

mestizos (mes-TEE-zos) People of Latin America who are part European and part Indian.

metics (MET-iks) Foreigners who settled in Greece.

Middle Ages The period from about A.D. 500 to 1500.

middle class The group of people, such as professional people and skilled crafts workers, who are neither rich nor poor.

migrated (MY-grayt-ed) Having moved from one country or territory to another to live.

migration (MY-gray-shun) The act of moving from one country, place, or locality to another.

military dictatorship (MIL-uh-ter-ee dik-TAYT-ur-ship) A government ruled by a soldier, usually of high rank.

millet (MIL-eht) A cereal grass whose grain is a food in Asia and Europe.

minaret (min-uh-RET) A tower attached to a mosque from which the call to prayer is made.

minority group (muh-NAWR-uh-tee) A group differing by race, religion, or ethnic background from the majority of a population.

missi dominici (MIS-see doh-MIH-nih-kee) Government representatives who traveled once a year throughout Charlemagne's empire to enforce the laws.

missionaries (MISH-un-er-eez) Religious persons who go to distant lands in order to convert people to their faith.

missions (MISH-uns) Government representatives sent to foreign lands; diplomatic delegation.

moat (MOHT) A deep, wide trench around the walls of a castle, usually filled with water.

mobilize (MOH-buh-lyz) To get an army and the army reserves ready to fight in a war.

moderate (MAHD-uhr-it) In the middle; not extreme.

Mogul (MOH-gul) One of the Mongolian conquerors of India or their descendants.

monarchs (MAN-arks) People who rule over empires or kingdoms.

monarchy (MAN-ark-ee) Government by monarch.

monastery (MAN-uh-ster-ee) A place where monks live away from the rest of the world.

monks (MUNKS) Persons who, for religious reasons, live away from the rest of the world in a monastery.

monochrome (MAN-uh-krom) Paintings done in only one color.

monotheism (MAN-uh-thee-izm) The belief in one god.

Monroe Doctrine (mun-ROE DOK-trin) The U.S. policy opposing European colonies in the Western Hemisphere.

monsoon (mon-SOON) The wind that blows across the Indian Ocean and Southern Asia.

Moors (MOORZ) North African followers of Islam.

mortgage (MOHR-gij) The transfer of rights in a piece of property until a debt is paid.

mosaic (moh-ZAY-ik) A picture made of small pieces of colored stone, glass, and tile.

mosque (mahsk) An Islamic place of worship.

mulatto (muh-LAHT-oh) A person of both European and African ancestry.

mummy (MUM-ee) In ancient Egypt, a body made ready for burial by embalming.

mural (MYOOR-ul) A painting applied and made part of the wall surface.

Muslim (MUZ-lim) A believer in, or follower of Islam.

mutiny (MYOOT-in-ee) Revolt by a military group against a superior officer.

myth (MITH) An unsupported belief that explains a natural phenomenon.

N

Napoleonic Code (nah-POH-lee-on-ik) (KOHD) A system of laws for France established by Napoleon.

national anthem (NASH-uh-nal AN-thum) A song or hymn officially adopted and played or sung on formal occasions as a mark of loyalty to the nation.

nationalism (NASH-uh-nal-izm) Devotion to the interests of one's own nation.

natural selection (NACH-ur-al suh-LEK-shun) A process that results in the survival of those individuals or groups that adapt best to the conditions in which they live. Those that don't adapt are naturally eliminated or don't survive.

navigate (NAV-i-gayt) To direct one's course in a ship or aircraft.

neutral (NOO-trul) A nation or person that does not take sides in a war or dispute.

New Economic Policy (NEP) Lenin's post-civil-war program of 1921 to restore food production and vital services, allowing some private enterprise.

nirvana (nir-VAH-nuh) A state of mind oblivious to care, pain, or external reality.

nobles (NOH-buls) Persons with title who belong to the upper class by birth.

nomads (NOH-mads) People who wander from place to place in search of better grazing land for their flock or herd.

non-cooperation (nan-koh-ap-uh-RAY-shun) Failure or refusal to cooperate, especially with the government of a country.

nuclear fusion (NOO-klee-ur FYOO-shun) A method for creating energy by combining atoms.

O

ocean currents (KUR-unts) Swift-moving streams in the ocean.

Old Regime (ray-ZHEEM) An earlier period of rule.

oligarchy (AHL-ih-gahr-kee) Government by a small group.

Open Door Policy A policy announced by the United States in 1899 to keep trade with China open to all nations.

opera (AHP-eh-ruh) A drama set to music, made up of vocal pieces and orchestral accompaniment.

oration (aw-RAY-shun) Elaborate speech given in a fanciful, pompous manner.

outrigger canoe (OUT-rig-uhr kuh-NOO) A projecting frame on a float attached to the side of a canoe to prevent its tipping over.

P

pact (PAKT) An agreement or treaty, especially one between nations.

paddies (PAD-ees) Wet lands in which rice is grown.

Paleolithic (pay-lee-uh-LITH-ik) Relating to the second period of the Stone Age, characterized by stone implements or tools.

papacy (PAY-puh-see) The office of pope.

papyrus (puh-PY-rus) A plant that when cut into strips and pressed together can be written on; used by the ancient Egyptians.

pariah (puh-RY-uh) A person occupying the lowest rank in the caste system of southern India and Burma. These people were despised and rejected.

parish (PA-rish) Local church or church group-members.

parliament (PAR-luh-munt) Lawmaking body, as in Canada or Great Britain.

pasteurize (PAS-tuhr-yz) To heat milk or other liquids to kill bacteria.

patricians (puh-TRISH-unz) Wealthy landowners in ancient Rome.

patrons (PAY-truns) Those who give generous support or guardianship.

Pax Romana (PAKS roh-MAH-nah) The "Roman Peace," 31 B.C.–A.D. 180, during which the Romans fought few outside enemies.

peaceful coexistence (PEES-ful koh-ig-ZIS-tehns) A state of living without hostilities between two or more governments.

Peninsulares (puh-NIN-soo-lers) People in the Spanish colonies who had been born in Spain; the small, privileged group at the top of colonial society.

perestroika (peh-ruh-STROI-kuh) A Russian word meaning "to rebuild."

peristylum (per-uh-STYL-um) An open courtyard lined with columns and filled with plants, statues and a bathing pool.

persecuted (pur-suh-KYOOT-ed) Being subject to harsh and unjust treatment.

persecution (pur-suh-KYOO-shun) The act of harassing, especially those who differ in origin, religion, or social outlook.

perspective (pur-SPEK-tiv) The consideration of things in their relationship to each other.

pesticides (PES-tuh-syds) Chemicals that are used to kill insects.

petty monarchy (PET-ee MON-ar-kee) A king or ruler of little significance or importance.

phalanx (FAY-lanks) An ancient military formation of infantry or soldiers in close ranks with shields joined together and spears overlapping.

pharaoh (FER-oh) Title of ancient Egyptian rulers.

philosopher (fi-LAS-uh-fur) One who seeks wisdom or enlightenment.

philosophes (fee-law-ZAWFS) A group of French thinkers in the Enlightenment.

philosophy (fuh-LAHS-uh-fee) The study of basic questions about people, society, and nature.

pilgrimage (PIL-grim-ij) A religious journey to a shrine or other sacred place.

plague (playg) A disease that kills large numbers of people in a short time.

Platt Amendment A part of the Cuban constitution that gave the United States the right to protect American lives and property in Cuba.

plebeian (plee-BEE-uhn) A poor person in ancient Rome.

plebiscite (PLEB-uh-syt) A popular vote by which the people indicate or express their wishes.

pocket boroughs (PAK-it BUR-ohs) Before 1832, any district or borough in Great Britain whose representation in Parliament was controlled by a family or person.

poet laureate (POH-ut LAWR-ee-ut) A poet with special recognition.

pogrom (poh-GRUM) Riots involving murder and pillage, aimed against Jews in Russia.

Politburo (PAH-lit-byoor-oh) The Political Bureau of the Communist Party, renamed the Presidium in 1952; the ruling group within the Party.

political (puh-LIT-i-kul) Having to do with government matters, such as elections, parties, rulers, and laws.

polo (POH-loh) A game originally from Persia, where teams of players on horseback use long-handled sticks to drive a ball across the playing field.

porcelain (PAWR-suh-lin) A hard, fine-grained, nonporous, and usually translucent white ceramic ware, such as cups, bowls, and dishes.

predestination (pree-des-tuh-NAY-shun) The belief that a person does not control the course of his own life since it has been planned by God.

prehistoric (pree-his-TAWR-ik) Before written history.

prime minister (PRYM MIN-is-tur) The chief officer, or leader of a government, as in Great Britain.

profit motive (PRAF-it MOH-tiv) An inner drive, impulse, intention or incentive that causes one to seek a gain, benefit or advantage in business.

profit (PRAF-it) Money earned from trade or business.

proletariat (proh-luh-TER-ee-ut) The largest class of people in any country, consisting mainly of workers, but including peasants.

propaganda (prop-uh-GAN-duh) The systematic spreading of ideas to influence the thinking of people.

prophet (PROF-it) One gifted with more than ordinary spiritual and moral insight, usually divinely inspired.

prose (PROZ) Ordinary written or spoken language.

prosperity (prah-SPER-uh-tee) A state of economic well being.

protective tariffs (pruh-TEK-tiv TAR-ifs) A means of safeguarding domestic goods from unfair competition by taxing goods coming from foreign countries.

protectorate (pruh-TEK-tur-it) A colony whose politics and military is controlled by a foreign power.

Protestant (PROT-is-tunt) A member of any of the Christians sects that separated from the Roman Catholic Church during the Reformation.

province (PRAHV-ins) An administrative district.

pyramid (PIR-uh-mid) A huge stone building, usually forming a square at ground level, with triangle shaped sides, meeting at a point on top, used as a tomb in ancient Egypt.

Q

Quadruple Alliance (kwah-DROO-pul uh-LY-uns) Agreement among Prussia, Great Britain, Austria, and Russia to put down revolutions in Europe after the Napoleonic Era.

quipu (KEE-poo) A device with bundles of knotted and colored string used by the Incas to keep records and send messages.

quota (KWOHT-uh) The number or amount constituting a proportional share.

R

radicals (RAD-i-kals) People who favor quick or revolutionary, changes in government.

radioactive (ray-dee-oh-AK-tiv) The spontaneous emission of alpha, beta and gamma rays by the disintegration of the nucleus of atoms.

rajah (RAH-juh) Prince or ruler of ancient India.

raw materials Natural resources, like wool, cotton, minerals, which can be turned into finished products.

realism (REE-uh-liz-um) The representation in literature and art of things as they are in life; the tendency to see situations as facts and to deal with them practically.

Realpolitik (ray-AL-poh-li-teek) The tough minded, hardnosed politics of the real world.

recession (ri-SESH-un) A downturn in business activity.

reform (ri-FAWRM) To make better by removing faults.

Reformation (ref-ur-MAY-shun) The sixteenth century religious movement which led to the establishment of the Protestant religion.

refugees (REF-yoo-jeez) People who flee from a country, usually because of war or religious or political persecution.

Reich (RYK) Germany or the German government.

reincarnation (ree-in-kar-NAY-shun) A belief in which the spirit takes on a new form after death.

Renaissance (REN-uh-sans) Rebirth or discovery of important ideas and events of the past; also, the period in Europe following the Middle Ages.

reparation (rep-uh-RAY-shun) The compensation that a nation defeated in war pays a victorious nation for damages or losses suffered during the war.

resident commissioner (REZ-i-dunt kuh-MISH-uh-nur) British official responsible for the local rulers of the Indian states, their relations with each other and with other nations.

Restoration (res-tuh-RAY-shun) The period in English history following the return of the monarchy when Charles II came to the throne.

resurrection (REZ-uh-REK-shun) Rising from the dead or coming back to life.

rhetoric (RET-ur-ik) The art of speaking or writing effectively.

Ringstrasse (RING-shtrah-suh) A series of eight boulevards forming a circle around the center of Vienna. The boulevards were lined with beautiful buildings, such as opera houses, libraries, and museums.

Risorgimento (ree-sor-jee-MEN-toh) Revival of the glory Italy had known during ancient Rome and the Renaissance.

rite (RYT) A ceremonial act or action.

romanticism (roh-MAN-tuh-siz-um) A literary, artistic, and philosophical movement marked by emphasis on the imagination and emotions.

Rome-Berlin Axis (AK-sis) Agreement of cooperation between fascist Italy and Nazi Germany.

Roosevelt corollary (KAWR-uh-ler-ee) U.S. policy of intervening in Latin America to make nations there pay their debts without interference from other nations.

ruling class A group of people with the power of authority.

Russify (RUS-uh-fy) Czarist policy in Russia to make people speak, dress and act like Russians.

S

sabotage (SAB-uh-tahj) Destructive or obstructive behavior by a person or persons against a nation's war efforts or defences.

sacrament (SAK-ruh-munt) A formal religious act, sign or symbol that is considered sacred.

Sahara (suh-HAR-uh) A vast desert region in northern Africa.

samurai (SAM-uh-ry) A warrior knight in feudal Japan.

sanction (SANK-shuhn) A measure designed to force a nation to change its policies.

Sanskrit (SAN-skrit) An early language of India.

satrap (SAY-trap) Governed province in ancient Persia.

savanna (suh-VAN-uh) Tropical or subtropical grassland containing scattered trees.

scandal (SKAN-dul) An offence against faith or morals that results in loss or damage to one's reputation.

scarcity (SKAIR-suh-tee) Not plentiful or abundant.

schism (SIZ-m) A formal division in or separation from a religious body or church.

scholars (SKAHL-urs) A formal word for students or those who are involved in serious study.

scientists (SY-un-tists) People learned in science, especially natural sciences.

scribe (SKRYB) A person who wrote and kept records in ancient times.

scripts (SKRIPTS) Styles of handwriting.

scurvy (SKUR-vee) A disease caused by a lack of vitamin C. Symptoms are weakness and bleeding gums.

Second Empire In France, the government of Napoleon III, 1852–1870.

Second Republic In France, the republican government established by the Revolution of 1848; replaced in 1852 by the Second Empire of Napoleon III.

segregation (seg-ruh-GAY-shun) The act of setting apart from or separating, usually referring to racial isolation.

seismograph (SYZ-muh-graf) An apparatus for measuring or recording the intensity, direction and duration of an earthquake.

self-determination (SELF di-tur-muh-NAY-shun) The act or power of deciding things for oneself.

senate (SEN-it) The supreme council of the ancient Roman republic and empire.

sepoy (SEE-poi) A native of India employed as a soldier by a European power.

serfs Farm peasants who owed their loyalty to a noble during the Middle Ages.

shards Fragments of something brittle, as in pottery.

Shinto (SHIN-toh) Japanese religion based on worship of the emperor.

shoguns (SHOW-guns) Military dictators who ran the government of Japan before the government was modernized.

Silk Road A trading route from China to Central Asia.

simony (SY-muh-nee) The buying and selling of church offices.

Slav (slahv) A person whose native language is one of the Slavic family of languages.

social contract (SOH-shul KON-trakt) The belief that government is based on an agreement made by the people.

social programs Government programs that help needy groups of people to improve their lives.

socialism (SOH-shul-izm) An economic system based on government ownership of industry and the end of private profit.

solar energy (SOH-lur EN-ur-jee) The sun as a source of power.

Solidarity (sahl-uh-DAIR-uh-tee) A Polish anti-Communist labor union and political party.

Sophists (SOF-ists) Special Greek teachers who were trained in the art of teaching rhetoric, grammar, logic, and philosophy.

soviets (SOH-vee-its) Local election districts in the Soviet Union.

speculators (SPEK-yuh-lay-tors) People who take business risks in hope of gain or profit.

sphere of influence (SFIR uv IN-floo-wuns) Territory over which a nation has power to affect political, social or economic outcomes.

stalemate (STAYL-mayt) A drawn contest or tie.

standard of living A level of subsistence for a nation, social class, or person.

steamboat A boat powered by a steam engine.

steam engine An engine driven by steam.

steles (STEE-lees) Tall stone shafts that were in front of pyramids and temples.

steppe (STEP) Large treeless plain that has cold winters and hot summers, and receives from ten to twenty inches of rain a year; called a prairie in the U.S.

stoicism (STOH-i-siz-um) Indifference to pleasure or pain; unmoved by joy or grief.

strait (STRAYT) Narrow body of water that connects two larger bodies of water.

strategy (STRAT-uh-jee) A plan of action.

submit (sub-MIT) To give in or yield to the power or will of another.

Sudan (soo-DAN) A region in Africa just south of the Sahara.

suffrage (SUF-rij) The right to vote.

sultan (SUL-ten) The sovereign or ruler of a Muslim state.

summit meeting (SUM-it) A gathering of top officials.

Super Powers The strongest militarily and most influential nations on earth.

suttee (suh-TEE) The act or custom of a Hindu widow allowing herself to be cremated or burned alive on the funeral pyre of her husband.

Swahili (swah-HEE-lee) The language spoken by many people of East Africa.

T

Tanzimat (TAHN-zee-maht) The period in Ottoman history during which the government and society were reorganized.

tariffs (TAR-ifs) Taxes on goods coming into a country.

telegraph (TEL-uh-graf) Method or system for communication at a distance using coded signals electrically transmitted over wires.

Tennis Court Oath The declaration that the Third Estate would serve as the National Assembly and that it would write a constitution for France. The meeting took place on the royal tennis court.

terrace (TER-us) Steps of earth cut into a hillside to increase the amount of land that can be farmed.

terra cotta (TER-uh KAT-uh) A brown-red clay used for sculpture by early West African artists.

terrorism (TER-ur-izm) Systematic use of fear and violence as a means of gaining some political end.

theory of evolution (THEE-uh-ree uv ev-uh-LOO-shun) The idea that animals and plants slowly evolve, or develop and change, over long periods of time. The theory was written by Charles Darwin.

theory of relativity (rel-uh-TIV-eht-ee) The relationship between matter, space, motion, and time. The theory was developed by Albert Einstein.

thermae (THUR-mee) Public baths built by the Roman government to provide citizens with an inexpensive place to exercise and relax.

thesis (THEE-sis) An unproven idea.

Third World The developing nations of Latin America, Africa, and Asia.

toleration (tal-uh-RAY-shun) The act of allowing different views, especially of religion.

trade deficit (DEF-uh-sit) An imbalanced amount of goods exchanged between nations.

translate (trans-LAYT) To change words from one language into another.

treaty (TREE-tee) A formal written agreement between nations about matters such as boundaries or trade.

Treaty of Versailles (TREE-tee uv vur-SY) The 1919 peace agreement between the Allies and Germany which ended World War I.

tribute (TRIB-yoot) To pay for the right to do something; also, to show respect.

Triple Alliance (TRIP-uhl ul-LY-uhns) An agreement of cooperation among Germany, Austria-Hungary, and Italy, signed in 1882.

Triple Entente (ahn-TANT) An agreement of cooperation between Britain, France and Russia.

troubadours (TROO-buh-dawrs) Poet-musicians who lived in the 11th, 12th, and 13th centuries. Traveling throughout southern France and northern Italy, they performed their poems of love and chivalry set to music.

truce (TROOS) A halt in fighting during a war.

Turkic (TUR-kik) A subfamily of Altaic languages including Turkish; also, the people who speak them.

tyrants (TI-runts) Rulers who exercise absolute power in an oppressive or brutal manner.

U

Ukiyo-e (OO-kee-oh-YAY) Inexpensive or affordable wood block drawings.

unification (yoo-nuh-fi-KAY-shun) The joining of different territories to form one nation.

Utopian Socialists (yoo-TOH-pee-un SOH-shuh-lists) People who believe in an ideal society in which all property and industry are owned in common and there are no private profits.

untouchables (un-TUCH-uh-blz) Members of the underclass in Hindu society.

V

vaccine (vak-SEEN) A serum given to humans or animals that promotes resistance to a disease such as smallpox.

vacuum (VAK-yoom) A space devoid of matter.

vassal (VAS-uhl) In feudalism, a person who owed loyalty to a lord.

vault (VAWLT) Arched stone roof.

vernacular (vur-NAK-yuh-lur) Using a language or dialect native to a region; the mode of expression of a group or class.

veto (VEE-toh) The rejection of a bill or law.

viceroy (VYS-roi) The governor of a country or province who represents a sovereign.

viceroyalties (vys-ROI-ul-tees) The offices or jurisdictions of a viceroy.

Victorian (vik-TOR-ee-un) Relating to the reign of Queen Victoria of England: the art, music, literature, taste, and conduct of her time.

Vietcong (VEE-eht KONG) The national front for liberation of Vietnam; they waged guerilla warfare and expressed the Communist philosophy. Politically they were known as the Provisional Regional Government of South Vietnam.

Vietnamization (vee-et-nuh-mi-ZAY-shun) Policy by U.S. president Richard Nixon that the job of fighting would be handed over to the South Vietnamese Army. The United States would continue to provide air support but American troops would gradually be withdrawn.

visionary (VIZH-uhn-air-ee) A person who knows how to act now to make things better later.

W

war guilt clause A treaty clause requiring Germany to take the blame for World War I.

Weimar Republic (WY-mar) In Germany, the democratic government from 1919 to 1933.

welfare state A state in which the government pays for many of the needs of the people.

Western Front In World War I, the front in Belgium and France between Germany on the one side and France and Britain on the other.

White Russian An opponent of the Bolsheviks in the Russian Civil War.

wireless telegraph (TEL-uh-graf) Instrument without connecting wires that operates by radio waves.

Z

zaibatsu (ZY-bat-soo) Wealthy business families in nineteenth century Japan.

zemstvo (ZEMST-voh) Administrative institutions of local government in Czanist Russia created by edict in 1864.

ziggurat (ZIG-oo-rat) In ancient Mesopotamia, a pyramid-like temple with steps to the top.

Zionism (ZY-uhn-izm) The movement to set up a Jewish national or religious community in Palestine.

Zollverein (TSUL-fer-eyn) (German word) A customs union which allowed states to trade freely with one another without having to pay taxes on traded goods.

Zulus (ZOO-loos) Members of the Bantu-speaking African people of Natal.

INDEX

as superpower, 596–609, 685
United States and, 688
uprisings in Eastern Europe
against, 613–14, 687
World War II and, 577–78
See also Russia
**Space exploration and
technology,** 601, 717–19
Spain, 229–31, 292–93, 294,
302–5, 344, 354, 359, 361, 479,
505–6, 538, 550–51
Spanish–American War (1898),
506, 512–13
Spanish Armada, 295
Spanish Civil War (1936), 549,
550–51
Spanish Inquisition, 292–93
Sparta (city–state), 114–15, 128
Sphere of influence, 477
Sputnik, 601
Sri Lanka (Ceylon), 90, 505, 632,
633–34
Stalin, Joseph, 544, 577, 580,
598, 604, 613, 614
Stalingrad, 577
Stanley, Henry, 478
**Strategic Arms Reduction Treaty
(START),** 688
Steam engine, 439
Stephenson, George, 454
Stock market crash in 1929, 536
Stoicism, 145
Sudan, 240, 241, 243, 244, 479
Sudetenland, 557
Suez Canal, 478–79, 518, 573,
641
Suharto, General, 650
Sukarno, 650
Suleiman I, 234, 236–37
Sumerian civilization, 18–20, 21,
23
Sunnis, 231
Sun Yat–sen, 487
Syria, 572, 641, 645
Szechenyi, Count Istvan, 417

T

Taft, William H., 513
Taiping Rebellion (1851–1864),
484, 485
Taiwan, Nationalist China in,
620, 621
Tajikistan, 689
Taj Mahal, 252
Tale of Genji, The **(Murasaki
Shikibu).** 96–97, 99

Tamerlane (Mongol prince), 250
Tamils, 633–34
Tanaka Memorial, 561
Tang dynasty, 81–83
Tanzimat period, 425, 427
Technology, 687–88, 694–95,
699–700, 715–19
Telegraph and telephone, 455
Telescope, 329
Ten Commandments, 37, 38, 39
Tennis Court Oath (1789), 347
Tenochtitlan, 266–67, 303
Terrorism, 633, 658
Tet Offensive, 652
Textile industry, 437, 438, 445,
447
Thailand, 92, 653
Thatcher, Margaret, 678–79
Theater, 260–61, 281, 353, 425
Thebes, Greek city of, 31, 129
Theodora (wife of Justinian I),
182–83
Theodosius, Emperor, 170
Theresa of Avila, 287
Thieu, Nguyen Van, 651
Third Reich, 556–57
Third Republic (France), 384–85
Third World nations, 622–23
**Thirteenth Amendment to the
Constitution,** 438
Thirty Years War (1618–1648),
312–13, 320
*Thoughts on the Education of
Daughters* **(Wollstonecraft),**
463
Tiananmen Square, 695
Tibet, 90
Tigris and Euphrates rivers, 14,
18, 19
Tikal, city of, 265, 304
Tilly, Count of, 313
Timbuktu, 242–43, 245
Tojo, General Hideki, 565
Tokugawa shoguns, 260–61, 491
Toltecs, 266
Tonga, 103
Torah, the, 39
Towns, medieval, 196–97, 198
Trade routes, 90, 198
Trade Union Act (1871), 461
Trajan, 143, 144
Transjordan, 572
Trans–Saharan trade, 240–41
Transvaal, 480
Triple Alliance, 406, 517
Triple Entente, 517

Troubadours, 199
Truman, Harry S., 581, 589,
604, 605
Truman Doctrine, 605
Trung Trac, Lady, 93
Tull, Jethro, 440
Tunisia, 478
Tupac Amaru II, 359
Turkestan, 249
Turks and Turkey, 205–7,
234–37, 569, 572, 605
Tuscany, 411
Tutankhamen, King, 30
Tutu, Desmond, 661
Two Sicilies, Kingdom of the,
411
Two Treatises on Government
(Locke), 335
Tyre, 35, 36
Tz'u-hsi, Empress, 487

U

Ukraine, 612, 689
United Arab Emirates, 644
United Arab Republic (UAR),
641
**United Nations Relief and Re-
habilitation Administration
(UNRRA),** 591
United Nations (UN), 593, 624
United States
China and, 486, 624
Cold War, 604–9, 612, 615,
617, 620, 623, 625, 709
Cuba and, 668–89
economy, 707, 709
foreign policy, 709
imperialism of, 506, 511,
512–13
industrialization, 447–49
Japan and, 564, 702–3
Persian Gulf War, 645, 709
Revolutionary War, 343–46
slavery in, 438
Soviet Union and, 688
as superpower, 596–609, 617,
620–21
trade budget deficit, 702,
709
Vietnam War, 651–52
World War I and, 519, 521
World War II and, 578, 589
Urban II, Pope, 205
Utopia **(More),** 281
Utopian socialists, 460

V

Varro, Marcus Terentius, 12
Vassals, 187, 188
Venetia, 411, 412, 413
Venezuela, independence for, 362–63
Venice, Italy, 211, 280, 291, 301
Verdi, Giuseppe, 398–99
Versailles, 290, 297, 347, 407
Versailles, Treaty of (1918), 524, 525–27, 535, 557
Via Appia, 145
Victor Emmanuel II of Sardinia, 413
Victoria, Queen, 378–79, 485, 500
Victorian Age, 378–79
Vienna, Congress of (1814–1815), 370–72, 383, 403, 411, 479
Vietnam War (1964–1973), 651–52, 653
Vikings, 176–77, 188
Vindication of the Rights of Women (Wollstonecraft), 463
Virgil, 151, 153, 277
Visigoths, 156, 159–61, 292
Volta, Allesandro, 467
Voltaire, 334, 335–36, 337

W

Wagner, Richard, 399
Wahballat, 157
Walesa, Lech, 688
Walker, Samuel and Aaron, 441
Wang Wei, 85
Warsaw Pact, 600, 608, 617, 687
Washington, George, 342, 343–44, 346
Waterloo, Battle of (1815), 355, 372
Watt, James, 439
Weimar Republic, 555
Wellington, Duke of, 355
West Africa, 59, 479, 481
West Berlin, 606–7
West Germany, 590, 606, 614–15, 679–81
  reunification with East Germany, 681
Westphalia, Treaty of (1648), 313
Whitney, Eli, 437–38
Wilhelm II, Emperor, 518, 521
William I of England, King (The Conqueror), 189, 293
William of Normandy, 293
William of Prussia (Emperor William I), King, 404, 406, 407
Wilson, Woodrow, 513, 521, 525, 526, 569
Wollstonecraft, Mary, 463
Women
  in U.S. politics, 708
  employment of, 445, 707
  Islam and status of, 227
  in Japanese society, 492
  leaders, 31, 82, 93, 157, 189–91, 296, 649–50
  rights of, 183, 378, 461–63
  in Turkey, emancipation of, 569
  World War I and status of, 516–17, 535
  writers, 96–97, 99
Women of Troy, The (Euripides), 123
World War I, 516–21, 524–27, 534, 543, 715
World War II, 539, 565, 571, 576–81, 588–93, 612–17, 642

Worms, Concordat of (1122), 205, 311
Worms, diet of (1521), 286
Wu Chao, 82

Y

Yahweh, 39
Yangtze River valley, 49
Yarmak, Battle of (A.D. 636), 229
Yellow fever, 467
Yellow (Huang) River, 14, 49–50
Yeltsin, Boris, 684–85, 689
Yong Le, 258–59
Yoritomo, 99
Yoruba, 59
Young Turks, 429, 572
Yuan Dynasty, 257
Yucatan Peninsula, 265, 304
Yugoslavia, 526, 599

Z

Zaghlul Pasha, Saad, 573
Zaibatsu, 493
Zaire, 477, 481
Zambezi River (Africa), 57, 476, 478
Zenobia, 157
Zeus (god), 123
Zhao Kuangyin, 83
Zhou Dynasty, 49, 50–51, 52, 79
Zhou Enlai, 624
Zhu Yuan-zhang, 257–58
Zia ul-Haq, Muhammad, 632, 634–35
Ziggurat, 20
Zimbabwe, 244, 245, 658
Zionism, 572–73, 642
Zola, Emile, 385
Zollverein (customs union), 403
Zulus, 480

ACKNOWLEDGMENTS FOR SPOTLIGHT ON SOURCES

Text credits are given below. Numerals in **boldface** refer to page numbers on which the selections of text appear.

UNIT 1

From *Lascaux: Paintings and Engravings*, p. **6**
By Annette Laming-Emplelaire, translated by Eleanor Frances Armstrong. (Penguin Books, 1959), p. 200. Copyright © Allen Lane, 1959. Reproduced by permission of Penguin Books.

From *Our Oriental Heritage*, p. **28**
The Story of Civilization: Part I, by Will Durant. Simon and Schuster. Copyright © 1935 Will Durant, renewed 1963, Will Durant.

From *The New English Bible*, p. **38**
© The Delegates of Oxford University Press and The Syndics of the Cambridge University Press 1961, 1970. Reprinted with permission.

From *Sources of Indian Tradition*, p.
Compiled by Wm. Theodore De Bary, et al. Copyright © 1958. Columbia University Press. Used by permission.

From *The Olmec World*, p. **64**
By Ignacio Bernal. University of California Press, 1969.

UNIT 2

From *The Travels of Fa-Hsien*, or *Record of the Buddhist Kingdoms*, p. **75**
Translated by H.A. Giles. Routledge & Kegan Paul.

From *Sources of Chinese Tradition*, p. **85**
Compiled by Wm. Theodore De Bary, et al. Copyright © 1960. Columbia University Press. Used by permission.

From *The Great Chinese Travelers: An Anthology*, p. **92**
Edited by Jeanette Mirsky. University of Chicago Press, 1964.

From *The Tale of Genji*, p. **96–97**
By Lady Murasaki. Translated by Arthur Waley. Anchor Books, 1955.

From *The Voyages of Captain James Cook Round the World*, p. **105**
Edited by Christopher Lloyd. Century, a division of Century Hutchinson Ltd., 1949.

UNIT 3

From *Readings in the History of the Ancient World*, p. **115, 120–121, 143**
Edited by William C. McDermott and Wallace E. Caldwell. Holt, Rinehart and Winston. Copyright © 1951 by William C. McDermott and Wallace E. Caldwell.

From *De Re Publica*, p. **165**
By Cicero, i. 44 (Loeb Classical Library No. 213). Copyright © by the President and Fellows of Harvard College. Reprinted by permission of Harvard University Press.

From *Caesar and Christ: A History of Roman Civilization from Their Beginnings to A.D. 325*, p. **158**
The Story of Civilization: Part III, by Will Durant. Simon and Schuster. Copyright © 1944 Will Durant, renewed 1972 Will Durant.

UNIT 4

From *The Women Troubadours*, p. **199**
By Meg Bogin. Paddington Press, 1976.

From *The Decameron of Giovanni Boccaccio*, p. **211–212**
Translated by Richard Aldington. Dell, 1962. Copyright © Catherine Guillaume.

UNIT 5

From *Readings in Russian History*, p. **223**
Vol. 1, 4th ed., edited by Warren B. Walsh. Syracuse University Press, 1953.

From *A Literary History of the Arabs*, p. **231**
By Reynold A. Nicholson. Copyright © 1953. Cambridge University Press. Used by permission.

From *"Süleyman the Magnificent,"* p. **234**
By Merle Severy and James L. Stanfield *National Geographic* 172, no. 5 (November 1987): 552–601.

From *History of West Africa*, p. **242–244**
By Basil Davidson. Anchor Books, 1966.

Adapted from *Discovering Our African Heritage*, p. **245**
By Basil Davidson, © copyright, 1971, by Ginn and Company. Used by permission of Silver, Burdett & Ginn Inc.

From *Memoirs of Babur*, p. **251**
Translated by Annette S. Beveridge. Luzac, 1969.

From *Full Moon Rising*, p. **261**
By Bashō Matsuo, translated by James D. Andrews, 1976. With permission of Branden Publishing Company, Boston, MA.

From *The Narrow Road to the Deep North and Other Sketches*, p. **261**
By Bashō Matsuo, translated by Nobuyuki Yuasa. London: Penguin Classics, 1966. P. 26. Copyright © Nobuyuki Yuasa, 1966. Reproduced by permission of Penguin Books.

From *Lost City of the Incas*, p. **269**
By Hiram Bingham. Duell, Sloan and Pearce, 1948.

UNIT 6

From *Institutes of the Christian Religion*, p. **290**
Vol. 2, by John Calvin, translated by Henry Beveridge. James Clarke, 1962.

From *Seven Britons in Imperial Russia, 1698–1812*, p. **317–318**
Edited by Peter Putnam. Princeton University Press, 1952.

UNIT 7

From *The Columbia History of the World*, p. **336**
Edited by John A. Garraty and Peter Gay. Copyright © 1972 by Harper and Row Publishers, Inc. Reprinted by permission of the publisher.

From *The Road to Independence: A Documentary History of the Causes of the American Revolution: 1763–1776*, p. **343**
By John Braeman. Copyright © 1963 by G.P. Putnam's Sons.

From *The Age of Napoleon: A History of European Civilization from 1789 to 1815*, p. **355**
The Story of Civilization: Part XI, by Will and Ariel Durant. Simon and Schuster. Copyright © 1975 by Will and Ariel Durant.

From *Bolivar*, p. **363**
By Donald E. Worchester. Little, Brown, 1977.

UNIT 8

From *Readings in European History Since 1814*, p. **385**
Edited by Alexander Baltzly and Jonathan F. Scott. F.S. Crofts, 1946.

From *Garibaldi*, p. **412**
By Jasper Ridley. Copyright © 1974 by Jasper Ridley. All rights reserved. Reprinted by permission of Viking Penguin, a division of Penguin Books USA, Inc., and Constable Publishers.

UNIT 9

From *Growing Up During the Industrial Revolution*, p. **439**
By Penny Clarke. B.T. Batsford, 1980.

From *"Steamboats on the Mississippi,"* p. **454**
By Joan W. Gandy and Thomas H. Gandy. *American History Illustrated* 22, no. 1 (March 1987). Reprinted through the courtesy of Cowles Magazines, Inc. Copyright © 1987 by *American History Illustrated*.

UNIT 10

From *African Past*, p. **480**
By Basil Davidson. Copyright © 1964 by Basil Davidson. Africa World Press. Reprinted by permission of Curtis Brown Ltd.

From *China's Response to the West: A Documentary Survey, 1839–1923*, p. **190**, p. **485–486**
By Ssu-Yu Teng and John K. Fairbank. Copyright © 1954, renewed 1982 by the President and Fellows of Harvard College. Reprinted by permission of Harvard University Press.

From *Japan: Selected Readings*, p. **491**
Edited by Hyman Kublin. Copyright © 1968, used with permission of Houghton Mifflin Company.

From *Modern Times*, p. **506**
By Carlton J. H. Hayes. Macmillan, 1983.

From *Testament of Youth*, p. **521**
By Vera Brittain. Putnam Publishing Group, 1980.

UNIT 11

From *Time to Spare*, p. **537**
Edited by Felix Greene. Unwin Hyman Ltd., 1935. Used by permission.

From *A History of Soviet Russia*, p. **545**
By Georg von Rauch, translated by Peter and Annette Jacobsohn, 5th rev. ed. (Praeger Publishers, New York, 1967), pp. 184–85. Copyright © 1967 by Frederick A. Praeger. Reprinted with permission.

From *Encyclopedia of Great Quotations*, p. **550**
Complied by George Seldes. Lyle Stuart, 1960.

From *Mein Kampf*, p. **555–556**
By Adolf Hitler, translated by Ralph Mannheim. Copyright 1943 and copyright © renewed 1971 by Houghton Mifflin Company. Reprinted by permission of Houghton Mifflin Company and Century, a division of Century Hutchinson Ltd.

From *Images of War*, p. **581**
By Robert Capa. Grossman. Copyright © 1964 by the Estate of Robert Capa.

UNIT 12

From *The Bells of Nagasaki*, p. **588**
By Nagai Takashi, translated by William Johnston, Kondansha International, 1984.

From *Khrushchev Remembers: The Last Testament*, p. **601**
Edited and translated by Strobe Talcott. Little, Brown, 1974.

From *Anatomy of China: An Introduction to One Quarter of Mankind*, p. **621–622**
2nd rev. ed., by Dick Wilson. New American Library, 1969.

UNIT 13

From *Blossoms in the Dust*, p. **636**
By Kusum Nair. Copyright © 1961 by Henry Holt. Used by permission.

From *The Fall of the Shah*, p. **645**
By Fereydour Hoveyda. Wyndham Books, 1980 and Simon & Schuster.

From *"New York,"* p.
By Léopold Senghor in *The Negritude Poets: An Anthology of Translations from the French*, edited by Ellen Conroy Kennedy. Viking Press, 1975. Reprinted by permission.

UNIT 14

From *Facts about Germany*, p
6th rev. ed., Bertelsmann Lexikon Verlag, Gütersloh 1988.

From *Perestroika: New Thinking for Our Country and the World*, p.
By Mikhail Gorbachev. Harper & Row Publishers, 1987. Reprinted by permission of the publisher.

Reprinted from *Policy Conflicts in Post-Mao China*, p.
Edited by John P. Burns and Stanley Rosen, 1986. M.E. Sharpe, Inc., Armonk, NY 105-04.

From *The Power Economy*, p.
John O. Wilson. Little, Brown, 1985.

From *The View from Space*, p.
By Ron Schick and Julia Van Haaften. Copyright © 1988 by Clarkson N. Potter, Inc.

PHOTO CREDITS